UNITED STATES ARMY IN WORLD WAR II

The War in the Pacific

OKINAWA: THE LAST BATTLE

by

Roy E. Appleman, James M. Burns
Russell A. Gugeler, and John Stevens

MILITARY INSTRVCTION

Special Editions

JM

BDD Special Editions
An imprint of BDD Promotional Book Company, Inc.
1540 Broadway
New York, N.Y. 10036

BDD Special Editions and the accompanying logo
are trademarks of the BDD Promotional Book Company, Inc.

This work is published by special arrangement
with William S. Konecky Associates, Inc.

First printed in 1948 by
The Center of Military History
United States Army
Washington, DC

ISBN 0-7924-5859-1

UNITED STATES ARMY IN WORLD WAR II

Kent Roberts Greenfield, General Editor

Advisory Committee

Historical Division, SSUSA

iii

. . . to Those Who Served

Foreword

The conflict with the Axis Powers confronted the United States Army with problems on a scale never faced before—problems as great in administration, training, supply, and logistics as in strategy and tactics. THE UNITED STATES ARMY IN WORLD WAR II sets forth in detail the nature of the problems faced, the methods used to solve them, and the mistakes made as well as the success achieved. The object is to provide a work of reference for military and civilian students as well as a record of achievements which deserve an honorable place in the pages of history. Its value to the thoughtful citizen as an aid to his comprehension of basic problems of national security has been a major consideration. Its preparation has also been prompted by the thought that in a faithful and comprehensive record all who participated in the Army's vast effort would find a recognition merited by their service and sacrifice.

The advantage to the Army and the scholar has been the decisive factor in proceeding with the least possible delay to the publication of such a series. No claim is made that it constitutes a final history. Many years will pass before the record of the war can be fully analyzed and appraised. In presenting an organized and documented narrative at this time, the Historical Division of the War Department has sought to furnish the War Department and the Army schools an early account of the experience acquired, and to stimulate further research by providing scholars with a guide to the mountainous accumulation of records produced by the war.

The decision to prepare a comprehensive account of military activities was made early in the war. Trained historians were assigned to the larger units of the Army and War Department to initiate the work of research, analysis, and writing. The results of their work, supplemented by additional research in records not readily available during the war, are presented in this series. The general plan provides for a division into subseries dealing with the War Department, the Army Air, Ground, and Service Forces, the technical services, and the theaters of operations. This division conforms to the organization of the Army during

World War II and, though involving some overlapping in subject matter, has the advantage of presenting a systematic account of developments in each major field of responsibility as well as the points of view of the particular commands. The plan also includes volumes on such topics as statistics, order of battle, military training, the Women's Army Corps, and other subjects that transcend the limits of studies focused on an agency or command. The whole project is oriented toward an eventual summary and synthesis.

The present volume concerns one of the most bitterly fought battles of the Pacific war, in which the Army, the Marine Corps, and the Navy all played a vital part. In order to make the Army's role and the campaign as a whole as intelligible as possible the historians have treated in detail the operations of the Marine Corps units attached to Tenth Army, and have also sketched the contribution of the Navy both in preliminary operations against Okinawa and in the campaign itself. Another characteristic of this as of other volumes on Pacific campaigns is that tactical action is treated on levels lower than those usually presented in the history of operations in the European theaters. The physical limitations of the terrain fought over in the Pacific restricted the number and size of the units which could be employed and brought into sharp focus the operations of regiments, battalions, and smaller units. A wealth of verified material on such operations is available for all theaters, but it is only that of the Pacific which can be used extensively, since in other theaters the actions of smaller units are lost in the broad sweep of great distances and large forces. The description of small-unit action has the merit of giving the non-professional reader a fuller record of the nature of the battlefield in modern war, and the professional reader a better insight into troop leading.

Okinawa: The Last Battle is the work of combat historians of the 1st Information and Historical Service, Tenth Army. The practice of dispatching trained historians to accompany troops into combat grew out of earlier experience, both in World War I and in the early part of World War II, which demonstrated that the paper records produced by units in battle were rarely, if ever, adequate for the writing of military history. Lower units, such as the infantry company and very often the battalion, do not write as they fight; hence the details of combat are not in their records. Even at higher levels many significant orders and reports, because they are communicated orally and by telephone, are noted in the record only sketchily if at all. An equally serious gap arises from the fact that the "why" behind the decision is almost never discernible in the documents.

The records must be supplemented by interviewing key participants in the action at all levels if anything approaching complete understanding of what happened is to be attained. Unless such quick on-the-spot study is made, memories will grow dim or the man who knows the answer may become a casualty in a subsequent operation. Thus the historians who took the field were given the mission of noting the messages, reports, and orders as they came in, of spotting the gaps in the story as it was thus unfolded, and of taking prompt steps to fill those gaps by asking questions.

At first, historians were sent to the theaters as individuals or teams. Later they were organized into units called Information and Historical Services, one of which was assigned to each field army. Though the 1st Information and Historical Service was the first of these to be activated, all the others were called on to deal with operations earlier. As a consequence the 1st Information and Historical Service not only benefited in some measure by the lessons they learned, but was the first which was fully organized and prepared to take the field at the very start of a major operation, with plans laid for a systematic coverage of the campaign.

In an organizational sense, therefore, the preparations for historical coverage of the Okinawa campaign were better than those for earlier operations. This explains why the history of the last operation has been issued first.

HARRY J. MALONY
Brigadier General, USA
Chief, Historical Division
War Department Special Staff

Washington, D. C.
1 July 1947

Preface

Okinawa: The Last Battle was written by U. S. Army historians who participated in the Ryukyus campaign as members of a group organized to accompany
the American forces to the Ryukyus and secure at first hand the materials for a
history of their operations. This group was formed in Hawaii as a section of the
1st Information and Historical Service, which was attached to Tenth Army in
January 1945.

Before the embarkation of troops for Okinawa, most of the Tenth Army's
combat historians, as they were called, had joined at various points in the Pacific
the units whose part in the coming battle they were to record. Similarly, Marine
historians were already with III Amphibious Corps headquarters and the Marine
divisions which were to take part in the action. Lt. Col. John Stevens was in
command of the Army historians; his chief assistant was M/Sgt. James M. Burns,
the author of *Guam* in the series AMERICAN FORCES IN ACTION.* Colonel
Stevens and Sergeant Burns accompanied Tenth Army headquarters. Capt.
Donald L. Mulford came from Leyte with XXIV Corps and remained with it
until late in May, when he was assigned to the 96th Division to replace its historian, Sgt. Bert Balmer, who had been wounded in action. At XXIV Corps
headquarters Maj. Roy E. Appleman succeeded Captain Mulford. Capt. Edmund
G. Love, an experienced historian of operations in the Central Pacific, was
attached to the 27th Division. Capt. Russell A. Gugeler and Capt. Paul R. Leach,
who had served respectively with the 7th and 77th Divisions on Leyte, accompanied these divisions to Okinawa. Capt. Jesse L. Rogers, on his arrival at Okinawa in June, was assigned to the 96th Division to assist Captain Mulford. The
Marine historians on Okinawa were Maj. Almet Jenks, III Amphibious Corps;
Sgt. Kenneth Shutts and Sgt. Paul Trilling, 1st Marine Division; and Capt.
Phillips D. Carleton, 6th Marine Division.

Army historians held frequent conferences during and after the campaign
for the purpose of coordinating their work. Liaison with the Marine historians

* Published by the Historical Division, War Department Special Staff.

was established soon after the initial landings at the target and was maintained throughout the operation. Further information and perspective were gained through conferences with Navy personnel at Okinawa and with Navy historians in Hawaii and Washington.

After the campaign, histories of the operations of the four Army divisions and of the 6th Marine Division were written by the respective division historians; a history of the XXIV Corps on Okinawa was written by Major Appleman; and a history of the 1st Marine Division on Okinawa was compiled by Capt. James R. Stockman, USMCR, from division records and from material supplied by the division historians.

In July 1945, after the battle of Okinawa ended, Colonel Stevens and Sergeant Burns were detached from the 1st Information and Historical Service and returned to Oahu to write the history of the Okinawa operation at Fort Shafter, where the records of all Amy units which had fought on Okinawa were subsequently brought together. Captain Love, who had completed his history of the operations of the 27th Division by July 1945, returned to Washington. The other Army historians remained with their units to complete their interrogations of the men who fought, write the division and corps histories for which they were responsible, and be available for prospective new assignments.

After the war ended, Captain Leach completed the history of 77th Division operations, and Captain Mulford and Captain Rogers the account of 96th Division operations; these three historians were then separated from the Army. Major Appleman and Captain Gugeler, who accompanied the XXIV Corps and the 7th Division to Korea, were ordered to Oahu late in the fall of 1945 to complete their respective corps and division histories at Fort Shafter. Sergeant Burns returned to the United States early in December and was separated from the Army.

By March 1946 Major Appleman had completed the narrative of XXIV Corps operations on Okinawa, and Captain Gugeler the history of the 7th Division in the campaign. At that time, although Colonel Stevens, Major Appleman, and Captain Gugeler were all eligible for separation, they returned with the Okinawa records to Washington to continue work in the Historical Division, WDSS, on the history of the Okinawa campaign. Together with Sergeant Burns, now a civilian, they completed the Okinawa manuscript by the end of June. Organization of the volume was developed at conferences of all the Army historians during and after the battle on the basis of studies by Sergeant Burns.

The manuscript was turned over to the Pacific Section of the Historical Division, WDSS. Dr. Charles B. Hirschfeld, a member of the Section, added material on high-level planning and logistics, revised and condensed certain portions of the manuscript, and aided in the preparation of the maps. The authors are especially indebted to Dr. Louis Morton, Chief of the Pacific Section, who supervised the preparation of the final manuscript and represented the authors during the editing process. The editing was performed by Dr. Albert K. Weinberg of the Editorial Branch, assisted by Miss Edith M. Poole and Miss Grace T. Waibel. The maps were prepared under the direction of Mr. Wsevolod Aglaimoff. Col. Allison R. Hartman acted as military editor, Major Charles F. Byars prepared the list of Tenth Army units in Appendix A, and Mr. George R. Powell compiled the charts and tables in Appendix C. Mr. W. Brooks Phillips prepared the index.

Capt. Robert L. Bodell selected the illustrations in this volume from material in the possession of the Signal Corps, Army Air Forces, U. S. Navy, U. S. Marine Corps, U. S. Coast Guard, and *Yank* magazine. The sketches on pp. 244–45 and 292–93 were drawn by S/Sgt. T. King Smith of the XXIV Corps Historical Section.

ROY E. APPLEMAN
JAMES M. BURNS
RUSSELL A. GUGELER
JOHN STEVENS

Washington, D. C.
1 July 1947

Contents

Tables

Charts

Maps

Illustrations

OKINAWA:
THE LAST BATTLE

CHAPTER I

Operation ICEBERG

On 3 October 1944 American forces in the Pacific Ocean Areas received a directive to seize positions in the Ryukyu Islands (Nansei Shoto). Okinawa is the most important island of the Ryukyu Group, the threshold of the four main islands of Japan. The decision to invade the Ryukyus signalized the readiness of the United States to penetrate the inner ring of Japanese defenses. For the enemy, failure on Okinawa meant that he must prepare to resist an early invasion of the homeland or surrender.

The Strategic Decision

Operation ICEBERG, as the plan for the Okinawa campaign was officially called, marked the entrance of the United States upon an advanced stage in the long execution of its strategy in the Pacific. Some 4,000 miles of ocean, and more than three years of war, separated Okinawa from Pearl Harbor. In 1942 and 1943 the Americans had contained the enemy and thrown him back; in 1944 their attack gathered momentum, and a series of fierce island campaigns carried them toward the Japanese inner stronghold in great strides.

The Allied advance followed two main axes, one through the islands of the Central Pacific, the other through the South and Southwest Pacific. Navy task forces and some other elements operated on both fronts as needed. The result was "unremitting pressure" against Japanese military and naval might, a major objective of American strategy.

Near the close of 1943, a thrust at the Gilbert Islands from the Central Pacific, in which Tarawa, Makin, and Apamama were seized, paved the way for the assault on the Marshalls on 31 January 1944. American forces captured Kwajalein, Majuro, and Eniwetok, and their fleet and air arms moved forward. At the same time, American carriers heavily attacked Truk, and that formidable enemy naval base in the Carolines was thenceforth immobilized. Saipan, Tinian, and Guam in the Marianas fell to American arms in the summer of 1944, and, in the First Battle of the Philippine Sea, the U. S. Navy administered a crushing

defeat to the Japanese fleet that tried to interfere with the American push west-
ward. In September and October the Americans occupied Ulithi in the western
Carolines for use as an anchorage and advanced fleet base, and took Angaur and
Peleliu in the Palau Islands, situated close to the Philippines.

Meanwhile, American forces in the South and Southwest Pacific were
approaching Mindanao, southernmost of the Philippine Islands, by advances
through the Solomons and New Guinea in which Japanese armies were neutralized and isolated on Bougainville, New Ireland, and New Britain. The
capture of Wakde on the northeastern coast of New Guinea in May 1944 was
followed by the seizure of Biak and Noemfoor. During the summer a Japanese
army attempting to break out from Wewak in Australian New Guinea was
subdued. The invasion of Morotai in September placed American forces within
300 miles of Mindanao.[1] (See Map No. I.)*

The ultimate goal of American operations in the Pacific was the industrial
heart of Japan, along the southern shores of Honshu between the Tokyo plain
and Shimonoseki. American strategy aimed to reach this objective by successive
steps and to take advantage, on the way, of Japan's extreme vulnerability to
submarine blockade and air bombardment. Throughout most of 1944 Army
and Navy staffs in the Pacific Ocean Areas had been planning for the invasion
of Formosa (Operation CAUSEWAY) in the spring of 1945. On the basis of
the Joint Chiefs of Staff directive of March 1944, the general concept of this
operation had been outlined, the availability of troops considered and reviewed
many times, and the assignment of task force commanders announced. On 23
August, a joint staff study for CAUSEWAY had been published. It was clear
that Admiral Chester W. Nimitz, Commander in Chief, U. S. Pacific Fleet
and Pacific Ocean Areas, intended to invade Formosa after Southwest Pacific
forces had established positions in the Central and Southern Philippines;
CAUSEWAY, in turn, was to be followed by operations against the Ryukyus
and Bonins, or against the China coast. Either course would lead eventually to
assault on the Japanese home islands.[2]

On 15 September the Joint Chiefs directed Gen. Douglas MacArthur to
seize Leyte on 20 October, instead of 20 December as planned, and to bypass

[1] *Biennial Report of the Chief of Staff of the United States Army, July 1, 1943 to June 30, 1945
. . .*, pp. 71, 73; see also maps, pp. 66–68.

[2] U. S. Army Forces, Middle Pacific, History of G–5 Section, pp. 169–76; JCS 713/4, 12 Mar 44;
JCS 924, 30 Jun 44: Opns against Japan Subsequent to Formosa.

*All maps numbered in Roman are placed in inverse order inside the back cover.

Mindanao. At the same time, Admiral Nimitz was instructed to bypass Yap.[3] On the next day Admiral Nimitz reconsidered the Formosa operation. He believed that the early advance into the Central Philippines, with the opportunity of acquiring the desired fleet anchorages there, opened up the possibility of a direct advance northward through the Ryukyus and Bonins rather than through Formosa and the China coast. He reviewed the objectives of CAUSEWAY— the establishment of air bases from which to bomb Japan, support China, and cut off the home islands from resources to the south—with reference to the new possibility and in a letter to his Army commanders requested their opinions on the subject.[4]

Lt. Gen. Robert C. Richardson, Jr., Commanding General, U. S. Army Forces, Pacific Ocean Areas, replied that only those steps should be taken which would lead to the early accomplishment of the ultimate objective—the invasion of Japan proper. From this point of view the occupation of Formosa as a stepping stone to an advance on Japan via the China coast did not, in his opinion, offer advantages commensurate with the time and enormous effort involved. He proposed instead, as a more economical course, a dual advance along the Luzon– Ryukyus and the Marianas–Bonins axes. He fully agreed with General Mac- Arthur's plan to seize Luzon after Leyte. The seizure of Luzon would provide air and naval bases in the Philippines from which enemy shipping lanes in the China Sea could be blocked and, at the same time, Formosa effectively neu- tralized. From the ample bases in Luzon, it would be possible and desirable to seize positions in the Ryukyus for the prosecution of air operations against Kyushu and Honshu. The occupation of bases in the Bonins would open another route from the Marianas for bomber operations against Japan. The air assaults on Japan would culminate in landings on the enemy's home islands.[5]

Lt. Gen. Millard F. Harmon, Commanding General, U. S. Army Air Forces, Pacific Ocean Areas, in his reply to Admiral Nimitz referred to a previous letter which he had written to the Admiral, recommending, as an alternative to the invasion of Formosa and the China coast, the seizure of islands in the Ryukyu chain, for development as air bases from which to bomb Japan. He restated these views and emphasized his opinion that if the objective of CAUSEWAY was the

[3] *Biennial Report Chief of Staff*, p. 71.

[4] Ltr CINCPOA to USAFPOA, Serial 000113, 16 Sep 44, sub: CAUSEWAY Objectives, cited in USAFMIDPAC G–5 Hist, pp. 176–77.

[5] Ltr HUSAFPOA to CINCPOA, Serial 0003, 27 Sep 44, sub: CAUSEWAY Objectives.

acquisition of air bases it could be achieved with the least cost in men and matériel by the capture of positions in the Ryukyus.[6]

The commander of the ground troops designated for CAUSEWAY, Lt. Gen. Simon B. Buckner, Jr., Commanding General, Tenth Army, presented the primary objection to the entire Formosa operation. He informed Admiral Nimitz that the shortages of supporting and service troops in the Pacific Ocean Areas made CAUSEWAY unfeasible. General Buckner added, about a week later, that if an invasion of Luzon was planned the need for occupying Formosa was greatly diminished.[7]

Admiral Nimitz communicated the substance of these views to Admiral Ernest J. King, Commander in Chief, U. S. Fleet. The latter, who had been the chief proponent of an invasion of Formosa, proposed to the Joint Chiefs of Staff on 2 October 1944 that, in view of the lack of sufficient resources in the Pacific Ocean Areas for the execution of CAUSEWAY and the War Department's inability to make additional resources available before the end of the war in Europe, operations against Luzon, Iwo Jima, and the Ryukyus be undertaken successively, prior to the seizure of Formosa. Favorable developments in the Pacific and in Europe might make CAUSEWAY feasible at a later date.[8] On the next day, 3 October, the Joint Chiefs of Staff issued a directive to Admiral Nimitz to seize one or more positions in the Ryukyu Islands by 1 March 1945.[9] On 5 October Admiral Nimitz informed his command that the Formosa operation was now deferred and that, after General MacArthur invaded Luzon on 20 December 1944, the Pacific Ocean Areas forces would seize Iwo Jima on 20 January 1945 and positions in the Ryukyus on 1 March.[10]

The projected Ryukyus campaign was bound up strategically with the operations against Luzon and Iwo Jima; they were all calculated to maintain unremitting pressure against Japan and to effect the attrition of its military forces. The Luzon operation in December would allow the Southwest Pacific forces to continue on the offensive after taking Leyte. The occupation of Iwo Jima in January would follow through with another blow and provide a base

---

[6] Ltr Hq AAFPOA to CINCPOA, 24 Sep 44, sub: CAUSEWAY Objectives, cited in USAFMIDPAC G–5 Hist, p. 177; USAFPOA Participation in the Okinawa Operation Apr–Jun 45, I, 143.

[7] Ltr Hq Tenth Army to CINCPOA, 26 Sep 44, sub: Feasibility of CAUSEWAY Opn; Ltr Hq Tenth Army to CINCPOA, 4 Oct 44, sub: CAUSEWAY Objectives. Both cited in USAFMIDPAC G–5 Hist, pp. 177, 179.

[8] JCS 713/18, 2 Oct 44.   [9] JCS 713/19, 3 Oct 44.

[10] CINCPOA dispatch 050644,—Oct 44, cited in USAFMIDPAC G–5 Hist, p. 180.

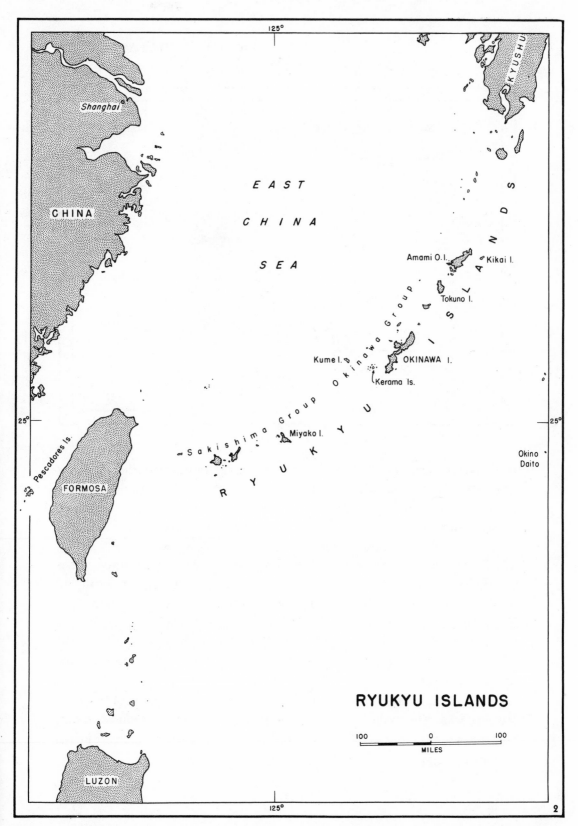

EAST

CHINA

SEA

Shanghai

CHINA

Amami O.I.   Kikai I.

Tokuno I.

Kume I.   OKINAWA I.

Kerama Is.

Miyako I.

Okino
Daito

Pescadores Is.

FORMOSA

LUZON

RYUKYU ISLANDS

125°

25°   25°

100   0   100
MILES

125°

MAP NO. 1

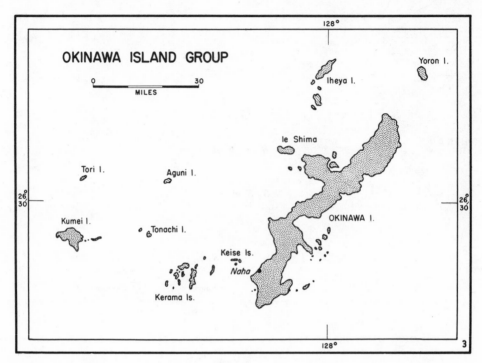

MAP NO. 2

for fighter support for the B–29's operating against Japan from the Marianas. The seizure of Okinawa in March would carry the war to the threshold of Japan, cut the enemy's air communications through the Ryukyus, and flank his sea communications to the south. Okinawa was, moreover, in the line of advance both to the China coast and to the Japanese home islands.[11]

The direct advance to the Ryukyus–Bonins line from the Luzon–Marianas was thus conceived within the framework of the general strategy of destroying by blockade and bombardment the Japanese military forces or their will to resist. The Ryukyus were within medium bomber range of Japan, and it was estimated that 780 bombers, together with the necessary number of fighters, could be based there. An advanced fleet anchorage was available in Okinawa. From these airfields and naval bases American air and naval forces could attack the main islands of Japan and, by intensified sea and air blockade, sever them from the Japanese conquests to the south. The captured bases could also be used to support further operations in the regions bordering on the East China Sea. Finally,

[11] JCS 713/18, 2 Oct 44.

the conquest of the Ryukyus would provide adequate supporting positions for the invasion of Kyushu and, subsequently, Honshu, the industrial heart of Japan.[12]

Nature of the Target

The Islands

The Ryukyu Islands lie southwest of Japan proper, northeast of Formosa and the Philippines, and west of the Bonins. (See Map No. 1.) The islands, peaks of submerged mountains, stretch in an arc about 790 miles long between Kyushu and Formosa and form a boundary between the East China Sea and the Pacific Ocean. The archipelago consists of about 140 islands, only 30 of which are large enough to support substantial populations. The climate is subtropical, the temperature ranging from about 60° F. to 83° F. Rainfall is heavy, and the high humidity makes the summer heat oppressive. The prevailing winds are monsoonal in character, and between May and November each year the islands are visited by destructive typhoons.[13]

Approximately in the center of the arc is the Okinawa Group (Gunto) of some fifty islands clustered around the island of Okinawa. The Kerama Islands lie in an area from ten to twenty miles west of southern Okinawa. Kume, Tonachi, Aguni, and Tori form a rectangle to the north of the Kerama Group. Ie Shima stands off the jutting tip of the Motobu Peninsula on northern Okinawa, while farther to the north lie the Iheya Islands and Yoron. A chain of small islands, called by the Americans the Eastern Islands, extends along the eastern shore of southern Okinawa. Lying in the path of the Japan Current, the entire Okinawa Group is surrounded by seas warm enough to allow the growth of coral, and hence all the islands are surrounded by fairly extensive reefs, some of which extend several miles off shore.   (See Map No. 2.)

Okinawa is the largest of the islands in the Ryukyus. Running generally north and south, it is 60 miles long and from 2 to 18 miles wide, with an area of

[12] JPS 404/14, 7 Oct 44.

[13] The description of the terrain of Okinawa is taken from the following sources: CINCPAC-CINCPOA Bull No. 161–44, 15 Nov 44: Okinawa Gunto; Office of the Chief of Naval Opns, Civil Affairs Handbook Ryukyu Islands, Op Nav 13–31, 15 Nov 44; Joint Amph Force Int Sec–Tenth Army G–2 Info Bull, Feb 45: Hagushi Landing Area; USAFPOA G–2 Objective Data Section, 1 Feb 45: Study of Okinawa Gunto; Tenth Army Tentative Opn Plan ICEBERG 1–45, 6 Jan 45, Annex 3; Tenth Army G–2 Int Monograph Ryukyus Campaign, Aug 45, Pt. I, Sec. A, p. 4; Interv 1st I & H Service Off with 1st Lt Robert Seeburger, Photo Interp Off, G–2 XXIV Corps, 4 Jul 45; personal obsn from air by Lt Col John Stevens, Tenth Army Historian, 9 Jun 45. All interviews and notes of personal observation are recorded in the Okinawa Diary kept by Lt Col John Stevens and M/Sgt James M. Burns of the 1st Information and Historical Service. The diary is on file in the Historical Division, WDSS.

OKINAWAN CUSTOMS *include the burial tomb and the veneration of ancestors. The burial tombs characteristic of the Okinawan landscape stand out clearly in this aerial view* (above) *just north of Shuri.*

OKINAWANS, *their head man, and a native priest (white hat) gather around an American soldier-interpreter as he asks questions.*

485 square miles. It is entirely fringed with reefs: on the western side the reef lies fairly close to shore and is seldom over a mile wide; on the eastern side, where the coast is more sheltered, the reef extends for some distance off shore, the widest and shallowest points being north of Nakagusuku Bay. (See Maps Nos. II and III.)

When Commodore Perry's ships sailed into Naha Harbor, on 26 May 1853, Okinawa was a semi-independent country, paying tribute to China and Satsuma. It was annexed in 1879 by Japan, which integrated the Okinawan people almost completely into the Japanese governmental, economic, and cultural structure. The racial origins of the Okinawans are similar to, but not identical with, those of the Japanese, and the Okinawan stock and culture had been subject to extensive Chinese influence. While the Okinawans generally resemble the Japanese in physique, they differ appreciably in their language, the native Luchuan tongue. The predominant religion among the Okinawans is an indigenous, animistic cult, of which worship of fire and the hearth is typical; veneration of ancestors is an important element in this religion and the burial tomb the most characteristic feature of the Okinawa landscape—a feature which the Japanese were to convert into a formidable defensive position.

The standard of living of the Okinawan people is low; the Japanese made no attempt to raise it, regarding the Okinawans as inferior rustics. Most of the inhabitants subsist on small-scale agriculture. When the invading Americans climbed up from the beaches, they found every foot of usable land cut into small fields and planted with sugar cane, sweet potatoes, rice, and soy beans. In 1940 the population of the island was 435,000.

The terrain in northern Okinawa, the two-thirds of the island above the Ishikawa Isthmus, is extremely rugged and mountainous. A central ridge, with elevations of 1,000 feet or more, runs through the length of the region; the ridge is bordered on the east and west by terraces which are dissected by ravines and watercourses, and it ends at the coast in steep cliffs. About 80 percent of the area is covered by pine forests interspersed with dense undergrowth. Troop movements are difficult in the region as the use of vehicles is confined to the poor road that hugs the western shore. The Motobu Peninsula, which is nearly square in shape and juts to the west, has also a mountainous and difficult terrain. Two mountain tracts separated by a central valley run east and west the length of the peninsula. Successive coastal terraces are well developed on the north, east, and west of the peninsula. About three and one-half miles off the northwest end of the Motobu Peninsula is the small flat-topped island of Ie Shima, with a sharp pinnacle about 500 feet high at the eastern end.

The southern third of Okinawa, south of Ishikawa, is rolling, hilly country, lower than the north but broken by terraces, steep natural escarpments, and ravines. This section is almost entirely under cultivation and contains three-fourths of the population of the island; here, too, are the airfields and the large towns—Naha, Shuri, Itoman, and Yonabaru. It was in this area that the battle for Okinawa was mainly fought. The limestone plateau and ridges are ideal for defense and abound in natural caves and burial tombs, easily developed into strong underground positions. Generally aligned east and west, the hills offer no north-south ridge line for troop movement, and thus they provide successive natural lines of defense, with frequent steep slopes created by artificial terracing. Rice paddies fill the lowlands near the coasts. The roads are more numerous than in the north, but, with the exception of those in Naha and its vicinity, they are mostly country lanes unsuited for motorized traffic. Drainage is generally poor, and heavy rains turn the area into a quagmire of deep, clay-like mud.

South of Zampa Point on the west there is a 15,000-yard stretch of coast line which includes nearly 9,000 yards of beaches, divided by the Bishi River. These are known as the Hagushi beaches, deriving their name from a small village at the mouth of the river. The beaches are not continuous but are separated by cliffs and outcropping headlands. They range from 100 to 900 yards in length and from 10 to 45 yards in width at low tide, and some are completely awash at high water. A shallow reef with scattered coral heads borders the entire stretch of beach and, in many places, is almost a barrier reef, with deeper water between its crest and the shore line than immediately to seaward. The beaches are for the most part coral sand and most have at least one road exit. A low coastal plain flanks the beaches from Zampa Point south to Sunabe; it is dominated by rolling hills which afford excellent observation, good fields of fire along the beaches, and extensive cover and concealment. Less than 2,000 yards inland on the plain lie the Yontan and Kadena airfields, north and south of the Bishi River. A 400-foot-high hill mass, rising southeast of Sunabe and extending across the center of the island, dominates the entire beachhead area. Composed of innumerable sharp ridges and deep ravines, it is a major obstacle to rapid troop movements and can be used effectively for a strong delaying action.

South of the Sunabe hills, down to the Uchitomari–Tsuwa line, the island narrows to 5,500 yards. The terrain is essentially similar to that behind the Hagushi beaches, with heavily wooded uplands and extensively terraced and cultivated valleys and lower slopes. The hills and ridges are generally low except for some high peaks in the general vicinity of Kuba on the east coast, from which observa-

OKINAWA'S LANDSCAPE *in the south is marked by fields of grain and vegetables, broken only by humps of coral, farmhouses, and villages. Navy plane flying over such terrain is shown dropping supplies to the fast-moving American troops early in the campaign.*

VILLAGES ON OKINAWA *consist of small clusters of houses surrounded by vegetation-covered stone and mud walls. Note camouflaged Japanese Army trucks.*

tion of the area is excellent.   Roads are adequate for light Japanese transport but not for the heavy strain of American military traffic.

On the east coast, the Katchin Peninsula on the north and the Chinen Peninsula on the south extend into the ocean to inclose the spacious fleet anchorage of Nakagusuku Bay, called by the American troops "Buckner" Bay. A low coastal plain from one-fourth to one mile wide runs along the shore of the bay from the Katchin Peninsula to Yonabaru. At Yonabaru the plain extends inland to the west through an area of moderate relief and joins another coastal flat extending northeastward from Naha. A cross-island road follows this corridor and connects the two cities. Naha, the capital of the island, with a population of 65,000, is Okinawa's chief port and can accommodate vessels up to 3,000 tons. Southwest of the city, on the Oroku Peninsula, was the Naha airfield, the most highly developed field on the island.

In the region north of the Naha–Yonabaru corridor and in the vicinity of Shuri, the ancient capital of Okinawa, lies the most rugged terrain in the southern part of the island.   From the high ground near Shuri and from many other vantage points in this area observation is excellent to the north and south and over the coastal regions. At the highest point the hills rise about 575 feet, but the lack of pattern, the escarpments, steep slopes, and narrow valleys characteristic of the region make the major hill masses ideal territory for defense. Many of the escarpments are sheer cliffs without topsoil or vegetation. The low ground is filled with twisting ridges and spotted with small irregular knolls, rendering observation difficult and providing excellent locations for minor infantry and antitank positions. The most prominent features of the region are the strong natural defensive line of the Urasoe-Mura Escarpment, rising from the west coast above the Machinato airfield and running for 4,500 yards across the island in a southeasterly direction, and the chain of hills through Tanabaru and Minami-Uebaru to the east coast southwest of Tsuwa.

South of the strong Shuri positions the terrain is rough, but there are few large escarpments. There are some broad valleys and an extensive road net which would facilitate troop movements. The terrain in the southern end of the island consists of an extensive limestone plateau, surrounded by precipitous limestone cliffs. The northern side of the plateau is a 300-foot escarpment which rises vertically from the valley floor in a jagged coral mass. On the top of the plateau major hills—Yuza-Dake and Yaeju-Dake—cover all approaches from the north, east, and west. Along the southeastern coast, much of the stretch from Minatoga to the eastern end of the Chinen Peninsula consists of beaches.

These are dominated by the rolling dissected terrace forming the body of the peninsula and by the high plateau to the southwest.

American Intelligence of the Enemy

American knowledge of the enemy and of the island of Okinawa was acquired slowly over a period of many months and in the face of many difficulties. With Okinawa isolated from the world by the Japanese, information of military value concerning this strategic inner defense line of the Empire was scarce and difficult to obtain. Limited basic intelligence was garnered from documents and prisoners captured on Pacific island battlefields, from interrogation of former residents of the Ryukyus, and from old Japanese publications. The great bulk of the data was obtained through aerial photographic reconnaissance. This, however, was often incomplete and inadequate, particularly for terrain study and for estimating enemy strength and activity. The distance of the target from American air bases—1,200 nautical miles—necessitated the use of B–29's and carrier planes for photographic missions; the former afforded only high-altitude, small-scale coverage, while the latter depended on the scheduling of carrier strikes. The relatively large land masses involved and the prevalence of cloud cover added to the difficulty of obtaining the large-scale photographs necessary for detailed study of terrain and installations.[14]

The target map prepared by American intelligence represented all that was known of the terrain and the developed facilities of the island. This map, scale 1:25,000, was based on aerial photographs obtained on 29 September and 10 October 1944 and was distributed about 1 March 1945. Incomplete coverage, varying altitudes of the planes, and cloudiness over parts of the island at the time prevented clear delineation, and certain portions of the map, including that of the high ground north of Shuri, had either poor topographic detail or none at all. Additional photographic coverage of the island was obtained on 3 and 22 January, 28 February, and 1 March 1945; that of 22 January was excellent for the proposed landing beach areas. To supplement aerial photography a submarine was sent from Pearl Harbor to take pictures of all Okinawa beaches. The submarine never returned.[15]

---

[14] Comdr Task Force 51, Comdr Amph Forces, U S Pac Flt, Rpt on Okinawa Gunto Opn from 17 Feb to 17 May 45, 25 Jul 45 (hereafter cited as CTF 51 Actn Rpt), Pt. V, Sec. A, Int Rpt; Tenth Army Actn Rpt Ryukyus 26 Mar to 30 Jun 45, 3 Sep 45, Ch. 11, Sec. II, G–2 Rpt; interv 1st I & H Service Off with Lt Col James R. Weaver, G–2 Sec, Tenth Army, 10 Jul 45.

[15] CTF 51 Actn Rpt, Pt. V, Sec. A, p. 6 (hereafter cited by part, section, and page as follows: V–A–6); interv 1st I & H Off with Lt Col James R. Weaver, G–2 Sec, Tenth Army, 10 Jul 45.

Hydrographic information was complete, but its accuracy could not be checked until the target was reached. As the data agreed with a captured Japanese map they were presumed to be accurate. The most reliable information on the depth of the water over the reefs was obtained from Sonne Strip photography and was made available to the troops in March.[16]

The first estimate of enemy strength, made in October 1944, put the number of Japanese troops on Okinawa at 48,600, including two infantry divisions and one tank regiment.[17] In January 1945 this estimate was raised to 55,000, with the expectation that the Japanese would reinforce the Okinawa garrison to 66,000 by 1 April 1945. At the end of February, however, the January estimate was still entertained. All these figures were based on interpretation of aerial photographs and on the use of standard Japanese Tables of Organization: there was no documentary evidence corroborating the estimate of the number of troops on the island.[18]

It was believed that the Japanese had moved four infantry divisions to the Ryukyus during 1944. These were identified as the *9th, 62d, 24th,* and *28th Divisions.* Army intelligence learned that one division, perhaps the *9th,* had been moved from Okinawa to Formosa in December 1944. In March 1945 American intelligence estimated that the Japanese forces on Okinawa consisted of the following troops, which included 26 battalions of infantry:

Headquarters 32d Army	625
24th Division (triangular)	15,000–17,000
62d Division (square)	11,500
44th Independent Mixed Brigade	6,000
One independent mixed regiment	2,500
One tank regiment	750
One medium artillery regiment, two mortar battalions, one antitank battalion, three antitank companies, and antiaircraft units	5,875
Air-ground personnel	3,500
Service and construction troops	5,000–6,000
Naval-ground troops	3,000
Total	53,000–56,000

[16] III Amph Corps Actn Rpt Ryukyus, 1 Jul 45, p. 10.

[17] Comdr in Chief Pacific Ocean Areas (CINCPOA) Joint Staff Study ICEBERG, Serial 00031, 25 Oct 44, p. 8.

[18] Tenth Army Tent Opn Plan 1–45, 6 Jan 45, Annex 3, G–2 Current Estimates, p. 10; CINCPAC-CINCPOA Bull No. 53–45, 28 Feb 45: Okinawa Gunto, p. 14. The only mention of possible civilian conscription is in Tenth Army Estimate of the Situation, 3 Nov 44, p. 2.

It was considered possible that elements of the *9th* and *28th Divisions* might also be present on Okinawa proper. Enemy forces were known to be organized under the *32d Army,* commanded, it was thought, by General Watanabe, with headquarters at Naha. Shortly before the landings the estimate of Japanese troops was raised to 65,000 on the basis of long-range search-plane reports of convoy movements into Naha.[19]

Calculations based on Japanese Tables of Organization indicated that the enemy could be expected to have 198 pieces of artillery of 70-mm. or larger caliber, including twenty-four 150-mm. howitzers.[20] The Japanese were presumed to have also about 100 antitank guns of 37-mm. and 47-mm. caliber in addition to the guns carried on tanks. The tank regiment on Okinawa had, according to Japanese Tables of Organization, 37 light and 47 medium tanks, but one estimate in March placed the total number of tanks at 90. Intelligence also indicated that rockets and mortars up to 250 mm. could be expected.[21]

Aerial photographs disclosed three main defense areas on Okinawa, centering in Naha, the Hagushi beaches, and the Yonabaru–Nakagusuku Bay area on the east coast. Prepared positions for four infantry regiments were noted along the bay; for one regiment, behind the Hagushi beaches; and for one battalion, along the beaches at Machinato above Naha. It was believed that a total of five or six battalions of troops would be found in the northern part of Okinawa and Ie Shima and that two divisions would be concentrated in southern Okinawa. The main strength of the Japanese artillery was believed to be concentrated in two groups—one about two miles east of Yontan airfield and the other about three miles due south of Shuri; the probable presence of guns was deduced from the spoil which had been deposited in front of cave or tunnel entrances on the slopes of ridges in a manner suitable for gun emplacements.[22]

At the end of March 1945 intelligence indicated that there were four operational airfields on Okinawa—at Naha, Yontan, Kadena, and Machinato; the first two were the best. All were heavily defended with numerous antiaircraft and dual purpose gun emplacements. The Yonabaru strip, which had been in an initial stage of construction in October 1944, was reported as having been aban-

---

[19] XXIV Corps G–2 Summary No. 3 ICEBERG, 6 Mar 45; XXIV Corps Actn Rpt Ryukyus, 1 Apr 45–30 Jun 45, p. 116.
[20] CINCPAC-CINCPOA Bull No. 53–45, p. 14.
[21] XXIV Corps G–2 Summary No. 3; CINCPOA Joint Staff Study ICEBERG; Comdr Amph Forces Pacific Fleet (CTF 51) Opn Plan A1–45, 16 Feb 45, Annex B: Int Plan.
[22] CTF 51 Opn Plan A1–45, Annex B: Int Plan; CINCPAC-CINCPOA Bull No. 53–45, pp. 8–12; CINCPAC-CINCPOA Bull No. 161–44, 15 Nov 44, pp. 110–12.

doned by February 1945. Apparently not intending to defend Ie Shima very determinedly, the Japanese, in the latter part of March, were reported to have rendered the airfield there unusable by digging trenches across the runways.[23] Land-based enemy aircraft on Okinawa was not expected to constitute a danger; the Americans fully expected that the airfields would be neutralized by the time they invaded the island. It was reported on 29 March, however, that enemy fighter and transport planes were being flown in at night to the Kadena airfield. On 31 March no activity was observed on any of the Okinawa airfields. It was constantly stressed that heavy enemy air attacks would probably be launched from Kyushu, 350 miles to the north. The potential threat of small suicide boats against shipping was also pointed out.[24]

Tenth Army believed that the most critical terrain for the operation was the area between the Ishikawa Isthmus and the Chatan–Toguchi line, particularly the high ground inland which dominates the Hagushi beaches and the valley of the Bishi River. The enemy could defend the beaches from prepared positions with one regiment, maintaining mobile reserves in the hills north and south of the river. Other reserves could be dispatched to the landing area within a few hours. It was expected that the Japanese would wait until the night of L Day to move their artillery. Alerted by American preliminary operations, they might have a division in position ready for a counterattack on the morning of the landings. From terrain 3,000 yards inland that offered both cover and concealment, the Japanese could launch counterattacks of division strength against both flanks of the landing area simultaneously. If the landings were successful, the enemy's main line of resistance, manned by a force of from nine to fifteen battalions, was expected to be at the narrow waist of the island, from Chatan to Toguchi, south of the landing beaches.[25]

The Plan of Attack

The plan for the conquest of the Ryukyus was in many respects the culmination of the experience of all previous operations in the Pacific war. It embodied the lessons learned in the long course of battle against the Japanese out-

---

[23] CINCPAC-CINCPOA Bull No. 53–45, pp. 15–24; USAFPOA G–2 Objective Data Section, 1 Feb 45: Study of Okinawa Gunto; Tenth Army Actn Rpt, Ch. 7, Sec. IV, p. 1 (hereafter cited by chapter, section, and page as follows: 7–IV–1).

[24] Tenth Army Tent Opn Plan 1–45, Annex 3: G–2 Current Estimates; 96 Div FO No. 12, 5 Mar 45, Annex 4, App. 1, p. 3; Tenth Army Opns Summary No. 10, 29 Mar 45, and No. 16, 31 Mar 45.

[25] Tenth Army Tent Opn Plan 1–45, Annex 3: G–2 Current Estimates.

AMERICAN COMMANDERS *in Operation ICEBERG: Admiral Raymond A. Spruance, Fleet Admiral Chester W. Nimitz, and Lt. Gen. Simon B. Buckner.*

posts in the Pacific—lessons of cooperation and combined striking power of the services, of the technique of amphibious operations, and of Japanese tactics and methods of meeting them. The plan for ICEBERG brought together an aggregate of military power—men, guns, ships, and planes—that had accumulated during more than three years of total war. The plan called for joint operations against the inner bastion of the Japanese Empire by the greatest concentration of land, sea, and air forces ever used in the Pacific.

Basic Features of the Plan

The immediate task imposed upon the American forces by the terms of the general mission was the seizure and development of Okinawa and the establishment of control of the sea and air in the Ryukyus. The campaign was divided into three phases. The seizure of southern Okinawa, including Keise Shima and islands in the Kerama Group, and the initiation of the development of base facilities were to constitute the first phase. In the next phase Ie Shima was to be occupied and control was to be established over northern Okinawa. The third phase consisted of the seizure and development of additional islands in the Nansei Shoto for use in future operations. The target date of the operation was set at 1 March 1945.[26]

Planning began in October 1944. The general scheme for Operation ICEBERG was issued in the fall of 1944 by Admiral Nimitz as Commander in Chief, Pacific Ocean Areas (CINCPOA). The strategic plan outlined was based on three assumptions. First, the projected campaign against Iwo Jima would have progressed to such an extent that naval fire-support and close air-support units would be available for the assault on Okinawa. Second, the necessary ground and naval combat units and assault shipping engaged in the Philippines would be released promptly by General MacArthur for the Okinawa campaign. Third, preliminary air and naval operations against the enemy would ensure control of the air in the area of the target during the operation.[27]

Air superiority was the most important factor in the general concept of the operation as outlined by Admiral Nimitz's staff. The CINCPOA planners believed that American air attacks on Japan, from carriers and from airfields in the Marianas, combined with the seizure of Iwo Jima, would force a concentration of enemy air strength around the heart of the Empire—on the home islands, Formosa, the China coast, and the Ryukyus. From these bases, strong

---

[26] CINCPOA Joint Staff Study ICEBERG, p. 1. This was not a directive but a basis for planning the operation.

[27] *Ibid.*

CHART I

Organization of Allied Forces for the Ryukyus Campaign, January 1945

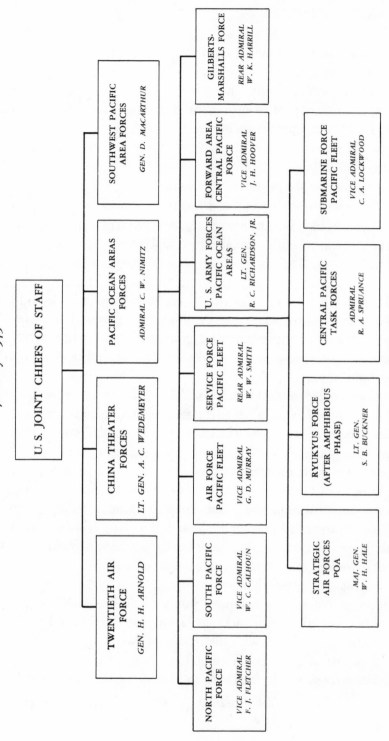

Source: Commander in Chief, U. S. Pacific Fleet and Pacific Ocean Areas, Operations in the Pacific Ocean Areas, April 1945, Plate I, opp. p. 76 (with adaptations).

and continuous air attacks would be made against the forces invading the
Ryukyus. It would be necessary, therefore, to neutralize or destroy enemy air
installations not only at the target but also at the staging areas in Kyushu and
Formosa. All available carrier- and land-based air forces would be called on to
perform this task and give the Americans the control of the air required in the
area of operations. On Okinawa itself, the scheme of maneuver of the ground
troops would be such as to gain early use of airfields that would enable land-
based planes to maintain control of the air in the target area. Control of the
sea was to be maintained by submarine, surface, and air attacks on enemy naval
forces and shipping.[28]

The American Forces

The isolation of Okinawa was to be effected with the aid of land-based air
forces of commands outside the Pacific Ocean Areas (POA). Planes from the
Southwest Pacific Area (SWPA) were to engage in searches and continuous
strikes against Formosa as soon as the situation on Luzon permitted. Twentieth
Air Force B–29's from China and the Marianas were to bomb Formosa, Kyushu,
and Okinawa during the month preceding the landings. The China-based XX
Bomber Command was to concentrate on Formosa, while the XXI Bomber
Command from the Marianas would attack Okinawa and then shift to Kyushu
and other vulnerable points in the home islands during the fighting on Okinawa.
The Fourteenth Air Force was to conduct searches along the China coast and
also, if practicable, bomb Hong Kong.[29]

All the forces in Admiral Nimitz's command were marshaled in support
of the ICEBERG Operation. (See Chart I.) The Strategic Air Forces, POA,
was assigned the task of neutralizing enemy air bases in the Carolines and the
Bonins, of striking Okinawa and Japan when practicable, and of providing
fighter cover for Twentieth Air Force bombing missions against Japan. The
Commander, Forward Areas Central Pacific, was to use his naval air strength
to provide antisubmarine coverage, neutralize bypassed enemy bases, and, in
general, furnish logistic support. Provision of intelligence on enemy naval units
and interdiction of the sea approaches from Japan and Formosa were the tasks
of the Submarine Force, Pacific Fleet. The enemy was to be contained in the
North Pacific Area, and the lines of communication were to be secured in the
Marshalls–Gilberts area. Logistic support was to be provided by General Rich-

[28] *Ibid.*, pp. 2–4.

[29] Fifth Fleet Opn Plan 1–45, 3 Jan 45, Annex E: Air Plan.

CHART II

Organization of Central Pacific Task Forces for the Ryukyus Campaign, January 1945

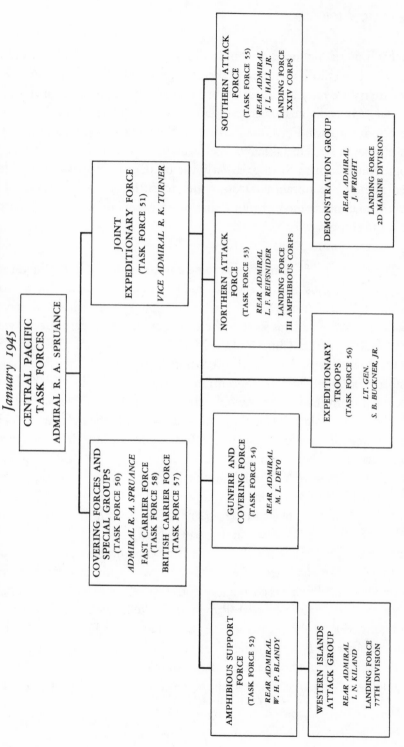

CENTRAL PACIFIC
TASK FORCES
ADMIRAL R. A. SPRUANCE

COVERING FORCES AND
SPECIAL GROUPS
(TASK FORCE 50)
ADMIRAL R. A. SPRUANCE
FAST CARRIER FORCE
(TASK FORCE 58)
BRITISH CARRIER FORCE
(TASK FORCE 57)

JOINT
EXPEDITIONARY FORCE
(TASK FORCE 51)
VICE ADMIRAL R. K. TURNER

AMPHIBIOUS SUPPORT
FORCE
(TASK FORCE 52)
REAR ADMIRAL
W. H. P. BLANDY

WESTERN ISLANDS
ATTACK GROUP
REAR ADMIRAL
I. N. KILAND
LANDING FORCE
77TH DIVISION

GUNFIRE AND
COVERING FORCE
(TASK FORCE 54)
REAR ADMIRAL
M. L. DEYO

EXPEDITIONARY
TROOPS
(TASK FORCE 56)
LT. GEN.
S. B. BUCKNER, JR.

NORTHERN ATTACK
FORCE
(TASK FORCE 53)
REAR ADMIRAL
L. F. REIFSNIDER
LANDING FORCE
III AMPHIBIOUS CORPS

SOUTHERN ATTACK
FORCE
(TASK FORCE 55)
REAR ADMIRAL
J. L. HALL, JR.
LANDING FORCE
XXIV CORPS

DEMONSTRATION GROUP
REAR ADMIRAL
J. WRIGHT
LANDING FORCE
2D MARINE DIVISION

Source: Commander in Chief, U. S. Pacific Fleet and Pacific Ocean Areas, Operations in the Pacific Ocean Areas, April 1945, Plates I and II, opp. p. 76 (with adaptations).

ardson's United States Army Forces, POA (USAFPOA), the Air and Service Forces, Pacific Fleet, and the South Pacific Force. All the armed forces in the Pacific Ocean Areas, from the West Coast to Ulithi and from New Zealand to the Aleutians, were directed to support the attack on Okinawa.[30]

The principal mission in seizing the objective was assigned to a huge joint Army-Navy task force, known as the Central Pacific Task Forces and commanded by Admiral Raymond A. Spruance, Commander of the Fifth Fleet. (See Chart II.) Admiral Spruance's forces consisted of naval covering forces and special groups (Task Force 50), which he personally commanded, and a Joint Expeditionary Force (Task Force 51), commanded by Vice Admiral Richmond K. Turner, Commander, Amphibious Forces Pacific Fleet. General Buckner, Commanding General, Tenth Army, was to lead the Expeditionary Troops (Task Force 56) under Admiral Turner's direction.[31]

Command relationships prescribed for the operation differed in some respects from those in previous operations against island positions remote from Japan. Because the campaign would entail prolonged ground combat activities by a field army on a large island close to the enemy's homeland, it was necessary to define clearly the relationships between Army and Navy commanders for the successive phases of the operation. Admiral Nimitz accordingly provided that initially the chain of command for amphibious operations would be Admiral Spruance, Admiral Turner, General Buckner. However, when Admiral Spruance determined that the amphibious phases of the operation had been successfully completed, General Buckner was to assume command of all forces ashore. He was thereafter to be directly responsible to Admiral Spruance for the defense and development of the captured positions. In time, Admiral Spruance would be relieved by Admiral Nimitz of these responsibilities, and General Buckner would take over complete command of the forces in the Ryukyus. As Commander, Ryukyus Force, a joint task force of ground, air, and naval garrison troops, he would be responsible only to CINCPOA for the defense and development of the newly won bases and for the protection of the sea areas within twenty-five miles.[32]

Admiral Spruance, as commander of Task Force 50, had at his disposal Vice Admiral Mitscher's Fast Carrier Force (Task Force 58), a British Carrier Force

[30] CINCPOA Opn Plan 14–44, 31 Dec 44, with changes to 20 Jul 45, p. 3; CINCPAC-CINCPOA Opns in the Pacific Ocean Areas during Apr 45, 16 Oct 45, Plate I.

[31] Rad CINCPOA to CG Tenth Army, 9 Oct 44, cited in Tenth Army Actn Rpt, 3–0–1.

[32] CINCPOA Opn Plan 14–44, Annex F: Command Relationships in Ryukyus Opn.

CHART III

Organization of Expeditionary Troops for the Ryukyus Campaign, January 1945

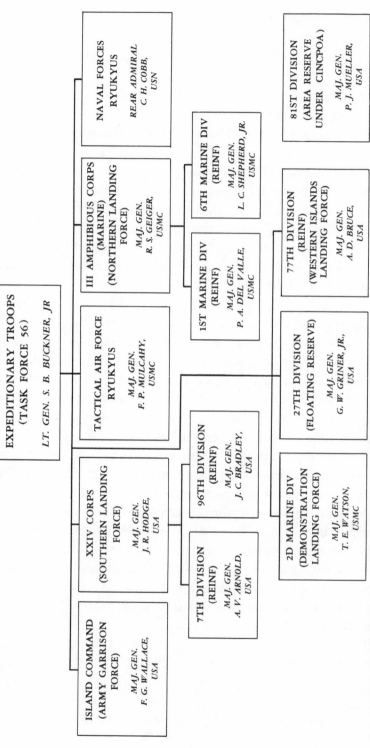

EXPEDITIONARY TROOPS (TASK FORCE 56)
LT. GEN. S. B. BUCKNER, JR

ISLAND COMMAND (ARMY GARRISON FORCE)
MAJ. GEN. F. G. WALLACE, USA

XXIV CORPS (SOUTHERN LANDING FORCE)
MAJ. GEN. J. R. HODGE, USA

TACTICAL AIR FORCE RYUKYUS
MAJ. GEN. F. P. MULCAHY, USMC

III AMPHIBIOUS CORPS (MARINE) (NORTHERN LANDING FORCE)
MAJ. GEN. R. S. GEIGER, USMC

NAVAL FORCES RYUKYUS
REAR ADMIRAL C. H. COBB, USN

81ST DIVISION (AREA RESERVE UNDER CINCPOA)
MAJ. GEN. P. J. MUELLER, USA

7TH DIVISION (REINF)
MAJ. GEN. A. V. ARNOLD, USA

96TH DIVISION (REINF)
MAJ. GEN. J. C. BRADLEY, USA

1ST MARINE DIV (REINF)
MAJ. GEN. P. A. DEL VALLE, USMC

6TH MARINE DIV (REINF)
MAJ. GEN. L. C. SHEPHERD, JR. USMC

2D MARINE DIV (DEMONSTRATION LANDING FORCE)
MAJ. GEN. T. E. WATSON, USMC

27TH DIVISION (FLOATING RESERVE)
MAJ. GEN. G. W. GRINER, JR., USA

77TH DIVISION (REINF) (WESTERN ISLANDS LANDING FORCE)
MAJ. GEN. A. D. BRUCE, USA

Source: Commander Task Force 51, Commander Amphibious Forces, U. S. Pacific Fleet, Report on Okinawa Gunto Operations from 17 February to 17 May 1945, Part I, pp. 2–4; Tenth Army Action Report Ryukyus, 26 March to 30 June 1945, Ch. 2; Commander in Chief, U. S. Pacific Fleet and Pacific Ocean Areas, Operations in the Pacific Ocean Areas, April 1945.

(Task Force 57), special task groups for aerial search and reconnaissance and antisubmarine warfare, and fleet logistic groups. Task Force 58 had a major share of the mission of neutralizing Japanese air strength. Its fast carriers were to strike Kyushu, Okinawa, and adjacent islands in the middle of March, to remain in a covering position east of the target area during the week preceding the invasion, to support the landings with strikes and patrols, and to be prepared for further forays against Kyushu, the China coast, or threatening enemy surface forces. The British carriers, the first to participate in Pacific naval actions with the American fleet, were given the task of neutralizing air installations on the Sakishima Group, southwest of the Ryukyus, during the ten days before the landings.[33]

The Joint Expeditionary Force (Task Force 51) was directly charged with the capture and development of Okinawa and other islands in the group. It was a joint task force of Army, Navy, and Marine units and consisted of the Expeditionary Troops (Task Force 56—see Chart III), shipping to transport them, and supporting naval and air units. Direct naval and air support for Task Force 51 was to be furnished by its Amphibious Support Force (Task Force 52), made up of escort carriers, gunboat and mortar flotillas, mine sweepers, and underwater demolition teams, and by the Gunfire and Covering Force (Task Force 54) of old battleships, light and heavy cruisers, destroyers, and destroyer escorts. The transports and tractor units of the Northern Attack Force (Task Force 53) and Southern Attack Force (Task Force 55) were to land the ground troops in the main assault on the Okinawa beaches, while a number of task groups were assigned the task of transporting the troops for subsidiary landings and the floating and area reserves. Task Force 51 also included a transport screen, a service and salvage group, and several specialized naval units.[34]

The troops who would assault the objectives constituted a field army, the Tenth Army, which had been activated in the United States in June 1944 and shortly thereafter had opened headquarters on Oahu. General Buckner formally assumed command in September 1944, having come to the new assignment from the command of the Alaskan Department, where for four years he had been organizing the American defenses in that area. His new staff included many officers who had served with him in Alaska as well as some from the European Theater of Operations. The major components of Tenth Army were

[33] Fifth Fleet Opn Plan 1–45, pp. 1, 5, Annex E: Air Plan.

[34] CTF 51 Opn Plan A1–45, 16 Feb 45, p. 1.

XXIV Army Corps and III Amphibious Corps (Marine). The former con-
sisted of the 7th and 96th Infantry Divisions and was commanded by Maj.
Gen. John R. Hodge, a veteran leader of troops who had met and defeated the
Japanese on Guadalcanal, New Georgia, Bougainville, and Leyte. III Amphibious
Corps included the 1st and 6th Marine Divisions and was headed by Maj. Gen.
Roy S. Geiger, who had successfully directed Marine operations on Bougainville
and Guam. Three divisions, the 27th and 77th Infantry Divisions and the
2d Marine Division, were under the direct control of Tenth Army for use in
special operations and as reserves. The area reserve, the 81st Infantry Division,
was under the control of CINCPOA. Also assigned to Tenth Army for the purpose of defense and development of the objectives were a naval task group, the
Tactical Air Force, and the Island Command.[35]

A total of 183,000 troops was made available for the assault phases of the
operation.[36] About 154,000 of these were in the seven combat divisions, excluding
the 81st Division, which remained in New Caledonia; all seven divisions were
heavily reinforced with tank battalions, amphibian truck and tractor battalions,
joint assault signal companies, and many attached service units. The five divisions
committed to the initial landings totaled about 116,000. The 1st and 6th Marine
Divisions, with 26,274 and 24,356 troops, respectively, each carried an attached
naval construction battalion and about 2,500 replacements in addition to their
other supporting combat and service units. The reinforced 7th, 77th, and 96th
Divisions averaged nearly 22,000 men per division but each was about 1,000
understrength in organic infantry personnel. The 27th, a reserve division, was
reinforced to a strength of 16,143 but remained nevertheless almost 2,000 understrength organically. The 2d Marine Division, also in Army reserve, numbered
22,195.[37] (See Appendix C, Table No. 4.)

Tenth Army, as such, had never directed any campaigns, but its corps and
divisions had all been combat-tested before the invasion of the Ryukyus. XXIV
Corps had carried out the conquest of Leyte, and III Amphibious Corps had
captured Guam and Peleliu. The 7th Division had seen action on Attu,
Kwajalein, and Leyte, the 77th on Guam and Leyte, and the 96th on Leyte.
The 27th had taken part in the battles for the Gilberts and Marshalls and for

---

[35] Tenth Army Tent Opn Plan 1–45, 6 Jan 45, pp. 1–10.

[36] CTF 51 Actn Rpt, Pt. V, Table 1.

[37] *Ibid.*, Tables 2a–2g: III Amph Corps Actn Rpt Ryukyus, 1 Jul 45, p. 28; XXIV Corps Actn Rpt
Ryukyus, p. 6; 7th Div Actn Rpt Ryukyus, 30 Jul 45, Annex I, App. B, pp. 1, 2; 27th Div Actn Rpt
Ryukyus, 19 Jul 45, p. 10; 96th Div Actn Rpt Ryukyus, Ch. IX, p. 21.

Saipan. The 1st Marine Division had been one of the first to see action in the Pacific, on Guadalcanal, and had gone through the campaigns of Western New Britain and Peleliu. The 6th Marine Division had been activated late in 1944, but its regiments were largely made up of seasoned units that had fought on Guam, the Marshalls, and Saipan. The 2d Marine Division had participated in the fighting on Guadalcanal, Tarawa, Saipan, and Tinian.

Plan for the Capture of Okinawa

Using the CINCPOA Joint Staff Study as a basis, each of the major commanders prepared his plans and issued his operation orders. Although each plan and operation order was derived from that of the next superior echelon, planning was always concurrent. The joint nature of the operation also required extensive coordination of the three services in all operational and logistical problems. Joint conferences thrashed out problems of troop lists, shipping, supplies, and strategy. Corps and task force commanders worked together on the plans for amphibious operations. Corps and division staffs were consulted and advised by Army for purposes of orientation and planning. To ensure interservice coordination, Navy and Marine officers were assigned to work with Tenth Army general and special staff sections.[38] In some cases planning was facilitated by utilizing the results of work on other operations. Thus the naval staff developing the gunfire support plans was able to use the operations at Iwo Jima to test and strengthen the general command and communications framework, which was generally similar for both operations; in the same way Tenth Army logistical planners took advantage of their work on the canceled Formosa operation, adapting it to the needs of the Okinawa campaign.[39]

Out of these planning activities came extremely important decisions that modified and expanded the scope of proposed operations. Tenth Army found it necessary to enlarge the troop list by about 70,000 to include greater numbers of supporting combat elements and service units. Its staff presented and supported a plan for initial assault landings on the west coast of Okinawa, just north and south of Hagushi, as the most feasible logistically and as consonant tactically with the requirements of CINCPOA. The naval staff insisted on the necessity of a sustained week-long naval bombardment of the target and on the consequent need for a protected anchorage in the target area where the fleet units could refuel and resupply. As a result it was decided to capture the Kerama Islands

[38] Tenth Army Actn Rpt, Ch. 3: Preliminary Planning.

[39] CTF 51 Actn Rpt, V–C–1; Tenth Army Actn Rpt, II–IV–3, 4.

just west of Okinawa, a week before the main landings, and the 77th Division
was assigned this task. At the suggestion of Admiral Turner a landing was to
be feinted on the eastern coast of the island, and the 2d Marine Division was
selected for this operation. The commitment of these two reserve divisions
impelled Tenth Army to secure the release of the area reserve division to the
Expeditionary Troops, and the 27th Division was designated the floating reserve.
In its place, as area reserve, the 81st Division was ordered to stand by in the South
Pacific. Finally, CINCPOA was twice forced to set back the target date because
delays in the Luzon operation created difficulty in maintaining shipping schedules and because unfavorable weather conditions appeared likely in the target
area during March. L Day (landing day) was set for 1 April 1945.[40]

As finally conceived, the plan for the capture of Okinawa gave fullest
opportunity for the use of the mobility, long range, and striking power of
combined arms. After the strategic isolation of Okinawa had been effected by
land- and carrier-based aircraft, the amphibious forces were to move forward
to the objective. Task Force 52 (the Amphibious Support Force) and Task Force
54 (the Gunfire and Covering Force), assisted by the fast carriers of Task
Force 58, were to begin operations at Okinawa and the Kerama Group on L
minus 8 (24 March). They were to destroy the enemy defenses and air installations by naval gunfire and air strikes, clear the waters around the objective and
the beaches of mines and other obstacles, and provide cover and protection
against hostile surface and air units to ensure the safe and uninterrupted
approach of the transports and the landings of the assault troops. After the
landings they were to furnish naval support and air cover for the land
operations.[41]

Mine sweepers were to be the first units of the Amphibious Support Force
to arrive in the target area. Beginning on L minus 8, they were to clear the way
for the approach of the bombardment units and then to sweep the waters in
the landing and demonstration areas to the shore line.[42] Underwater demolition
teams were to follow the mine sweepers, reconnoiter the beaches, and demolish
beach obstacles.[43]

Naval gunfire was to support the capture of Okinawa by scheduled destructive bombardment in the week before the landings, by intensive close support

[40] Tenth Army Actn Rpt, Ch. 3: Preliminary Planning.
[41] CTF 51 Opn Plan A1–45, p. 35.
[42] *Ibid.*, Annex A; CTF 52 Actn Rpt Okinawa, 1 May 45, V–H–1.
[43] CTF 52 Actn Rpt, V–G–1.

of the main and subsidiary landings and the diversionary feint, and thereafter by delivering call and other support fires. The fire support ships with their 5- to 16-inch guns were organized into fire support units, each consisting of 2 old battleships, 2 or 3 cruisers, and 4 or 5 destroyers, that were to stand off the southern part of the island in accordance with definite areas of responsibility. In view of the size of the objective and the impossibility of destroying all targets, fire during the prelanding bombardment was to be laid on carefully selected targets; the principal efforts were to be directed to the destruction of weapons threatening ships and aircraft and of the defenses opposing the landings. Profitable targets were at all times to be sought by close observation, exploratory firing, and constant evaluation of results. Covering fires were to be furnished in conjunction with fire from gunboats and mortar boats in support of mine-sweeping operations and beach demolitions.[44]

On L Day, beginning at 0600, the naval guns were to mass their fires on the beaches. Counterbattery and deep supporting fires were to destroy the defense guns and keep enemy reinforcements from moving up to oppose the landings. As the assault waves approached the beaches, the fires of the big guns would lift to targets in critical areas inland and to the exterior flanks of the troops. Mortar boats and gunboats were to lead the boat waves to the shore, delivering mortar and rocket fire on the beaches. All craft would begin 40-mm. fire on passing the line of fire support ships and would fire at will until H Hour.[45] After the landings scheduled fire on areas 1,000 yards inland and on the flanks would be continued, but top priority would be given to call fires in direct support of the assault elements.[46]

All scheduled bombardments until H minus 35 minutes were to be under control of the commander of Task Force 52. After that time, because of the size of the landing forces and the extent of the beaches, the commanders of the Northern and Southern Attack Forces would assume control of the support of their respective landing forces. The commander of Task Force 51 was to remain responsible for the general coordination as well as the actual control of bombardment in the Army zone. By 1500 each day he would allocate gunfire support vessels for the succeeding twenty-four hours in accordance with approved requests from Army and Corps.[47]

[44] CTF 51 Opn Plan A1–45, Annex G: Ship's Gunfire Support Plan.
[45] Ibid., App. III.
[46] Tenth Army Tent Opn Plan 1–45, Annex 6: Naval Gunfire Support.
[47] Ibid., CTF 51 Opn Plan A1–45, Annex G: Ship's Gunfire Support Plan.

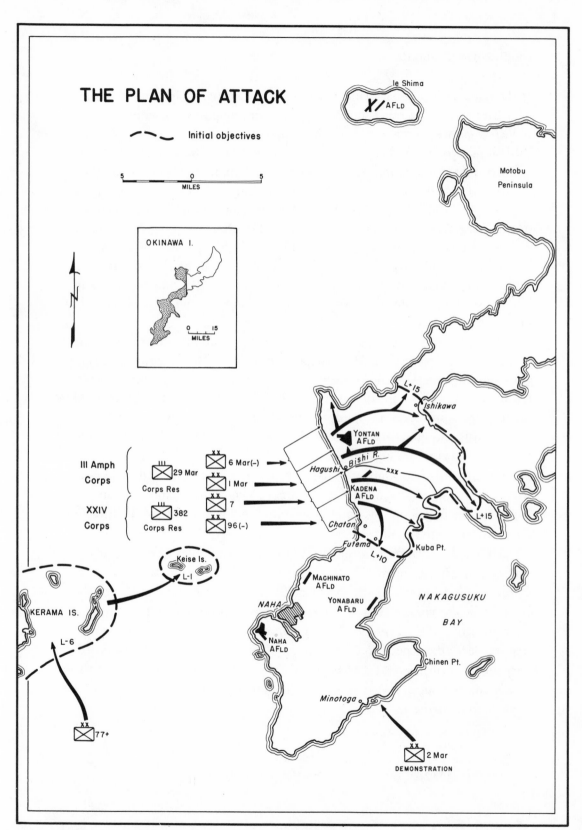

THE PLAN OF ATTACK

- - - Initial objectives

5   0   5
MILES

OKINAWA I.

0   15
MILES

Ie Shima

✗ AFLD

Motobu Peninsula

L+15
Ishikawa

YONTAN AFLD

III Amph Corps { 29 Mar   6 Mar(−) →
               Corps Res

XXIV Corps { 382   7 →
            Corps Res   96(−) →

Hagushi   Bishi R.   xxx

KADENA AFLD

L+15

Chatan

Futema   L+10   Kuba Pt.

Keise Is.
L-1

KERAMA IS.

L-6

77+

MACHINATO AFLD

NAHA

YONABARU AFLD

NAHA AFLD

NAKAGUSUKU

BAY

Chinen Pt.

Minotoga

77   2 Mar
DEMONSTRATION

MAP NO. 3

Air support was to be provided largely by the fast carriers of Task Force 58 and by the escort carriers of Task Force 52. The fast carriers were for the first time to be available at the target area for a prolonged period to furnish support and combat air patrols. They were to cover mine-sweeping operations, hit targets on Okinawa which could not be reached by naval gunfire, destroy enemy defenses and air installations, and strafe the landing beaches. The escort carriers would provide aircraft for direct support missions, antisubmarine patrols, naval and artillery gunfire spotting, air supply, photographic missions, and the dropping of propaganda leaflets. After L Day additional support was to be furnished by seaplane squadrons based on the Kerama Islands and by the shore-based Tactical Air Force of the Tenth Army.[48] The latter was eventually to be responsible for the air defense of the area, being charged with gaining the necessary air superiority and giving tactical support to the ground troops.[49]

Provision was made for the careful coordination of all naval gunfire, air support, and artillery both in the assault and in the campaign in general. Target information centers, to be established at army, corps, and division levels, would collect and disseminate data on all targets suitable for attack by the respective arms and keep a record of attacks actually carried out. In addition, at every echelon, from battalion to army, representatives of each support arm—artillery, naval gunfire, and air—were to coordinate the use of their respective arms for targets in their zones of action and advise their commanders on the proper employment of the various types of supporting fires. Requests for support would thus be coordinated and screened as they passed up through the various echelons for approval.[50]

Under cover of the sustained day and night attacks by the naval and air forces, the first phase of the campaign—the capture of the Kerama and Keise Islands and of the southern part of Okinawa—was to begin. On L minus 6, the Western Islands Attack Group was to land the reinforced 77th Division on the Kerama Islands. The seizure of these islands was designed to give the Joint Expeditionary Force, prior to the main assault on Okinawa proper, a base for logistic support of fleet units, a protected anchorage, and a seaplane base. Two regimental combat teams were to land on several of the islands simultaneously and to proceed from the southeast end of the group to the northeast by island-

[48] CTF 51 Opn Plan A1–45, Annex H: Air Support Plan.

[49] Tenth Army Tent Opn Plan 1–45, Annex 7: Air Support Plan.

[50] Tenth Army Tent Opn Plan 1–45, Annex 5: Planning and Coordination of Artillery, Naval Gunfire and Air Support.

hopping maneuvers, capturing Keise Island by L minus 1. All hostile coastal defense guns that could interfere with the construction of the proposed naval bases were to be destroyed. Organized enemy forces would be broken up without attempting to clear the islands of snipers. Two battalions of 155-mm. guns were to be emplaced on Keise in order to give artillery support to the landings on the coast of Okinawa. Then, after stationing a small garrison force in the islands, the division would reembark and be prepared to execute the Tenth Army's reserve plans, giving priority to the capture of Ie Shima.[51] (See Map No. 3.)

While the 77th Division was taking the lightly held Kerama Islands, the preliminary operations for softening up Okinawa would begin; they would mount in intensity as L Day approached. Beginning on 28 March fire support units would close in on the island behind the mine sweepers and demolition teams. The Northern and Southern Attack Forces would arrive off the west coast early on L Day and land their respective ground forces at H Hour, tentatively set for 0830. III Amphibious Corps would land, two divisions abreast, on the left flank, north of the town of Hagushi at the mouth of the Bishi River: XXIV Corps would land, two divisions abreast, on the right flank, south of Hagushi. The four divisions in landing would be in the following order from north to south; 6th Marine Division, 1st Marine Division, 7th Division, and 96th Division. The two corps were then to drive across the island in a coordinated advance. The 6th Marine Division was first to capture the Yontan airfield and then to advance to the Ishikawa Isthmus, the narrow neck of the island, securing the beachhead on the north by L plus 15. The 1st Marine Division was to head across the island and drive down the Katchin Peninsula on the east coast. South of the Corps' boundary, which ran eastward from the mouth of the Bishi, the 7th Division would quickly seize the Kadena airfield and advance to the east coast, cutting the island in two. The 96th was required initially to capture the high ground commanding its beaches on the south and southeast; then it was to move rapidly down the coastal road, capture the bridges near Chatan, and protect the right of the Corps. Continuing its attack, it was to pivot on its right flank to secure the beachhead on the south by L plus 10 on a line running across the isthmus below Kuba and Futema.[52]

The choice of the beaches north and south of Hagushi for the initial assault was made after a study by Tenth Army of all the landing beaches in southern

---

[51] CTF 51 Opn Plan A1–45, Annex A, pp. 35, 38; 77th Div Opn Plan ICEBERG, 18 Feb 45, Opn Plan I (Preferred Plan).

[52] Tenth Army Tent Opn Plan 1–45, pp. 12–13; XXIV Corps FO 45, 8 Feb 45: Preferred Plan, pp. 2–6.

Okinawa and a survey of several plans of action. The various plans were weighed in the light of the requirements of the CINCPOA Joint Staff Study and considerations of tactical and logistical feasibility. The preferred plan was finally chosen for a number of reasons. First, it would secure the necessary airfields by L plus 5. Second, it would provide the unloading facilities to support the assault. The Hagushi beaches were considered the only ones capable of handling sufficient tonnage to sustain a force of two corps and supporting troops, and this seemed to outweigh the disadvantages of not providing for the early capture of the port of Naha and the anchorage in Nakagusuku Bay. Third, the plan would result in separating the enemy forces. Fourth, it would concentrate the troops on one continuous landing beach opposite the point where the greatest enemy resistance was expected. Fifth, it would use the terrain least advantageous for enemy resistance to the landings. Finally, it would permit maximum fire support of the assault.[53]

The scheme of maneuver was designed to isolate the initial objective, the southern part of the island, by seizing the Ishikawa Isthmus, north of the landing beaches, to prevent enemy reinforcement from that direction. At the same time the establishment of a general east-west line from Kuba on the south would prevent reinforcement from the south. Thereafter, the attack was to be continued until the entire southern part of the island was occupied.[54] Ground commanders hoped that, for the first time in the Pacific, maneuver could be used to the utmost. The troops would cut across the island quickly, move rapidly to the south, break up the Japanese forces into small segments, bypass strong points, and mop up at leisure.[55]

While the troops were landing on the west coast, the 2d Marine Division would feint landings on the southeast coast. This demonstration, scheduled for L Day and to be repeated on L plus 1, would be as realistic as possible in order to deceive the enemy into believing that landings would be made there as well as on the Hagushi beaches. After the demonstration the division would be prepared to land on the Hagushi beaches in support of the assault forces.[56]

The 27th Division, as floating reserve, was to arrive at Ulithi not later than L plus 1 and be on call of the Commander, Joint Expeditionary Force. It was

[53] Tenth Army Estimate of the Situation ICEBERG, 3 Nov 44, pp. 6–11.

[54] Tenth Army Tent Opn Plan 1–45, p. 12.

[55] Interv 1st I & H Off with Gen Buckner, CG Tenth Army, 21 Mar 45, and with Gen Hodge, CG XXIV Corps, 12 Mar 45.

[56] Tenth Army Tent Opn Plan 1–45, p. 13.

to be prepared to seize the islands off the east coast of Okinawa and then to land on that coast in support of XXIV Corps.[57]

In case the preferred plan for landing on the west coast proved impracticable, an alternate plan was to be used. In this plan, the capture of the Kerama Islands was to be followed by a similar sweep through the small islands east of southern Okinawa that guarded the entrance to Nakagusuku Bay. On L Day two Marine divisions would land on the southeast coast of Okinawa, between Chinen Point and the town of Minatoga. During the next three days the marines were to seize high ground in the area in order to support a landing by two divisions of XXIV Corps on the lower part of Nakagusuku Bay, between Kuba and Yonabaru. Although the alternate plan met most of the requirements for a successful landing operation, it was distinctly a second choice because it would allow the enemy reserves to offer maximum opposition to the second landings and would require a prolonged assault against all the enemy forces on the island to complete the first phase of the mission.[58]

Psychological Warfare and Military Government

Despite general skepticism as to the effectiveness of psychological warfare against the Japanese,[59] an attitude which resulted from its failure in many previous operations, the American plan called for an intensive effort to weaken the enemy's will to resist. Intelligence agencies prepared 5,700,000 leaflets to be dropped over Okinawa from carrier planes. More millions of leaflets were to be printed at the target and scattered over specific areas by bombs and shells. Tanks with amplifiers, an airplane with an ultraloud speaker, and remotely controlled radios dropped behind enemy lines would also tell the enemy why and how he should surrender.[60]

The plans for psychological warfare were also directed toward influencing the Okinawans, and in this connection there was greater optimism. Because the Okinawans were of a different stock and culture from the Japanese, and had been treated by their rulers as inferiors rather than as elements to be assimilated to Japanese nationalism and militarism, it was hoped that the civilians would not be as hostile, or at any rate as fanatical, as the Japanese.

[57] *Ibid.*, pp. 13–14.

[58] *Ibid.*, Annex 18; Tenth Army Estimate of the Situation ICEBERG, pp. 9, 11. Plan Baker was the basis for the alternate plan.

[59] Interv with Gen Buckner, CG, Tenth Army, 21 Mar 45, Command Ship *El Dorado*, off Leyte, and with Gen Hodge, CG, XXIV Corps, 12 Mar 45, Leyte; interv with 2d Lt Alfred S. Yudkoff, Combat Propaganda Team en route to Okinawa,—Mar 45.

[60] *Tentative Opn Plan, ICEBERG*, Annex 5, "Intelligence Plan," pp. 1–15.

The Okinawans also presented the American planners with the problem of military government. The problem was twofold—that of removing the Okinawans from the front lines and that of caring for them; it was necessary to handle the problem in such a way as to facilitate military operations and to make available to the occupying forces the labor and economic resources of the areas. Approximately 300,000 natives lived in southern Okinawa; thousands of others were in the north and on near-by islands. Never before in the Pacific had Americans faced the task of controlling so many enemy civilians.

Basic responsibility for military government in the conquered Japanese islands devolved on the Navy, and Admiral Nimitz was to assume the position of Military Governor of the Ryukyus. However, in view of the fact that most of the garrison forces were Army troops, Admiral Nimitz delegated the responsibility to General Buckner. The latter planned to control military government operations during the assault phase through his tactical commanders; corps and division commanders were made responsible for military government in the areas under their control and were assigned military government detachments whose mission was to plan and organize civilian activities behind the fighting fronts. As the campaign progressed and increasing numbers of civilians were encountered, teams attached to military government headquarters of Tenth Army would assume charge, organize camps, and administer the program on an island-wide basis. During the garrison phase the Island Commander, on order of General Buckner, would exercise command over all military government personnel. Maj. Gen. Fred C. Wallace would act through a Deputy Commander for Military Government, Brig. Gen. W. E. Crist.[61]

The major problem of Military Government was to feed and provide emergency medical care for the approximately 300,000 civilians who were expected to be within the American lines by L plus 40. Each of the combat divisions mounted out with 70,000 civilian rations of such native staples as rice, soy beans, and canned fish and also with medical supplies. Military Government personnel would land in the wake of assault units to handle a huge "disaster relief" program. Additional supplies of all kinds were to be included in the general maintenance shipments.[62]

[61] CINCPOA Opn Plan 14–44, Annex G; Tenth Army Tent Opn Plan 1–45, Annex 15: Military Government; Tenth Army Opnl Directive No. 7, 6 Jan 45; Tenth Army Tech Bull Mil Govt, 25 Feb 45, p. 5; Tenth Army Mil Govt Opn Rpt, 2 Aug 45.

[62] *Tentative Opn Plan, ICEBERG,* "Military Government Plan," Annex 15, pp. 1–5. Cf. App. I, Table of Population.

Mounting the Attack

Organizing the Supply Line

The planning and execution of ICEBERG presented logistical problems of a magnitude greater than any previously encountered in the Pacific. For the assault echelon alone, about 183,000 troops and 747,000 measurement tons of cargo were loaded into over 430 assault transports and landing ships at 11 different ports, from Seattle to Leyte, a distance of 6,000 miles. (See Appendix C, Tables Nos. 4 and 5.) After the landings, maintenance had to be provided for the combat troops and a continuously increasing garrison force that eventually numbered 270,000. Concurrently, the development of Okinawa as an advanced air and fleet base and mounting area for future operations involved supply and construction programs extending over a period of many months subsequent to the initial assault. Close integration of assault, maintenance, and garrison shipping and supply was necessary at all times.[63]

Factors of distance dominated the logistical picture. Cargo and troops were lifted on the West Coast, Oahu, Espiritu Santo, New Caledonia, Guadalcanal, the Russell Islands, Saipan, and Leyte, and were assembled at Eniwetok, Ulithi, Saipan, and Leyte. The closest Pacific Ocean Area bases were at Ulithi and the Marianas, 5 days' sailing time to Okinawa (at 10 knots). The West Coast, which furnished the bulk of resupply, was 6,250 nautical miles away, or 26 days' sailing time. Allowing 30 days to prepare and forward the requisitions, 60 days for procurement and loading on the West Coast, and 30 days for sailing to the target, the planners were faced with a 120-day interval between the initiation of their calculations and the arrival of supplies. This meant in practice that requisitioning had to be started before a Troop Basis had been fixed and the details of the tactical plans worked out. Distance, moreover, used up ships and compelled the adoption of a schedule of staggered supply shipments, or "echelons," as well as a number of other improvisations. Mounting the troops where they were stationed, in the scattered reaches of the Pacific Ocean and Southwest Pacific Areas, required close and intricate timing to have them at the target at the appointed moment.[64]

Broad logistic responsibilities for the support of ICEBERG were assigned by Admiral Nimitz to the various commanders chiefly concerned. Admiral Turner, as commander of the Amphibious Forces Pacific Fleet, furnished the

---

[63] CTF 51 Actn Rpt, I–5, 6, 7, and V–I–12; Tenth Army Actn Rpt, 11–IV–1, 2.

[64] CINCPOA Joint Staff Study, p. 29; Tenth Army Actn Rpt, 11–IV–1–12; Com Phibs Pac Op Ord A1–45.

shipping for the assault troops and their supplies, determined the loading schedules, and was responsible for the delivery of men and cargo to the beaches. General Buckner allocated assault shipping space to the elements of his command
and was responsible for landing the supplies and transporting them to the
dumps. The control of maintenance and garrison shipping, which was largely
loaded on the West Coast, was retained by CINCPOA. Responsibility for both
the initial supply and the resupply of all Army troops was assigned to the Commanding General, Pacific Ocean Areas, while the Commanders, Fleet Marine
Force, Service Force, and Air Force of the Pacific Fleet were charged with
logistic support of Marine, Navy, and naval aviation units. The initial supplies
for the troops mounting in the South Pacific and the Southwest Pacific were
to be furnished by the commanders of those areas.[65]

The first phase of supply planning involved the preparation of special lists
of equipment required for the operation, which included excess Tables of Equipment items, equipment peculiar to amphibious operations, and base development
materials. Such lists, or operational projects as they were known, had been prepared for the projected Formosa operation; when this was canceled the projects
were screened and reduced to meet the needs of ICEBERG.[66]

At a very early stage in the planning it became evident that there was a shortage of available shipping. The number of combat and service troops included in
the initial Troop Basis far exceeded the capacity of allocated shipping. As a
result, tonnage had to be reduced for some units while other units were eliminated entirely from the assault echelon and assigned space in the next echelon.
Later, in January 1945, it became apparent that there was still not enough shipping space in the assault echelon to transport certain air units and base development materials designed for early use. It was necessary to request CINCPOA to
increase the over-all allocation of LST's and LSM's, as well as to curtail cargo
tonnage and provide for the quick return of LST's to Saipan to load eight naval
construction battalions.[67]

Providing the assault troops with their initial supplies was not a difficult
problem as generally there were sufficient stocks on hand at each of the mounting
areas. When the assault units embarked, they took with them a 30-day supply of
rations, essential clothing and equipment, fuel, and medical and construction

[65] CINCPOA Opn Plan 14–44, Annex D, pp. 1, 2, 20, 21.

[66] Tenth Army Actn Rpt, 11–IV–3, 4.

[67] *Ibid.*, 5–0–4, 11–IV–8.

supplies. Initial ammunition quotas consisted of five CINCPOA units of fire.[68] On Leyte, XXIV Corps found that SWPA logistics agencies did not have sufficient rations on hand to supply it as required, and the shortage was overcome by having the Corps joined at Okinawa by two LST's loaded with rations from Tenth Army reserve stocks in the Marianas.[69]

Equipment issued to the troops included weapons and instruments of war never before used against the Japanese. New-type flame-thrower tanks, with an increased effective range and a larger fuel capacity, were available for the invasion. Each division was issued 110 sniperscopes and 140 snooperscopes, devices for seeing in the dark by means of infrared radiation; the former were mounted on carbines and permitted accurate night firing, while the latter were on hand-held mounts and could be used for night observation and signaling. Army artillery and antiaircraft units used proximity (VT) fuzes over land areas for the first time in the Pacific. During the campaign tests were conducted with a new mortar-locating device, the Sound Locator Set GR–6, and the 57-mm. and 75-mm. recoilless rifles and 4.2-inch recoilless mortars.[70]

Supplies to maintain the troops at the target were scheduled to arrive in twenty-one shipments from the West Coast. Loaded ships were to sail from Pacific ports at 10-day intervals, beginning on L minus 40 (20 February 1945), and to arrive at the regulating stations at Ulithi and Eniwetok beginning on L minus 5, there to await the call of General Buckner. These maintenance shipments, planned to provide automatic resupply until L plus 210 (31 October 1945), were based on the estimated population build-up at the scheduled time of arrival. The principal emergency reserves were kept at Saipan and Guam.[71]

The main logistical task of the operation, in Admiral Nimitz's opinion, was the rapid development of air and naval bases in the Ryukyus to support further operations against Japan. The Base Development Plan for Okinawa, published by CINCPOA, provided for the construction of eight airfields on Okinawa, two of which were to be operational by L plus 5, a seaplane base, an advanced fleet

---

[68] A CINCPOA U/F was a balanced assortment of ammunition based on Central Pacific experience. It included, among other types, 100 rounds for the M1 Rifle, 1,500 for the .30-caliber machine gun, 600 for the .50-caliber machine gun, 275 for the 60-mm. and 81-mm. mortars, 250 for the 105-mm. howitzer M2, and 150 for the 155-mm. howitzer. See Tenth Army Tent Opn Plan 1–45, Annex 13, App. B, Incl 1, for the complete description of CINCPOA U/F, 6 Dec 44.

[69] CINCPOA Opn Plan 14–44, Annex D, pp. 4–11; Tenth Army Actn Rpt, 11–IV–11; interv 1st I & H Off with Brig Gen David H. Blakelock, ACofS G–4, Tenth Army, 22 May 45.

[70] Tenth Army Actn Rpt, 11–III–8, 9; 11–XIV–15; USAFPOA, Participation in the Okinawa Operation, I, 63, 240. See also below, pp. 256–57.

[71] CINCPOA Opn Plan 14–44, Annex D, pp. 8–12; Tenth Army Actn Rpt, 11–IV–5.

base at Nakagusuku Bay, and the rehabilitation of the port of Naha to accommodate support shipping. Base development responsibilities also included immediate support of the assault by the early construction of tank farms for the bulk storage of fuel and for the improvement of waterfront unloading facilities and of roads. Later a large construction program was planned that included roads, dumps, hospitals, communications facilities, water supply systems, and housing and recreational facilities. A plan for the development of Ie Shima as an advanced air base was also prepared.[72]

General Buckner was charged with the responsibility for base development in the Ryukyus. Assigned to Tenth Army for the execution of the Base Development Plan was the Island Command Okinawa, or Army Garrison Force, with Maj. Gen. Fred C. Wallace in command. Some of the Island Command troops were to land in the assault echelon and to provide logistic support for the assault troops during and immediately after the landings. At the conclusion of the amphibious phase, the Island Command was to act as Tenth Army's administrative and logistical agency, operating in effect as an Army service command and an advanced section of the communications zone. As such, it was to be in charge of the base development program as well as of the garrisoning and defense of the captured positions. Garrison troops and base development materials were scheduled to arrive at Okinawa in seventeen echelons. These were based primarily on the unloading capacity of the Hagushi beaches; the tonnage in each echelon was kept within the estimated discharge capacity between the arrivals of the echelons. Most of this garrison shipping was loaded on the West Coast and Oahu, but some originated in the South Pacific and the Marianas.[73]

Training and Rehearsal of Troops

The great distances that separated the elements of its command, together with the limited time available, precluded combined training or rehearsal by Tenth Army of the maneuver which would land two corps abreast on a hostile shore. To the extent that circumstances permitted, however, the scattered units of the Tenth Army engaged in individual training, combined-arms training, and special training in amphibious, cave, and mountain warfare. Particular efforts were made to train ground troops in the use of the new snooperscopes

---

[72] CINCPAC-CINCPOA Opns in the POA during May 45, p. 46; CINCPOA Joint Staff Study, App. E; CINCPOA Base Development Plan LEGUMINOUS, Serial 000221, 10 Feb 45 (LEGUMINOUS was the code name for the base development of Okinawa); Tenth Army Actn Rpt, 11–IV–7.

[73] CINCPOA Opn Plan 14–44, Annex D, p. 36, and Annex F, pp. 1, 2; Tenth Army Tent Opn Plan 1–45, Annex 12: Island Command Plan; Tenth Army Actn Rpt, 5–0–8, 9; 11–IV–6, 9, 10; 11–XXVI–1.

and sniperscopes, and the one standard tank battalion which was converted to an armored flame thrower battalion received instruction in the use and maintenance of its tanks. Many service units received little specialized training because of the pressure of their regular duties and, in some cases, the circumstance that they had been released to Tenth Army only a few days before mounting from Hawaii.[74]

When, in December 1944, XXIV Corps received its warning order, it was in action over a large part of southern Leyte, engaged in virtually separate operations on the east and west coasts of the island. The Corps was not released from tactical responsibility until 10 February 1945, and it did not complete the assembly of all its units in the staging area at Dulag until 18 February. Training and rehearsals had to be sandwiched between the rehabilitation program for its combat-weary units and the mounting-out for the new operation. The 7th, 77th, and 96th Divisions were able to engage only in a very limited amount of training specifically oriented to the Okinawa operation, but all managed to train in the use of the sniperscope and of flame throwers. The Corps was, however, able to engage in a full-scale nonfiring rehearsal with the 7th and 96th Divisions and amphibious elements of the Southern Attack Force in Leyte Gulf from 15 to 19 March 1945. In addition to training in the techniques of amphibious landings, the troops practiced the breaching and scaling of sea walls. Assault regiments of the two divisions landed and moved inland for 1,000 yards in a simulated attack, after which critiques were held and the exercise repeated. The 77th Division conducted practice landings separately in Leyte Gulf from 9 to 16 March. The 27th was able to engage in intensive training in Espiritu Santo between October 1944 and 25 March 1945, when it embarked for the target; four landing rehearsals were also held between 20 and 25 March.[75]

All the Marine divisions scheduled for the Okinawa campaign had several months in which to train and rehearse. The 1st Marine Division, finding training facilities restricted in the Russell Islands, arranged for each of its regiments to take a month's training on Guadalcanal, where adequate artillery, mortar, and small-arms ranges were available. The 6th Marine Division trained on Guadalcanal, conducting numerous division problems and field exercises. On Saipan the 2d Marine Division had the advantage of practicing against the Japanese still holed up in the hills. The III Amphibious Corps conducted a combined

[74] Tenth Army Actn Rpt, 4-0-1-6, 11-III-8, 9.

[75] XXIV Corps Actn Rpt, pp. 4, 6, 8, 18; 7th Div Actn Rpt, pp. 4, 28, 29; 96th Div Actn Rpt, Ch. V, pp. 1, 2; 77th Div Actn Rpt, pp. 8, 19; 27th Div Actn Rpt, pp. 18-21.

rehearsal with the 1st and 6th Marine Divisions at Guadalcanal from 2 to 7 March; full-scale problems were worked out, troops and token supplies were landed, and a communications net established.[76]

Mounting Out

Responsibility for the loading of the assault units was decentralized through delegation to the commanders at the various mounting points; the Commanding General, Tenth Army, however, retained control of the mounting of units from Oahu. The commanders of the III Amphibious Corps and XXIV Corps were responsible for embarking their respective troops in the South Pacific and Leyte. The 2d Marine Division supervised the loading of its own troops and other units mounting from Saipan. Units which originated on the West Coast were moved to the assigned mounting points for integration with the assault echelon.[77]

All loading was conducted according to the transport doctrine of the Amphibious Forces Pacific Fleet and the logistical directives published by Tenth Army. One transport squadron of fifteen APA's (transports) and six AKA's (cargo ships), together with the requisite number of LST's and LSM's, was allocated to each division, and additional allocations were made for Corps and Army troops. (See Chart IV.) Altogether, 111 APA's, 47 AKA's, 184 LST's, and 89 LSM's were loaded in mounting the Joint Expeditionary Force. Transport Quartermaster Teams were activated and assigned to Army units to load their troops and equipment, while Marine units used the teams which had functioned in previous operations. Admiral Turner also sent two combat loading teams, trained in embarkation procedures and familiar with the policies of his command, to aid in the loading of the two corps at Leyte and the Guadalcanal–Russells area and of the 27th Division at Espiritu Santo. All loading plans and operations were subject to the approval of the captain of each ship as well as of the transport squadron commander concerned.[78]

Tenth Army headquarters and most of its attached troops mounted out of Hawaii, while the 7th, 77th, and 96th Divisions embarked at Leyte, where the largest number of ships was loaded. Each division did its own loading under general supervision of the Corps. The chief difficulty encountered was the necessity of loading across the open beaches in the Dulag area on the east coast of Leyte. Piers were nonexistent or of too flimsy a construction to withstand the battering which they took in the high surf and tide. LST's and LSM's were

[76] III Amph Corps Actn Rpt, pp. 23, 24.
[77] Tenth Army Actn Rpt, 5-0-1, 2, 6.
[78] CTF 51 Actn Rpt, V–I–14, 21; Tenth Army Actn Rpt, 5-0-1, 3, 6, 7.

LOADING SUPPLIES FOR OKINAWA—*not only arms, ammunition, and food but also great quantities of construction material (above). Barrels of fuel and boxes of other matériel are shown below being loaded at Leyte.*

beached as near shore as possible and vehicles had to be driven through the water; 105-mm. artillery was loaded by means of DUKW's and ponton causeways. Transports were loaded in the stream by ships' boats, LCT's, and LSM's. Many lighters and landing craft on Leyte had been diverted to the needs of the Luzon campaign in February when loading began, and a hurry call was sent to Tenth Army for additional lighterage. Loading plans also went awry because of the lack of accurate advance information on the characteristics of ships to be loaded. Much time was consumed by the necessity of unloading newly arrived supplies across the open beaches and reloading them in the assault shipping. The 27th Division loaded separately at Espiritu Santo, where it met difficulties of transportation and misunderstandings with naval officials.[79]

III Amphibious Corps and its units mounted out in the Guadalcanal–Russells area. Loading was out in the stream but was facilitated by an ample supply of lighterage and by excellent sandy beaches. Assault troops were embarked on transports initially and were transferred to landing ships at the staging point at Ulithi, a method which shortened the time to be spent in the uncomfortable, crowded LST's and LSM's.[80]

Movement to the target got under way on 18 March 1945, when the slow tractor group carrying the assault troops which were to take the Kerama Islands left San Pedro Bay, Leyte. Transports with other 77th Division troops sailed from Leyte three days later, and the remainder of the division followed on 24 March. The tractor groups of the Southern Attack Force sailed from Leyte on 25 March, and the faster transports followed two days later. The course from Leyte was approximately NE by N to a point about 300 miles south of Okinawa, when it was changed to N by NW directly to the target. Units of III Amphibious Corps in the Northern Attack Force sailed from the Guadalcanal area on 12 March, arriving on 21 March at Ulithi, where four days were spent in topping off supplies and effecting the transfer of troops to landing ships. The Northern Tractor Flotilla left from Ulithi on 25 March. The tractor groups carrying the 2d Marine Division to the demonstration beaches left Saipan the same day. When the remainder of the Northern and Southern Attack Forces and the Demonstration Group set forth on 27 March, Americans and Japanese were already engaged in land fighting in the Kerama Islands.[81]

[79] *Ibid.;* see also sections on loading in the Actn Rpts of XXIV Corps and the 7th, 27th, 77th, and 96th Divisions.

[80] III Amph Corps Actn Rpt, pp. 31, 32.

[81] CTF 51 Actn Rpt, II–7–13; XXIV Corps Actn Rpt. Ch. VI.

CHAPTER II

Invasion of the Ryukyus

Operations preliminary to the landing on Okinawa were as protracted and elaborate as the tactical and logistical planning. From October 1944 to April 1945 American forces from the Pacific Ocean Areas, the Southwest Pacific Area, and the China Theater conducted an intensive campaign to neutralize Japanese air and naval strength.[1] In the last week of March, while the Kerama Islands were being seized, the Navy concentrated on a furious bombardment of the main target. Before the troops for the assault mounted out American forces had invaded Luzon and Iwo Jima.

Preliminary Neutralization of Enemy Strength

The first attack on Okinawa was made by Vice Admiral Marc A. Mitscher's Fast Carrier Task Force, operating as part of the Third Fleet, in the preliminary operations for the landings on Leyte. Nine carriers, 5 fast battleships, 8 escort carriers, 4 heavy cruisers, 7 light cruisers, 3 antiaircraft cruisers, and 58 destroyers arrived off Okinawa early on 10 October. Admiral Mitscher made every effort to achieve surprise. The force followed the track of bad weather caused by a typhoon moving toward Okinawa from the southeast. A smaller force of cruisers and destroyers made a diversionary attack on Marcus Island, 1,500 miles to the east, in such a way as to simulate a large force. Aircraft based on the Marianas intensified attacks on Iwo Jima, to hamper searches from that direction, and flew interdiction patrols ahead of the Third Fleet forces.

Wave after wave of carrier planes swept over Okinawa shortly after dawn of 10 October. The first strikes bombed, rocketed, and strafed airfields at Yontan, Kadena, Ie Shima, and Naha. Later waves made intensive attacks on shipping, installations, harbor facilities, and similar targets. The attack con-

[1] The data for this account were taken from monthly reports of operations by Admiral Nimitz entitled "Operations in the Pacific Ocean Areas during the Month of ———." Copies of the reports are available in the Historical Division, WDSS.

tinued throughout the day. Many enemy aircraft were caught on the ground, dispersed and revetted, but only a few in the air. A fighter-bomber from the *Bunker Hill* dropped a bomb between two midget submarines moored side by side. Other islands in the Ryukyus were reconnoitered and attacked, including Kume, Miyako, Amami-O, Tokuno, and Minami.

The attack was one of the heaviest delivered by the Fast Carrier Force in a single day up to that time. In 1,356 strikes, the planes fired 652 rockets and 21 torpedoes and dropped 541 tons of bombs. Naha was left in flames; four-fifths of the city's 533 acres of closely built-up area was laid waste. Twenty-three enemy aircraft were shot down and 88 more destroyed on the ground or water. Twenty cargo ships, 45 smaller vessels, 4 midget submarines, a destroyer escort, a submarine tender, a mine sweeper, and miscellaneous other craft were sunk. "The enemy is brazenly planning to destroy completely every last ship, cut our supply lines, and attack us" was the gloomy observation of a Japanese soldier on the island on that day.[2]

Admiral Mitscher's estimate of results was probably conservative. A Japanese Army report on the attack listed in addition a destroyer and a mine sweeper as sunk. According to the report, almost 5,000,000 rounds of machine-gun ammunition and 300,000 sacks of unpolished rice were among the supplies destroyed. The report noted that antiradar "window" had been used by the Americans, and that propaganda leaflets had been dropped. Nowhere did the Japanese report mention one of the most significant accomplishments of the task force during the day—photographic coverage of important areas throughout the Ryukyus.[3]

Okinawa was not assaulted again until 1945, when carrier planes raided the Ryukyu and Sakashima Islands on 3 and 4 January during a heavy attack on Formosa by the Fast Carrier Task Force. The primary objective of the task force was the destruction of enemy air strength on Formosa in preparation for the invasion of Luzon, and the attack on Okinawa was limited in extent because of the long distance the fighters had to fly to the target. On 22 January, Admiral Mitscher's carrier force moved a second time against the Ryukyus, with the primary mission of photographing the islands. Unfavorable weather interfered with some of the sorties, but pilots obtained photographic coverage of 80

[2] ONI Weekly, Vol. IV, No. 30, 25 Jul 45, pp. 2276–77, Translated Diary of Miyashita Kuraji.
[3] CINCPAC-CINCPOA Bull No. 170–45, 7 Jul 45, Transl and Interrog No. 35: Effects of First Carrier Plane Attack on Okinawa, Ishi Condition Rpt No. 1, *62d Div* Hq, 17 Oct 44, pp. 89–93.

percent of priority areas and attacked ground installations, aircraft, and shipping. The operations were small compared to those of 10 October but to the enemy they must have seemed impressive. A Japanese superior private in the infantry wrote indignantly in his diary on 22 January:

> Grumman, Boeing, and North American Planes came over one after another continuously. Darn it, it makes me mad! While some fly around overhead and strafe, the big bastards fly over the airfield and drop bombs. The ferocity of the bombing is terrific. It really makes me furious. It is past 1500 and the raid is still on. At 1800 the last two planes brought the raid to a close. What the hell kind of bastards are they? Bomb from 0600 to 1800! I have to admit, though, that when they were using tracers this morning, it was really pretty.[4]

On 1 March the Fast Carrier Task Force, now operating as Task Force 58, a part of Admiral Spruance's Fifth Fleet, delivered another strike on the Ryukyus at the end of a 3-week battle cruise in Japanese home waters which included an attack on Tokyo. Sweeping down the long Ryukyu chain, American planes hit Amami, Minami, Kume, Tokuno, and Okino as well as Okinawa. Cruisers and destroyers shelled Okino Daito, 450 miles from Kyushu, in the closest surface attack to the Japanese homeland made by the fleet up to that time. The carrier planes sank a destroyer, 8 cargo ships, and 45 more craft of various sizes, destroyed 41 enemy planes, and attacked airfields and installations, particularly in the Okinawa Group. Enemy opposition was meager and American losses were small.

During February and March 1945, aircraft based in the Southwest Pacific and in the Marianas made almost daily runs over the Ryukyus and adjacent waters. Army and Navy search planes and patrol bombers hunted the waters for Japanese shipping and helped to isolate Okinawa by destroying cargo vessels, luggers, and other craft plying between Okinawa and outlying areas. One or two bombers flying high over Okinawa became so familiar a sight to the Japanese that they called it the "regular run" and dispensed with air raid alarms.[5] During March American submarines also tightened the shipping blockade around the Ryukyus.

On 14 March 1945, Task Force 58 steamed out of Ulithi and headed north. Its objective was the Inland Sea, bounded by Kyushu, western Honshu, and Shikoku; its mission was to prepare for the invasion of the Ryukyus by attacking

---

[4] CINCPAC-CINCPOA Bull No. 147-45, 16 Jun 45, Transl and Interrog No. 32: Translation of Diary Captured on Okinawa, p. 71.

[5] *Ibid.,* Extracts from an Okinawa Diary, p. 49.

PRELIMINARY BOMBARDMENT *of Okinawa and supporting islands began months in advance of the landings. Naha (above) was a prize target because of its port installations and was leveled long before the invasion. Also important were bridges (below) along the island's lines of supply.*

JAPANESE KAMIKAZE ATTACKS *were a constant menace to the American fleet. Here a Kamikaze* plane, *falling short of its target, plunges into the sea after being riddled by antiaircraft fire from an American cruiser. But the aircraft carrier* Franklin *(below) was not as fortunate. Hit off Kyushu by two 550-pound armor-piercing bombs, the Franklin's fuel, aircraft, and ammunition went up in flame; more than a thousand of her crew were lost. Gutted and listing badly, the carrier limped back to New York for repairs.*

airfields and naval bases in the Japanese homeland. The formidable task force was composed of 10 large aircraft carriers, 6 smaller carriers, 8 fast battleships, 16 cruisers, and dozens of destroyers and other vessels; included were famous names like *Hornet, Yorktown, Enterprise, New Jersey,* and *Missouri.*[6]

As Task Force 58 neared Kyushu on 17 March, it was spotted by Japanese search planes but was not attacked. At dawn on the 18th the destroyers formed two radar patrol groups, one 30 miles north and the other 30 miles west of the main force, each with carrier-based fighter protection. At 0545, when Task Force 58 was about 100 miles east of the southern tip of Kyushu, the first fighters took off from their carriers and headed for Kyushu airfields. Within an hour more fighters were launched, then the bombers and torpedo bombers. During the forenoon American planes attacked aircraft and fields near the coasts of Kyushu. When the enemy air opposition proved ineffective, the planes were ordered to strike farther inland, at targets originally scheduled for the next day. The move was profitable; during the day 102 aircraft were shot down, 275 more on the ground damaged or destroyed, and hangars, shops, and other airfield installations heavily bombed.

The Japanese counterattacked during the day. Their attack was not heavy, but it was carried out in an aggressive and determined manner. Single enemy aircraft using cloud cover effectively launched bombing attacks on American carriers. Radars were not of much help, but visual sightings by destroyers were invaluable. Although patrol planes shot down twelve of the enemy, and anti-aircraft fire accounted for twenty-one more, the *Yorktown* and *Enterprise* were hit by bombs. Fortunately, damage to the former was minor, and the bomb that hit the *Enterprise* failed to explode. Both could continue flight operations.

The next day, 19 March, Admiral Mitscher concentrated the attack on the enemy warships at Kobe, Kure, and Hiroshima in western Honshu, as well as on the airfields in Honshu and Shikoku. Major Japanese fleet units, including the battleship *Yamato,* were at Kure and Hiroshima harbors. The attack against the enemy fleet was only moderately effective, mainly because of extremely heavy and accurate antiaircraft fire. One group alone lost thirteen planes over Kure. The *Yamato* was slightly damaged, an escort carrier severely damaged, and fourteen other warships damaged in varying degrees. Merchant ships and coastal vessels were sunk or damaged in the Inland Sea.[7]

[6] CTF 58 Actn Rpt, pp. 2–3, Incl A, p. 1.

[7] *Ibid.,* pp. 4–5.

Soon after the first planes were launched on 19 March, enemy aircraft appeared over Task Force 58, concentrating their attack as usual on the carriers. Two 550-lb. bombs hit the *Franklin* while she was in the course of launching a strike. She burned fiercely amid shattering explosions and enveloping clouds of black smoke, finally becoming dead in the water. A bomb hit the *Wasp* and exploded between her second and third decks, but the fire was quickly put out and the carrier was able to work her aircraft within an hour. The weather was perfect for the enemy: a thin layer of clouds at 2,500 feet. Antiaircraft gunnery was, however, excellent. Six Japanese planes attacked one group, coming in at cloud level at an angle of 45 degrees; all six were blown to pieces.

Task Force 58 retired during the afternoon of 19 March. Carriers covered the burning *Franklin,* which was being towed at five knots, and launched fighter sweeps against Kyushu airfields in order to disrupt any planned attack on the force as it withdrew slowly south. Eight enemy planes attacked in the evening but were intercepted 80 miles away; five were shot down. The total number of Japanese planes shot out of the air during the day by planes and anti-aircraft fire was 97, and approximately 225 additional enemy aircraft were destroyed or damaged on the ground. Installations at more than a score of air bases on Honshu, Shikoku, and Kyushu were left in ruins by the operations of the day.

Japanese "bogeys" shadowed Task Force 58 on 20 March, and enemy planes attacked during the afternoon and evening. The *Enterprise* was hit by American gunfire which started a fire. Eight planes were destroyed and flying operations were halted. A plane narrowly missed the *Hancock* and hit and crippled a destroyer. The Japanese delivered an 8-plane torpedo strike against the force during the night, without success. On the 21st the enemy launched a final heavy attack on the retiring ships, with a force of 32 bombers and 16 fighters. Twenty-four American fighters intercepted the enemy planes about sixty miles from the force and quickly shot down every enemy plane, with the loss of only two American fighters. Task Force 58 met its supply ships south of Okinawa on 22 March, and spent a busy day fueling, provisioning, and taking on replacement pilots and aircraft, in preparation for the decisive phase of the campaign soon to come. In the entire course of its foray from 18 to 22 March, Admiral Mitscher's force had destroyed 528 enemy planes, damaged 16 surface craft, and hit scores of hangars, factories, warehouses, and dock areas. The success of the operation was indicated by the subsequent failure of the Japanese to mount a strong air attack for a week after the American landing on Okinawa.

Seizure of the Kerama Islands

The first landings in the Ryukyus were on the Kerama Islands, fifteen miles west of Okinawa. The boldly conceived plan to invade these islands six days prior to the landing on Okinawa was designed to secure a seaplane base and a fleet anchorage supporting the main invasion. An additional purpose was to provide artillery support for the Okinawa landing by the seizure of Keise Shima, eleven miles southwest of the Hagushi beaches, on the day preceding the Okinawa assault. The entire operation was under the control of the Western Islands Attack Group. The force selected for the landings in the Keramas was the 77th Division, commanded by Maj. Gen. Andrew D. Bruce; the 420th Field Artillery Group was chosen for the landing on Keise Shima.[8]

Steaming from Leyte, where the 77th Division had been engaged in combat since November 1944, the task force moved toward the objective in two convoys. The 22 LST's, 14 LSM's, and 40 LCI's, organized into a tractor flotilla with its own screen, left on 20 March. Two days later twenty transports and large cargo vessels followed, screened by two carrier escorts and destroyers. En route, the training begun on Leyte was continued. Operational plans were discussed and the men were thoroughly briefed with the aid of maps, aerial photographs, and terrain models. Booklets on habits, customs, government, and history of the Okinawans were distributed. After an uneventful voyage, broken only by false submarine alarms, the entire task force arrived on 26 March in the vicinity of the Kerama Islands.

Naval and air operations against the Keramas had begun two days earlier. Under the protection of the carriers and battleships of Task Force 58, which was standing off east of Okinawa, mine sweepers began clearing large areas south of the objective area on 24 March. On 25 March Vice Admiral William H. Blandy's Amphibious Support Force arrived, and mine sweeping was intensified. By evening of 25 March a 7-mile-wide lane had been cleared to Kerama from the south and a slightly larger one from the southwest. Few mines were found. Underwater demolition teams came in on the 25th and found the approaches to the Kerama beaches clear of man-made obstacles, though the reefs were studded with sharp coral heads, many of which lay only a few feet beneath the surface at high tide and were flush with the surface at low tide.[9]

[8] CTF 51.1 Rpt, I-1-19, III-5-17.   [9] CTF 52 Actn Rpt Okinawa, II-C-1, 4; V-H-1; V-G-1.

While the demolition teams surveyed the approaches, observers from 77th Division assault units studied their objectives. A fringing reef of irregular width surrounds each island. The coasts of the islands are generally steep and irregular. Narrow benches of coral rock lie along the coasts in many places. The beaches are narrow and are usually bulwarked by 4-foot sea walls. The only beaches of any considerable length are at the mouths of steep valleys or within small bays. All but the smallest of the islands are for the most part masses of steep rocky slopes, covered with brush and trees and from about 400 to 800 feet in height. Wherever possible the inhabitants grew sweet potatoes and rice on the terraced slopes of the hills and in small valley flats near the beaches. There are no roads and only a few pack-animal trails. No island in the group is suitable for an airstrip; none can accommodate large masses of troops or extensive base facilities. The military value of the Keramas lies in two anchorages, Kerama Kaikyo and Aka Kaikyo, separated from each other by Amuro Islet, in the center of the group, and bounded on the east by Tokashiki and on the west by Aka, Geruma, and Hokaji. These anchorages inclosed 44 berths, from 500 to 1,000 yards long, ranging in depth from 13 to 37 fathoms.[10] (See Map No. IV.)

Four battalion landing teams (BLT's) of the 77th Division made the first landings in the Kerama Islands on the morning of 26 March. The sky was clear, visibility good, and the water calm. Escorted by Navy guide boats, waves of amphibian tractors moved from LST's to four central islands of the group— Aka, Geruma, Hokaji, and Zamami. Cruisers, destroyers, and smaller naval craft swept the beaches with 5-inch shells, rockets, and mortar shells. Carrier planes strafed suspected areas and guarded against interference by enemy submarines and aircraft. Amphibian tanks led the amtracks to the beaches.[11]

The first unit ashore was the 3d BLT of the 305th Regimental Combat Team (RCT). At 0804[12] the 3d BLT hit the southern beaches of Aka, an island of irregular shape, measuring 3,400 by 3,000 yards at its extreme dimensions and rising in a series of ridges to two peaks, one 539 feet and the other 635 feet high. Aka, "Happy Corner Island," lies near the center of the group. The 200 boat operators and Korean laborers on Aka put sporadic mortar and machine-gun fire on the Americans, without inflicting damage, and then re-

---

[10] CINCPAC-CINCPOA Info Bull No. 161–44, 15 Nov 44; Okinawa Gunto, pp. 56–58; Supplement, 17 Dec 44: Okinawa Gunto, pp. 35–46.

[11] CTF 52 Actn Rpt Okinawa, II–C–3; 77th Div Opn Rpt, pp. 25–26.

[12] 77th Div G–3 Jnl and Msg File, 26 Mar 45. This time is erroneously reported as 0904 in the Opn Rpt.

TERRAIN IN THE KERAMA RETTO *was rugged. In particular the coastal terrain was precipitous, appearing formidable to the 2d BLT, 306th Infantry, 77th Division, as it approached Hokaji Island on 26 March. Below is an aerial view of Tokashiki Island.*

treated into the steep central area as the invaders rapidly overran the beaches and the town of Aka.

The next island invaded—and the first to be secured—was Geruma, a circular island five-eighths of a mile in diameter, lying south of Aka. The 1st Battalion Landing Team of the 306th Regimental Combat Team landed on the narrow beach at 0825, meeting no opposition except for long-range sniper fire. Within three hours it wiped out a score of defenders and secured the island. Before the engagement was over, DUKW's began unloading 105-mm. howitzers of the 304th and 305th Field Artillery Battalions for use in operations scheduled for the next day.

The easiest conquest of the day was that of Hokaji, an island one mile by 800 yards, lying a few hundred yards south of Geruma and linked to it by an encircling reef that follows the contours of the two land masses. The 2d BLT of the 306th landed on Hokaji at 0921 and secured it without resistance.

At 0900 on 26 March the 1st BLT of the 305th invaded Zamami, initially meeting little resistance. A two-legged, humpbacked island, approximately 5,500 yards long east-west and 400 yards at its narrowest point, Zamami is formed, except for a few low flat areas along the southern coast, by a group of wooded hills which rise about 450 feet. Amtracks carried the troops ashore in a deep bay that cuts into the southern coast. A sea wall fifteen feet from the water's edge held up the amtracks and forced the men to continue by foot. The assault elements received sporadic mortar and sniper fire until they reached the town of Zamami, just to the rear of the beach. Then a group of Japanese estimated to be of company strength, together with about 300 Korean laborers, fled north from the town to the hills.

It became apparent to General Bruce by late morning of 26 March that the rapid progress of the landing teams would permit the seizure on the first day of an additional island. Accordingly the 2d BLT of the 307th, a reserve unit, was directed to seize Yakabi, northwesternmost islet of the Keramas, which was nearly oval in shape and a little more than a mile long. At 1341 the battalion landed on Yakabi and, meeting only slight opposition, quickly overran it.[13]

On both Aka and Zamami the invading forces met stiffer resistance as they pressed up the steep slopes into the interior of the islands. On Aka a group of Japanese of platoon strength was routed by naval gunfire. During the afternoon the troops killed fifty-eight Japanese in a series of brief skirmishes

[13] 77th Div Opn Rpt, p. 25.

on the eastern heights of the island. Though the enemy fought from caves and pillboxes with small arms, he had no effective defense. By 1700 of 26 March two-thirds of Aka was secured; 300 Japanese troops and 400 civilians were still at large on the island.

On Zamami advance elements of the 1st BLT of the 305th pushed up into the high ground during the afternoon without closing with the enemy. From midnight until dawn of the next day, however, groups of Japanese armed with rifles, pistols, and sabers tried to break into the American perimeters near the beach. Company C bore the brunt of the attack, repulsing nine local thrusts supported by automatic weapons and mortars. One American machine gun changed hands several times. In a series of night fire fights that at times developed into savage hand-to-hand combat, the 1st Battalion killed more than 100 of the enemy at a cost of 7 Americans killed and 12 wounded.[14]

On 27 March the Americans took without opposition Amuro, an islet between the two anchorages and Kuba, the southwesternmost of the Keramas. Fitful action was still in process on Aka and Zamami on the morning of 27 March. On Aka the 3d BLT of the 305th isolated seventy-five Japanese who were dug in on a ridge and its reverse slope and were fully supported by mortars and automatic weapons. After a period of aerial strafing, bombing, rocketing, and mortar fire, the Americans drove the enemy from their position into the brush. On Zamami patrols of company size reconnoitered the island and eliminated scattered groups of the enemy. One organized position was located but could not be assaulted until the following day, when amtracks blasted frontally the caves where the last Japanese to be found were dug in.

After a preparation by artillery firing from Geruma, the 1st BLT of the 306th landed on the west coast of Tokashiki at 0911 of 27 March, and a few minutes later the 2d BLT landed to the south of the 1st. Tokashiki was the largest island in the group, six miles long from north to south and averaging about one mile in width. Closest of the islands to Okinawa, it formed the eastern barrier of the Kerama anchorages. Its coasts rise for the most part as cliffs or steep slopes cut by narrow ravines, the hill masses reaching heights of more than 650 feet in the center of the island and at the northern and

---

[14] Terrain descriptions are from 77th Div G–2 Estimate of the Situation ICEBERG, 15 Mar 45; Capt Paul R. Leach (77th Div Historian), Opns of 77th Div in Kerama Retto; Narrative of Actn from 77th Div Opn Rpt Kerama Retto; G–2 and G–3 Periodic Rpts, 27–31 Mar 45; and G–2 and G–3 jnls and msg files for the same period.

southern ends. At the backs of two sheltered bays near the center of the west coast there are two settlements, Tokashiki and Aware; the sandy beaches near these bays were selected by the invaders for the landings.

Operations on Tokashiki followed the pattern of those on the other major islands of the Keramas. Resistance at first was negligible, the Americans being hindered more by the rugged terrain than by the scattered sniper fire. The two battalions abreast drove north over narrow trails. The 3d BLT of the 306th, initially in reserve, was landed with the mission of clearing the southern portion of the island. By nightfall the 1st and 2d Battalions were set for the next day's attack on the town of Tokashiki on the east coast; 3d Battalion patrols had reached the southern tip of the island.

On the following day, 28 March, the two battalions of the 306th renewed their drive to the north. After a 500-round artillery preparation the troops occupied Tokashiki, which had previously been leveled by air and surface bombardment. The area near the bay was overrun without opposition. The advance continued to the north, meeting only scattered resistance. On 29 March, after the three battalions had sent patrols throughout the island, Tokashiki was declared secured.

By the evening of 29 March all islands in the Kerama Retto were in American hands. In all, combat elements of the 77th had made fifteen separate landings, involving five ship-to-shore movements by LVT's, two ship-to-shore movements by DUKW's, three ship-to-shore movements by LCVP's with subsequent transfer to LVT's, and five shore-to-shore movements by LVT's. Despite the complexity of the maneuvers, the veterans of Guam and Leyte operated with little confusion. Casualties were low. From 26 to 31 March the 77th killed 530 of the enemy and took 121 prisoners, at a cost of 31 Americans killed and 81 wounded.[15]

The operations on Aka and Tokashiki had interesting consequences. Although 77th Division patrols scoured the islands, hundreds of Japanese soldiers and civilians managed to evade discovery in caves, ravines, and brush throughout the hilly central parts of the islands. After the Okinawa operation, representatives from Tenth Army tried unsuccessfully to induce the Japanese commander on Aka to surrender. The Japanese soldiers and sailors were not as stubborn, and most of them escaped from the island and surrendered. On Tokashiki teams of Nisei and Japanese officer prisoners negotiated with the Japanese commander, who refused to surrender his garrison of 300 officers and men. He offered, how-

[15] 77th Div Opn Rpt, pp. 26, 30–32, 41.

ever, to allow Americans to swim on Tokashiki beaches provided they kept away from the Japanese camp in the hills. Only after many months, when he was given a copy of the Imperial rescript announcing the end of hostilities, did the Japanese commander surrender, claiming that he could have held out for ten more years.[16]

The capture of the Kerama Islands was followed by the landings on Keise Shima. Lying about eleven miles southwest of the Hagushi beaches and about eight miles west of Naha, the group of four tiny coral islets that make up Keise had an importance in the attack on Okinawa far out of proportion to its size and topography. From Keise 155-mm. guns could command most of southern Okinawa. Employing tactics used with great success on Kwajalein, Tenth Army ordered XXIV Corps artillery to emplace two battalions of 155-mm. guns on Keise to support the attack.

On 26 March the Fleet Marine Force Amphibious Reconnaissance Battalion, attached to the 77th Division, scouted Keise without encountering enemy troops or civilians. On the morning of 31 March a convoy of LST's and LSM's bearing the 420th Field Artillery Group and attachments arrived off the islets. Over floating caisson docks set up by Seabees the heavy guns and other equipment were unloaded. Twenty-four 155-mm. guns were emplaced on the low, sandy islets, and a cub strip and a bivouac area were established. By dawn of L Day the batteries were ready to execute their mission of firing counterbattery, interdiction, and harassing fires deep into enemy territory.

The guns were set up in full view of the Japanese occupying high ground on Okinawa. General Ushijima ordered a "surprise shelling" of Keise to begin at midnight of 31 March, after which army and navy commands were to dispatch "raiding infiltration units" to Keise, "thereby wiping out the enemy advanced strong point in one blow."[17] For an hour after midnight, Japanese 150-mm. shells exploded on the islets. There were no casualties or damage. The infiltration party never appeared. This attempt to destroy the artillery on Keise was only the first of several, the enemy being keenly aware of the threat offered by the artillery in this flanking position.[18]

The assault on Kerama and Keise had come as a surprise to the Japanese commanders on Okinawa Gunto. The enemy commanders on Okinawa had

---

[16] 77th Div Opn Rpt, pp. 33, 35; 870th AAA AW Bn Actn Rpt Kerama Retto, p. 5.

[17] Tenth Army Transl No. 248, 8 Jul 45: *32d Army* Ord, 31 Mar 45.

[18] 420th FA Gp Actn Rpt, 31 Mar to 30 Jun 45, pp. 4–6; 531st FA Bn Actn Rpt, pp. 1–2; 532d FA Bn Actn Rpt, p. 1.

expected that the Americans would land first on the Hagushi beaches and that their ships would deploy just east of the Kerama Islands.[19]

Since the enemy considered the Keramas as bases for special attack units rather than as defensive positions, there were few prepared defenses on the beaches or inland when the Americans appeared. At one time 2,335 Japanese troops occupied the islands, engaged in installing and operating facilities for the *Sea Raiding* units. When, in late 1944 and early 1945, the need for combat troops on Okinawa became acute, most of these troops were moved to the larger island. There remained on the Kerama group only about 300 boat operators of the *Sea Raiding Squadrons,* approximately 600 Korean laborers, and about 100 base troops. The garrison was well supplied not only with the suicide boats and depth charges but also with machine guns, mortars, light arms, and ammunition.[20]

In Kerama Retto, "Island Chain between Happiness and Good," the Japanese tradition of self-destruction emerged horribly in the last acts of soldiers and civilians trapped in the hills. Camping for the night of 28 March a mile from the north tip of Tokashiki, troops of the 306th heard explosions and screams of pain in the distance. In the morning they found a small valley littered with more than 150 dead and dying Japanese, most of them civilians. Fathers had systematically throttled each member of their families and then disemboweled themselves with knives or hand grenades. Under one blanket lay a father, two small children, a grandfather, and a grandmother, all strangled by cloth ropes. Soldiers and medics did what they could. The natives, who had been told that the invading "barbarians" would kill and rape, watched with amazement as the Americans provided food and medical care; an old man who had killed his daughter wept in bitter remorse.[21]

Only a minority of the Japanese, however, were suicides. Most civilians straggled into American positions, worn and dirty. In all, the 77th took 1,195 civilian and 121 military prisoners. One group of 26 Koreans gave up on Zamami under a white flag. On Aka one Japanese lieutenant surrendered voluntarily because, he said, it would be "meaningless" for him to commit suicide.[22] A Japanese

---

[19] Interrog Yahara; 77th Div G–2 Periodic Rpt No. 4, 30 Mar 45; XXIV Corps PW Interrog No. 71, 20 Apr 45.

[20] 77th Div Opn Rpt Kerama Retto, pp. 38–39; G–2 Periodic Rpt, 26–31 Mar 45.

[21] Personal Obsn of Capt Leach, 77th Div Historian, and Cpl Alexander Roberts, 1st I & H Service.

[22] XXIV Corps PW Interrog No. 71, 20 Apr 45; 77th Div G–2 Periodic Rpt No. 3, 29 Mar 45: Order of Battle Rpt.

LANDINGS IN THE KERAMAS, *made by the 77th Division, met little opposition. Zamami Island (above) was taken by the 1st BLT, 305th Infantry, some soldiers of which are shown just before they started inland. Amtracks were unable to negotiate the seawall and were left at the beach. Below is a scene on a beach at Tokashiki, captured by the 1st BLT, 306th, on 27 March. Soldier (right) seems puzzled by the absence of opposition.*

major captured by a patrol on Zamami late in May assisted in efforts to induce Japanese remaining in the islands to surrender.

More than 350 suicide boats were captured and destroyed by the 77th in the Kerama Islands. They were well dispersed throughout the islands, many of them in camouflaged hideouts. These plywood boats were 18 feet long and 5 feet wide. Powered by 6-cylinder Chevrolet automobile engines of about 85 horsepower, they were capable of making up to 20 knots. Two depth charges weighing 264 pounds each were carried on a rack behind the pilot and were rolled off the stern of the boat when released. According to captured instructions, three boats would attack a ship simultaneously, each seeking a vital spot to release its charge. Strictly speaking, manning the boats was not suicidal in the same sense as piloting the *Kamikaze* planes or the "Baka" bombs. Delay time for the depth-charge igniters was five seconds. According to a Japanese officer, it was considered possible to drop the depth charges against a ship and escape, but the fragility of the boats made survival highly unlikely. As a result, the pilots were promoted two grades upon assignment and received preferential treatment. After completion of their missions they were to receive promotion to second lieutenant; obviously, most such promotions would be posthumous.

From hideouts in the small islands, the "Q-boats" with their charges were to speed to the American anchorages. "The objective of the attack," General Ushijima ordered, "will be transports, loaded with essential supplies and material and personnel. . . . The attack will be carried out by concentrating maximum strength immediately upon the enemy's landing."[23] The Japanese had carefully mapped out possible assembly areas of American transports and had prepared appropriate routes of approach to each area, especially those around Keise.[24] The initial thrust into the Keramas completely frustrated the enemy's plan. In the opinion of General Bruce, the destruction of the suicide boat base alone was well worth the cost of reducing the Kerama Islands.[25]

In a campaign that found the Japanese prepared for the major moves of the invading forces, the initial seizure of their "Western Islands" not only caught them off guard but frustrated their plan of "blasting to pieces" the American transports with a "whirlwind" attack by suicide boats.[26] The Americans gained

---

[23] Tenth Army Transl No. 231, 6 Jul 45: *32d Army* Opn Ord No. 115, 23 Mar 45.

[24] Tenth Army Transl No. 210, 11 Jul 45: *20th Sea Raiding Bn* Opn Ord No. 26, 16 Feb 45.

[25] 77th Div Opn Rpt, p. 40.

[26] 77th Div Opn Rpt Kerama Retto [n. d.], p. 38; Interrog Yahara; Tenth Army G–2 CICA Transl No. 231, 6 Jul 45: *32d Army* Opn Ord No. 115.

"SUICIDE BOATS" *wrecked by their crews were found by the 77th Division as it mopped up in the Keramas. They looked like small speedboats but were poorly constructed and quite slow. These two craft (below) were captured in their cave shelters by American troops on Okinawa. Note booby trap warnings and crude depth charge racks at stern.*

SOFTENING UP THE TARGET *was the task of the Allied fleet. It stood off Okinawa to place accurate fire on known Japanese installations and to support underwater demolitions teams clearing the beaches. At the same time the fleet's air arm conducted aerial bombardment. This low-level bombing attack on L minus 1 (below) hit enemy shipping in the mouth of the Bishi River.*

even more than the Japanese lost. In American hands, this sheltered anchorage became a miniature naval base from which seaplanes operated and surface ships were refueled, remunitioned, and repaired.

Softening Up the Target

While operations were proceeding in the Kerama Islands, Task Force 52, under the command of Admiral Blandy, supervised the specialized tasks that were an essential prelude to the invasion of Okinawa itself—the mine sweeping, underwater demolition work, and heavy, sustained bombardment of the target by ships and aircraft. Task Force 58 stood off to the north and east of Okinawa, ready to intercept any Japanese surface force approaching from the east, while Task Force 52 guarded against enemy attack from the west and against any "express runs" from the north either to reinforce or to evacuate Okinawa. During the day the ships bombarding Okinawa stayed close enough together to be able to concentrate for surface action without undue delay. At night 80 percent of Task Force 52 deployed to the northwest of Okinawa and 20 percent to the northeast. The northwest group was considered strong enough to cope with any surface force which the Japanese could bring against it; the northeast element was to deal with "express runs," and could count on the support of Task Force 58 if the enemy dispatched a larger, slower, and more easily detected force to the area east of Okinawa. In case of emergency, one force could join the other by passing through the unswept waters north of Okinawa.[27]

Bombardment of Okinawa began on 25 March when ships of the Amphibious Support Force shelled the southeast coast. The fire was executed only at long range, however, for mine-sweeping operations which had commenced the previous day were still proceeding well offshore. During the following days, as the mine sweepers cleared areas progressively nearer the coast of Okinawa, the bombardment ships were able to close in for heavier and more accurate fire. The Japanese had planted a mine field of considerable strength along the approaches to the Hagushi beaches, and until mine-sweeping operations were completed the American ships could not bring the beaches within range. Not until the evening of 29 March were the approaches to Hagushi and other extensive areas cleared in what Admiral Blandy called "probably the largest assault sweep operation ever executed." Operating under inter-

[27] CTF 52 Actn Rpt Okinawa, I–C–1, 2.

mittent air attack, American mine sweepers cleared about 3,000 square miles in 75 sweeps.

From 26 to 28 March the naval bombardment of Okinawa was at long range; targets were located with difficulty because of the range and occasional poor visibility, and few were reported destroyed. Effective bombardment of the island did not begin until 29 March when battleships, cruisers, destroyers, and gunboats closed the range and hit their objectives with increasing effectiveness. Then for the first time the large concentration of targets in the Naha-Oroku Peninsula area was taken under effective fire. On the 30th heavy shells breached the sea walls along the coast line in many places. Ten battleships and eleven cruisers were now participating in the attack. On 31 March four heavy ships, accompanied by destroyers and gunboats, supported the final underwater demolition operation off the Hagushi beaches. This was completed before noon. Then the ships concentrated on sea walls and on defensive installations behind the beaches. Even at the shortest range, however, it was difficult to locate important targets, and ships had to explore with gunfire for emplacements and similar structures.

During the seven days before L Day, naval guns fired more than 13,000 large-caliber shells (6-inch to 16-inch) in shore bombardment. Including several thousand 5-inch shells, a total of 5,162 tons of ammunition was expended on ground targets. All known coast defense guns in the area were destroyed or severely damaged. The enemy had established a few heavy pillbox-type installations and numerous emplacements along the beaches and farther inland, but most of them were empty. Naval guns fired extensively into cliffs and rocky points overlooking and flanking the beaches to disclose defensive positions such as the enemy had frequently used in the past; few, however, were found.[28] By the afternoon of 31 March, Admiral Blandy could report that "the preparation was sufficient" with the exception of certain potentially dangerous installations still in the Naha area. Enemy shore batteries did not open up on ships during the preliminary bombardment.[29]

Aircraft from Task Force 58 and from the escort carriers flew 3,095 sorties in the Okinawa area prior to L Day. Their primary objective was enemy aircraft based on the islands. Second priority was given to small boats and "amphibian tanks," which later were discovered to be suicide attack boats

[28] Ibid., V–C–1, 7.
[29] CINCPAC-CINCPOA Opns in POA, Apr 45, pp. 35–36. See below under "The Japanese Plan of Defense," p. 93.

fitted with depth charges. After these, they gave preference to installations such as coastal defense guns, field artillery, antiaircraft guns, floating mines, communications facilities, and barracks areas.

Planes from Task Force 58 concentrated on targets that could not be reached by naval gunfire. Escort carrier aircraft protected the mine sweepers and underwater demolition teams, conducted preliminary attacks against Kerama and Keise, and supported the assault generally. The preliminary air assault got under way on 25 March with bombing, napalm, and rocket attacks on Tokashiki Island in the Keramas and attacks on air installations on Okinawa. On the 26th, 424 sorties were made against suicide boat and midget submarine bases, airfields, and gun positions. On the following day attacks continued on these targets, and barracks areas were also worked over with bombs, napalm, and rockets.

From 28 to 31 March air missions were closely coordinated with projected ground operations as the escort carriers executed missions requested by Tenth Army. Aircraft concentrated on gun positions at scattered points throughout southern Okinawa. They bombed a bridge along the northern shore of Nakagusuku Bay and broke it in ten places. They scored fifteen direct hits with napalm on installations near the Bishi River. Operations against enemy air and naval bases continued. On 29 March carrier planes destroyed 27 enemy planes on Okinawa airfields and probably destroyed or damaged 24 more; planes hit on the ground during the period totaled 80. Barges, wooden boats, and other small enemy craft were systematically gutted. At least eight submarine pens were demolished at Unten Ko on the north coast of Motobu Peninsula.[30]

Under cover of carrier planes and naval gunfire, underwater demolition teams performed reconnaissance and necessary demolitions on Keise, on the demonstration beaches of southeastern Okinawa, and on the Hagushi landing beaches. Planes made strafing, bombing, and rocket runs on the beaches, and smoker planes, where needed, concealed the teams with smoke. Three lines of ships, increasing in fire power from the beach out, gave the underwater demolition teams formidable support. LCI(G)'s (Landing Craft, Infantry, Fire Support) armed with 40-mm. guns stood approximately 1,200 yards off the beach; then a line of destroyers at about 2,700 yards covered the shore to 300 yards inland with 40-mm. and 5-inch gunfire; and 1,000 yards behind the destroyers were battleships and cruisers ready with secondary and antiaircraft batteries to neutralize all ground from 300 to 1,000 yards inland.

---

[30] CTF 52 Actn Rpt, pp. V–E–1–7; CINCPAC-CINCPOA Opns in POA, Apr 45, pp. 37–38.

Underwater demolition teams first reconnoitered the Hagushi beaches on 29 March, after a delay of a day because of the large number of mines found in the areas off the beaches. Three battleships, 3 cruisers, 6 destroyers, and 9 LCI(G)'s supported the operation. The machine-gun and mortar fire encountered was silenced by the fire support units. The swimmers found approximately 2,900 wooden posts, from 6 to 8 inches in diameter and from 4 to 8 feet high, most of them off beaches north of the Bishi River. In some places there were four rows of these posts. On 30 and 31 March underwater demolition teams destroyed all but 200 of the posts, using tetratol tied in with primacord. A demolition operation was carried out on the demonstration beaches under gunfire coverage; several tons of tetratol were detonated on the edge of the reef even though no obstacles had been found.[31]

As the Americans closed in on Okinawa from 26 to 31 March, the enemy suddenly found itself confronting another adversary—the Royal Navy. A British carrier force, under the command of Vice Admiral H. B. Rawlings and assigned to the Fifth Fleet, struck at the Sakishima Islands on 26, 27, and 31 March. Its planes made 345 sorties over Sakishima, dropped more than 81 tons of bombs, and fired more than 200 rockets. The British labored under several handicaps. They lacked night fighters, and their ships carried a much smaller number of planes than did the large American carriers. Also, their supply resources afloat were rudimentary. Nevertheless, the British rendered valuable assistance to the assault forces by considerably reducing the magnitude and number of enemy air attacks staged from Sakishima airfields.[32]

Task Force 58 remained in a constant state of readiness, and on 28 March it demonstrated its fast striking power in convincing fashion. Word was received from Admiral Spruance of a reported sortie of enemy fleet units from the Inland Sea on a southwesterly course. Immediately a task group headed north at high speed to attack the enemy ships. The Japanese force, however, was not found. On the 29th another task group joined in the search, but without success. The foray was not allowed, however, to be useless. On their way back to the carriers, planes from both groups bombed airfields in the Kagoshima Bay area of Kyushu and attacked miscellaneous shipping with good results.[33]

[31] CTF 52 Actn Rpt, V–G–1, 2, 3; CINCPAC-CINCPOA Opns in POA, Apr 45, pp. 32–33.

[32] CINCPAC-CINCPOA Opns in POA, Apr 45, pp. 67–68.

[33] *Ibid.,* p. 61.

Despite American attacks on enemy airfields and installations, approximately 100 Japanese planes made 50 raids in the Okinawa area during the period from 26 to 31 March. Many of the attacking planes tried to suicide-crash the American ships—an omen of the basic Japanese tactics in the tremendous sea-air war soon to come. With few exceptions, the attacks came during early morning or by moonlight. Already the Japanese were using a considerable assortment of new- and old-type planes. As they approached, the enemy raiders generally split up into single planes or 2-plane groups, which made individual, uncoordinated attacks. There was some evidence that planes flew in from outlying bases and landed on fields in Okinawa at night. Favorite targets of the Japanese were pickets and patrols, including small craft, but several planes attacked formations of heavy ships. Of the enemy planes that suicide-crashed, nine hit their targets and ten made near misses. Much of the damage from these attacks was superficial, but several ships suffered serious damage and casualties. Ten American ships, including the battleship *Nevada* and the cruisers *Biloxi* and *Indianapolis,* were damaged in the period from 26 to 31 March, eight of them by suicide planes; two other vessels were destroyed by mines. The defending ships and planes shot down approximately forty-two of the attackers.[34] In addition to the suicide attacks the Japanese conducted a few bombing, strafing, and torpedo attacks during the period, but these were without significant results.

On the afternoon of 31 March naval auxiliary vessels delivered the latest aerial photographs of the beaches to the transports approaching the target area. As night fell, the vast armada of transports, cargo ships, landing craft, and war ships ploughed the last miles of their long voyage. Before dawn they would rendezvous off the Hagushi beaches in the East China Sea. Weather for 1 April promised to be excellent.

[34] Com Amphib-Gp 1, CTF 52 Actn Rpt, IV–B–10.

CHAPTER III

Winning the Okinawa Beachhead

Dawn of Easter Sunday, 1 April 1945, disclosed an American fleet of 1,300 ships in the waters adjacent to Okinawa, poised for invasion. Most of them stood to the west in the East China Sea. The day was bright and cool—a little under 75°; a moderate east-northeast breeze rippled the calm sea; there was no surf on the Hagushi beaches. Visibility was 10 miles until 0600, when it lowered to from 5 to 7 miles in the smoke and haze. More favorable conditions for the assault could hardly be imagined.

The Japanese doubtless marveled at the immensity of the assemblage of ships, but they could not have been surprised at the invasion itself. The Kerama Islands had been seized; Okinawa had been heavily bombarded for days; and underwater demolition teams had reconnoitered both the Hagushi beaches and the beaches above Minatoga on the southeast coast, indicating that landings were to be expected at either place or both. Moreover, Japanese air and submarine reconnaissance had also spotted the convoys en route.[1]

The Japanese had been powerless to interfere with the approach to the Ryukyus. Bad weather, however, had caused not only seasickness among the troops but also concern over the possibility that a storm might delay the landings. It was necessary for some convoys to alter their courses to avoid a threatening typhoon. The rough seas caused delays and minor damage and resulted in other deflections from planned courses. Thus on the evening before L Day various task forces converging on Okinawa were uncertain of their own positions and those of other forces. All arrived on time, however, and without mishap.[2]

For the men, observing the outline of the strange island in the first rays of light before the beaches became shrouded in the smoke and dust of naval and air bombardment, this Easter Sunday was a day of crisis. From scale models

[1] Comdr Amph Gp 12 (CTF 55), Actn Rpt Okinawa, II–2; Comdr Transport Sq 14, Actn Rpt Okinawa, II–5.

[2] Capt Donald Mulford and 1st Lt Jesse Rogers (96th Div Historians), 96th Div Actn on Okinawa (cited hereafter as Mulford and Rogers, 96th Div Hist), Introduction, p. 6 (available in Hist Div WDSS); 381st Inf Actn Rpt Okinawa, p. 15; CTF 53 Actn Rpt, II–B–1; CTF 55 Actn Rpt Okinawa, II–2.

of Okinawa studied on shipboard they had seen that the rising ground behind the landing beaches, and even more the island's hills and escarpments, were well suited for defense. They had read of the native houses, each protected by a high wall, and of the thousands of strange Okinawan tombs which might serve the enemy as pillboxes and dugouts. They had been encouraged by the weakness of Kerama Retto's defenses, but the generally held expectations of an all-out defense of the beaches on the first Japanese "home" island to be invaded was one to appall even the dullest imagination. And behind the beaches the men were prepared to meet deadly snakes, awesome diseases, and a presumably hostile civilian population.[3]

The Landing

H Hour had been set for 0830. At 0406 Admiral Turner, Commander of Task Force 51, signaled, "Land the Landing Force." [4] At 0530, twenty minutes before dawn, the fire support force of 10 battleships, 9 cruisers, 23 destroyers, and 177 gunboats began the pre-H-Hour bombardment of the beaches. They fired 44,825 rounds of 5-inch or larger shells, 33,000 rockets, and 22,500 mortar shells. This was the heaviest concentration of naval gunfire ever to support a landing of troops. About seventy miles east of Okinawa, Task Force 58 was deployed to furnish air support and to intercept attacks from Kyushu. In addition, support carriers had arrived with troop convoys. At 0745 carrier planes struck the beaches and near-by trenches with napalm.[5]

Meanwhile LST's and LSM's, which had carried to the target both the men composing the first assault forces and the amphibian vehicles in which they were to ride, spread their yawning jaws and launched their small craft, loaded and ready for the shore. Amphibian tanks formed the first wave at the line of departure, 4,000 yards from the beach. Flagged on their way at 0800, they proceeded toward land at four knots. From five to seven waves of assault troops in amphibian tractors followed the tanks at short intervals.[6]

[3] Capt Russell Gugeler (7th Div Historian), The Opns of the 7th Inf Div on Okinawa (hereafter cited as Gugeler, 7th Div Hist), pp. 10–11.

[4] Tenth Army Actn Rpt, 7–III–1; 1st Marine Div Actn Rpt, Nansei Shoto Opn, 1 Apr–30 Jun 45, Ch. VII, p. 2; CTF 51 Actn Rpt, V–B–II–2, 3; Comdr Amph Gp 4 Pac Flt (CTF 53), Actn Rpt Okinawa Gunto, 20 Jul 45, III–12; III Amph Corps Actn Rpt, p. 69.

[5] CTF 51 Actn Rpt, II–15; Tenth Army Actn Rpt. 11–V–6; CTF 58 Actn Rpt Okinawa, Incl A, p. 3, and II–5; CTF 53 Actn Rpt, III–13.

[6] Gugeler, 7th Div Hist, p. 17; III Amph Corps Actn Rpt, p. 69; CTF 53 Actn Rpt, III–13; XXIV Corps Actn Rpt, Fig. 3, following p. 19.

Opposite each landing beach, control craft, with pennants flying from the mast, formed the assault waves of amphibious vehicles in rotating circles. At 0815 the leading waves of amtracks uncoiled and formed a line near their mother control craft. Five minutes later the pennants were hauled down and an almost unbroken 8-mile line of landing craft moved toward the beaches.

Gunboats led the way in, firing rockets, mortars, and 40-mm. guns into prearranged target squares, on such a scale that all the landing area for 1,000 yards inland was blanketed with enough 5-inch shells, 4.5-inch rockets, and 4.2-inch mortars to average 25 rounds in each 100-yard square. Artillery fire from Keise added its weight. After approaching the reef, the gunboats turned aside and the amphibian tanks and tractors passed through them and proceeded unescorted, the tanks firing their 75-mm. howitzers at targets of opportunity directly ahead of them until landing. Simultaneously, two 64-plane groups of carrier planes saturated the landing beaches and the areas immediately behind with machine-gun fire while the fire from supporting ships shifted inland. When the assault wave moved in, the landing area had been under constant bombardment for three hours.[7]

As the small boats made their way steadily toward the shore the men kept expecting fire from the Japanese. But there was no sign of the enemy other than the dropping of an occasional mortar or artillery shell, and the long line of invasion craft advanced as though on a large-scale maneuver. The offshore obstacles had either been removed by the underwater demolition teams or were easily pushed over by the amphibian tractors. Some concern had been felt as to whether, despite the rising tide, the Navy landing boats would be able to cross the coral reef, and the first waves were to inspect the reef and send back information. The reef did not hinder the first waves, in amphibian vehicles, but those who followed in boats had difficulty and were therefore ordered to transfer at the edge of the reef and cross in LVT's.

Beginning at 0830, the first waves began to touch down on their assigned beaches. None was more than a few minutes late. The volume of supporting fire had increased until a minute or two before the first wave landed; then suddenly the heavy fire on the beach area ended and nothing was to be heard except the rumble of the shells that were shifted inland. Quickly the smoke and dust that had shrouded the landing area lifted, and it became possible for the troops to see the nature of the country directly before them. They

[7] CTF 51 Actn Rpt, V–C–7 and III–9, 10; III Amph Corps Actn Rpt, pp. 70, 76; XXIV Corps Actn Rpt, p. 34; 1st Mar Div Actn Rpt, Ch. VII, p. 2.

BOMBARDING THE BEACHES *directly preceded the landings. It was carried on at closest range by rocket gunboats of the U. S. fleet. These boats led the way to the Hagushi beaches, turned aside just outside the reefs, and allowed amphibian tanks and tractors (below) to proceed ashore unescorted. Meanwhile the* Tennessee *and other American battleships kept up a steady support barrage.*

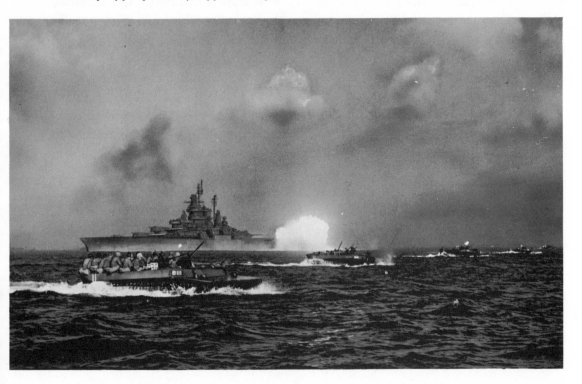

were on a beach which was generally about twenty yards in depth and which was
separated by a 10-foot sea wall from the country beyond. There were few shell
holes on the beach itself, but naval gunfire had blown large holes in the sea
wall at frequent intervals to provide adequate passageways.[8] Except at the
cliff-bordered Bishi River mouth, in the center of the landing area, the ground
rose gradually to an elevation of about fifty feet. There was only sparse natural
vegetation, but from the sea wall to the top of the rise the coastal ground was
well cultivated. In the background, along the horizon, hills showed through
the screen of artillery smoke. Farther inland, in many places, towns and
villages could be seen burning and the smoke rising above them in slender
and twisted spires. These evidences of devastation, however, made less impression upon the men than did the generally peaceful and idyllic nature of the
country, enhanced by the pleasant warmth, the unexpected quiet, and the
absence of any sign of human life.

New waves of troops kept moving in. Before an hour had passed III Amphibious Corps had landed the assault elements of the 6th and 1st Marine
Divisions abreast north of the Bishi River, and XXIV Corps had put ashore those
of the 7th and 96th Infantry Divisions abreast south of that river. The 6th Marine
Division and the 96th Division were on the flanks. Two battalion landing teams
from each of two assault regimental combat teams in the four divisions, or more
than 16,000 troops, came ashore in the first hour.[9] (See Map No. V.)

The assault troops were followed by a wave of tanks. Some were equipped
with flotation devices, others were carried by LCM(6)'s which had themselves
been transported by LSD's, and still others were landed by LSM's. After debark-
ing the assault waves, the amphibian tractors returned to the transfer line to
ferry support troops, equipment, and supplies across the reef onto the beach.
LVT, DUKW, and small-boat control points were established at the transfer
line.   Amphibian vehicles preloaded with ammunition and supplies proceeded
inland as needed.[10]

The entire landing on Okinawa had taken place with almost incredible ease.
There had been little molestation from enemy artillery, and on the beaches

[8] Tenth Army Actn Rpt, 7–III–1 and 11–IX–7; III Amph Corps Actn Rpt, pp. 69, 101; XXIV Corps
Actn Rpt, p. 24; 1st Mar Div Actn Rpt, Ch. VII, p. 3; 32d Inf Actn Rpt, p. 3; 780th Tank Bn Actn Rpt, p. 24.

[9] Maj Roy E. Appleman (XXIV Corps Historian), The XXIV Corps in the Conquest of Okinawa
(hereafter cited as Appleman, XXIV Corps Hist), p. 89; III Amph Corps Actn Rpt, p. 69; 1st Mar Div
Actn Rpt, Ch. VII, p. 3.

[10] Gugeler, 7th Div Hist, p. 18; Appleman, XXIV Corps Hist, p. 91; Tenth Army Actn Rpt, 11–IX–6;
III Amph Corps Actn Rpt, pp. 69, 70, 99, 101.

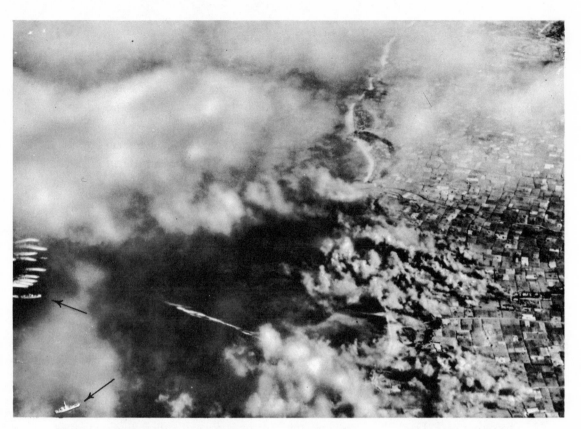

THE LANDINGS *were made in amphibian craft which were shepherded to shore by control craft (arrows). Heavy support fire which had blanketed the beaches with smoke and dust lifted seconds before the first troops touched down. Absence of enemy opposition to the landings made the assault seem like a large-scale maneuver as troops (below) left their craft and quickly consolidated. Other waves followed closely.*

no enemy and few land mines had been encountered. The operation had taken place generally according to plan; there was little disorganization and all but a few of the units landed at the beaches assigned to them. The absence of any but the most trivial opposition, so contrary to expectation, struck the men as ominous and led them to reconnoiter suspiciously. After making certain that they were not walking into a trap, the troops began moving inland, according to plan, a very short time after they had landed.

Spirits rose as the marines and soldiers easily pushed up the hillsides behind the beaches. The land was dry and green with conifers and the air bracing—a welcome change from the steaming marshes and palm trees of the islands to the south. An infantryman of the 7th Division, standing atop a hill just south of the Bishi River soon after the landing, expressed the common feeling when he said, "I've already lived longer than I thought I would." [11]

Simultaneously with the landing Maj. Gen. Thomas E. Watson's 2d Marine Division feinted a landing on Okinawa's southeast coast, above Minatoga, with the hope of pinning down the enemy's reserves in that area. This diversion simulated an actual assault in every respect. The first part of the demonstration group left Saipan on 25 March, and the main body arrived at Okinawa early in the morning of L Day. The Japanese attacked the force with their suicide planes, and one transport and an LST were damaged. Under cover of a smoke screen, seven boat waves, each composed of twenty-four LCVP's, carried 2d Marine Division troops toward the beach. As the fourth wave crossed the line of departure at 0830—H Hour for the main assault on the Hagushi beaches—all boats reversed course. By 1500 all the landing vessels had been recovered by their parent vessels. The only enemy reaction to the demonstration was one salvo of four rounds. The next day the demonstration was repeated, and the marines retired from the area. Proudly the Japanese boasted that "an enemy landing attempt on the eastern coast of Okinawa on Sunday morning [1 April] was completely foiled, with heavy losses to the enemy." [12]

Moving Inland

Having ascended the slight hills at the landing beaches, the troops moved inland cautiously. Their immediate objectives were the two airfields, Kadena and Yontan, each about a mile inland. At 1000 the 17th RCT of the 7th Divi-

---

[11] Gugeler, 7th Div Hist, p. 24; Tenth Army Actn Rpt, 11–IX–6; III Amph Corps Actn Rpt, p. 99.
[12] CINCPOA Operations in POA, April 1945, p. 42.

sion had patrols on Kadena airfield, which was found to be deserted, and at 1030 the front line was moving across the airstrip. A few minutes later it was 200 yards beyond. With similar ease the 4th Marines of the 6th Marine Division captured the more elaborate Yontan airfield by 1130. Wrecked Japanese planes and quantities of supplies were strewn about on both fields.[13]

By nightfall the beachhead was 15,000 yards long and in places as much as 5,000 yards deep. More than 60,000 men were ashore, including the reserve regiments of the assault divisions. All divisional artillery landed early, and, by dark, direct-support battalions were in position. Numerous tanks were ashore and operating, as well as miscellaneous antiaircraft artillery units and 15,000 service troops. Kadena airfield was serviceable for emergency landings by the evening of the first day. The 6th Marine Division halted for the night on a line running from Irammiya to the division boundary below Makibaru. The 7th Division had pressed inland nearly three miles, knocking out a few pillboxes and losing three tanks to mines. On the southern flank, the 96th Division had established itself at the river south of Chatan, on the high ground northwest of Futema, in the outskirts of Momobaru, and in the hills northwest and southwest of Shido. There were gaps in the lines in many places, but before nightfall they had been covered by reserve units or by weapons.[14]

Although in the hills around Shuri the enemy had superb observation of the Hagushi beaches and of the great American armada that stood off shore, he had been content for the time being to leave the burden of opposition to the Japanese air force. Some delaying actions were fought by small groups of Japanese, and some rounds of artillery and mortar fire were directed at the landing craft and the beaches, but the total resistance was negligible.

In the air the enemy did his best, but did not inflict much damage. Thrown off balance by the strikes of Task Force 58 against the airfields on Kyushu on 18–19 March, Japanese air resistance to the landings was aggressively pressed home but was small in scale. Suicide hits were scored on the battleship *West*

---

[13] Gugeler, 7th Div Hist, p. 25; Capt Phillips D. Carleton (6th Mar Div Historian), The 6th Marine Div in Northern Okinawa (hereafter cited as Carleton, 6th Mar Div Hist), p. 11; Steven–Burns, Okinawa Diary, entry 15 Apr 45; III Amph Corps Actn Rpt, p. 33.

[14] CTF 51 Actn Rpt, III–9, and Tenth Army Actn Rpt, 7–III–2, give the number of troops landed as 50,000. A survey of unit reports indicates a figure of 60,000 as more accurate. See 382d Inf (96th Div) Actn Rpt, Ch. VII, p. 1; 7th Div Opn Rpt, p. 38; III Amph Corps Actn Rpt, p. 33; 1st Mar Div Actn Rpt, Ch. VII, p. 3; Gugeler, 7th Div Hist, p. 26. On the Kadena airfield, see CTF 55 Actn Rpt, III–7. For the front lines at the end of L Day, see III Amph Corps G–3 Periodic Rpt, 1 Apr 45; 1st Mar Div Actn Rpt, Ch. VII, pp. 2, 3; 17th Inf (7th Div), Actn Rpt, map opp. p. 14, Ch. VII; 32d Inf (7th Div) G–3 Periodic Rpt, 1 Apr 45; Mulford and Rogers, 96th Div Hist, Pt. I, pp. 5, 7, and Pt. II, pp. 5, 9, 10.

Virginia, two transports, and an LST; another LST was damaged by a suicide plane's near miss, and two ships were damaged in other ways.[15] An indefinite number of Japanese planes were shot down during the day by ships' fire and defending fighters.[16]

Favored by perfect weather and light resistance, American forces moved swiftly during the next two days, 2 and 3 April. By 1400 on 2 April the 17th Infantry, 7th Division, had established itself on the highlands commanding Nakagusuku Bay, on the east coast, and had extended its patrols to the shore of the bay. The speed of its advance had left the units on its flanks some distance behind. To the south the 32d Infantry came abreast late in the afternoon of 2 April, after reducing a strong point south of Koza with tanks. To the north, where the 1st Marine Division had encountered rugged terrain and difficult supply problems, a 6,000-yard gap was taken over by the 184th Infantry. Okinawa was now cut in two, and units of the Japanese Army in the northern and southern parts of the island were separated.[17]

The 96th Division made slow progress during the morning of 2 April in the country around Shido. Here it found heavily forested ridges, empty caves and dugouts, and mines and tank traps along the rough trails. Before evening the 381st Infantry had pushed through Shimabuku but had been stopped by enemy opposition in and around Momobaru. After a sharp fight the 383d Infantry took a hill just south of Momobaru, and with the help of an air strike, artillery, and tanks it reduced a ridge northeast of Futema. That night its lines stretched from the west coast just north of Isa to a point southwest of Futema on the Isa–Futema road and along the northern edge of Futema.[18]

On 3 April XXIV Corps turned its drive southward. Leaving the 17th Infantry to guard and consolidate its rear, the 32d Infantry pushed all three of its battalions southward along Nakagusuku Bay. After gaining 5,000 yards it occupied Kuba and set up its lines in front of Hill 165, the coastal extremity of a line of hills that swept southwest of the village. Fire was received from the hill, and a few Japanese were killed in a brief fire fight. Ten rounds of enemy artillery were received in the regiment's sector, a sign of awakening resistance.[19]

[15] CINCPAC-CINCPOA Opns in POA, Apr 45, p. 42; CTF 51 Actn Rpt, IV–75ff; CTF 58 Actn Rpt, I–7.

[16] CTF 51 Actn Rpt, IV–75ff; CTF 53 Actn Rpt, I–A–1; XXIV Corps Actn Rpt, p. 24; 1st Mar Div Actn Rpt, Ch. VII, p. 2.

[17] Gugeler, 7th Div Hist, p. 29.

[18] Mulford and Rogers, 96th Div Hist, Pt. I, pp. 10ff, and Pt. II, pp. 11ff.

[19] Gugeler, 7th Div Hist, pp. 32ff.

Coordinating their advance with that of the 32d Infantry on their left, elements of the 96th Division moved toward Hill 165 and Unjo. An unsuccessful attempt was made to take the hill. Other 96th Division units advanced to positions in the vicinity of Kishaba and Atanniya and northeast of Nodake. Futema and the high ground 600 yards south of it were taken. On the west flank the division's line went through Isa to the southeastern edge of Chiyunna.[20]

Having completed its wheeling movement to the right, the 96th Division was ready to drive south in conjunction with the 7th Division. Civilians and prisoners of war stated that Japanese troops had withdrawn to the south. XXIV Corps now changed the boundary line between its two assault divisions. On the next day, 4 April, four regiments were to move into line across the narrow waist of the island—the 32d and the 184th of the 7th Division on the east, and the 382d and the 383d of the 96th Division on the west. The real battle for Okinawa would then begin.[21]

Meanwhile, in the zone of III Amphibious Corps, the 1st Marine Division continued on 2 April 1945 to the line Ishimmi–Kutoku and Chatan. It met a few small pockets of resistance but was slowed mainly by the primitive roads and rough terrain. On the following day this division again advanced against little opposition, its forward elements reaching Nakagusuku (Buckner) Bay by 1600. At the same time its reconnaissance company explored Katchin Peninsula and the east coast roads north to Hizaonna. On 4 April all three regiments of the 1st Marine Division were on the eastern shore of Okinawa, and the division's zone of action was completely occupied.[22]

On L plus 1, the 6th Marine Division continued its advance into the foothills of Yontan-Zan, patrolled the peninsula northwest of the Hagushi beaches, and captured the coastal town of Nagahama. In this mountainous sector, well-worn trails crisscrossed the wooded hills and ridges, and caves pitted the coral walls and steep defiles. By manning both ridge tops and caves, the Japanese put up tenacious resistance. The 6th Marine Division killed about 250 of the enemy in two such strong points on 2 April. Next day it advanced 7,000 yards, the 22d Marines on the left maintaining supply through rough wild country by "weasels." One more day's march would bring this division to the L-plus-15 line drawn from Nakodamari to Ishikawa.[23]

[20] Mulford and Rogers, 96th Div Hist, Pt. I, pp. 12ff.
[21] Gugeler, 7th Div Hist, p. 35; Mulford and Rogers, 96th Div Hist, Pt. I, pp. 17, 18.
[22] 1st Mar Div Actn Rpt, Ch. VII, pp. 4–5, and maps.
[23] Carleton, 6th Mar Div Hist, pp. 15–18; Tenth Army Actn Rpt, 7–III–3.

MOVING INLAND, *American troops at first met little or no opposition. South of Kadena airfield, in coral crags deeply scarred by naval bombardment, 96th Division infantrymen engaged in their first hill and cave fighting in Okinawa. Other 96th Division troops, in amphibian tanks (below), turned south on the right flank and paused just north of Sunabe to reconnoiter; here they raised the American flag.*

The tempo of Japanese air attacks increased somewhat during the first three or four days after L Day, and many ships were damaged and some lost during this period. Vessels not actually engaged in unloading withdrew some distance from Okinawa each night, but this did not make them proof against attack. The *Henrico,* an assault transport carrying troops and the regimental staff of the 305th Infantry, 77th Division, was crashed by a suicide plane south of the Keramas at 1900 on 2 April. The plane struck the commodore's cabin and plunged through two decks, its bomb exploding on the second deck. The commodore was killed, as were also the commanding officer, the executive officer, the S–1, and the S–3 of the 305th. The ship's total casualties were 30 killed, 6 missing, and 50 injured.[24]

Organizing the Beachhead

The first waves of the troops were no sooner across the beaches and moving up the slopes than the complex machinery of supplying them, planned in intricate detail over long months, went into action. The problem was to move food, ammunition, and equipment for more than 100,000 men across beaches with a fringing reef from 200 to 400 yards wide[25] to dumps in rear areas, and then to the troops; to widen the native roads; to repair the captured airfields; and to alleviate the inevitable distress of the civilian population while rendering it incapable of interference.

While the beaches varied widely in serviceability, they were in general well adapted to unloading purposes. LCM's and LCVP's could cross the reef for four or five hours at each flood tide and unload directly on the beach; during middle and low tides their cargoes had to be transferred to amphibian vehicles at transfer barges. LST's, LSM's, and LCT's were beached on the reef at high tide to enable vehicles and equipment to be discharged during the next low tide, and the bulk cargo by DUKW's and LVT's at any tide. Various expedients were used to hasten the unloading. Night unloading under floodlights began on 2 April, and the work proceeded without interruption except when enemy aircraft was in the vicinity. Ponton causeways accommodating LST's were established at predetermined sites. By 4 April a T-pier, with a 300-foot single-lane approach and a 30- by 170-foot head, and a U-pier,

---

[24] Fifteen ships of Task Force 51 were damaged and three others lost from 2 to 5 April. CTF 51 Actn Rpt, IV–75ff, 94–98, and III–10, 12, 13; 305th Inf Opn Rpt, 1–27 Apr 45, p. 3.

[25] III Amph Corps Actn Rpt, p. 125.

with two 500-foot approaches and a 60- by 175-foot wharf section, had been set up on the beaches. The piers were soon supplanted by six single-lane causeways. By the same day an L-shaped pier, with a 1,400-foot single-lane approach and a 45- by 175-foot head, had been completed. Several sand piers were also constructed. As the marines rolled northward, additional unloading points were established as far north as Nago. Ponton barges carried to Okinawa on cargo ships were assigned varying jobs from day to day. By 11 April, 25 had been equipped with cranes and were operating as transfer barges, 53 were operating as lighters, and 6 as petroleum barges, while 8 were being used for evacuating casualties. A crane barge was capable of handling 400 tons in a 20-hour day when enough amphibian vehicles were available to make the runs ashore.[26]

Control of operations on the beaches, initially in the battalion landing teams, passed step by step through the echelons of command until Tenth Army, acting through the Island Command and the 1st Engineer Special Brigade, assumed responsibility on 9 April. Navy beachmasters maintained liaison with the ships and scheduled the beaching of landing ships and the assignment of lighterage. General unloading began on 3 April. It was soon apparent that the limiting factor was the availability of transport from the beaches to the dumps. The shortage of service units and equipment due to space limitations was immediately felt, especially in the Army zone; the problem was eased for the Marines by the use of 5,000 replacements landed with the Marine divisions. The rapidity of the advance and the immediate uncovering of Yontan and Kadena airfields required a rearrangement of supply priorities. The difficulties in initiating so intricate an undertaking near the enemy's homeland were prodigious, and it required time and the process of trial and error to overcome them. Suicide planes and suicide boats were a constant menace, and on the afternoon of 4 April the weather came to the aid of the enemy. A storm, bringing with it from 6- to 10-foot surf on the Hagushi beaches, lasted through the night and the following day. All unloading ceased, and some landing craft hit against the reef and were damaged. Again on 10 April surf backed by a high wind brought work to a standstill, and on 11 April conditions were but slightly improved. Rain accompanying these storms made quagmires of the roads and further complicated the supply problems. Despite these handicaps, the assault shipping was 80 percent unloaded by

[26] *Ibid.*, CTF 51 Actn Rpt, V–I–23–26 and V–J–14–16; Tenth Army Actn Rpt, 11–IV–14.

16 April, and 577,000 measurement tons had crossed the Hagushi beaches, a larger amount than had been anticipated in the plans.[27]

In addition to beach installations, base facilities necessary for the immediate success of the operation had to be developed quickly. Existing roads had to be improved and new roads built; the two airfields required repairs and expansion; and facilities for bulk storage of petroleum products, especially aviation gas, with connections to tankers off shore, were urgently needed. It was not long before the road down the west coast of Okinawa blossomed with markers which proclaimed it "US 1," and route numbers were similarly assigned to all main roads as they were taken, in accordance with the Engineers' plans. Okinawa's roads were, for the most part, unsurfaced and only one or one and one-half lanes in width. On L Day beach-exit and shore-party dump roads were improved; next, the main supply routes to the troops and roads to permanent and semipermanent supply installations. During the rains of 4–5 and 10–11 April the spinning wheels of endless lines of trucks soon tore through the crusts of the more traveled highways and became mired. In dry weather the surface became pulverized, and the heavy military traffic raised clouds of dust that sometimes cut visibility to the length of the hood. Engineers widened and resurfaced the main thoroughfares, using coral from existing and newly opened pits, coral sand, rubble from destroyed villages, and limestone. Bridges that were too narrow or too weak to carry American trucks and tanks were soon replaced by Bailey bridges, which could be set up and taken down much in the fashion of an Erector span. It was late in April before equipment was available for the construction of gasoline tank farms.[28]

An area 30 feet by 3,000 feet on the Yontan runway was cleared and the bomb craters filled on L Day; by the evening Kadena was also ready for emergency landings.[29] Nineteen artillery spotting planes were flown in from CVE's and LST's on 2 April and began operations on 3 April.[30] The work of conditioning the two fields began in earnest the following day.[31] Land-based fighter groups arrived at Yontan on 7 April and at Kadena two days later, improving local control of the air and making more aircraft available for support. Air

[27] CTF 51 Actn Rpt, V–I–22–26; Tenth Army Actn Rpt, 11–IV–12, 14, 17; personal observation of road conditions by Lt Col John Stevens.
[28] Tenth Army Actn Rpt, 11–IV–24–29 and 11–XI–7; personal observation of traffic conditions by Lt Col John Stevens.
[29] Tenth Army Actn Rpt, 11–VII–3; CTF 55 Actn Rpt, III–7.
[30] CINCPAC-CINCPOA Opns in POA, Apr 45, pp. 47, 48.
[31] III Amph Corps Actn Rpt, p. 114; personal observation at Kadena airfield by Lt Col John Stevens.

SUPPLYING AND DEVELOPING THE BEACHHEAD *had by L plus 3 made substantial progress. Supply ships were run in to the reef's edge, where they unloaded into trucks or amphibian vehicles. Indentation in shore line is Bishi River mouth, with Yontan airfield on horizon beyond; one runway (below) had been sufficiently repaired to allow use of land-based fighter planes.*

evacuation of the wounded to the Marianas by specially equipped C–54's began on 8 April.[32] At the same time a C–47 equipped for spraying DDT was brought into Yontan to take over the sanitation mission performed since 2 April by carrier-based aircraft.[33] The 69th Field Hospital landed on 3 April and received its first casualties two days later. Until it was established, the divisions had evacuated their casualties immediately by LCVP's and DUKW's to one of eight LST(H)'s lying off the Hagushi beaches. Each hospital ship could take care of 200 patients and perform emergency surgery. By 16 April Army and Marine hospitals ashore had a capacity of 1,800 beds.[34]

Thousands of destitute Okinawans, dazed by the preinvasion bombardment of their island and the swift advance of the Americans, entered the custody of the Military Government authorities almost at once. Initially placed in stockades to keep them out of the way, they were quickly moved to selected villages which had escaped destruction. Thus by 5 April 1,500 civilians held in a barbed wire enclosure just south of Kadena were being moved by truck to Shimabuku, where they would have freedom of movement within boundaries established by the military police. Other collection points were similarly emptied and closed.[35]

Thus, in an amazingly short time the beachhead had been won and the supply lines established. By 4 April Tenth Army held a slice of Okinawa 15 miles long and from 3 to 10 miles wide. The beachhead included two airfields of great potentialities, beaches that could take immense tonnage from the cargo ships, and sufficient space for the dumps and installations that were rapidly being built. The months of planning and preparation had borne their first fruit.

[32] Appleman, XXIV Corps Hist, p. 136.
[33] Tenth Army Actn Rpt, 11–VII–4.
[34] Tenth Army Actn Rpt, 11–XV–8.
[35] Stevens–Burns, Okinawa Diary, 5 Apr 45.

CHAPTER IV

Where Is the Enemy?

The ease with which American forces landed and established themselves on Okinawa gave rise to widespread speculation as to the whereabouts of the Japanese Army. The most optimistic view was that the enemy had been strategically outguessed and had prepared for the Americans at some other island, such as Formosa. Or, if Okinawa was not to be another Kiska, there was the possibility that the Marine diversion in the south had drawn the Japanese forces to that area. While the real attack forces approached by a roundabout route, covered by an early morning fog and artificial smoke, the approach of the diversion troops had been in full view of the enemy. Again, the Japanese might be conserving their strength for a bold counterattack as soon as American forces should be irrevocably committed to the beaches; but the time for such a counterattack came and went and still the enemy gave no sign.

The truth was, as the Americans were soon to discover, that the enemy was indeed on Okinawa in great strength, and that he had a well-thought-out plan for meeting the invasion.[1]

The Japanese Forces

The task of defending the Ryukyus was entrusted to the Japanese *32d Army,* commanded by Lt. Gen. Mitsuru Ushijima.[2] General Ushijima had assumed command in August 1944, relieving Lt. Gen. Masao Watanabe who had activated the *32d Army* in the preceding April. On assuming command, General Ushijima and his chief of staff, Lt. Gen. Isamu Cho, had reorganized the staff of the *Army,* replacing the incumbents with bright young officers from Imperial Headquarters. As reconstituted, the staff was distinguished by its youth, low rank, and ability. Col. Hiromichi Yahara, the only holdover from the old staff, was retained as senior staff officer in charge of operations.

[1] Stevens–Burns, Okinawa Diary, entries for 3 and 4 April.

[2] Unless otherwise noted, the account of the Japanese units and weapons on Okinawa was taken from Tenth Army G–2 Combat Intelligence Collecting Agency (CICA), Prisoner of War Interrogation Summaries, Nos. 1–19, Jul–Aug 45. These summaries are based on extensive interrogations of a large number of prisoners captured for the most part at the end of the campaign. A good deal of the material in Tenth Army G–2 Intelligence Monograph, Ryukyus Campaign, Aug 45, Pts. I–V, is based on these summaries. The original typescript summaries are, however, fuller and more accurate sources.

General Ushijima, according to the members of his staff, was a calm and very capable officer who inspired confidence among his troops. He had commanded an infantry group in Burma early in the war and came to his new assignment from the position of Commandant of the Japanese Military Academy at Zama. General Cho was a hard-driving, aggressive officer who had occupied high staff positions with the troops in China, Malaya, and Burma and had come to Okinawa from the Military Affairs Bureau of the War Department in Tokyo. Colonel Yahara enjoyed the reputation of being a brilliant tactician, conservative and calculating in his decisions. The combination of Ushijima's mature judgment, Cho's supple mind and aggressive energy, and the shrewd discernment of Yahara gave the *32d Army* a balanced and impressively able high command.[3]

Prior to the activation of the *32d Army* on 1 April 1944, Okinawa had been defended by a small and poorly trained garrison force. In June, before the American landings in the Marianas, the Japanese planned to reinforce the garrison with nine infantry and three artillery battalions.[4] The first reinforcement to reach Okinawa was the *44th Independent Mixed Brigade,* which arrived late in June. The *9th Division* landed on the island in July and was followed in August by the *62d Division* and the *24th Division.* Artillery, supporting troops, and service elements arrived during the summer and fall of 1944.

The Japanese plans for the defense of the Ryukyus were disrupted when the veteran *9th Division* left Okinawa for Formosa early in December, as part of the stream of reinforcements started toward the Philippines after the invasion of Leyte. It was intended to replace the division, but shortage of shipping made this impossible. Of the remaining combat units, the *62d Division* was considered by the commanding general and his staff to be the best in the *32d Army.* Commanded by Lt. Gen. Takeo Fujioka, the division was formed from the *63d* and *64th Brigades,* each consisting of four independent infantry battalions which had fought in China since 1938. It lacked divisional artillery but by April 1945 had been brought up to a strength of about 14,000 by the addition of two independent infantry battalions and a number of *Boeitai* (*Okinawa Home Guards*).

[3] See Tenth Army G-2 PW Interrog Rpt No. 28, 6 Aug 45 (hereafter cited as Interrog Yahara). This is a verbatim report of the interrogation of Col. Hiromichi Yahara, senior staff officer, the most important Japanese officer captured on Okinawa. Also Tenth Army G-2 PW Interrog Rpt No. 27, 24 Jul 45 (hereafter cited as Interrog Shimada), a verbatim report of the interrogation of Akira Shimada, civilian secretary to General Cho.

[4] CINCPAC-CINCPOA Bull No. 194–45: Empire Defense Opns Plan, Special Transl No. 86, 7 Aug 45, pp. 5, 6. The Japanese plan was dated 15 Jun 44.

JAPANESE COMMANDERS on Okinawa (photographed early in February 1945). In center: (1) Admiral Minoru Ota, (2) Lt. Gen. Mitsuru Ushijima, (3) Lt. Gen. Isamu Cho, (4) Col. Hitoshi Kanayama, (5) Col. Kikuji Hongo, and (6) Col. Hiromichi Yahara.

As finally organized, each of the independent infantry battalions was composed of five rifle companies, a machine gun company, and an infantry gun company, with a total battalion strength of approximately 1,200 men. (See Chart V.)

Unlike the *62d Division,* the *24th* was a triangular division, consisting of the *22d, 32d,* and *89th Infantry Regiments* and the *42d Field Artillery Regiment;* it had never seen combat. In January 1945 each of the infantry regiments had incorporated 300 Okinawan conscripts into its ranks and had been reorganized. After the reorganization a regiment consisted of three battalions of three rifle companies each, with each company reduced from 290 to 180 men. The total strength of the division, including Okinawans, was more than 15,000.

The *44th Independent Mixed Brigade* consisted of the *2d Infantry Unit* and the *15th Independent Mixed Regiment* and had a strength of about 5,000 men. The brigade had lost most of its original personnel by American submarine action while en route to Okinawa in June 1944, and it had been reconstructed around a nucleus of 600 survivors. The latter, plus replacements from Kyushu and conscripted Okinawans, were reorganized into the *2d Infantry Unit,* of approximately regimental strength but without a full complement of weapons and equipment. The *15th Independent Mixed Regiment* was flown to Okinawa at the end of June 1944 and assigned to the brigade. In addition to its three battalions of infantry, it had engineering troops and an antitank company; by the addition of native conscripts and *Boeitai* it had been brought by April 1945 to a strength of almost 2,800 men.

To add to the three major combat infantry units, General Ushijima in February 1945 converted seven sea-raiding battalions, formed to man suicide boats, into independent battalions for duty as infantry troops to fill the serious shortage resulting from the withdrawal of the *9th Division.* These battalions had a strength of approximately 900 men each and were divided among the major infantry commands. Counting these additions there was a total of thirty-one battalions of infantry on Okinawa, of which thirty were in the southern part.

Independent artillery units constituted an important part of the reinforcements sent to Okinawa. Two regiments of 150-mm. howitzers, one regiment of 75-mm. and 120-mm. guns, and one heavy artillery battalion of 150-mm. guns were on the island by the end of 1944 to supplement the organic divisional artillery and infantry cannon. For the first time in the Pacific war, Japanese artillery was under a unified command; all artillery units, with the exception of divisional artillery, were under the control of the *5th Artillery Command.* Most of the personnel of the command, which numbered 3,200, had served in other cam-

CHART V

Organization of the Japanese 62d Division in Okinawa

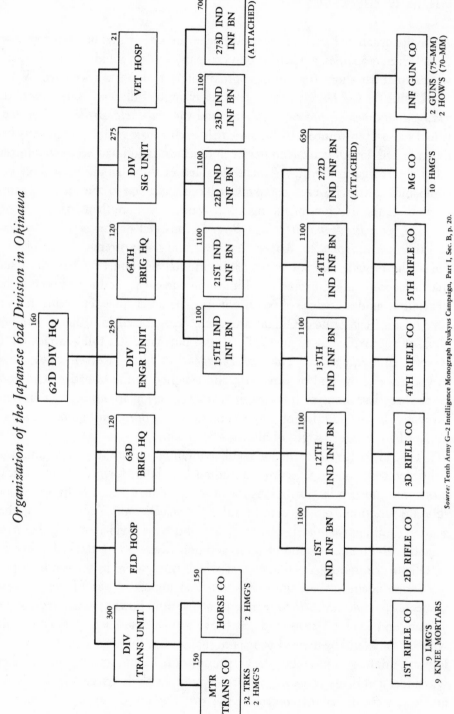

Source: Tenth Army G–2 Intelligence Monograph Ryukyus Campaign, Part I, Sec. B, p. 20.

paigns and had been with their units for three or four years. They were well trained by Japanese standards and were considered among the best artillerymen in the Japanese Army.

About 10,000 naval personnel were organized into the *Okinawa Naval Base Force,* commanded by Rear Admiral Minoru Ota, which had control of all naval establishments and activities in the Ryukyus. The unit was largely concentrated on Oroku Peninsula and just before the American landings was reorganized as a ground combat force for the defense of the peninsula. Only about 200 of the *Force,* however, had had more than superficial training in ground combat.

Other important units on Okinawa included the *27th Tank Regiment* of about 750 men, 4 independent machine gun battalions totaling over 1,600 men, an independent mortar regiment of 600 men, 2 light mortar battalions comprising 1,200 men, 4 antiaircraft artillery battalions totaling 2,000 men, 3 machine cannon battalions with 1,000 men, and 3 independent antitank battalions and 4 independent antitank companies totaling about 1,600 men. There were also from 22,000 to 23,000 service troops of various kinds.

At the time of the American landings on Okinawa, about 20,000 *Boeitai* had been mobilized by the Japanese for duty as labor and service troops. Though these men were for the most part not armed, they performed valuable services as ammunition and supply carriers at the front lines and also engaged in numerous front-line and rear-area construction and other duties. Some eventually saw combat. The *Boeitai* are not to be confused with the Okinawan conscripts and reservists who were called up and assimilated into the regular army just as were the Japanese in the home islands. The first group of *Boeitai* was assembled in June 1944 to work on the construction of airfields, but the general mobilization of natives into "National Home Defense Units" was not ordered until January 1945, after the departure of the *9th Division.* About 17,000 Okinawans between the ages of seventeen and forty-five were drafted to serve as *Boeitai.* In addition, about 750 male students of the middle schools, fourteen years of age and over, were organized into *Blood and Iron for the Emperor Duty Units* and trained for guerilla warfare. Further drafts of *Boeitai* were made at various times during the battle. In addition to the *Boeitai* a large number of Okinawan civilians were conscripted into the Japanese forces either to increase the strength of existing units or to organize new units. While the actual number of Okinawans serving with the *32d Army* has not been determined, available evidence indicates that they represented a large proportion of the total,

50–mm. Grenade Discharger

Hand Grenade

320–mm. (Spigot) Mortar Shell

Satchel Charge

JAPANESE WEAPONS

increasing the Japanese strength by perhaps as much as one-third or more.[5]

When the Americans invaded Okinawa, the total strength of the *32d Army* amounted to more than 100,000 men, including the 20,000 *Boeitai* draftees and an unknown number of conscripted Okinawans. The army proper totaled 77,000, consisting of 39,000 Japanese troops in infantry combat units and 38,000 in special troops, artillery, and service units. (For the troop list of the *32d Army*, see Appendix B.)

Weapons of the 32d Army

The armament of the Japanese on Okinawa was characterized by a high proportion of artillery, mortar, antiaircraft, and automatic weapons in relation to infantry strength. Their supply of automatic weapons and mortars was generally in excess of authorized allotments; much of this excess resulted from the distribution of an accumulation of such weapons intended for shipment to the Philippines and elsewhere but prevented by the shortage of shipping and the course of war from leaving the island. The Japanese also had an abundant supply of ammunition, mines, hand grenades, and satchel charges.[6]

On Okinawa the Japanese possessed artillery in greater quantity, size, and variety than had been available to them in any previous Pacific campaign. Utilizing naval coastal guns, they were able to concentrate a total of 287 guns and howitzers of 70-mm. or larger caliber for the defense of the island. Of this total, sixty-nine pieces could be classified as medium artillery, including fifty-two 150-mm. howitzers and twelve 150-mm. guns. The smaller pieces included 170 guns and howitzers of calibers of 70- and 75-mm. In addition, seventy-two 75-mm. antiaircraft guns and fifty-four 20-mm. machine cannon were available for use in ground missions.

The principal mortar strength of the *32d Army* was represented by ninety-six 81-mm. mortars of the two light mortar battalions. The Japanese also possessed, in greater numbers than had previously been encountered, the large 320-mm. mortars, commonly called spigot mortars; the *1st Artillery Mortar Regiment,* reputed to be the only one of its kind in the Japanese Army, was armed with twenty-four of these. Standard equipment of the ground combat units of the army included about 1,100 50-mm. grenade dischargers (knee mortars).

[5] Tenth Army G–2 CICA Transl No. 83, 19 May 45: Standard for Establishment of Nansei Shoto Garrison Plan, 1 Jan 45; Transl No. 228, 6 Jul 45: *32d Army* Op Ord A #110, 3 Mar 45; Transl No. 76, 15 May 45: *62d Div* Op Ord A25, 8 Mar 45; Tenth Army G–2 Wkly Summary, 15 Aug 45; XXIV Corps G–2 Summary No. 16, 24 Jun–1 Jul 45, Incl 3: OB Summary. See also Tenth Army PW Interrog Summary No. 18, 31 Jul 45: Civilian Defense Organizations.

[6] See n. 2. See also *32d Army* equipment and weapons chart, 1 Dec 44, in Tenth Army Int Monograph, Pt. I, Sec. B, Order of Battle, pp. 4–7.

To counter American tank strength, the Japanese relied, among other things, on an unusually large number of antitank guns, especially the 47-mm. type. The independent antitank units had a total of fifty-two 47-mm. antitank guns, while twenty-seven 37-mm. antitank guns were distributed among the other units of the *Army*. The entire Japanese tank force, however, consisted of only fourteen medium and thirteen light tanks, the heaviest weapon of which was the 57-mm. gun mounted on the medium tanks.

The *32d Army* relied heavily on a great number of automatic weapons, well emplaced and plentifully supplied with ammunition. Its units possessed a total of 333 heavy and 1,208 light machine guns. In the course of the battle many more were taken from tanks being used as pillboxes and from wrecked airplanes. The *62d Division* alone wielded nearly half the automatic weapons of the *32d Army* and was by far its most potent unit.

The Japanese Plan of Defense

The active formulation of a defense plan for the Ryukyus dates from the American capture of the Marianas in June and July 1944. The first plan for the ground defense of the Ryukyus was established in a *32d Army* directive of 19 July 1944. This document outlined a plan to destroy the Americans at the water's edge; that failing, to "annihilate" them from previously constructed positions, embodying a fortified defense in depth. In accordance with this directive, construction of cave and underground positions began in the summer of 1944. The command on Okinawa was convinced that the situation was urgent and informed the troops that "the Empire is determined to fight a show-down battle with an all-out effort for the preservation of national unity when the enemy advances to the Nansei Shoto." [7] In instructions issued in August *32d Army Headquarters* stated:

The enemy counteroffensive has become increasingly severe and they have infiltrated into our central Pacific defense area and are now boldly aiming toward the Nansei Shoto. Should we be unable to defend the Nansei Shoto, the mainland and the southern frontier would become isolated. Thus, the execution of the present war would be extremely difficult and would become a life-and-death problem for our nation. [8]

In the early part of 1945 important changes were made in the original defense plan. It was decided not to attempt the destruction of the invading

[7] Tenth Army Transl No. 4, 17 Apr 45: *32 Army* Ord No. 82, 19 Jul 44.
[8] Tenth Army Transl: *32d Army* Instructions, 6 Aug 44.

forces at the beaches, but to have the *32d Army* offer a strong resistance around a central fortified position; a decisive land battle would be avoided until the *Kamikaze* planes and the Japanese fleet should destroy the American warships and transports. The general character of the final plan reflected the critical situation that faced General Ushijima with the departure of the *9th Division* for Formosa and with the fading of prospects for reinforcements. He had to alter his plans to fit his resources, so depleted by now that he had to mobilize virtually the entire civilian population of the island.

The Japanese high command was determined to hold Okinawa and planned to employ the major portion of the Empire's remaining air strength as well as a large portion of its fleet in an attack on the American sea forces. The Japanese hoped to isolate and weaken the invading ground forces by destroying the American naval units and support shipping lying off Okinawa. To accomplish this, they relied chiefly on bomb-laden planes guided to their targets by suicide pilots, members of the Japanese Navy's *Special Attack Corps* known as the *Kamikaze (Divine Wind) Corps*. This desperate measure was expected to equalize the uneven ground battle by cutting off the Americans from supplies and reinforcements. It would enable the *32d Army* to drive the invaders into the sea.

Despite the hopes of the Japanese high command, planning of the *32d Army* for the defense of Okinawa proceeded on the assumption that it was impossible to defeat the enemy and that the most that could be done was to deny him the use of the island for as long a period as possible and inflict the maximum number of casualties.[9] Acting on this assumption, General Ushijima drew his forces together into the southern part of Okinawa and, from the strongly fortified positions around Shuri, prepared to make his stand there as costly to the enemy as possible. He would not go out to meet the invaders; he would wait for them to come to him, and force them to fight on his own terms. The *32d Army* artillery was instructed not to fire on the invading ships and landing forces, in order to avoid revealing its positions and exposing them to the devastating naval gunfire of the Americans. Units were not to oppose landings in their sectors until enough enemy troops had been brought ashore to render escape by sea impossible. The *32d Army* planned to defend only the southern third of Okinawa strongly. The principal defenses would be established in the rugged ground north of Naha, Shuri, and Yonabaru. Landings north of this line would not be opposed; south of it the Americans would be met on the beaches.

[9] Interrog Yahara.

Wherever the Americans landed, they would eventually come up against the Shuri defenses, where the main battle would be fought.[10]

The Japanese estimate of American plans was very accurate. The enemy expected the Americans to land across the Hagushi beaches on the west coast, with from six to ten divisions, and to strike out for the Yontan and Kadena airfields. He anticipated that American landing forces would form large beach-heads of 2-division strength each, hold within these perimeters until sufficient supplies were unloaded to permit a strong attack, and then advance behind massed tanks and concentrated artillery fire. The Japanese estimated that it would take the Americans about ten days to launch their attack against the main Shuri defenses. They believed that the Americans intended to draw the main Japanese force into the Shuri lines so that a not too costly secondary landing could be effected with perhaps one division on the east coast somewhere south of Shuri, near Minatoga.[11]

The *32d Army* disposed its available troops in accordance with its general plan of defense and its estimate of the enemy's capabilities. Only two battalions of the *2d Infantry Unit* were left in the north to defend not only the Motobu Peninsula but also Ie Shima, where they destroyed the island's airfield.[12] The only force stationed in the area immediately behind the Hagushi beaches was the *1st Specially Established Regiment, Boeitai,* which was ordered to fight a delaying action and then, after destroying the two airfields in the sector, to retreat.[13] The *62d Division* manned the defensive belt across the island north of the Naha–Shuri–Yonabaru line. Its *63d Brigade* was to absorb the shock of the American attack southward at the narrow waist of the island between Chatan and Toguchi, while the main line of resistance was established from Uchitomari to Tsuwa north of the Shuri defenses. Deployed to support the *63d,* the *64th Brigade* was dug in to fight in the successive positions around Shuri. Artillery attached to the *62d Division* was emplaced in direct support on the west side of the line.[14] (See Map No. VI.)

[10] Interrog Yahara; Interrog Shimada; U. S. Strategic Bombing Survey (Pacific), Naval Analysis Division, *The Campaigns of the Pacific War,* pp. 324, 325.   [11] *Ibid.*

[12] Tenth Army PW Interrog Summary No. 4; Int Monograph, Pt. I, Sec. A, General Tactical Essay, p. 10: *32d Army* Op Ord A H 111, 11 Mar 45.

[13] Tenth Army Transl No. 149, 17 Apr 45: *32d Army* Ord 82, 19 Jul 44; Transl No. 237, 7 Jul 45: *32d Army* Op Ord 127, 28 Mar 45; XXIV Corps G–2 Transl, Batch No. 70, Item No. 11, 17 Apr 45: *32d Army* Op Ord A 113, 21 Mar 45; Item No. 14: *1st Specially Established Regt* Op Ord 1, 30 Mar 45.

[14] Tenth Army PW Interrog Summary No. 1, 5 Aug 45: *32d Army;* Summary No. 2, 2 Aug 45: The *62d Division;* Transl No. 214, 3 Jul 45: *32d Army* Op Ord A 98, 26 Jan 45; Transl No. 232, 6 Jul 45: *32d Army* Op Ord A 116, 24 Mar 45; Int Monograph, Pt. V, Special PW Interrog, p. 5; CINCPAC-CINCPOA Bull No. 186–45; Transl Interrog No. 37, 24 Jul 45, pp. 43–50: *63d Brigade* Defense Plans, 20 Feb 45.

Having selected the Shuri area as their main battle position, the Japanese with shrewdness and great industry organized the ground for a strong defense. The main zone of defense was planned as a series of concentric positions adapted to the contours of the area. Caves, emplacements, blockhouses, and pillboxes were built into the hills and escarpments, connected by elaborate underground tunnels and skillfully camouflaged; many of the burial tombs were fortified. The Japanese took full advantage of the terrain to organize defensive areas and strong points that were mutually supporting, and they fortified the reverse as well as the forward slopes of hills. Artillery and mortars were emplaced in the caves and thoroughly integrated into the general scheme of defensive fires.[15]

To meet the threat of landings in the south, the *32d Army* stationed the *24th Division* in defensive positions covering the Minatoga beaches and extending across the southern end of the island.[16] The *44th Independent Mixed Brigade* was moved to the Chinen Peninsula and was ordered to cooperate with the *24th Division* in repelling any landings in the area. Artillery was registered on the Minatoga beaches, and some of the 320-mm. mortars were moved to this sector.[17]

During the long period of planning the Imperial General Staff and the *32d Army* were constantly concerned with fixing the probable date of the American invasion; each changed its view several times and on occasion they were not in agreement. It was during and after the invasion of Saipan, Tinian, and Guam, in the summer of 1944, that the Japanese first expected an immediate invasion of Okinawa and, accordingly, began to pour troops into the island. But after the invasion of the Palaus and Leyte in September and October 1944 the Imperial General Staff in Tokyo considered it unlikely that sufficient American troops would be immediately available for another major operation.[18] During the Philippines operations at the end of 1944 the Imperial General Staff in Tokyo was in doubt as to whether the next blow would fall on the south China coast or on Formosa,[19] although the command of the *32d Army* was still convinced that Okinawa would be invaded and pushed forward preparations for its defense.[20]

[15] Tenth Army Int Monograph, Pt. I, Sec. A, General Tactical Essay, pp. 4–8.
[16] Tenth Army PW Interrog Summary No. 3, 2 Aug 45: *24th Division;* Transl No. 214, 3 Jul 45.
[17] Tenth Army Transl Nos. 214, 238, PW Interrog Summary No. 11.
[18] Interrog Yahara.
[19] 1st Demobilization Ministry Tokyo, Answers to Questions Regarding the Okinawa Operation, 22 Dec 45. These were answers to questions submitted by the Tenth Army historian and were based on the memory of a staff officer in charge in Imperial Headquarters, fragmentary documents, and statements of participants in the operation.
[20] Tenth Army Transl No. 4, 17 Apr 45: *32d Army* Ord No. 82, 19 Jul 44.

Again, at the beginning of 1945 the Imperial General Staff was uncertain whether the next American attack would be against Formosa or Okinawa. By the end of February, as a result of the invasion of Iwo Jima, which pointed to the American strategy of cutting off the Japanese home islands from the mainland and the Indies, the Japanese concluded that Formosa would be bypassed and that Okinawa would be the next target.[21] Their aerial reconnaissance and intelligence reports revealed an increase in west-bound American shipping to the Philippines and the Marianas during the latter part of February—an increase that swelled to large proportions early in March; this seemed a clear indication of the imminence of another American operation.[22] When the invasion fleet appeared off Iwo Jima, it was considered by some to be a feint for the invasion of Okinawa.[23] With the Iwo Jima battle in progress and submarine activity increasing around the Ryukyus, it was taken for granted that the invasion of Okinawa would soon follow, on or about 1 April 1945.[24]

As one of the last steps in preparing for the expected struggle, the Japanese command on Okinawa on 21 March ordered all air, shipping, and rear-echelon units to "prepare for ground combat." On 27 March, the day after the American invasion of the Keramas, *32d Army* advised its units that "the enemy is planning to land his main strength tomorrow, the 28th, on the western coast of southern Okinawa, in particular in the Yontan-Kadena sector."[25] When the American forces invaded Okinawa, a few days later than had been predicted, the *32d Army* adhered strictly to its plan of offering little resistance until the invaders should come up against their outposts at the Shuri line. The Japanese Combined Fleet Commander, meanwhile, prepared to execute his plan, delayed by Task Force 58's foray into the Inland Sea in March, to destroy the American fleet by air and surface action. Before many days had passed, the enemy was to react to the invasion with a fury never before encountered.

Enemy Counterattacks by Air and Sea

The American command was aware of the likelihood of formidable attacks by both air and sea on the assault forces. Okinawa was close to the Japanese home-

---

[21] Answers to Questions Regarding the Okinawa Operation.

[22] *Ibid.;* Tenth Army Transl No. 168, 20 Jun 45: *32d Army* Op Ord A 106, 15 Feb 45; PW Interrog Rpt No. 23.

[23] Interrog Yahara; XXIV Corps G–2 PW Interrog Rpt No. 54, 6 May 45.

[24] Answers Regarding the Okinawa Operation; Tenth Army PW Interrog Rpt No. 16, 14 Jun 45.

[25] XXIV Corps G–2 Transl Batch No. 70, Item No. 11, 17 Apr 45, *32d Army* Op Ord A 113, 21 Mar 45; Tenth Army Transl No. 310, 11 Jul 45, *32d Army* Op Ord A 114, 27 Mar 45.

land, where the remaining strength of the enemy's naval and air forces was concentrated. To meet the expected air offensive from the near-by fields of Kyushu. Shanghai, and Formosa, the Americans relied upon Task Force 58, the Tenth Army's Tactical Air Force, the guns of the fleet and supply ships, the British task force, and land-based antiaircraft artillery. To ensure early warning of Japanese raids, the Navy established around Okinawa a ring of picket stations, manned by destroyers and destroyer-type vessels, to which gunboats (LCS) and later LSM(R) types were added to give increased fire power. These stations were all less than 100 miles from Zampa Point, the peninsula just north of the Marine beaches; some were only a few miles off the coasts of the island. Combat air patrols were maintained day and night over the picket stations, which could also call for aid from the routine combat air patrol of from 48 to 120 planes aloft during the daytime, orbiting in depth in a circle around Okinawa. Task Force 58, deployed just to the east of Okinawa, with its own picket group of from 6 to 8 destroyers, kept 13 carriers (7 CV and 6 CVL) on duty from 23 March to 27 April and a smaller number thereafter. Until 27 April from 14 to 18 converted carriers (CVE's) were in the area at all times, and until 20 April British Task Force 57, with 4 large and 6 converted carriers, remained off the Sakishima Islands to protect the southern flank. Two Marine Fighter Groups were installed and operating at Yontan and Kadena airfields by 9 April, and other Marine and Army Air Groups were added later. All assault antiaircraft artillery of the XXIV Corps was ashore by the night of 4 April, and that of III Amphibious Corps by 12 April. Japanese airmen were to find these combined defenses formidable.[26]

Enemy air opposition had been relatively light during the first few days after the landings. On 6 April the expected air reaction materialized with a fierce attack of 400 planes which had flown down from Kyushu to drive the invaders from Okinawa. The raids began at dawn, and by noon Task Force 58 had shot down seven possible suicide planes. Throughout the afternoon the battle increased in intensity. Patrol and picket ships, which throughout the operation proved an irresistible attraction to enemy planes, were a favorite target. Japanese planes also appeared from time to time over the Hagushi beaches and transport area and were taken under fire by the ship and shore

[26] CINCPAC-CINCPOA Opns in POA, Apr 45, pp. 47, 51, 52, and Plates VII, XIX; CTF 58 Actn Rpt, Incl H; CTF 51 Actn Rpt, II-17, 18, 19. For operational dates of Yontan and Kadena airfields, see Tactical Air Force (TAF) Actn Rpt Ryukyus, 5-0-2; interv 1st I & H Hist Off with Lt Col Eugene H. Hawkins, Tactical Air Force, 13 Apr 45; see, however, Tenth Army Actn Rpt, 11-X-4, 5, and TAF Actn Rpt, 6-III-1, which give operational dates as 7 and 10 April respectively.

KAMIKAZE ATTACKS *resulted in many hits, more near misses. U. S. S.* Sangamon *(above) was just missed but was hit in a later attack.   Another near miss (below) sent U. S. battleship* Missouri's *gunners scurrying from upper turret while those in Turret 9 looked to see what was going on.*

batteries. On such occasions the raider, ringed with bright streams of tracer bullets from automatic weapons, would streak across a sky filled with black puffs of smoke from hundreds of bursting shells, and in the course of seconds would plunge into the sea in a geyser of water and smoke, or crash into a ship with an even greater explosion of smoke and flame. Directed against such raiders, friendly fire killed four Americans and wounded thirty-four others in the XXIV Corps zone, ignited an ammunition dump near Kadena, destroyed an oil barge, and in the late afternoon shot down two American planes over the beaches. Some ships also suffered damage and casualties from friendly fire. Twenty-two of twenty-four suicide crashes were successful, sinking two destroyers, a mine sweeper, two ammunition ships, and an LST. A ship rescuing survivors from the lost LST was itself struck by a suicide plane soon after but was not seriously damaged. The attack cost the Japanese about 300 planes; 65 were splashed by fliers from the *Essex* alone. Unloading continued on the Hagushi beaches almost without pause, and the American fleet, although it had taken severe blows, was still intact.[27]

On the night of 6–7 April the Japanese fleet came out for the planned surface attack on the American sea forces. An American submarine lying off Kyushu reported the movement of the Japanese warships, and forty planes of Task Force 58 began a far-flung search at dawn on 7 April. At 0822 a plane from the *Essex* sighted the enemy force, which consisted of the battleship *Yamato,* the light cruiser *Yahagi,* and eight destroyers, in the East China Sea on a course toward Okinawa. Task Force 58, which had started northeastward at 0400 that morning in order to close with the enemy, launched its planes at a point estimated to be 240 miles from the enemy fleet. The first attacks through heavy but inaccurate antiaircraft fire scored at least eight torpedo and five bomb hits on the *Yamato,* the *Yahagi,* and three of the destroyers. Subsequent attacks succeeded in sinking the *Yamato,* the *Yahagi,* and four destroyers; one destroyer was seriously damaged and one left burning. Task Force 58 lost only 10 planes out of the 386 that participated. Okinawa was now safe from surface attack.[28]

While the strike on the *Yamato* was in progress, Task Force 58 was busy warding off enemy air attacks and in the course of the day shot down fifty-four planes. A suicide plane dropped its bomb from a height of fifty feet onto the *Hancock's* flight deck, then itself plowed through a group of planes aft. Although

[27] CINCPAC-CINCPOA Opns in POA, Apr 45, pp. 50, 52; CTF 51 Actn Rpt, II–18 and III–20, 21, 22; CTF 58 Actn Rpt, I–7, 8; personal obsn Lt Col John Stevens, 6 Apr 45.
[28] CTF 58 Actn Rpt, I–8, 9.

SINKING OF THE YAMATO, *last of Japan's super-battleships, was accomplished by Task Force 58 before the* Yamato *had ever fired her main batteries in World War II. With her escorts near by, she went up in a blast of smoke and flame.*

seriously damaged, the carrier landed her own planes when they returned at 1630. British Task Force 57 was able to keep the airfields of Sakishima largely inoperative during the Japanese air and sea offensive of 6–7 April.[29]

The enemy continued during April to deliver periodic heavy air attacks. Daytime raids were generally staged against Task Force 58, the picket ships, and shipping beyond the range of land-based antiaircraft artillery. At night, when the supply ships shrouded themselves in artificial fog as raiders approached, the enemy usually struck Yontan and Kadena airfields, with the Hagushi beaches a secondary target. Most of these raids were made between 2100 and 2300, and 0200 and 0400. The Japanese, clever at deception, sometimes shelled one of the airfields with their artillery, leading the Americans to expect an attack at that point, and then followed with an air raid on the other field. On occasion enemy planes would follow American planes in at dusk, circle the fields with their lights on, and then bomb and strafe the runways and storage areas.[30]

Task Force 58 was heavily engaged on 11 April, and near misses by four suicide planes sent the carrier *Enterprise* to Ulithi for repairs. On the next day the main weight of the attack shifted to the picket ships and the Hagushi anchorage. Seventeen Allied ships were hit and two sunk. The destroyer *M. L. Abele* was sent to the bottom when hit by both a suicide plane and a Baka bomb; the latter was a potentially dangerous but not often successful piloted, rocket-driven projectile launched by a twin-engined bomber. Again on 15–16 April, despite strikes by Task Force 58 against Kyushu airfields, Japanese airplanes appeared in strength at Okinawa. On the 16th a *Kamikaze* plane crashed the *Intrepid's* flight deck, and other suicide planes damaged 10 ships and sank a destroyer; 270 enemy planes were shot from the air and many more destroyed on the ground. Eventful days, too, were 22, 27, and 28 April. On the last of these, starting at 1400, a force of 200 Japanese planes attacked Okinawa in 44 raids. Several American ships were damaged, but 118 of the attacking planes were destroyed. The hospital ship *Comfort,* although following hospital procedure, was crashed by a suicide plane 50 miles south of Okinawa. The *Comfort's* casualty list was 63, of whom 29 were killed and 1 missing.[31]

American planes too had struck hard. During the month the XXI Bomber Command had hit Japan with 15,712 tons of bombs; 36 percent of the tonnage

[29] *Ibid.,* pp. 9, 10; CINCPAC-CINCPOA Opns in POA, Apr 45, pp. 63, 68.

[30] Tenth Army Actn Rpt, 11–VI–21 and 11–X–8, 12, 13; interv 1st I & H Off with Brig Gen Chas. S. Harris, Tenth Army AAA Off, 11 Jul 45.

[31] CTF 51 Actn Rpt, II–16, 17, 18, and III–67, 68, 69; CTF 58 Actn Rpt, I–12, 13.

had been dropped on Kyushu airfields in support of the Okinawa operation, 29 percent on the Japanese aircraft industry, and 34 percent on other Japanese urban industrial areas. Formosa was being struck from the Philippines.

During the period 26 March–30 April, 20 American ships were sunk and 157 damaged by enemy action. Suicide attacks accounted for the sinking of 14 ships and the damaging of 90, while other air attacks damaged 47 ships and sank 1. Two of the largest carriers—the *Hancock* and the *Enterprise*—one CVL, the *San Jacinto,* and the British carrier *Intrepid* sustained serious damage from suicide planes. Picket ships suffered especially heavy attrition, and as quickly as land-based radar could be installed on Okinawa and neighboring islands the number of picket stations was reduced. Five picket stations remained after completion of radar installations at Hedo Point on 21 April and in Ie Shima on 23 April. Although the seizure of the Kerama Islands had substantially reduced this threat, suicide boats continued to be active on a small scale, particularly in the Naha and Yonabaru areas at night. Up to 30 April suicide boats sank one ship and damaged six. Navy casualties were heavy; during April they totaled 956 killed, 2,650 wounded, and 897 missing in action.[32]

For their part, the Japanese had lost up to 30 April more than 1,100 planes in the battle to Allied naval forces alone, and many more to land-based antiaircraft artillery and planes of the Tactical Air Force. Not only had the task force led by the *Yamato* been defeated and for the most part sunk, but a considerable number of other Japanese combatant and auxiliary vessels had also been sunk or damaged.

More important, the Japanese plan to destroy or drive off the fleet and isolate the troops, thus winning the battle for Okinawa, had been frustrated. Instead, the Japanese on the island were completely cut off and isolated from their near-by homeland. The invading warships and transports remained and, despite the weight of the blows delivered against them, continued to pour supplies into Okinawa and to keep the lanes open for fresh supplies from the other side of the Pacific Ocean. Thus American ground troops could work their way inland with the assurance of an unbroken supply line.[33]

[32] CINCPAC-CINCPOA Opns in POA, Apr 45, pp. 50, 66, 70–76; CTF 51 Actn Rpt, II–15, 16, 17.

[33] CINCPAC-CINCPOA Opns in POA, Apr 45, pp. 1, 2, 5, 6, 17, 50.

CHAPTER V

Coming to Grips With the Enemy

American intelligence, handicapped as it was by various circumstances, had not succeeded in ascertaining all the salient facts regarding the enemy's forces and his plans. It had underestimated substantially the number of Japanese soldiers on Okinawa, largely through not taking into account the possibility of conscripting Okinawan natives. It had also not foreseen the great concentration of Japanese troops in the Shuri defense line or suspected its array of formidable defenses; these had not been indicated by the aerial photographs because most of the Shuri area had been cloud-covered during the photographic missions. But in the course of the fighting between 4 and 14 April the real nature of the Japanese defense on Okinawa was to become clear. In particular the 96th Division, grappling during 9–12 April with one of the strongest enemy positions in Okinawa, was to experience the full potency of the carefully prepared Japanese defensive plan.

For General Ushijima and his staff, this was still a time of watchful waiting as they were not certain that the pattern of the American attack was yet fully revealed. A new landing in the Machinato–Oyama area was considered possible. A Japanese field order of 4 April noted that "the tempo of enemy operations in the Minatoga area is increasing," and that vigilance was necessary against landings in this sector. Above all, the Japanese were concerned over the possibility of American operations in the Yonabaru area—either a new landing covered by American warships already operating in Buckner Bay or, more likely, a vigorous drive down the eastern flatlands by ground troops heavily supported by tanks and naval guns.[1] Because of these American capabilities, General Ushijima continued to follow his basic plan of centering his main forces in and around the Shuri defenses, leaving outposts to slow up the American attack.

The Japanese braced themselves for the shock of battle as XXIV Corps, after cutting the island in two, turned south on 3 April for the drive toward Shuri. "Do your utmost," the enemy troops were told; "the victory of the century lies

---

[1] Tenth Army Transl No. 182, 23 Jun 45; No. 199, 1 Jul 45; No. 264, 12 Jul 45.

in this battle." [2] Orders went out to hold ground "regardless of whether the communications are severed or any other unfavorable conditions." [3]

Through the Outposts, 4–8 April

General Hodge ordered both his divisions to continue the attack southward on 4 April—the 7th on the east and the 96th on the west. The Corps' objective was the hill mass extending from Urasoe-Mura to Hill 178 and Ouki. This was a larger assignment than anyone realized at the time, and much blood was to be shed before it could be carried out. The objective was not to be gained for three weeks, and then only partially.

XXIV Corps Drives South, 4–5 April

The 96th Division made sweeping gains on 4 April. Its advance carried it through much of the outpost area immediately north of the Uchitomari–Tsuwa line. In the center of the island, troops of the 382d Infantry advanced more than two miles south from Nodake along the division's east boundary. On the west coast, the 96th's right-flank units swept along the flatlands from Isa to Uchitomari. Progress was only a little slower in the division's center along Route 5. Enemy resistance, which included artillery fire from the area to the south, varied from sniper fire to intense machine-gun and mortar fire directed out of scattered Japanese strong points. Rapid maneuver by infantry units supported by tanks reduced the enemy positions. Risks were taken for the sake of rapid advance, with the result that adjacent units often lost contact with one another, and advance elements occasionally were cut off by fire from supporting units.[4]

The deepest penetration of the Japanese area was on the west, where the 3d Battalion, 383d Infantry, preceded by elements of the 96th Reconnaissance Troop, drove rapidly from Isa to Uchitomari during the morning of 4 April. Between Mashiki and Uchitomari the troops ran into heavy fire from the south and from the ridges on their left (east). Three medium tanks from the 763d Tank Battalion ran afoul of a carefully sited and well-concealed 47-mm. antitank gun. Firing twenty rounds, Japanese gunners set the three tanks afire. The enemy later described this feat as an illustration of the effectiveness of 47-mm. guns. "Great results," Japanese combat instructions stated, "can be

---

[2] 7th Div G–2 Periodic Rpt No. 10, 11 Apr 45.

[3] *Ibid.*

[4] The account of operations of the 96th Division is based on Mulford and Rogers, 96th Div History, Pts. I and II, and 96th Div G–2 and G–3 Periodic Rpts for the period 4–14 Apr 45.

obtained by concealing the guns and opening surprise fire on the tanks at close range." [5] As a result of continuing Japanese fire in the rough ground east of Mashiki and Oyama, the 3d Battalion, 383d Infantry, pulled back under smoke to Mashiki, where the troops dug in under artillery fire. (See Map No. VII.)

For the 96th Division, 5 April marked the beginning of iron resistance on Okinawa. The 383d estimated at one time during the day that its forward elements were receiving fire from 20 machine guns and from 15 to 20 mortars, besides artillery pieces. Driving through the green, rolling country east of the Ginowan road, the 382d unmasked a series of fortified positions, many of them protected by mine fields. Each position caused American casualties and required enveloping movements. Well-camouflaged Japanese troops, supported by tanks, attacked the 1st Battalion during the afternoon, but the attack was broken up by artillery, mortar, and machine-gun fire. During the day, the 382d gained about 400 yards on the left (east) and 900 yards on the right.

The 383d on the west made little progress on 5 April. Its efforts centered on Cactus Ridge, 600 yards southeast of Mashiki, which commanded much of the ground between Uchitomari and Oyama. An infantry company supported by tanks made a direct assault on Cactus Ridge under heavy fire. The ridge was protected by a tank ditch, barbed wire, and a long mine field. When American tanks tried to pass through a gap in the mine field, they came under 47-mm. fire. Two were hit and had to be abandoned. The infantry soon came to a halt under almost continuous machine-gun, rifle, and mortar fire, and were forced to withdraw.

By the evening of 5 April the 7th Division had pulled up almost abreast of the 96th. The 7th had fallen about two miles behind on the preceding day, when its center elements encountered a high, wooded ridge paralleling the coast line just west of Kuba and defended by a group of Japanese estimated as of company strength. On this ridge a great castle had been built in the sixteenth century by a feudal lord who chose the commanding height as a vantage point from which he could observe movement through this narrow part of the island. Now there remained only attractive green terraces encased on several levels within massive stone walls intricately pieced together by Okinawans of a former day, 10,000 of whom labored for ten years to build this castle for their lord. [6]

---

[5] 7th Div G–2 Periodic Rpt No. 10, 11 Apr 45; *32d Army* Combat Instructions, 5 Apr 45.

[6] The account of operations of the 7th Division is based on Gugeler, 7th Div History, pp. 36–57; Tenth Army Int Monograph, Pt. I, Sec. C, Ch II: Japanese Defense of the Pinnacle (prepared in part by Lt Gugeler); 7th Div G–2 and G–3 Periodic Rpts for the period 4–14 Apr 45.

XXIV CORPS TURNS SOUTH *on 4 April and meets greater opposition. Antitank gunners of the 383d Infantry, 96th Division, fire at Japanese positions in the Mashiki area, the approaches to Cactus Ridge. About the same time, on the Ginowan road, men and armor of the 382d Infantry, 96th Division (below), move through a wooded area, alert for concealed enemy positions.*

Whatever its strength in feudal times, the castle was good now only for one day's defense by the Japanese. On the morning of 5 April, the 7th Division found that the heights had been deserted before daylight. The division registered long advances during the day. The 32d Infantry moved more than two miles along the coast to a point east of Ukuma. The 184th advanced through Arakachi, and then was brought to a standstill by heavy and accurate fire from a rocky pinnacle located about 1,000 yards southwest of Arakachi. Company B, 184th Infantry, assaulted the hill on the 5th but was driven back. The reduction of this position—called the Pinnacle after a thin coral spike that rose 30 feet above the 450-foot ridge and served as a watchtower for the Japanese—was to be the main task of the 7th Division on the following day.

The Pinnacle: Capture of an Outpost

It was probably on this very hill that a party of Americans from Commodore Perry's expedition in 1853 raised the American flag "with hearty cheers" while exploring the island.[7] The Japanese had selected the Pinnacle as an important outpost position because it dominated the adjoining ground and afforded excellent observation in all directions. Holding the Pinnacle was 1st Lt. Seiji Tanigawa's *1st Company, 14th Independent Infantry Battalion,* composed of company headquarters and two rifle platoons, a total of 110 men. The third platoon was a mile to the rear in battalion reserve.

Lieutenant Tanigawa had built his defenses around eight light and two heavy machine guns sited at the base of the hill. In trenches and pits riflemen well-supplied with grenades covered the dead spaces in front of the machine guns. The defenses were connected by the usual tunnels and trenches, affording underground mobility. On the top of the ridge were four 50-mm. mortars, and on the reverse slope to the south were three more. Artillery check points had been established for *62d Division* field pieces to the south. Barbed wire and mine fields protected the major approaches. Lieutenant Tanigawa could hardly have hoped to stop the Americans, but undoubtedly he expected to make the price of victory high. (See Map No. VIII.)

After a 10-minute artillery preparation on the morning of 6 April, Company B, 184th Infantry, made a frontal assault on the Pinnacle, supported on the right (west) by Company C. Two platoons climbed almost to the top of the ridge, but when they started dropping grenades into caves and underground positions they stirred up a hornet's nest. The Japanese fought back with grenades,

[7] See Francis L. Hawks, *Expedition of an American Squadron to the China Seas and Japan* (Washington, 1856), pp. 167–69.

satchel charges, and mortars. The troops held on for fifteen minutes, until mounting casualties forced a withdrawal. An hour later another infantry assault was
attempted, supported by 105-mm. artillery, light tank fire, antitank guns, heavy
machine guns, 60-mm. and 81-mm. mortars, 4.2-inch chemical mortars, and
bazookas; but the attack was again stopped by Japanese who hid underground
during the heavy fire and then rushed back to their firing positions to meet the
oncoming Americans.

For the third attack of the morning, Lt. Col. Daniel G. Maybury, commanding the 1st Battalion, 184th Infantry, decided to push Company C up a draw
just beyond the ridge used by Company B, but the latter was still expected to
seize the peak. Company B moved up the ridge quickly to catch the enemy out
of his holes, but again the troops were driven back. Company C was now working its way up the western approaches along a difficult but partially covered
route. Lieutenant Tanigawa had directed the repulse of Company B from the
Pinnacle watchtower but he did not know of Company C's approach on his
flank. Colonel Maybury directed supporting fire in front of Company C, which
quickly moved to the top without losing a man. It then proceeded leisurely and
methodically to destroy the remaining Japanese with white phosphorus grenades
and flame throwers. Only 20 of the 110 defenders escaped to the south. With the
Pinnacle reduced, the entire 7th Division line could move forward.

The Pinnacle had been a tough position to crack, yet it was only an outpost.
The Pinnacle was undermanned, and no reinforcements were provided. During
the action Lieutenant Tanigawa pleaded with his superiors for artillery support,
but he was provided with neither the artillery nor an explanation of the refusal.
By 6–7 April the XXIV Corps had unmasked the Shuri fortified zone, composed
of many positions as fanatically defended as Pinnacle outpost and also heavily
supported by artillery and fed by an almost endless stream of reinforcements
from local reserve units.

XXIV Corps Halted on the West, 6–8 April

Assault units of the XXIV Corps had by 6 April penetrated the outposts
held by the *12th Independent Infantry Battalion* and were in contact with two
other battalions of the *63d Brigade* of the *62d Division*. In general, the *13th
Independent Infantry Battalion* faced the 96th Division; the *14th* opposed the
7th Division; and remnants of the *12th,* which had suffered heavily in its outpost
actions to the north, straddled the division boundary in the center of the island.
The Japanese *Independent Infantry Battalion* was well adapted for outpost
action. Each of its five rifle companies was equipped with nine light machine

EAST COAST BATTLES *of the 184th Infantry, 7th Division, in early April centered about the hill called the Pinnacle. Its western approaches, over which Company C moved to capture it, are shown above. At high point on right is watchtower. From the Pinnacle the 2d Battalion, 184th, attacked toward Tomb Hill along the finger ridge shown in the center of the picture below. A white phosphorus shell had just burst on the hill beyond.*

guns and nine grenade dischargers; the machine gun company operated ten heavy machine guns; and the infantry gun company was furnished with two 75-mm. regimental guns and two 70-mm. howitzers. Each of the three battalions had originally a strength of about 900, but Okinawan conscripts and *Boeitai* swelled the total to approximately 1,200.[8]

On 6 April the strong enemy positions on Cactus Ridge continued to hold up the Corps' west flank. An air strike early in the morning put bombs squarely on the ridge, but the assaulting troops of the 96th Division found enemy fire as intense as ever. The 2d Battalion, 383d Infantry, made frontal assaults through intense mortar fire to gain the ridge. "We figured," S/Sgt. Francis M. Rall later wrote, "that the way to get out of that knee mortar fire was to get to where it was coming from. So we stood up in waves, firing everything we had and throwing hand grenades by the dozen, and charged the Jap position." [9] By such tactics the 2d Battalion gained the western half of Cactus. On the next day, 7 April, more American "banzai charges" won the rest of the ridge.

The capture of Cactus Ridge brought the 383d Infantry up against the formidable Japanese positions in the Kakazu area. On 7 and 8 April the regiment pushed down toward Kakazu Ridge, supported by planes, light and medium artillery, and naval gunfire from the battleship *New York*. Col. E. T. May, commanding the 383d, at this time had no conception of the enemy's strength on Kakazu. Small-scale attacks along the approaches to Kakazu by the 1st Battalion on 7 and 8 April failed with heavy losses. Spigot mortar fire was met on the 8th for the first time. The 320-mm. shells had little fragmentation effect but a terrific concussion and dug craters fifteen feet across and eight feet deep. The spigot mortar shells were dubbed "flying box cars" by the American troops, who claimed that they were able to see the huge missiles in time to run to safety.

From 6 to 8 April the 382d Infantry advanced slowly east of the Ginowan road. The enemy fought stubbornly from hilly ground north and west of Kaniku and delivered heavy fire from his strong positions on Tombstone Ridge, just south of Kaniku, and from Nishibaru Ridge, southwest of Tombstone. Quantities of rifle, machine-gun, mortar, and artillery fire were poured on the troops as they moved south. Savage hand-to-hand encounters marked the slow progress of the regiment, which suffered numerous casualties. By night of 8 April the

---

[8] Tenth Army Int Monograph, Pt I, Sec B: Japanese Order of Battle, p. 9; XXIV Corps G–2 Summary No. 4, 12 Apr 45; XXIV Corps PW Interrog Rpt No. 54, 6 May 45.

[9] Mulford and Rogers, 96th Div History, Pt II, pp. 25–26.

regiment was strung out on a wide front just north of Kaniku and Tombstone Ridge. Heavy fire from the front, from the Kakazu area on the right (west), and from its exposed left (east) flank, where the 184th was slowed by strong opposition, had brought the 382d virtually to a dead stop.

XXIV Corps Halted on the East, 7–9 April

After the fall of the Pinnacle, the 184th Infantry continued to move southward over broken eroded ground on its right (west) and rocky finger ridges on the left. On the flatlands along the coast the 32d Infantry advanced with little difficulty, keeping contact with the 184th. Only when forward elements of the 32d tried to push out ahead of the 184th in force did its assault units encounter aggressive Japanese opposition, in the form of heavy fire from the heights on the right. Thus the rate of advance of the 184th governed that of the XXIV Corps' left. By 7 April it was clear to the 7th Division commander, studying the ground ahead from his observation post on the Pinnacle, that the 184th was now meeting the main Japanese defenses.

The fighting in the 7th Division's sector on 7 April centered on a low, bare hill 1,000 yards west of the town of Minami-Uebaru, called Red Hill because of its color. The enemy had made a fortress of the hill by constructing his usual system of caves and connecting trenches. A frontal assault on Red Hill by troops of the 3d Battalion, 184th Infantry, failed in the face of machine-gun and mortar fire. In a second attempt, three platoons of tanks supported the attack. Ten medium and five light tanks advanced through a cut toward Red Hill; two tanks were blown up by mines and one was satchel-charged as the column moved toward the hill and up the sides. Intense enemy artillery and machine-gun fire drove the infantry back and disabled more tanks. Japanese swarmed in among the armor and tried to destroy the tanks with satchel charges and flaming rags. Two medium tanks held off the attackers, the defending crews resorting to hand grenades, while the rest of the operative tanks withdrew.[10]

The *14th Independent Infantry Battalion* headquarters proudly described this action as a perfect example of how to separate troops from tanks and thus break up the American infantry-tank team. The enemy dispatch stated: "The above method of isolating the troops from the tanks with surprise fire followed by close combat tactics is an example in the complete destruction of enemy tanks and will be a great factor in deciding the victories of tank warfare." [11]

[10] See 711th Tank Bn (7th Div) Actn Rpt, pp. 7–9.
[11] Incl to 7th Div G–2 Periodic Rpt No. 10, 11 Apr 45.

After these two reversals the 3d Battalion, 184th, made a wide enveloping maneuver to the right. Behind fire from artillery and supporting weapons, the troops drove toward Red Hill from the west and occupied it, suffering only two casualties in the move. Once more a Japanese outpost had shown its strength against a frontal attack and its vulnerability to a flanking maneuver. The capture of Red Hill left another sector of enemy territory open for the taking. The troops advanced 100 yards south before digging in. A platoon of tanks conducted a remarkable 4,000-yard foray almost to Hill 178 and withdrew safely, despite a bombing attack by two single-engined Japanese planes.

The 184th continued to make the main effort on the Corps' east flank during the next two days, 8 and 9 April. Two formidable enemy positions built around strong points lay between Red Hill and Hill 178—Tomb Hill, 1,000 yards northwest of Ouki, and Triangulation Hill, 1,000 yards northwest of Tomb Hill. Enemy artillery fire was the heaviest yet encountered by the 7th Division. Tank-infantry teams were the special target of the Japanese shells. The heavy enemy fire drove off infantry and demolished tanks; then the attacking Japanese satchel-charged the exposed tanks and bayoneted crews when they tried to escape. The enemy reoccupied abandoned tanks and converted them into pillboxes.

Triangulation Hill fell on 8 April after two bloody assaults. Tomb Hill, so named after the numerous burial vaults along its sides, held out until the 9th, when infantry and tanks, closely supported by artillery and planes, managed to seize and hang onto the crest of the hill. Its capture enabled the 32d to seize finger ridges east of Tomb Hill that dominated the approaches to Ouki. Japanese clung tenaciously to the reverse slope of Tomb Hill, and direct enemy observation from Hill 178, now only 1,500 yards to the southwest, hindered the efforts to clean out the area south of Tomb Hill.

An ambitious flanking maneuver around the Japanese right (east) was tried on the 10th, but it was a dismal failure. The 7th Division had come up against the hard rim of the Shuri fortified zone, and maneuver was impossible. The 7th now paused, while the XXIV Corps made its main effort in the Kakazu area.

The Japanese outpost units had done their work well. They had held the XXIV Corps off from the Shuri fortified zone for eight days. For its work during this and later periods, the *14th Independent Infantry Battalion* was cited by Lt. Gen. Takeo Fujioka, commander of the *62d Division,* who stated: "Burning with the determination to annihilate the enemy, the soldiers carried

out counterattacks, followed by close combat, and crushed the continuously reinforced enemy who was attacking with fierce artillery and bombardment." [12] By
the night of 8 April, XXIV Corps had suffered 1,510 battle casualties and had
accounted for 4,489 Japanese killed and 13 captured.[13] The 96th had taken the
bulk of the American casualties and was about to suffer further serious losses
in abortive attempts to reduce the Kakazu positions.

Assaulting the Shuri Defenses, 9–12 April

On 8 April Colonel May ordered the 1st and 3d Battalions of the 383d
Infantry to seize the Kakazu hill mass the next day, and on the morning of
9 April the two battalions were drawn up in position for the attack. (See Map
No. IX.)

The Japanese-held area in front of the 383d Infantry offered the enemy an
ideal combination of defensive features. A deep moat, a hill studded with natural
and man-made positions, a cluster of thick-walled buildings behind the hill—
these were the basic elements of Kakazu stronghold. The enemy had exploited
each one of them. Moreover, Kakazu, unlike such outposts as the Pinnacle, was
an integral element of the Shuri fortified zone and a vital rampart that could
expect reinforcements and heavy fire support from within the ring of positions
that surrounded the *32d Army* headquarters, only 4,000 yards to the south.

The 1st and 3d Battalions were drawn up on the high ground several hundred yards northeast of the main hill of Kakazu. Between the Americans and
Kakazu lay a deep gorge, half hidden by trees and brush, which could be crossed
only with difficulty. The Kakazu hill mass itself, on the other side of this gorge,
stretched northwest-southeast for 1,000 yards, sloping on the west toward the
coastal flat and ending on the east at Highway 5. Kakazu was made up of two
hills connected by a saddle. On the east was the larger of the two hills, about 500
yards long and topped by a fairly level strip of land averaging 25 yards in width;
it came to be known to the American troops as Kakazu Ridge. At the western
end of this ridge was a north-south saddle, sloping gently up toward the south.
This saddle was dotted with tombs, as were the sides of Kakazu Ridge. West of
the saddle was another portion of the Kakazu hill mass, forming the head of a T
in relation to Kakazu Ridge, and stretching north-south for about 250 yards.
This hill was later called "Crocker's Hill" by the 27th Division, but to the 96th

---

[12] 7th Div G–2 Periodic Rpt No. 62, 1 Jun 45.
[13] XXIV Corps G–3 Periodic Rpt No. 9, 9 Apr 45.

KAKAZU WEST *and the west end of Kakazu Ridge, viewed from high ground north of the gorge. Tombs used by the 1st Battalion, 381st Infantry, 96th Division, and a Japanese cave position can be seen. Below are caves along north slope of Kakazu West used by the 2d Battalion, 381st, while entrenched on the reverse slope of the knob.*

it came to be known as "Kakazu West." On the northern slope of Kakazu West the ground fell away sharply in a steep cliff pockmarked with caves; on the east it was steep but not precipitous.

Kakazu was not formidable in appearance. It was not high, nor jagged, nor especially abrupt. Kakazu was overshadowed by the Urasoe-Mura Escarpment, 500 yards to the south, which, from the position of the American forces, seemed like a towering, insurmountable cliff, preventing passage beyond. Compared to Urasoe-Mura, Kakazu was simply an ugly, squat hill, originally covered with vegetation but soon left only with bare tree trunks standing gaunt against the skyline. Just below Kakazu Ridge on the southeast was the town of Kakazu, a compact group of tile-roofed structures, each surrounded by hedges and stone walls and somewhat in defilade to the adjoining open fields.

In and around the Kakazu hills the Japanese had created one of their strongest positions on Okinawa. Mortars dug in on the reverse slope were zeroed-in on the gorge and on vulnerable areas between the gorge and the crest of Kakazu. Several spigot mortars also protected the hill. In an intricate system of coordinated pillboxes, tunnels, and caves Japanese machine guns were sited to cover all avenues of approach. The enemy was also supported by many artillery pieces within the Shuri fortified zone. The heavy walls and the hedges of the town of Kakazu—and eventually its rubble—afforded the Japanese countless defensive positions.

The 1st Battalion of the 383d, commanded by Lt. Col. Byron F. King, was to capture Kakazu Ridge; the 3d Battalion, commanded by Lt. Col. Edward W. Stare, was to take Kakazu West.[14] The companies were to attack before dawn without an artillery preparation in order to surprise the enemy. The men had only a vague conception of the ground over which they were to attack. The air photographs and maps were inaccurate or lacking in detail. From the jump-off position the gorge between the men and Kakazu was not visible.

Rifle Companies Storm Kakazu

The predawn darkness hid the movement of the troops as they moved out. From east to west the companies were C and A of the 1st Battalion and L and I of the 3d Battalion. Companies C and A crossed the gorge, picked their way up the slopes of Kakazu Ridge, and were on the top by dawn without being discovered. Company L's forward elements killed several Japanese on the way up Kakazu West without arousing the bulk of the defenders. Company I on

---

[14] 383d Inf (96th Div) FO No. 21, 8 Apr 45.

the far west was delayed in its jump-off and by daylight was in open ground 150 yards south of Uchitomari.

Shortly after 0600 the enemy was alerted. A lone Japanese in a pillbox spotted Company A and opened fire. Almost immediately a terrific hail of mortar fire fell along the entire front, punctuated by staccato bursts from machine guns. The Americans were in poor positions. Most of Companies A and C were on the ridge, but they had separated in the approach and had not yet regained contact. Likewise there was no contact between Company A and Company L, which was part way up Kakazu West. Company L at first escaped most of the fire, which blanketed the gorge after L had crossed it, but the same fire cut off Company I in the open ground to the west and thus left L isolated on Kakazu West.

While the men of Companies A and C huddled in holes on the crest and forward (northeast) slopes of Kakazu Ridge to escape the murderous fire, Company L made a dash to gain the top of Kakazu West. In the face of machine-gun fire 1st Lt. Willard F. Mitchell, commander of Company L, a stocky Louisianian whose favorite expression was "Watch out! Here comes 'the Hoss' and God's on the Hoss's side," urged his men to the top. They made it with fixed bayonets and immediately became engaged in a close-quarters fight that was to last all morning.

Just as Company L gained the top of Kakazu West the situation was becoming desperate on Kakazu Ridge. The Japanese charged through their own mortar barrage into the American lines. Hand-to-hand fighting, especially in Company A's section, raged without a lull until 0745. Since the support platoons were pinned down in the open ground between the gorge and the hill, reinforcement was impossible; yet more and more of the enemy closed in.

Capt. Jack A. Royster, commander of Company A, reported that it would be forced to withdraw or would be wiped out unless reinforcements could be brought up or the 3d Battalion could come abreast on the right (west).[15] He evidently did not know that only Company L of the 3d Battalion had made the top of Kakazu West and that it was now fighting for its life. Company B was ordered to move up behind A but was stopped by the fire blanketing the gorge. The enemy was keeping over the gorge a curtain of steel and explosive which prevented more Americans from moving up, while Japanese counterattacking elements were attempting to finish off the small force on the top.

---

[15] 1st Bn, 383d Inf, Unit Jnl, Entry No. 5, 9 Apr 45.

"Hold the Ridge at All Costs!"

At 0830 Company C was being heavily attacked on its exposed left (east) flank. Colonel King, 1st Battalion commander, had ordered Captain Royster to hold at all costs, but now knew that the game was up. He radioed Colonel May:

Have 50 men on ridge. Support elements pinned down. Heavy concentrations of mortars and artillery being laid down on troops beside MG crossfire. If we do not get reinforcements, we will have to withdraw.[16]

Colonel May was acting under a division field order which called for a "vigorous" attack to the south.[17] He was unwilling to relinquish his toe hold on Kakazu; to do so meant giving up vital high ground. Furthermore, he felt that the 1st Battalion would lose as many men in attempting a retreat as in trying to hang on. Colonel May therefore radioed to the 1st Battalion:

Sending G Company to reinforce you . . . if the Battalion CO is jumpy, have the executive officer take over. Hold the ridge at all costs.[18]

He then ordered the 2d Battalion to fill the gap between the 1st and 3d Battalions by sending Company G forward. Company G, however, was 1,000 yards to the rear and did not arrive in time to help the 1st Battalion out.

Up on Kakazu Ridge, Captain Royster felt his position was untenable. Although almost blind from a mortar burst, he kept rallying his men until a smoke barrage gave them concealment for the move back. The first smoke from a chemical company blew over the lines, but at 1000 it was effective enough for C and A to begin their withdrawal. A rear guard held the crest while the wounded men were carried out. The remaining troops on Kakazu, along with those who had been pinned down in the open ground near the gorge, moved back through mortar fire.

The first members of A and C to reach the gorge were met there at 1030 by Capt. John C. Van Vulpen of Company B, who had been trying to move up to reinforce them. Under orders from battalion to attack, Captain Van Vulpen led the forty-six able-bodied men of his company up the south bank of the gorge onto the open ground. They had gone only a few yards when a hail of mortar shells and machine-gun fire wounded seven of the men. Advance was impossible as the enemy had both the gorge and the area north of the gorge under artillery and mortar fire. During the afternoon the survivors of the three companies

[16] 383d Inf Jnl, Msg No. 8, 9 Apr 45.

[17] 96th Div FO No. 14, 3 Apr 45; FO No. 15, 7 Apr 45.

[18] 383d Inf Jnl, Msg No. 9, 9 Apr 45.

straggled back to the battalion lines. For many the trip was a nightmare of hair-breadth escapes; the battalion surgeon considered none of the survivors fit for further duty.

Company L Fights On

With the withdrawal of Companies C and A during the morning of 9 April, Company L was the sole American unit on Kakazu. Lieutenant Mitchell and his men held the northernmost of two knolls that made up Kakazu West. Although Mitchell and his men had seized enough of the saddle to set up machine guns in its slight defilade, they were unable to seize the southern knoll. The Japanese, who were making their main effort against Companies C and A on Kakazu Ridge, were unable to push the Americans off the northern knoll of Kakazu West, although they drove in close enough to engage in hand-grenade and even satchel-charge duels.

About noon the enemy apparently realized that the American force on Kakazu West was not as strong as its fierce resistance had seemed to indicate. He launched four hard counterattacks during the afternoon with forces of from platoon to company strength. The Japanese infantry attacked through their own mortar fire, throwing potato mashers and satchel charges. Lieutenant Mitchell's booming voice could be heard above the din of battle as he directed the defense.

Heroism was commonplace on Kakazu West that afternoon. Both machine gunners took their weapons out into the open for better fields of fire; one of them, Sgt. James Pritchard, fired six boxes of ammunition and killed many Japanese charging up the west slopes of Kakazu West before he was mortally wounded. When ammunition was exhausted in the mortar section, which was supporting the company from a position at the base of the steep cliff on the north of Kakazu West, S/Sgt. Erby L. Boyd, section leader, volunteered to go to the rear through the fire-swept gorge for more ammunition. He was killed in the attempt. Pfc. Joseph Solch stood up in full view of the enemy and emptied three BAR clips into their midst, killing fifteen Japanese. Solch was the only survivor of six men who earlier in the day had knocked out a spigot mortar at the base of the reverse slope of Kakazu West, after watching four enemy soldiers pull the huge launcher out of a cave on a 40-foot track, fire the mortar, and pull the launcher back into the cave.

Desperate efforts to relieve the pressure on Company L were fruitless. Colonel May had ordered the 2d Battalion to send Company G on Kakazu between L on Kakazu West and A on Kakazu Ridge. Company G did not reach the gorge until midafternoon. By this time Company I, which had been pinned down in the open area just south of Uchitomari, had managed to work its way forward by one's and two's to more covered positions. Together Companies I and G tried at 1400 to reach L's left (east) flank. But because of heavy Japanese fire they were not able to cross the ravine. The enemy's curtain of fire along the gorge was still impassable.

Retreat From Kakazu West

By 1600 Lieutenant Mitchell realized that his position was hopeless. Of eighty-nine men who had reached the top of Kakazu West, fifteen had now been killed and only three were uninjured. One man had just been blown thirty feet into the air by what Lieutenant Mitchell suspected was American naval gunfire. Worst of all, the company was almost out of ammunition. Those who still had a few rounds had obtained them by stripping the dead and wounded of ammunition; others had none at all. The machine guns stood idle, their belts empty. The last counterattack at 1530 had been launched by from 100 to 150 Japanese, and Lieutenant Mitchell knew that his small force could not withstand another such onslaught.

Deciding to withdraw, Lieutenant Mitchell called for supporting fires, and these were expertly handled. The 4.2-inch chemical smoke on the south side of Kakazu West was interspersed with high explosive artillery shells to keep the enemy pinned down. Under cover of the smoke the survivors of Company L pulled back off the hill to the gorge, carrying their wounded with them. Lieutenant Mitchell then had the concentration moved to the top and north slopes of Kakazu West. Nevertheless Japanese machine gunners, firing blindly into the smoke, killed two of the men on the way back.

It had been a black day for the 383d Infantry. The regiment had suffered 326 casualties—23 killed, 256 wounded, 47 missing.[19] The 1st Battalion was at half strength and was considered ineffective. Colonel May had relieved Colonel King of the 1st Battalion and had placed the battalion's executive officer, Maj. Kenny W. Erickson, in command. Company L had only thirty-eight men left, including the company headquarters. The regiment had gained no ground. However, it had killed about 420 of the enemy. Company L was later awarded the Distinguished Unit Citation for its tenacity in holding on against great odds.[20]

[19] 383d Inf Jnl, Msg No. 24, 9 Apr 45.
[20] Tenth Army GO No. 104, 23 Jun 45.

"Powerhouse Attack" on Kakazu, 10 April

Even before the attack of 9 April disintegrated, Brig. Gen. Claudius M. Easley, assistant division commander, Colonel May, commander of the 383d, and Col. M. E. Halloran, commander of the 381st, had met at the 383d command post to plan a "powerhouse attack" for 10 April.[21] One regiment had assailed Kakazu unsuccessfully on 9 April; now two regiments were to do the job, under the direction of General Easley. The 381st was to assault Kakazu West from positions south of Uchitomari; the 383d was to attack Kakazu Ridge from positions north of the gorge. (See Map No. X.)

No tanks were to move out with the assault battalions. They could not negotiate the gorge at the base of Kakazu; if the tanks tried to make a wide flanking move on the right (west) south of Uchitomari, they would encounter a jumble of rice paddies and terraced fields under direct fire from the enemy; similarly a wide sweep on the left, east of the deepest part of the gorge, would bring the tanks into the open, fire-swept ground where the 382d was inching ahead. As a result, the infantry-tank team, which proved to be so indispensable a weapon in the final reduction of the Shuri defenses, could not be used in the attack on Kakazu. The two regiments, however, were to have exceptionally heavy artillery support from seven battalions of field artillery, including Marine battalions attached to the 96th.[22] Naval gunfire and three squadrons of Navy fighter planes were also on call.

Artillery opened a 15-minute preparation at 0645 on 10 April, but, as General Easley felt that it had not fallen close enough to the lines to be effective, he ordered another 15-minute bombardment. The 2d Battalion, 381st Infantry, then jumped off from the outskirts of Uchitomari toward Kakazu West; it soon came under intense mortar and machine-gun fire. The 1st Battalion, 381st, moved up behind the 2d. At first the 383d met little resistance; thus during the morning the attack on Kakazu revolved around the efforts of the 381st.

A part of the 2d Battalion, 381st Infantry, soon was pinned down by fire in the open area north of the gorge—about the same place where Company I, 383d, had been stopped on the previous day—but some troops managed to reach it. Already the enemy had his curtain of fire established along the length of the gorge, and the men of the 2d Battalion were forced to cling to overhanging rocks on the south side to escape the fire. A heavy mortar barrage dropped on the gorge as more troops moved up.

[21] 383d Inf Jnl, Msg No. 16, 9 Apr 45.
[22] 96th Div FO No. 16, 9 Apr 45.

At 0805 leading elements of the 2d Battalion moved out of the gorge and started up the north slope of Kakazu West in a skirmish line. Resistance was not strong; machine guns on the crest of Kakazu West were knocked out by small flanking movements. By 0930 the troops were on the crest of Kakazu West, where they hastily consolidated their position, knowing that Company L of the 383d had been forced off this very height on the previous day. Soon two companies were on the hill. Here they waited for the 383d to move up on their left (east) flank onto Kakazu Ridge.

Checkmate at Kakazu Ridge

The 383d, however, was not making much progress. Both battalions, the 3d on the right (west) and the 2d on the left, advanced until they were stopped by enemy fire just short of the gorge, which on 10 April, as on 9 April, was the dominant element of the action. Although Colonel May believed that enemy fire was negligible and radioed both battalions to move forward toward Kakazu Ridge, the battalions could not advance.[23] As a result, both battalions became involved in flanking movements. Part of the 2d Battalion never left the area north of the gorge, but other elements moved southeast along the Uchitomari–Kaniku road, turned right (south) on Highway 5, and infiltrated through houses along the highway to flank the gorge. They were still no better off, however, for the enemy had the open area here under control by fire. The 2d Battalion stayed in this position, at the eastern end of the gorge in front of Kakazu Ridge, for the rest of the day.

When stopped at the gorge, the 3d Battalion, 383d Infantry, made a flanking move in a direction opposite to that taken by the 2d Battalion, moving west toward the 381st regimental sector. The 3d Battalion managed to cross the gorge at the north base of Kakazu West in the 381st sector. It then attacked up the north slopes of that hill, connecting with the 2d Battalion, 381st, in the latter's sector on the northeast side. By 1100 elements of the 381st and 383d held the top of Kakazu West, its northern slopes, and part of the saddle between Kakazu West and Kakazu Ridge. The hold was none too secure, for the enemy had troops available for counterattack and was placing intermittent machine-gun and mortar fire on Kakazu West.

Kakazu Ridge was still unconquered. About noon the 2d Battalion, 383d, attacked east along the saddle connecting Kakazu Ridge and Kakazu West, in an effort to take the ridge. The attempt was abortive; the troops advanced about

[23] 383d Inf Jnl, Msg Nos. 18 and 19, 10 Apr 45.

KAKAZU GORGE *from the saddle between Kakazu Ridge and Kakazu West, giving an idea of its depth. Path shown was used by the 381st Infantry, 96th Division, to reach Kakazu hills. (Photo taken some time after action.)*

100 yards and then were pinned down by machine-gun and mortar fire from Kakazu Ridge. It was now raining, and movement was more difficult than ever. The 2d Battalion, 381st, tried to push south along the crest of Kakazu West in order to gain ground dominating the town of Kakazu and the reverse slope of Kakazu Ridge. The troops made a small gain; then quickly a vicious counterattack drove them back to their original positions on the north knob of Kakazu West.

At this point the struggle for Kakazu had become a stalemate. The Japanese had stopped the American troops, but they could not mount enough power to drive them off Kakazu as they had done the previous day. The Americans were facing a situation that was to be repeated many times on Okinawa: the enemy had more strength on the reverse slope of the hill than on the crest or forward slope, since on the reverse slope he had considerable concealment and cover from hostile fire.

The situation was now critical, for the 3d Battalion, 383d, had suffered many casualties during the day, especially among the small-unit commanders, and was now being vigorously attacked. At 1345 General Easley attempted to break the deadlock. He ordered the 1st Battalion, 381st Infantry, to pass through the right (west) flank of the 383d in the saddle, and instructed the latter to hold on until help arrived.

By 1400 the 1st Battalion, 381st, was on the move in a column of companies, following the same route of approach that had been used by the 2d Battalion in the morning. About half the battalion was across the gorge when the enemy again placed his prearranged mortar concentrations and machine-gun fire on this vulnerable point. Cut off from some of their supporting elements, the forward troops of the 1st Battalion made their way up the steep slopes of Kakazu West in the pouring rain. Some of the near elements later joined them; others never reached Kakazu West that day.

At about 1530 the 1st Battalion of the 381st finally arrived to relieve the 3d Battalion of the 383d in the saddle. But it was too late for an effective relief. A part of the 3d Battalion had given way before the fierce enemy attack, and the relieving troops discovered a horde of Japanese where they had expected to find only Americans. Nevertheless, the 1st Battalion attacked southeast along Kakazu Ridge. The attack was not delivered in strength, however, and it failed. Later, some of the elements of the 1st Battalion which were cut off at the gorge rejoined the unit, and by darkness the troops had worked their way up the north slopes of Kakazu Ridge to within twenty yards of the crest.

The Enemy Clings to Kakazu Ridge, 11–12 April

Under regimental orders to seize Kakazu Ridge, the 1st Battalion, 381st Infantry, attacked across the saddle at 0700 on 11 April. The troops worked up the western slope of the ridge but then came under severe flat trajectory gunfire from the area south of Kakazu and under high-angle mortar fire from the reverse (southern) slope of Kakazu Ridge. The Japanese also threw satchel charges at them from the crest of Kakazu Ridge. Although the attacking troops were supported by fire from the top of Kakazu West, they finally were forced to dig in short of the crest of the ridge. Here the enemy made two sharp counterattacks, which were stopped mainly by one man, T/Sgt. Alfred C. Robertson. With BAR, rifle, grenades, bayonet, and trench knife Robertson killed about twenty-eight of the enemy, and in addition directed mortar fire when his radio operator was seriously wounded.

The 3d Battalion, 383d Infantry, spent the morning in its position on the north slope of the saddle, receiving rations and ammunition brought through the gorge under heavy fire. At 1300 this battalion, with the 1st Battalion, 381st, on the right (southwest), drove up the northwest slopes of Kakazu Ridge. Since the commander of the 1st had been unable to cross the gorge, Colonel Stare, commander of the 3d Battalion, directed the attack.

After advancing about 150 yards the attacking troops came under severe mortar and machine-gun fire from the crest and reverse slope of Kakazu Ridge. Even heavier fire was coming from the reverse (south) slope of Kakazu West, which was still in enemy hands. Colonel Stare decided that his assault could continue only if the 2d Battalion of the 381st, occupying the northern part of the top of Kakazu West, attacked and destroyed the Japanese who still clung to the southern portion of Kakazu West.

Through heavy fire Colonel Stare made his way to the 2d Battalion command post to plan this attack with Lt. Col. Russell Graybill, 2d Battalion commander. Just as the attack was about to be launched the Japanese counterattacked on Kakazu West, and Colonel Graybill's men had all they could do to hold their positions. Colonel Stare then called off further attacks on Kakazu Ridge and ordered casualties evacuated under a smoke screen. The two battalions on the northwest slopes of Kakazu Ridge drew back to their original positions. Once again the enemy had retained his grip on the main portions of Kakazu.

During the night of 11–12 April the Japanese bombarded the Uchitomari–Kakazu area with huge mortar shells, some of them 320-mm. One fell squarely on the aid station of the 1st Battalion of the 381st, killing the two medical officers and eleven soldiers and wounding nine others. On 12 April the 96th Division made its final attempt to take Kakazu. After planes bombed and rocketed the crest and reverse slope of Kakazu Ridge, the 1st Battalion, 381st, attacked up the northwest slopes of the ridge. The Japanese waited for the planes to leave and then opened up with one of the heaviest mortar concentrations the 96th had ever met. For over an hour mortar shells burst on the rocky slopes at a rate faster than one a second. Three times the troops of the 381st attacked; each time, in the face not only of this mortar fire, but also of machine-gun and rifle fire, grenades, and satchel charges, the attack disintegrated. The battalion lost forty-five men. Although the mortar fire stopped as soon as the Americans pulled back, the enemy was still very much in control of the situation on Kakazu Ridge.

In the midst of the bitter struggle for the Shuri line the troops received almost unbelievable news. Early on 12 April word flashed through the bivouac areas and along the front lines on Okinawa that President Roosevelt had died. The enemy also heard the news, and attempted to capitalize on it. Shortly afterward a Japanese propaganda leaflet was found which stated:

> We must express our deep regret over the death of President Roosevelt. The "American Tragedy" is now raised here at Okinawa with his death. You must have seen 70% of your CV's and 73% of your B's sink or be damaged causing 150,000 casualties. Not only the late President but anyone else would die in the excess of worry to hear such an annihilative damage. The dreadful loss that led your late leader to death will make you orphans on this island. The Japanese special attack corps will sink your vessels to the last destroyer. You will witness it realized in the near future.[24]

American Attack on the East Flank Halted, 10–12 April

While elements of the 96th Division were attempting fruitlessly to take Kakazu Ridge, other elements of that division, together with units of the 7th Division, were trying to continue the advance on the east flank that had begun with the success of the 184th Infantry on 8–9 April. The capture of Tomb Hill by the 184th on 9 April, after an infantry attack supported by the massed fire of mortars and guns, made it possible for the 7th Division to advance several hundred **yards** on 9 and 10 April. The 32d Infantry continued to push ahead on the east along the flat coastal plain, while the 184th moved along the rough high ground farther inland. Despite bad weather conditions the troops were supported by naval gunfire and artillery. Enemy resistance was stiffening.

[24] 7th Div G–2 Periodic Rpt No. 23, 23 Apr 45.

Japanese artillery fire increased in intensity, and the 7th experienced several small but well-organized counterattacks. (See Map No. XI.)

On 10 and 11 April the 32d Infantry tried to advance into the town of Ouki, while the 184th on the heights warded off small counterattacks, sealed up caves, and consolidated its positions. The Japanese had made Ouki into a strong point, covered by their artillery and protected on the north by a well-laid mine field, pillboxes, and trenches. A chill, penetrating rain made advance difficult and the troops miserable. The 2d Battalion of the 32d, coordinating with the 184th Infantry on the west, moved slowly over a series of small spurs overlooking the plain, while the 1st Battalion of the 32d advanced against Ouki below.

On 11 April troops of the 1st Battalion entered Ouki on the heels of an artillery preparation, killing forty-five Japanese soldiers in the attack. The supporting tanks, however, were held up by a mined antitank ditch north of Ouki. Japanese heavy weapons opened up on the tanks and mine-clearing squads, cutting off the troops in Ouki from their supporting elements just as they had done in the Kakazu fight when they covered the gorge with fire. The troops in Ouki had to retreat from their exposed position. On 12 April the 1st Battalion sent patrols into Ouki, and the 2d Battalion reconnoitered Ishin, 400 yards to the west, but neither made advances. The 7th Division lines were now stabilized a few hundred yards northeast of Hill 178, a strongly held enemy position.[25]

The 382d Infantry of the 96th Division, in the center of the XXIV Corps line, also came to a standstill during 9–12 April. The 382d had three battalions on line by 10 April—the 2d on the right (west), the 1st in the center, and the 3d on the left. On the west the 2d Battalion tied in loosely with the 383d Infantry on Highway 5; on the east a large gap lay between the 184th Infantry of the 7th Division and the 382d. The terrain fronting the 382d was notable for its irregularity but had a few prominent features lending themselves to defense. The enemy had fortified Tombstone Ridge, a long low hill running northeast-southwest just south of Kaniku, as well as high ground south of Nishibaru. Kakazu Ridge extended across much of the regiment's right (west) front; and the upper part of the gorge, east of Highway 5, was an effective obstacle even if less precipitous here than on the other side of the highway north of Kakazu.

The main effort of the 382d during this period was made on 10 April, while the 381st and 383d on the west were attempting their "powerhouse" attack on

[25] 7th Div Actn Rpt, pp. 49–50; 184th Inf Actn Rpt, pp. 12–13; 32d Inf Actn Rpt, pp. 10–12; XXIV Corps G–3 Periodic Rpts Nos. 9–14, 9–14 Apr 45.

Kakazu. The 382d attacked southwest with three battalions in line. On the west the 2d Battalion advanced several hundred yards and crossed the gorge, only to halt in the face of heavy fire from its front and flanks. On the regimental left (east) the 3d Battalion gained one of the knobs east of Tombstone Ridge, but continual rain, which bogged down the tanks and decreased visibility, combined with heavy enemy mortar, machine-gun, and 47-mm. fire to force the battalion to withdraw to its original position north of the Ginowan road.

The 382d suffered its worst setbacks of 10 April in the center of its line. The 1st Battalion, commanded by Lt. Col. Charles W. Johnson, attacked Tombstone Ridge, which dominated the ground across the entire regimental front. By 0840 Company A had seized the northern nose of the ridge, but it was stopped by small-arms fire from the steep slopes of the ridge and by heavy artillery and mortar fire. Colonel Johnson then swung Companies B and C around west of Kaniku for an assault on the ridge from the northwest. The Japanese were unusually quiet while Companies B and C advanced to the crest, but shortly afterward they delivered a 15-minute concentration of mortar and artillery fire, at the conclusion of which they swarmed out of pillboxes, trenches, and caves.

A furious struggle followed. From the reverse slope of Tombstone machine guns opened up on the Americans at almost point-blank range. The Americans used portable flame throwers, but the Japanese brought forward flame throwers of their own. Spigot mortar shells burst on the hill. Colonel Johnson, who had previously extricated Company A from its deadlocked position on the north of Tombstone, now committed it on the right (southwest) of the other two companies. It was of no avail. On the northeast flank, now open, the Japanese overran a machine-gun position; only one man was able to escape. The American troops on the right made a few more yards in a desperate effort to gain a firm foothold on the ridge. By 1415 it was obvious to Colonel Johnson that further attack would be fruitless, and he secured permission from regiment to pull out of the fire-swept area. The men made an orderly retreat to high ground north of Kaniku. More spigot mortar fire fell during the withdrawal, but the troops remained calm; they were "too tired to give a damn." [26]

The abortive attacks of the 382d Infantry on 10 April were its last attempts to move forward until the Corps' offensive opened on 19 April. On 11 and 12 April this regiment, like the 7th Division to the east, mopped up small bypassed

[26] Mulford and Rogers, 96th Div History, Pt. I, pp. 41–42, 49–55; 96th Div Actn Rpt, pp. 11–13; 382d Inf Actn Rpt, pp. 2–4.

TOMBSTONE RIDGE AREA (*photographed 10 July 1945*).

groups of the enemy and sent out patrols to probe enemy positions on the front and flanks. Intelligence sections of the combat units redoubled their efforts to discover the strength and the weaknesses of the Shuri defensive system.

From 8 to 12 April the enemy had delivered intense fires, concentrating on the American front lines, observation posts, and forward command posts. The 7th Division reported that more than 1,000 rounds of 75-mm., 105-mm., and 150-mm. artillery fell in its sector on 8 April, and more than 2,000 rounds on 10 April. Evidently in order to minimize counterbattery fire, artillery units received orders from General Ushijima to cooperate "secretly"—that is, with all precautions to conceal their location—in the *62d Division* fighting.[27] Some of the enemy's fires were extremely accurate. He knocked out one medium tank with a series of direct hits, damaged the control tower at Kadena airfield seven miles from his front lines, and dropped a concentration on a battalion command post and aid station that took a toll of forty-one casualties. The Japanese showed themselves fully aware of the value of artillery in supporting a coordinated attack. A captured map, showing artillery position areas, indicated a well-conceived plan for use of artillery and mortars. However, because of the great dispersion of their pieces and the inadequacy of their communications, they did not show themselves capable of massing the fires of more than one battery. Moreover, the Japanese did not exploit the capabilities of their heavy artillery by delivering persistent harassing or interdictory fires deep within opposing lines.[28]

Despite the effective defensive fighting of the enemy during 9–12 April, his strategy, as he was fully aware, was essentially a negative one. He was losing men faster than the Americans; by 1600 on 12 April about 5,750 of the enemy were estimated to have been killed, as against 451 of the XXIV Corps. The Corps had suffered approximately 2,900 casualties, including 2,198 wounded and 241 missing. The enemy had lost heavily in some of his key combat units. The *12th Independent Infantry Battalion* had been reduced to 475 effectives by 12 April, little more than one-third of its original strength.[29] XXIV Corps had captured or destroyed 17 artillery pieces, 40 mortars, including 32 knee mortars, 20 antitank guns, 79 machine guns, 262 rifles, and moderate amounts of ammunition and supplies. Although these losses represented only a small

[27] Tenth Army Transl No. 265, 12 Jul 45: *32d Army* Ord No. 146, 9 Apr 45.

[28] Tenth Army Int Monograph, Pt. I, Sec. D, Ch. I: Artillery, p. 2; XXIV Corps G–2 Summary No. 5, 17 Apr 45, pp. 5–6.

[29] XXIV Corps G–2 Summary No. 9, 15 May 45: JOB Summary.

decrease in over-all strength, they were irreplaceable, whereas American losses both in personnel and in equipment, though moderately heavy, could be replaced.

American control of the air and sea meant that the enemy's capabilities rested on an ever-diminishing supply of men, weapons, and ammunition. Probably it was this consideration which in April, and again in May, strengthened the hands of the aggressive members of the *32d Army* staff with their visions of victory through all-out attack.

The Enemy Takes the Offensive

Eager for offensive action, aggressive-minded members of the staff of the Japanese *32d Army* proposed at a conference on 6 April that an all-out attack be made to drive the Americans out of southern Okinawa. In the proposed plan, the *62d Division* was to spearhead the attack and advance northeast of Yontan airfield. The *24th Division* was to drive up the east coast, and the *44th Independent Mixed Brigade* would be held in reserve. The plan was vigorously opposed by Colonel Yahara and other cooler heads among the staff officers. They reasoned that, even if the attacks should succeed initially, the Japanese troops would be at the mercy of American bombardment since no positions had been prepared in the area. Furthermore, the south would be left defenseless against new landings. The majority of the staff members were convinced that only a madman could envision the success of such a venture. Accordingly the plan was dropped—reluctantly by the so-called radical element.[30]

The decision did not dispose of the basic issue between the radicals and the conservatives in the *32d Army* staff. The "fire-eaters," as Colonel Yahara called them, continued to chafe at the static defensive strategy followed by the Japanese during early April. When, on 9–10 April, the Americans came to a virtual standstill at the approaches to the Shuri defenses, those who had favored aggressive action continued to advocate an all-out offensive despite their earlier rebuff at the hands of the more cautious staff members. At a staff meeting on the night of 9 or 10 April, General Ushijima gave in, over Colonel Yahara's protests, to this aggressive element. It was decided that three battalions of the *62d Division* and three of the *24th* would attack toward Kishaba on the evening of 12 April.[31]

---

[30] Tenth Army PW Interrog Rpt No. 28 (cited hereafter as Interrog Yahara), 6 Aug 45.

[31] *Ibid.*

The enemy's choice of the time of attack seemed a shrewd one. The American forces had suffered heavy casualties, and reinforcements were not yet in line. The events of 9-12 April, not only at Kakazu but across the entire front, had seen the American drive lose momentum in the face of the Shuri defenses. The failure of the American attack and the unyielding Japanese defense set the stage for an enemy counteroffensive during 12-13 April.

The Enemy Prepares to Attack

The main obstacle to a successful attack, the *32d Army* staff believed, would be American field artillery and naval gunfire. In previous campaigns Japanese offensives had failed largely because the area over which the troops advanced was smothered with gunfire within a few moments of the opening of the attack. As a result, the enemy plan for 12-13 April called for a mass infiltration in force through American lines across almost the entire front. After a bombardment by Japanese artillery, three battalions of the *62d Division* on the west and three of the *22d Regiment* of the *24th Division* on the east were to penetrate the American lines during the night of 12-13 April; then the troops were to scatter through the American-held area as far north as Kishaba, one and a half miles northeast of Futema, each battalion taking an assigned area. The Japanese were to hide in caves and tombs, awaiting an opportunity to fall upon Tenth Army rear elements on 13 April. They would then be able to engage the Americans in hand-to-hand combat, at which they considered themselves superior. American guns would be silent since their fire would endanger friendly troops as much as Japanese.[32] (See Map No. XII.)

The *62d Division,* already in line, pulled some of its units to the west to enable the *22d Regiment* to move into position. The *22d* was located on Oroku Peninsula south of Naha. Moving into line was in itself a major effort since the entire route was exposed to bombardment. Lt. Col. Masaru Yoshida, commander of the *22d,* on 10 April instructed his troops on the importance of secrecy:

Although you will be traveling in darkness over bad roads and under severe shelling, the secrecy of our plans must be maintained to the last. March in a sinuous "eel line." Although you are going to an unfamiliar place, do not make any noise when you arrive, but dig foxholes in hard ground, and camouflage them skillfully by dawn tomorrow.

Carrying 110-lb. packs and hiding in canefields during the day, the troops pushed east and north along slippery roads in heavy rain.[33]

[32] *Ibid.*

[33] 96th Div Periodic Rpt No. 48, 19 May 45, Translations: *22d Regt* Ord, 11 Apr 45; No. 45, 16 May 45, diary of member of *22d Regt.*

The *62d Division* was ordered to maintain its existing line from Kakazu to Ouki "at all costs." While the *22d Regiment* passed through the *62d Division* positions on the east for a "sweeping attack" toward Kishaba, the *63d Brigade* was to "advance the Army's attack by recapturing and holding front-line positions after the Army's offense had developed." [34] By this means the enemy presumably hoped to maintain pressure on American forward combat elements while his infiltration units went to work on rear echelons. Meanwhile, the *272d Independent Infantry Battalion,* attached to the *62d Division,* together with other elements of that division, were to attack in the Kakazu area in coordination with the move of the *22d Regiment.*

At the last minute there was a change in plans. Colonel Yahara and the other conservatives, considering the entire scheme too bold, succeeded in reducing the forces participating to four battalions. There was also some fear that the Americans might attempt a landing in the Yonabaru area, and it was therefore considered necessary to hold forces in reserve near that town. [35] Nevertheless, Colonel Yoshida's order to his *22d Regiment* on the eve of the attack showed no change in the objective of the audacious plan. At 1900 on 12 April Japanese artillery was to open up a 30-minute bombardment. Supported by a "maximum of infantry fire power," forward infiltration squads were to penetrate American lines and seize strategic points on the ridge line along Buckner Bay. Other infiltration squads were to follow. By dawn the Japanese would be infiltrating into American bivouac areas as far north as Kishaba, and the close-quarters combat would be under way. [36]

Enemy Attack Crushed, 13 April

Brilliant enemy flares exploded over the battle lines shortly after dusk on 12 April. Two of them were red parachute flares; another seemed to be a dragon flare. American intelligence officers consulted a Japanese signal code, captured a few days before. The red bursts meant, "We are attacking with full strength tonight"; the dragon flare stood for, "Make all-out attack." [37]

Shortly after the first flare Japanese artillery opened up an intense bombardment. Hundreds of enemy 105-mm. and 150-mm. shells burst throughout areas just behind the American lines—most of them around command posts,

[34] 7th Div G–2 Periodic Rpt No. 27, 27 Apr 45.

[35] Interrog Yahara; see also XXIV Corps PW Interrog Rpt No. 54, 6 May 45, and No. 36, 6 May 45.

[36] Tenth Army Transl No. 198, 1 Jul 45: *22d Regt* Op Ord No. 63, 12 Apr 45.

[37] 96th Div G–2 Periodic Rpt No. 13, 14 Apr 45; for the captured signal code, see 7th Div G–2 Periodic Rpt No. 7, 7 Apr 45.

observation posts, and artillery positions. Regiments reported receiving the heaviest barrages in their experience. In the 96th Division area, more than 1,000 rounds fell on the 381st Infantry, approximately 1,200 on the 383d. The troops were well dug in, however, and losses were light. The 3d Battalion of the 184th Infantry, 7th Division, estimated that 200 rounds of 105-mm. fire landed in front of them within the space of five minutes, but no casualties resulted.

The attack on the 32d and 184th Infantry was not in regimental strength, as planned. Two infiltration attempts by about a squad each were repulsed by the 184th before midnight. Two squads also attacked the 3d Battalion of the 382d Infantry, just to the west of the 184th, and a savage fight ensued, during which an American private killed a Japanese officer with his bare hands, but the enemy did not follow through with this assault. While groups of two or three tried to infiltrate behind the 7th Division front, the only attack of any weight came shortly after midnight against Company G of the 184th. By the light of flares it discovered to its front from thirty to forty-five Japanese, carrying rifles and demolitions; the company opened fire and sent the enemy running for the cover of caves and trenches. Perhaps, as Colonel Yahara later said, the *22d Regiment,* which was not familiar with this part of the island as was the *62d Division,* was bewildered by the terrain and became too broken up for a coordinated attack. Perhaps another change of plans further weakened the enemy's attack on the east. Possibly the *22d Regiment* moved by design or by chance to the west and ended by taking part in the attacks on the 96th Division.

The assault on the 96th was heavy, sustained, and well organized. The enemy artillery and mortar preparation began promptly at 1900 as planned and continued in heavy volume until about midnight, when it lifted over the center of the division line. Japanese in groups ranging from platoon to company size, with radio communications to their own command posts, began to infiltrate in strength into the American lines in the general area between Kakazu Ridge and Tombstone Ridge. (See Map No. XIII.)

The 96th Division front in the area under attack was thinly held by the 382d and 383d Regiments. There was a large bulge in the lines where the 382d had been held up by strong enemy positions in the Nishibaru–Kaniku–Tombstone Ridge area. A series of fire fights broke out as the Japanese closed with elements of the 382d strung along Highway 5 and with troops of the 383d just west of the highway. Troops of the 2d Battalion, 383d Infantry, saw a group of sixty soldiers coming down the highway in a column of two's. Thinking they were troops of the 382d, the 383d let twenty of them through before realizing that they were Japanese; then it opened fire and killed most of the enemy group. At 0100 the 2d Battalion of the 382d, calling for artillery fire, repulsed an attack by a group estimated as of company strength. Although troops of the two regiments in this sector killed at least a hundred Japanese during the night, a number of the enemy managed to make their way into the Ginowan area.[38] These Japanese proved to be the only ones who attained any measure of success in the entire offensive of 12–13 April.

By far the heaviest blow was delivered by the *272d Independent Infantry Battalion,* commanded by Captain Shimada and operating under control of the *62d Division.* The *272d* had the mission of attacking Kakazu and breaking through at that point. This was no banzai charge; the battalion had a precise knowledge of American positions and a carefully drawn-up plan. It was a fresh unit, having moved up for the attack from the Shuri area on 10 and 11 April. Composed of three rifle companies and a machine gun unit, the *272d* was smaller than the other independent infantry battalions. The men were well supplied with grenades and carried sacks of food.[39]

From dusk of 12 April until past midnight a terrific artillery and mortar barrage blanketed the 1st Battalion, 381st Infantry, on the north slopes of Kakazu Ridge, and the 2d Battalion, 381st, on Kakazu West. The barrage knocked out the dual wire communication of the 1st Battalion but casualties were slight. At 0300 the enemy fire intensified on the north slopes of Kakazu West and Kakazu Ridge. This was the signal for the *272d Battalion* to move out of Kakazu town up into the draw separating Kakazu Ridge from Kakazu West, in an effort to break through the American lines, while smaller groups tried to flank Kakazu West on the west.

Naval illumination was asked, but because of an air raid alert an hour passed before it was provided. During that hour, as the Japanese advanced up the south slopes of Kakazu and through the draw, a handful of men guarding the draw on its lower northern end fought off the attackers until heavier fire power could be brought to bear.

As the enemy, carrying knee mortars and machine guns, advanced down the draw into the American lines on the northwest slopes of Kakazu Ridge, a

[38] Interrog Yahara. Colonel Yahara's statement that a battalion reached the Ginowan area is probably highly exaggerated.

[39] Mulford and Rogers, 96th Div History, Pt. I, p. 62; XXIV Corps G–2 Summary No. 7, 30 Apr 45, App. I, p. 3.

mortar squad of the 1st Battalion of the 381st, led by S/Sgt. Beauford T. Anderson, holed up in a tomb where it commanded the draw. Ordering his men to stay under cover, Anderson went out into the dark to face the enemy alone. He grenaded the enemy column until his supply of grenades was exhausted, but the Japanese kept advancing. In desperation Anderson turned to his squad's mortar ammunition. He tore a mortar shell from its casing, pulled the safety pin, banged the projectile against the wall to release the set-back pin, and threw it football-fashion into the midst of the enemy. Its explosion was followed by screams. Anderson threw fourteen more shells and the enemy advance in this area came to a halt. In the morning twenty-five dead Japanese were found here, weighted down with ammunition and explosives. For this feat Anderson was later awarded the Congressional Medal of Honor.

Other Japanese infiltrated into the lines of the 2d Battalion on Kakazu West. A BAR man was in position along its rocky crest when a Japanese officer approached him and asked whether he was a Jap. The BAR man said "No," then shot the Japanese officer and ten more of the enemy who were following single-file behind him. Personnel of a company command post sallied forth from their position in a tomb to kill twenty of the enemy. On the west slopes of Kakazu West, an American killed twenty-three more Japanese with his heavy machine gun.

Bright naval illumination robbed the enemy of protective darkness and allowed effective use of support fire on the general Kakazu area in front of the Americans. The 1st Battalion brought the fire of its 81-mm. mortars to bear on the positions of its own forward elements, hoping that American troops would remain in their holes. More than 800 rounds of high explosive were successfully used in this fashion. The 2d Battalion ordered fire from its attached Marine artillery to within 150 yards of its front, successfully risking a clearance of 15 feet.

A member of the *272d Independent Infantry Battalion* who tried to storm Kakazu during the night and later escaped by cutting back across American territory east of Kakazu wrote in his dairy:

We started to move again at 0800, and entered the shelter on Hill 70, after advancing individually under enemy aerial attack. The other side of the hill is enemy territory. . . . Two platoons were organized, including the wounded, etc., for infiltration. Before we crossed the hill, the master sergeant was killed and two others were wounded. I was leader of the first team of the platoon and started out with four other men. Since the company commander got lost on the way, we were pinned down by concentrated mortar

SADDLE BETWEEN KAKAZU WEST AND KAKAZU RIDGE, *through which enemy advanced on the night of 12–13 April. Tomb (left) was used by S/Sgt. Beauford T. Anderson and his mortar squad. Sergeant Anderson is shown below (center) displaying trophies of the battle.*

fire before we could cross the hill. Continuous mortar and machine-gun fire lasted until dawn, when we, having suffered heavy casualties, withdrew, taking heavy punishment from concussions. . . . Only four of us . . . were left. . . . The Akiyama Tai (1st Company, 272d) was wiped out while infiltrating. The Shimuzu Tai (2d Company) also suffered heavy losses. The company fell apart during withdrawal.[40]

After several hours of fighting, during which a few Japanese tried to come in across the sea wall near Uchitomari, the remnants of the enemy force withdrew. In the morning 317 enemy dead were counted in the 381st and 383d areas. Patrols sent to the crest of Kakazu, which had been a target for American artillery and mortar fire, reported that "dead were stacked up like cordwood." Nine light machine guns, 4 knee mortars, 125 rifles, and 1 radio were captured in the Kakazu area. Casualties in the 381st and 383d during the fight totaled about 50.[41]

During the day of 13 April the 7th Division noted several large concentrations of Japanese in front of its lines but it was not attacked. The 96th continued to hunt down and destroy Japanese who had infiltrated into its rear areas; some enemy soldiers blew themselves up when cornered. Just before midnight the *9th Company, 22d Regiment,* which that day had been held in reserve in the Kuhazu area, attacked the 184th after an artillery preparation. The assault was quickly broken up by artillery, mortars, and machine guns. The enemy intensified his artillery fire on Kakazu at dusk and launched an attack in the same direction as on the previous night, but this attempt also was soon frustrated by artillery. At 0315 on 14 April the enemy attacked for the last time. The attackers, estimated at company strength, had heavy supporting fire but were repulsed, 116 Japanese being killed. Infiltration attempts were made across the Corps line, with little success.

By dawn of 14 April the Japanese counterattack on the XXIV Corps was over. It had been almost a total failure and had confirmed the worst fears of the *32d Army* staff. Its chief effect had been to bring the enemy out of his stout positions and render his troops vulnerable to the enormous fire power of the Americans. On the 14th there was practically no enemy activity; it was clear that the Japanese had reverted to the defensive. A survivor of the *272d Battalion* well summarized the situation in his diary entry for that day: "Back to the trenches," he wrote. "Heavy mortar fire continues as usual." [42]

[40] CINCPAC-CINCPOA Bull No. 147–45, 16 Jun 45, p. 52, transl Interrog No. 32.

[41] XXIV Corps G–3 Periodic Rpt No. 13, 13 Apr. 45; 96th Div G–2 Periodic Rpt No. 13. 14 Apr 45; Mulford and Rogers, 96th Div History, Pt. I, pp. 59–64.

[42] CINCPAC-CINCPOA Bull No. 147–45, p. 53.

CHAPTER VI

The Conquest of Northern Okinawa

"All restrictions removed on your advance northward."[1] This message from General Buckner reached General Geiger, commander of III Amphibious Corps, on 3 April as the 6th Marine Division was approaching the Nakadomari–Ishikawa line. The message marked an important change in the Okinawa plan. Originally, as part of Phase II, the capture of Motobu Peninsula and the neutralization of northern Okinawa were to come after the seizure of southern Okinawa. General Buckner's order placed the northern operations in the first phase and permitted the III Amphibious Corps to attack the enemy in the north while the XXIV Corps was closing with the Shuri defenders in the south.

There were good reasons for attacking northward without delay. The sooner this was done the less chance the enemy would have to organize his forces and fortify his positions. Colonel Udo, commander of the Japanese forces in the north, was known to be organizing the Okinawans for guerilla warfare. There was also the threat of counterlandings in the small ports of northern Okinawa by Japanese moving in from other Ryukyu islands or from Japan itself; by securing the ports this threat could be removed.[2]

Drive up the Ishikawa Isthmus, 4–7 April

By early afternoon of 4 April columns of the 6th Marine Division were moving down off the high coral cliffs that overlook Ishikawa Isthmus, the narrow waist of the island leading off to the north, and were advancing to the long beach that faces the sea at the town of Ishikawa on the east coast. Here the forces of the division gathered. The marines were footsore and weary, but their spirits

---

[1] Tenth Army G–3 Jnl, Msg No. 7, 3 Apr 45.

[2] The account of Marine operations in the north is based on Carleton, 6th Mar Div History; III Amph Corps G–3 Periodic Rpts for the period; and III Amph Corps Action Rpt. Captain Carleton was the official historian attached to the 6th Marine Division on Okinawa; he witnessed much of the action, interviewed participants, and used official records.

were high. North of the Nakadomari–Ishikawa line scattered groups of Japanese were straggling toward Motobu Peninsula; south of it American tanks were moving up to assembly areas while engineers were organizing dumps and bulldozing wide roads toward the isthmus. (See Map No. 4.)

This "rear area" work by the engineers was vital, for the advance up the isthmus was to be primarily a logistical effort. From the Nakadomari–Ishikawa line to the base of Motobu Peninsula there were two narrow roads, one along each coast, which were difficult to widen because they frequently ran along sea walls or wound around steep hills. Aerial reconnaissance had indicated that many bridges were out. Between the coastal roads was a rugged mountain range, covered with brush and grass. At long intervals roads and trails crossed the isthmus. The 6th Marine Division's hardest task was to move troops, vehicles, supplies, tanks, and guns over these one-way roads without losing the momentum that had been moving the division ahead at the rate of 7,000 yards a day.

The advance up the isthmus was spearheaded by the 22d Marines. Its tank-infantry teams moved along the coasts, making short patrols inland. Along the high ground in the center its 1st Battalion proceeded more slowly, patrolling trails and intercepting enemy stragglers. When the 22d reached the Atsutabaru–Kin line, the regiment paused while the 4th Marines passed through on the east and the 29th on the west. The marines encountered only stragglers except during the night of 5–6 April, when from thirty to forty Japanese blundered into their lines and were killed or driven off.

Both regiments continued to advance with great rapidity. The division prescribed a method of leapfrogging that at the same time freed the roads and provided security. As the battalions pressed ahead, platoons peeled off to patrol in advance or on the flanks. Their mission completed, they returned to the rear of the column. Trucks and supplies followed swiftly as engineers cleared roads and repaired bridges. LVT's and LST's waited for the troops to secure likely inlets or bays where they could unload.

The 29th Marines reached Chuda on 6 April and threw a line across the isthmus on the road there. In its sector the enemy's destruction of bridges had been inept; frequently only a span of the bridge had been dropped or cracked. The engineers cut hasty bypasses for the vehicles, repairing the broken spans later. The 4th Marines, however, was delayed by blown bridges, since destruction had been more effective in its sector on the east coast; at one point engineers had to set in a 120-foot bridge.

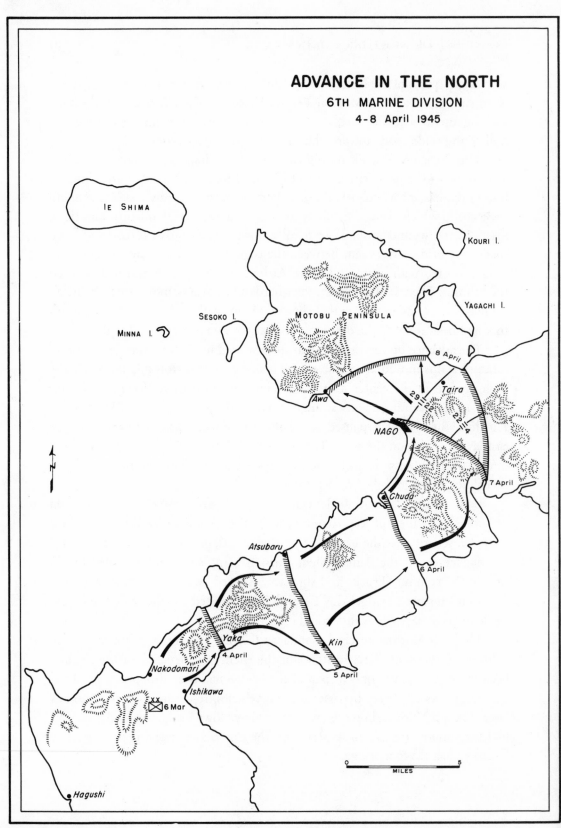

ADVANCE IN THE NORTH
6TH MARINE DIVISION
4-8 April 1945

IE SHIMA

KOURI I.

YAGACHI I.

MOTOBU PENINSULA

SESOKO I.

MINNA I.

Awa

8 April

Taira

29–22

22–4

NAGO

7 April

Chuda

Atsubaru

6 April

Yaka

Kin

4 April

Nakodomari

5 April

Ishikawa

XX 6 Mar

Hagushi

0   MILES   5

MAP NO. 4

Behind reconnaissance units and tanks the 29th Marines advanced on 7 April into Nago, a medium-sized town nestling in the deep bend where Motobu juts out westward from the island. A spearhead drove north to Taira, cutting Motobu off from the rest of Okinawa; other troops started west from Nago along the coast road to Awa. Here for the first time there was evidence that he troops were meeting not stragglers but outposts of an organized defense, for the marines became involved in a few small fire fights and met some organized rifle fire. They had reached Motobu Peninsula, which for some time was to be the focus of the III Amphibious Corps' effort.

Probing the Motobu Defenses, 7–13 April

Motobu Peninsula was largely unknown territory to the Americans. Much of the interior was cloud-covered when the first photographs were taken; later photographs failed to disclose important trails hidden under the trees; it was only after a Japanese map had been captured that the complete road network was made clear. To gain a better idea of the terrain of Motobu and the nature of the enemy positions, the 6th Marine Division conducted an intensive reconnaissance of the peninsula.

The Reconnaissance Company on 7 April followed the road around the southern and western coasts of Motobu. Broken bridges forced the troops to leave the tanks behind and to proceed on foot. Just offshore five LCI's moved slowly along, firing into the hills and cliffs ahead of the troops. The company rounded the southwestern corner of Motobu and drew up abreast of the silent island of Sesoko. After exploring the deserted town of Suga the troops marched back. Not a shot had been fired at them. A prisoner of war said later that the Americans had been under constant observation but that the Japanese had let them pass, waiting for bigger game.

The marines found the peninsula to be virtually a country in itself, inhabited by mountain farmers who dug out their plots on steep slopes. As Motobu broadened out, the area inland rose in a series of slopes topped by a sprawling, twisted mass of rocky ridges and ravines called Yae-Take, the highest points of which were close to 1,500 feet. This mass was to prove the critical terrain feature of the peninsula. The lower ridges were heavily wooded; the upper areas were covered with grass and a few stunted trees. Hills bordered Motobu Peninsula on its western end, broken only where the Manna River ran through to the inlet on which Toguchi was located. On the northern side a small group

FIRE BOMBING *aided the advance in northern Okinawa. A Marine fighter plane (F4U) has flown low and dropped its fire bomb on an enemy-held slope in the rugged north.*

of islands formed a protecting harbor; here the Japanese had established a midget submarine base, a torpedo station, and an operating point for suicide boats. The more important towns lay on the flatlands along the coast. Two towns in the interior were to prove tactically important: Manna, one and a half miles east of Toguchi, and Itomi, two miles northeast of Yae-Take. (See Map No. XIV.)

From 8 to 11 April the 29th Marines made efforts to fix the position of the enemy on Motobu. The 2d Battalion struck out to the north coast of the peninsula but encountered only occasional Japanese soldiers. The other battalions of the 29th found a different situation in the area around Yae-Take. The 3d Battalion reached Toguchi on 10 April, despite a brief shelling en route by two enemy artillery pieces and heavy mortars which caused sixteen casualties. From Nago the 1st Battalion drove inland in a northwesterly direction to Itomi, overcoming a small ambush at the approaches to the town. The 1st and 3d Battalions, 29th Marines, were now separated from each other only by the 3-mile trail between Itomi and the Toguchi area; they had almost surrounded Yae-Take.

Closing the ring around Yae-Take proved to be difficult. When the 3d Battalion of the 29th tried to push inland east from Toguchi, the marines were stopped in the narrow defiles in the Manna area by mortar and machine-gun fire. The 1st Battalion of the 29th picked its way from Itomi along a winding trail bordered by steep slopes. When the men were close to Manna and could see the ocean, Japanese mortars and machine guns opened up from the heights. The enemy fire split up the column, and the marines withdrew to Itomi, forcing their way past another ambush on the way back.

By 11 April the intelligence officer of the 6th Marine Division could draw a great red oval on his map of Motobu and set up fairly accurately the outermost limits of enemy resistance. After further intense patrolling around Yae-Take on 12 and 13 April, during which the marines had frequent brushes with enemy groups, more information came in on the enemy's defenses and probable plan. Colonel Udo, apparently adopting a passive defense, was not sending his men out of the Yae-Take area; moreover, he was cautiously husbanding his troops and ammunition by not engaging the American forces until late in the afternoon, when it was too late for them to send an expedition into the hills. It was already apparent that he hoped to keep alive a center of guerilla resistance and to delay the Americans rather than destroy them.

Colonel Udo's command post in a ravine on Yae-Take had excellent radio and telephone communications with strategically located outposts. The Japanese were well prepared for mountain warfare; they knew the trails and had horses, the best means of transportation over this terrain. The enemy was especially strong in automatic weapons, among them 25-mm. naval guns set in emplacements in the hill masses. Though the forces in the north were generally weak in equipment and supplies, the best of what was available had been concentrated in Motobu. With mortars and machine guns that were easily carried, with fixed 25-mm. guns, and with at least a battery of field artillery, Colonel Udo might well have hoped to maintain for a considerable time his control of this mountain stronghold.

Closing In on Yae-Take, 14–15 April

Under orders to "destroy remaining enemy forces on Motobu," the 6th Marine Division on 13 April laid plans for the assault on the Yae-Take positions. The plan was for the 1st and 2d Battalions, 4th Marines, and the 3d Battalion, 29th, all under the command of Col. Alan Shapley, to attack Yae-Take from the west. From the east the 1st and 2d Battalions of the 29th were to march from Itomi and occupy the high hills north of the Itomi–Manna road. A battle of maneuver and of opportunity was in prospect since units could not maintain contact. Company and battalion leaders would have to decide methods of approach up the ridges and narrow valleys, and to change those methods on their own initiative when necessary. The infantry would have to depend on its organic weapons; artillery and air strikes would prove more effective when the heights were taken, but tanks were out of the question.

The 6th Marine Division could now focus its effort on the Yae-Take defenses without fear of major diversion to its rear on northern Okinawa. On 13 April, after a fast trip along the west coast by foot, LVT, and truck, the 2d Battalion, 22d Marines, reached Hedo Point at the north tip of Okinawa. On the way the marines had met virtually no opposition. Other elements of the 22d worked along the east coast of northern Okinawa. From bivouac areas on the coast, company patrols penetrated deep into the mountainous interior of the island. The patrols reconnoitered the interior on trips lasting several days; they then returned to the coast, where they were picked up by LVT's.

Nago, the site of the division command post, was now a nerve center; supplies for the operations were being brought to its harbor by LST's as the long road haul over the isthmus had been largely abandoned. Control of roads south of Nago had been transferred to Corps; division engineers were now assembling bridging material for use on Motobu. The rapid advance strained every resource of the shore parties, who had based their plans on the expectation that the divi-

PUSHING TO YAE-TAKE, *infantrymen of the 6th Marine Division pause on a mountain top while artillery shells a Japanese position. Meanwhile another group of marines (below) makes its way up a hillside, probing cave openings and watching for Japanese to show themselves.*

sion would be near the Hagushi beaches for the first fifteen days; supplies and gear, however, rolled ahead with the troops.

On 14 April Colonel Shapley's three battalions attacked east toward Yae-Take, and by evening they had a firm hold on the first ridges. The marines met running opposition from small groups of machine gunners and riflemen. The enemy had good observation of the marines' movements; his machine guns and mortars covered the approach routes; and he followed his custom of allowing a few troops to pass across an open saddle and then firing on the group from behind. American officers were his favorite target. It was dangerous to hold a map, to wave a directing arm, or even to show a pistol rather than a carbine or rifle. Under the circumstances the companies deployed rapidly, and on many occasions the approach march became a series of assaults as fire teams engaged with enemy outposts. The marines, accustomed to grappling with solid defense lines on small islands, now had to use tactics of maneuver "right out of the book."

More maneuvering on 15 April brought the marines into position for a final assault. On the same day the 3d Battalion of the 29th attacked east from the left (north) of the American line west of Yae-Take, over a ridge just below the heights. One company of the 3d Battalion remained in place, while another circled behind the ridge and assaulted it under covering fire of riflemen and machine gunners in the third company. After sharp hand-to-hand fighting the marines took the ridge.

In the center of the line, the 2d Battalion, 4th Marines, attacked another hill just west of Yae-Take. One company gained the crest but was driven off by enemy fire. This attack, however, protected the advance of the 1st Battalion on the right (south). Companies A and C moved southeast all day across the hills and saddles. By nightfall of 15 April the battalion was entrenched along a curving ridge which faced Yae-Take. On its left rear (northwest) were Colonel Shapley's other battalions. Japanese soldiers were withdrawing to the heights of Yae-Take as the Americans contracted their area.

Conquest of Motobu Peninsula, 16–18 April

The attack on Yae-Take on 16 April was designed to take full advantage of the position gained by the 1st Battalion, 4th Marines, on the previous day. While the 3d Battalion of the 29th Marines and the 2d Battalion of the 4th maintained pressure along a line west of Yae-Take, the 1st and 3d Battalions of the 4th were to attack north across their fronts to seize the crests. The 29th Marines, moving southwest along the Itomi–Manna road, would be in position to attack the north part of the sprawling hill mass from the east. The 1st Battalion, 22d Marines, then in reserve, was placed on the line on the 16th to close the gap on the south between the 4th and 29th Marines.

Early on 16 April the 1st Battalion of the 4th Marines, supported by planes, artillery, and naval guns, moved up the steep slopes of Yae-Take. Mortar observers in the foothills directed a heavy pounding on the areas ahead. Forward elements of the battalion climbed up the wooded slopes, apparently unobserved. As the marines moved out on steep bare rock 100 yards from the crest, knee mortar shells and hand grenades exploded over the face of the slope. Lacking cover, the troops pulled back into the woods. On the right (southeast) other troops of the battalion worked their way up a small valley under rifle fire; then both forces made a charge that carried them over the summit and into the defending Japanese. By late afternoon the 1st Battalion had secured the crest and the defenders were dead or dispersed.

Below them on other ridges of Yae-Take the marines that evening could see Japanese hurrying about—sign of a counterattack forming. Heavy mortar and artillery fire protected the Americans while everyone available at battalion headquarters helped to rush ammunition up the mountain. At 1850 the expected charge came. The marines held their ground and killed about one hundred Japanese. That night the battalion was still there, although one company stretched precariously down the steep east and west slopes. The marines had little food and were exposed to enemy fire, but there was no enemy activity.

The greater part of Yae-Take was still to be captured. While Colonel Shapley's troops were taking the southern and western ridges, the 29th Marines were moving toward Yae-Take from the northeast. Originally the 29th was to occupy hills north of the Itomi–Manna road, but the columns had been diverted to the southwest as they clashed with enemy patrols in the Yae-Take area. The mountain was well defended against attack from this direction. The 29th spent most of 16 and 17 April probing the enemy positions. Although on several occasions its patrols were driven back by storms of mortar fire, the 29th slowly pushed up the ridges.

On 17 April the attack toward the northeast heights of Yae-Take was spearheaded by the 1st Battalion, 29th Marines, commanded by Lt. Col. Jean W. Moreau. From his position Colonel Moreau could see the high ground from which the Japanese had fired on his company patrols. His objective was a mountain which rose sharply from a defile to the south and dropped off to the north in steep but smooth grades to the Itomi–Manna road. When the Americans moved, the Japanese opened up from the mountain with machine guns and rifles; their guns poured regular patterns of explosive shells on the Marine positions.

Colonel Moreau decided to assault this mountain from the rear. On the morning of 17 April he swung one company around the ridge on the left (south) with the plan of climbing the almost sheer face of the mountain. He ordered two squads to march along a trail that led to the north of the mountain, then to return to the starting point and repeat the process. He hoped by this method to deceive the enemy as to the point of the attack. The stratagem succeeded. The attacking elements disappeared in the undergrowth. Colonel Moreau directed artillery and mortar fire on the enemy gun positions on the north face of the mountain. At noon a smoke grenade at the top announced that his troops had reached their objective. They had suffered one casualty. By nightfall two companies were entrenched on the summit and dominated much of the northern heights of Yae-Take. Artillery killed about ten Japanese during the assault, and five 25-mm. guns were taken intact.

On the same day the 4th Marines swept north over Yae-Take. The enemy put up little effective resistance, and about 700 Japanese were killed as they withdrew before the 4th Marines over ridges covered by the fire of the holding forces. The marines found large stores, the command post of Colonel Udo, and the elaborate telephone switchboard through which he had controlled his once far-flung units. On 18 April the 4th and 29th Marines joined ranks and pushed north abreast across the Itomi–Manna road in pursuit of the fleeing enemy.

The 6th Marine Division had broken the main enemy defenses north of the landing beaches, but enough Japanese remained to participate in organized guerilla warfare. Until the 6th moved south in May, the marines patrolled and reduced enemy pockets in Motobu and northern Okinawa.

In its special action report the division summarized its experience in the campaign in northern Okinawa as follows:

During that period the Division had moved 84 miles, seized 436 square miles of enemy territory, counted over 2,500 enemy bodies and captured 46 prisoners. Our losses during the period were 236 killed, 1,061 wounded, and 7 missing. During the rapid advance of the Division from Yontan Airdrome to the northern tip of Okinawa practically every type of maneuver was employed and all types of supply problems encountered. The successful execution of the mission assigned gives conclusive evidence that a Marine Division is capable of extended operations ashore.[3]

---

[3] 6th Marine Division Special Actn Rpt, cited in Carleton, 6th Marine Div History, p. 55.

CHAPTER VII

The Capture of Ie Shima

When III Amphibious Corps succeeded in making a rapid advance to the Motobu Peninsula and neutralizing the Japanese forces there, Tenth Army decided that early operations against Ie Shima were both feasible and desirable. Originally, both the capture of this island and the conquest of the northern part of Okinawa had been scheduled for Phase II of the campaign, but the possibility of an early seizure of Ie Shima had nevertheless been considered. On 11 April, after the successful development of operations in the north, Tenth Army merged completely Phases I and II and ordered the 77th Division to seize the island on 16 April. The main purpose of the operation was the acquisition of additional airfields to support the assault on Okinawa and the strikes against the Japanese homeland.[1]

Ie Shima lies about three and one-half miles off the western tip of Motobu Peninsula and twenty miles north of the Hagushi beaches on Okinawa. It is oval in shape, about five miles long and two miles wide, the longer dimension lying east and west. Coral reefs fringe the entire island. Along the north and northwest coasts the land rises abruptly in steep sea cliffs containing hundreds of caves, but along the southern shores are numerous beaches from which the terrain slopes gently upward. The best of these for landing heavy equipment, designated as Red 3 and 4 by the invading forces, lay on the southeast coast southwest of the town of Ie. The approaches were clear to the reef, the beaches were sandy and free of obstacles, and a number of roads led inland over gently rising ground. Other beaches on the southeast coast, as well as those on the south and southwest coasts, were less satisfactory because of the character of the reef and other conditions offshore, the bluffs behind the beaches, and the lack of roads.

The island is spotted with small clumps of scrub trees, sparse areas of knee-high grass, and a few cultivated fields and patches of sugar cane. Almost its

[1] Tenth Army Opn Ord 4-45, 11 Apr 45; Tenth Army Tent Opn Plan 1-45, p. 13; Tenth Army Actn Rpt, 3-0-4, 7-IV-I; 77th Div Actn Rpt Ie Shima, p. 1.

entire interior is occupied by a plateau approximately 165 feet in altitude, broken on the east by Iegusugu Mountain, which rises abruptly for about 600 feet above the level terrain and was appropriately called "the Pinnacle" by the soldiers. South of the Pinnacle lies the town of Ie, consisting of about 300 houses. Together, the plateau and the Pinnacle were the distinctive terrain features of Ie Shima and also the most important from a military point of view. Iegusugu was surrounded by clear fields of fire, and from it one could see the entire island. On the plateau the Japanese had established three landing strips, which together formed the pattern of the Roman numeral XI. No obstructions interfered with the approaches to these mile-long strips; aircraft had unlimited expanses of open water over which to gain altitude. With its pinnacle and oval plateau, Ie Shima resembled a huge, immovable aircraft carrier.[2]

Plans and Preparations of the Enemy

In November 1944 only the *50th Airfield Battalion* was stationed on Ie Shima,[3] but toward the end of the year the Japanese began to make intensive preparations for defense. The *1st Battalion, 2d Infantry Unit, 44th Independent Mixed Brigade*—called the *Igawa Unit* after its commander, Major Igawa—was sent back from Motobu Peninsula to Ie where it had been stationed originally. As part of the *32d Army* plan to convert members of special units into ground combat troops, the *50th Airfield Battalion,* which was composed largely of veterans of Manchuria, became the *50th Specially Established Infantry Battalion.* An Okinawan conscripted labor battalion, 580 strong, arrived at Ie in February 1945. The airfield battalion had originally been scheduled to return to Okinawa to work there after helping to destroy the Ie strips, but it was caught on Ie Shima by the invasion and took part in its defense.[4] Likewise, only 3,000 of the 8,000 civilians were evacuated to Okinawa, Allied air attacks having destroyed nearly all the shipping in the Okinawa group of islands.

These forces, approximately 2,000 in number and aided by hundreds of civilians, spent the first quarter of 1945 fortifying Ie Shima. Expending human labor on a vast scale, they made pillboxes out of houses and tombs, honeycombed ridges and reverse slopes with trenches, tunnels, and emplacements, and con-

---

[2] Capt. Paul R. Leach, Operational History of 77th Inf Div on Ie Shima (hereafter cited as Leach, 77th Div Ie Shima History), pp. 2–3; 77th Div G–2 Estimate of the Situation ICEBERG, 16 Jan 45.

[3] 77th Div G–2 Summary No. 7, 28 Apr 45.

[4] Tenth Army Transl No. 230, 6 Jul 45: *32d Army* Ord No. 113, 21 Mar 45.

IE SHIMA, *looking east over 77th Division landing beaches, toward the Pinnacle. Marked are Green Beach 1, where the 1st and 2d Battalions, 306th, landed, and Red 1 and Red 2, landing beaches of the 3d and 1st Battalions, 305th, respectively. Heaviest fighting took place on the eastern end of the island (below), where the town of Ie can be seen between southern beaches and the Pinnacle.*

cealed rifle pits and machine-gun and mortar positions in hedgerows. The numerous natural caves were strengthened by tunnels and holes dug into the limestone rock. Some caves were three stories deep and had outlets for firing positions on each level. Mortar emplacements were made twenty feet deep; cave mouths were fitted with sliding steel doors.[5]

Early in March the Japanese command on Okinawa, believing that Ie Shima could not be held for more than a few days, ordered that all airfields on the island be destroyed by the end of the month "because of tactical requirements."[6] Thorough demolitions followed. The runways were ditched and blasted and the entire central area sown with mines, as defense against possible airborne attack. The enemy showed his usual resourcefulness; the mines included bombs rigged variously as pressure-detonating or controlled charges, wood and terra cotta antitank and antipersonnel charges, and fougasse mines made from drums of gasoline.

The Japanese defense plan was based on an elaborate attempt to trick the Americans. The defensive positions were concentrated in and around the town and the Pinnacle because the terrain and the structures there were well adapted for fortification. Consequently, the central east sector of Ie became by far the strongest area; the western part of the island was merely outposted and mined. Furthermore, the best landing beaches were near the southeast end of the island and were commanded by the strong positions in the Ie–Iegusugu area. The Japanese hoped to lure the invaders in over these exposed southeastern beaches and then to destroy them by intense fire from hundreds of concealed positions in the Pinnacle and the town of Ie. They tried to deceive the Americans into thinking that the good southeastern beaches were not defended while the poorer beaches were heavily defended; if the ruse succeeded and the Americans landed on the southeast, the Japanese could exact a heavy price. Consequently, when American reconnaissance parties operated off the southeastern beaches, they were not fired on and could see no indication of the enemy; one American actually strolled along the beach without drawing fire. Pilots flying 100 feet over the area saw no sign of activity. But on the less desirable southern and southwestern beaches the situation was reversed. Here, in accordance with the Japanese stratagem, beach reconnaissance parties drew considerable small-arms fire from the shore.[7]

[5] 77th Div Actn Rpt Ie Shima, pp. 8–9, 50–52.
[6] Tenth Army Transl No. 225, 5 Jul 45: *32d Army* Ord No. 111, about Mar 45.
[7] 77th Div Actn Rpt, p. 5.

American Plans and Preparations

The ruse failed. The 77th Division staff relied on photo interpretation and map study, which provided an accurate means of plotting the development of defensive installations on Ie. After studying photo intelligence reports of 1 March, the G–2 of the 77th stated on 15 March that the nature of the defenses on Ie made a landing on the southeast undesirable, since such a landing would encounter maximum initial resistance:

Therefore, from a consideration of both terrain and enemy action, a landing over the beaches on the southwest end of the island should meet with the greatest initial success. An attack from the west enters the back door of the defensive organization east of the airport. However, the capture of key terrain and the best beaches for bringing in heavy equipment will be delayed.[8]

Plan of Attack

This analysis set the pattern of the attack. General Bruce, in a field order issued 12 April 1945, ordered the 305th Regimental Combat Team (RCT) to land on Red 1 and 2 on the south coast of Ie Shima on 16 April and the 306th RCT to invade Ie simultaneously over Green Beach at the southwest end of the island. While the 305th advanced eastward to seize additional landing beaches, the 306th was to swing around on the 305th's left (north) flank and overrun the airfield. Together the two regiments would reduce the strong points at the eastern end of the island. The troops would be supported by the 105-mm. howitzers of the 305th and 902d Field Artillery Battalions and by the 155-mm. guns of the 306th, which on the day before the landing were to be emplaced on Minna Shima, a sand islet four miles south of Ie.[9] (See Map No. XV.)

This plan was adopted over the objections of supply officers of the 77th, who pointed out that reef conditions off the selected beaches would prevent the use of landing craft except for a short time at high tide. The surfaces of the wide coral reef offshore were so rough and broken that nothing but LVT's and DUKW's could negotiate them.[10] It was planned, however, to unload only a minimum of supplies over these beaches and to unload the heavy equipment over the more desirable beaches farther east—Red 3 and 4—once they had been secured by the 305th RCT.[11]

[8] 77th Div G–2 Estimate, 15 Mar 45, App. IV: Discussion of Ie Shima Defenses; see also G–2 Estimate, 16 Jan 45, 26 Feb 45, 14 Apr 45.

[9] 77th Div FO No. 26, 12 Apr 45.

[10] 77th Div G–2 Estimate, 16 Jan 45.

[11] 77th Div Actn Rpt, pp. 9–10, 42–44.

Although the Japanese failed to lure the invaders onto the best-defended beaches, they did succeed, through excellent camouflage, in concealing their strength on Ie. During early April the 77th received a series of reports from air observers which indicated that Ie was almost deserted. On 6 April General Bruce, explaining his plan to General Buckner, wrote as follows:

. . . original estimate of enemy is considerably reduced. It is planned to take entire division to target area; secure island quickly with minimum forces, less heavy equipment. . . . This plan places sufficient forces in immediate target to quickly and unquestionably complete mission with minimum casualties.[12]

Actually, the entire division was not available to General Bruce. The 2d Battalion of the 305th Infantry was garrisoning the Kerama Islands. The 307th RCT was being held in readiness by Tenth Army to feint a landing on the southern beaches of Okinawa in connection with an attack planned for 19 April. All but the 1st BLT of the 307th, however, was made available to General Bruce during the operation. The 77th had suffered some casualties in the Keramas, but the number was doubled by *Kamikaze* attacks on division shipping during the early part of April. On 2 April, during a night retirement, the 77th Division convoy was caught twelve miles south of Kerama Retto by a flight of Japanese suicide planes which attacked from the clouds. Four ships were crash-dived before fighters and antiaircraft drove off the enemy craft.[13]

Preparations for the Assault

In preparation for the landings, units of the Fifth Fleet bombarded Ie Shima intermittently from 25 March through 16 April. Systematic bombardment of the island began on 13 April when the battleship *Texas,* two cruisers, and four destroyers fired on targets throughout the island, concentrating on the strong points in the east. That evening six rocket LSM's began a night interdiction and harassing patrol of Ie, firing rockets and 40-mm. shells and executing illuminating missions. A similar schedule was followed on the 14th; on the 15th the daylight bombardment of Ie was canceled to prepare for other required dispositions of the fire support ships.[14]

During the first ten days of April, Navy fighters and light bombers attacked caves, buildings, and installations on Ie Shima. After a spell of bad weather from 10 to 12 April, the air strikes were intensified. During the period 13–15 April

---

[12] 77th Div G–3 Msg File, Msg No. 3, 7 Apr 45; see also Msgs No. 9, 7 Apr 45, and No. 23, 13 Apr 45.
[13] 77th Div Actn Rpt, pp. 7–8.
[14] The account of preliminary support operations is taken from Comdr Amph Group 4 PACFLT (CTF 53), Actn Okinawa Gunto, 20 Jul 45, Pt. V.

ROCKETS OVER IE SHIMA, *fired by a Navy airplane toward the Pinnacle. Beyond, to the south, are Ie and Government House, almost obscured by smoke of preinvasion softening-up. Dark area (upper right) is nose of plane.*

54 strikes comprising 292 sorties were flown; 830 rockets, 35 tons of bombs, and full loads of .50-caliber ammunition struck all targets that could be located by observation and by study of aerial photographs. All remaining emplacements around Ie were neutralized and two aircraft found on the field were destroyed.

Under the cover afforded by these air and surface strikes, Navy underwater demolition teams conducted daylight reconnaissance of all beaches on Ie during 13 and 14 April. Except for light and inaccurate enemy fire on the western beaches, the swimmers met no opposition. The teams provided the earliest first-hand information on Ie; although their observations were made from the water line, their reports on beaches and terrain immediately inland proved to be accurate.

On the night of 12–13 April the Amphibious Reconnaissance Battalion of the Fleet Marine Force, Pacific, landed on Minna Island and secured it without resistance. On 15 April, the 305th, 902d, and 306th Field Artillery Battalions went into position on Minna to support the Ie operations. Each battalion quickly registered on base points and check points established on the target. Three cub planes, operating from a field constructed within a few hours after the landing, conducted registration missions for the battalions. There were no preparatory or neutralizing fires, however, until the attack began on the following day.[15]

It had been the enemy's original plan to cover Ie Shima with his own artillery on Okinawa. During the operations on Motobu the marines overran a battery of two 150-mm. guns, complete with prime movers and ammunition, near the west coast of the peninsula. The guns were in a steep draw which opened directly toward Ie Shima. They were to be fired from the mouths of caves and to be pulled back when not in use. Late in March, General Ushijima had ordered the naval detachment in charge of the guns to prevent American use of the airfields on Ie; the two guns completely covered the island.[16] By the time of the invasion of Ie, the situation had been neatly reversed; the enemy had lost his guns, and Ie Shima was exposed to American medium and heavy land artillery as well as to the powerful guns of the Pacific Fleet.

Invasion of Ie Shima, 16–17 April

Two battleships, four cruisers, and seven destroyers of the Fifth Fleet opened up a heavy bombardment of Ie Shima at dawn of 16 April. LCI's swept the

[15] 77th Div Actn Rpt, pp. 16–17.
[16] Tenth Army Transl No. 233, 6 Jul 45: *32d Army* Ord No. 117, 24 Mar 45.

landing beaches with rockets and mortar shells. Thousands of rounds of 40-mm., 20-mm., and .50-caliber ammunition arched into the beaches from support craft and from guide boats escorting the first landing waves. Planes bombed and rocketed the island and dropped tanks of napalm on and behind the beaches. Billowing clouds of smoke and dust rose from the flaming napalm, exploding ammunition dumps, and burning gasoline stores. Within a few minutes Ie Shima was blacked out. Puffs of white smoke against the gray pall over the island showed where the rocket and mortar ships were preparing the beaches. A Japanese soldier wrote in his diary: "After fierce air and naval bombardment, the enemy began his landing in front of the 4th Company, using amphibian tractors. Their fire power is so great we dared not show our heads." [17]

Debarkation of the landing craft from the LST's went smoothly. By 0650 boat waves were forming in the assembly area. Soon afterward amphibian tanks, followed by waves of amphibian tractors, roared toward the landing beaches from the line of departure 3,600 yards offshore. The weather was clear and bright and the sea was calm. The tanks and tractors moved past the cruisers, destroyers, and LCI's to the smoking beaches. As the first waves neared the shore, support fire was directed inland.[18]

At 0758—two minutes ahead of schedule—the forward elements of the 1st BLT of the 305th landed on the southern coast of Ie directly south of the airfield. Three minutes later the 3d BLT of the 305th started landing on a separate beach 600 yards to the left (west). The troops pushed rapidly inland over high dunes. On reaching a road which ran along high ground 400 yards north of the beaches, the 1st Battalion swung east. From this high ground to the town of Ie there were extensive mine fields which, although hurriedly laid and crudely camouflaged, slowed the movement of amphibian tanks and self-propelled guns. The 3d BLT moved inland and then swung east toward Ie, its left flank passing just south of the easternmost air strip.

At 0807 the first waves of the 306th RCT landed on a 600-yard-wide beach at the southwest end of Ie, with the 1st BLT on the left (north). Within three

[17] 77th Div G–2 Periodic Rpt No. 26, 21 Apr 45.

[18] The account of the landings and ensuing action on Ie Shima is based on the following sources: Leach, 77th Div Ie Shima History; 77th Div Actn Rpt Ie Shima, a superior after-action report; G–2 Periodic Rpts, Summaries, Jnls, Msg Files; G–3 Periodic Rpts, Jnls, Msg Files; Tenth Army Jnl and Msg Files, 15–22 Apr 45. Particularly valuable sources are: (1) Memo CG 77th Div for CG Tenth Army, in 77th Div G–3 Msg File, Msg No. 32, 20 Apr 45, in which General Bruce discusses the problems of the Ie Shima campaign; (2) Memo CG 77th Div for Capt Leach, 26 Oct 45, in which General Bruce answers questions submitted to him by the 77th Div historian.

INVASION OF IE SHIMA *was well prepared but met considerable opposition. Assault boats (above) approach the island as supporting shell fire is lifted from the beaches and moved inland. Eight hundred yards inland from Red Beach 2 were these cave positions (below), around which the 305th RCT, 77th Division, was engaged in an infantry-demolition fight until nightfall of 16 April.*

hours the assault battalions advanced 2,000 yards inland to the western edges of the airfield. The 3d BLT of the 306th completed its landing at 1015 and, as the reserve battalion, patrolled the western end of the island. After mopping up small groups of Japanese in caves and entrenchments, the 3d BLT resumed its advance to the east, echeloned to the left rear of the 1st BLT of the 306th.

The rapid advance of the 306th continued during the afternoon of the 16th. The troops quickly overran the airfield. Although the open, level expanse of the runways offered clear fields of fire for the defenders, the only opposition came at the east end of the airfield, where American troops and amtracks knocked out several pillboxes. After pushing on regardless of phase lines, in accordance with division orders, the 306th Infantry by nightfall had gained 5,500 yards for the day and had overrun about two-thirds of the length of the island which lay in its zone of action. The 306th, with three battalions abreast, held a line which began at a point just north of Ie, about 600 yards from the base of Iegusugu, and ran northwest to the north coast. The 306th advanced so rapidly during the day that a gap developed between its right (south) and the left (north) flank of the 305th. To cover this area by fire and prevent attack from the east, Company K of the 306th took a position on three Japanese-built bunkers about 300 yards east of the airfield.

Slow Progress on the South Coast

After advancing inland and wheeling to the east in the morning, the 305th RCT attacked east in a zone parallel to the coast, extending about 800 yards inland. Progress during the afternoon was slow. The enemy delivered rifle and machine-gun fire from coral emplacements west of the town of Ie and from caves and fortified tombs in the hillside below the plateau. It was mainly an infantry-engineer fight; armor and self-propelled guns were held up by mines, including many buried 500-pound aerial bombs. By nightfall the 1st Battalion had advanced only 800 yards from its beachhead; the 3d Battalion, which made the wide turn on the left of the regiment, had moved about 1,800 yards.

During the night of 16 April the enemy launched a coordinated attack on the 3d Battalion of the 305th. The attack came with suicidal recklessness. The Japanese were supported by mortars and 70-mm. guns, and were armed with small arms, sharpened stakes, bags of hand grenades, and literally hundreds of satchel charges, some of which had been improvised from mortar shells. Japanese worked up to the perimeters in small groups and either threw their satchel charges at close range or blew themselves up in an effort to take Americans with them. Some of the human bombs were successful, but most of the

Japanese were killed before they came within effective range. One American had his arm broken by the flying leg of a Japanese soldier who had blown himself up. After hours of wild fighting in the dark the enemy withdrew, leaving 152 of his dead in and around the 3d Battalion's position. Meanwhile the 1st Battalion of the 305th RCT fought off a number of small harassing attacks, but the 306th had a relatively quiet night.

The next day, 17 April, the 305th resumed its attack in an attempt to seize the high ground behind Red Beaches 3 and 4. Following preparations by the two light artillery battalions on Minna Shima and by one light battalion which had landed on Ie, the 1st and 3d Battalions pushed off to the east. Apparently the enemy had concentrated his defenses in front of the 3d Battalion sector, for the 1st Battalion, moving along the coast, met only scattered opposition and made substantial gains during the morning. By noon the 1st Battalion had advanced another 800 yards and had partially secured the area behind Red Beaches 3 and 4.

The 3d Battalion of the 305th quickly seized high ground in its sector, about 800 yards short of the town, after a brief fire fight during which Lt. Col. Edward Chalgren, Jr., the battalion commander, was wounded. The attack was slowed down by heavy machine-gun fire coming from caves in the coral slopes on the left (north) side of the regiment's zone of action. A flanking movement followed by infantry-tank action reduced this enemy position, and the advance continued. Although intermittent mortar, rifle, and machine-gun fire made progress of the troops during the rest of the morning slow, by 1245 the 3d Battalion had generally secured the ground behind the central beaches and had reached the immediate outskirts of Ie.

During the 17th the 306th Infantry held its lines in place to enable the 305th to come abreast and to assist its advance by fire. The regiment probed the enemy's defenses around Iegusugu with combat patrols. The enemy appeared to have anchored his right (north) flank on Iegusugu and to have extended his line generally southeast to the coast. His strongest defenses seemed to lie south of the Pinnacle in Ie town; his defense in depth here was holding the 305th to small gains.

Entrance of the 307th Infantry

When the 305th met increasing resistance on 16 April, General Bruce decided to commit the 307th Infantry on the beaches southwest of Ie. Several considerations underlay this decision—one of them the supply situation. The whole plan of attack assumed that the superior beaches to the east of the 305th's

FIGHTING TOWARD IE, *American troops were held up close to the town by strong Japanese positions. The morning of 17 April the 305th Infantry, 77th Division, paused while artillery pounded Japanese positions in the western outskirts (smoke-covered area). At the same time the right flank of the 305th was attempting to reduce these enemy pillboxes (below) along road parallel to Red Beaches 3 and 4.*

landing beaches would be seized quickly in order to land tanks and other heavy equipment. Moreover, with the capture of the airfield the first day it was advisable to land heavy aviation engineering equipment as soon as possible. General Bruce's main reason for committing the 307th, however, was his desire to capture the island as quickly as possible. Reports indicated that about 1,000 of the enemy had withdrawn to the Pinnacle area for a last stand. General Bruce knew that the 307th might be available to him for only a day or two, being scheduled to make a demonstration off the beaches at the southern end of Okinawa on 19 April. At 1615 on 16 April, General Bruce asked General Buckner for two assault battalions of the 307th, promising to return them by noon of the 18th "or earlier" if they were needed for the demonstration. General Buckner assented.

The 2d and 3d Battalions of the 307th landed on the beaches southwest of Ie during the morning of 17 April, with the 3d Battalion on the east. The plan called for these two battalions to attack abreast northeast toward Ie. They were to pass through the 1st Battalion of the 305th Infantry, which was holding the ground inland to the west of the two beaches over which the 307th landed. The attack was to cut across the front of the 3d Battalion of the 305th, which would provide supporting fire from its flank position on the outskirts of Ie.

The 307th jumped off at 1300. Both battalions made about 400 yards in two hours against steadily increasing resistance. The troops had to move uphill over open ground. From his positions on the Pinnacle and on intervening high ground, the enemy had perfect observation of their movements. The strongest Japanese positions, aside from those in or around the Pinnacle, were along a prominent ridge and in a small rise on the ridge topped by a large concrete building, about 700 yards southwest of Iegusugu. These positions came to be known as "Bloody Ridge" and "Government House Hill."

The 307th made limited gains during the afternoon of 17 April. In the town the 3d Battalion came up against an organized position protected by wire entanglements and mines. A house-to-house fight ensued. The mined and debris-filled streets prevented the self-propelled guns from coming up in support; when engineers tried to clear the way, the enemy opened up on them with machine guns. The 3d Battalion moved east several hundred yards along gently sloping ground south of the town.

By late afternoon both battalions were receiving heavy mortar and small-arms fire from dominating ground ahead of them. The numerous mine fields slowed the movement of self-propelled artillery, and since tanks had not yet been landed the foot soldiers and the engineers bore the brunt of the close-in action. Division artillery kept the rear enemy areas under attack. Elements of the 307th fought their way to a point 600 yards south of Government House Hill, but, being unable to consolidate their position for the night so close to Bloody Ridge, they withdrew to more favorable terrain about 400 yards inland from the beach. Casualties were mounting. Hopes for a quick victory were fading.

Stalemate at Bloody Ridge, 18–19 April

After receiving an urgent request from the assistant division commander, Brig. Gen. Edwin H. Randle, for retention of the 307th RCT on Ie Shima to avoid serious delay in its capture, General Bruce secured permission from Tenth Army to keep the regiment. The plan for 18 April called for continuation of the attack by the 307th, supported by the 305th, against the defense in depth established by the enemy in the town south of the Pinnacle. The 306th Infantry, pivoting on its right (south) flank, was to attack toward the Pinnacle from the west and north. Although this move would continue the encirclement of the enemy's main positions around Iegusugu, the main effort was to be the attack from the south and west. For two days the 305th and 307th were to batter in vain against Bloody Ridge south of the Pinnacle. In the fierce fighting south and west of the Pinnacle during 18 and 19 April, the 77th Division was to meet the stiffest opposition in its experience and to sustain the bulk of its casualties on Ie Shima.

The enemy detachments concealed behind American lines had tragic consequences for Ernie Pyle, war correspondent, as well as for many troops of the 77th. On 18 April Pyle was on his way to the front in a jeep, accompanied by a regimental commander. At the outskirts of Ie, a Japanese machine gun hidden in the terraced coral slopes along the side of the road sent both men into a ditch for cover. When Pyle raised his head a few moments later, another burst caught him full in the temple just below the rim of his helmet, killing him instantly. Only after three hours of intense patrol action was the enemy position destroyed. Pyle was buried in the 77th Division's cemetery on Ie under a crude marker which the Division later replaced by a monument. The inscription reads: "At this spot the 77th Infantry Division lost a buddy, Ernie Pyle, 18 April 1945."

Attack of 18 April

The 306th Infantry moved out at 0730 on 18 April and the 307th an hour later. The 2d Battalion of the 306th on the right (south) and the 3d Battalion on the left met initially little opposition as they pushed generally east in their zones of action north of Iegusugu. The 307th Infantry, however, met heavy resistance from the beginning. From the rubble of Ie and from positions dug into Bloody Ridge the enemy fought back with heavy mortar, machine-gun, and rifle fire. Infantrymen, closely backed by engineer blasting teams, often had to fight their way into the enemy positions and clean them out with grenades and bayonets. (See Map No. XVI.)

The 2d Battalion, 307th, had especially hard going, for it was moving directly into the strongest enemy positions on Bloody Ridge. At first it was planned that the 3d Battalion of the 305th would follow the 2d of the 307th and take over the attack, and the 3d actually moved to a position behind it. Resistance was so strong, however, that the plan was altered; the 3d Battalion was recalled and sent in on the left (north) of the 307th to attack east toward Iegusugu. The battalion was also to maintain contact with the 306th, which was swinging around north of the Pinnacle.

After a heavy preparation by the artillery on Minna Shima, the 3d Battalion, 305th, attacked at 1130 on an 800-yard front. A house-to-house fight ensued amid the rubble of Ie. "Every street became a phase line," one observer reported.[19] The necessity of forming a connecting link over the wide area between the 306th and the 307th made the fight harder. Artillery was ineffective against many enemy positions and could not be used freely because other friendly units were so close by. Self-propelled guns were held up by mines and debris in the narrow streets. After working about halfway through the northwestern section of the town, the troops withdrew to a more secure position on the outskirts, their right (south) flank then being 500 yards west of Government House Hill, and their left (north) flank 700 yards west of the base of Iegusugu. They had made a net gain of only about 350 yards for the day.

When the attack of the 307th came almost to a standstill directly south of Government House Hill about midday of 18 April, it was decided to send the 3d Battalion of the 307th around to the right, where it could attack toward the northeast in the eastern section of the town. The Americans hoped that resistance east of Government House Hill would be less severe than that encountered south of it, and such proved to be the case. The 3d Battalion made moderate progress and advanced to a point 300 yards north of the village Agarii-mae. Medium tanks and self-propelled guns covered the gap that developed between

---

[19] Leach, 77th Div Ie Shima History, p. 17.

DEATH OF ERNIE PYLE, *American war correspondent, took place while he was observing the fighting on Ie Shima. Above he is pictured talking to a Marine infantryman on Okinawa a few hours after its invasion. After the close of the Ryukyus campaign Brig. Gen. Edwin R. Randle, assistant commander of the 77th Division, unveiled a monument (below) over Pyle's grave.*

MINNA SHIMA

AGARII - MAE
VILLAGE

BLOODY RIDGE

GOVERNMENT HOUSE

RED 4

RED 3

IEGUSUGU

IE AND THE SOUTHERN BEACHES *viewed from directly over the Pinnacle.*

the two battalions of the 307th. These weapons put direct fire into caves, pill-boxes, and enemy gun positions in the town of Ie and the Pinnacle. They could not be moved close to the enemy positions, however; deadly machine-gun and mortar fire held the infantry back and left the armor vulnerable to suicide attacks by Japanese armed with satchel charges, who hid in holes until the tanks and guns came within range.

In order to protect the right (southeast) flank of the 307th Infantry, the 1st Battalion, 305th, moved into position on the right of the 3d Battalion, 307th. The 1st Battalion, having passed to the control of the 307th at 1500 on 18 April, attacked to the north abreast of it, covering a zone from the flank position of the 307th to the beach. Meeting little more than scattered sniper fire, forward elements had moved about 1,000 yards by the end of the day. This battalion had advanced farther than the 307th, however, and in order to protect the latter's right (east) flank it withdrew to a position about 600 yards east of the village of Agarii-mae.

In its advance north of Iegusugu the 306th made good progress during the day, despite almost continual mortar fire from positions on the Pinnacle from which the enemy had unlimited observation of all movements. The regiment pivoted on the 2d Battalion, which in its attack toward the base of the Pinnacle had by the end of the day occupied positions as close as 300 yards to its base on the northwest side. In the center of the regimental zone the 1st Battalion encountered four pillboxes, which were finally reduced by hand-placed charges. The 3d Battalion, moving along the north coast, reduced enemy positions in caves in the bluffs after hours of fighting at close range. The 306th could have pressed farther east against scattered groups of the enemy, but instructions were received to cease advance in order to avoid fire which was supporting the 305th and 307th Regiments. By the end of the day the line of the 306th extended from the northeast base of Iegusugu to the northeast coast of the island.

Crisis at the Beaches

Meanwhile a crisis had developed at the beaches. From the very beginning of the operation supplies for the troops on Ie Shima had been a touch-and-go affair. As had been expected, the initial assault beaches were suitable only for DUKW's, LVT's, and small boats, and even then for only a few hours at high tide. The superior beaches southwest of the town of Ie, Red 3 and 4, were not secured on the 16th as planned; reconnaissance parties were driven off by heavy enemy fire. It was only after the 307th landed on Red 3 and 4 on 17 April that unloading of heavy equipment could be undertaken. The first cargo was not

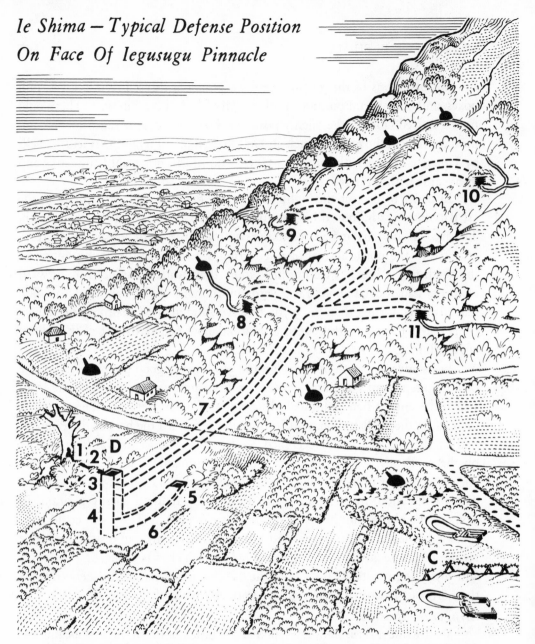

This diagram of a typical defense system on the face of Iegusugu Pinnacle was adapted from a sketch appearing in CINCPAC-CINCPOA *Weekly Intelligence,* Volume 2, Number 5, 13 August 1945. The diagram does not show all the defensive positions in the area depicted and is designed only to indicate the method by which the enemy attained mobility even in fighting from positions underground. In describing this position the bulletin states:

About 50 yards south of the approach road was the camouflaged entrance to a typical tunnel system within the hill. The entrance was a square log-shored shaft 30 feet deep.

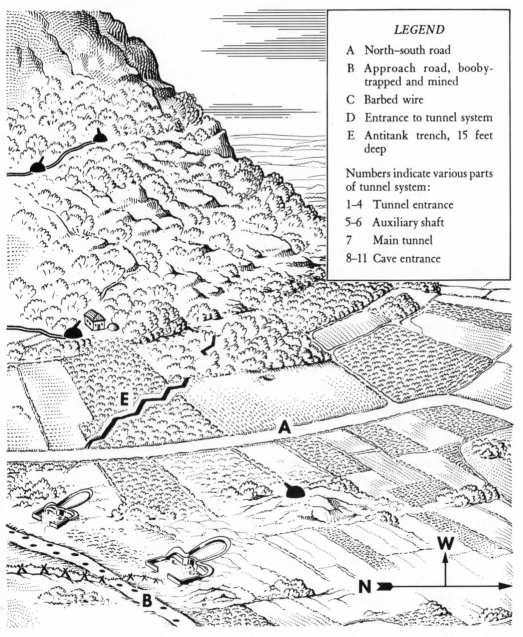

A smaller curved shaft which came to the surface about 15 feet away was probably designed for ventilation purposes.

The main tunnel to the hill installations ran from this shaft, under the road to the first of a series of caves approximately 100 feet from the shaft entrance. This tunnel was from four to five feet high and three feet wide. Walls were reinforced with logs six to eight inches in diameter. Loose coral rock on the ceilings was held in place by logs. The tunnel apparently was used for ammunition storage as well as communication.

on shore until the evening of 17 April. For the first two days of the operation the supply level maintained by the shore parties was only barely adequate.[20]

The difficulties were by no means over when Red 3 and 4 were captured. From his positions in Ie, on Bloody Ridge, and on the Pinnacle, the enemy could put mortar fire on the beaches to the south and on the area directly behind them. During the night of 17–18 April numerous enemy infiltration attempts supported by mortar and machine-gun fire had to be repulsed by shore party engineers. On the 18th the enemy seriously delayed the organization of the beach by firing on the exit roads. The beach became congested with supplies. A platoon of the 233d Engineers had to abandon its shore duties and clear a proposed dump area of snipers who were harassing unloading operations. Late on the 18th unloading was temporarily halted because of the enemy fire. The building up of adequate supply levels was again delayed.

Not until 21 April was the eastern exit free of Japanese fire. In the meantime shore parties continued to improve the beach, establish water-supply points, land tanks and other heavy equipment, and move supplies to beach dumps. Although superior to the other beaches, Red 4 was far from ideal. The deep sand made it necessary for tractors and bulldozers to tow in wheeled vehicles. Until two causeway sets were established on 20 April, LST's had to come in through a narrow, crooked channel, and there were many vexing delays. Unloading schedules were also disrupted when sudden squalls arose and when frequent *Kamikaze* attacks forced ships to disperse and maneuver.

Heavy expenditures of ammunition by artillery, tanks, and self-propelled mounts (SPM's) as they hammered at strong positions on Ie necessitated selective unloading of ships; considerable cargo had to be moved in the holds of ships to get at the ammunition reserves. Despite temporary shortages, however, the combat troops received the needed supplies. By 24 April, the 77th Division shore party, in addition to supplying the division, had unloaded 14 LST's carrying 18,331 measurement tons.

Reversal at Bloody Ridge, 19 April

On 19 April, as on the two previous days, the plan called for the main effort to be directed against the strongest Japanese positions on Bloody Ridge in an attack by the 305th and 307th from the southwest. No attack was ordered for the 306th because any advance might bring it under naval gunfire supporting the

---

[20] See CTF 53 Actn Rpt, V–F–3.

main attack; the lines of the 306th would remain substantially unchanged for the day.

The continuation of this attack after failure on the two preceding days was due largely to the critical situation at the beaches; American forces were attacking toward Bloody Ridge and the Pinnacle, with Red Beaches 3 and 4 a few hundred yards to the south. The protection of these beaches was the decisive element of the tactical plan. The rapid establishment of Ie airfield was highly important in the strategic concept of the Ryukyus campaign, and equipment for the airfield, as well as for a badly needed air warning service, was coming in over these exposed beaches. General Bruce stated in a message to General Buckner: "I know emergency exists for air warning service and airfields. My tactical plans for 17, 18, 19 April based on necessity of securing Red Beaches 3 and 4 for unloading garrison troops even though not required for my supplies and even though other ground maneuver would have been preferable." General Bruce believed that the enemy might stage a banzai attack on the vital beach area if only a holding force were left south of Bloody Ridge while the main thrust was delivered against the Japanese from a different direction.[21] (See Map No. XVII.)

After a half-hour artillery preparation, three battalions attacked at 0900 on 19 April. The 3d Battalion, 305th Infantry, moved east against the northern part of Ie; the 2d and 3d Battalions, 307th, attacked north from their positions south of Bloody Ridge, moving abreast with the 3d Battalion on the east. By massing all the 81-mm. mortars and heavy machine guns of its 2d and 3d Battalions and those of the 1st Battalion, 305th, the 307th built up a heavy base of fire for the advancing assault troops. The infantrymen along the line fought their way from one strong point to another in a series of bloody skirmishes marked by hand-to-hand combat. From the high ground the enemy poured mortar and small-arms fire on the troops; there seemed to be more of it than ever. The controlling factors on the 19th were the same as on the 17th and 18th—heavy and accurate enemy fire from all the high ground and especially from Bloody Ridge; the ineffectiveness of artillery against many of the Japanese positions; and the restricted use of self-propelled artillery because of the rough terrain, the narrow roads, and numerous mines.

Once again some progress was made on the east flank, less on the west, and practically none in the center. On the east the 3d Battalion of the 307th, bypassing the main enemy positions to the west, managed to advance 800 yards north. A

---

[21] 77th Div G–3 Msg File, Msg No. 85, 19 Apr 45.

gap thereby developed between the two battalions of the 307th, and to fill it the 1st Battalion, 305th, pulled out of its position north of Agarii-mae, swung south and west, and attacked north at 1330.

The 3d Battalion of the 305th Infantry, on the west, ran into heavy fire from pillboxes and the ruins of Ie as it pressed east. Since the battalion was to maintain contact with the 307th on the right (south) and the 306th on the left (north), its commander had to extend his line into parallel zones of advance, with platoons taking a street apiece. In the maze of smashed buildings and rubble, fields of fire averaged only from 10 to 20 feet. Because of the width of the front and the channelized fighting, the unit could not mass its strength for a drive in any one zone. The battalion gained about 250 yards, lost 100 yards on the right in a Japanese counterattack, and then withdrew to the outskirts of Ie for a safer night position.

Companies F and G of the 2d Battalion of the 307th, in the center, attacked at 0900 and slowly fought their way up the slopes of Government House Hill. After a frontal attack had failed because of heavy enemy fire, the two companies turned to the west, pushed into the edge of the town on the high ground, and then swung back to the nose of the ridge and proceeded to assault the large buildings there during the afternoon. Meanwhile the 1st Battalion, 305th, on the east flank of the 2d Battalion, 307th, had attacked through heavy fire at 1330 and had reached high ground 300 yards east of Government House Hill.

Two battalions were now on Bloody Ridge, but they were not to stay for long. An enemy counterattack supported by mortar and automatic fire drove the men of the 1st Battalion, 305th, off the high ground and back to their original position near the beach. At this time the 2d Battalion, 307th, was still fighting for Government House Hill 300 yards to the west. The Americans could not, however, consolidate their hold on the buildings. Their ammunition was running low; an amtrack started up the hill with resupply, but the drivers fled when a group of Japanese ran out of a small draw and flung a satchel charge into the vehicle. The troops on the hill were now receiving fire from the high ground just lost by the 305th as well as from the area to the north. Their commander received permission to withdraw. Despite intense fire, Pfc. Martin O. May, a machine gunner of Company H, voluntarily held his post and covered the withdrawal. Another assault on Bloody Ridge had netted only heavy casualties.

The Japanese on Ie Shima were using the defensive methods that had characterized their fighting on other Pacific islands: a house-to-house, cave-to-cave, yard-by-yard linear defense, supported by vicious counterattacks of from platoon to company strength; ingeniously concealed detachments that harassed rear elements after the assault troops had passed by; and night infiltrators who even reactivated mines that had been collected by American troops during the day. Although they had few heavy weapons on Ie, the Japanese effectively used mortars, antitank guns, and light and heavy machine guns; when these were not available, they fought with satchel charges, grenades, and crude spears. The soldiers on Ie, unlike those on Kerama, had the fanatical support of the civilians, including even women with babies, who took part in suicide raids and helped defend caves and tunnels.

On Ie Shima the Japanese sowed thousands of mines, most of them on the airfield, along the beaches and beach roads, and in the heavily defended area west of the town of Ie. Many mines were adapted from aerial bombs and set up in a crude manner: the bomb was fixed at the bottom of a hole, fuze up, and a rock was balanced on two poles at the top of the hole. A pull wire ran from one of the poles to a Japanese soldier concealed near by who set off the contraption when an American vehicle approached. Such a bomb-mine could flip a 15-ton amtrack over on its back. Most of the mines, however, were of a more standard type.

Capture of Iegusugu, 20–21 April

General Bruce determined to break the deadlock. On 19 April he reconnoitered the eastern approaches to Iegusugu by sailing around the eastern end of Ie Shima in a Navy control boat. Aerial reconnaissance had failed to give an accurate picture of the terrain, but from his floating observation post General Bruce was able to study the terrain as it would appear to attacking infantrymen. He concluded that the most promising direction for the attack on Iegusugu would be across the favorable terrain north and east of the Pinnacle. His plan of attack for 20 April shifted the main effort from the 307th Infantry, south of the Pinnacle, to the 306th, north of it, while the division as a whole tightened the ring around Iegusugu. (See Map No. XVIII.)

By nightfall of 19 April the regiments of the 77th were in an advantageous position to execute this plan. The lines of the 306th Infantry extended from the Pinnacle northeast to the coast, and the 306th had patrolled extensively southeast of its lines. After its easy advance on 19 April, the 3d Battalion of the 307th was directly at the base of Iegusugu on the east. South and west of the mountain and the town were the battalions that had been hammering at Bloody Ridge: from southeast to west, the 1st Battalion, 305th; the 2d Battalion, 307th; and the 3d

ATTACK ON BLOODY RIDGE *of 20 April was marked by severe fighting. Infantrymen of the 307th Infantry, 77th Division (above), move on the double toward Government House Hill, on the ridge. During the fighting on Bloody Ridge two medium tanks (below) were knocked out by Japanese artillery fire from the Pinnacle.*

Battalion, 305th. Since the noose around the enemy bastion was not yet tight, the 2d Battalion, 307th, and the 1st Battalion, 305th, were ordered to recapture the ground they had lost on the previous day, while the 306th made the main assault from the northeast.

Closing the Ring

At 0850 on 20 April artillery fired an intense preparation on enemy-held areas ahead of the troops. At 0900 the fires stopped. For ten minutes, as part of a strategem to draw the Japanese out of their position, the infantry remained in place. Then at 0910 the artillery loosed an even heavier concentration, lasting fifteen minutes.

The three regiments attacked on the heels of the second bombardment. The 306th jumped off with the 1st Battalion in assault, supported by tanks and combat engineers. The 2d Battalion of the 306th remained in position on the north slopes of the Pinnacle, and the 3d Battalion followed the 1st, echeloned to the left (southeast) of the 1st to protect its flank. The 3d Battalion of the 307th, east of Iegusugu, pulled back to the south to give the attacking troops greater freedom of action. The 2d Battalion of the 307th, with the 1st Battalion of the 305th abreast of it on the east, again drove up the steep slopes toward the top of Bloody Ridge and the town and mountain beyond. The 3d Battalion, 305th, attacked east into Ie—for the fourth consecutive day.

All the assault units closing in on the Japanese came almost immediately under heavy fire. Enemy resistance seemed no less stubborn than on the previous days. The 305th and 307th, respectively south and west of the town of Ie, were soon involved in another bitter, yard-by-yard advance. Once again the 3d Battalion, 305th, had to fight through a maze of rubble and narrow streets amid the ruins of Ie. Under intense mortar and small-arms fire, the 2d Battalion, 307th, and the 1st Battalion, 305th, pushed up once again toward the top of Bloody Ridge, the key to the enemy's defenses south of the Pinnacle. The two battalions moved out across open terrain dominated by the enemy, who had perfect observation of all their movements.

Leading elements of the 306th came under intense mortar and small-arms fire as they left the line of departure 600 yards northeast of the base of Iegusugu. The Pinnacle loomed above them, its slopes covered with masses of torn and twisted vegetation. Describing the Pinnacle on the morning of the 20th, General Randle, assistant division commander of the 77th, stated: "It is a damned highly fortified position with caves three stories deep, each house concrete with machine guns in and under. Whole area of village and circumference of mountain a maze of machine gun, mortar, and gun positions little affected by artillery fire we have poured on." [22]

Even as this message was on its way to the 77th Division command post, the 306th was winning a hold on the formidable position.

Assault by the 306th

Company B of the 306th Infantry, on the right (northwest), and Company C, on the left, advanced straight into the Japanese positions on the north slopes of Iegusugu. A deep tank ditch lay 300 yards from the base of the Pinnacle. Mortar and antitank fire was coming from this ditch, from the peak of Iegusugu, and from a string of concealed pillboxes and deep caves on the lower slopes. The area over which the assault troops moved was mined and was swept by crossed grazing machine-gun fires. The action that ensued was singled out by the division report as worthy of note:

> The attack of the 306th Infantry was as close to being a perfect Fort Benning demonstration problem as one could expect to see in actual combat. Maximum use was made of organic and attached supporting weapons on a ridge overlooking the advance and their fire was closely coordinated with the steady advance of the infantry: 37-mm. guns emplaced in positions from which gunners had good observation of the terrain were used to blast pillboxes and to designate targets with tracers for the more powerful guns of the SP Guns M18 and the medium tanks. The Infantry advance frequently was accomplished only by creeping, crawling, and infiltration, but it continued steadily forward. Engineers and infantry, covered by overhead machine gun fire and direct fire of self-propelled guns of infantry regiments and tanks, opened a lane through the minefields which ringed the mountain, and through this bridgehead succeeding waves of tanks and infantry poured to fan out on the other side of the field and resume the offensive.[23]

The 3d Battalion of the 306th, echeloned to the left (southeast) of the 1st, came under flat trajectory 37- and 47-mm. gunfire as it neared the base of Iegusugu. Infantrymen supported by the direct fire of medium tanks crept up to a group of concrete tombs converted into strong points and blew them out with satchel charges, killing twenty-four Japanese. By early afternoon the attack of the 306th had secured all ground to within 200 yards of the base of the Pinnacle. The regiment halted to reorganize; in its 4-hour fight Company B, which had the hardest going on the right (northwest), had lost its commander and twenty-six men dead or wounded.

After a preparation by the 304th Field Artillery Battalion, the 306th launched a second attack at 1430, supported by self-propelled mounts (SPM's) and tanks.

[22] 77th Div G–3 Msg File, Msg No. 97, 20 Apr 45.
[23] 77th Div Actn Rpt, p. 32.

Company C of the 306th was passed through B to continue the attack. By a series of rushes through intense machine-gun and mortar fire, the troops gained the slopes of the Pinnacle. In twenty minutes the leading troops were halfway up the northeast side. Supported by direct gunfire from the area below, the infantry and engineers assaulted cave after cave. Higher up on the Pinnacle infantrymen trained in mountain climbing scaled sheer rock walls, hauling up flame throwers and charges to blast the enemy out of his holes.

By the end of the day the 1st Battalion, 306th, was spread over the northern slopes of Iegusugu. A patrol from Company A had climbed up the face of a cliff and thrown a colored smoke grenade over the peak to inform the troops on the south of their position. The battalion pulled its lines back for the night but stayed on the slopes. The 3d Battalion, 306th, had during the day gained positions within 400 yards of the peak on the east side. The 2d Battalion had pivoted south to keep abreast of the other elements of the 306th.

General Bruce notified General Buckner at noon on 20 April: "Base of Pinnacle completely surrounded despite bitterest fight I have ever witnessed against a veritable fortress." [24]

Capture of Bloody Ridge

While the 306th Infantry was assailing Iegusugu from the north on 20 April, the 305th and 307th were attacking up the southern slopes of Bloody Ridge. After a bitter fight lasting several hours and resembling the yard-by-yard advances of previous days in this area, the 2d Battalion, 307th, again seized the buildings on Government House Hill, and the 1st Battalion, 305th, reoccupied the knob overlooking Government House Hill from the east. Knowing that it would be even harder to hold their positions than it had been to gain them, the Americans hastily fortified them against counterattack. Machine guns were mounted on the second floor of Government House, covering the area toward the Pinnacle, and the troops occupied the ground north of the buildings up to a shallow draw that led to the mountain. Company G was to the west, Company E to the east, and Company F in the center. Engineers and guns were brought up to strengthen the weakened units on Bloody Ridge, who were determined not to lose these positions again. Even as they consolidated their ground the Americans fought off two small but vigorous counterattacks and lost two tanks to Japanese carrying satchel charges.

The 3d Battalion of the 307th, east of Ie, and the 3d Battalion of the 305th, on the west, attacked into the town during the day from opposite directions.

[24] 77th Div G–3 Msg File, Msg No. 64, 20 Apr 45.

After fighting over difficult terrain covered with thick undergrowth and dotted with pillboxes and caves, the 3d Battalion, 307th, held a line at the base of Iegusugu running to newly won Bloody Ridge. The 3d Battalion, 305th, made a slow advance through the ruins of Ie in an easterly direction, keeping visual contact with the 306th on the left (north) and physical contact with the 307th on the right (south). The increasing restriction of its zone by the advance of the 2d Battalion of the 307th, on the south, together with the continued resistance of the enemy in Ie, limited the battalion to small gains.

During the night of 20–21 April small groups of Japanese probed the American lines around Government House Hill on Bloody Ridge, evidently looking for a weak spot in the defenses of the 2d Battalion. At 0430 on 21 April the enemy began an hour-long mortar concentration on the positions. At 0530, from 300 to 400 of the enemy stormed the American lines on the left (west) flank. Supported by intense mortar and small-arms fire, the Japanese advanced in columns—one from the north, another from the northwest, and a third from the west. Among them were women armed with spears. The enemy came through his own mortar fire in a last desperate attempt to knock the Americans off Bloody Ridge.

Company G, 307th Infantry, felt the chief weight of the attack. Its right platoon held fast, but the left (west) platoon gave way. The Japanese drove in to the battalion command post just under the rim of Government House Hill on the west side. Here the command post personnel, attached engineers, and the remaining members of Company G fought for their lives. The battalion commander, staff officers, clerks, cooks, and drivers formed a line along the crest of the hill. In a suicide attack Japanese rushed into the line and exploded satchel charges. Some of them came within fifteen feet of the center of the command post area before they were shot down or grenaded by the defending troops. The improvised line held. It did so largely because of the action of Private May, who was still supporting the riflemen after two days of almost continual action under heavy fire. He fired his machine gun until it was knocked out by a mortar burst and he was severely wounded. May, who later was awarded the Congressional Medal of Honor for this action, resorted to hand grenades, which he threw at the Japanese until he was again wounded, this time mortally. After an hour of struggle at close quarters, the Americans drove the enemy back and regained the lost position.

By dawn the counterattack had slackened off. Most of the attacking Japanese had been killed within the American lines. In the area of Company G there were

GOVERNMENT HOUSE HILL, *western end of Bloody Ridge, viewed after the battle from beach road at east end of Red Beach 4. Scarcely any vestige of the town of Ie remained. The Pinnacle looms behind ridge. Government House (below) was only a concrete shell after both American and Japanese fire power had worked it over. The 2d Battalion, 307th Infantry, 77th Division, used the second floor as machine-gun position to cover 305th and 307th troops moving up Bloody Ridge on right.*

280 bodies; in front of F and E were 84 more. The American troops also suffered heavy casualties. Company G, already depleted by the previous fighting for Bloody Ridge, had only 36 effectives left on the morning of 21 April. Company H had 49; Company E, 57. Of the two machine gun platoons of Company H, 19 men were available for duty, and two guns were left of the original eight. In the 2d Battalion, 307th, 30 officers had been killed or wounded by 21 April—almost all its original officer complement.

However great the cost, Bloody Ridge was now won for good. There was little fight left in the scattered groups of Japanese still occupying the center of the town below Iegusugu. The 3d Battalion, 307th Infantry, relieved the 2d during the morning and began mopping up positions and sealing caves around Government House Hill. The 3d Battalion, 305th, which had broken up an attack on its north flank by two platoons of Japanese at dawn of 21 April and killed thirty of the enemy, finally made a successful attack east into the town of Ie. The troops moved forward again after a short artillery preparation. In three hours the battalion destroyed twelve separate emplacements, chiefly by means of flame throwers, bazookas, and pole charges, and gained a line running south from the small lake at the southwest base of Iegusugu. The Pinnacle at last lay open to attack from the south.

Conquest of the Pinnacle, 21 April

The three battalions of the 306th tightened their grip on Iegusugu during the morning of 21 April. The 3d Battalion assaulted the east slopes at 0830, and the 1st and 2d Battalions continued to reduce caves and pillboxes on the north and northwest slopes. Early in the morning a patrol from the 1st Battalion scaled a 50-foot cliff under sniper fire, and at 1025 a member of the patrol flew the American flag from his hands at the very tip of Iegusugu. Increased sniper fire from the lower slopes prevented others from bringing up a flagpole and ultimately forced the men off the peak.

Fierce fighting continued on the sides of the Pinnacle as the infantrymen tightened their grip during the remainder of 21 April. The battalions were now so close to one another that careful coordination was necessary to prevent troops from firing on friendly units. General Randle ordered successive attacks so that one battalion could attack while others took cover. The 3d Battalion, 306th, reduced a strong position on its left (south) flank, and at 1030 established contact with the north flank of the 1st Battalion, 305th. Shortly after noon the 3d Battalion of the 307th, on the west, and the 1st Battalion of the 305th, on the east, attacked north from their positions on Bloody Ridge to gain the southern slopes of Iegusugu. Resistance was slight and the slopes were reached at 1300. The attack crossed the front of the 3d Battalion, 305th, which was pinched out. The 1st Battalion, 305th, was also pinched out when its zone of action narrowed. The 3d Battalion, 307th, was now between the 2d Battalion, 306th, on the left (west), and the 3d Battalion, 306th, on the right. "All organized resistance crushed," General Randle notified General Bruce at 1345.[25]

Disorganized resistance, however, continued. The southwest slopes of Iegusugu were still in enemy hands. At 1400 Company E on the right (south) flank of the 2d Battalion, 306th, made a coordinated attack with elements of the 3d Battalion, 305th, to push on to the southwest side. The attacking troops immediately came under fire from emplacements still occupied by the enemy. It was no longer possible to use artillery, the area still held by the Japanese being too small. Naval gunfire support had ceased on 19 April for the same reason. Even the use of self-propelled 75-mm. howitzers was limited. With small arms, grenades, flame throwers, and demolitions, the troops cleaned the Japanese from their positions on the steep slopes. Two tanks were brought up to help knock out a large fortified cave about halfway up the mountain. By 1445 the troops attacking from the west had seized their assigned area.

By midafternoon of 21 April all units on the Pinnacle were engaged in mopping up. The exterior of the Pinnacle was secure, but Japanese still remained in subterranean passages and strongholds from which they made sallies against the troops. The openings were systematically blown out and sealed off. The 307th alone captured or destroyed during the day five 81-mm. mortars, five knee mortars, one 75-mm. howitzer, and two 47-mm. antitank guns. These were some of the weapons that had held the Americans off Bloody Ridge for three days.

At 1730 on 21 April, Ie Shima was declared secure. "The last three days of this fighting were the bitterest I ever witnessed," General Bruce stated when the operation was over.[26]

Last Phase

For five days after Ie Shima was declared secure, elements of the 77th mopped up remaining groups of the enemy, sealed caves, destroyed pillboxes, marked or removed the thousands of mines that were still on the island, and buried the dead. During this period hundreds of Japanese were killed in and around the

[25] 77th Div G–3 Msg File, Msg No. 70, 21 Apr 45.
[26] 77th Div G–3 Msg File, Msg No. 97, 22 Apr 45.

Pinnacle, in the town of Ie, and in caves along the coast line. Removal of mines on the airfield and on the roads feeding it was given priority in order to speed up airfield construction. The last noteworthy encounter on Ie Shima came during the night of 22–23 April, when a group of Japanese soldiers and civilians, including women, all armed with rifles, grenades, and demolitions, rushed from caves on Iegusugu toward the lines of the 306th. They were all cut down without loss to American troops.

During the 6-day battle on Ie Shima the Americans killed 4,706 Japanese and took 149 prisoners. Many of the dead were civilians; it was extremely hard to distinguish between soldiers and civilians during the fighting or when inspecting the bodies afterwards. It was estimated that 1,500 civilians had been armed and supplied with Japanese Army uniforms. Some others were in American uniforms. The amount of enemy matériel destroyed will never be known, since so much of it was buried by gunfire, sealed up in caves, or simply blown to pieces. Among the destroyed or captured matériel actually counted were 34 mortars, 44 light machine guns, 8 heavy machine guns, 4 antitank guns, 5 antiaircraft guns, more than 5,000 mines of assorted types, and several crates of parts for suicide rocket planes.

American casualties through 24 April were reported as 172 killed in action, 902 wounded, and 46 missing—a total of 1,120. According to the division surgeon, "casualties on Ie Shima were unusually severe, many of them compound fractures of the extremities and penetrating head wounds caused by small-arms fire." Out of 944 cases, he reported, 412 wounds had been caused by small-arms fire, 511 by shell fragments, and 21 by other causes.[27] Losses in matériel and ammunition expenditures also were high for such a short engagement. Of sixty medium tanks and six 105-mm. assault guns, five were completely destroyed by enemy mines, hand-placed satchel charges, or antitank guns, and many others were temporarily neutralized. During the operation almost 5,000 75-mm. and 105-mm. shells were fired from tanks and SPM's and over 2,500 rounds of 37's and 75's from amtracks. Despite restrictions on the use of heavier fire because of the proximity of the units during the latter part of the fighting, division artillery fired 16,023 rounds of 105-mm. and 155-mm. shells.

"We have gained at relatively low cost in men, materials, and time what will soon be the most valuable eleven square miles of land in the far western Pacific," the 77th Division reported optimistically at the conclusion of the engagement.[28]

[27] 77th Div Actn Rpt, p. 42.
[28] 77th Div G–3 Msg File, p. 55.

Base development proceeded rapidly once the mopping up was completed. Although initially delayed by the large number of mines, the engineers quickly repaired the enemy airfield and began the construction of new strips. The coral foundation of the island and the rubble of the town of Ie facilitated the work. There was ample room for dispersal area, and the sloping ground on the sides and ends of the central plateau provided space for housing base personnel. Civilians were evacuated to Tokashiki in the Keramas. Engineers discovered a large limestone basin on the north coast which produced 100,000 gallons of fresh water; at high tide each day the basin filled up with water filtered by nature. Under these conditions work proceeded rapidly and by 10 May one fighter group was based on the island. By the middle of the month all taxiways and runways were fully operational and radar and air warning facilities installed, although much construction work remained. By 14 June three fighter groups and one night fighter squadron were operating from the airfield. As expected, Ie Shima proved to be an ideal base for the support of operations on Okinawa and for preparing later attacks on the Japanese homeland.

CHAPTER VIII

The Attack of 19 April on the Shuri Defenses

Under a bright warm sun on the afternoon of 18 April, infantrymen of the 27th Division in their bivouac area north of Uchitomari inspected their weapons and struggled with their belts, harness, and bandoleers. At 1500 they began to stroll off toward Uchitomari in long, halting lines. At 1540 several men, without jackets or helmets, picked up a machine gun on O'Hara's Knob, north of Machinato Inlet, and sauntered over to the north edge of the inlet, where they set up the weapon. There was little stir or bustle. Small groups of soldiers moved here and there, settling down at various spots to look across the inlet and wait.[1]

Such was the opening move in an action that was soon to swell into a heavy attack across the entire Corps front. This seemingly random movement was carefully planned. The 27th was going into position to launch a surprise penetration of the enemy's west flank as a preliminary to the attack of the whole XXIV Corps on 19 April. For more than a week the Corps had been making feverish preparations for this attack, in the hope that one powerful assault by three divisions abreast might smash through the Shuri defenses.

Plans and Preparations

American Plan of Attack

General Hodge's plan was to break through the enemy's intricate defense system around Shuri and to seize the low valley and highway extending across the island between Yonabaru and Naha. He ordered the 7th Division on the east to take Hill 178, then to press south to that section of the Naha–Yonabaru road in its zone. The 96th Division, less the 383d Infantry, in Corps reserve, was to drive straight through the heart of the Shuri defenses, seizing the town of Shuri as far as the highway beyond. For these two divisions H Hour would be 0640, 19 April. The 27th was to attack at H plus 50 minutes from positions taken

---

[1] The account of the operations of the 27th Division is based almost wholly on Capt. Edmund G. Love, The 27th Division on Okinawa (hereafter cited as Love, 27th Div History).

during the previous night; its mission was to seize Kakazu Ridge, the western portion of the Urasoe-Mura Escarpment, and the hilly country and coastal plain beyond to the Naha–Yonabaru highway. The 27th Division's delayed entrance was to allow for progressive massing of artillery fire from east to west along the line as the attack developed.[2] (See Map No. XIX.)

Perhaps the most striking element of the plan was its provision for a tremendous artillery preparation beginning 40 minutes before the assault groups moved out. Twenty-seven battalions of artillery, nine of them Marine, were to be prepared to mass fire on any section of the front. After 20 minutes of pounding the enemy's front lines, artillery would lift its fire and hit his rear areas for 10 minutes, in an effort to induce the Japanese to emerge from their underground positions; then the shelling would shift back to the enemy's front lines for the 10 minutes remaining until H Hour. This procedure was to be repeated for the attack of the 27th Division. During the preparation, aircraft and naval guns were to pound the Japanese rear areas. Rockets and 1,000-pound bombs were to be directed against the headquarters installations in Shuri. A landing force, covered by planes and naval guns and embarked in transports, was to feint a landing on beaches along the southeastern coast of southern Okinawa.

General Hodge viewed the prospect with high hopes, mingled with grim appreciation of the difficulties ahead. "It is going to be really tough," he said two days before the attack; "there are 65,000 to 70,000 fighting Japs holed up in the south end of the island, and I see no way to get them out except blast them out yard by yard." He saw no immediate possibility of large-scale maneuvers, but he did foresee opportunity for "small maneuver thrusts within the divisions," and possibly later within the Corps if the Americans broke through the Shuri fortified zone.[3]

Terrain Features

Terrain which became increasingly formidable confronted each of the three divisions. In front of the 27th lay Machinato Inlet on the right; a low flat area covered with rice paddies and dissected by streams, later called "Buzz Bomb Bowl," in the center; and the Kakazu hill mass and town on the left. The 96th faced several inconspicuous but strongly defended hills, such as Tombstone and Nishibaru Ridges, as well as the bold face of Tanabaru Escarpment. The 7th Division was confronted by the stout defenses of Hill 178 and the town of Ouki, which had brought it to a full stop.

[2] XXIV Corps FO No. 47, 16 Apr 45.
[3] Ltr CG XXIV Corps to COMGENPOA, 17 Apr 45.

NAHA
AIRFIELD

KOKUEA
HILLS

NAHA

KOKUBA
GAWA

SHURI

MACHINATO
AIRFIELD

MAEDA
ESCARPMENT

URASOE
MURA

MACHINATO
INLET

KAKASU

HWY 5

TSUKASAN

CHAN

KOCHI

ONAGA

KUHAZU

CONICAL
HILL

HWY 13

YONABARU

BUCKNER BAY

STRATEGIC AREA OF SOUTHERN OKINAWA *seen from an altitude of 7,500 feet.*

These terrain features were merely points of the initial barrier; beyond them lay even stronger obstacles. The most prominent of these was the Urasoe-Mura Escarpment, which stretched across the 27th Division's front and most of the way across that of the 96th. The escarpment rose from the East China Sea in a jagged coral spine that steadily gained height as it extended southeastward. At its highest point, near the center of the island, Urasoe-Mura jutted upward 215 feet from the jumbled ground at its base. From this point, called Hill 196, and from most of the escarpment itself, the enemy had excellent observation in all directions. Although the escarpment came to an abrupt end near the center of the island, Japanese defenses in the rough ground around Kochi, Onaga, and Unaha extended almost to Buckner Bay. Behind this line lay the inner Shuri defenses. The core of the Japanese defensive system on Okinawa, this ground was utterly without pattern; it was a confusion of little mesa-like hilltops, deep draws, rounded clay hills, gentle, green valleys, bare and ragged coral ridges, lumpy mounds of earth, narrow ravines, and sloping finger ridges extending downward from the higher hill masses.[4]

American Preparations

There was virtually no change in the lines from 14 to 19 April. Patrols probed the enemy's defenses; artillery, naval guns, and aircraft searched out and destroyed enemy mortars, artillery pieces, and installations. Ground and air observers studied the ground in front of XXIV Corps and pinpointed caves, trenches, supply points, and emplacements which were to be demolished during the artillery preparation on the 19th.

Behind the lines there was unceasing activity. General Hodge had remarked that the attack would be "90 percent logistics and 10 percent fighting";[5] the truth of this observation was borne out by the intensified activity along the beaches, the continuous bulldozing of the main supply routes, and the long lines of trucks and DUKW's laden with ammunition and supplies rolling toward the front night and day. Among the array of weapons poised for the attack were armored flame throwers, which were to be used for the first time on Okinawa in the attack of 19 April.

Fresh troops also were brought in. The 27th Division, previously in floating reserve, had landed at the Hagushi beaches on 9 April to serve as reinforcements

[4] Appleman, XXIV Corps History, pp. 161–65. The authors reconnoitered this terrain by jeep and on foot at frequent intervals during and after the operation and studied the area from observation planes.

[5] Interv 1st I & H Off with Gen Hodge, 12 Apr 45.

OUKI TOWN

SKYLINE

OUKI HILL

HILL 178

TOMB HILL

RED HILL

OUKI HILL–SKYLINE AREA *on the east coast, which was attacked 19 April (photographed 10 July 1945).*

MACHINATO INLET, *seen shortly after the action of 19 April. Three Weasels on the road (left) were knocked out. In background (left) Buzz Bomb Bowl slopes up to Urasoe-Mura Escarpment.*

in the attack. It was assigned to XXIV Corps and proceeded to relieve the 96th Division in the western part of its zone. By 15 April the 27th was in position. The attack was further reinforced by about 1,200 replacements sent in to the 7th and 96th Divisions. Processed and equipped in Saipan, the new arrivals had been dispatched through the replacement battalion on Okinawa in a few hours. They were uniformly young and healthy, and mentally above average. Their arrival heightened the morale of the men in the infantry companies, but XXIV Corps still remained understrength for the heavy fighting ahead.[6]

Japanese Preparations

The Japanese were not idle. A *62d Division* order on 14 April warned of the attack: "The enemy is now preparing to advance on all fronts. Our front lines will necessarily be subjected to fierce bombardments." Unit commanders were ordered to strengthen positions. Strong points were to be so distributed that the loss of one point would not mean the break-up of the whole line. Units were to "secure their weapons by placing them under cover or in a position of readiness, so that they will not be prematurely destroyed." The enemy evidently anticipated the necessity of withdrawing, however, for he ordered secret documents to be burned "as the situation becomes untenable."[7]

During the lull before the attack, the enemy redoubled his attempts to teach his troops the proper defense against American tactics and weapons. The *44th Independent Mixed Brigade* on 13 April issued a "battle lesson—urgent report" describing defenses against American flame-throwing tanks and "yellow phosphorus incendiary shells." The *22d Regiment* on 15 April described American night defensive positions and how to infiltrate through them. The *32d Army* emphasized the importance of careful selection of points from which to make close-quarters attacks on American tanks.[8]

Admitting that American fire power was their main concern, the Japanese paid special attention to their underground defenses. Units were cautioned to build reserve positions into which troops could move quickly from caves under attack. Simple rules were issued on 15 April for protecting the health and morale of Japanese troops in caves undergoing severe bombardment:

Spiritual training within the cave must be intensified. . . . Useless work should be avoided; whenever there is free time, get as much sleep as possible. . . . Have the men go outside the cave at night at least once or twice and perform deep breathing and physical

[6] XXIV Corps Actn Rpt, p. 100.
[7] Tenth Army Transl No. 65, 11 May 45, and No. 115, 31 May 45.
[8] Tenth Army Transl No. 111, 2 Jun 45, No. 163, 18 Jun 45, and No. 122, 2 Jun 45.

exercises. . . . Latrines should be built inside and outside the caves and, above all, kept clean. . . . Take precautions against diarrhea and epidemic diseases resulting from drinking water which has been left untreated because of the inconvenience of having fire.[9]

Preliminary Attack of the 27th Division, 18 April

The 27th Division, on the right of the Corps line, was faced by a situation that called for the utmost ingenuity if it were to succeed in its assignment of a preliminary surprise attack. Holding the sector on the northern side of Machinato Inlet, this division, and particularly the 106th Infantry on the extreme right, was wholly under the observation of the enemy on the other side of the inlet. Any movement by the Americans, or even preparation for movement, could be clearly observed from the Japanese positions on a bluff overlooking the inlet and on the escarpment about a mile farther back. The success of any attack depended on its being prepared and executed in complete secrecy from the enemy.

Plan of Attack

A captured Japanese document gave Maj. Gen. George W. Griner, Jr., commander of the 27th, an idea for the tactics to employ. This document, issued by the *62d Division,* informed the Japanese troops that "the enemy generally fires during the night, but very seldom takes offensive action." A copy of the translation reached 27th Division headquarters as the plans for the attack were being laid, and impelled the division staff to decide on a night attack to surprise the enemy. The 27th had trained in night maneuvers shortly before embarking for Okinawa. Moreover, the terrain in front of the division made a night attack most desirable. More than 1,000 yards of open ground lay between its front lines in the Uchitomari area and the Urasoe-Mura Escarpment, which was an initial objective of the 27th. An attack during daylight across this ground, obstructed as it was by Machinato Inlet on the west, rice paddies and streams in the center, and rough ground on the division's left (east), would enable the enemy to exploit his complete observation of the area and to bring in prearranged fires on the exposed troops. A night attack would avoid this peril and might catch the enemy napping.[10]

General Griner's plan also took advantage of the fact that the Machinato area was not held in strength by the enemy but merely outposted. Accordingly, the 106th Infantry on the right (west) was to cross Machinato Inlet, advance

[9] Tenth Army Transl No. 47, 7 May 45.
[10] Love, 27th Div History, pp. 36–38.

under cover of darkness during the night of 18–19 April toward the escarpment, and by daylight reach Urasoe-Mura where Route 1 cuts through it; then the assault troops were to push down the escarpment to the southeast and seize the vital high ground in its sector. On the division's left (east), the 105th Infantry was to undertake an entirely different type of attack—a powerful daylight push, lacking deception or maneuver, designed to obliterate Japanese opposition by main force. The 105th was to attack from its positions before Kakazu on the morning of the 19th, clean out the town of Kakazu, and advance straight ahead to gain the crest of Urasoe-Mura Escarpment, where the regiment would hook up with the 106th on its right (west). "Nothing must be allowed to stop the forward movement," General Griner ordered.[11]

Mounting the Attack

The mounting of the attack furnished a ticklish engineering problem, which was complicated by the need for secrecy. Four bridges at Machinato Inlet were to be built during the night of 18–19 April—a footbridge for the assault troops to move across during the night, two Bailey bridges, totaling ninety feet, for supporting weapons, and a rubber ponton bridge strong enough to carry 2½-ton trucks loaded with supplies. Erecting these bridges in the dark would be difficult enough, but, to make matters worse, the 102d Engineer Combat Battalion, the division engineers, had had no experience with the Bailey bridge. The division had left the United States before the adoption of this type of structure and had fought on small islands where large spans were not required. Fortunately, an officer who had helped construct several Baileys in Tunisia, 1st Lt. Irving S. Golden, had recently joined the division. Under his direction the engineers spent several days building, tearing down, and rebuilding Bailey bridges in a division rear area.

Secrecy was vitally important, but very difficult to maintain because of the excellent enemy observation and the intense activity necessary for the attack. The appearance of stock piles of bridge equipment near Machinato Inlet would alert the Japanese to the plan of crossing the inlet in strength. Consequently the 102d Engineers assembled its equipment in rear areas in readiness for instant transportation. Pontons were inflated, and bridge sections were assembled to the maximum size that trucks could carry.

Another piece of deception was also executed cunningly. The route leading to the proposed ponton bridges was a shell-pocked, deeply rutted little jeep road

[11] *Ibid.*, p. 42.

which ran by O'Hara's Knob and ended in a rice paddy 250 yards short of the objective, the northeast edge of the inlet. The road had to be made ready to carry the traffic of trucks loaded with bridge equipment, but attempts to improve it might arouse Japanese suspicions. During daylight hours in the period before the attack a bulldozer puttered about on this road, in plain view of the enemy. When an occasional jeep became bogged down, the bulldozer chugged over to extricate the vehicle, remaining to push dirt and rocks into the ruts. The operator alternately slept, tinkered with the engine, and expressed his annoyance with sweeping gestures when still another jeep became bogged down. But at night he worked feverishly. By 18 April the road had been extended and improved and reached almost to the edge of the inlet, although it would have been difficult for an observer to estimate just what had been done to the road and when.

As the time for the attack approached, the plans took final form. General Griner hoped for a break-through and insisted that "no matter what else happens, we must advance. We do not have time to wait for units on our flanks. If they cannot move, we will push forward anyway. I do not want to hear any unit commander calling me and telling me that he cannot advance because the unit on his flank cannot advance." [12] Maj. Gen. Archibald V. Arnold, Commanding General of the 7th Division, and Maj. Gen. James L. Bradley, commanding the 96th, also instructed their commanders to push their attacks "vigorously and rapidly," even though casualties became severe and logistical problems resulted. They believed that by this means an early success could be ensured and an extended and costly battle avoided. [18]

Night Attack on the Escarpment

At 1607 on 18 April a lone smoke shell, like a tentative mistaken shot, landed 200 yards east of Machinato Inlet. A breeze wafted the smoke west toward the sea and spread a thin haze over the inlet. Assault troops who had assembled casually on the northeast side of the inlet during the afternoon now waited tensely. Within a few minutes other shells landed. Veiled by smoke, infantrymen sprinted along a pipeline to the western edge of the inlet. In a few minutes Company G, 106th Infantry, had crossed the inlet in this manner and had assembled under cover of the cliffs that border the inlet on the west.

Company G's mission was to clean out the enemy outposts in the Machinato village area in order that the bridge construction and the movement of troops across the inlet during the night might proceed without detection. Operating

[12] *Ibid.*, p. 43.
[18] 7th Div FO No. 32, 17 Apr 45; 96th Div FO No. 17, 17 Apr 45.

by platoons, the company scaled the cliffs and maneuvered around the enemy outposts. By midnight, after a series of skirmishes, ambushes, and brief fire fights in the dark, the Japanese in the Machinato area had been cleaned out.

The 27th Division was now on the move. At 1930 trucks carrying Bailey bridge equipment began moving out of a coral pit in the village of Isa and rolling south to the inlet. The last truckload of Bailey equipment was followed at 2000 by the first full load of material for the footbridge. The ponton bridge was shuttled forward at 2030. Shortly after dark the bulldozer began to put the finishing touches on the approaches to the footbridge and ponton bridge to enable the trucks to drop their loads at the edge of the inlet. Working in the darkness, quietly and without interruption, the engineers completed the 128-yard footbridge by midnight and both Bailey bridges by 0300, 19 April. Only the ponton bridge caused trouble; the receding tide carried away the anchor line and some of the pontons, delaying completion of the bridge until noon of 19 April.

The 106th Infantry moved out shortly after midnight. Throughout the night a steady stream of men trudged across the footbridge. The enemy made no move to stop the crossing; Company G had done its work well. Company F of the 106th passed through Company G's lines just before dawn and quietly advanced single file along Route 1 toward the road cut at the northwest end of Urasoe-Mura Escarpment. Since the cut was believed to be defended, a frontal assault up the highway would be costly, even during darkness. Near the base of the escarpment, one platoon of the company turned off the road to the right (west) and started climbing the brush-covered slope. Half an hour later the troops reached the top, still undetected by the enemy.

The platoon swung left (southeast) on the crest and silently moved down the ridge line of the escarpment toward the cut. It was now daylight. Near the cut they found Japanese soldiers sitting around fires, preparing their breakfast. The Americans immediately opened fire. Some of the enemy dropped; others fled toward the cut, leaving their weapons behind. The enemy was now alerted. Soon mortar fire began dropping on the rest of Company F as it moved up the highway. The platoon on top of the escarpment began sweeping rapidly toward the cut. For thirty minutes there was a brisk fight as the Americans closed in on the enemy; then, outflanked, the Japanese gave way and fled south from the cut.

The 106th began consolidating its hold on the northwest end of Urasoe-Mura. By 0710 additional platoons were arriving on the crest near the cut and the few remaining Japanese were being flushed out of their hiding places. The 106th prepared to push down the escarpment toward an eventual junction with the 105th. The attack had started auspiciously for the 27th Division. But by now the whole front was alive with thundering conflict.

The General Attack

As the morning mists cleared, the campaign's largest single air strike was delivered. By 0900 Yonabaru had been hit by 67 planes spreading napalm that burned everything above ground, Iwa had been devastated by a strike of 108 planes, and Shuri by a strike of 139. A total of 650 Navy and Marine planes bombed, rocketed, napalmed, and machine-gunned the enemy. Six battleships, six cruisers, and six destroyers of the Fifth Fleet added their fire power to that of the planes and artillery. These sledge-hammer blows fell on about 4,000 combat veterans of the Japanese *62d Division* who were manning the positions.[14]

The greatest concentration of artillery ever employed in the Pacific war sounded the prelude to the attack at dawn. Twenty-seven battalions of Corps and division artillery, 324 pieces in all, ranging from 105-mm. to 8-inch howitzer, fired the first rounds at 0600. This concentration represented an average of 75 artillery pieces to every mile of front, and actually it was even greater as the firing progressed in mass from east to west. The shells thundered against the enemy's front lines for twenty minutes, then shifted 500 yards to the rear while the infantry simulated a movement as if beginning the attack; at 0630 the artillery shifted back to spray the enemy's front lines for the next ten minutes with time fire. In forty minutes American artillery placed 19,000 shells on the enemy's lines. Then, at 0640, the artillery lifted to enemy rear areas.

The assault platoons advanced, hopeful that the great mass of metal and explosive had destroyed the enemy or had left him so stunned that he would be helpless. They were soon disillusioned; for the Japanese, deep in their caves, had scarcely been touched, and at the right moment they manned their battle stations.[15] Brig. Gen. Josef R. Sheetz, Commanding General, XXIV Corps Artillery, later said he doubted that as many as 190 Japanese, or 1 for every 100 shells, had been killed by the morning artillery preparation.[16]

---

[14] XXIV Corps Arty Actn Report, Annex C, Incl 2: Daily Air Missions for XXIV Corps, 1 Apr to 21 Jun 45, p. 5; XXIV Corps G–3 Periodic Rpt, 19 Apr 45; 381st Inf Jnl, Msg No. 40, 19 Apr 45; Tenth Army PW Interrog Summary No. 2, 2 Aug 45: *62d Division*, pp. 5–6.

[15] XXIV Corps Actn Rpt, p. 37; Appleman, XXIV Corps History, pp. 151–52, 168.

[16] *Ibid.*, p. 179.

OPENING ACTION, 19 APRIL, *was the crossing of Machinato Inlet on footbridge in the early morning. Supporting artillery included this 8-inch howitzer unit (below), one of the first used against the Japanese in the Pacific fighting.*

The 7th Division Is Stopped on the East

The 7th Division faced the *11th Independent Infantry Battalion,* which occupied a line extending from the east coast through the high ground immediately inland. The 7th was deployed with the 32d Infantry on the left and the 184th on the right. The plan of attack called for the 32d Infantry to seize Skyline Ridge, the eastern anchor of the Japanese line, and for the 184th to capture Hill 178 and the area westward to the division boundary, which lay just beyond a long coral spine later known as the Rocky Crags. The main effort was to be made by two battalions down the center, along the lip of high ground leading to Ouki Hill, an extension of Skyline Ridge, high on the eastern slope of Hill 178. Once this point was reached the 2d Battalion, 32d Infantry, was to turn downhill along Skyline Ridge to the left (east), and the 2d Battalion, 184th Infantry, was to turn right (west) uphill against the crest of Hill 178.[17]

Two medium tanks and three armored flame throwers rumbled southward from the 7th Division's lines on the coastal flats, passed through Ouki, and quickly moved into position at the tip of Skyline Ridge. They poured shot and flame into the cluster of enemy-occupied tombs and emplacements at the lower extremity of the ridge. The long jets of orange flame probed all openings in the face of this part of Skyline, and dark, rolling masses of smoke billowed upward. This was a new spectacle for the waiting infantry, who watched fascinated. For the enemy who died in the searing flame inside their strong points, there was hardly time to become terror-stricken. This phase of the attack lasted fifteen minutes, and then, just after 0700, the infantry moved up. All the Japanese on the forward face of the tip had been killed by the flame, but there were others on the reverse side who denied any advance across the crest. The battle of the infantry quickly erupted and smoldered along the narrow knife-edge line of Skyline Ridge. American troops clung desperately to the forward slope through two Japanese counterattacks, in which the enemy crowded forward into his own mortar fire to hurl grenades and satchel charges.

Higher up along the slope leading to Ouki Hill, the assault troops advanced about 500 yards without a shot being fired at them. Then suddenly, as they moved into a belt of ground covered by preregistered Japanese mortar and machine-gun fire, enemy weapons let loose and all forward movement stopped. Efforts to advance were unavailing throughout the **day,** and at 1620 the men pulled back to their former positions. The 3d Battalion was now compelled to

---

[17] The account of 7th Division operations on Skyline Ridge is based on Gugeier, 7th Div History.

give up its slight hold on the lower end of Skyline Ridge, where it had suffered almost one hundred casualties, including thirteen killed, during the day.

On the division's right, the coral spine of the Rocky Crags, so named for the two dominating, jagged knobs, extended southward several hundred yards. It paralleled the direction of the American attack, pointing directly at the bold, white face of the Tanabaru Escarpment almost a mile away. For two days this ridge had been pounded by artillery. Company K of the 184th Infantry was directly in front of the northern point of the Crags. Patrols had not been molested. Observers had seen Japanese running about among the tombs on the slope but had not guessed that the coral outcropping was honeycombed with tunnels and caves stocked with weapons and alive with troops. Nor was it known that this area was an impact zone for artillery, mortar, and machine-gun fire from pre-registered enemy weapons. All this was discovered on the morning of 19 April. Company K advanced 200 yards. Then, at 0730, it entered the forbidden zone and was pinned to the ground by the enemy fire. The adjoining company on the left, raked by enfilading fire from the Crags, was also stopped. Shortly after noon, Company K pulled back from along the eastern slope of the northernmost of the crags. At the end of the day there had been no gain.

96th Division Attack Stalls

Meanwhile the 96th Division was attacking farther west, with the 382d Regiment on the left (east) and the 381st on the right (west). The 382d Infantry had the task of taking Tombstone Ridge and the Tanabaru Escarpment; the 381st, that of seizing Nishibaru Ridge and the Urasoe-Mura Escarpment beyond. The 3d Battalion, 381st Infantry, on the division right at the saddle between Kakazu and Nishibaru Ridges, was a mile ahead of the division left. Facing the 96th in the Kaniku–Nishibaru sector, the *12th Independent Infantry Battalion,* which had absorbed the depleted *14th Independent Infantry Battalion,* defended the center. It had the *1st Light Machine Gun Battalion* attached, and altogether numbered about 1,200 men.[18]

On the left, the 2d Battalion of the 382d Infantry moved out at 0640 and began occupying the series of small hills to the front, only a few of which were held by the enemy. Sniper and mortar fire from the Rocky Crags on the left was a source of trouble and caused casualties. A few spots of resistance developed but were easily overcome. At one point a Japanese popped out of a small roadside cave and satchel-charged the lead tank of a column; by a strange quirk the tank

---

[18] The account of 96th Div operations is based on Mulford and Rogers, 96th Div History, Pt. III.

toppled over against the hole and closed it. The road was now effectively blocked to the other tanks. A few scattered grenade fights took place but did not prevent a gain of 800 yards on the division's left.

Immediately to the right there was no opposition to the advance of the 1st Battalion until Company C on the left and Company A on the right started a pincer move against the northern tip of Tombstone Ridge, so named because of the large number of burial tombs on either side. About seventy-five feet high and half a mile long, it was the dominating terrain feature of the vicinity. As soon as the two companies moved forward the Japanese positions on the ridge broke their silence. Company C was stopped on the east side by machine-gun and mortar fire, Company A on the west side by grenades. Artillery and tank fire was brought on the position to neutralize it. At noon Company A charged up the west slope only to find that it could neither stay on top nor go down the other side. The company commander was killed on the crest. In the midst of this action a supporting tank was lost to a 47-mm. antitank gun. At the end of the day the 1st Battalion held only a precarious position across the northwest nose of the ridge and along a portion of the west slope. The crest was nowhere tenable and the east side was wholly in the hands of the Japanese. Though Tombstone Ridge was unimposing from a distance, it harbored a maze of mutually supporting underground positions that opened on either face and made it a formidable strong point.

Up ahead and to the west, Nishibaru Ridge was under attack. This ridge was separated by a depression and a ravine, upper Kakazu Gorge, from the southern end of Tombstone Ridge, to which it ran at right angles for a mile in a generally east-west direction. Nishibaru Ridge was an extension of Kakazu Ridge, separated from it by only a wide, shallow saddle, through which passed Route 5, the Ginowan–Shuri road. The stream which emptied into Machinato Inlet began in the hills northeast of Tanabaru and ran along the northern base of Nishibaru and Kakazu Ridges the entire way to the sea, forming at times, as in front of Kakazu, a gorge-like bed.

The 1st Battalion, 381st Infantry, moved from its position just north of Kaniku through the western part of the town and pressed forward into the open, despite machine-gun fire from southeast Kaniku. Company C on the left was only a short distance from Tombstone Ridge and had a difficult time because of enemy fire from this elevation paralleling its course. The company fell behind, and soon some of the men were pinned down in the open, unable to continue until dark. Huge spigot mortar shells began falling at 1045, adding their tre-

BATTLE FOR TOMBSTONE RIDGE, *like many others on Okinawa, did not permit much use of heavy armored weapons because of uneven terrain.   Above an M-7 self-propelled 105-mm. howitzer, supporting 96th Division troops, fires at a Japanese position. Below, men of the 1st Battalion, 381st Infantry, bend low as they run through burning ruins of western Kaniku, 19 April.*

mendous explosions to the din. A part of the battalion reached the northern face of Nishibaru Ridge, but even this slight gain was lost when the battalion withdrew from the exposed position at the end of the day.

On the division's right, the 3d Battalion of the 381st Infantry waited for thirty-five minutes in its place along the southern bank of the gorge for the 1st Battalion, still not in sight; the assault troops of the 3d Battalion then moved out, Company K on the left and Company I on the right. As soon as they passed over the lip of the gorge embankment, the troops from Company K drew knee-mortar, machine-gun, and rifle fire from cave and tomb positions in Nishibaru Ridge. One squad rushed an enemy position, killing five Japanese and destroying a machine gun and two knee mortars. But immediately above it a second and then a third machine gun opened up, killing four and wounding two of the small group. Despite these difficulties two platoons managed by 0830 to advance over the crest of the ridge as far as the upper edge of the village of Nishibaru. Here all progress ended when showers of mortar shells and hand grenades formed a frontal barrier and enfilade machine-gun fire from both flanks was added. The survivors drew back over the crest and dug in on the forward slope, hoping that if they held out there help would come during the day. Company K had its third commanding officer in twenty-four hours; the first had been killed, the second wounded.

On the right, the first three men of Company I who tried to cross the hump of ground in front of Nishibaru Ridge were one after the other killed. Machine-gun fire came from the western end of Nishibaru Ridge directly in front and from the nose of Kakazu Ridge across the road to the right front. Exposure for even a moment meant death or a wound. It was here that the 96th Division joined the 27th Division, the boundary running just west of the Ginowan–Shuri road at the saddle between Kakazu and Nishibaru Ridges. Lt. Col. D. A. Nolan, Jr., commanding officer of the 3d Battalion, 381st Infantry, realized the necessity for coordinated effort after the morning of death and failure. He crossed over to the adjoining unit, Company C, 105th Infantry, 27th Division, to discuss with Capt. John F. Mulhearn, its commanding officer, the possibility of a joint attack using five tanks which Colonel Nolan had available. But this proposal could not be acted upon because Captain Mulhearn was then preparing, as part of a battalion movement, to start his men around Kakazu to the right. It was now midafternoon, and, realizing that he could not hope to advance with the Kakazu area on his right front vacated, Colonel Nolan obtained authority from his regimental commander, Col. M. E. Halloran, to

DEATH OF A TANK, *series of photos enlarged from a movie film of Okinawa fighting. Sherman tanks, supported by riflemen, are assaulting Japanese cave positions, and in the engagement a tank is overturned by a Japanese land mine. One of the crew is thrown clear by the blast. Infantrymen fight flame with fire extinguishers in an effort to rescue four tankmen trapped in vehicle. Before rescue can be effected fire reaches ammunition in the tank, and the resulting explosion leaves only a battered metal hulk.*

move his men back into the protection of the gorge.[19] Before this withdrawal began, one of the five tanks ventured through the saddle between Kakazu and Nishibaru Ridges and was immediately destroyed by a swarm of Japanese attacking with satchel charges from the nose of Nishibaru Ridge.

Company L came up from reserve to close the gap between the 1st and the 3d Battalions. This movement drew enemy fire, and on reaching the gorge the company dug in along the edge. From there it gave fire support for the withdrawal of the other companies in front. While it was thus engaged three spigot mortar shells fell on the company and buried several men. The number of 81-mm. mortar shells that fell on the 381st Infantry during the day in front of and on Nishibaru Ridge was estimated at 2,200. By 1700 the 3d Battalion had suffered eighty-five casualities, including sixteen killed.[20]

Kakazu Ridge Is Bypassed

Meanwhile various maneuvers were taking place on the right in the 27th Division zone. Following the two battalions of the 106th Infantry that had crossed Machinato Inlet under cover of darkness and had established themselves before dawn on the western end of the Urasoe-Mura Escarpment, the 3d Battalion of the 106th left Kakazu West at 0600; it was crossing Machinato Inlet when the general attack got under way elsewhere. The battalion mounted the escarpment and took a position along the crest between the other two battalions. The Reconnaissance Troop was now on the extreme right of the escarpment.

The only other 27th Division unit on the front line ready to join in the initial assault was the 1st Battalion of the 105th Infantry. This battalion was deployed along Kakazu Gorge, with Kakazu Ridge, immediately in front, its initial objective. Company C was on the left, next to the Ginowan–Shuri road; Companies B and A, in the order named, were to the west, the latter being initially in reserve. The attack of the 1st Battalion was planned to combine a frontal assault against the ridge with a sweeping tank attack around the east end of Kakazu Ridge. The two forces were to meet behind the ridge near the village of Kakazu and to join in a drive to the Urasoe-Mura Escarpment beyond.

The troops began moving up to the ravine on schedule at 0730, fifty minutes after the attack began on the east and in the center. At 0823 the leading elements were on the crest of a little fold of ground lying a short distance beyond the ravine, facing Kakazu Ridge 200 yards away across open ground. Now, as they started to move quickly down into the open swale, machine-gun and mortar fire from close

---

[19] 3d Bn, 381st Inf, Unit Jnl, Msg No. 20, 19 Apr 45.
[20] Ibid., Msg No. 21, 19 Apr 45; 381st Inf Jnl, Msg No. 90, 19 Apr 45.

range struck them. At once there were casualties, and casualties kept mounting. Those in the open were pinned down; those behind could not reach them. The tip of Kakazu and the western slope of the saddle were ablaze with enemy guns.

At 0830, just before the infantry left the protection of the little fold in front of Kakazu, tanks in groups of three and four in column formation began moving across Kakazu Gorge; they then continued southward through the saddle between Kakazu and Nishibaru Ridges. Altogether about thirty tanks, self-propelled assault guns, and armored flame throwers moved out of the assembly area that morning for a power drive against the Japanese positions, Company A of the 193d Tank Battalion making up the major part of the force. Three tanks were lost to mines and road hazards in crossing the gorge and the saddle. As the tanks moved down the road in column, a 47-mm. antitank gun, firing from a covered position to the left on the edge of Nishibaru Ridge, destroyed four tanks with sixteen shots, without receiving a single shot in return. The tank column hurried on south to look for a faint track leading into Kakazu that had shown on aerial photographs: the column missed it, lost another tank to antitank fire, and then in error took a second little-used trail farther south and began working over enemy positions encountered in the face of the escarpment and in the relatively flat country to the east of Kakazu. Discovering that they could not reach the village from this point, the tanks retraced their way to the main road, turned back, found the right trail, and were in Kakazu shortly after 1000. They moved around and through the village, spreading fire and destruction; Kakazu was completely shot up and burned during the next three hours. Fourteen American tanks were destroyed in and around the village, many by mines and 47-mm. antitank guns, others by suicide close-attack units, and more by artillery and mortar fire. During the day six tanks in the Kakazu–Nishibaru area were destroyed by suicide attackers using 22-lb. satchel charges, which were usually thrown against the bottom plate. A majority of the tank crew members were still living after the tanks had been disabled, but many were killed by enemy squads that forced the turret lids open and threw in grenades.[21]

[21] The account of the tank action is based on Love, 27th Div History; discussion and critique on the ground by 1st I & H Off and Co Comdrs, 1st Bn, 105th Inf, and personnel of Co A, 193d Tank Bn, and attached flame-thrower units, 5 Jul 45; interv XXIV Corps Hist Off with Col Walter A. Jensen, CO, 20th Armd Gp, and Maj Harley T. Kirby, S–2, 20th Armd Gp, 4 Jul 45, recorded in Okinawa Diary, XXIV Corps, kept by Maj Roy E. Appleman, XXIV Corps Historical Officer, on file in Hist Div WDSS. Japanese sources for the action are the following: 7th Div PW Interrog Rpt, No. 48, 2 Jul 45; Tenth Army Transl No. 118, 1 Jun 45: *62d Division* Battle Lesson Dispatch No. 19, 20 Apr 45; Transl No. 189, 28 Jun 45; *Furuta* Combat Intelligence Rpt No. 11, 20 Apr 45; 27th Div G–2 Periodic Rpt No. 13, 22 Apr 45.

At 1330, since it was now evident that infantry would not be able to reach them, the tanks received orders to return to their lines. Of the thirty tanks that had maneuvered around the left end of Kakazu Ridge in the morning, only eight returned in the afternoon. The loss of twenty-two tanks on 19 April in the Kakazu area was the greatest suffered by American armor on Okinawa in a single engagement.[22] The tanks had operated wholly without infantry support. Four of the twenty-two were armored flame throwers, and this was their first day in action. Some crew members of tanks destroyed by antitank gun fire dug pits under their tanks and remained hidden forty hours before they escaped, incredibly unmolested by the scores of Japanese within 100 yards.

The Japanese had guessed that a tank-infantry attack would try to penetrate their lines between Nishibaru Ridge and Kakazu Ridge, and they had prepared carefully for it. Their plan was based on separating the infantry from the tanks. The 272d Independent Infantry Battalion alone devised a fire net of four machine guns, two antiaircraft guns, three regimental guns, and the 81-mm. mortars of the 2d Mortar Battalion to cover the saddle between the two ridges. The machine guns were sited at close range. In addition, two special squads of ten men each were sent forward to the saddle for close combat against the infantry. One group was almost entirely wiped out; the other had one noncommissioned officer wounded and three privates killed. The enemy defense also utilized the 47-mm. antitank guns of the 22d Independent Antitank Gun Battalion and close-quarters suicide assault squads. So thorough were these preparations that the Japanese boasted "Not an infantryman got through." (See Map No. XX.)

It was here in the Kakazu–Urasoe-Mura Escarpment area that the most extensive reorganization of Japanese units had taken place just before the American attack. The remnants of badly shattered battalions were combined into a composite unit of about 1,400 men that consisted largely of members of the 272d Independent Infantry Battalion but also included elements of the 13th, 15th, and 23d Battalions. The 21st Independent Infantry Battalion stood ready to support the 272d. The 2d Light Machine Gun Battalion added its fire power.[23]

While the tanks were operating alone behind the enemy's lines, the 1st Battalion, 105th Infantry, was pinned to the ground in front of Kakazu Ridge. A 34-man platoon from Company A that moved out ahead of the main attack

[22] Interv XXIV Corps Hist Off with Gen Hodge, 6 Jul 45; 713th Tank Bn Actn Rpt Ryukyus, entry 19 Apr 45.
[23] Tenth Army PW Interrog Summary No. 2, 2 Aug 45: 62d Division, pp. 5–6; XXIV Corps PW Interrog Rpt No. 54, 6 May 45.

was allowed to pass over Kakazu Ridge undisturbed only to walk into a trap. When the platoon reached the northern edge of Kakazu village, the trap was sprung. None of the men in the platoon returned during the day, but by separating into small groups and hiding in rubble and in tombs most of them escaped death. Six men returned to the American lines that night, seventeen made their way out the next day, and two more were rescued on 25 April. Eight had been killed and others badly wounded.[24]

With the 1st Battalion of the 105th Infantry completely stopped, the 2d Battalion was ordered at 0907 to move up on the boundary at the extreme left and apply pressure along the Ginowan–Shuri road. In coming up to reconnoiter this ground, the battalion commander was hit four times when he jumped over a low stone wall into the open ground opposite the tip of Kakazu. When the 2d Battalion finally attacked at 1225 in an attempted movement around to the left, it was turned back at the east end of Kakazu Ridge. Simultaneously with the movement of the 2d Battalion, the 3d Battalion, which had relieved the 3d, 106th Infantry, in the morning, moved down from Kakazu West, bypassed Kakazu village, and by 1535 had two companies, L and I, on top the Urasoe-Mura Escarpment, on the east side of the 106th Infantry. During the afternoon the weather had become increasingly unsettled, with high wind and some rain.

At 1530 Capt. Ernest A. Flemig, who had assumed command of the 2d Battalion, 105th Infantry, earlier in the day, asked to be allowed to move around the west end of Kakazu Ridge to join the 3d Battalion on the escarpment. This permission was given by Col. W. S. Winn, the regimental commander, at approximately 1600. The battalion moved off and by 1800 had taken up a position on the slope at the base of the escarpment below the 3d Battalion, 105th Infantry. At the same time, the 1st Battalion, 105th, was ordered in front of the village of Kakazu to become regimental reserve. "Front" as represented by the position actually taken by the 1st Battalion was southwest of the village in front of the escarpment. Thus by late afternoon the entire Kakazu Ridge front had been abandoned by the 105th Infantry. It was just before this shift of positions that Colonel Nolan made his suggestion for a joint attack. In front of Kakazu Ridge during the day, two battalions of the 105th Regiment had suffered 158 casualties: the 1st Battalion, 105, and the 2d Battalion, 53.

On the western end of the Urasoe-Mura Escarpment, the 2d Battalion of the 106th Infantry tried to work south after its successful night attack; but it ran

WEST END OF URASOE-MURA ESCARPMENT, *area of 27th Division attack (photographed 10 July 1945).*

into a series of cave, tomb, and tunnel positions along the ridge to the west of Route 1 and was fought to a standstill. This was the beginning of what later became known as the Item Pocket battle. Elsewhere on the escarpment the 106th was, in general, stopped after its presence was discovered at daybreak. Elsewhere on the escarpment the 106th was also unsuccessful in advancing to the south, but it did extend its lines to the east to join the 3d Battalion, 105th.

The bridges across Machinato Inlet were subjected to Japanese artillery and mortar attack shortly after daybreak. Direct tank fire silenced a gun firing from a cave position in the face of the escarpment, but 320-mm. mortar shells then began dropping in the crossing area, known as "Buzz Bomb Bowl." An enemy artillery barrage on the crossing area began at 1530, and by 1600 one of the Bailey bridges and the ponton bridge were out, only the footbridge remaining. This was the beginning of a week-long struggle to keep bridges across the inlet.

The big attack of 19 April had failed. At no point had there been a break-through. Everywhere the Japanese had held and turned back the American attack. Even on the west, where the front lines had been advanced a considerable distance by the 27th Division, the area gained was mostly unoccupied low ground, and when the Japanese positions on the reverse slopes of the escarpment were encountered further gain was denied. Everywhere the advance made early in the morning represented only an area lying between the line of departure and the enemy's fortified positions. As a result of the day's fighting the XXIV Corps lost 720 dead, wounded, and missing.

CHAPTER IX

Fall of the First Shuri Defense Ring

The mood of the American troops on the morning of 20 April was far different from what it had been the morning before. The feeling now was one of weariness and awareness that breaking through would be slow and costly. The most immediate and pressing objective was to consolidate the line for further advance and, in particular, to eliminate the gap of approximately a mile that existed between the 96th and 27th Divisions when darkness fell. The strong Japanese position at Kakazu Ridge lay in the middle of this gap, bypassed by the 27th Division, and the heart of the Japanese stronghold was behind it to the south. If the enemy could take advantage of the gap he might counterattack and reach the rear of both the 27th and 96th Divisions. Two points of view existed with regard to bypassing Japanese positions. One was represented by General Griner, 27th Division commander, when he ordered that the movement must be forward even if it meant bypassing Japanese and mopping them up later. The other was expressed by Colonel Halloran, the commanding officer of the 381st Infantry, 96th Division, when he said on a later occasion: "You cannot bypass a Japanese because a Jap does not know when he is bypassed." [1]

The primary responsibility for ensuring that dangerous gaps did not develop between units, and that the attack along unit boundaries was coordinated, rested upon the unit commander on the right. [2] The large gap in the 27th Division zone must have alarmed General Griner, since after dark, at 1930, he ordered Company B, 165th Infantry, to take up a position in front of Kakazu Ridge.

Item Pocket

In accordance with General Griner's plan, Col. Gerard W. Kelley, commander of the 165th Infantry, on 20 April had two battalions abreast and ready to attack on the right of the 27th Division line. The 1st Battalion, commanded

---

[1] Love, 27th Div History, p. 180.
[2] XXIV Corps FO No. 47, 16 Apr 45, p. 6.

by Lt. Col. James H. Mahoney, was on the left, and the 2d Battalion, under Lt. Col. John McDonough, on the right. A mile southwest of the 165th lay Machinato airfield and three miles beyond the airfield was Naha—both important objectives. Although photographs and maps did not reveal to any precise degree the strength of the Japanese or the nature of the terrain, regimental headquarters was optimistic. On the morning of the 20th Lt. Col. Joseph T. Hart, regimental executive officer, brought out a large green sign, "CONROY FIELD," in honor of the 165th's commander killed on Makin, and announced that he expected to nail it up at Machinato airfield by evening. He added that the regiment would "hold a dance in Naha on Saturday night." [3]

Item Pocket Blocks the Way

Such hopes proved to be illusory before the fighting of 20 April was more than a few hours old. Almost immediately the regiment hit intense resistance in rough ground north of Gusukuma. When the 1st Battalion drove south along Route 1, the Japanese entrenched in this area cut off the forward elements with heavy mortar and machine-gun fire, killing five and wounding twenty-two. Only by dogged efforts was the battalion able to reach a point east of Gusukuma by nightfall. It had then lost contact with the 2d Battalion, which was meeting equally stiff resistance west of the Japanese position. (See Map No. XXI.)

The center of the Japanese resistance lay in the I section of Target Area 7777, which came to be called "Item Pocket"—in military terminology I is called Item. Actually, the pocket was the hub of the enemy position; from it, like spokes of a giant wheel, extended four low ridges, separated from each other by ravines and rice paddies. Potter's Ridge ran north from the hub, Charlie Ridge to the northeast, Gusukuma Ridge to the southeast, and Ryan Ridge to the southwest. Lying between Gusukuma and Charlie Ridges and sloping to the east was a cone-shaped hill called by Americans "Brewer's Hill." A gulch ran along each side of the hill—Anderson's Gulch on the north and Dead Horse Gulch on the south. Both ran in an easterly direction, crossing Route 1 at small bridges just north of Gusukuma. The ground was superbly suited for active defense. Typical Japanese positions were connected by tunnels along the sides and under the crests of the ridges; Ryan Ridge, in particular, was honeycombed with such defenses. From Item Pocket the enemy had excellent command both of the coastal areas to the north and west and of the open land to the east where Route 1 ran north-south. The Japanese had long been aware of the defensive value of this position against

---

[3] The account of the 165th Infantry in Item Pocket is taken from Love, 27th Div History, Pt. VI.

either a beach landing on the northwest or an attack from the north. Months before the Americans landed, Japanese troops and Okinawan laborers were boring tunnels and establishing elaborate living quarters and aid stations. The area was held by two companies of the *21st Independent Infantry Battalion* of the *64th Brigade, 62d Division,* supported by an antitank company, a machine gun company, and elements of antiaircraf, artillery, and mortar units. At least 600 Japanese occupied the Pocket, reinforced by several hundred Okinawans.

Infantrymen of the 2d Battalion, 165th Infantry, operating on the right of the 1st Battalion, cleaned out a system of dugouts and tunnels on the southeast nose of Potter's Ridge on the 20th but Colonel McDonough's men made little more progress after that day. When the 2d started a pivoting movement to join up with the 1st Battalion on its left, the troops came under intense flanking fire from the left rear out of the Pocket. Japanese mortars on Ryan Ridge knocked out the machine gunners when they tried to lay down covering fire. The troops retreated to Potter's Ridge after several hours' fighting which cost them twelve casualties.

Farther to the west infantrymen managed to reach Fox Ridge, a low rise due west of the hub of the Pocket. Colonel McDonough then ordered Company E on his extreme right to use Fox Ridge as cover and to attack south to seize Ryan Ridge. The leading platoon was well up on the slope of Ryan when Japanese on top opened up with mortars, machine guns, and artillery, cutting off the rest of Company E. While the company commander, his clothes torn by bullets, and the rest of the company straggled back to Fox Ridge, the leading platoon continued doggedly ahead. Its leader, T/Sgt. Earnest L. Schoeff, managed to reach the top with eight of his men despite almost constant fire. He was ordered by radio to hold until relief came. The men hugged the ground as darkness slowly descended. Then from three directions from fifty to sixty heavily armed Japanese set upon the Americans. In wild hand-to-hand fighting the nine men beat off the attack. Pfc. Paul R. Cook fired four cases of ammunition into the enemy, shooting down at least ten before he was killed. With grenades, rifle butts, and the enemy's own weapons, Schoeff and his men killed another dozen before the Japanese withdrew. With two of his men killed, another missing, and two wounded, Schoeff led the survivors back to his company during the night.

At 0630 on 21 April the 2d Battalion launched another attack across the mouth of Item Pocket. The troops were supported by antitank guns which had been unloaded at the sea wall, hand carried almost 1,000 yards, and set up to fire directly into the hub of the Pocket. Within ten minutes the entire left of the battalion line was pinned down. Efforts to advance against interlocking lanes of fire were fruitless and the men withdrew to Potter's Ridge later in the morning. During the afternoon troops on the battalion's right, protected from Item Pocket by Fox Ridge, moved several hundred yards along the coast on amphibian tractors. But an attack east toward the Pocket was abortive. As soon as the infantry climbed over the sea wall, the enemy blazed forth from Ryan Ridge with light artillery pieces and small arms. The first rounds were wild, and every man scrambled back safely over the wall. Another attempt under such conditions seemed out of the question. Again the troops pulled back to Fox Ridge. (See Map No. XXII.)

Thus with little difficulty the Japanese defending the western approaches of Item Pocket repulsed the Americans on 21 April. The enemy's defense was equally effective on the east. Here the 1st Battalion had a major supply problem on its hands. Two blown bridges along Route 1 east of the Pocket were holding up vehicles of support units. During the previous night, fire from the Pocket had driven off an engineer platoon working at the site and killed the platoon leader. Early on the 21st Lieutenant Golden, the Bailey bridge expert, came up with ten truckloads of material. His engineers worked for an hour but had to stop in the face of almost ceaseless fire from the Pocket.

Colonel Kelley then ordered scouts to find another stream crossing. A bulldozer cut a bypass around Anderson's Gulch near the railroad, but when, about 1000, the operator nosed his machine out in the open, he was shot in the ear. General Griner, in Colonel Kelley's observation post at the time, ordered Lt. Col. Walter F. Anderson, commander of the 193d Tank Battalion, to push the bypass through. Anderson himself climbed into his battalion's sole remaining "tank-dozer" and completed the bypass. A 47-mm. antitank gun, hitherto silent, scored a direct hit on Anderson's tank, killing him and a guide. The bypass was now blocked and had to be abandoned.

This break-down in supply over Route 1 seriously affected operations east of Gusukuma. Colonel Mahoney's 1st Battalion attacked southwest early on the 21st into Gusukuma, but without tanks or cannon the troops made little ground against machine guns in the village and fire from Item Pocket on the right rear. Mahoney's left company did reach a point 400 yards north of the village of Yafusu—the farthest advance yet registered by XXIV Corps since 19 April—but here the troops were stopped by a network of enemy positions.

Fight of Dead Horse Gulch

Colonel Kelley, back at his headquarters, was becoming increasingly worried about the wide vertical gap between his 1st and 2d Battalions. Early on 21 April

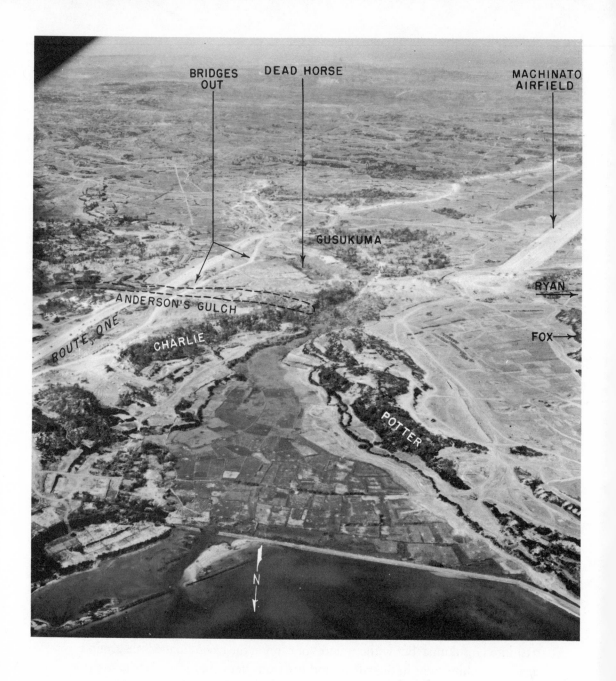

BRIDGES OUT   DEAD HORSE   MACHINATO AIRFIELD

GUSUKUMA

RYAN

ANDERSON'S GULCH

FOX

ROUTE ONE

CHARLIE

POTTER

N

ITEM POCKET AREA *(photographed 10 July 1945), which the 27th Division spent nine days in taking.*

he decided to commit his 3d Battalion, under Lt. Col. Dennis D. Claire, in a move designed to plug the gap and break into Item Pocket in one blow. Using Route 1 as its line of departure, Company L was to push west through Dead Horse Gulch, outflanking the Japanese covering Anderson's Gulch. Simultaneously Company K, on L's left, would attack northwest toward the Pocket along Gusukuma Ridge. Even moving into the line of departure was so difficult in this area swept by fire from artillery, spigot mortars, and light arms that it was 1515 before the battalion attacked.

Under a heavy smoke screen, Company L advanced along Dead Horse Gulch. In forty-five minutes the infantry was pinned flat to the ground under a hail of light-arms fire. The men could only crawl into holes. When the smoke cleared, Japanese machine gunners worked over the area. At dusk the company retreated down the gulch.

Company K, commanded by Capt. Howard E. Betts, Jr., was the other prong of the battalion attack. The company skirted the eastern edge of Gusukuma under heavy fire and drove up to the crest of Gusukuma Ridge. From here Captain Betts launched an attack down into Dead Horse Gulch with one platoon and sent the other along the crest of the ridge to cover the men on the low ground. In a savage encounter Company K fought its way almost into the heart of the Pocket. But the odds were against it; within an hour it had lost 6 men killed, 3 missing, and 15 wounded. The troops could advance no farther against the virtually intact Japanese defenses. Under cover of smoke and twilight, Betts pulled his men back to the crest of Gusukuma Ridge. He was forced to leave behind several of his wounded, who crawled into caves. A squad leader, himself wounded twice, tried to evacuate these men, but he was hit four times in the attempt and later died.

Company K had hardly begun digging in on the rocky crest of Gusukuma Ridge when the Japanese began a series of attacks that lasted four hours. The first, well-supported by enemy artillery, was driven off by the troops and artillery, but all men still in the gulch were killed in the onslaught. Low on ammunition and unable to evacuate the wounded, the men of Company K hung on under heavy fire and incessant sniping. At 2300 the enemy launched an all-out attack, striking simultaneously from Gusukuma and from the gulch. The Japanese overran and captured two machine guns and turned them on the outnumbered and disorganized Americans. Betts managed to pull his remaining men back to the 1st Battalion line, 200 yards to the south. Company K was now down to half-strength.

The engagement had a grim aftermath. Early the next morning the Japanese attacked the caves in Dead Horse Gulch where some wounded Americans had hidden. With grenades and bonfires the Japanese forced some of the Americans into the open, where they were shot; the others were stifled to death inside.

On 22 April General Griner, who was mainly concerned with coordinating the movements of his 105th Infantry with the 96th Division on the left (east) and was not too much impressed by the strength of the enemy in Item Pocket, ordered Colonel Kelley to hold and improve his positions. In conjunction with the 106th on his left, Kelley therefore shortened his 1st Battalion line to present a more compact front. A heavy air strike was delivered on the Pocket without major effect. Patrol action was intensified. All remaining Japanese were cleared out of Potter and Charlie Ridges. Artillery, well registered in, prevented the enemy from retaking any ground. (See Map No. XXIII.)

The patrols brought back information on Japanese dispositions, providing the basis for the next day's plan. Under that plan Company I was to attack from the nose of Potter's Ridge across the mouth of the Pocket and seize the face of Ryan Ridge. Meanwhile Company C would send a platoon over Brewer's Hill and down into the heart of the Pocket. Then Company I was to consolidate its hold on Ryan and, together with Company K, drive along Ryan Ridge to Machinato airfield. A special assault squad was set up to establish the all-important "beachhead" on the face of Ryan Ridge. Commanded by S/Sgt. Howard Lewis, this squad consisted of twelve men, heavily armed with BAR's, rifles, bazookas, demolitions, and a portable flame thrower.

Early next morning, the 23d, Sergeant Lewis worked his squad through the tombs on the nose of Potter's Ridge to the bare flat ground at the base. A Japanese mortarman opened fire on them from the top of Ryan Ridge just above the center of the Pocket. Sergeant Lewis spotted the position and sent his men toward it as their first objective. One by one the men sprinted toward Ryan Ridge. Two Japanese machine guns opened up. The lead man, together with most of the squad, took cover at the base of Ryan. Below, other enemy machine guns were firing. Lewis was now cut off from reinforcement.

Climbing from rock to rock on the craggy nose of Ryan Ridge, the squad made its way to within forty yards of the mortar position. A shower of potato-masher grenades stopped the advance. Lewis deployed his squad, sending four to the right and two to the left and bringing up his bazooka man for direct fire into the position. Advance was impossible; the area now seemed to be swarming with Japanese trying to move in to finish off the squad. Crawling from rock to rock in Indian fashion, the Americans held them off. Lewis called for artillery fire within forty yards of his position. The rest of Company I, still waiting on Potter's Ridge, put long-range fire on the enemy. The enemy replied with machine guns and mortars. The Pocket was an inferno of bursting shells and of rifle and machine-gun fire.

For three hours Lewis and his men held out, but it was a hopeless fight. At 1300 he called his company on the radio and said that he had only three men left capable of fighting, three being dead and seven wounded. The supporting platoon from Company I had been stopped short. The platoon from Company C had reached the crest of Brewer's Hill but had not been able to climb down the steep side. The troops lowered charges on ropes over the side and set them off at the cave entrances, but the charges seemed to make little impression. Lewis received orders to pull back with his wounded. Two more Americans were hit on the way back, but most of the wounded were brought out. Only Lewis and one other man returned unwounded.

Item Pocket—on the fourth day of the assault—was still in enemy hands.

Captain Ryan's Raiders, 24–25 April

The man on whom most now depended was Capt. Bernard Ryan, commanding Company F, 165th Infantry. Subjected nightly to intense artillery concentrations, harassed by numerous enemy patrols in force, compelled to evacuate his wounded and bring in his supplies by water around Kezu Point, lacking direct fire support except from his own mortars, Captain Ryan had operated largely on his own initiative. From 20 to 24 April he had watched Companies E, G, K, and I assault the Pocket from different directions. He correctly reasoned on 24 April that his turn would be next.

Captain Ryan proposed to Colonel Claire a plan calling for an attack by Company F at 0200 on the following day, 25 April, along the same general route as had been followed by Company E on 20 April. This plan was accepted by higher headquarters. Ryan was therefore astonished to receive a telephone call from Colonel Claire at 1900 on 24 April, ordering him to attack Ryan Ridge in one hour over an entirely different route—that followed by Sergeant Lewis on the 23d. There had been a hopeless mix-up of orders.

It was now necessary for Captain Ryan to execute a complete change of dispositions and attack preparations in the dark. He was calling together platoon leaders for a new briefing when the regular evening barrage began landing in his company. Soon his communications were out and his men pinned down.

POTTER

CHARLIE

GUSUKUMA

DEAD HORSE
GULCH

HEART OF ITEM POCKET, *looking north from Gusukuma Ridge.*

Later, a series of patrol actions by the enemy slowed his reorganization. In the morning, when Colonel Kelley discovered that Ryan Ridge was still in enemy hands, he ordered Colonel Claire to attack immediately and secure the ridge. Claire felt that the task was impossible and demurred. Kelley thereupon relieved Claire, and Maj. Herman M. Lutz, executive officer, assumed command. Kelley ordered Lutz to attack at 0630; Lutz decided to use Ryan's original plan.

Captain Ryan realized that the chief obstacles were the Japanese positions in Ryan Ridge and in the heart of the Pocket. From these positions the enemy dominated much of the area between Ryan and Fox Ridges. Captain Ryan's key to the problem was artillery fire. He reasoned that, since the direction of fire of supporting artillery would be perpendicular to his direction of attack, and the greatest possible lateral deviation would be fifteen yards, he need not worry about overs or shorts. He ordered a 20-minute preparation on the slopes of the ridge. In briefing his company Ryan stressed the need for a speedy ground attack to exploit the artillery support. The mission would put heavy demands on a company that was tired, undermanned, and low on food, water, and ammunition.

The two assault platoons of Company F started off at a dead run the moment the first shells were fired on the morning of the 25th. Mortars, machine guns, and antitank guns supported them. The attacking infantry was thinned out by enemy fire and natural obstacles, but thirty-one reached the top of Ryan Ridge. They found themselves perched atop a rugged razorback, full of rocks, holes, and blasted vegetation. As the artillery fire receded, Japanese began emerging from "spider holes," pillboxes, caves, and tunnels. The thirty-one Americans were ready for them. In twenty minutes of fighting similar to previous encounters on Item Pocket ridge tops they killed thirty-five Japanese and chased a larger number off the ridge. Five of the Americans were killed and two were wounded.

The crux of the situation lay in Captain Ryan's ability to consolidate his position; repeatedly units had gained footholds on these ridges, only to lose them to the enemy. By late afternoon the twenty-four effectives on the ridge had an average of only six rounds of rifle ammunition. They had no medical supplies, and all the aid men were casualties. Radio communication was out. The Japanese, after their first unsuccessful sortie, had rigged a noose around the perimeter and were slowly tightening it. Holding the ridge now depended on Ryan's initiative.

Ryan fully understood the critical situation. He arranged for Company I to be moved around to his right flank. He planned to repeat the move that had worked so well in the morning. At 1605, fifteen minutes after artillery support opened up, Ryan and the rest of the company reached the crest, suffering five casualties on the way. Company I failed to make the top, having been cut off on the slopes. After reorganizing his company Ryan departed with two men to find reinforcements—a risky mission in the dark. Company I was still unable to move up, but Captain Betts of Company K was quick to help. By midnight all of Company K were on the ridge.

With more than a hundred men now on the ridge, Ryan and Betts could take the offensive. During the morning of the 26th they swept along the crest of Ryan Ridge in opposite directions. Company F advanced rapidly southwest to a point just opposite the north end of Machinato airstrip. Betts made some progress, then ran into heavy fire near the nose of Ryan Ridge and built up a defensive position. The main task now was systematic burning out and blowing up of caves on the western slope of the ridge. The Japanese still held several areas in Item Pocket, but the Americans were on Ryan Ridge to stay. The 165th could now establish an unbroken regimental line and prepare to continue the advance south.

Item Pocket Reduced, 26–27 April

Captain Ryan's attack on the 25th coincided with an assault launched southwest of Ryan Ridge on Gusukuma by other companies of the 165th. In bitter fighting that lasted all day the troops moved from wall to wall and tree to tree into the debris of Gusukuma. At one time Company A was receiving fire from eight machine guns, at least one 47-mm. antitank gun, and mortars. Much of it came from the eastern slope of Ryan Ridge, not yet reduced. Riflemen made the main effort. One of them, Pfc Richard King of Company A, killed a Japanese tied in the crotch of a tree, sat on a limb beside the dead sniper, and killed ten enemy soldiers before nightfall.

Fighting in and around Item Pocket raged on through the 26th. American troops were now pressing in on the heart of the Pocket from all directions. Casualties were still running high. On the 26th, a full week after the 165th began its attack, the regiment, as a result of enemy fire on Route 1, was still operating without tanks or self-propelled mounts. Attack after attack by the infantry slowly constricted the Japanese-held area. By the night of the 26th the enemy had been cleaned out of Gusukuma, Ryan Ridge, and all the area west of the Pocket. Cave positions commanding the key bridges on Route 1 were sealed off, and engineers then resumed work.

The first two tanks to arrive south of the Pocket on the 27th were quickly knocked out by 47-mm. gunfire. Succeeding tanks worked with the infantry in reducing the remaining positions. Pfc. Alejandro C. Ruiz of Company A administered the final blow to Item Pocket. Exasperated by machine-gun fire and grenades which had wounded seven of his comrades, Ruiz seized a BAR and charged headlong into the remaining Japanese positions. He moved from cave to cave, killing the enemy within. At 1637 on 27 April the Pocket was declared secure. Many Japanese, however, remained; weeks later they were still emerging from the deep caves and tunnels.

General Griner had become increasingly distressed over the slow progress of the 165th. He was especially disturbed by the confused disposition of the regiment; disorganization had begun as early as 21 April and had increased as Colonel Kelley was forced to split up battalions and detach companies for various missions. On 27 April General Griner, on authority from General Hodge, relieved Colonel Kelley from command of the 165th.

Assaulting the Outer Shuri Defense Ring

While the reduction of Item Pocket was in progress, the 7th, 27th, and 96th Divisions were trying to break through the outer Shuri defense ring. The results of the intense action of 19 April had been disappointing. The day's fighting had shown that further advance would be very difficult, and this was confirmed by the difficult fighting between the 20th and 24th.

The Japanese outer defenses to the Shuri line were anchored along a hilly mass which extended across the island in a northwesterly direction from the village of Ouki on the east to Machinato Inlet on the west. Behind this mass and echeloned to the right was the formidable Urasoe-Mura Escarpment, the western anchor of the Japanese line. A series of dominating hills which formed natural defensive positions—Skyline Ridge, Hill 178 (the highest point), Tanabaru, and Nishibaru and Kakazu Ridges—stretched along the crest of this hilly mass, and formed the core of the Japanese defense system. The approaches to this system were covered by a number of forward positions which, like Rocky Crags and Tombstone Ridge, were well adapted to the terrain. (See Map No. XIX.)

Facing the 7th Division on the east was Skyline Ridge, barring passage along the coast. On the right of the division was Rocky Crags. Between the two was a series of concrete blockhouses and strong points which guarded the approaches to Hill 178. In the center of the Corps line, on the 96th Division front, was Nishibaru Ridge—an extension of Kakazu Ridge—and Tombstone Ridge, the northwestern slopes of which were held by the 382d Infantry. On the west, in the area held by the 27th Division, was Kakazu Ridge. The Japanese atop this ridge commanded Nishibaru's western slopes and covered the 96th Division's right flank. In the Kakazu area a gap had developed between the two divisions, and the closing of this gap was to entail the reduction of Kakazu Ridge.

The fighting between 20 and 24 April was to be as difficult as any during the campaign. These days were marked by incessant heavy attack against cave, tomb, tunnel, and dug-in positions with mutually supporting fields of fire. Mortar and artillery fire and armored flame throwers were used extensively, and the infantry engaged in costly assaults and hand-grenade duels at close range. The enemy did not give a single foot of ground; he fought until he was killed. During the first four days there was no material gain over most of the line, except for a few local penetrations. But on the 24th, after a sustained onslaught of four days of heroic effort against Skyline Ridge, Rocky Crags, and equally formidable barriers, the Americans moved into positions—among them Kakazu Ridge—in the first Shuri defense ring.

Skyline Battle

The attack of the 7th Division on Ouki Hill had been stopped on 19 April after hard and bitter fighting.[4] This was only the beginning of the struggle for Skyline Ridge, and, in order to see in proper perspective the events of 20 to 24 April, the action of the 7th on 19 April must be reconsidered in detail. (See **Map No. XXIV.**)

At 0640 on 19 April, with Company G on the left and Company F on the right, the 2d Battalion of the 184th Infantry, 7th Division, led the advance along high ground toward Ouki Hill.[5] Company G of the 32d Infantry trailed at the left rear. The troops had advanced 500 yards when the first mortar shells fell. Quickly the number increased, and machine-gun fire was added; at 0830, 400 yards short of Ouki Hill, the advance stopped. The troops had reached the forbidden zone. The Japanese *11th Independent Infantry Battalion* with attached units was defending Skyline Ridge, the anchor of the enemy line, which fell off from Ouki Hill to Buckner Bay. This battalion had received a unit citation during the China war. Composed of five rifle companies and attached gun, machine gun, and mortar companies, it had numbered about 1,400 men on 1 April, but by 19 April it had been reduced to from 800 to 1,000 men. In arranging

---

[4] See above, pp. 196–97.

[5] The account of operations of the 7th Division at Skyline Ridge is, unless otherwise noted, taken from Gugeler, 7th Div History; 7th Div G–3 Jnl, G–2 Jnl, and Periodic Rpts; 32d Inf Unit Jnl and Opn Rpt; Tenth Army PW Interrog Summary No. 2, 2 Aug 45: *62d Division;* XXIV Corps PW Interrog Rpt No. 54, 6 May 45 (Kimura).

SKYLINE RIDGE *as seen from an observation plane. Ouki Hill and Hill 178 are beyond the top of Skyline. Photo below shows smoke cover being placed on reverse slope of Skyline during the fighting of 22 April. Note tanks (arrows) and American troops on lower knob of Tomb Hill (foreground).*

TANKS

TOMBS

the defenses of Skyline Ridge the Japanese placed most of their machine guns on the forward (north) face and on the northern and eastern slopes of Ouki Hill. The 81-mm. mortars were on the reverse (southern) slope of Hill 178 to the west of the battalion guns.

After a delay of fifteen minutes, 1st Lt. Daniel R. Leffel, commanding Company G, 184th Infantry, sent a squad under S/Sgt. Gordon P. Foster to feel out the enemy. Keeping close to the ground, the men had moved slowly forward fifty yards when a Japanese machine gun and enemy riflemen a few yards away fired point-blank into them, killing Foster and four others with the first spray of bullets. Pfc. Kenneth J. Klawitter was wounded seriously but could not be reached by the rest of the squad. Lieutenant Leffel radioed for a flame tank. T/Sgt. Garret Schultz, acting 1st Sergeant, tried to rescue Klawitter but was shot in the side as he started to bring him back. Both men then hugged the earth for such protection as it gave. Each move of Company G brought an enemy mortar concentration immediately. Company G, 32d Infantry, on the left (east), also was stopped.

Down below along the coastal flat Company I, 32d Infantry, 7th Division, went through Ouki and, following tanks and armored flame throwers, moved against the lower tip of Skyline Ridge, while Company L maneuvered into position on the right (west) for a frontal attack against the ridge. One platoon of Company I assaulted the nose of the ridge after the flame tanks backed away, found that all Japanese at this point had been killed, and occupied the forward face of the tip at 0710. Mortar fire covered the crest and prevented further gain. By this time the leading platoon of Company L, under 1st Lt. Lawrence T. O'Brien, had climbed up the slope of Skyline to the right (west) and started west along the side of the ridge. One hundred yards ahead a northward jog in the ridge and a dip in the crest allowed the enemy on the reverse slope to fire eastward through the dip to the forward face of Skyline. Machine-gun fire, directed against O'Brien's platoon, now came through the depression, and O'Brien and his men dashed to an abandoned pillbox on the crest. This brought the platoon within grenade range of Japanese on the other side, and the men were forced to scatter. Knee mortar shells began to fall, plummeting almost straight down. Watching the sky, the men could see the descent of the small black objects in time to dash from the calculated point of impact.

To the right of O'Brien's men another platoon of Company L started up the slope and came into the line of fire of a machine gun that kept silent until the men were exposed. With its first burst the gun wounded nine men, almost half the platoon, which fell back disorganized to the base of the ridge. Meanwhile the third platoon of Company L, which had taken refuge from mortar fire in burial tombs near the lower tip of the ridge, was trapped inside by a Japanese machine gun that put a band of fire across the entrances of the tombs when anyone tried to get out. In the Ouki coastal area combat patrols of Company B protected the regiment's left flank, encountering several strong points and killing numerous enemy soldiers.

Just before 1200 a platoon from Company K, west of O'Brien's position, reached a point within ten feet of the crest of Skyline Ridge. Japanese on the reverse slope made it impossible to occupy the crest, which was just wide enough for a footpath, and only glimpses of the southern side could be secured by a momentary raising of the head. Fortunately the slope of the ridge was so steep that most of the grenades coming over the top rolled down the incline before they exploded. The Company K platoon was hit almost immediately by a counterattack of about fifty Japanese who crawled up on the reverse slope and began to throw grenades. Artillery was called for to help repel the counterattack, but four rounds fell short and killed or wounded most of the platoon. Another platoon was sent forward at once to replace it. Before it could dig in it was struck by a second counterattack of more than a hundred Japanese. The attackers pressed forward through their own mortar fire to a point just under the crest on the south side and engaged in a close-quarters grenade battle. The knife-edge crest of Skyline Ridge now looked from a distance as though it were smoldering. This close fight lasted for an hour, and at the end all of the second platoon had been killed or wounded but six men, who dropped back to the base of the ridge.

Meanwhile enemy pressure against O'Brien's men down the ridge to the left had not lessened, and it was evident at 1330 that the 3d Battalion did not have enough strength to push ahead. There were not more than twenty-five men of Companies L and K left on Skyline Ridge. These men were trying grimly to hold on in the hope that the 2d Battalion, higher up on the approach to Ouki Hill, could get through and start a drive down toward them, or that the platoon cooped up in the tombs below could escape and help.

During all this time the troops in front of Ouki Hill had made no progress. A flame tank had come up and burned out the position encountered by the unlucky squad in the morning, and on its way back it had picked up Klawitter and Schultz, who, badly wounded, had been near the enemy machine gun. Schultz died on the way to the rear.

At 1525 the G Companies of the 32d and 184th Regiments undertook to resume the attack which had been stalemated since early morning, but with no great promise of success. Along the base of Ouki Hill both companies were pinned to the ground at 1620 by an extremely heavy enemy 81-mm. mortar concentration. Amid the din of exploding mortars slivers of flying metal filled the air. In small groups or singly the men dashed back in short spurts toward their former position. Many were killed instantly while in flight. One man running wildly back toward safety stopped suddenly and assumed what appeared to be an attitude of prayer. In the next instant he was blown to bits by a direct hit.[6]

There was now no hope that the remnant of the 3d Battalion near the bottom of Skyline Ridge could stay there, and by 1730 the exhausted men had pulled back to their starting point of the morning. The 3d Battalion had lost approximately one hundred men along Skyline Ridge during the day. At 2000 the 32d Infantry was ordered by General Arnold to resume the attack at 0730 the next morning. Rain, which had begun in the afternoon, continued steadily on into the night.

Though American disappointment was keen and losses heavy in the Skyline Ridge fight on 19 April, it was not a one-sided affair. During the day the *1st* and *5th Companies* of the defending Japanese battalion had been all but annihilated. The *1st Company* was wiped out when a tank fired into a cave, setting off satchel charges and killing most of the men, whereupon the company commander committed suicide. The other three companies of the battalion were reduced to about fifty men each in the battles for Hill 178, Ouki Hill, and Skyline Ridge. The machine gun and battalion gun companies each had about eighty men left.

On 20 April the attack centered against Ouki Hill. Skyline Ridge itself was left alone after the experience of the day before. The 2d Battalion, 184th Infantry, and Company G, 32d Infantry, moving out at 0730, were checked almost at once by enemy mortar and machine-gun fire, and the situation remained stalemated all morning. Two armored flame throwers, however, successfully penetrated 400 yards in front of the infantry to burn out an enemy mortar position on the west slope of Ouki Hill. This led Lt. Col. Roy A. Green of the 184th to call Col. John M. Finn of the 32d Infantry and obtain his approval of a plan for covering the Japanese positions on Ouki Hill and the eastern part of Hill 178

[6] Personal Obsn of Capt Gugeler, 7th Div Historian.

with a mortar concentration and smoke while blanketing Skyline Ridge with a 4.2-inch chemical mortar barrage, as a prelude to an attack on Ouki Hill in which tanks would precede the infantry. Company G of the 184th, now down to nineteen riflemen, was attached as a platoon to Company G of the 32d Infantry for the assault. It was launched at 1445.

The Japanese, blinded by the smoke, apparently did not see the advancing troops until they were on the lower slopes of Ouki Hill. Heavy mortar fire then began to fall, threatening to break up the American attack. At the critical moment 1st Lt. John J. Holm and S/Sgt. James R. W. McCarthy, the platoon leader and the platoon sergeant of the leading platoon, scrambled on toward the top of the hill, yelling to the others to follow. Individually and in groups of two's and three's the men responded, and a feeble line was built up just under the crest. It was none too soon, for a counterattack struck immediately from the other side. Both Holm and McCarthy were among those killed, but the Japanese were repulsed and lost thirty-five killed. Just before dark a platoon from Company F, 184th Infantry, joined the little group on Ouki Hill from the American lines 400 yards to the rear. Tanks brought supplies to the isolated men, and half-tracks evacuated the wounded. The Japanese shelled the forward face of the hill throughout the night. Five men were killed and eighteen wounded, all in their foxholes; the two company commanders and several platoon leaders were among the casualties. Before dawn the enemy made another counterattack; although some Japanese came close enough to throw satchel charges, the attack was repulsed.

During the night Japanese with light machine guns infiltrated behind Company G's lines, and at an opportune moment on the morning of 21 April they opened fire, killing or wounding nine men before being killed themselves by tanks and armored flame throwers. It was nearly 0900 before Company F, hampered by enemy mortar and artillery fire, was able to start the attack down Skyline Ridge. At first there was no resistance, and within forty-five minutes the men reached a deep road cut through the middle part of the ridge. Here they were halted by mortar fire. Company E, 32d Infantry, coming up on the left (east), was stopped in the cut by a Japanese machine gun emplaced on the narrow crest and by grenades that were rolled down on the leading third platoon. The mortar section then adjusted on a point where Japanese had been seen, not more than twenty yards ahead of the foremost man. (See Map No. XXV.)

At 1230 General Arnold, 7th Division commander, arrived at Colonel Finn's observation post. A discussion of the situation led these commanders to conclude that it would be best to delay assault on the lower half of Skyline Ridge until the fall of Hill 178, which would make the enemy's position on the lower ground untenable. Orders to this effect were received by Maj. John H. Duncan, commanding the 2d Battalion, 32d Infantry, a few minutes after 1400. The order was nullified, however, by an incident then taking place.

When, east of the road cut, a man in the stalled third platoon, Company E, was killed, Sgt. Theodore R. MacDonnell, a 91st Chemical Mortar Company observer, was impelled to drastic action. MacDonnell had frequently joined men on the line and shown qualities of a determined infantryman. Now, infuriated, he gathered up a handful of grenades and ran in the face of the machine-gun fire along the slope to a point underneath the spot where he believed the enemy gun to be located, and then started up the 20-foot embankment. When he looked over the crest he failed to spot the gun, but he did see three enemy soldiers and grenaded them. He made two trips to the bottom of the embankment for fresh supplies of grenades, but it was not until his third trip to the crest that he located the machine gun. MacDonnell then slid back to the bottom, grabbed a BAR, and mounted the embankment with it, only to have the weapon jam after the first shot. He skidded to the bottom, seized a carbine, and went back up for the fifth time. On reaching the crest he stood up and fired point-blank into the machine-gun position, killing the gunner and two covering riflemen. MacDonnell then hurled the machine gun down the slope behind him. A mortar that he found in the position was also sent crashing down the hillside. Sergeant MacDonnell was later awarded the Distinguished Service Cross for his heroism on this occasion.[7]

Lt. Fred Capp, commanding Company E, sent troops to reinforce MacDonnell immediately, and the position was consolidated. Then Company F, on orders given as a result of this sudden development, pressed the attack down Skyline Ridge, and by 1800 the entire forward face of the ridge was occupied and only a knob at the lower tip was causing trouble. As evening fell a lone 105-mm. shell from friendly artillery landed short on Company E along the ridge, killing 4 and wounding 9 men, 3 of whom died later.

The next day, 22 April, the 32d Infantry held the forward face of Skyline Ridge but made no effort to advance. Patrols, however, worked over large sections of the southern slope and one patrol reached the eastern face of Hill

[7] See the account in *Gunto Graphic,* 24 Jun 45, which differs from Gugeler's account. The *Gunto Graphic* was a news bulletin issued by XXIV Corps and its account of MacDonnell's exploit was based on interviews with MacDonnell and several witnesses. See also Tenth Army GO No. 141, 1 Aug 45.

178, finding few Japanese. Three sets of trench lines were found on the southern slope of Skyline Ridge, one of them at the very top. There was a maze of caves, and, though many were blasted shut, others could be examined. On the lower tip of Skyline Ridge one cave contained approximately 200 Japanese dead, another about 100, a third 50, and a fourth 45. Bodies had been neatly stacked. Altogether, about 500 dead Japanese were counted on Skyline Ridge. Most of the bodies showed artillery and mortar wounds; many others had neat rifle holes or had been burned by flame. Approximately 200 rifles, 4 heavy machine guns, and a number of knee mortars were found piled in a cave, apparently salvaged from the battlefield. These circumstances seemed to indicate that the Japanese had intended to bury their dead and use the weapons at a later time. Japanese weapons destroyed or captured on Skyline Ridge totaled 250 rifles, 4 heavy machine guns, 19 light machine guns, 20 knee mortars, a 20-mm. gun, and a 75-mm. field piece.

On the night of 22–23 April Skyline Ridge was well covered by enemy artillery. On 23 April the 32d Infantry remained on the north slope of the ridge except when patrolling or closing caves. An enemy pillbox 400 yards away, which had survived three direct hits by a 37-mm. gun, restricted movement on the south slope until it was destroyed the following day.

The *11th Independent Infantry Battalion* had defended Skyline Ridge effectively and well; for this, together with subsequent action in the vicinity of Maeda on the other side of the island, it was to receive a unit commendation from the commanding general of the *62d Division*. The battalion had only about three hundred men by the night of 22–23 April and was relieved by elements of the *22d Regiment*. This was the first appearance of *24th Division* troops in front-line combat positions. The remnants of the *11th Battalion* crossed the island and fought on ensuing days in the Maeda area.

During the night of 23–24 April a heavy fog set in over southern Okinawa. Under its protection, while delivering heavy artillery fire against the American front lines, the Japanese withdrew from their remaining positions around Hill 178.

The Battle of the Crags

The 7th Division's attack against the Rocky Crags on 19 April had uncovered a formidable position. The height of the crags was such that they covered from the northwest the approaches to Hill 178. They themselves were protected by machine guns emplaced on elevated ground 200 yards east and by long-range machine-gun fire and mortars on Hill 178 to the southeast, on the Tanabaru

Escarpment to the south, and on high ground to the west. The tall, blunt coral pinnacle itself was honeycombed with caves and connecting tunnels.[8]

An attack against the crags on 20 April gained no ground. General Arnold then came to the conclusion that the position was the key to Hill 178. The 7th Division's main effort was now shifted to the right, and, to give strength here, Company B, 17th Infantry, was attached to the 184th Infantry and came into the line at 1630, 20 April. After a limited advance the company pulled back to escape enemy hand grenades and dug in for the night.

Company B resumed the attack on 21 April, but it was soon stopped by machine-gun fire. Tanks and armored flame throwers then worked over the western face of the northernmost crag at close range. This enabled infantry to gain the west side of the northern crag. Just over the crest, on the other side, Japanese could be heard talking. An effort was made to move over to the east side, but the first man to show himself was shot through the face, and no advance was possible. A tank and infantry attack on the western face of the southernmost crag also failed. Company B fell back to its starting point of the morning.

The next day Battery B of the 31st Field Artillery Battalion rolled a 155-mm. howitzer to a point within 800 yards of the crags. Here, firing against the eastern face, it quickly shot seven rounds. Great chunks of coral were blown loose. The Japanese swung a machine gun on the howitzer and raked the point of the hill, hitting two of the gun crew and pinning the remainder and General Arnold, who happened to be present at this time, to the ground.

Tanks and infantry started forward and crossed the open ground on the western side of the crags. The flame tanks moved up to the base of the southern crag and sprayed its face with great jets of liquid flame. Eight Japanese hurled themselves at the armored flame throwers with satchel charges but were cut down before they could reach the tanks.[9] Immediately after the billows of black smoke had cleared, the infantrymen, who had followed the tanks closely, moved up to the base of the hill. But the Japanese again emerged from within the crag to man machine guns and to drop grenades and knee mortar shells from the coral crest. All but twelve men of the platoon were wounded in a few minutes. Another platoon, working along a ledge near the crest, was driven back in a close-quarters grenade fight. Artillery hit one of the tanks and set it on fire. At

[8] The account of operations of the 7th Division at Rocky Crags is, unless otherwise noted, taken from Gugeler, 7th Div History. See also Appleman, XXIV Corps History, p. 182.

[9] See also 713th Tk Bn Actn Rpt, 21 Apr 45.

ROCKY CRAGS *west slope was attacked by flame thrower tanks shortly before capture of the point shown above. The heart of the Japanese defenses in Rocky Crags appears below. It had been chipped and scarred by artillery fire and demolitions directed against enemy lodged deep inside the hill.*

noon Capt. Charles Murphy halted the attack, planning to resume it at 1600 after reorganizing the company and evacuating the wounded.

In the meantime the 155-mm. howitzer, which had been immobilized by machine-gun fire early in the day, was moved to another position under protection of smoke. It now went back into action, firing forty-three rounds, each a target hit. The shape of the coral peak was altered, and the newly pulverized rock glistened white.

At 1600 two platoons attacked again along the west side. Three medium tanks and three armored flame throwers led the way, shelling and burning the crag. The infantry then moved in so close to the Japanese soldiers that one could hear the enemy rifle bolts click. Enemy artillery became active and once again hand grenades and knee mortar shells were dropped on the attackers from above. In this attack 18 out of 31 men were casualties, and only 5 were left fit for duty. At the end of the day, 22 April, Company B of the 17th Infantry had been reduced to 40 percent strength as a result of two days' fighting at the crags. At the same time elements of the 184th Infantry east of the crags had been held to virtually no gain by the network of fire from the crags and supporting positions.

With Company B exhausted, the remainder of the 1st Battalion of the 17th Infantry took up the attack on 23 April after the crag had been pounded once more by all available weapons and burned by the flame tanks. There was almost no opposition. At 1030 the Rocky Crags were in American hands. The price had been 186 casualties in four days to the 3d Battalion, 184th Infantry, and 57 casualties in two days to Company B, 17th Infantry—a total of 243 men.

The Fight for Nishibaru Ridge

To the west of the 7th Division, in the center of the line, the 96th Division was having a difficult time.[10] (See Map No. XXVI.) Early on 20 April the 1st Battalion, 382d Infantry, fought off an attempt by the Japanese to wrest from them the toe hold gained the day before on Tombstone Ridge. The 3d Battalion relieved the 1st at 0730 and attacked south from the northern part of Tombstone Ridge. Company L ran into trouble at a small, tree-covered, conical hill just east of the southern end of Tombstone Ridge. A bitter fight lasting all afternoon took place there. The Japanese held firm and finally even counterattacked with bayonets through their own knee-mortar fire. Company L withdrew at 1700 after suffering thirty-two casualties. On succeeding days this particular Japanese

---

[10] The account of operations of the 96th Division at Nishibaru Ridge is, unless otherwise noted, taken from Mulford and Rogers, 96th Div History, Pt. III; 96th Div Actn Rpt, Ch. VII; 382d Inf Actn Rpt, Ch. VII; 383d Inf Actn Rpt.

strong point was to hamper operations against Nishibaru Ridge. Meanwhile Company I fought down the length of Tombstone Ridge, wiping out the enemy in caves and tombs, and reached the southern end in time to help Company L by supporting fire. But because of the strong point in front of Company L the battalion was unable to cross the draw between Tombstone and Nishibaru Ridges.

The 3d Battalion, 382d Infantry, having drawn abreast at the southern end of Tombstone Ridge, and the 1st Battalion, 381st Infantry, in position to the right (west), attacked Nishibaru Ridge at 1100. The attack, launched without artillery support, surprised the Japanese, and Companies A and B were on the crest of Nishibaru Ridge at 1125. The inability of the 3d Battalion of the 382d to cross the draw from Tombstone Ridge left the 1st Battalion of the 381st exposed on the left. Company C of the 1st Battalion, ordered up to protect this exposed flank, was met by heavy enemy fire and suffered many casualties in the three and a half hours it took to cross the draw, but at 1600 it was abreast of Company A on Nishibaru Ridge. During the afternoon the commander of Company A was killed; only four officers were left in the three rifle companies now on the northern slope of the ridge.

The success of the 1st Battalion of the 381st in reaching Nishibaru Ridge led Colonel Halloran, the regimental commander, to order the 2d Battalion of the 381st to attack at 1300 and come abreast on the right. Japanese guns on the tip of Kakazu covered much of the ground over which the attack had to be made, and the platoon nearest Kakazu lost half its strength in crossing the 250 yards to Nishibaru Ridge. The 3d Battalion, 381st, still farther over on the division right, was unable to move at all because of the bypassed Kakazu position. Spigot mortar fire was heavy all day in the Nishibaru Ridge area, for it was here that the Japanese had one of their main concentrations of these huge mortars.[11] In the afternoon one of the big "flying boxcars" lazily wobbled down into the midst of Company E, 381st Infantry, on the northern slope of the ridge, killing four and wounding six men.

Severe punishment was meted out to the 2d Battalion of the 381st, exposed on its right flank to automatic weapons fire from Kakazu Ridge and to a heavy mortar barrage, but Companies E and G held firm. By nightfall the 96th had five rifle companies dug in along the northern slope of Nishibaru Ridge.

The tremendous explosions of the spigot mortars, the showers of knee mortars, and the drumming of enemy automatic fire caused many cases of combat

---

[11] See Tenth Army PW Interrog Summary No. 11, 4 Aug 45: *1st Artillery Mortar Regiment.*

fatigue during the day. In the fighting of 20 April both the 96th and the 27th Divisions suffered more casualties than did the Japanese. This was the only time during the campaign that American casualties in two army divisions exceeded those of the enemy facing them.[12]

In the fighting for Nishibaru Ridge maneuver was difficult. On the division left flank, enemy positions in the Rocky Crags dominated the 2d Battalion, 382d, and limited activity to patrols. On the division right flank, Japanese fire power located on the tip of Kakazu Ridge in the 27th Division zone immobilized the 3d Battalion, 381st Infantry. This meant that the division's effort had to be made in the center. The foothold gained on 20 April on the western part of Nishibaru Ridge indicated that the logical move would be to attack to the left (east) along the ridge from the positions already gained.

The 1st Battalion, 382d Infantry, replaced the 3d Battalion, 382d, at the southern end of Tombstone Ridge, and at 0720, 21 April, the latter began a circling march to the rear and westward to reach Nishibaru Ridge through the 381st Infantry. Once on the ridge to the left of Company C, the battalion reorganized and attacked eastward. It gained ground steadily until 1245, when the first of three Japanese counterattacks struck. The first counterattack, of platoon strength, was beaten off. A second counterattack, of company strength, was launched at 1330 from the village of Nishibaru and developed into a bitter close battle. Lt. Col. Franklin W. Hartline, battalion commander, went from company to company encouraging the men. The heavy machine guns of Company M were carried up the steep northern slope and aided greatly in beating back the attack. The tripod of the first gun had just been set up when the gunner was killed. S/Sgt. David N. Dovel seized the weapon and fired it from the hip, dodging from one point to another to escape knee-mortar fire. A short distance away another gun was set up, but it was hit almost immediately and put out of action. The gunner, Sgt. John C. Arends, and 1st Lt. John M. Stevens then took BAR's and dashed over the crest, firing point-blank into the attacking enemy. The weapons platoon leader of Company I was killed while directing fire from his mortars, which were only thirty-five yards below the crest of the ridge. At another point American 60-mm. mortars used an elevation of 86 degrees to fire on Japanese knee mortars only 30 yards away. In repulsing this counterattack the 3d Battalion, 382d Infantry, killed approximately 150 Japanese.[13] A

[12] Appleman, XXIV Corps History, p. 187.
[13] See also 3d Bn, 382d Inf, Unit Jnl, 21 Apr 45.

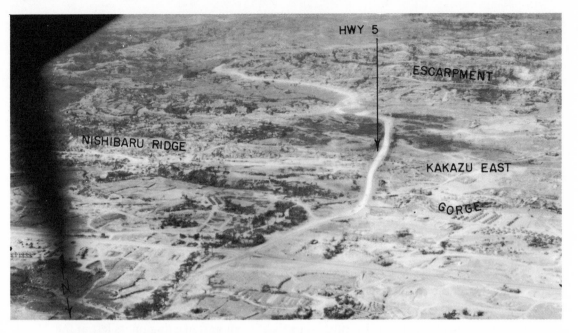

NISHIBARU ESCARPMENT AREA, *which the 96th Division took. On 21 April the 3d Battalion, 382d (below), attacked eastern end of escarpment by moving through the 381st's zone to the ridge, then turning east. Men of the 3d Battalion are shown moving forward in support of this attack.*

third counterattack at 1515 from Hill 143, 400 yards south of Nishibaru, was easily stopped. During the day the 3d Battalion, 382d, accounted for 198 of the enemy. The 3d Battalion, 383d Infantry, had tried to come up on the left of the 3d Battalion, 382d, while the latter was under counterattack to give help, but hidden machine guns and mortar fire had stopped it at the gorge.

On the right portion of the division's center, the 1st and 2d Battalions, 381st Infantry, undertook a coordinated attack at 0630, 21 April, to capture Nishibaru village. The 1st Battalion was on the left and the 2d Battalion was on the right. Because the slope of the ridge was too steep to negotiate, tanks could not be used. The 1st Battalion and Company E on its right had just cleared the crest of Nishibaru Ridge when they were stopped in their tracks by intense enemy fire. Company G, on the right of the two battalions, moved down to the southwest corner of the village of Nishibaru. Here it received a hurricane of mortar fire and discovered enemy troops infiltrating on its right front and massing on its left in the village. In the fight that followed, the heavy machine guns attached to Company G were fired like BAR's, braced without tripods against a low stone wall. Cross machine-gun fire from the tip of Kakazu on the west and from the southern slope of Nishibaru Ridge to the east laced across Company G's position. At 1400 a smoke screen was laid, and the battalion withdrew to a line just over the crest of the ridge, carrying its dead on hastily improvised sapling-and-poncho litters. At the end of the day the reverse (southern) slope of Nishibaru Ridge and the village of Nishibaru were still in enemy hands.

By the evening of 21 April the heavy casualties inflicted on the 382d Infantry had reduced its combat efficiency about 50 percent, and it was relieved by the 383d Regiment on 22 April. The 2d Battalion, 382d, having suffered little in the preceding days, was now attached to the 383d Regiment for operational control.

The 383d Infantry picked up the attack against Nishibaru Ridge, directing its assault against the "Gate," a saddle in the ridge. To the left (east) of the Gate the ridge line rose again to the bold Tanabaru Escarpment. The 2d Battalion of the 383d, on the right, attacked at 1100 down the Ridge toward the Gate. Nishibaru, a hornet's nest the day before, was occupied by Company E without difficulty, and Company G occupied high ground facing Hill 143 to the south. Company F, advancing against the front of the ridge, encountered heavy fire and lost four company commanders, killed or wounded, in half an hour. Satchel charges, hand grenades, and knee mortar shells hurled into the company by the Japanese forced it back beyond throwing range of the coral pinnacles.

The 3d Battalion, attacking the Gate on the left, made no appreciable gain. Of one group of ten men, including the Company L commander, on the side of a small hill, all were wounded except the officer. Company I, farther to the left, ran into fire from ten enemy machine guns emplaced near the Tanabaru Escarpment. The foremost platoon leader was killed just as he ordered his men to withdraw from this overwhelming volume of fire. Light tanks came up to the gorge in front of the ridge, and since they were unable to cross they remained there and poured thousands of rounds of machine-gun fire at the slope in a vain effort to silence the enemy guns.

On 23 April an armored bulldozer came up and prepared a crossing over the gulch. Medium tanks of Company B, 763d Tank Battalion, then crossed over and took the ridge and the Tanabaru Escarpment under direct attack. Armored flame throwers joined in the assault and burned the north face of the escarpment and the slope of the ridge as far west as the Gate. The infantry made only limited gains despite the effective work of the armor. The Japanese held out on the high points and repulsed the attacks by grenades and satchel charges. Elsewhere in the division zone the fighting tapered off sharply.

It was clear on the evening of 23 April that the Nishibaru–Tanabaru line was nearly broken. Four battalions were on the ridge line, and all the high ground had been occupied except the Tanabaru Escarpment and the extreme western part of Nishibaru Ridge opposite the tip of Kakazu. These were taken the next day with ease because the bulk of the Japanese forces had withdrawn to the south.

The Battle of the Pinnacles

The long, high Urasoe-Mura Escarpment was a natural defensive position that became progressively more difficult to breach eastward from the coast. Toward the middle of the island it was higher and its northern face was almost sheer cliff. This part of the escarpment fell within the left end of the 27th Division zone and continued on into that of the 96th Division. The village of Iso, which lay just beyond the crest of the escarpment, was a key Japanese defensive position occupied by the *21st Independent Infantry Battalion* and by elements of the *1st Heavy Mortar Regiment,* armed with spigot mortars. On 20 April the Japanese *64th Brigade* took over the line from the crippled *63d Brigade* as far east as Nishibaru. Its troops, deployed from the west coast eastward, consisted of the *23d,* the *21st,* the *15th,* and the *273d Independent Infantry Battalions.* The *4th Independent Machine Gun Battalion,* cooperating with the *22d Antitank Bat-*

talion, supported the *62d Division* in the Kakazu-Ginowan area. In the fighting from 19 to 22 April the *4th Independent Machine Gun Battalion* was to be more successful than at any other time on Okinawa.[14]

The heart of the defensive network around Iso was a high, rocky pinnacle, designated "West Pinnacle," which rose from forty to fifty feet above the ridge itself, just northeast of the village of Iso. Studded with caves, crevasses, and scores of little nooks and crannies, this pinnacle was difficult to approach from any direction and was impervious to artillery and mortar fire. Tunnels branched out from it in all directions; some emerged in Iso, others as far away as 200 yards to the west. The other strong point was a towering height on the escarpment, the "East Pinnacle," located from 450 to 600 yards southeast of the West Pinnacle. The crest of the escarpment here was hollowed out with burial vaults, most of which had courtyards in which the Japanese had carefully placed machine guns interdicting all approaches. Midway between the two pinnacles a road climbed to the top of the escarpment and cut through the crest in a sharp turn. A strong road block filled the cut, and the road itself was mined.[15]

On the night of 19 April the 3d Battalion, 105th Infantry, was on the top of the escarpment, spread around one end of the West Pinnacle. The 2d Battalion, 105th, was not on top of the escarpment but joined the 3d at the road cut through the ridge and then bent its line eastward down the slope. On the morning of 20 April heavy fighting developed quickly around the two pinnacles. Colonel Winn, 105th regimental commander, ordered his 2d and 3d Battalions to continue the attack south after the 2d Battalion came up on the escarpment abreast of the 3d Battalion. Enemy guns from the pinnacles, however, interdicted the crest of the escarpment in this area and the 2d Battalion was unable to reach the top. Colonel Winn came up to look over the situation, and at 1200 he ordered the two battalions to attack at 1230, regardless of fire conditions. Colonel Winn himself organized the 2d Battalion and launched an attack by a new route. Company E was left to attack as before, but Companies F and G were sent along the base of the escarpment to a point beyond the East Pinnacle, where they turned west and scaled the cliffs to reach the top north of the village of Nakama. Both companies immediately started south down the reverse slope toward a road at the bottom. In this rapid movement they approached the Japanese in the area from the rear and surprised them. (See Map No. XXVII.)

---

[14] Tenth Army PW Interrog Summary No. 2, 2 Aug 45: *62d Division;* No. 5, 27 Jul 45: The *Independent Machine Gun Battalions;* No. 11, 4 Aug 45: *Artillery Mortar Regiment.*

[15] The account of operations of the 27th Division at the Pinnacles is, unless otherwise noted, taken from Love, 27th Div History, Pt. VIII.

At the road both companies halted, F on the left and G on the right, to organize for an attack on Nakama to the south. While the two company commanders were discussing by radio the tactics to be used in the attack, Company F received the first blow—an intense mortar barrage that fell on its left flank, nearest Nakama. Japanese could be seen swarming through the town. After half an hour Capt. Edward C. Kidd, commanding Company F, radioed Capt. Louis F. Cudlin, who commanded Company G, that the enemy was working around Company F's left flank and into the rear. The two company commanders decided to pivot their lines to face eastward to meet the threat. From his position Cudlin could see only part of one platoon of Company F. He decided to make the shift when these men changed position.

Just after the two company commanders finished their radio conversation, Captain Kidd was wounded and his radio destroyed. Machine-gun and mortar fire was now coming from directly behind Company F. Within only a few minutes all the remaining officers and most of the noncommissioned officers were killed or wounded. Without leaders and smothered with fire, Company F lost all organization and most of the men ran for the edge of the escarpment. But the little group out front on the right in view of Company G was oblivious to what was happening behind them; it held fast and fought on, and the Japanese soon turned their attention to them. Shortly the group discovered that they were all alone, and one of them came running over to Captain Cudlin, shouting, "Where the hell is F Company?" This was the first inkling Cudlin had that anything was seriously wrong.

Captain Cudlin immediately ordered his platoon leaders to execute the swinging movement to face east, but it was too late; Japanese were already closing in on his right rear from the East Pinnacle, and the force which had just finished off Company F was closing in from the other side. The two assault platoons of Company G were deployed along the forward (south) edge of the road, which was cut into the reverse slope of the escarpment. The north side of the road was a 6-foot embankment, and in trying to escape the men had to dash across the road, scramble up the embankment, and then climb a 100-yard slope that ran at a 35- to 50-degree angle to the top of the escarpment. Enemy machine guns set up on either side swept this ground with enfilading fire as soon as the first man started back. Mortars and grenades filled the area with flying metal fragments, and enemy riflemen fired as fast as they could reload. In the dash up the slope some of the men were killed and others wounded; still others dropped down to hide behind rocks and bushes.

The 3d Platoon and the machine guns had been left on the edge of the escarpment when the two assault platoons of Company G moved to their advanced positions. Disorganized elements of Companies F and G now fell back through these men. It was discovered at this time that Japanese had infiltrated to the low ground below the escarpment on the north, and this added to the prevailing consternation. The Japanese, now in a good position on the flanks along the escarpment, set up a merciless fire on the men stampeding down the cliff. Men were hit and fell to the bottom to lie still; others stumbled and went sprawling headlong to the ground below. Still others, running with all their might, reached the lines of the 1st Battalion, which had come up and had faced east to meet the Japanese. Companies F and G had been completely surrounded and badly mauled by enemy from the bypassed East Pinnacle and by Japanese, estimated at two companies, who had turned Company F's left flank.

The 3d Battalion, 105th, with the 1st Battalion, 106th, abreast, had meanwhile, after some initial delay, advanced without too much opposition some 200 yards southwest of Iso and had taken up positions there for the night.

During this disastrous day the 2d Battalion lost fifty men killed and forty-three wounded, nearly all of them in Companies F and G. Total casualties of the 27th Division on 20 April amounted to 506 men—the greatest loss for an Army division during any single day on Okinawa.[16]

On the next day, 21 April, the struggle for control of the escarpment continued, still centering on the fight for the two pinnacles. The 1st and 2d Battalions, 105th Infantry, were reorganized overnight and operated against the East Pinnacle. Both the 3d Battalion, 105th, and the 1st Battalion, 106th, turned back to deal with the West Pinnacle. Neither of these efforts met with success. At one time four different groups were working on the West Pinnacle, while a Japanese sniper sat somewhere in the folds of coral, picking off men one by one.

The day, however, saw one definite improvement. On the day before a Japanese officer had been killed and a map was found on his body showing the location of mine fields on the road from Machinato to the top of the escarpment. By 0900, 21 April, the road was cleared of mines and a supply line opened as far as the road block on top of the escarpment, and by noon the road block itself had been removed. At 1400 tanks went through the cut, and armor was at last on the escarpment. In the meantime the problem of supplies on the crest of the

[16] See 27th Div Actn Rpt, p. 39.

THE PINNACLES, *center of the 27th Division's fighting on Urasoe-Mura Escarpment.*

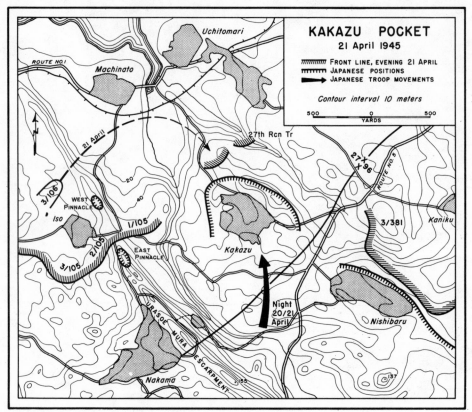

MAP NO. 5

escarpment had become critical, and air drops for the 2d Battalion of the 106th Infantry were necessary on 21 and 22 April.[17]

On 22 April the 1st Battalion, 106th Infantry, supported by self-propelled guns of the 106th Cannon Company, which moved over a path prepared by an armored bulldozer, systematically searched out and destroyed enemy positions in its rear along the escarpment. Japanese soldiers were still hidden somewhere in the West Pinnacle, which the enemy used as an observation point and as a control center for spigot mortar fire. But the enemy machine guns behind the lines at this point had been destroyed, and supply lines to Iso were for the first time free from serious harassing fire. The 1st Battalion, 106th, now had pulled back 600 yards to straighten and shorten the lines along the escarpment

[17] See 106th Inf Actn Rpt, pp. 13–14.

and to establish contact with the 105th Infantry on the east. In the 105th Infantry zone, Colonel Winn continued to reorganize the 1st and 2d Battalions.

On 23 April two assault companies of the 1st Battalion, 105th, which had relieved the 2d Battalion, climbed on top of the escarpment to the east of the East Pinnacle in much the same manner as had the 2d Battalion on 20 April, and similarly caught the enemy by surprise. Company C reached the crest of the escarpment at the edge of the East Pinnacle stronghold and found itself in the midst of the enemy. A wild hand-to-hand fight ensued in which bayonets, clubs, and grenades were used, and more than a hundred Japanese were killed within an hour. S/Sgt. Nathan S. Johnson led the battle and was himself credited with killing more than thirty of the enemy. On one occasion he jumped over a small mound of earth and found himself among a dozen Japanese. He killed eight with his rifle and clubbed the other four to death.[18] At the end of the day the 27th Division held the escarpment as far east as the edge of Nakama, the division boundary.

The end of the West Pinnacle fight came abruptly, on the night of 23 April. Precisely on the hour of midnight the enemy bugler within the pinnacle, who had in previous days and nights frequently sounded his bugle as a signal, blew a call, and thirty Japanese soldiers emerged in a wild yelling banzai charge, rushing straight into the lines of the 1st Battalion, 106th Infantry, dug in south of Iso. There they were wiped out.

The Kakazu Pocket

On 20 April, while the 2d and 3d Battalions, 105th Infantry, were involved in the disastrous battle on the escarpment, it was left to the 1st Battalion to mop up the Kakazu Pocket. All three rifle companies of the battalion were involved by noon in a grim fight for the village. The 96th Division had complained about the bypassed Japanese stronghold on its right flank, and General Hodge, XXIV Corps commander, had ordered General Griner to have Kakazu Ridge cleared by nightfall.[19] By 1635 the 1st Battalion had fought its way to the western edge of Kakazu village and had swept Kakazu Ridge almost to its eastern tip.

Just when it seemed that the 1st Battalion, 105th, might be able to clear the Kakazu Pocket, it was ordered to the escarpment to support the 2d Battalion and prevent a break-through. Company A was left behind to clean up the village of Kakazu. A 16-man patrol went into the village and passed through its rubble-

[18] Sgt Johnson received the DSC for his gallantry.   Tenth Army GO No. 255, 14 Oct 45.
[19] 27th Div G–3 Jnl, entry 61, 20 Apr 45.

strewn streets without receiving a shot. At 1700 it reported to Colonel Winn that there were no enemy troops in Kakazu. He was not satisfied for he could hear small-arms fire from the direction of the village, and he instructed Capt. Louis F. Ackerman, commander of Company A, to make another check of the village. The patrol was not fired on as it retraced its steps toward the village, but Captain Ackerman had barely stepped into the street when he went down with a shot in the back. Four men in succession were killed trying to rescue him, and then the entire patrol was scattered. Only one man returned that day, although three other survivors were rescued on 24 April. Kakazu was still a death trap.

During the night of 20–21 April, Japanese in large numbers came from the escarpment, moved around the left flank of the 27th Division, set up mortars and machine guns in the Kakazu area, and occupied the pocket in strength.[20] Against this increased opposition the division Reconnaissance Troop slowly fought its way toward the village of Kakazu and reached its edge at 1145, 21 April. There the entire troop was pinned down, and a platoon of tanks was called up. In three more hours of creeping and of fighting into the rubble of Kakazu only fifty yards were gained. The troop then pulled back, and at 1600 division artillery placed mass fire on the village. Later it tried to enter, but the Japanese emerged from underground and stopped it with a wall of fire. (See Map No. 5.)

The events of 21 April in the Kakazu Pocket placed the 27th Division in a bad situation. The enemy was in force behind its lines; the division had no reserve; and there was a broad gap between it and the 96th Division. Available combat strength was stretched thin. While retiring from the front lines as division reserve, the 3d Battalion, 106th Infantry, was ordered into position on Kakazu West, "that damned hill," as the men called it.[21] There they had dug in by nightfall.

On the evening of 21 April General Hodge ordered Brig. Gen. William B. Bradford, Assistant Division Commander, 27th Division, to take command of operations in Kakazu Pocket with full authority to coordinate action with the 96th Division. At the same time General Hodge directed that the right-flank elements of the 96th Division should not "be moved out of their own zone except by agreement with CG 96th Div. or specific orders from this Headquarters." XXIV Corps considered the enemy positions holding up the right flank of the 96th Division to be within the 27th Division zone of action.

[20] XXIV Corps G–2 Periodic Rpt No. 22, 22 Apr 45.
[21] 106th Inf Actn Rpt, p. 13.

During the night of 21–22 April the Japanese placed heavy artillery fire on the lines of the 105th Infantry, and before daylight they started an attack around the regimental left flank. Naval star shells illuminated the front, and naval fire was called in to break up the attack.[22]

On the afternoon of 22 April General Griner requested a battalion from XXIV Corps reserve to help deal with the enemy in Kakazu Pocket, estimating the Japanese force there to be at least a battalion. General Hodge ordered the 3d Battalion, 17th Infantry, to proceed at once from the 7th Division zone on the east to the Kakazu area. In the steadily worsening situation, General Griner in the afternoon of 22 April directed the 102d Engineer Battalion to assemble near Machinato Inlet as division reserve and to be prepared to fight as riflemen. By night, there was not only a 1,200-yard gap between the 96th Division and the 3d Battalion, 106th Infantry, at Kakazu, but also a gap between the 3d Battalion, 106th, and the 1st Battalion, 105th, at the bottom of the escarpment. If the enemy broke through in either place he could cut through to the coast and the service installations in the rear. At 2000 General Griner ordered the 2d Battalion, 165th Infantry, less Company F, to leave its position near Machinato and move to the left flank. With the aid of these troops the gap between the 105th Infantry and the 3d Battalion of the 106th was closed by 2110. The larger gap between divisions, however, remained open. At 2130, 22 April, the 27th Division had every rifle company committed to a defensive line that stretched southeast of Kakazu village to the west coast beyond Gusukuma.

On the night of 22 April General Hodge decided to form a special force to eliminate Kakazu Pocket once and for all. A formidable force of four battalions of infantry was assembled from the 27th, 7th, and 96th Divisions, supporting units of tanks, armored flame throwers, self-propelled assault guns, and 4.2-inch chemical mortars, and was given the mission of taking the ridge and town of Kakazu. These units were placed under the command of General Bradford, Assistant Division Commander, 27th Division, and were known as the Bradford Task Force. On 23 April plans were completed and the troops moved into place for an attack to take place the next day.

The 24th of April dawned dark and rainy after a night marked by unusually heavy enemy artillery fire. After a 13-minute artillery preparation the Bradford Task Force attacked at 0730, determined to fight its way through the Kakazu Pocket. No enemy resisted it; the Japanese had vacated their

---

[22] 105th Inf Actn Rept, p. 20.

URASOE-MURA ESCARPMENT

KAKAZU VILLAGE, *center of Kakazu Pocket, looking south to Urasoe-Mura Escarpment.*

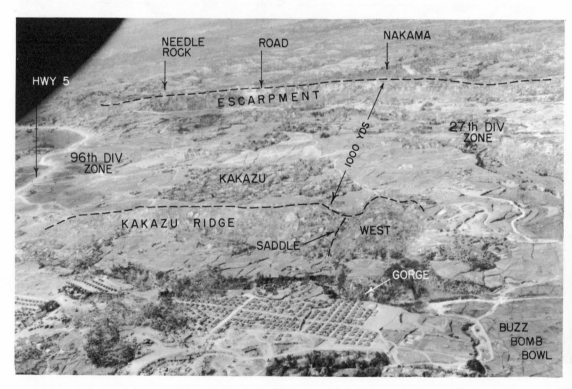

KAKAZU POCKET *area (photographed 10 July 1945), looking south.*

positions in the Pocket during the night. Within two hours all battalions reached their objectives. In the afternoon, adjacent battalions of the 96th and 27th Divisions dug in along the division boundary at the foot of the Urasoe-Mura Escarpment and had solid contact with each other for the first time since 19 April. On 24 and 25 April, when it was at last possible to examine the Kakazu area, approximately six hundred Japanese bodies were counted, and there was evidence of mass burials and of many dead in sealed caves.

Never again on Okinawa did the Japanese have such an opportunity of inflicting major damage on the American Army as in the period from the evening of 19 April through 22 April in the Kakazu area. That they could not take advantage of it was due to the fact that almost all their infantry reserves were in the southern part of the island. A landing feint off the Minatoga beaches simultaneously with the attack of 19 April had been designed to keep them there.[23]

The First Line Falls

The ease with which the Bradford Task Force gained its objectives the morning of 24 April was no isolated phenomenon. On the eastern side of the island the 7th Division walked up to the top of Hill 178 with only a few scattered, random rounds of artillery dropping in the area. There was no small-arms or automatic fire. All but a few enemy bodies had been removed or buried; the usual litter of war was largely missing and weapons and stores had been removed, indicating a planned and orderly withdrawal. (See Map No. XXVIII.)

In the middle of the front in the 96th Division zone, the only Japanese found were stragglers and those behind the lines. The Americans occupied the Tanabaru Escarpment, the 1,500-yard-long ridge to the south of it, the village of Tanabaru, all of Nishibaru Ridge, and Hill 143. Other units advanced farther, crossing the draw and the Ginowan–Shuri road (Route 5) to take up positions at the foot of the eastern end of the Urasoe-Mura Escarpment. The day was not altogether without incident; scattered enemy were encountered, and occasional sudden bursts of long-range machine-gun fire exacted a toll.

The pattern of easy and uncontested advance across the line was broken only on the west coast, where the 27th Division was unable to advance, and by the fierce and confused battle of Item Pocket which was raging behind the division's lines.

[23] Tenth Army PW Interrog Rpt No. 27, 24 Jul 45 (Shimada); No. 28, 6 Aug 45 (Yahara); PW Interrog Summary No. 2, 2 Aug 45: *62d Division.*

During the night of 23–24 April, when a heavy mist and then a fog settled over southern Okinawa, Japanese artillery stepped up its rate of fire to reach a new peak of intensity along the entire front; every front-line American regiment received at least 1,000 rounds during the hours of darkness.[24] As the day of 24 April wore on it became apparent that the heavy enemy artillery barrage, together with the fog which formed during the night, had covered a Japanese withdrawal from the remaining positions in the first ring of the Shuri defenses. The Japanese had fought doggedly for five days after the American attack of 19 April was launched, limiting gains to yards daily and in some places, such as Kakazu, denying any gain. But on the evening of 23 April his positions had been penetrated at so many places, and the remaining strong points were so badly battered and were so rapidly becoming untenable, that it was unprofitable to fight longer in these positions.

Both the disappointments and the hopes of the Japanese front-line troops at this time are reflected in the diary of a Japanese superior private fighting in the Nishibaru–Kakazu area. On 23 April, date of the final entry, he wrote:

Although nearly a month has passed since the enemy landed, a terrific battle is still going on day and night. I am really surprised at the amount of ammunition that the enemy has. When friendly forces fire one round, at least ten rounds are guaranteed to come back. There is not one of our friendly planes. If some come, I think we can win the fight in a short while. We want planes! We want planes![25]

[24] XXIV Corps G–2 Periodic Rpt No. 25, 25 Apr 45.

[25] CINCPAC-CINCPOA Bull No. 147–45, 16 Jun 45; Transl Interrog No. 32.

CHAPTER X

Tactics and Tactical Decisions

While General Buckner knew soon after the initial landings that the Japanese had concentrated their forces on southern Okinawa and had elected to fight the battle there, he did not then know the true extent of these defenses. The strength of the Shuri fortifications was first fully revealed in the heavy fighting between 8 and 23 April, when the Japanese positions held against furious American onslaughts. Across the entire front line evidence fast accumulated that the Japanese held tightly, from coast to coast, a dug-in, fortified defense line, reaching in depth as far as Yonabaru–Shuri–Naha. The failure of the American attack to break through the Shuri line led to a review of the tactical situation and of the tactics required to overcome Japanese resistance with the least possible cost and time.

Tactics and Weapons on Okinawa

Elements of Japanese Power

As the Americans came up against the Shuri line veteran fighters in the Pacific noted many familiar tactics and techniques in the Japanese defense. Intricate and elaborate underground positions, expert handling of light mortars and machine guns, fierce local attacks, willingness of Japanese soldiers to destroy themselves when cornered, aggressive defense of reverse slopes, full exploitation of cover and concealment, ceaseless efforts to infiltrate the lines—all these were reminiscent of previous battles with the Japanese from Guadalcanal to Leyte.

The enemy had shown all his old ingenuity in preparing his positions underground. Many of the underground fortifications had numerous entrances connected by an intricate system of tunnels. In some of the larger hill masses his tunneling had given him great maneuverability where the heaviest bombs and shells could not reach him. Such underground mobility often enabled him to convert an apparent defensive operation into an offensive one by moving his troops through tunnels into different caves or pillboxes and sometimes into the rear of attacking forces. Most remarkable was the care he had lavished on positions housing only one or two weapons. In one place a 47-mm. antitank gun had a clear field of fire to the east from a pillbox embrasure set into the hill and constructed of heavy stone slabs and coral blocks faced with mortar; a tunnel braced with heavy timbers ran from this embrasure fifteen feet into the hill, where it met another tunnel running out to the north slope of the hill. A heavy machine-gun emplacement near Oyama consisted of two pillbox-type dugouts looking out to the north, strongly constructed and connected with the southwest slope of the hill by a long, unbraced tunnel cut through the coral and lime formation. A cave 400 yards north of Uchitomari, with an opening only 3 by 4 feet, led into a 70-foot tunnel that adjoined two large rooms and received ventilation through a vent extending 30 feet to the top of the ridge. Some pillboxes had sliding steel doors. Experienced officers described such positions as "both artful and fantastic." [1]

The most striking aspect of the enemy's resistance was his strength in artillery. Never had Pacific veterans seen Japanese artillery in any such quantity or encountered such effective use of it, especially in coordination with infantry attacks. Together with hundreds of mortars from 50 mm. to 320 mm. the enemy had quantities of light and medium artillery and dual purpose guns. He was strongest in 70-mm. and 75-mm. guns, 75-mm. and 150-mm. howitzers, and 5-inch coast defense guns. The 2d Battalion of the Japanese 1st Medium Artillery Regiment, located initially south of Kochi and Onaga, typified his artillery organization. It was composed of three batteries, each with four 150-mm. howitzers, the best Japanese weapons of that type, which could fire 80-pound projectiles at a maximum range of 11,000 yards. Each battery had four prime movers—6-ton, full-tracked vehicles that could be used for hauling ammunition as well as for towing the howitzers. [2]

Usually widely dispersed as defense against American bombing and shelling, the Japanese artillery was nevertheless closely integrated into the general tactical scheme of the Shuri defenses. The keynote of the enemy's defensive tactics around Shuri was mutual support through coordination of fire power. The enemy command indoctrinated the defenders of each position with the importance of protecting adjacent positions as well as their own. "It must be borne in mind that one's own fire power plays an important part in the defense of the neighboring positions and vice versa," a 44th Brigade order read. "If one's own

---

[1] Tenth Army Int Monograph, Ryukyus Campaign, Ch. III, "Engineer," pp. 16–18; XXIV Corps G–2 Periodic Rpt No. 9, 10 Apr 45.

[2] Captured and Destroyed Enemy Weapons and Equipment Chart, Incl 2 to XXIV Corps G–2 Summary No. 15, 26 Jun 45; Tenth Army Int Monograph, Ryukyus Campaign, Pt. I, Sec. D, Ch. I, "Artillery," pp. 2–3.

12-cm. British gun in concrete emplacement

Concrete pillbox in hillside

Double pillbox, earth and bamboo

Tank trap across a road

Reverse-slope caves, two levels

JAPANESE FORTIFICATIONS

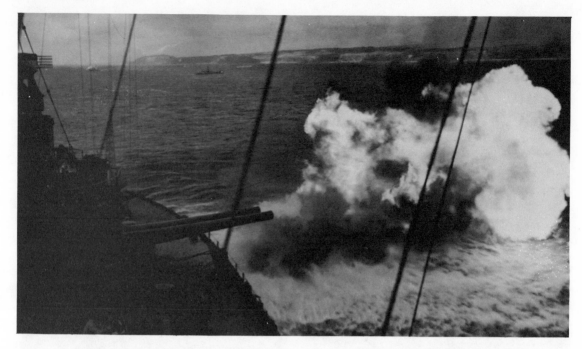

NAVAL FIRE *was directed into Japanese positions from all sides of Okinawa. Here the U. S. battleship* Maryland *fires an after battery at a target near southern tip of the island.*

AIR SUPPORT *helped in taking some stubborn and inaccessible enemy positions. This is in the Love Hill area above Yonabaru. Ridge from lower left to upper right divided opposing troops, with Japanese on the side where bomb burst is seen.*

fire power is not fully brought to bear, neighboring positions will be destroyed, and their supporting fire power lost against an advancing enemy, thus exposing oneself to danger." [8]

Blowtorch and Corkscrew

The American forces had brought to bear against the enemy their great superiority in armor and self-propelled assault guns, the weight of massed artillery, and supremacy in the air over the scene of battle. Added to all this was something new to warfare. The continuous presence of the tremendous fleet, aligned on the enemy's flanks, provided the ground forces with the constant support of its great mobile batteries, capable of hurling a vast weight of metal from a variety of weapons ranging from rockets to 16-inch rifles.

Naval gunfire was employed longer and in greater quantities in the battle of Okinawa than in any other in history. It supported the ground troops and complemented the artillery from the day of the landing until action moved to the extreme southern tip of the island, where the combat area was so restricted that there was a danger of shelling American troops. Naval fire support ships normally were assigned as follows: one for each front-line regiment, one for each division, and one or more for deep-support missions designated by the Corps. Whenever possible, additional ships were employed along the east coast to neutralize Japanese gun positions on the Chinen Peninsula, which dominated the entire coast line of Nakagusuku Bay and the left flank of XXIV Corps.

Night illumination fires were furnished on about the same basis as gun-fire—one ship to a regiment, with additional ships available to Corps for special illumination missions. The night illumination provided by the ships was of the greatest importance. Time and again naval night illumination caught Japanese troops forming, or advancing, for counterattacks and infiltrations, and made it possible for the automatic weapons and mortars of the infantry to turn back such groups. Often the Japanese front lines were almost as well illuminated at night as during the daytime. It was very difficult for the Japanese to stage a night counterattack of any size without being detected.

Many different kinds of ships were used in providing naval support. A typical day would see the use of 3 battleships, 3 heavy cruisers, 1 light cruiser, and 4 or 5 destroyers to support the Corps. Later LCI rocket boats were used extensively. During the night of 18–19 April, 5 battleships, 1 heavy cruiser, 1 light cruiser, and 4 destroyers furnished night fires and illumination. During the 19th,

[8] Tenth Army G–2 Summary No. 2, 4 Jun 45, Notes on Construction of Positions, *44th IMB,* 7 May 45.

BLOWTORCH—*flame sears a Japanese-held cave.*

CORKSCREW—*demolition team runs from cave blast.*

the day of the big attack, more heavy naval gunfire was made available than usual. On call for each division were 4 battleships, 1 heavy cruiser, and 1 destroyer. In addition, 1 battleship, 1 heavy cruiser, and 1 destroyer were used for deep support behind the lines.[4]

Both carrier-based and land-based air support was given the troops throughout the battle when weather conditions permitted the planes to take to the air. During the first week all air support was carrier-based, but after Kadena and Yontan airfields became operational, Marine fighters gave daily support from these fields. The largest single air strike of the Okinawa battle was on 19 April in support of the coordinated attack. On this day 139 aircraft were used, most of them armed with 1,000- and 2,000-pound bombs and rockets.

Literally, the Japanese were enveloped by fire power, from the ground in front, from the air above them, and from the water on their flanks—fire power and explosives the like of which had never before been seen in such concentrated form in so restricted an area. Surely, all this fire power must have pulverized the Japanese positions and rendered the enemy incapable of prolonged resistance. But it had not. The enemy was denied freedom of movement, but even 16-inch naval shells as they penetrated the surface concrete or coral and exploded sounded like ping-pong balls to those who were kept deep underground.

The American answer to the enemy's strong and integrated defenses was the tank-infantry team, including the newly developed armored flame thrower, and supported by artillery; each team generally worked in close coordination with assaults of adjacent small units. Although rockets, napalm, mortars, smoke, aerial bombing, strafing, naval bombardment, and all the others in the array of American weapons were also important, the tank-infantry team supported by 105's and 155's was the chief instrument in the slow approach on Shuri. A captured Japanese commander of a 47-mm. antitank battalion stated that in view of the success of this combination he did not see why any defense line, however well protected, could not be penetrated.[5]

A pattern of tank-infantry attack had been developed in wresting the outer main ring of Shuri defenses from the enemy. There the fighting had dissolved into numerous small-unit actions, with assault groups of tanks and riflemen, demolition squads, BAR men, and machine gunners, each trying by all the means their wits could devise, and acting with high courage, to take a given

[4] Actn Rpt XXIV Corps, p. 45; G–3 Periodic Rpt XXIV Corps, 19 Apr 45.

[5] Sgt Bert Bamer, USAFMIDPAC G–2 Hst Sec, Japanese Counter-Tactics against U. S. Infantry-Tank Teams Okinawa. (On file in Hist Div, WDSS.)

single position in front of them. Guns and howitzers battered Japanese cave openings, dugouts, and pillboxes, forcing enemy gunners back into tunnels for protection and decreasing their fields of fire. Taking advantage of the resulting "dead spaces," infantry and tanks crept up on the most exposed strong point; the tanks attacked the position point-blank with cannon, machine guns, and flame, while the infantry prevented Japanese "close-quarters attack troops" carrying explosives from closing in on the tanks. Once the troops gained a foothold in the enemy position, they could move down on cave openings from above, in maneuvers which the Japanese called "straddle attacks" and greatly feared.

Each small action, a desperate adventure in close combat, usually ended in bitter hand-to-hand fighting to drive the enemy from his positions and there to hold the gains made. In these close-quarters grenade, bayonet, and knife fights, the Japanese frequently placed indiscriminate mortar fire on the melee. The normal infantry technique in assaults on caves and pillboxes involved the coordinated action of infantry-demolition teams, supported by direct-fire weapons, including tanks and flame throwers. Cave positions were frequently neutralized by sealing the entrances. In some instances Tenth Army divisional engineers employed a 1,000-gallon water distributor and from 200 to 300 feet of hose to pump gasoline into the caves. Using as much as 700 gallons for a single demolition, they set off the explosion with tracer bullets or phosphorus grenades. The resulting blast not only burned out a cave but produced a multiple seal. The complete destruction of the interconnected cave positions sometimes took days.[6]

The tank-infantry team waged the battle. But in the end it was frequently flame and demolition that destroyed the Japanese in their strongholds. General Buckner, with an apt sense for metaphor, called this the "blowtorch and corkscrew" method.[7] Liquid flame was the blowtorch; explosives, the corkscrew.

Okinawa saw the use by ground troops of important new American weapons: the armored flame thrower, Sound Locator Sets, GR–6, and VT fuzes. The first was perfected at Oahu, after experimentation by the Marines with cruder types, in time for use by the troops on Okinawa. The 713th Tank Battalion was equipped with, and trained in the use of, the new weapon, which was installed in the standard medium tank. The flame-thrower gun was mounted in the 75-mm. gun tube and was operated under high pressure. Fuel

---

[6] Engineers of the Southwest Pacific, 1944–45, Vol. I: Engineers in Theater Operations. OCofEngr, GHQ Army Forces, Pacific.

[7] Journal, Hist Off XXIV Corps, 1 May 45; Appleman, XXIV Corps History, p. 257.

tank capacity was 300 gallons and effective range was 80 to 100 yards, although a maximum range of 125 yards could be obtained. The fuel used was a mixture of napalm and ordinary gasoline. Napalm is a granular soapy substance giving consistency and weight to the mixture and restricting the area of the flame. The greater the quantity of napalm, the heavier the viscosity of the mixture.

The fifty-five armored flame throwers of the 713th Tank Battalion were unloaded at Okinawa on 7 April and were attached to the divisions. Although they were committed in the fighting of 8–12 April, they used only their machine guns and not their flame throwers. In the attack of 19 April the Japanese experienced the full effects of this terrifying weapon for the first time.[8]

New sound-locator devices were also used for the first time on Okinawa. Sound locator teams were rushed from Fort Benning at the last minute to join the invasion. There were initially five teams of eight men, with two Sound Locator Sets, GR–6, per team. The locators, set up at each end of a base line about 700 yards in length, determine the direction from which the fire of a gun is coming, locating the weapon by intersection. One can then either place counterbattery over the general area, or else pinpoint the weapon by aerial observation and destroy it by direct hit.[9]

The VT or proximity fuze, placed in the nose of an artillery shell, consists of a tiny transmitting and receiving radio set which automatically detonates a shell at a predetermined distance from its target. The fuze transmits a radio beam, which, when it strikes a solid object, is reflected by that object and picked up by the receiver of the fuze. The beam then trips a switch within the fuze which detonates the shell. The fuze was first used on 5 January 1943 by the Navy in the Pacific. Employed first by the Army in the air defense of London in the summer of 1944, the fuze was used in ground combat during the German break-through of December 1944 in the Ardennes. In ground combat against the Japanese it was first utilized on Okinawa, in 105-mm., 155-mm., and 8-inch howitzers. Its most lethal effect was produced by bursts over the heads of troops at a predetermined distance above the ground. Trenches and foxholes provided little protection against these bursts; the Japanese were safe from the fuze only when holed up in caves, concrete pillboxes, tunnels, and other types of deep underground fortifications.[10]

[8] Actn Rpt 713th Tank Bn, Jul 45; Appleman Diary, 15 Jun 45.

[9] Actn Rpts Sound Location Teams Nos. 1–5; Appleman Diary, 13 Jun 45.

[10] Appleman Diary, 11 Jun 45.

Tactical Decisions

The proved strength of the Japanese defenses, and the costliness of reducing them even with the aid of so powerful an arsenal of weapons as the American forces possessed, raised the question of making an amphibious landing south of the Shuri line to envelop the enemy's Shuri positions. It had been hoped that the 7th, 27th, and 96th Divisions, supported by massed artillery, could penetrate the Shuri line.[11] But failure of the attack of 19 April dispelled the expectation of an early and easy penetration of the enemy defenses. If any doubt remained about the kind of fighting that lay ahead before Okinawa could be won, it was dissipated by the heavy combat and high casualties experienced from 19 to 24 April in penetrating the first main ring of the Shuri defense zone. Even this gain was small, and it was evident that it would take a long time to reach Shuri at the rate of progress of the first three and a half weeks of the operation.

The question of a second landing in southern Okinawa was considered by Tenth Army most seriously before 22 April. General Bruce, commander of the 77th Division, knew that his division would be committed in the Okinawa fighting as soon as Ie Shima was secured. At Leyte the amphibious landing of the 77th Division behind the Japanese line at Ormoc had been spectacularly successful. General Bruce and his staff wished to repeat the move on Okinawa and urged it on the Tenth Army command even before the division sailed from Leyte. As the Ie Shima fighting drew to a close, General Bruce pressed his recommenda-

[11] This section is of necessity based primarily on statements by and interviews with various commanders and staff officers. No contemporary records were found of the numerous discussions of the subject, which were largely informal. As is evident, it has been impossible to fix the time and content of the discussions with any great degree of accuracy. The sources used are as follows: statements of Brig Gen Elwyn D. Post, CofS, Tenth Army, 10 Jun 46; Brig Gen Laurence E. Schick, DCofS, Tenth Army, 13 Jun 46; Brig Gen David H. Blakelock, ACofS, G-4, Tenth Army, 8 Feb 46; Col Virgil Shaw, ACofS, G-3, Tenth Army, 6 Feb 46; Brig Gen Oliver P. Smith, Marine DCofS, Tenth Army, 30 Jul 46; Lt Gen John R. Hodge, CG XXIV Corps, 1 Feb 46; Lt Col Max Meyers, ACofS, G-2, 77th Div,—Apr 46; Capt Edmund G. Love, 27th Div Hist Off, 23 Feb 47; interv 1st I & H Off with Gen Buckner, CG Tenth Army, 15 Jun 45; with Maj James H. McMullen, G-3 Sec, Tenth Army, 18 Jun 45; with Brig Gen Walter A. Dumas, ACofS, G-3, Tenth Army, 9 Jul 45; with Lt Col James R. Weaver, ACofS, G-2, 13 Jun 45; interv XXIV Corps Hist Off with Col John W. Guerard, ACofS, G-3, XXIV Corps, 1 Jul 45; with Col Cecil W. Nist, ACofS, G-2, XXIV Corps, 15 Jun 45; with Brig Gen Josef R. Sheetz, CG XXIV Corps Arty, 23 Jun 45; with Col Kenneth C. Strothers, DCofS for Opns, XXIV Corps, 27 Jun 45; with Capt Mervin A. Elliott, G-2 Sec, XXIV Corps, 27 Jun 45. Interviews conducted by the XXIV Corps Hist Off are recorded in the Okinawa Diary, XXIV Corps, kept by Maj Roy Appleman, on file in the Hist Div, WDSS; Appleman, XXIV Corps History, Vol. IV, Annex II, has a useful discussion of the entire problem. For Japanese plans and dispositions see Interrog Yahara; Tenth Army Transl No. 246, 8 Jul 45: *32d Army* Ord No. 170, 22 Apr 45; Transl No. 244, 7 Jul 45: *32d Army* Ord No. 172, 23 Apr 45; Transl No. 273, 13 Jul 45: *32d Army* Ord No. 175, 26 Apr 45.

tion to land his division on the southeast coast of Okinawa on the beaches just north of Minatoga. He believed that it would be necessary to effect a juncture with American forces then north of Shuri within ten days if the venture was to be successful. His plan was either to drive inland on Iwa, a road and communications center at the southern end of the island, or to push north against Yonabaru.

General Buckner rejected the idea. His assistant chief of staff, G–4, stated that he could supply food but not ammunition for such a project at that time. The Minatoga beaches had been thoroughly considered in the planning for the initial landings and had been rejected because of the impossibility of furnishing adequate logistical support for even one division. The reefs were dangerous, the beaches inadequate, and the area exposed to strong enemy attack. Although beach outlets existed, they were commanded both by the escarpment to the west and by the plateau of the Chinen Peninsula. The Tenth Army intelligence officer reported that the Japanese still had their reserves stationed in the south. Both the *24th Division* and the *44th Independent Mixed Brigade* were still in the area and could move quickly to oppose any landings. Artillery positions on the heights overlooking the beaches were fully manned. The 77th Division would be landing so far south that it would not have the support of the troops engaged to the north or of XXIV Corps artillery. (See Map No. III.)

Moreover, at the time the 77th Division was available, around 21 April, all three Army divisions in the line—the 7th, 27th, and 96th—were in a low state of combat efficiency because of casualties and fatigue. The Tenth Army commander felt that it was of paramount importance to relieve these divisions as far as possible in order to maintain the pressure against the Japanese. Furthermore, the full strength of the 77th would not have been available: the division had left garrison forces on the Kerama Islands and Ie Shima which would not be replaced immediately. General Buckner felt that any landing on the southeast coast would be extremely costly, "another Anzio, but worse." Unless a juncture between the diversionary force and the main body of his troops could be made within forty-eight hours of the landing he felt that he could not endorse the plan. A juncture within such a period of time being obviously impossible, the general's disapproval was patent.

Looming even larger than the question of where to commit the 77th Division was that of how best to use the 1st and 6th Marine Divisions in conquering southern Okinawa. The 2d Marine Division, which had been sent back to Saipan, was scheduled to invade Kikai, north of Okinawa, in July;

thus its employment on Okinawa was to be avoided if possible. The 6th would not be available for the southern front until relieved of its security mission in north Okinawa; this was effected early in May by the 27th Division. The 1st Marine Division, however, could be moved south to enter the line at any time, except for one consideration. In Phase III of the original plan for ICEBERG, the island of Miyako, in the Sakishima Group just north of Formosa, was to be invaded after Okinawa had been taken. The V Amphibious Corps, scheduled for this operation, had suffered so severely at Iwo Jima that Tenth Army was directed on 13 April to keep III Amphibious Corps free from heavy commitment that would interfere with its possible use at Miyako. Reconnaissance of Okinawa after the American landings had disclosed that the island had far greater potentialities for development as an air base than had been thought, and the strategical aspects of the entire operation were therefore reconsidered. On 26 April Admiral Nimitz sent a dispatch notifying Tenth Army that the Miyako operation of Phase III had been postponed indefinitely by the Joint Chiefs of Staff in Washington, thus freeing the III Amphibious Corps for full use on Okinawa.

Doubtless in anticipation of this decision, Tenth Army had already considered the problem of where and how to commit the two Marine divisions standing by in northern Okinawa. Landings on the Minatoga beaches were rejected for the same reasons as were adduced in the case of the 77th Division. The beaches from Machinato airfield to Naha were not considered suitable because their use would create supply problems and because the strong Japanese positions west of Shuri overlooked the coastal flat. The vicinity of Itoman farther south on the west coast was studied, but the formidable reef there discouraged such a plan. The southern tip of the island was sheer cliff along the shore. Landings along lower Buckner Bay were considered impracticable because Japanese artillery on the Chinen Peninsula and on the hills east of Shuri completely dominated the area and could prevent naval gunfire support ships from entering the bay. The commanding general of XXIV Corps Artillery believed that landings here would end in catastrophe, that artillery could not be put ashore, and that if it could be, it would be largely destroyed. In addition the time element was unfavorable: it would take an appreciable time to obtain shipping from the 1st Marine Division and mount it out, while the 2d Marine Division, which still had its shipping, would have to be brought back from Saipan. If Marine troops were to be committed in the south, it would be much quicker to move the 1st Marine Division down the island by road to the established front.

SOUTHERN COAST LINE *of Okinawa is marked by jumbled masses of rock and vegetation, fronted by wide reefs. Cliff in picture is over 50 feet high.*

Later, about 26–28 April, three staff officers of Tenth Army visited XXIV Corps headquarters and talked over with Col. John W. Guerard, G–3, XXIV Corps, the tactical problems involved in committing III Amphibious Corps to the battle in southern Okinawa. Colonel Guerard had noticed that identifications of Japanese *24th Division* troops had been found during the past few days of fighting. These seemed to indicate that the enemy command had moved the *24th* to the Shuri front and that the Japanese rear areas, accordingly, were more lightly held than formerly. Colonel Guerard believed therefore that a landing in the south, to which he had hitherto been opposed, was now feasible. He urged this view on the Tenth Army officers and recommended landing the marines on the Minatoga beaches at the southern base of the Chinen Peninsula. When informed of this discussion by Colonel Guerard, General Hodge agreed that a landing of the marines in the south was tactically desirable. Early the next morning General Hodge went to Tenth Army headquarters to urge this view. The proposal was rejected on the ground that a major landing in the south could not be supported logistically.

Tenth Army staff officers, advising against additional landings, contended that there were no suitable landing beaches on the west coast; that it would be very difficult to supply even one division on the southeastern beaches; that two diversionary landings, one on each coast, would result in a dispersion of force with each division being contained in its beachhead. They considered the entire plan too hazardous; the troops would come up against strongly held Japanese positions in an area where the terrain favored a strong defense, and the landings could not be supported by artillery. General Buckner believed that the need for fresh troops was greatest on the Shuri front, where they could relieve the bat-tered divisions already on the line.

Relying on the advice of his staff, General Buckner made his final decision against amphibious landings at some time between 17 and 22 April; thereafter the matter, although raised again, was not given serious consideration by Tenth Army. General Buckner came to the conclusion that the landings were not feasible either tactically or logistically. Admiral Nimitz later flew with his staff members from Guam to Okinawa to confer with General Buckner and other commanders present and concurred in the decision which had been made.[12]

The chief reason for the rejection of a second landing seems to have been

[12] New York *Herald Tribune,* June 18, 1945. Admiral Turner, in conferences recalled by Col. V. F. Shaw, G–3 Plans, Tenth Army, also expressed opposition to a second landing, because of lack of sufficient combat ships to screen another anchorage. Interv Hist Div, SSUSA, with Col. Shaw, 19 Jan 48.

logistical—the judgment that a landing in the south could not be supplied. This judgment was confirmed during the later stages of the campaign when the 7th Division, in possession of the Minatoga area, was supplied by landing craft over the beach; despite the relatively quiet conditions, the tonnage unloaded never reached a satisfactory level because of the inherently unfavorable beach conditions, and landing craft had to be supplemented by overland supply from Yonabaru. Aggressive forward movement after a landing might have eased the initial logistical difficulties but not to a very great extent. A second major consideration was the danger that any beachhead might be contained by the strong Japanese forces in the area. The truth was, indeed, that the Japanese fully expected and almost hoped for another landing in the south, foreshadowed by the L-Day feint, and kept a large body of alerted troops there to meet just such a contingency. After having committed most of these troops to the Shuri front, they prepared a substitute plan to oppose landings in the south, whereby from 2,000 to 3,000 troops in the area were to fight a delaying action while the main forces consolidated a strong perimeter defense around Shuri.

While before the end of April any attempted landings in the south with one or two divisions might have failed—and certainly would not have succeeded except with heavy losses—later the situation became more favorable. The Japanese *24th Division* was committed piecemeal to the Shuri front between 23 April and 4 May, and the *44th Independent Mixed Brigade* was brought up on 26 April, although it did not enter the battle immediately. These changes weakened Japanese strength south of the Shuri line, and the Japanese counterattack of 4–5 May brought about a still greater depletion of the enemy's resources. The prospect of success for a southern amphibious landing thus greatly improved between 5 and 21 May; a landing then would have been justifiable could it have been supplied. By that time, however, the Marines had already been committed to the Shuri front. Moreover, after Tenth Army turned the enemy's right flank on 21 May [13] there was no longer any need for a second landing.

The Japanese command, expecting American landings in the south and prepared to meet them, could not understand why they were not made. The prevailing opinion among the Japanese was that the American command wished to obtain as cheap a victory as possible by wearing down the Shuri line rather than to risk troops in a hazardous landing in the south, though the latter course might bring the campaign to a speedier end.

[13] See below, pp. 358–59.

By their decision General Buckner and his staff committed themselves to the alternative basic tactics of the battle for Okinawa—a frontal assault by the two corps against the Shuri line and an attempt to make a double envelopment of Shuri. The choice was a conservative one: it avoided the risks inherent in another landing under the conditions which would have attended it. It was definitely decided to bring the III Amphibious Corps from northern Okinawa and the 77th Division from Ie Shima. Efforts were also made to speed up the logistical preparations necessary for another general attack. Until sufficient troops and supplies should be at hand the Tenth Army would continue its attack against the second Shuri defense ring with as much force as available resources permitted. For the time being the tactical aim would be to consolidate and advance the American lines for the purpose of gaining a better position for the big attack.

CHAPTER XI

Assaulting the Second Shuri Defense Ring

The forward surge of the American lines on 24 April marked the fall of the first Shuri defense ring everywhere but on the extreme right, in the Item Pocket area. The enemy had withdrawn to the next ring of prepared positions of the Shuri defense zone and was ready to repeat the process of making the invader pay for every foot of ground.

On 24 April General Hodge radioed his division commanders that "operations today indicate enemy withdrawn his forces from the strong positions he has fought so desperately to hold," and ordered aggressive patrolling to determine the new enemy dispositions. At 1100 of the same day he directed the division commanders to regroup their forces and improve their positions by aggressive action, seizing all advantageous ground to their front and pushing in enemy outposts. They were to prepare for a general attack at 0600, 26 April.[1]

While the attack against the second ring of Shuri defenses was under way, there was a major regrouping of the weary American forces at the end of April everywhere on the line except on the 7th Division front. The 27th Division on the west was relieved by the 1st Marine Division, and the 96th Division in the center of the line was relieved by the 77th. These changes were completed by 30 April. The 7th Division was to remain on the line until relieved by the 96th after its 10-day rest.

By the end of April a shift of troops in the line had become necessary. The Japanese position was still strong and there was no indication that it would soon be reduced. The 96th Division, which had gone into Okinawa understrength, had suffered very heavy casualties. It needed a rest and an opportunity to assimilate its replacements; on the other hand, the 77th was relatively fresh, although it had fought in the Kerama Retto and on Ie Shima. The 27th Division had not been intended for combat duty on Okinawa but had been loaned temporarily to XXIV Corps when it became evident that the 7th and 96th could not

---

[1] XXIV Corps CofS Jnl, 24 Apr 45; Appleman, XXIV Corps History, p. 207.

ASA RIVER AREA, *where marines drove south.* (*Photo taken 10 July 1945.*)

break through the Shuri defenses alone. After the cancellation in the middle of April of Phase III for the Okinawa campaign, the conquest of Miyako, the III Amphibious Corps became available to General Buckner for use on the southern front. The 1st Marine Division in the north was to go south first since it was closer to the Shuri line and could be moved into position more quickly than the 6th Marine Division.

Despite this redisposition, the use of fresh troops, and some of the most intensive efforts that the campaign had yet seen, the Americans fought for an entire week without making any significant gain except in the center of the front. In large measure their failure was due to the difficulty of appraising correctly the nature of the interlocking Japanese defenses that they now faced.

Stalemate on the West Coast

On the west coast, in the 27th Division zone, the Item Pocket fighting was practically over by 27 April. The 165th Infantry spent the remaining days of the month patrolling the Kuwan Inlet south of Machinato airfield. On the division left, the 105th Infantry regrouped after the battles of the Pinnacles, pushed to the southern edge of Nakama on 26 April, organized a line, and held there until relieved on 1 May. In the division center the 2d Battalion, 106th Infantry, engaged in hard fighting on 27–28 April around Yafusu in an effort to straighten the line. But the division, overextended and all but exhausted, made no major offensive effort during the last days of April.[2]

On 30 April the 1st Marines of the 1st Marine Division relieved the 165th Infantry on the west coast, and the next day the 5th Marines of the same division completed the relief of that part of the line held by the 105th and 106th Infantry. Maj. Gen. Pedro A. del Valle, commanding general of the 1st Marine Division, which had been attached to XXIV Army Corps, assumed responsibility for the former 27th Division zone of action at 1400, 1 May.[3]

The enemy also reinforced his line in this area. On 26 April General Ushijima ordered the *44th Independent Mixed Brigade* to take a position west of Shuri and north of Naha at the Asa River, behind the remnants of the *62d Division*. Thus the *62d Division* would be supported if a break-through threatened on the west coast.

[2] Love, 27th Div History, Pt. IX.
[3] Capt James R. Stockman, USMC, *The First Marine Division on Okinawa,* published by Historical Division, Hq USMC, 1946 (hereafter cited as Stockman, 1st Mar Div History); 27th Div Actn Rpt, p. 49.

Asa River Battle

The initial objective of the 1st Marine Division was the north bank of the Asa River. Immediately in front of the division, between it and the Asa River, was a series of hills and ridges. On this high ground the Japanese had prepared defensive positions in depth which were to occupy the Marines well into May. On 30 April, and again on 1 May, while the 5th Marines were moving into the line, the 1st Marines tried to push south, but on each day it was repulsed with considerable loss of life; on 1 May one company alone suffered twenty-four casualties.

The 2d of May was wet and chilly, but the marines, two assault regiments abreast, pressed the attack. On the left, next to the 77th Division, the 5th Marines met stubborn resistance. Again, for the third day, the 1st Marines met trouble trying to cross the draw south of Nakanishi village to reach the Jichaku ridge mass. Marines of Company B, one at a time, attempted to cross over a blown bridge. Three of the first five men were hit in the attempt. One man negotiated the top of the south bank. The next three men to follow him were shot in the head. After this bloody reception the company hugged the southern bank of the draw until 1300, when it was ordered to withdraw. In the confusion of the withdrawal, a large number of men were left behind. Eighteen men, five of them wounded, who had not known of the withdrawal order were brought back after dark.

Advance Along the Coast

Farther to the west along the coast, Company F moved forward under fire along Machinato airstrip and dug in after dark by the light of flares. On the regimental left (east), Companies L and K made limited advances but developed gaps of as much as 200 yards between platoons. Weapons jammed with mud, and the situation quickly became precarious. At 1800 the men began to withdraw behind a white phosphorus grenade screen. That night Company K was in an unenviable position, with an exposed left flank. Practically all its weapons were unusable because of mud in the mechanisms. The perimeter defense had only, in addition to grenades, two rifles and one BAR that would work. In repelling a counterattack which struck it that night at 0200, Company K used rifles as clubs. During the day and night Company K suffered forty-two casualties. By 2 May the 1st Marine Division had lost 54 men killed, 233 wounded, and 11 missing—total casualties of 298.[4]

---

[4] XXIV Corps G–3 Periodic Rpt, 3 May 45; Stockman, 1st Mar Div History.

The fighting on 3 May followed closely the pattern of the previous days. The marines continued to advance along the coastal flats. However, it was soon realized that if the advance continued the troops would be flanked by automatic and mortar fire from the finger ridges to the east. It became clear that enemy positions in the high ground eastward from the coast would have to be destroyed before any general advance was possible. Accordingly, after 3 May, the direction and plan of attack pivoted to the southeast toward this commanding ground.[5]

The 7th Division at Kochi Ridge

On the eastern side of the Corps line, the 7th Division, although not realizing this immediately, faced a new enemy combat unit. On 23 April the *22d Regiment* of the *24th Division* took over the eastern part of the Shuri defense zone. At last the *62d Division,* which for three weeks had borne the brunt of the American attack, was to have help. It was time, for the *62d* was but a remnant of its former self. The boundary between the *24th Division* and the *62d Division,* which now was assembled in the western half of the line, ran generally from Shuri Castle north to the front lines west of Kochi and Tanabaru. The Ginowan–Shuri road (Route 5) marked roughly the boundary between the two major units of the Japanese *32d Army.* The change in command along the front was effective at 1100, 23 April. The order directing the new deployment of *24th Division* troops stated that "in particular, liaison forces with the 62d Division near Kochi, must be strongly protected." The front lines of the *22d Regiment* extended from the east coast northwestward through the villages of Gaja, Kuhazu, Onaga, and Kochi. The rest of the *24th Division* was in reserve northeast of Shuri or in the Oroku area. The *22d Regiment,* fresh and never before in combat except for small groups that had participated in the abortive counterattack of 13 April, faced the 7th Division at Kochi and eastward to the sea.[6]

Directly south of Hill 178, two miles away, stood dominant Conical Hill, guarding the coastal passage. Hill 178 and Conical sent long ridges downward toward each other which terminated, 800 yards short of meeting, in a low, flat area, an inward bulge of the coastal flat which reached at this point as far as

[5] 1st Mar Div Special Actn Rpt, Nansei Shoto, 10 Jul 45, Ch. VII: Assault Narrative Phase III, p. 2; XXIV Corps G–3 Periodic Rpt, 3 May 45.

[6] Tenth Army PW Interrog Summary No. 3, 2 Aug 45: *24th Division;* Transl No. 246, 8 Jul 45; *32d Army* Ord No. 170, 22 Apr 45; Transl No. 244, 7 Jul 45; *32d Army* Ord No. 172, 23 Apr 45; 7th Div G–2 Periodic Rpt Nos. 26–28 and 34, 26–28 Apr and 4 May 45, especially PW Interrog Rpt No. 14 in G–2 Periodic Rpt No. 28, and Transl No. 23 in G–2 Periodic Rpt No. 27.

CONICAL HILL   KUHAZU   ONAGA   SHURI HEIGHTS   KOCHI RIDGE   HWY 5

KOCHI AREA, *where the 96th and 77th Divisions attacked vital Japanese positions. Attempting to reach Kochi through Onaga, south of Skyline Ridge, these tanks (below) were lost 29 April when the American lead tank blocked the road forward.*

Onaga. A half mile west of Onaga was the village of Kochi. Between these two villages was high ground, the northern part of which was known as Horseshoe Ridge, and the 500-yard-long southern arm as Kochi Ridge. Beyond Kochi Ridge the ground rose in ever higher broken ridges and hills southwestwardly toward Shuri.[7] (See Map No. XXIX.)

To the southwest of Kochi Ridge was Zebra Hill, a long, high stretch of ground which climbed toward the still higher ground north of Shuri. A deep road cut separated the lower extremities of Kochi Ridge and Zebra. Opposite the road cut on the east, the Onaga side, were How and Item Hills, both of them flanking this important area. On the other side (west) of Kochi Ridge, and paralleling it, was Hill 138. This high ground surrounding Kochi Ridge on three sides was held by the Japanese. From these points the enemy had observation of the Kochi area, and from the same circle of high ground mortars and machine guns could concentrate their fire on Kochi Ridge, which was also a well-organized strong point.

The 17th Infantry Attacks Kochi Ridge

On 25 April the 1st Battalion, 17th Infantry, against surprisingly little resistance, advanced 600 yards across the flat ground on the 7th Division right (west) to occupy the slope of Horseshoe Ridge. The next day the 1st Battalion tried to advance along the west side of Kochi Ridge, and the 2d Battalion along the east side. As soon as this effort began, the reverse-slope fighting technique of the Japanese came into play, and prearranged mortar and machine-gun fire from surrounding heights swept over the area. The attack was stopped and all the troops fell back to their former positions except one platoon of Company G that dug in on the east side of the ridge for a precarious foothold. Neither battalion had observation of the other's movements; neither could gain possession of the crest of the ridge; each fought essentially an isolated action on its own side of the ridge. By the evening of 26 April, it was evident that the 17th Infantry had come up solidly against the Japanese manning the Kochi sector of the line. The next day, a rainy, muddy day, efforts to establish physical contact between the 1st and 2d Battalions failed. There was no gain but there were many casualties.

Before dawn of 28 April the 3d Battalion, 17th Infantry, relieved the 1st Battalion on the west side of Kochi Ridge and took up the attack under the command of Lt. Col. Lee Wallace. Colonel Wallace hoped to move men around Kochi Ridge into the cut between the ridge and Zebra, and then to take the

[7] The account of operations of the 7th Division in the Kochi sector is taken from Gugeler, 7th Div History, Ch. 5.

Kochi Ridge defenses in the rear and flank. He succeeded in getting Company K through Kochi to the cut, while Company L moved southward along the west slope. But once at the cut the company received a blast of machine-gun fire that killed four and wounded eight. Thereafter Company K kept under cover until it could work its way back. In the meantime Company L was unable to reach the crest.

The attack remained stalled on 29 April. Whenever any serious movement threatened, the Japanese concentrated the fire of from twelve to fourteen mortars on the endangered spot and denied it to the attackers. To add to the misfortunes of the men, twelve rounds of friendly 105-mm. artillery shells fell short, landing in the midst of Company G on the east side of Kochi Ridge. Five men were killed and eighteen wounded in one platoon, and an adjacent platoon was left with only twelve men. In addition to the killed and wounded, there were eighteen cases of concussion and shock. Company G now had only twenty-seven men left in the rifle platoons.

On the morning of 30 April, Company E took the place in the line formerly held by Company G and started forward. Suddenly, at 0845, it was hit by cross fire from about eight machine guns located on both flanks and to the front. This was followed by a mortar concentration. Losses were heavy. Twenty men were killed, and in one squad only two men were left. The wounded were helpless. Smoke placed over the men was blown away quickly by a brisk wind and offered almost no protection; even those not wounded were unable to withdraw, and relief parties could not come forward. Medical supplies were finally dropped by a cub plane from a height of fifty feet, in the face of small-arms fire. After dark most of the wounded were brought back .

Farther down the slope toward Onaga, Company I was struck by a Japanese counterattack of about 25 men at 1100, and 5 men were killed and 11 wounded. On the same day a carrier-based Corsair strafed behind the lines of the 17th Infantry, killing 6 and wounding 19 in a tragic blunder. Unquestionably, 30 April was a bad day for the 17th Infantry Regiment. Since 26 April the regiment had suffered more than 60 casualties from friendly fire.

While the 17th Infantry was trying vainly to find some way of taking Kochi Ridge, the 32d Infantry to its east was delayed in opening an attack by lack of success around Kochi. On 28 April an attack on the ridge southwest of Kuhazu put armored flame throwers into the village, but the infantry was stopped by heavy mortar concentrations. On the 29th, when tanks tried to reach Onaga from the coast, one of them hit a mine on a narrow road among the rice paddies near Unaha and was knocked out, blocking the road. Three of the remaining four tanks turned over or threw their tracks and were lost in trying to turn around. The 32d Infantry was now trying to help the situation at Kochi by putting pressure on enemy positions to the southeast.

In a predawn attack on 30 April the 1st Battalion, 32d Infantry, successfully placed Company C on "Chimney Crag" and Company A in the "Roulette Wheel" on the ridge southwest of Kuhazu. Japanese in large numbers infiltrated behind the lines of these companies during the night and disrupted the relief of the 32d by the 184th, the completion of which was to take place before dawn of 1 May but was not accomplished until 1730 in the afternoon. In fighting its way back after being relieved in the line, the 1st Battalion, 32d Infantry, lost eleven men killed and twenty-two wounded.

That night, 1–2 May, a penetration was made by Company L, 184th Infantry, to Gaja Ridge just in front of Conical Hill. The advantage gained by this surprise move was lost at the end of the day when the men were withdrawn by company officers in direct violation of orders to hold the ground despite heavy casualties.

The Kochi Fight Continues

The fight at Kochi Ridge continued during the early days of May, the 17th Infantry making only negligible gains. On 1 May an armored bulldozer prepared an approach from the west to the top of Kochi Ridge between Knobs 1 and 2. An armored flame thrower moved up the approach and twice burned the area, but it was unable to reach the enemy strong points on the east side just over the crest. Onaga was mopped up during the day, but otherwise the infantry undertook no movement and remained in their dug-in positions, engaging in intermittent grenade duels.

At dawn of 2 May the 1st Battalion, 17th Infantry, relieved the 2d Battalion on the east side of Kochi Ridge. It was a bad day, dark with mist and rain. Once again the flame thrower climbed to the saddle between Knobs 1 and 2 and spurted flame at enemy positions. Troops of the 1st Battalion then tried to take Knob 1 from the east side but failed, largely because of the heavy mortar fire which fell on them. During the night sniper positions were dug through the ridge by both battalions to give observation of areas that were hidden from view.

On 3 May, after a dawn artillery preparation, the 1st Battalion on the east and the 3d Battalion on the west side moved forward for a coordinated attack, which included a movement by Company C against How Hill on the east flank of Kochi Ridge. The entire effort came to nothing as the enemy soon halted all forward movement by a mass of artillery and mortar fire, together with intense machine-gun and rifle fire. Grenades also were brought into play.

General Hodge, XXIV Corps commander, was disturbed by the continued failure of the 7th Division to make gains at Kochi Ridge. This failure was largely caused by the fact that limited knowledge of the mutually supporting Japanese positions hindered the launching of a coordinated divisional attack. Here, as in so many other sectors on Okinawa, the thorough integration of the Japanese defenses across the entire front brought combined fire power on one American regimental sector so great that the troops were denied the freedom of movement necessary to effective attack.[8]

The Maeda Escarpment Barrier

The eastern end of the Urasoe-Mura Escarpment dominated the 96th Division front in the center of the line. It loomed directly ahead on the division right—a huge, forbidding, sheer cliff. The part of the escarpment lying within the 96th Division zone was called by the division the "Maeda Escarpment" after the village of Maeda, situated just over the crest on the reverse (south) slope. It was also called "Hacksaw Ridge" and the "Big Escarpment." The hill mass centering on the eastern end of the Urasoe-Mura Escarpment was often called Hill 196 in the official reports.[9] (See Map No. XXX.)

At its eastern end the escarpment terminates abruptly in a gigantic sentinel-like monolith, called "Needle Rock." To the left (east) of Needle Rock a 200-yard saddle dips toward Hill 150, and 400 yards east of Hill 150 across another saddle is Hill 152, which marks the corner where the high ground of the Urasoe-Mura Escarpment formation turns at right angles to the southwest. The Ginowan–Shuri road (Route 5) bends around the corner of Hill 152 and then heads southwest toward Shuri, following the slope of the high ground on the west.

On 25 April the 96th Division was deployed with the 383d Regiment on the left, extending from the vicinity of Kochi to Hill 150; on the division right (west) the 381st Regiment stood in front of the escarpment. All of 25 April was spent by the 96th Division in studying this formidable terrain and in pounding known or suspected enemy positions in it. Thirty-six artillery concen-

[8] Appleman, XXIV Corps History, pp. 274–75.

[9] The account of operations of the 96th Division at Maeda Escarpment is, unless otherwise noted, taken from Mulford and Rogers, 96th Div History, Pt. III.

trations, comprising 1,616 rounds, were fired in the zone of the 381st Infantry alone. Air strikes burned the escarpment with napalm bombs.

The Japanese Rampart Holds

On 26 April the attack against the Maeda Escarpment was launched. The infantry had little trouble in moving up the forward face, but when Company G of the 381st Infantry clambered to the top of the escarpment it suffered eighteen casualties in a matter of minutes. The Japanese on the Maeda Escarpment used to perfection their technique of reverse-slope defense. It was not difficult to occupy the forward slope of the ground, but the crest and the reverse slope were forbidden land. There the battle was to be fought.

Company F at Needle Rock tried to place men on the point of the escarpment by means of a human ladder, but the first three men to reach the top were killed at once by machine-gun fire. Just before dark Company E attempted to occupy some small knolls in Maeda, south of the Hill 150 saddle, but once the men were on the ground the knolls were swept by fire from about a dozen machine guns, which immediately killed two men and wounded six. Four hundred rounds of 81-mm. and 4.2-inch smoke shells were used in screening the withdrawal of the company in the gathering dusk.

Farther to the east there was, for a time, promise of considerable success. Elements of the 383d Regiment reached the crests of Hills 150 and 152 to find the ground below alive with Japanese. They estimated that they could see 600 of the enemy, who were unaccountably exposed. Machine gunners, BAR men, and individual riflemen had a field day. One BAR man was reported to have killed thirty Japanese. Tanks and armored flame throwers were able to move into the edge of Maeda and wreak havoc. Scores of the enemy were driven from caves by flame and then shot down as they fled.

This action on the crest and reverse slopes of Hills 150 and 152, and the penetration of the armor to Maeda on 26 April, had immediate and violent repercussions at *32d Army* headquarters. At 1600 in the afternoon General Ushijima issued a terse order:

> The enemy with troops following tanks has been advancing into the southern and eastern sectors of Maeda since about 1300. The 62d Division will dispatch local units . . . attack the enemy advancing in the Maeda sector and expect to repulse him decisively.[10]

At the same time, adjacent *24th Division* units were ordered to cooperate in this effort regardless of division boundary. Two hours later the Japanese command-

[10] Tenth Army Transl No. 272, 13 Jul 45: *32d Army* Ord No. 174, 26 Apr 45.

ing general issued another order: "The army will crush the enemy which has broken through near Maeda. The 24th Division will put its main strength northeast of Shuri this evening." [11] In these orders can be seen the underlying reason why in the ensuing four days the 96th Division gained only yards. The Japanese meant to hold at Maeda and they did.

Reverse Slope Classic

On the left of the escarpment, at the corner where the high ground turns sharply southwest, the 1st Battalion, 381st Infantry, and elements of the 383d Infantry on 27 April worked their way through the saddle between Hills 150 and 152, supported by tanks of the 763d Tank Battalion and armored flame throwers of the 713th. In a notable example of tank-infantry action they engaged in hours of carnage. The tanks and flame throwers burned and blasted enemy positions, flushing out of their underground positions hundreds of Japanese who were then cut down by the infantry or by the machine guns of the tanks. Tanks and infantry penetrated to the south edge of Maeda, but here the infantry was stopped by enemy fire. On top of the escarpment an all-out effort was made to reduce the large underground pillbox that separated Companies F and G, but the attempt failed.[12] Although many Japanese were killed southeast of the escarpment, no ground was won permanently this day except for very slight advances in Maeda near Hills 150 and 152.

On 28 April Company K of the 381st Infantry, in an effort to weaken resistance at the escarpment, moved through the 27th Division zone to the west and attacked southeast through Nakama toward the "Apartment House." This was a large concrete school building, used as barracks, which was a center of Japanese strength; it was situated south of the escarpment between the villages of Nakama and Maeda. In a half hour of hand-to-hand fighting, Company K was repulsed with heavy losses, and survivors withdrew under smoke. Company K was now down to twenty-four effectives. Because both were greatly reduced in numbers, Companies K and I, 381st Infantry, were combined into one company which had a consolidated strength of only 70 men, 4 machine gunners from the heavy weapons company, and 1 artillery observer.[13]

During the early morning of 29 April, Japanese counterattacks were common across the entire 96th Division front. At 0515 the 2d Battalion, 383d Infantry, was attacked heavily by enemy armed with grenades and spears. One platoon of

[11] Tenth Army Transl No. 273, 13 Jul 45: *32d Army* Ord No. 175, 26 Apr 45.

[12] See also 713th Tk Bn Actn Rpt, Ch. 1, pp. 6–7; 96th Div Actn Rpt, Ch. VII, pp. 25–26.

[13] See also 96th Div Actn Rpt, Ch. VII, pp. 26–27.

HWY 5   HILL 152   HILL 150   NEEDLE ROCK   PILLBOX

MAEDA ESCARPMENT *viewed from east end of Kakazu Ridge.*

TANK-INFANTRY ATTACKS *marked the battle for the escarpment. An armored flame thrower of the 713th Tank Battalion, protected by infantry against enemy satchel-charge attacks, sprays flame over a knob on the crest of the escarpment.*

MAEDA ESCARPMENT STRONG POINTS *included the Apartment House and a cave-tunnel-pillbox network. The Apartment House barracks area (above), just east of Nakama, was captured 5 May as the 307th Infantry, 77th Division, cleaned out reverse slope of Maeda Escarpment. Demolitions played a large part in capture of the maze of caves, tunnels, and pillboxes some 200 feet from the east end of the escarpment. Great sections of the hilltop were blasted away (below), blocking cave entrances in the escarpment's face.*

Company G was reduced from 30 to 9 men in this fight. In repulsing two counter-attacks, the 383d Infantry killed approximately 265 Japanese.[14] Later in the day tanks and armored flame throwers spearheaded the action, during which they killed more than 200 of the enemy.[15]

The left (east) flank of the division on 29 April surged ahead to thrust a salient closer to Shuri than any other point of the Corps line. The crest of Hill 138 was seized again by Company L of the 383d Infantry in furious close combat. One machine-gun position on the crest was destroyed in banzai fashion by Pfc. Gabriel Chavez, who rushed it with a grenade in his hand and took five Japanese and himself to death in the grenade explosion. Tanks worked into position near the top of Hill 138 and engaged in duels with enemy 47-mm. antitank guns to the south; for the first time in the month-old Okinawa battle direct fire was placed in Shuri, a little over a mile to the southwest.[16]

On 29 April the 307th Infantry of the 77th Division took over the Maeda Escarpment part of the line from the 381st Infantry, and the next morning the 306th relieved the 383d Infantry on the 96th Division left. At noon on 30 April, General Bruce, Commanding General of the 77th Division, assumed responsibility for the former 96th Division zone of action on the Corps front. The end of April also witnessed a regrouping among the Japanese units on the line. In response to the urgent orders of the Japanese commander on 26 April, when the Maeda sector was threatened, the *32d Regiment* of the *24th Division* hurried northward to the Maeda sector but apparently did not take over front-line duty until 28 April. It then went into the middle sector between the *22d Regiment of the 24th Division* on the east and the badly mauled *62d Division,* which was now occupying the western third of the front.

By the time it was relieved, the 381st had been reduced to about 40 percent combat efficiency and had suffered 1,021 casualties, 536 of them in the Maeda Escarpment fighting of the past four days. Some platoons were down to five or six men.[17] Many of the men were so exhausted that they did not have the energy to carry their equipment down the slope to the road below where trucks were waiting to take them to the rear.

[14] *Ibid.,* p. 27.

[15] See also 713th Tk Bn Actn Rpt, Ch. I, p. 8.

[16] 96th Div Actn Rpt, Ch. VII, p. 27.

[17] 381st Inf Actn Rpt, pp. 36–37.

Demolition Battle

When the 307th Infantry moved into the line on 29 April, it found itself on the flat top of an escarpment which at its eastern end at the Needle Rock was not more than two feet wide. From this point westward the escarpment crest gradually widened until it was from 100 to 150 feet across. The reverse slope dropped abruptly, but its height was not as great as that of the northern face. It was on this reverse (southern) slope of the escarpment that the Japanese had their intricate network of caves and tunnels connecting with pillboxes on top of the escarpment. The nature of this underground fortress is illustrated by an incident of 2 May. On that day a tank fired six phosphorus shells into a cave and within fifteen minutes observers saw smoke emerging from more than thirty other hidden openings along the slope.[18]

There were innumerable attacks and counterattacks, grenade duels, satchel-chargings of dugouts and caves, horrifying night encounters, and many little strategems used by both sides to win advantages in the hand-to-hand demolition battle of the Maeda Escarpment. Air strikes, employing both demolition and napalm bombs, were made almost daily against the escarpment positions. Tanks and armored flame throwers worked against the southeastern slope. Yet the top of the escarpment, in the words of the men who fought there, was "all hell rolled into one." It took Lt. Col. Gerald D. Cooney's 1st Battalion, 307th Infantry, on the left side of the line, five days to gain control of Needle Rock. Men of the battalion were driven from Needle Rock and the top of the escarpment nine times before they held them for good.

During the night of 30 April–1 May, the 1st Battalion, 307th, brought up to the escarpment four 50-foot ladders and five cargo nets, the latter borrowed from the Navy. On 1 May Company A troops mounted the ladders at the eastern end of the escarpment, but every man who stood up was killed or wounded. Farther to the west, however, Company B, using the cargo nets, had two platoons on the edge of the escarpment by nightfall. About midnight Japanese counter-attacked in this area and drove the men off the escarpment.

On the division right the 3d Battalion, 307th Infantry, on 1 May moved through the 27th Division zone behind the escarpment to Nakama village, from where it attacked eastward toward the Apartment House barracks area. During this action a Japanese shell exploded an ammunition dump in Nakama, killing

[18] The account of operations of the 77th Division at Maeda Escarpment is based on the following: Leach, 77th Div History, Vol. II; 77th Div Actn Rpt Okinawa, pp. 35–43; Appleman, XXIV Corps History, pp. 259–64.

five men and disrupting ammunition supply for hours. On 2 May, Companies A and B placed men back on the edge of the escarpment but made no real gain. Machine-gun fire was so intense that one man was decapitated. During 3 May the 1st Battalion, 307th Infantry, fought a desperate grenade battle to win the top of part of the escarpment. The Japanese showered the top with grenades and knee mortars from the reverse slope and with 81-mm. mortar fire from a distance. Men came back across the narrow top of the escarpment to the north side, swearing and crying, saying they would not go back into the fight. "Yet," observed one platoon leader, "in five minutes' time those men would go back there tossing grenades as fast as they could pull the pins." [19]

Maeda Escarpment Bastion Falls

The fighting was especially fierce on top the escarpment on 4 May. Colonel Cooney's 1st Battalion successfully executed a complicated demolition assault on the big cave-tunnel-pillbox network about 200 feet west of the eastern end of the escarpment. The battalion then held the newly won ground against repeated counterattacks from the southern side. It was estimated that 600 enemy were killed by the 307th Infantry in the fighting at the escarpment on 4 May. Slowly, on 5 May, the reverse slope was taken and caves blasted and closed. On the night of 5–6 May the Japanese staged several counterattacks in an effort to win back the escarpment. An especially severe attack struck the 3d Battalion, 307th Infantry, on the regimental right. In repelling it the 3d Battalion killed 250 enemy troops, largely in hand-to-hand fighting. During 6 May all battalions of the 307th Infantry advanced southward to the slopes of Hill 187. The battle of the escarpment was over.

One of the most remarkable incidents of the battle for the Maeda Escarpment was the performance of Pfc. Desmond T. Doss, a medical aid man attached to Company B, 307th Infantry. Doss was a Seventh Day Adventist and would not touch a gun, but time after time he remained on top of the escarpment after the others had been driven off, lowering the wounded over the side in a rope litter. He went repeatedly to within a few yards of caves to administer first aid to men who had been cut down trying to assault the positions, and then carried these men to safety under the very guns of the enemy. For his valor Doss later received the Congressional Medal of Honor. [20]

The losses in the escarpment battle had been heavy. In the 1st Battalion, 307th Infantry, no less than eight company commanders were wounded in one

[19] Leach, 77th Div Hist, Vol. II, p. 13.
[20] WD GO 97, 1 Nov 45.

36-hour period. It had gone up on the escarpment on 29 April with a strength of about 800 men; it came down on 7 May with 324. The 77th Division estimated that it had killed upwards of 3,000 Japanese in the 7-day battle for the escarpment.[21]

While at the Maeda Escarpment and in a few other sectors the American attack continued through the first week of May, yet, in general, this attack was brought to an unexpected pause after 3 May. (See Map No. XXXI.) On 4 May the enemy launched a surprise counteroffensive by which he hoped to wrest back from the invaders all that they had so painfully gained. For a time most American troops had all they could do to hold their own.

[21] Appleman, XXIV Corps History, p. 264; 77th Div Actn Rpt, p. 43.

CHAPTER XII

The Japanese Counteroffensive and Its Aftermath

A hundred feet below Shuri Castle, in a small chamber shored up with heavy beams, the top commanders of the Japanese *32d Army* met on the night of 2 May to make a fateful decision. General Ushijima's staff was still divided over strategy. General Cho, the chief of staff, continued to press for an immediate large-scale attack. The time was ripe, he said, for a decisive blow. Colonel Yahara, clinging to his faith in defensive tactics, opposed the attack as premature.

Sake was flowing freely, and the meeting became tense and quarrelsome. When it was proposed that the *63d Brigade* of the *62d Division* come under command of the *24th Division* for an attack, the brigade commander, General Nakashima, retorted hotly with a pointed and biting comparison of the abilities of the *62d* and *24th Divisions*. His brigade would not fight as a mere branch of a weak tree; rather it would die where it stood. General Nakashima won his point, and the meeting moved quickly to a decision. General Fujioka, commander of the *62d Division,* vehemently backed up Cho. Most of the Japanese commanders were impatient with defensive fighting and saw no prospect of success in a battle of attrition. Colonel Yahara's warnings were unavailing, and once again he was overruled. General Ushijima ordered an all-out offensive by *32d Army* for 4 May.[1]

Planning the Offensive

Plan for Combined Operations

Even before the Japanese commanders conferred at Shuri headquarters, their operations officers had been framing attack orders and telephoning the gist of them to unit commanders. The final plan was ambitious. The enemy aspired to destroy the XXIV Corps on Okinawa and to disable the Allied fleet offshore in a series of heavy, coordinated blows. To this end he committed a sizeable portion of his ground, air, and amphibious forces.

[1] The account of the conference is based on Interrog Yahara; Interrog Shimada; Tenth Army Int Monograph, Pt. II, Sec. D: *32d Army* Hq, Shuri; PW Interrog Summary No. 2, 2 Aug 45: *62d Division*.

The *24th Division* was to make the main effort in the ground attack. This unit, comprising approximately 15,000 men under the command of General Amamiya, was largely intact on 3 May except for its *22d Regiment,* which had seen extended action. Amamiya's mission was to drive strong spearheads through the center and left (east) of the American lines. Once the XXIV Corps front was disrupted, his remaining forces, supported by other Japanese units pouring through the gaps, would systematically destroy the Corps in a series of day and night attacks.

The amphibious attack was to come in the form of landings from barges over the beaches behind the American front lines. Several hundred men of the *26th Shipping Engineer Regiment,* loaded with light arms and satchel charges, were ordered to land on the west and destroy American tanks and artillery. The *23d Engineers* had a similar mission on the east coast. The raiders were formally detached from their units and ordered not to return.[2]

The Japanese offensive was to coincide with a major attack by *Kamikaze* planes and suicide boats against the American ships off Okinawa. The enemy was convinced that a successful assault against American supply lines would be a decisive blow in the campaign. The unending stream of supplies and ships was demoralizing to him. "There were so many they looked like an island," a member of the *24th Division* wrote plaintively on the eve of the attack after he viewed the American ships. "I wish we could somehow get air superiority back."[3]

Plan for the Ground Attack

The Japanese planned their ground attack with extreme care. This was to be no banzai charge. The enemy's intelligence had formed an accurate estimate of American dispositions, and his orders were clear and explicit. Divisions, regiments, battalions, and companies were given definite objectives and precise boundaries. Units in close support followed designated routes. Commanders were ordered to dispatch infiltrating squads to gain up-to-date information. The efforts of supporting arms, such as artillery, tanks, and engineers, were thoroughly integrated with the infantry action.[4]

[2] Tenth Army PW Interrog Summary No. 6, 3 Aug 45: Shipping Engineers.

[3] 96th Div G–2 Periodic Rpt No. 45, 16 May 45.

[4] Seven Japanese orders for the attack were later captured. Two were *24th Division* orders covering the entire ground attack; the others were regimental and battalion orders. The *32d Army* orders were not recovered. For copies of the orders see Tenth Army Int Monograph, Pt. I, Sec A, p. 13; 96th Div G–2 Periodic Rpt, No. 42, 13 May 45, and No. 44, 15 May 45; 7th Div G–2 Periodic Rpt No. 36, 6 May 45. See also Interrog Yahara and Shimada; Tenth Army PW Interrog Summary No. 4, 1 Aug 45: *44th Independent Mixed Brigade.*

The *24th Division,* occupying the eastern half of the front, was to open the attack at daybreak of "X Day," 4 May. "After effecting a quick rupture of the enemy front lines," General Amamiya's order read, "the division will continue penetration and annihilate him at all points by continuous night and day attacks." By sunset of the first day the Japanese were to have penetrated two miles into the opposing lines to a point northeast of Tanabaru. The final objective was an east-west line at Futema, site of the 96th Division command post, which the Japanese mistakenly thought to be General Buckner's headquarters.

The attack was to be two-pronged. Following a 30-minute artillery preparation at daybreak, the *89th Regiment* on the east was to break through in the Onaga area. The *32d Regiment,* also supported by artillery, was to penetrate American lines in the Maeda area. Tanks were to support both prongs. Raiding and infiltration units were ordered to follow in the wake of the "break-through troops." Once the *24th Division* was established at the first objective northeast of Tanabaru, the Japanese troops were to dig in against American counterattacks, set up antitank traps, and prepare to continue the attack northward.

The *22d Regiment* and the *44th Independent Mixed Brigade* had special missions. Located in the center of the *24th Division's* line, the *22d Regiment* was to screen the advance of the other two regiments with smoke and fire. Then, echeloned to the left rear of the *89th Regiment,* the 22d would join in the attack. The *44th Independent Mixed Brigade,* a fresh unit, was ordered to protect the Japanese left flank during the attack. Following the expected break-through east of Maeda, the *44th* was to turn left toward Oyama on the west coast and thus cut off the 1st Marine Division. The enemy high command evidently considered the break-through at Maeda to be the critical blow, for his troops were especially well supported by tanks, artillery, and antitank elements. (See Map No. XXXII.)

Rear Echelon Support

The Japanese reasoned that success depended on the extent to which they could support their front-line troops with artillery, tanks, supplies, and communications. Their plans specified in detail the role that each of the support units was to play in the projected operations.

Artillery units were ordered to regroup in preparation for the attack. Guns and howitzers were pulled out of cave positions and set up farther south in more open emplacements for greater flexibility. They were to open fire thirty minutes before the attack. When the infantry had driven through the American front lines, artillerymen were to move their weapons forward. The *27th Tank Regiment*, hitherto uncommitted, was ordered to move from its position near Yonabaru during the night over several routes and support the attack in the Maeda area.

Japanese signalmen had the task of putting in a trunk line between the Shuri headquarters and a point behind the front. As the troops moved forward, the line was to follow. Before dawn on the 4th, a signal net was to connect "break-through units" with artillery and transport elements. First-aid sections, two of which were assigned to each of the spearheads, would collect the wounded in caves and send the worst cases to the rear on trucks and carts. Engineers were responsible for road maintenance and for "mopping up" behind the assault troops.

Ammunition and other supplies were carefully allotted. The infantry was allowed rations for ten days. Trucks were to follow the troops closely, working out of designated supply points. General Amamiya ordered that "critical materials will be supplied with caution when required, and captured stores will be used to best advantage. The division's fighting strength will be constantly maintained and cultivated." [5]

The offensive was to open at dawn of 4 May. "Display a combined strength," final orders read. "Each soldier will kill at least one American devil." [6]

The Offensive Under Way

All these preparations the Japanese concealed with remarkable skill. On 2 May Col. Cecil W. Nist, XXIV Corps intelligence officer, noted a definite decrease in the volume and intensity of enemy artillery fire, and sound-plots located Japanese pieces nine miles south of their front lines. Colonel Nist conjectured that the enemy was withdrawing his guns farther south—a move which could foreshadow a general Japanese withdrawal. No one divined the enemy's real intent. General Buckner believed that the enemy's rigid type of defense made it impossible for him to launch more than minor counterattacks. [7]

Japanese rear areas, quiescent during the daylight hours when there was constant air observation, burst into activity soon after sundown on 3 May. Artillery opened up with heavy concentrations on American front lines. Enemy

[5] Tenth Army Transl No. 116, 1 Jun 45: *24th Div* Ord No. 179, 2 May 45; 77th G–2 Periodic Rpt No. 51, 16 May 45.

[6] 7th Div G–2 Periodic Rpt No. 36, 6 May 45.

[7] XXIV Corps G–2 Periodic Rpt No. 32, 3 May 45; interv 1st I & H Off with Gen Buckner, 1 May 45.

troops moved up to their appointed positions. Small units of three or four men, variously designated as "reconnaissance raiding" and "rear harassing" teams, proceeded toward the American lines to attack command posts, heavy weapons, communications, and depots and to send back information by means of smoke signals. The *27th Tank Regiment* rumbled up to Ishimmi, several of its tanks being severely damaged by American artillery fire en route.[8] On beaches south of Naha and Yonabaru, men of the shipping engineer regiments piled into barges and assault boats.

"The time of the attack has finally come," a Japanese infantryman wrote in his diary during the evening. "I have my doubts as to whether this all-out offensive will succeed, but I will fight fiercely with the thought in mind that this war for the Empire will last 100 years."[9]

Sorties in the Night

The *Kamikazes* struck at American shipping at dusk on 3 May. Five suicide planes crashed into the *Aaron Ward* inside of one hour, firing the ship and killing or wounding ninety-eight men. Three others carrying bombs sank the *Little*. Two vessels were sunk and four damaged, but American planes and anti-aircraft fire accounted for fourteen suicide planes and twenty-two other enemy aircraft before dark. The Japanese also bombed shore installations, concentrating on Yontan airfield.[10]

Armed with antitank guns, heavy machine guns, light arms, and thousands of satchel charges, several hundred men of the *26th Shipping Engineer Regiment* headed under overcast skies for landing places below Yontan and Kadena air-fields. They miscalculated their position and turned into the shore at a point where it was heavily defended. At 0200 riflemen of the 1st Marine Division on the sea wall near Kuwan caught sight of ten barges and opened up with con-centrated fire. Naval flares lighted up the area. One company fired 1,100 rounds from 60-mm. mortars. Several enemy barges burst into flames. One platoon of marines used fifty boxes of ammunition and burned out six machine-gun barrels as it sprayed the Japanese trying to cross the reef. (See Map No. XXXIII.)

Many of the enemy managed to reach the shore; some of these fled back to the Japanese lines and others were cornered in Kuwan, where the marines mopped them up at leisure. All the landing boats were destroyed. A smaller group of Japanese advanced almost as far as Chatan, landing one and one-half

[8] Tenth Army PW Interrog Summary No. 8, 25 Jul 45: *27th Tank Regiment*.
[9] 7th Div G–2 Periodic Rpt No. 38, 8 May 45.
[10] CTF 51 Actn Rpt, III–75, 76.

JAPANESE AIR AND SEA ATTACK *on transports left supply craft beached and still burn-ing the morning of 4 May. Scene above is near mouth of the Bishi River. Some 48-foot folding landing craft (below), a type used by the Japanese in their attempted surprise landing during the night of 3–4 May, were found at Naha after its capture.*

miles south of there at Isa, but they were contained without major difficulty and during the following day were destroyed.[11]

The shipping engineers were even less successful on the east coast of Okinawa. After a trip northward in various types of boats, including native-type boats rowed by *Boeitai,* several hundred tried to land behind the 7th Division lines, but most of them were killed by fire from ships in Buckner Bay or by the 7th Division Reconnaissance Troop and 776th Amphibious Tank Battalion on land.[12]

The amphibious attack was a complete fiasco. The enemy lost from 500 to 800 men and almost all their landing craft. The engineer regiments never mounted another amphibious attack of any proportion; the survivors fought as infantry in the final operations on Okinawa.

The 24th Division Attacks

Never had the 7th Infantry Division in its long combat in the Pacific experienced such shelling as swept its front lines during the night of 3–4 May. The enemy, using all types of weapons down to 20-mm., fired more than 5,000 rounds on the division during the night. To reach the Americans in their foxholes, he used airburst artillery and 70-mm. barrage mortar shells which burst in the air and in turn scattered more explosives to blow up on the ground. With their field pieces now in the open enjoying wide fields of fire, the Japanese artillerymen were gambling that the infantry attack would overwhelm XXIV Corps artillery before it could search out and destroy their weapons.[13]

In the pitch darkness Japanese troops made their way toward the American front lines. At 0500 two red flares ordered them to attack. As the artillery fire became heavy, a guard of Company A, 17th Infantry, on a hill just north of Onaga, dropped back below the crest for cover. He thought that the enemy would not attack through his own artillery, but the enemy did just that. A few Japanese appeared on the crest and set up a light machine gun. Pfc. Tillman H. Black, a BAR man, killed the gunner, and as more of the enemy came over the crest he killed four Japanese who tried to man the machine gun. The enemy advanced over the crest in ragged groups, enabling Black to hold his own. Soon the whole company was in action and drove the enemy off the

[11] XXIV Corps PW Interrog Rpt No. 82, 14 May 45; G–2 Summary No. 8, 29 Apr–5 May 45, p. 4; Tenth Army PW Interrog Summary No. 6, 3 Aug 45: Shipping Engineers; Stockman, 1st Mar Div History.

[12] 7th Div G–2 Periodic Rpt No. 34, 4 May 45; Gugeler, 7th Div History, p. 243; Tenth Army PW Interrog Rpt No. 10, 2 Jun 45.

[13] 7th Div G–2 Periodic Rpt No. 34, 4 May 45.

crest. The Japanese abandoned three light machine guns, four mortars, and much ammunition.[14]

At another point a surprise attack nearly succeeded. On high ground 1,000 yards east of Onaga a group of Japanese crept up the hill in front of Company I, 184th, commanded by Capt. James Parker. In the sudden onslaught that followed, two heavy machine gun crews abandoned their positions. One of them left its weapon intact, and the Japanese promptly took it over and swung it around on the company. Parker, watching the attack from the ridge, had anticipated the move. The Japanese managed to fire one burst; then Parker destroyed the usurped weapon with his remaining heavy machine gun. For an hour or two longer the Japanese clung to the forward slopes, firing their rifles amid shrill screams, but they made no further progress.

By dawn the general pattern of the Japanese attack on the left (east) of the XXIV Corps line was becoming clear. In the 184th's sector the enemy's *89th Regiment,* following instructions to "close in on the enemy by taking advantage of cover," [15] had advanced around the east slopes of Conical Hill, crept across the flats, and assembled in force around the "Y ridges" east of Onaga. They had outflanked three companies of the 184th on Chimney Crag and the Roulette Wheel north of Kuhazu, and had also managed to evade the forward battalions of the 17th around Kochi. Another Japanese element had attacked 7th Division lines on the high ground north of Unaha.

At dawn 1st Lt. Richard S. McCracken, commanding Company A, 184th, observed 2,000 Japanese soldiers in the open area east and north of Kuhazu. They were perfect "artillery meat." Unable to get through to his artillery support, McCracken called his battalion commander, Colonel Maybury, and described the lucrative targets. Maybury was equally pleased. McCracken suggested, however, that the Colonel should not be too happy—a group of Japanese at that moment was within 100 yards of Maybury's observation post.

"Oh no," Maybury said, "that's a patrol from Company K down there."

"I don't know who the hell it is," McCracken said, "but there's a lot of them and they've got two field pieces that are pointed right at your OP."

There was indeed a party of Japanese busily unlimbering two 75-mm. howitzers just below Maybury. But Company C, 17th Infantry, had spotted this activity, and within a few minutes maneuvered tanks into position and scattered

---

[14] The account of the operations of the 7th Division during the Japanese attack is taken from Gugeler, 7th Div History.

[15] 7th Div G–2 Periodic Rpt No. 36, 6 May 45.

the enemy group. Artillery eliminated the Japanese caught in the open.

The 3d Battalion, 184th, beat off an attack by 200 Japanese, who thereupon withdrew to the ruins of Unaha and set up mortars. A mortar duel ensued, sometimes at ranges of 250 yards. The 3d Battalion, 32d, also poured fire on the enemy there. After the impetus of the attack was lost, a Japanese officer stood out on open ground and waved his saber to assemble his men for an attack. American mortarmen waited for a worth-while target to develop, then put mortar fire on it. Four times the officer assembled a group, only to have his men killed or scattered, before he was finally killed.

By 0800 the Japanese had been driven beyond grenade range on the entire 7th Division front. But they did not abandon their attack, perhaps because they had been ordered to advance "even until the last man." [16] They made the mistake of milling about in the exposed flatland, where they became perfect targets; they neither pressed the attack nor essayed an organized withdrawal. American heavy weapons fenced off avenues of retreat in order to contain the enemy in open areas. "We laid them down like ducks," a platoon sergeant reported.

Tank-Infantry Attack in the Center

While the 7th Division was repelling the Japanese attack in the eastern sector of the XXIV Corps line, the 77th Division was blunting the other enemy "spearhead" in the center. Here the Japanese *32d Regiment,* supported by tanks and engineers, attacked behind intense artillery fire. This sector was the critical point of attack, for a break-through here would enable the supporting *44th Independent Mixed Brigade* to cut west and isolate the 1st Marine Division.

Transportation difficulties beset the *32d Regiment* almost from the start. During the night light tanks drove out of Shuri up the Ginowan road (Route 5), but American artillery interdicting the road prevented medium tanks from following. The mediums had to take a long detour, which was in such poor condition that only two of the tanks could enter into the attack. Trucks and artillery also were slowed down. Even foot troops had trouble in moving. One Japanese infantryman recorded that his column was shelled on the way and that everyone except himself and one other was wounded. Another wrote of encountering "terrific bombardment" on the way to Kochi. These difficulties severely handicapped the *32d Regiment* in ensuing operations.[17]

[16] *Ibid.*

[17] Tenth Army PW Interrog Summary No. 8, 25 Jul 45: *27th Tank Regiment;* Transl No. 154, 15 Jun 45; Interrog Shimada; 96th Div G–2 Periodic Rpt No. 45, 16 May 45.

POSITION OCCUPIED BY THE JAPANESE IN THEIR PENETRATION TO
TANABARU ESCARPMENT, 4–7 MAY

JAPANESE LAND OFFENSIVE of 4–5 May was opened by rocket barrages. The erratic paths of enemy fire shown above are in sharp contrast with those of the more accurate American weapons. Below, a knocked-out Japanese light tank is examined by a 96th Division soldier. All enemy tanks used in the predawn offensive 4 May were destroyed.

Supported by nine light tanks, the *3d Battalion* led the assault of the *32d Regiment* against the 306th Infantry, 77th Division, before dawn on 4 May. The enemy mounted his assault from southeast of Hill 187 and hit the 77th where Route 5 curled around the east end of Urasoe-Mura Escarpment. The Japanese drove into the front lines of the 1st Battalion, 306th, near Maeda. Although the enemy found the weak points of the line, American automatic fire split up the attacking forces. As in the case of their right "spearhead," the Japanese were unable to move into the American lines at any place with sufficient force to break through. The enemy's only success consisted of driving a platoon off one of the hills. American artillery was called in against the Japanese tanks. Several were knocked out, and, as the infantry stalled, the rest withdrew.[18]

Shortly before daylight, when the Japanese infantry had failed to take its initial objectives east of Hill 187, Colonel Murakami, commanding the *27th Tank Regiment,* became impatient and recklessly committed his own infantry company, a standard element of a Japanese tank regiment. American artillery fire destroyed one platoon, disrupting the attack, and daylight found the surviving troops in a precarious position across from the American lines. Colonel Murakami ordered the company to withdraw, but artillery fire prevented a retreat during the day. When the Japanese used smoke for concealment, the Americans simply blanketed the obscured area with shell fire. The survivors straggled back to their front lines after nightfall. All the light tanks that had supported the attack were lost.[19]

By 0730 the 306th Infantry had driven off the enemy. Broken up into small groups, the Japanese tried to pull back over ground swept by tremendous volumes of artillery and mortar fire, but few got through. Continued attack was impossible. At 0800 the commander of the Japanese *3d Battalion* radioed the *32d Regiment* command post at Dakeshi: "Although the front lines on the high ground southeast of Maeda advanced to the line of the central sector and are holding, further advance is very difficult due to enemy fire. There is no tank cooperation." [20]

Artillery and Air Attack

On 4 May, for the first time in the campaign, whole batteries of enemy artillery were visible. By bringing his field pieces out into the open the enemy was

---

[18] The account of the operations of the 77th Division during the Japanese attack is, unless otherwise noted, based on Leach, 77th Div History, Vol. II, Ch. II.

[19] Appleman, XXIV Corps History, pp. 310–11; XXIV Corps PW Interrog Rpt No. 144, 15 Jun 45.

[20] 77th Div G–2 Periodic Rpt No. 51, 16 May 45.

able to deliver more than 13,000 rounds onto American lines in support of the attack. He ringed his artillery with antiaircraft guns, chiefly 75-mm., to keep off cub planes, and he used smoke pots to hide the flashes of the firing. This gamble proved to be a costly failure. By taking advantage of area artillery barrages which drove Japanese antiaircraft crews to cover, American cub planes were able to pinpoint many Japanese artillery positions for precision fire. During 4 May American counterbattery destroyed nineteen enemy artillery pieces and during the next two days forty more. The Japanese thereupon moved their remaining weapons back into caves. With the lessening of Japanese artillery fire, the number of combat fatigue cases among American troops dropped correspondingly.[21]

The Japanese effort in the air on 4 May was more successful. From dawn to 1000 American naval forces were under continuous attack by enemy planes using *Kamikaze* tactics, and many of the light units were sunk or damaged. Four planes crashed into the U. S. destroyer *Morrison,* and the ship sank in eight minutes, with 154 casualties. A Baka bomb hit and fired the *Shea,* killing twenty-five and flooding the forward compartments, but the ship stayed afloat. A plane over the transports in the Hagushi area, after receiving fire from many ships, dived straight down into the *Birmingham* just aft of Number 2 turret. The impact carried the motor of the plane through three decks, and the 250-pound bomb burst in the sick bay. There were ninety casualties. More Japanese planes attacked at dusk. A suicide flyer hit the escort carrier *Sangamon,* destroying twenty-one planes on the flight deck. Her entire hangar deck was gutted by fire, and all radar and bridge control was knocked out. From the evening of 3 May until that of 4 May the Japanese had sunk or damaged 17 American ships and inflicted 682 naval casualties, while American planes and naval gunfire had destroyed 131 enemy planes. The enemy's air attack, which was simply one phase of his unceasing air campaign against the invading forces, amounted to 560 raids by 2,228 enemy planes between 1 April and 17 May and was probably the most profitable effort of his entire counteroffensive.[22]

Japanese Penetration to Tanabaru, 5 May

General Amamiya refused to abandon the attack. Although both "spearheads" of his *24th Division* had smashed vainly against the American defenses,

[21] Appleman, XXIV Corps History, pp. 305–06; XXIV Corps Actn Rpt, p. 112; G–2 Summary No. 8, p. 5; Tenth Army PW Interrog Summary No. 12, 3 Aug 45: Army AAA Units on Okinawa.
[22] CTF 51 Actn Rpt, III–75–79; IV–2–65; V–H–2–10.

suffering heavy losses in the process, he ordered another assault for the night of 4–5 May. The *1st Battalion, 32d Regiment,* and the attached *26th Independent Infantry Battalion* were directed to penetrate XXIV Corps lines northwest of Kochi in a night attack. The *1st Battalion* had been used in support of the Japanese left "spearhead" on the 4th, but it had not been fully committed and was still relatively intact.

The reason for Amamiya's persistence after the morning's debacle is not clear, but one event of the day may well have led to his decision. Unknown to XXIV Corps, elements of the *1st Battalion, 22d Regiment,* had penetrated more than 1,000 yards behind the American lines near Kochi. After dusk on the 4th these elements were ordered to pull back to their regimental lines. Amamiya may have reasoned that he had found a weak point in the American defenses. In any event the *1st Battalion* of the *32d* was given a similar route of approach, lying near the boundary between the 7th and 77th Divisions.[23]

Break-through at Night

The Japanese, having shelled the lines of the 306th Infantry during the night of 4–5 May, at 0200 launched an attack on the 306th where it straddled Route 5 northwest of Kochi. American artillery broke up this attempt. Three hours later the enemy attacked in battalion strength, supported by tanks. Although six tanks were soon knocked out, the Japanese pressed on through artillery and mortar fire to engage the 306th in close combat. They isolated a battalion observation post and killed or wounded its five occupants. Despite hostile heavy mortar fire, the Japanese set up knee mortars and heavy machine guns close to the American lines and even tried—unsuccessfully—to emplace a 75-mm. gun.[24]

Fierce fire fights developed along the regiment's entire line. One enemy force, moving up a draw in close column formation, marched squarely into a company and was destroyed by automatic weapons fire. Most of the Japanese, unable to close in for hand-to-hand fighting, took refuge in ditches just in front of the American positions. Grenade duels and exchanges of automatic fire continued until midday. By dawn, however, the 306th had the situation in hand. American tanks moved along the ditches and machine-gunned the enemy. Some of the surviving Japanese, using smoke for concealment, managed to withdraw to their lines. They left 248 dead in the 77th Division's sector,

[23] 7th Div G–2 Periodic Rpt No. 37, 7 May 45, and No. 38, 8 May 45; Tenth Army PW Interrog Summary No. 3, 2 Aug 45: *24th Division;* 96th Div G–2 Periodic Rpt No. 41, 12 May 45.

[24] Leach, 77th Div History, Vol. II, Ch. II, pp. 37–40; Appleman, XXIV Corps History, pp. 313–15.

TANABARU ESCARPMENT *viewed from position of the 17th Infantry, 7th Division, on a finger of Hill 178. Company E, 17th, moved back to the secondary crest (right) on morning of 6 May after enemy had counterattacked in force. Below appear the north and west sides of the escarpment, where Company F, 17th, regained the hill 7 May.*

together with numerous machine guns, mortars, rifles, and several hundred rounds of 75-mm. ammunition for the gun they had failed to get into action.

Behind this noisy fire fight along Route 5, a large portion of the Japanese *1st Battalion, 32d Regiment,* managed to infiltrate through the XXIV Corps line. The Japanese made their penetration at a point between Route 5 and Kochi. This route lay within the 77th Division sector but close to the divisional boundary between the 7th and 77th. About ninety of the infiltrating Japanese made their way into the command post of the 306th Infantry, but they did little damage and were killed during the following day. Most of the Japanese, numbering approximately 450, crossed the divisional boundary and reoccupied the town of Tanabaru and Tanabaru Ridge. The deepest penetration was more than a mile behind the Corps front.[25]

The town and ridge had constituted a strong point on the first Shuri defense line, dominating much of the adjacent area. This position had never actually been taken by American troops; the Japanese had abandoned it on the night of 23 April when the rest of the line cracked. The escarpment dropped abruptly in a steep coral cliff on the north. The town stretched along the southeast slope of the ridge and was divided by a road running south to Onaga and Kochi. The front-line battalions of the 17th Infantry, 7th Division, were supplied over this road. While the Japanese held at Tanabaru, this supply road was effectively cut.

Battle Behind the Lines

Through field glasses sentries of the 17th Infantry could see in the moonlight a column of troops moving northwest against the skyline on Tanabaru Escarpment. The 17th fired on some of the troops but was handicapped by fear of endangering friendly troops. Other Japanese columns apparently passed undetected. The enemy quickly located and cut the telephone wires between regimental headquarters and the three battalions, but the regiment was able to record enemy movements through its units in the rear areas. The Japanese also surrounded and attacked supply dumps at the base of the ridge and were barely prevented from destroying them.[26]

The job of cleaning out the infiltrating Japanese fell to Company E, which sent a patrol of platoon strength up the east slope of the escarpment. When the Japanese on the heights held up this patrol with fire, 1st Lt. Walter J. Sinkiewicz,

[25] Appleman, XXIV Corps History, pp. 316–17.

[26] The account of the operations of the 7th Division in retaking Tanabaru Escarpment is, unless otherwise noted, based on Gugeler, 7th Div History, pp. 255–63.

commanding Company E, committed the rest of his unit. One platoon almost reached the top, but the enemy drove it back with mortar, machine-gun, and light-arms fire, killing two and wounding seven. A sharp fire fight developed, during which Sinkiewicz and his three platoon leaders were all wounded.

The Japanese were meanwhile making the most of their position. Their fire covered the 1st Battalion's supply dump and motor pool on the north side of the ridge, rendering them inaccessible to the Americans. Enemy groups in Tanabaru mined the supply road through the town and blanketed the road with machine-gun fire. A half-track carrying medical supplies was disabled by a mine, and a medical officer was killed as he tried to escape. The Japanese occupied the vehicle and converted it into a pillbox. An American patrol killed eleven Japanese in and around the vehicle. S/Sgt. Carl W. Johnson volunteered to retrieve the weapons in the half-track; he made three successful trips across exposed ground but was killed on the fourth.

By noon of 5 May there was apprehension at the regimental command post, which had not fully appreciated the strength of the infiltration. From a hill near the command post Lt. Col. Albert V. Hartl, executive of the 17th Infantry, could plainly see several Japanese soldiers 600 yards away on Tanabaru Escarpment. The Japanese were in turn watching American activity. Lying on his stomach, Colonel Hartl fired some shots from an M1 at the Japanese to "neutralize" them. While he was so engaged, a soldier ran up with a radio report that the German armies had surrendered. "Well now," Hartl said, "if we just had the Japs off the escarpment we'd be all right, wouldn't we?"

With Company E stalled on the east slope of the escarpment, Company F attempted a broad flanking attack. Two of its platoons on the line, supported by tanks, pushed through Tanabaru and knocked out hastily established defenses. Beyond the town the company drew heavy fire from numerous caves, and it spent the rest of the day destroying the Japanese in these positions. Company E thereupon took over the burden of the attack, and by 1730 it had reached the top of Tanabaru Escarpment behind a mortar preparation. This move enabled the 1st Battalion to transfer its vehicles and supplies to a safer location, but the supply route was still blocked.

Early in the morning of 6 May a force of Japanese just below Company E pressed in on the Americans with grenades and satchel charges. After suffering sixteen casualties in half an hour, Company E retreated off the top to a protected ledge just below. Here the survivors formed a line and bombarded the top of the hill with grenades to deny it to the enemy. While some members of the company hauled new boxes of grenades up the steep trail, the others lobbed several hundred grenades on the Japanese, who withdrew from the exposed top at dawn.

Company F returned to Tanabaru the same morning for a second sweep through the town and killed eight Japanese. Supported by mortar fire and aided by small-arms fire from Company E, Company F initially made rapid progress on the slope but then ran into a series of coral outcroppings. With portable flame throwers, mortar fire, and quantities of grenades, the troops eliminated all resistance on the slope by evening.

On the following day, Company F attacked the crest of Tanabaru Escarpment from the west behind mortar fire and quickly gained the top. Trenches were littered with Japanese dead, most of them killed by 81-mm. mortar fire. The amount of Japanese and American equipment found on the escarpment explained the ability of the enemy to hold out so tenaciously. Enemy equipment included one 75-mm. pack howitzer with ammunition, 2 heavy machine guns, 6 light machine guns, 2 knee mortars, 3 magnetic mines, and a large quantity of ammunition. Their American weapons consisted of 1 light machine gun, 2 BAR's, 3 carbines, and 3 Tommy guns. A total of 462 Japanese were killed in the area of Tanabaru during the 3-day battle, most of them on the escarpment and others as they tried to make their way back to their lines.[27]

Failure of the Offensive

By midnight of 5 May it was clear to General Ushijima that the offensive had failed. He had suffered tremendous casualties and had made no headway except in the Tanabaru area. Even there his troops were being compressed. General Ushijima realized that he must revert to defensive warfare. "The Army will temporarily halt its offensive," he ordered, "because of the opportunity offered by the painful blows against the enemy. . . . The battle plan in the Shuri area sector will be an attrition of enemy strength until he has lost his endurance. The 24th Division . . . will shift to a holding basis."[28]

Despite Ushijima's bravado, *32d Army Headquarters* was sunk in gloom over the failure of the offensive. During the day Ushijima called Colonel Yahara to his office and declared with tears in his eyes that henceforth he would be guided by Yahara's opinions. Yahara felt that the battle had been the decisive event of the campaign. Even General Cho, who was considered by many officers to be the incarnation of the fighting will of the Japanese Army, gave up hope

[27] XXIV Corps G–3 Periodic Rpt No. 37, 7 May 45; 7th Div G–2 Periodic Rpt No. 37, 7 May 45.
[28] Tenth Army Transl No. 243, 7 Jul 45.

for victory and said that defeat was only a matter of time. This pessimism was reflected down the line. One Japanese lieutenant wrote in his diary, "We realized that we were doomed when we heard of the failure of the 24th Division." [29]

The Japanese lost in the attack approximately 5,000 troops, including those killed in the counterlandings. The *24th Division* was greatly reduced in strength. On 5 May the combat strength of its *32d Regiment* was down to 30 percent; two battalions of the *32d* were at 15 percent. The *27th Tank Regiment* never fought as a mobile unit again; its six remaining medium tanks were converted to stationary artillery and pillboxes northwest of Shuri. Japanese artillery and shipping engineers also went into decline. The *44th Independent Mixed Brigade* was still intact, however, for it had not been committed after it became apparent that the *24th Division* would be unable to break through. [30]

American casualties during the enemy offensive were heavy. On 4 May 335 were killed or wounded, excluding 352 casualties of the 1st Marine Division, which was not involved in the enemy ground attack. On 5 May the two divisions hit hardest by the counterattack and penetration, the 7th and 77th, suffered 379 casualties. These losses are comparable to those previously incurred during the heaviest fighting in the Kakazu Ridge struggles and in the first few days of the general attack starting 19 April. [31]

Notwithstanding their heavy losses during the Japanese offensive, the Americans, in general, suffered less from Cho's aggressive tactics than from Yahara's defensive methods. The 1st Marine Division, for example, which was barely touched by the Japanese offensive on 4 May, had more casualties on that date than the two other divisions of the Corps combined; most of the losses had been suffered in making an attack west of Machinato airfield against strong enemy defenses. Colonel Yahara had hoped to exact such losses for every small advance by the Americans across the entire line week after week. The Japanese counteroffensive of 4–5 May showed the superiority of Yahara's tactics to Cho's. Overambitiously conceived and ineptly executed, the offensive was a colossal blunder.

The Americans Resume the Offensive

The XXIV Corps now resumed its attack, which in several sectors of the front had hardly been interrupted by the Japanese offensive. Because the Jap-

---

[29] Interrog Yahara; Interrog Shimada; Tenth Army G–2 Weekly Summary, 15 Aug 45.
[30] Appleman, XXIV Corps History, p. 326; 77th Div G–2 Rpt No. 51, 16 May 45.
[31] Appleman, XXIV Corps History, p. 324.

anese had used almost all their fresh reserves in the counterattack, General Buckner could feel confident of the launching sometime in May of a general attack on the Shuri defenses. On 7 May General Hodge ordered that preparatory to this coordinated Tenth Army attack the advance was to continue to the Asa–Dakeshi–Gaja line, to be seized by the evening of 8 May. Upon reaching this line, "a bare minimum," the attack was to continue in order to gain as much ground as possible for later offensive action.[32]

After the failure of their offensive, the Japanese turned all their energies toward waging a prolonged battle of attrition. Their losses did not impair immediately their defensive capacities; thus the XXIV Corps found no weak point in the Shuri defenses resulting from the ill-starred offensive. By throwing fresh troops into the attack of 4 May Ushijima had been able to maintain his strength all along the line. Nor was there any breakdown in his command and staff operation. Front-line units were reorganized without seeming loss of effectiveness; available reinforcements were carefully allotted to existing regiments; local counterattacks were timed for maximum effect.[33]

General Ushijima's chief task now was to keep sufficient combat troops at the front to man his Shuri defenses. It was apparent by 7 May that the strength of the remaining regular infantry was not great enough for this task. Consequently, Ushijima converted service units into infantry combat groups. By mixing service troops with the "regulars," he exacted from them their maximum combat effectiveness. "One man in ten will continue with his rear-echelon duties. The remaining nine men will devote themselves to antitank combat training," one order stated.[34]

The reorganization of the *32d Regiment, 24th Division,* was typical of the resourcefulness of the Japanese. The regimental headquarters received 5 men from the *24th Transport Regiment.* The *1st Battalion* kept its own surviving members and was allotted all the survivors of the *2d Battalion,* 20 men from the *7th Shipping Depot,* 90 from the *24th Transport Regiment,* and 9 from the *26th Sea Raiding Squadron.* The *2d Battalion* was totally reconstituted from the *29th Independent Infantry Battalion* and other units. The *3d Battalion* was reorganized in a manner similar to that used with the *1st.* It was by this process of piecing units together that the *32d Army* was able to stay intact long after the original

---

[32] XXIV Corps FO No. 49, 7 May 45.

[33] Gugeler, 7th Div History, p. 269; 96th Div G–2 Periodic Rpt No. 43, 14 May 45.

[34] XXIV Corps G–2 Transl Batch No. 473, Sec. 1, 1 Jun 45.

combat units had been virtually destroyed—a capability which at the time American intelligence officers found "baffling." [35]

After his offensive failed, the enemy formed a line in which the relative position of the major units was to remain roughly the same until the end of the battle. On the east the *24th Division,* reinforced by two independent battalions, held the line as far as Shuri, with its *89th Regiment* on the east, its *22d* in the center, and its *32d* on the west. The remnants of the battered *62d Division* were stretched from a point north of Shuri almost to the west coast, holding about one-third of the line. Along the Asa River estuary was a battalion of the *44th Independent Mixed Brigade.* [36]

The Japanese husbanded their remaining heavy weapons, especially their artillery, as carefully as they meted out their manpower. On 6 May the Japanese *5th Artillery Command* directed its units to "revert to the [defensive] situation which held prior to the attack situation of 3 May." Once again the protection of individual pieces was a cardinal feature of enemy operations. Artillery units were ordered to "use ammunition with the utmost economy" and to "wait and fire for effect against vital targets." [37]

Marines Fight for Hill 60

Turning east to seize the high ground that dominated the Asa River estuary, the 1st Marines on 6 May drove toward Hill 60, a small hump one-half mile southeast of Yafusu. (See Map No. XXXIV.) The mission was an extremely difficult one. Hill 60 was commanded by Japanese fire from Dakeshi Plateau and Ridge, Wana Ridge, and high ground south of the Asa River. Moreover, Nan Hill, a hillock 200 yards north of Hill 60 from which the attack was to be supported, was not yet wholly in Marine hands. In a classic demonstration of reverse-slope tactics, the Japanese had relinquished the crest and northern slope of Nan to the Americans but still held numerous caves on the southern slope as well as tunnels underground. Men of the 2d Battalion, 1st Marines, had to ward off incessant forays on Nan during the night; some of them were bayoneted or knifed to death in their foxholes. [38]

The 2d Battalion attacked Hill 60 at 1000 on 6 May, supported by mortar, artillery, and naval fire. The Japanese dug in on the reverse slope of Nan

[35] Appleman, XXIV Corps History, pp. 335–37; XXIV Corps G–2 Summary No. 9, 15 May 45.

[36] XXIV Corps G–2 Summary No. 9, 15 May 45; 96th Div G–2 Periodic Rpt No. 46, 17 May 45.

[37] XXIV Corps G–2 Transl Batch No. 502, Item 1, 6 Jun 45.

[38] The account of operations of the Marines on Nan Hill and Hill 60 is taken from Stockman, *1st Mar Div History.*

ATTACKS ON HILL 60 *by marines developed into a tank, flame, and demolitions battle. Above, tank-infantry team attacks northwest slope of Hill 60. Below, marines await result of a blasting charge, prepared to pick off any Japanese who might attempt escape.*

opened up on the attackers from their flank and rear. The Marine platoons quickly lost contact with one another and left a trail of casualties in their wake. Tanks met Japanese mortar and 47-mm. fire as soon as they moved onto open ground; two were destroyed and left burning and another disabled, after receiving a total of ten hits. One platoon reached the crest of Hill 60, only to come under a holocaust of grenades, satchel charges, white phosphorus shells, and knee mortar shells. Marines on Nan Hill were unable to move off to support the attack because of the Japanese just below them. At 1227, after the marines on Hill 60 had suffered thirty-five casualties without consolidating their position, the 2d Battalion commander ordered them to withdraw.

Next day a second attack on Hill 60 by the 2d Battalion was equally unsuccessful. Although four battalions of artillery, a fire support ship, and 81-mm. and 60-mm. mortars put concentrated fire on the slopes and crest of Hill 60, the marines who gained the top again came under concentrated enemy fire. The fighting was at such close range that it was impossible to keep enough grenades on the line, and the marines used rifle butts against Japanese who tried to storm their position. One wounded sergeant directed his squad until the moment he died. The troops lost their hold at one point, then fought their way to the top again. But the continuing Japanese fire from the reverse slope of Nan Hill was the decisive factor, and at 1700 the marines pulled back after losing eight killed and thirty-seven wounded.

The 2d Battalion now redoubled its efforts to destroy enemy positions on Nan Hill. The marines found the task hazardous and often disheartening. Demolition charges placed in one cave sometimes blew out several other openings as well. Rushing for defilade during blasting, a marine might find himself in another part of a tunnel. In several instances caves were unsealed by Japanese digging out from the inside. But the work went steadily on. With relays of tanks and flame-thrower tanks, demolitions, and hundreds of gallons of napalm, the marines cleaned out Nan Hill by 9 May.

With Nan completely "processed," marines attacked Hill 60 again on 9 May. While the 1st Battalion assaulted the northwest portion of Dakeshi Plateau, the 2d Battalion moved on Hill 60. Careful coordination of tanks, infantry, and supporting weapons brought quick results, and by the end of the day Hill 60 was securely in Marine hands.

XXIV Corps Advances on the Left

After extensive patrolling during 5–6 May, the 184th Infantry, 7th Division, resumed its southward drive. The initial objective of Colonel Green, command-

ing officer, was Gaja Ridge, which had been won and lost on 2 May. On 7 May
this ridge was occupied with astonishing ease. A platoon-sized patrol having
operated freely along the tip of Gaja Ridge, infantrymen of the 3d Battalion
started across the flats southwest of Unaha in deployed formation and were in
place along the length of the ridge an hour later. The Japanese, who may well
have been surprised by the speed of the attack, brought in a few artillery rounds
but no small-arms fire.[39]

Further moves by the 184th into the western approaches of Conical Hill
were more difficult. One patrol, cut off by machine-gun fire and shelled by mortars, had to fight its way back. A drive into Kibara stalled at the very edge of the
town in the face of artillery and mortar fire. Mines in Kuhazu and Onaga prevented tanks from coming up in support. Infantry attacks on hills at the western
terminus of the flatlands were more successful. William Hill fell on 7 May; the
forward slope of Easy Hill, on the 8th.

During this period the chief obstacle to the 7th Division's advance was a
network of Japanese positions around Kochi Ridge and Zebra Hill just south
of the town of Kochi. Previous attacks had demonstrated that the defenses here
could not be overrun in a single attack but required a tedious, methodical destruction of individual enemy soldiers and positions. Any large-scale attack by the
17th Infantry, even though coordinated among battalions, was doomed to fail
because of the combined fire power of enemy positions stretching from Shuri
to Conical Hill—a volume of fire greater than a regiment could control.

The struggle for the Kochi positions, which had started on 26 April, was
resumed after the Japanese counteroffensive failed. By 6 May the 3d Battalion,
17th Regiment, was fighting for Knob 2 on Kochi Ridge and was trying to
burn the Japanese out of the east side by rolling 10-gallon cans of napalm, gasoline, and motor oil over the top. On the same day two platoons of infantry seized
a small portion of How Hill but, contrary to orders, retreated in the face of
heavy fire from Kochi Ridge. At this point the 7th Division was under heavy
pressure from XXIV Corps to push more aggressively. Accordingly, Brig. Gen.
Joseph L. Ready, the assistant division commander, ordered Colonel Pachler's
17th Infantry to attack Zebra Hill on the next day, 7 May.

Tanks and infantry of the 3d Battalion moved out the next morning
through Kochi. Their initial objective was an enemy strong point in the road
cut between Zebra Hill and Kochi Ridge. This strong point formed the western

[39] The account of operations of the 7th Division from 5 to 10 May is taken from Gugeler, 7th Div
History, pp. 264–85.

AMERICAN ADVANCE DOWN THE CENTER *of the line, 77th Division sector, was slow and costly. Every knob of ground was fortified and fanatically defended. This photograph, taken from an artillery spotting plane 6 May, shows American tanks burning out a strong point on the edge of a village.*

anchor of the Japanese line running toward Kibara, from which the Japanese *22d Regiment* was ordered on 7 May "to exact as heavy a toll of the enemy as possible." [40] Heavy artillery fire held up the infantry, but the tanks plunged through Kochi to the west end of the road cut, and the troops followed as soon as the artillery slackened off. The strong point was a cave in the north side of the cut. Japanese fire from Knob 4 and neighboring heights, combined with the steep walls of the narrow passage, made this position almost inaccessible. Tanks poured flame and shells into the road cut, but when they prepared to return for resupply the enemy on Knob 4 opened up on the troops. After exchanging fire with the Japanese until midafternoon, the 3d Battalion withdrew.

Meanwhile the 1st Battalion again seized How Hill and gained more ground on Kochi. Rain began on the afternoon of the 7th and continued into the next day, but the tired men of the 17th Infantry did not give up the attack. The platoon of 2d Lt. William T. Coburn, who had joined Company G nine days before as a replacement, followed him to Knob 4 but was soon driven back by mortars and machine guns. Infuriated by the loss of two men killed and three wounded, Coburn and S/Sgt. George Hills returned to Knob 4 and hurled grenades at an enemy mortar crew in the road cut below. Although a mortar shell had severely wounded Hills, he and Coburn killed the Japanese in the cut.

By 9 May, when the 17th was relieved by the 382d Infantry, 96th Division, the hold of the Americans on Kochi was almost complete. A straight and firm regimental line ran from How Hill to the crest of Kochi Ridge and thence to the southern end of Kochi town. However, the cave in the road cut, as well as all of Zebra Hill, was still in enemy hands. On 9 May the battalion of the Japanese *22d Regiment* which had held this area for three days was relieved by other units and commended by the regimental commander for "inflicting heavy casualties on the enemy." [41]

Inching Along in the Center

In the very center of the island the 77th Division, after taking Maeda Escarpment, made step-by-step advances along Route 5 in its advance on Shuri. General Bruce used all weapons available, including air strikes, naval gunfire, and 8-inch howitzers, only to find the enemy still capable of putting up a fierce fight when the infantry and tanks moved up. The troops made use of seesaw tactics by which heavy weapons softened up a small area, permitting troops to

[40] 96th Div G–2 Periodic Rpt No. 47, 18 May 45.
[41] *Ibid.*

extend a salient from which they could support a similar effort in the adjoining sector. Nevertheless, progress was agonizingly slow.

The 5th Marines, 1st Marine Division, on the right (west) of the 77th, met equally stout resistance. The enemy positions to the immediate front of this regiment were organized around an area of rough ground known later as Awacha Pocket, northeast of Dakeshi and south of the town of Awacha. Here again the close teamwork of tanks and infantry, supported by heavy weapons, provided the only means of advance. Encircling this pocket required a week and was not finally accomplished until 11 May. By that time the marines had uncovered even more formidable positions to the south.

By 11 May XXIV Corps, though still far from the minimum line set by General Hodge, had eliminated many Japanese positions in preparation for the full-scale attack that was to follow. The week of 3–10 May had been one of general consolidation of the line that ran from Ouki on the east coast to Asa-Kawa on the west. At the expense of more than 20,000 casualties, including nonbattle,[42] the American forces on the Shuri line had extended their line at Maeda, Kochi, and Awacha, thus making their lines of communication more secure and gaining more favorable terrain for the Tenth Army attack scheduled for 11 May.

---

[42] XXIV Corps G–3 Periodic Rpt No. 41, 11 May 45. The figure cited in the text is only approximate because 1st Marine Division losses during 7–10 May were estimated on the basis of previous losses during 30 April–6 May, when the division was under XXIV Corps.

CHAPTER XIII

The May Attack on the Shuri Defenses

Although by 10 May the American troops were still short of the line set by Tenth Army as the point of departure for a general offensive, there was no time to spare in launching this offensive. Admiral Turner was somewhat impatient because of the heavy naval losses, particularly in picket ships. On 4 May Brig. Gen. Elwyn Post, Tenth Army Chief of Staff, had declared that the situation was serious and that immediate action was imperative.[1] After the failure of the Japanese offensive, General Buckner felt that the moment was opportune because the enemy had used almost all his fresh reserves in the counterattack; both his divisions were in the front lines and the *44th Independent Mixed Brigade* also had been partly committed.[2] Accordingly, General Buckner on 9 May ordered a coordinated Tenth Army attack for the 11th.

With both corps now on the line, Tenth Army on 7 May assumed direct control of operations on the southern front for the first time. By 11 May the III Amphibious Corps in the north (consisting of the 6th Marine Division and Corps troops) had been relieved by the 27th Division and had moved into position on the right of the southern front. The Corps assumed control again of the 1st Marine Division, which had been attached to XXIV Corps since the latter part of April. The XXIV Corps' zone of action now extended eastward from the 1st Marine Division boundary to Yonabaru. From west to east, the 6th Marine Division, the 1st Marine Division, the 77th, and the 96th occupied successive positions on the line. The 7th Division was in XXIV Corps reserve, enjoying a period of rest and rehabilitation.

The plan of attack called for Tenth Army to renew the assault on the Shuri defenses with its two corps abreast, III Amphibious Corps on the right, XXIV Corps on the left. The initial scheme of maneuver was an envelopment of Shuri by the Marine divisions on the west and the Army divisions on the east, while a

---

[1] Notes on Tenth Army staff meeting, 4 May 45, in Okinawa Diary kept by Stevens and Burns, entry 4 May 45.

[2] Tenth Army G-3 Jnl, outgoing Msg No. 7, 3 May 45; Opns Ord 7-45, 5 May 45; XXIV Corps FO No. 50, 9 May 45; interv 1st I & H Off with Gen Buckner, 10 May 45.

strong holding attack was maintained in the center.[3] The Tenth Army staff believed that the Japanese positions were weaker on the right and that the fresh Marine divisions had a chance for a quick break-through on that flank. Moreover, the terrain was more favorable along the western coast. The wide flanking maneuver around Shuri that later developed was not projected in the original plans. General Buckner explained on 10 May that there would be nothing spectacular. He added:

It will be a continuation of the type of attack we have been employing to date. Where we cannot take strong points we will pinch them off and leave them for the reserves to reduce. We have ample firepower and we also have enough fresh troops so that we can always have one division resting.[4]

The initial order for the attack provided for a 30-minute general preparation by the artillery just before the ground attack. This provision was revoked two days later in favor of pinpointing of targets. The new order stated that "the maximum practicable number of known enemy guns and strong points will be destroyed or neutralized" prior to the infantry assault. This change resulted, in all probability, from recognition of the failure of the mass preparation for the attack of 19 April. The elaborate system of Japanese underground positions across the entire front made it necessary to use precision fire, hitting each cave entrance.[5]

In preparation for a renewed American attack the Japanese bolstered their Shuri defenses. Ready at last to commit almost all his reserves to action, General Ushijima ordered that "the Army will immediately move its main strength into the Shuri area." He established a central defense zone with his front lines running from a point north of Asato on the west coast, through Wana and the high ground near Ishimmi, to the east coast just north of Conical Hill. Aware of the entrance of the 6th Marine Division on the west, he shifted his forces

[3] Tenth Army Opns Ord 8–45, 7 May 45; interv 1st I & H Off with Brig Gen Walter A. Dumas, ACofS, G–3, Tenth Army, 9 Jul 45. There is still some question as to the precise scheme of maneuver. The Tenth Army operation plan overlay, which according to the text of the plan was to show the scheme of maneuver more precisely than the order itself, indicated a very close envelopment of Shuri by the two divisions immediately north of the Japanese headquarters city. The XXIV Corps field order indicated pressure across the line by both its divisions rather than major effort near the center of the Army line. Despite the scheme of maneuver outlined on the Tenth Army overlay, it seems that the actual plan was for uniform pressure across the line which would crack the Japanese defenses at some point and be immediately exploited wherever the particular break might come.

[4] Interv 1st I & H Off with Gen Buckner, 10 May 45.

[5] Change No. 1, to Tenth Army Opns Ord 8–45, 9 May 45; interv XXIV Corps Hist Off with Brig Gen Josef R. Sheetz, CG XXIV Corps Arty, 23 Jun 45.

for an iron defense on both his flanks. General Ushijima ordered roads and bridges to be destroyed east of Naha. His continued fear of an attack behind Japanese lines by American parachute troops, however, restrained him from bringing all available forces up to the front.[6]

The attack launched on 11 May, although coordinated initially along the entire front, soon broke down into a series of intense battles for particular points with the western, central, and eastern sectors presenting relatively distinct situations. At many places the American efforts were merely an intensification of assaults that had begun on previous days. For ten days of continuous fighting, from Sugar Loaf on the west coast to Conical Hill on the east, the Japanese, except for local and relatively minor retreats, held tenaciously to their long-prepared positions. Finally, on 21 May, after some of the bitterest action of the battle of Okinawa, the American forces were to seize the eastern slope of Conical Hill, close to the east coast, and thereby to make an opening in the enemy lines which permitted an attempt at envelopment.

The Attack in the West

On 8 May the 22d Marines, 6th Marine Division, relieved the 7th Marines, 1st Marine Division, on the bluffs north of the Asa River. The enemy held positions south of the Asa, which was too deep to ford at the mouth and which had a bottom too soft to support any type of vehicle. The enemy-held ground rose gently to the horizon 2,000 yards away. To the west barren coral ridges formed a barrier to the sea; to the south a long clay ridge dominated the road to Naha; to the southeast a group of low grassy hills, set close together, commanded the ground between the Asa River basin and the Asato River corridor. On the east were the rough folds of Dakeshi Ridge, Wana Ridge, and Wana Draw, positions toward which the 1st Marine Division was driving.[7] (See Map No. XXXV.)

Maj. Gen. Lemuel C. Shepherd, Jr., commander of the 6th Marine Division, had warned his troops that the battle in southern Okinawa would be different from anything they had previously encountered in the Pacific. In a training order read twice by every platoon leader to his men, he described the enemy's intel-

---

[6] Tenth Army Transl No. 294, 10 Jul 45: *32d Army* Ord No. A 10, 11 May 45; Transl No. 176, 21 Jun 45: *32d Army* Ord No. A 23, 14 May 45; Transl No. 300, 10 Jul 45: *32d Army* Ord No. A 19, 12 May 45; Interrog Shimada.

[7] The account of operations of the 6th Marine Division is taken from Carleton, 6th Mar Div History, Ch. II, supplemented and corrected by III Amph Corps G–3 Periodic Rpts for the period and 6th Mar Div Actn Rpt, a detailed and well-balanced narrative.

ligent use of artillery, his ample supplies, his defensive line "which cannot be breached by simple frontal attack without heavy losses," and his willingness to counterattack by every available means. General Shepherd urged his commanders and troops to take advantage of cover and camouflage, to use maneuver in outflanking the Japanese rather than to try to "outslug" them, and to keep driving. "Your enemy can't think as fast as you can and he is no match for a determined aggressive Marine who has confidence in himself and his weapon." [8]

6th Marine Division Advances in the West

The 22d Marines began crossing the Asa estuary in the early hours of 10 May over a footbridge completed during the night. An enemy suicide squad destroyed the bridge with satchel charges after the first three companies had crossed, but other marines reached the south bank by wading. During the morning the troops advanced into the town of Asa against steadily increasing resistance. Movement west of the town was difficult in the confusion caused by heavy fog and smoke. Direct fire from self-propelled 105-mm. howitzers and LVT's supported the attack. Despite heavy enemy artillery fire and strong local counterattacks on the infantry, the 22d Marines had established by dark a "beachhead" 350 yards deep and almost a mile wide. (See Map No. XXXIV.)

The Drive Along the Coast

During the night of 10–11 May the 6th Marine Division engineers, working under fire, laid across the Asa a Bailey bridge which enabled tanks and other heavy weapons to support the attack. The marines advanced under almost continual artillery fire delivered from the western face of Shuri Heights, where the enemy had excellent observation of the coastal area. Japanese infantry opposition was well coordinated with this fire. A company commander of the 1st Battalion, 22d Marines, led a squad up to the summit of a strongly defended hill 800 yards south of Asa, but all his troops were killed or wounded in the assault except the flame-thrower man. A concentration from the main battery of a fire support ship broke loose great blocks of coral from the top of the hill and rolled them down the face, but without much damage to Japanese positions. An infantry charge by Company C, closely supported by tanks, finally won the hill. Although Company C was now reduced to eighty men, the marines clung to the hill in the face of counterattacks.

On the regimental right (west) the 3d Battalion seized a cliff on the coast north of the town of Amike by a tank-infantry-flame-thrower assault late in

[8] 6th Mar Div Tng Ord No. 23–45, 6 May 45, cited in Carleton, 6th Mar Div History, Ch. II, pp. 5–7.

HILL 45 AMIKE NAHA HWY ONE

ASATO GAWA

ASA TOWN

BAILEY BRIDGE
ERECTED HERE

ASA RIVER

WEST FLANK ZONE, *where the 22d Marines, 6th Division, crossed Asa River toward Naha. (Photo taken 5 May 1945.)*

KOKUBA

←SHURI (1 MILE) ←— RAILROAD —→

NAHA —→

MACHISHI

SUGAR LOAF

HORSE SHOE

SUGAR LOAF AND HORSESHOE HILLS, *photographed after the battle had moved on into Machishi and almost to Naha. Between Sugar Loaf and the hillock in foreground, where Marine attack centered, 10 knocked-out American armored vehicles can be seen.*

the afternoon. This advance placed the Marines on the northern outskirts of Amike overlooking the devastated city of Naha, capital of the Ryukyus. Had this city, the largest in the islands, been the objective of Tenth Army the 6th Marine Division would have held an excellent position from which to capture it. Since Naha was not their objective, however, the marines who reached the north bank of the Asato near its mouth simply consolidated their position during the next two weeks, sending patrols into Naha, while the marines to the east continued to press in on the flank of Shuri.

Progress of the other troops of the 22d Marines during 12 and 13 May was slow. The 1st and 2d Battalions were now moving into the rough ground a mile east of Amike—ground which the Japanese had been ordered to hold as a key point in the defense of Shuri. This area was occupied by the *15th Independent Mixed Regiment, 44th Independent Mixed Brigade,* supported by the *7th Independent Antitank Battalion,* a Navy mortar company, and an independent battalion of approximately 700 men formed from a *Sea Raiding Base Battalion.* These forces were well supplied with light mortars, machine guns, and light arms. As the battle developed, reinforcements streamed in from the rest of the *44th Brigade.*[9]

Closing In on Sugar Loaf, 12–13 May

The first encounter of the Marines with the Japanese guarding Sugar Loaf came on 12 May, almost inadvertently. Company G, 22d Marines, advanced southeast with eleven tanks toward the Asato River. Heading directly toward Sugar Loaf, which was known to be a strong point, the infantry and tanks met increasing rifle fire but pushed ahead. When the Marines reached Sugar Loaf, a number of Japanese soldiers fled from their positions. It was not clear whether this action was a ruse or resulted from panic at the sudden arrival of the Americans. Four men on the crest of Sugar Loaf and the company commander frantically radioed battalion for reinforcements. Because of his many casualties, the commander was ordered to withdraw. As the Americans withdrew, the enemy opened up with heavy fire. Three tanks were quickly knocked out. Slowly the troops pulled back, suffering more casualties in the process. By evening Company G's total strength was down to seventy-five.

The 6th Marine Division now planned an attack in force on the Sugar Loaf area. The hills there were so small that they did not show up on the

---

[9] Tenth Army PW Interrog Summary No. 4, 1 Aug 45: *44th Independent Mixed Brigade*, p. 4.

standard military map with its 10-meter contour interval. Sugar Loaf and the other hills supporting it were formed in such a way, however, as to offer exceptionally advantageous positions to the enemy. The crest, running generally east-west, curved back slightly at each end, affording the Japanese weapons on the reverse slope excellent protection from American flanking fire as well as from frontal attack. Supporting Sugar Loaf on its right rear was Crescent Hill, also known as Half Moon Hill; on its left rear was the Horseshoe, a long curved ridge harboring many mortar positions. These three hills supported one another, and any attack on Sugar Loaf would bring fire from the others. The Japanese here had excellent fields of fire to the northwest, obstructed only slightly by several tiny humps of ground which had their own reverse-slope defenses. Japanese on Shuri Heights commanded most of the ground.[10]

On the morning of 13 May the 3d Battalion, 29th Marines, entered the battle east of the 22d Marines. The day was spent in slow costly moves in an effort to seize the high ground overlooking the upper reaches of the Asato. The Marines made advances of several hundred yards on the division left, but resistance steadily increased. By the evening of 13 May the 6th Marine Division had committed the 29th Regiment for a renewed attack. Supporting aircraft made many sorties during 13 May against artillery positions, buildings, and storage areas, using rockets and hundreds of 100- and 500-pound bombs. One battleship, four cruisers, and three destroyers also supported the attack. This heavy fire power was available to the ground troops throughout the attacks.

The enemy's skillful use of his remaining artillery greatly handicapped the Marine advance from the Asa to the Asato. Artillery of the *44th Brigade* consisted of eight 100-mm. howitzers and four mountain guns, and these were supplemented from time to time by artillery and heavy mortars of adjacent units. Having excellent observation, the Japanese used their weapons singly or in pairs with great precision against marines and tanks. On one occasion a shell landed squarely amid several men at an observation point; the commander of the 1st Battalion, 22d Marines, 3 radio men, and 2 tank officers were killed, and 3 company commanders were wounded.

"Banzai Attack" on Sugar Loaf, 14-15 May

The plan for 14 May called for the 2d Battalion, 22d Marines, commanded by Lt. Col. Horatio C. Woodhouse, to seize high ground west and north of

---

[10] Personal obsn of Lt Col John Stevens, Tenth Army historian, and Maj Roy Appleman, XXIV Corps historian.

Sugar Loaf, and from this ground to launch an assault against Sugar Loaf. (See Map No. XXXVI.) The marines were able to seize the forward slopes of the protecting hills north of Sugar Loaf, but intense fire met them whenever they tried to move around or over these hills. Of fifty men who made an attempt to advance, only ten returned, and most of the morning was spent in evacuating casualties on amtracks. Nevertheless, the marines launched a successful attack on Queen Hill which protected Sugar Loaf to the north. The first attack on Sugar Loaf stalled under heavy fire. One platoon, consolidated from the remnants of two platoons, made another attempt at dusk. By 2000 the platoon leader was dead and most of the platoon had been killed or wounded as a result of intense mortar fire, but the survivors clung to the slope. The executive officer of the 2d Battalion then rallied the available members of Company G, 22d Marines, numbering twenty, and twenty-six marines from supply elements for an attempt to reinforce the survivors. He and his men moved across the little valley and advanced up the slopes of Sugar Loaf. About forty feet up the hill they set up two machine guns with fire teams to support each. Twenty replacements arrived from the shore party with two officers who had never seen combat. Grenades and knee mortar shells were falling among the troops so heavily that the executive officer moved his force to the crest of the hill. "The only way," he declared, "we can take the top of this hill is to make a Jap banzai charge ourselves."

The small Marine force on Sugar Loaf was now so close to the reverse slope that the enemy could not effectively throw grenades, but the mortar shelling increased. The executive officer, crouching in his foxhole, was killed instantly when a fragment hit him in the neck. One of the platoon leaders on the hill was also killed, and another was wounded as he was bringing up reinforcements. Four or five men grouped together for a moment froze as a shell dropped among them.

Mortar fire and infiltration steadily cut down the small force, until at dawn on 15 May the position on Sugar Loaf was held by only one officer and nineteen exhausted men. Daylight made the situation even more precarious, for now the enemy entrenched on the Horseshoe and on Crescent Hill could put accurate fire on the Americans. Orders arrived from Battalion at 1000 stating that relief was on the way. The marines had already given some ground; the enemy was now massing fire on the crest and Japanese infantrymen were creeping up the hill from their caves on the reverse slope. The relief was exceptionally difficult because of the heavy fire. A platoon of Company D, 29th Marines, attempting to reach the crest, quickly discovered that an effective relief would require an attack against the Japanese who were trying to retake the crest of the hill. The platoon leader, 1st Lt. George Murphy, ordered an assault with fixed bayonets. The marines reached the top and immediately became involved in a grenade battle with the enemy. Their supply of 350 grenades was soon exhausted. Lieutenant Murphy asked his company commander, Capt. Howard L. Mabie, for permission to withdraw, but Captain Mabie ordered him to hold the hill at all costs. By now the whole forward slope of Sugar Loaf was alive with gray eddies of smoke from mortar blasts, and Murphy ordered a withdrawal on his own initiative. Covering the men as they pulled back down the slope, Murphy was killed by a fragment when he paused to help a wounded marine.

Captain Mabie advanced his company to protect the survivors as they withdrew. He at the same time notified Colonel Woodhouse: "Request permission to withdraw. Irish George Murphy has been hit. Has 11 men left in platoon of original 60."

Two minutes later Colonel Woodhouse replied: "You must hold."

In five minutes the answer came from Mabie: "Platoon has withdrawn. Position was untenable. Could not evacuate wounded. Believe Japs now hold ridge."

By now the Japanese were shelling the area around Sugar Loaf and were attacking the left sector of the 6th Marine Division in at least battalion strength. By midmorning the enemy effort had spread over a 900-yard front. As a result of the bitter fighting for Sugar Loaf and in front of Crescent Hill the entire left sector of the division was weak. The 2d Battalion gave up the ground immediately north of Sugar Loaf, but the enemy did not press through with his advantage. By 1315 his attack had lost momentum. Later in the day the 2d Battalion, 22d Marines, was withdrawn from the action; it had suffered 400 casualties during the preceding three days.

Attacks on Sugar Loaf Continue, 16–17 May

Another attack, more heavily supported, was made on 16 May, but this was also a failure. (See Map No. XXXVII.) At 0800 five companies on a 1,000-yard front advanced on the Sugar Loaf–Crescent Hill area. Affairs went badly from the beginning. Support planes were half an hour late, delaying the attack, and several tanks lost their way in the approach. Two platoons reached the crest of Sugar Loaf after moving up the steep north slope under mortar, grenade, and automatic weapons fire. Immediately the difficulties of the previous days presented themselves again. The Japanese on the reverse slope could not be dislodged by mortar or artillery fire; tanks were unable to creep around the west slope of Sugar Loaf because of antitank fire from several directions; and infantrymen accompanying the tanks were helpless under that fire. The integration of the Japanese position was fully evident; marines on Sugar Loaf could not advance over the crest because of fire from adjacent hills; marines fighting for those hills were held up by fire from Sugar Loaf. Maneuver was impossible. After savage close-in fighting around the crest of Sugar Loaf, the marines withdrew to their positions of the previous night.

The veterans of the 6th Marine Division who fought in this action later called 16 May their bitterest day of fighting during the Okinawa campaign. Two regiments had attacked with all their available strength and had failed. Intelligence officers reported that the Sugar Loaf defenses had been greatly strengthened in the previous twenty-four hours. Marine casualties continued to be heavy.

The plan for 17 May called for a flanking attack on Sugar Loaf from the east. The 1st and 3d Battalions, 29th Marines, were to assault Crescent Hill, then to hold there and support the 2d Battalion, 29th Marines, in an attempt to seize Sugar Loaf. A heavy bombardment by 16-inch guns, howitzers, and planes carrying 1,000-pound bombs preceded the attack. At 0830 elements of the 1st and 3d Battalions attacked the western end of Crescent Hill. Tank-infantry teams supported by artillery destroyed many fortified positions. As this advance uncovered the east side of Sugar Loaf, Company E of the 2d Battalion began a flanking attack around the left of that key terrain feature.

While the attack on Crescent Hill was still going on, elements of the 2d Battalion moved toward Sugar Loaf. The first effort was a wide movement attempting to employ the railroad cut, but this proved unsuccessful because of fire received from the left. An attempt at a close flanking movement failed because of the precipitous slopes. Then, using the northeast slopes of the hill, two platoons of Company E gained the top. On reaching the crest the attacking force was struck by a heavy enemy charge which drove them back off the hilltop. A platoon of Company F also tried to advance along the ridge toward the west, but the leader was killed and the platoon withdrew under heavy mortar fire. Three times more Company E drove to the hilltop. Twice they were thrown back after hand-to-hand fighting. The third time the marines beat off the Japanese, but in doing so they exhausted their ammunition. The company was forced to withdraw, relinquishing the position for which 160 marines had been killed or wounded during the day.

Capture of Sugar Loaf, 18–19 May

Throughout the four seemingly fruitless days of battle for the Sugar Loaf area the tedious work of destroying Japanese positions had been proceeding everywhere in the area. Progress in this work steadily reduced the amount of fire which the Japanese could place on Sugar Loaf. On 18 May a skillful, coordinated attack by Company D, 29th Marines, took advantage of the progress of the past days and succeeded in reducing Sugar Loaf. (See Map No. XXXVIII.)

Captain Mabie, commanding Company D, maneuvered his company onto the edge of the low ground north of Sugar Loaf on the morning of the 18th. Artillery and mortars placed a heavy preparation on the objectives. Immediately afterward three tanks moved around the eastern slope of Sugar Loaf and fired into the reverse slope as the Japanese swarmed out of their caves to repel an expected attack. The tanks retired, shooting down two satchel teams that dashed out of caves. Then Captain Mabie opened up with a rocket barrage; trucks carrying rocket racks came over a saddle, loosed their missiles, and raced away to escape artillery fire. Field pieces opened up again as the troops moved forward.

One platoon climbed the west nose, peeling off fire teams to keep a continuous line from the base of the hill. Another platoon drove directly up the northeastern slope. The two parties reached the summit at about the same time, then moved on to destroy positions on the reverse slope. The position was secure by 0946. A few minutes later Captain Mabie received word to "send up the PX supplies." The rest of Company D soon followed to the crest. By noon the wounded had been evacuated and a line firmly established. Meanwhile Company F seized part of the Horseshoe, thereby decreasing fire from that point and enabling positions to be consolidated on the north slopes of Crescent Hill.

That night 60-mm. mortars of three companies on and behind Sugar Loaf shot up flares every two minutes to illuminate the area. At 2300 the marines heard yelling and jabbering southwest of Sugar Loaf, and enemy mortar fire increased. At 0230 the full force of a Japanese attack hit the marines on Horseshoe. Enemy troops along the road cut west of Sugar Loaf set up a machine gun that could enfilade the Marine lines. Marine machine gunners knocked out this gun, but the Japanese manned others. Two platoons pulled back to the forward (north) slope of Sugar Loaf, and fire teams, using their own reverse-slope tactics, killed thirty-three Japanese as small groups attempted to reoccupy the hill. The counterattack was stopped by dawn.

On the next day, 19 May, the 4th Marines relieved the exhausted 29th Marines. During the 10-day period up to and including the capture of Sugar

Loaf the 6th Marine Division had lost 2,662 killed or wounded; there were also 1,289 cases of combat fatigue. In the 22d and 29th Marines three battalion commanders and eleven company commanders had been killed or wounded. On 20 May the 4th Marines gained more of the Horseshoe but were still unable to reach the crest of Crescent Hill. An attack by an enemy force estimated as of battalion strength was repulsed by the combined fire of six artillery battalions and infantry weapons. Although forced to commit part of its regimental reserve, the 4th Marines broke up the attack and inflicted on the enemy more than 200 casualties.

On 21 May the 4th Marines continued the attack toward the Asato River line. Troops advanced 250 yards into the Horseshoe but were unable to complete the seizure of Crescent Hill because of intense enemy artillery and mortar fire. Much of this fire came from Shuri Heights. The next moves of the 6th Marine Division would depend on the outcome of the fierce struggle for those heights that was still being waged by the 1st Marine Division.

Attack of the 1st Marine Division on Shuri Heights

While the 6th Marine Division was advancing slowly toward the Asato River from 11 to 20 May, the 1st Marine Division was making vigorous efforts to seize Shuri Heights. The key Japanese positions in this area were built into Dakeshi Ridge, Wana Ridge, Wana Draw, and the towns of Dakeshi and Wana, all protecting Shuri on the northwest. Although other ground around Shuri was higher and even more precipitous, the term "Shuri Heights" was used by III Amphibious Corps to denote the Japanese positions in this area which afforded a view of almost the entire Marine front. (See Map No. XXXV.)

The ridges, draws, and ruins of Shuri Heights gave the enemy a perfect combination for his type of defensive warfare. Dakeshi Ridge, which the marines had reached by 10 May, had typical reverse-slope defenses supported by many positions in the town of Dakeshi. The Japanese had exploited this situation as fully as they had capitalized on the relationship of the town and ridge of Kakazu and on that of the town of Maeda and Urasoe-Mura Escarpment. Another ridge, Wana, lay directly south of the town of Dakeshi. West of these positions steep declivities of from 50 to 100 yards protected the Japanese against a flank attack from their left. South of Wana Ridge was Wana Draw, which began as a narrow, rocky defile just north of Shuri and widened out broadly to the west, giving its defenders a full view of the ground below.[11]

[11] Personal Obsn of Lt Col John Stevens, Tenth Army historian.

CRESCENT HILL *held out until 21 May. Troops of the 4th Marines, 6th Division, crossing open ground to Crescent were under constant observation and fire from Japanese positions on Shuri Heights to the east.*

FIGHTING AT SUGAR LOAF *cost the Americans many armored vehicles. They are shown wrecked and abandoned in this photo taken from a Japanese gun position after fall of Sugar Loaf 18 May.*

These positions in the Dakeshi–Wana area were considered by General Ushijima a vital sector of the Shuri perimeter, which his forces were to "hold without fail." The *62d Division,* which by 11 May had seen continuous action for five weeks, still held this area. The entire *11th Independent Infantry Battalion* and most of the *21st* and *23d Battalions* had been destroyed. Only 600 troops remained of the original division. General Ushijima transferred the survivors of the *64th Brigade* to the *63d Brigade* and reconstructed the latter by assigning to it airfield construction troops, a machine cannon unit, and a suicide boat group, bringing the *63d* up to a strength of 6,700. He bolstered the Dakeshi sector with elements of the *44th Brigade,* whom he ordered to defend the ridge to the last man.[12]

Capture of Dakeshi Ridge, 10–13 May

In the Tenth Army attack of 11 May the part played by the 7th Marines, 1st Marine Division, represented an intensification of the attack on Dakeshi Ridge begun on the previous day. The regimental attack of 10 May had been abortive. The enemy had put intense mortar and machine-gun fire on the attacking marines from his positions on and behind the long ridge. By nightfall the 7th Marines had been forced back to its original lines.[13]

The plan for 11 May was designed to take advantage of the natural formation of Dakeshi Ridge, which was shaped roughly like a horseshoe, with the prongs extending north along the boundaries of the 7th regimental sector. The bowl between the ends of the ridge was impassable because of enemy fire; the routes of attack were along the extensions of the ridge. The 2d Battalion attacked the western end of the ridge on the regimental right, while the 1st Battalion attacked on the left. Both battalions had to move over rough ground.

Using tank-infantry teams, the 1st Battalion slowly pushed up the eastern slope of Dakeshi under heavy enemy fire and reached the ridge line during the afternoon. The 2d Battalion also managed to reach the crest of the ridge in its sector but immediately came under intense fire from Wana Ridge directly to the south. It was impossible to continue the attack; a marine could hardly raise his head without receiving fire. Evacuating casualties was extremely difficult. When one marine was set on fire by a Japanese flame thrower, several of his comrades tried to cross open ground to put out the flames, but each one was

[12] Tenth Army Transl No. 176, 21 Jun 45: *32d Army* Ord No. A 23, 14 May 45; PW Interrog Summary No. 2, 2 Aug 45: *62d Division;* 96th Div G–2 Periodic Rpt No. 55, 26 May 45.

[13] The account of operations of the 1st Marine Division is based on Stockman, 1st Mar. Div History, and III Amph Corps G–3 Periodic Rpts for the period.

wounded in the attempt. The Americans were forced back a short distance but held most of their gains. The attacking company had lost its commander and every squad leader in the two assault platoons.

The 7th Marines extended its hold on Dakeshi during 12 May. The fighting in the 1st Battalion sector revolved around a pinnacle on the east end of Dakeshi Ridge. As usual, the enemy occupied the reverse slope in such favorable positions that flank or frontal assault attacks were virtually impossible. There was room enough only for a platoon to maneuver. Well supplied with grenades, four marines tried to occupy the pinnacle by stealth, but the attempt failed. After a 60-mm. mortar concentration, twelve marines assaulted the position only to find the enemy waiting unscathed; they pulled back under a hand-grenade barrage. Then demolitions men put 400 pounds of charges below the position. The blasting was an exciting spectacle to watch but ineffective.

There was still another trick in the Marine repertory, and this one worked. The platoon secured a medium tank and two flame-thrower tanks and directed them through the saddle on the right (west) of the pinnacle to a point where they could operate against the reverse slope. While the tank put 75-mm. shells and machine-gun fire into the enemy positions, the flame thrower sprayed fire over the whole slope. Immediately afterward the infantry assaulted the pinnacle and won it without much difficulty.

By nightfall the 7th Marines held firmly most of Dakeshi Ridge. Shortly before midnight the Japanese made a counterattack against the 2d Battalion on the ridge. This was the third counterattack against this regiment in as many nights. The Americans killed about forty of a force estimated as of company strength, including two Japanese officers with excellent maps of the area. Tank-infantry teams secured the rest of Dakeshi Ridge on the 13th.

A savage fight developed on 13 May when the 2d Battalion tried to move through the town of Dakeshi in preparation for an assault on Wana Ridge. Dakeshi was a network of tunnels, shafts, and caves—ideal for a large defending force. Snipers were among ruins, behind walls, and in cisterns and wells. The forward platoon was caught in the open by mortar and automatic fire from the front and both flanks. The radio broke down. Tanks and artillery supported the men and tried to screen them with smoke, but the Japanese crawled forward through the smoke and grenaded the platoon. One marine, wounded so badly that he begged to be shot, was being helped by two comrades when a grenade exploded among them, killing all three. The platoon pulled back after thirty-two of its original forty-nine had been killed or wounded.

DAKESHI RIDGE *was attacked by these tank-infantry teams of the 7th Marines, 1st Division, in attempting to reach the eastern slope. Below, 7th Marine troops closing in on a Japanese-held cave in Dakeshi Ridge hug the ground as an enemy mortar shell bursts on crest. Cave is in the depression to right of shell burst.*

On 14 May the 1st Battalion relieved the 2d Battalion, which had been in the attack for four days. On the next day the 1st Battalion consolidated ground already taken, and artillery, naval guns, and air strikes were directed against Japanese defenses on Shuri Heights. Wana Ridge was the next objective of the 1st Marine Division elements on the high ground. Operations against the ridge were to be coordinated with the fighting around Wana Draw.

The 1st Marines Advances on the Right

While the 7th Marines fought for Dakeshi Ridge during 10–13 May, the 1st Marines moved south along the rolling ground below Shuri Heights. After capturing Hill 60 on 9 May, the 1st Marines found its zone of action sloping downward and exposed to enemy observation and fire from Shuri Heights and from Hill 55, which was just below Wana Draw. Immediately before the regiment lay the low basin drained by the Asa River. On the marines' right the railroad from Naha ran along an embankment.

When the 1st Marines attempted to push past the western nose of Dakeshi Ridge on 10 and 11 May, fire from Shuri Heights was so severe that the advance stalled. Consequently the attack was reoriented, and the marines, giving Dakeshi Ridge a wide berth, advanced west of the railroad. Here the 1st Marines made good progress in coordination with the 6th Marine Division. The farther the troops advanced on the right, however, the greater was the difficulty in supplying the forward elements; all routes of approach were under fire. Japanese artillery shelled the area between Dakeshi Ridge and the railroad. On 12 May it was necessary to use air drops, but these were only partially successful because some of the parachutes drifted into areas under enemy fire.

The attack of the 1st Marines on 13 May was coordinated with the moves of the 7th Marines on Dakeshi Ridge. Artillery, naval guns, mortars, and 37-mm. guns pounded the areas in front of the marines. By noon the 3d Battalion was near Hill 55. This hill, forming part of the south wall of Wana Draw, presented to the marines a steep incline. Its defenses were well integrated with those of Wana Ridge and Draw. One company, supported by tanks, assaulted Hill 55 during the afternoon but was hit by heavy fire from the heights. Japanese machine guns, mortars, and 20-mm. automatic guns forced the company to withdraw under a smoke screen.

The plan for 14 May was an attack on Wana Ridge in coordination with the 7th Marines. Wana Ridge formed the northern wall of Wana Draw. The ridge, a long coral spine running out of the northern part of Shuri, was lined on both sides with fortified tombs, many of which looked out on the low ground below. The 1st Marines was a part of the way up the ridge by noon of the 14th, but was unable to make contact with the 7th Marines. The ridge seemed to be swarming with Japanese. Before dusk the enemy launched a counterattack which for a time threatened to cut off the forward company. The marines pulled back to lower ground under cover of smoke.

Fight for Wana Draw

The 5th Marine Regiment relieved the 1st Marines during the evening of 14 May. The plan now was to attack Wana Draw and the neighboring heights with all available weapons. Four self-propelled guns and twelve tanks for direct fire arrived on 16 May. The tanks, working in relays and escorted by infantry fire teams, moved into the low ground at the mouth of Wana Draw and began firing into the high ground. The enemy responded almost immediately with 47-mm. antitank fire, destroying two tanks; he also dropped in mortar shells to kill the accompanying infantry. The marines pulled back with their casualties. Observers, however, had spotted two of the Japanese antitank gun positions and main batteries of the *Colorado* destroyed both of them later in the afternoon.

The tanks and M–7's (self-propelled guns) continued to press up into Wana Draw. On the 17th the 2d Battalion attempted to storm Hill 55, but the attack was premature. Japanese machine guns and mortars in Wana Ridge stopped the infantry, and 47-mm. guns knocked out two tanks. The marines were able to hold only the west slope of the hill. On the next day tanks and self-propelled guns fired more than 7,000 rounds of 75 mm. and 105 mm. into the Japanese positions. Engineers with demolitions and flame throwers destroyed enemy weapons on the lower slopes of Wana Ridge.[14]

Naval guns, field artillery, tanks, and M–7's pounded Shuri Heights and Hill 55 as the marines moved to the crest of the hill on the morning of 20 May. The infantry destroyed some Japanese on the crest after a brief hand-to-hand encounter. Tank-infantry teams moved up into Wana Draw and with point-blank fire killed many Japanese dug in on the reverse slope of Hill 55. Seizure of this position made possible some further advances on the ground below Hill 55. Marines overran many spider traps manned by Japanese soldiers equipped with satchel charges. By 21 May the 1st Marine Division was attacking Shuri Ridge, the high barrier which was the last natural feature protecting Shuri Castle on the west.

[14] Some confusion had arisen as to the location of the town of Wana because the standard target map showed it on the southwest slopes of Wana Ridge. Study of the ground by historians indicated that the town actually may have been located southeast of Dakeshi and northeast of Wana Ridge.

Deadlock at Wana Ridge, 16–21 May

Despite the advances of the 5th Marines in the Wana Draw and Hill 55 area and the firm grip of the 7th Marines on Dakeshi Ridge, the Japanese continued to hold Wana Ridge. Their positions on this ridge overlooked both regimental sectors. On the 16th the 1st Battalion, 7th Marines, sent patrols to probe around the west nose of Wana Ridge. When infantrymen moved up behind the patrol, the Japanese launched a series of counterattacks which drove the marines back to the northern base of Wana Ridge.

After relieving the 1st Battalion on the morning of 17 May, the 3d Battalion attacked up Wana Ridge on three successive days; each time it was forced to fall back to its positions on the southern edge of Dakeshi town. The attackers were usually able to reach the top, but were subjected immediately to intense mortar and automatic fire from front and both flanks, making the crest untenable. On 19 May the 7th Marines was replaced by the 1st Marines. The 7th, which had lost more than 1,000 killed, wounded, and missing since 10 May, was later awarded the Presidential Unit Citation for its participation in the battle for Shuri Heights.

By the time the 1st Marines took over, progress in the Wana Draw–Hill 55 area was beginning to make itself felt in the Wana Ridge fighting. Tanks, M–7's, and artillery had been pounding the northern wall of Wana Draw, which was the reverse slope of Wana Ridge. Nevertheless, Japanese artillery and lighter weapons that were "zeroed in" on Wana Ridge from Shuri town still controlled the craggy ridge line. Some Japanese positions were built into the sheer, 200-foot walls of the upper part of Wana Draw and were almost unassailable.

The 1st Marines opened a two-pronged assault on Wana Ridge on the morning of 20 May. The 3d Battalion was to attack southeast up Wana Ridge, while the 2d Battalion was to advance against 100 Meter Hill, the eastern extension of the ridge. Supported by tanks, self-propelled guns, and 37-mm. guns, the 2d Battalion advanced rapidly to the base of 100 Meter Hill. Three forward platoons were stopped on the slope by fire from Wana Ridge and from the south, but another company passed through them and continued the attack. By dusk the 2d Battalion held part of the ridge but not 100 Meter Hill. In heavy close-range fighting the 3d Battalion gained only 200 yards on the west slope.

The attack continued on 21 May, but progress was even slower than on the day before. Like so many previous attempts on Okinawa, the attack faltered as troops were forced to make the most strenuous efforts to destroy particular

REVERSE SLOPE OF WANA RIDGE *as it appeared from slope of Wana Draw. High, treeless point on right side of photo is 100 Meter Hill. Below appear remains of a Japanese 47-mm. antitank gun and a crewman burned by flame-throwing tank.*

positions with shell fire, grenades, and demolitions. The 2d Battalion poured napalm into Wana Draw and then ignited it; this drove some of the enemy into the open, where they were exposed to mortar fire. Bazookas, rifle grenades, and hundreds of white phosphorus and fragmentation grenades were used against the caves on the reverse slope of Wana. Japanese mortar and sniper fire was intense, forcing the marines to take cover in native tombs and coral formations. The 3d Battalion advanced seventy-five yards through the broken ground on Wana Ridge, but then had to pull back to previous positions for the night. The 2d Battalion had been stopped short in another attempt to take 100 Meter Hill.

Shortly after midnight of 21 May an enemy force of about 200 troops tried to drive the 1st Marines off the forward slope of Wana Ridge. After climbing the steep reverse slope by means of ropes, picks, and ladders, the Japanese surged through a small cut on the ridge and charged the Marine positions. Company C, holding a thin line between the 2d and 3d Battalions, used automatic and rifle fire, but the most effective weapon at such short range was the grenade. The marines threw them until their arms ached; at the same time, mortarmen put heavy concentrations on the reverse slope of Wana. The Japanese attack was checked. Company C lost 4 killed and 26 wounded in the attack, but counted 140 dead Japanese in its sector in the morning.

The Attack in the Center

In the 77th Division's sector the Tenth Army's attack of 11 May marked a resumption of the snail-like frontal advance on Shuri. The division's two regiments, fighting on opposite sides of a long open valley southeast of Route 5, had to coordinate more closely with neighboring divisions than with each other. The progress of the 305th on the 77th's right (west) was dependent largely on the advance of the 1st Marine Division on Dakeshi Ridge; the 306th, on the division left, worked closely with the 96th Division along high ground west and southwest of Kochi Ridge. (See Map No. XXXV.) Enemy forces facing the 77th consisted of two battalions of the *32d Regiment, 24th Division*, supported by elements of four independent battalions, including a Shuri guard unit.[15]

The sector of the 305th Infantry was a jumble of ground extending south from Hill 187 toward Shuri. In contrast to the bold terrain features east and

[15] 77th Div G–2 Periodic Rpt No. 48, 13 May 45; Appleman, XXIV Corps History, p. 338.

northwest of Shuri, this area was a rough plateau pitted with innumerable knolls, ravines, and draws. By the middle of May the ground was even more broken by shell holes, trenches, and gaping cave mouths. Hardly a living plant was visible. The 305th pressed on, although every advance of a few yards uncovered more positions to be destroyed. The attack took a steady toll of Americans; by 15 May the 305th was fighting at about one-fourth strength.[16]

Ordinarily on Okinawa the Americans attacked in the morning, dug in on the new position late in the afternoon, and held a tight perimeter defense during the night. On a few occasions, however, the 77th Division made night attacks. Such an attack was made on 17 May by the 307th Infantry, which had relieved the 306th on the division left on 15 May in an attempt to capture Ishimmi Ridge, lying west of the town of Ishimmi. This attack, which developed into a desperate effort to hold a position surrounded by the enemy, was typical of the ordeal that many infantrymen had to go through on Okinawa to register even minor gains.

Through the Japanese Lines to Ishimmi Ridge

Shortly before dark of 16 May 1st Lt. Theodore S. Bell, commanding Company E, 307th Infantry, took his platoon leaders up to the 2d Battalion observation post atop a coral pinnacle, pointed out Ishimmi Ridge, dimly visible in the dusk, 1,200 yards to the south, and announced that Company E had been ordered to make a surprise night attack on the ridge. In the few minutes remaining before dark the officers studied the lay of the land. A heavy machine gun section from Company H and a reinforced rifle platoon from Company C were attached to Company E for the attack. The members of the reinforced company, many of them replacements without previous combat experience, were ordered to load and lock their weapons and to fix bayonets.[17]

Company E moved out in the dark at 0300, 17 May. Going down through the west part of the valley, the troops at 0400 reached the line of departure, where they were joined by the platoon from Company C. Fifteen minutes later the reinforced company was silently picking its way along low ground. Several gaunt trees on Ishimmi Ridge, showing dimly in the light of the frequent flares, served as guide points. Although Japanese controlled the ground, the Americans were not detected. Troops froze in their tracks whenever flares exploded over-

---

[16] Appleman, XXIV Corps History, p. 353; XXIV Corps G–3 Periodic Rpt No. 45, 15 May 45.

[17] The account of the night attack of Company E, 307th Infantry, is based entirely on the signed statement of 2d Lt Robert F. Meiser, commanding 2d Platoon, Company E. This statement is recorded in Leach, 77th Div History Okinawa, Vol. II, Ch. III, pp. 67–82.

head. The sound of battle—rifle and automatic fire and the whir of artillery shells—was always around them.

The company reached Ishimmi Ridge just before dawn and began taking up positions along a 125-yard sector of the flat crest. Digging in was difficult because of the coral and rock formation. The crest of Ishimmi was hardly ten yards wide at the center but flared out on either end. The 3d Platoon moved to the left, the 2d Platoon formed the center, the platoon from Company C took the right flank, and the 1st Platoon protected the rear. Lieutenant Bell established his command post in a pocket twenty yards north of the narrow part of the ridge.

By dawn the men were in position but the enemy was still unaware of their presence. A Japanese officer and his aide, talking and laughing as they emerged from a tunnel, were killed before they noticed the Americans. The 2d Platoon found a dozen sleeping Japanese in one trench and dispatched them with bayonets and rifle fire. By 0530, however, the enemy was fully alerted. Japanese troops began to pour out of tunnels in a ridge south of Ishimmi and tried to cross the intervening valley. American machine-gun fire cut them down. Soon enemy artillery, mortar, machine-gun, and rifle fire was sweeping the bare crest, forcing the troops to lie flat in their shallow holes. The Japanese were firing from all directions, including the rear, and were delivering mortar fire even from tunnel openings along the lower slopes of Ishimmi Ridge itself.

The First Day

The Japanese quickly spotted Company E's automatic weapons. One heavy machine gun was blown to pieces as its crew was setting it on the tripod; the other heavy was destroyed before it had fired one box of ammunition. Almost all the members of the crews were killed. Both light machine guns had been knocked out by 0700, one being completely buried. All but one of the light mortars were out of action by 1000. Lieutenant Bell's communications with Battalion were also a target. Of five radios brought along by his company and by the artillery forward observer, one was smashed by mortar shells, another was set on fire, and two had their aerials shot off. Only one remained intact.

As the American fire power was reduced, the Japanese tried to close in to destroy the beleaguered force. The 3d Platoon, occupying an exposed position on the eastern part of the ridge, repulsed three bayonet charges on its left. The Americans suffered many casualties from grenades. Japanese in the ridge south of Ishimmi took a heavy toll of the 2d Platoon, occupying the center. Two knee mortars, firing in unison 100 yards off either flank, systematically swept the

ISHIMMI RIDGE, *extending from right foreground almost to spinner of airplane from which this picture was taken, rises out of flat ground northeast of Shuri. Immediately behind the ridge are village of Ishimmi and the draw before Okinawa's ancient capital. From these positions the enemy could pour mortar fire into the small group of the 307th Infantry, 77th Division, on the hill.*

American positions from one end to another. The dead lay in pools of blood where they fell, or were pushed from the holes to make room for the living. An aid man, although wounded himself, continued his work until his supplies were exhausted.

During the day the 307th Infantry could not reinforce the company over the fire-swept approaches, but supported the force with artillery and self-propelled guns. Cannon company weapons put direct fire on Japanese trying to storm the hill. Many American shells landed so close to the encircled troops that the men were showered with rock. The one remaining radio enabled Lieutenant Bell to pinpoint targets for support fire. Mortars and heavy machine guns also helped to break up enemy charges.

The combined fire piled up the Japanese on the slopes of Ishimmi, but their attacks continued. By midday the 2d and 3d Platoons were at half strength and the rest of the company also had suffered heavily. Realizing that he could not possibly hold his extended positions during the night, Lieutenant Bell ordered the 2d and 3d Platoons late in the afternoon to pull into the command post and form a perimeter around it. Withdrawal was difficult, for the 2d Platoon had six badly mangled men in its sector. These were placed on ponchos and dragged out sled-fashion. One casualty was killed by machine-gun fire on the way out.

During the night a rescue force tried to get through to Company E, but the Japanese ambushed it and the survivors turned back. The Americans on Ishimmi Ridge, bombarded during the night by artillery, mortars, and "buzz bombs," repelled several attempts at infiltration. Flares kept the area well lighted and enabled Company E to see the approaching Japanese. Sleep was impossible. The tired, tense men hunched in their foxholes and waited for the dawn.

The Second Day

The order came by radio in the morning of 18 May to stay at all costs. Lieutenant Bell said firmly, "We stay." The men resigned themselves to a last-ditch stand. Their grenades exhausted and their machine guns and mortars destroyed, the remaining men salvaged every clip of ammunition from the bandoleers of the dead. Spare workable rifles were loaded and bayonets laid alongside. Enemy pressure increased steadily during the day. Some Americans were shot at close range as they darted from hole to hole to escape grenades. At one time eight knee mortars were pounding the ridge, firing in pairs. Friendly artillery could to some extent keep off the charging Japanese but seemed unable to ferret out the enemy mortars, which were well protected.

The moans of wounded men, many of whom were in pitiful condition from lack of water and of medical aid, added to the strain. All canteens had been emptied the previous night. Nevertheless, battle discipline remained excellent. The worst problem concerned the replacements, who were courageous but inexperienced. Thrust suddenly into a desperate situation, some of them failed at crucial moments. One man saw two Japanese attacking a sergeant thirty feet away, but his finger froze on the trigger. Another shouted wildly for a comrade to shoot some Japanese while his own rifle lay in his hands. Another saw an enemy soldier a few yards from his hole, pulled the trigger, and discovered that he had forgotten to reload. By the end of the ordeal, however, the replacements who survived were battle-hardened veterans.

During the afternoon the 307th attempted to reinforce the small group. Elements of Company C tried to cross the open ground north of Ishimmi Ridge. Only the commander and five men reached Company E. The men scrambled safely into foxholes, but the commander, shot through the head while racing toward the command post, fell dead on the parapet of the command post foxhole. Spirits rose considerably when word came later in the afternoon that a litter-bearing unit of eighty men would try to get through in the evening.

Enemy fire slackened after dark, and the first of the litter bearers arrived at about 2200. They immediately started back carrying casualties. Walking wounded accompanied them. The litter bearers moved swiftly and managed to avoid being seen in the light of flares. Through splendid discipline and good luck eighteen men were carried out in two and a half hours, and others walked out. The litter teams had brought some water and ammunition and the troops drank for the first time since the day before. The second sleepless night on the ridge passed.

The Third Day

On 19 May the enemy seemed to intensify his efforts to recapture Ishimmi Ridge. The besieged troops wondered whether his supply of men and ammunition was inexhaustible. The Japanese launched several attacks which were repulsed with great difficulty. Only the support of artillery and mortars, together with self-propelled mounts firing with precision on both flanks of Ishimmi Ridge, prevented the enemy from making an attack in strength which would have overrun the American positions. One enemy attack of platoon strength was dispersed by mortar and machine-gun fire and by a four-battalion time-on-target artillery concentration. Japanese mortar fire continued to fall on Ishimmi, however, and took its toll during the day.

A message arrived during the morning that Company E would be relieved that evening. By noon the radio had become so weak that further communication with the company was impossible. The day wore slowly on. By 2100 there was still no sign of the relief. Shortly afterward, however, rifle fire intensified to the rear, a sign of activity there. At 2200 Company L, 3d Battalion, 306th Infantry, arrived. The relief was carried out in pitch darkness; each member of Company E left as soon as a replacement reached his position. As the haggard survivors were about to descend the ridge at 0300, a bursting shell hit two of the newcomers; one of them had to be evacuated on a poncho. Carrying its own wounded, Company E followed a white tape to the rear and arrived safely.

Of the 204 officers and men of the reinforced company that had made the night attack on Ishimmi, 156 had been killed or wounded. There were 28 privates, 1 noncommissioned officer, and 2 officers left of the original 129 members of Company E. The platoon sent in relief by Company C had gone out with 58 effectives and returned with 13. Of the 17 men in the heavy weapons section only 4 came back. Company E had spearheaded a several-hundred-yard advance toward Shuri, however, and with the help of supporting weapons had killed hundreds of Japanese around Ishimmi.

During the battle to hold Ishimmi Ridge, the 305th Infantry had continued its attack along Route 5. The enemy held tenaciously to his positions in the finger ridges running west from the highway. Fierce fire fights flared up, often holding up the advance for a substantial time. The network of small hills and ridges afforded the Japanese almost complete interlocking fire; many positions were covered by five or six others. Even though the 305th utilized all its supporting arms, including medium tanks, self-propelled howitzers, antitank guns, and armored flame throwers, it was almost impossible to keep all the supporting strong points neutralized at the same time. The 306th Infantry relieved the 305th on 21 May, as the troops were reaching the northern outskirts of Shuri.[18]

The Reduction of Chocolate Drop Hill

Of all the strongly defended terrain features that made up the concentric ring of defenses around Shuri, Chocolate Drop Hill was undoubtedly the most insignificant in appearance. Its name, which was coined by 77th Division troops while headquarters was still calling it Hill 130, was aptly descriptive. The hill,

---

[18] 77th Div G–3 Periodic Rpts Nos. 54–57, 18–21 May 45; Leach, 77th Div History Okinawa, Vol. II, Ch. III, pp. 85–86.

a bare, brown hump of earth with a slightly peaked crest, rising abruptly from a flat expanse of ground, did indeed resemble a chocolate drop resting on a slightly tilted saucer.[19]

Several circumstances made the "Drop" an almost impregnable position. Movement across the saucer was extremely difficult. Except for low scrub growth in a few spots there was no cover on the surrounding ground. The west part of the saucer, near Route 5, was low and marshy—unsuited for tanks and other heavy weapons. Near Chocolate Drop was one of the largest mine fields on Okinawa. This area was covered by fire from Flattop Hill on the east, from Ishimmi Ridge on the southwest, and from other heights the entire way around the circle except to the north where the Americans were advancing. The Japanese also had the usual reverse-slope defenses on Chocolate Drop and on Wart Hill, a knob 500 yards east of Chocolate Drop on the long ridge running southwest between Flattop and Chocolate Drop.

At 0700 on 11 May, immediately after the 30-minute artillery preparation, the infantry moved out. The 3d Battalion, 306th Infantry, was to make the main effort on the left (east) of the 77th Division sector. The troops had advanced a little more than 200 yards when they were stopped by a hail of artillery and mortar fire. Fields of crossed machine-gun fire, converging just north of Chocolate Drop, also barred the way. By 0900 one company was engaged in close-in fighting near the north base of the hill. Other troops tried to advance on the left but were stopped by enemy entrenched around the base of Wart Hill.[20]

Tanks, self-propelled guns, artillery, mortars, and other infantry heavy weapons supported the attack, but no weapon seemed capable of reaching the Japanese dug in on the reverse slope of the Drop. Japanese weapons on Flattop took a heavy toll. One platoon, exposed to Flattop, sustained eleven casualties in the first few minutes of its attack. Japanese 47-mm. antitank guns raised havoc with tanks attempting to cross the open ground. Two tanks were destroyed and six others damaged by this fire. Another tank threw a track and was later destroyed by a Japanese satchel charge. After sustaining fifty-three casualties during the day, the battalion was withdrawn to the previous night's positions.

---

[19] Personal Obsn of 1st I & H Off. The precise location of Chocolate Drop Hill is not clear. While XXIV Corps and 77th Division records place it in Target Area 8073P of the 1:25,000 map of Okinawa, observation of the ground and study of photographs indicate that the hill is located from 200 to 300 yards northeast of that point.

[20] The account of the capture of Chocolate Drop is taken from Leach, 77th Div History Okinawa, Vol. II, Ch. III, pp. 48–87; Appleman, XXIV Corps History, pp. 341–51; 77th Div Actn Rpt Okinawa; 306th Inf Actn Rpt; 307th Inf Actn Rpt; 706th Tk Bn Actn Rpt.

CHOCOLATE DROP HILL *under attack 13 May from the west by tanks and armored flame throwers. Tanks which moved through the draw (below) between the "Drop" and Flattop were knocked out by fire from reverse slopes of these hills.*

On the following day, 12 May, the 306th held its position and aided the advance of friendly forces on both flanks. The 2d Battalion, 306th, supported by a platoon of tanks, anchored the right flank of the 96th Division. The 1st Battalion, 306th, supported the advance of the 305th Infantry. This regiment was having extremely hard going in the broken ground west of Route 5. Japanese here held positions in large, well-protected caves. One such cave had two Japanese 2½-ton trucks parked end-to-end inside it.

The plan for 13 May was a combined attack on Flattop Hill and Chocolate Drop. After a short but intense artillery preparation, the 306th renewed its attack on the Drop. The 2d Battalion led the assault, moving down the high ground on the northeast. The leading company reached the hill in thirteen minutes, only to stall at its northern base under intense artillery and mortar fire. An effort to swing left into the area between Chocolate Drop and Flattop was stopped quickly: there the troops were more exposed than ever. The infantry managed to secure part of the slope of Chocolate Drop but was soon forced back to the base of the hill. At 1400 the enemy scored twenty hits with 150-mm. artillery in the area just north of Chocolate Drop. Supported by all available artillery pieces, tanks, and self-propelled guns, the battalion made a third attempt to seize the hill. The troops, however, could not gain a tenable position, and they withdrew 300 yards to a fold of ground north of the hill. Two American medium tanks, one of them equipped with a 105-mm. howitzer, were destroyed during the day.

Some troops managed to dig in at the base of Wart Hill and to hold their position despite withdrawal of the forces on Chocolate Drop. Japanese who occupied trenches on the other side of Wart attacked this small group during the night. The fight was so fierce that the Americans were driven out of their holes. In the dark they did not dare to shoot for fear of hitting comrades. With grenades, bayonets, and entrenching tools, the men stormed back to their holes, now occupied by a dozen Japanese, and quickly regained their position.

By 14 May the 306th Infantry was so depleted in strength that the remaining riflemen were grouped into one battalion. Led by five tanks, this composite battalion attempted to advance beyond Wart Hill. As soon as the assault platoon reached the slope of Wart, a holocaust of fire from the front and both flanks hit the troops. In a few minutes the platoon was cut down to half strength, and the platoon leader, a platoon sergeant, and a squad leader were all casualties. Enemy antitank fire hit six tanks soon after they appeared on the crest. The line of dead infantrymen at one place near Chocolate Drop looked to one observer like a skirmish line that had lain down to rest. Further efforts to take Chocolate Drop and the high ground to the east were fruitless. On the next morning the 306th Infantry, which had suffered 471 casualties since 6 May, was replaced by the 307th.

The 307th Infantry attacked through the 306th at 0900 on 15 May. The scheme of maneuver was a simultaneous assault on Flattop on the left (east) and on Chocolate Drop on the right. The troops moved slowly toward their objectives under heavy fire from rifles, machine guns, and mortars. Simultaneously elements of the 96th Division were making progress in their sector east of the 77th, and this aided the 77th's advance. By noon the 3d Battalion was at the north base of the Drop and was working up the north slopes of Flattop. The 2d Battalion moved around to the right of the 3d Battalion and advanced about 500 yards before being held up by intense mortar and machine-gun fire. But the Americans were still unable to capitalize on their advances. To move through the saddle between Chocolate Drop and Flattop was to invite fire from the reverse slope of the Drop as well as from the entire system of defenses to the south. Several more tanks were disabled before the advance ended.

For the first time, however, the assault elements of the 77th Division were able to hold their positions directly north of Chocolate Drop and just below the crest on the north slope of Flattop. During the night the enemy tried to break the 307th's hold on the immediate approaches to Chocolate Drop. From huge caves on the reverse slope of the hill, groups of Japanese armed with knee mortars attacked the Americans twice during the dark. These attacks were warded off. During the night, however, the Japanese discovered in a ditch just east of Chocolate Drop five men who had been cut off after the assault company withdrew from the hill on the previous evening; they killed two of the group and wounded one.

The 307th continued the attack on 16 May, but this was another day of frustration. One platoon of the 3d Battalion reached the crest of Flattop; then enemy mortar and machine-gun fire forced the troops back. Four times more during the day the 3d Battalion reached and attempted to hold the crest, but each time the troops fell back to the north slope. The 2d Battalion continued to probe around the sides of Chocolate Drop in an effort to reach the enemy on top and on the reverse slope. One platoon was forced off Chocolate Drop late in the afternoon, but other infantrymen were able to hold positions gained during the day on the saddle east of the hill.

Slowly the 77th Division forces between Flattop and Route 5 were reducing enemy positions bearing on the area in front of the 307th Infantry. By 17 May this progress began to show in the advances of the foot troops around Chocolate Drop. Covered by company heavy weapons out on both flanks, infantrymen worked around both sides of the hill to the huge caves on the reverse slope. Inside were 4 antitank guns, 1 field piece, 4 machine guns, 4 heavy mortars, and 2 American 60-mm. mortars. By nightfall the caves had been partially sealed off. During the night an enemy force launched a counterattack against the American positions around the hill but was repulsed with the loss of twenty-five Japanese killed.

During the next two days the 3d Battalion consolidated and expanded its positions around Chocolate Drop. Reducing the tiny hill continued to be ticklish work because enemy positions to the south still overlooked the area. The fighting was still so confused that three wounded Americans lay south of Chocolate Drop for two days before relief arrived. By that time two had died and the third was so delirious that he thought he was still fighting Japanese and had to be forcibly subdued. By 20 May the caves were completely sealed off. The enemy made a final attempt to retake Chocolate Drop, attacking in company strength, but was repelled with the loss of half his force. On the same day the 3d Battalion, using tanks, flame throwers, and demolition teams, finally secured the crest of Flattop.

Some days later Tokyo Radio broadcast a message in English to the American troops on Okinawa:

Sugar Loaf Hill . . . Chocolate Drop . . . Strawberry Hill. Gee, those places sound wonderful! You can just see the candy houses with the white picket fences around them and the candy canes hanging from the trees, their red and white stripes glistening in the sun. But the only thing red about those places is the blood of Americans. Yes, sir, those are the names of hills in southern Okinawa where the fighting's so close that you get down to bayonets and sometimes your bare fists. Artillery and naval gunfire are all right when the enemy is far off but they don't do you any good when he's right in the same foxhole with you. I guess it's natural to idealize the worst places with pretty names to make them seem less awful. Why Sugar Loaf has changed hands so often it looks like Dante's Inferno. Yes, sir, Sugar Loaf Hill . . . Chocolate Drop . . . Strawberry Hill. They sound good, don't they? Only those who've been there know what they're really like.[21]

Flattop and Dick Hills

The right elements of the 96th Division were still fighting for Zebra Hill when the Tenth Army attack order went into effect on 11 May. Southwest of Zebra were other formidable positions that were to engage elements of both

[21] Appleman, XXIV Corps History, p. 347.

the 96th and 77th for ten days. These positions were built into Flattop and into the Dick Hills, east of Flattop. The Dick Hills and Flattop were so close to one another that their reduction depended on close coordination of troops of the 96th and 77th across the divisional boundary. A captured Japanese map showed these hills to be on the perimeter of the inner core of the Shuri defenses.

The Japanese had a miscellaneous collection of troops in the Flattop–Dick Hills area. Although heavily reduced during the past weeks, the *22d Regiment, 24th Division,* was still ably commanded and capable of effective defense in the scores of available positions in the Flattop area. Supporting the *32d Regiment* were troops of the *24th Transport Regiment,* the *29th Independent Battalion,* and the *27th Tank Regiment.* The remaining six tanks of the *27th* were dug in behind Flattop and used as stationary pillboxes. Engineers from the tank regiment had mined roads and other approaches and had constructed bell-shaped foxholes from which satchel charges could be thrown against American tanks. The Japanese had salvaged a number of 7.7-mm. machine guns from destroyed tanks to round out their defenses.[22]

The Dick Hill mass consisted of four heights, known officially as Dick Baker, Dick Able, Dick Right, and Dick Left. The highest and most heavily fortified of these was Dick Right (ordinarily called Dick Hill), which was a companion hill mass to Flattop and lay just southeast of it. Dick Baker was close to Zebra and just west of the narrow road running southwest from Onaga along the southeast slope of Zebra. Dick Able was southeast of Dick Baker. Dick Left, another well-fortified and strongly defended height, was the southern elevation of the ridge running south from Dick Right. (See Map No. XXXIX.)

During the night of 10–11 May a fight raged on the crest of Zebra Hill as the Japanese tried to oust the Americans from positions occupied on the previous day. Not until 0730 was the enemy forced off the hill, leaving 122 of his number dead. During the 11th, the 382d Infantry, 96th Division, commanded by Col. M. L. Dill, consolidated its positions on Zebra. Operating on the reverse slope of the hill was difficult since Japanese positions in the Dick Hills area commanded that slope. An attempt to move over open ground to Dick Baker, undertaken later in the day, proved abortive because of accurate enemy fire. One assault platoon lost all its noncommissioned officers and a private first class was in command at the end of the day.[23]

---

[22] 96th Div G–2 Periodic Rpt No. 47, 18 May 45; Appleman, XXIV Corps History, pp. 369–70.

[23] The account of operations of the 96th Divisions at Dick Hills is based on Mulford and Rogers, 96th Div History, Pt. IV, pp. 25–31, 58–62, 64–67, 72–74.

DICK HILLS AND FLATTOP, *photographed 23 May 1945, two days after reduction of these positions. Enemy was still dropping harassing fire on farther slopes, with battle moving closer to Shuri. American foxholes, some covered by shelter halves, can be seen in profusion on the hillsides.*

The 382d attacked again on 12 May, with the 1st Battalion on the right (west) and the 3d Battalion on the left. Block and tackle were used to haul 37-mm. antitank guns up to the top of Zebra for direct fire into Japanese positions on heights to the south. Artillery fire and the 37-mm. fire enabled the attack of the 3d Battalion to get off to a good start toward Baker Hill. While the tank-infantry teams of the 1st Battalion cleared out the reverse slope of Zebra, the 3d Battalion advanced slowly between Zebra and Item Hills. The 1st Battalion attacked toward Dick Baker but was surprised by fire from its rear. Despite the efforts of the two battalions, some Japanese on the reverse slope of Zebra had survived. Nevertheless, assault troops of the 1st Battalion reached Dick Baker and dug in on the crest under a heavy smoke screen. Heavy fire soon forced them to withdraw.

In the afternoon Company A attacked up the east slope of Dick Baker. The troops were halfway to the top when most of them were pinned down by heavy fire from the south. Lt. Woodrow W. Anderson and three soldiers continued the assault. Anderson covered two huge caves on the east face of Dick Baker by fire while Pfc. Amador G. Duran made a dash between them to the crest. Anderson and the two other men joined him. Suddenly a terrific mortar barrage descended on the hill. Anderson and Duran were killed instantly when a shell landed squarely in their foxhole; the two survivors ran down the northwest slope to friendly territory. No further progress was made during the day. The regiment's only success of the day was the 3d Battalion's capture of Baker Hill, 600 yards south of Zebra.

The effort of 13 May was closely coordinated with the advance on the right made by the 306th Infantry, 77th Division. The 1st Battalion, 382d Infantry, pushed off shortly after 1100. The plan was for Company A, leading, to attack Dick Baker while Company B swung out to the left toward Dick Able. For a time everything went smoothly. Both companies reached the crests of their objectives, meeting little fire, and they promptly began blowing up caves and pillboxes. But Japanese gunners were waiting. Suddenly a storm of explosives hit the forces on Dick Able. Over 200 rounds of 90-mm. mortar fire, together with 150-mm. artillery rounds and knee mortar shells, fell on the small, exposed crest. The commander of Company B and all but one or two of the fourteen men with him were killed. Company A was able to hold its position on Dick Baker. (See Map No. XL.)

The Japanese reinforced their positions in the Dick Hills area during the night of 13–14 May. On the next morning enemy fire was so strong that tanks had to be used to transport supplies to the forward troops. It was a risky procedure to leave a foxhole on Dick Baker even to receive supplies from tanks at the base of the hill. In the afternoon, after coordinating with the 306th Infantry on his right, Colonel Dill launched an attack on Dick Able and Dick Right. Supported by Company A on Dick Baker, Company B managed to reach the crest of Able without difficulty. The heavy pounding of support weapons during the morning had evidently knocked out many of the mortars covering this position. A platoon of Company C then attacked Dick Right from the north. Five infantrymen advanced halfway up the slope, but the first three were killed by rifle fire. The enemy also opened up on the platoon with mortars, and the Americans were forced to withdraw.

The 3d Battalion also attacked Dick Right, advancing from the Baker Hill area toward the east fingers of Dick. Company K managed to reach the military crest on the north slopes of the fingers. As Company L, supported by a platoon of tanks, started up a draw leading to Dick Right, a barrage of mortar shells descended on it. Some of the rounds hit the tanks and had the same effect on the accompanying foot troops as air bursts. All but two of the twenty-three men in the leading platoon were killed or wounded. Despite the continuing mortar fire, the company commander rallied his remaining men and led them to the military crest on Dick Right, where they tied in on the right of Company K. In obtaining this precarious hold on Dick, the 3d Battalion had lost six killed and forty-seven wounded.

During the night heavy rain fell, adding to the difficulties the troops already were having with the steep terrain. Before the rain the soft earth had made climbing much like scaling a sand dune; now the hillsides were slick with wet clay. During the morning the 3d Battalion, 382d, was able to consolidate its position. It was still difficult, however, to move from the military crest to the topographical crest of Dick Hill; one platoon made seven attempts to seize and hold positions on the skyline but each time was forced back just below the crest. Troops were able only to extend their hold westward along the north slope of the long ridge. These attacks brought the 382d Infantry into close conjunction with the fighting around Flattop on the west, toward which the left elements of the 77th had been driving for several days. (See Map No. XLI.)

Seen from the north, Flattop resembled what its name implied—a long, tabletop ridge, dropping abruptly to narrow saddles at both ends. It stood on the right flank of the rugged hill masses extending southeast to Conical Hill and constituting the eastern defenses of Shuri. Flattop dominated the Kochi Valley for 1,300 yards to the north, including Chocolate Drop on the northwest. Just to the east, on the other side of a saddle deepened by a road cut, was Dick Hill, objective of the 96th Division. Flattop had a fairly steep reverse slope with the usual profusion of enemy defenses.[24]

Flattop was one objective of the 306th Infantry, 77th Division, when that regiment moved out in the Tenth Army attack of 11 May. Chocolate Drop was the other objective. Flattop commanded both Chocolate Drop and the west slopes of Dick Hill, and only after Flattop was taken could the others be entirely reduced. On 11 May elements of the 3d Battalion started to work slowly along the extended swell of ground north of Flattop. On the 12th, tank-infantry teams tried to reach Flattop but failed. Japanese fire power prevented the troops from coming within range of the height. Similar efforts on the 13th and 14th were frustrated, but each day artillery and other support weapons heavily pounded the hill. The 307th relieved the 306th Infantry on the morning of 15 May.

Throughout the rainy night of 14-15 May, artillery pounded Flattop and the neighboring hills. The 3d Battalion, 307th Infantry, attacked at 0900 in the morning. Troops moved up the slippery face of Flattop with grenades, satchel charges, and portable flame throwers. Tanks put direct fire on the crest and face of the hill. The troops spent the afternoon in a grenade battle with the enemy and dug in for the night just below the crest. On the next day a platoon reached the top of the hill, but shortly afterward a heavy mortar concentration from enemy positions on Tom Hill, 1,000 yards to the south, forced the Americans off the crest. Meanwhile, support tanks had quickly knocked out the six enemy tanks dug in around Flattop. A member of the Japanese *27th Tank Regiment,* amazed by the accuracy of American tank fire, described it as "100 shots—100 bulls eyes." The destruction of these tanks with their 37-mm. guns scarcely affected the Flattop fighting. The real trouble was with mines and 47-mm. anti-tank fire, which together knocked out three American tanks during the day.

On the 17th another bitter struggle raged on Flattop. The struggle swayed back and forth across the narrow crest of the hill. Company K, the assaulting unit, had been reduced to fourteen infantrymen by the end of the day; finally it was forced back off the top. Tanks tried to go through the road cut between Flattop and Dick Hill, but two of them were disabled by mines, leaving the cut blocked. The road cut was later blown along its entire length by seven tons of bangalore torpedoes to remove the mines. The infantry continued its close-in

[24] The account of operations of the 77th Division at Flattop Hill is based on Appleman, XXIV Corps History, pp. 366-77, and Leach, 77th Div History Okinawa, Vol. II.

fighting with the enemy on 18 May while more tanks tried to move through the cut. A 47-mm. antitank gun destroyed one of the first tanks to emerge from the cut, but it was knocked out in turn by an American 105-mm. self-propelled gun. Other tanks of the 77th and 96th Divisions came up in support.

Now for the first time the Americans could place direct fire on the reverse slopes of Flattop and Dick Hill. This was to prove decisive. Tanks and assault guns put destructive fires on Japanese positions throughout the next day, 19 May. Bayonet charges by the enemy from southwest of Flattop were dispersed by artillery and mortar fire. On 20 May the final American attack started with a saturation shower of grenades. A chain of men extending from the base of Flattop passed hand grenades to the troops lined up along the crest, who threw the missiles as fast as they could pull out the pins. Having seized the advantage, the infantry moved down the reverse slope blasting caves with satchel charges and flame throwers. Tanks along the road cut accounted for many of the Japanese. By 1545 Flattop had fallen. More than 250 enemy bodies lay on the crest and reverse slope of the hill.

In the zone of the 382d Infantry, 96th Division, the bitter struggle for Dick Hill continued from 15 to 20 May. All attempts to move over the crest of the hill were met by grazing machine-gun fire from Oboe Hill to the left (east) and from Flattop to the right. The 2d Battalion relieved the 1st Battalion on the morning of the 16th. During the previous night the American lines had been pushed back down the south slope of Dick Hill; thus a part of the work had to be done over again. There seemed to be no decrease in Japanese resistance, and the battle raged into the night. Efforts to hold the crest of Dick Hill on the west exposed the men to fire from Flattop. The 382d made little more progress on the 17th.

The seizure of the road cut between Flattop and Dick Hill on 18 May was the turning point in the Dick Hill fighting as it had also been in the struggle for Flattop. On 19 and 20 May the hold of the 382d on the reverse slope of Dick Hill was steadily enlarged. Despite continuing heavy antitank fire from enemy positions to the south, tank-infantry teams methodically destroyed Japanese strong points in the immediate Dick Hills area. On one occasion an armored flame thrower flushed fifty Japanese out of a cave; all fifty were cut down as they fled. Pockets remained to be cleaned out as late as 21 May. By that time, however, the 382d was involved in another grinding effort to take Oboe Hill on the regimental left.[25]

[25] Mulford and Rogers, 96th Div History, Pt. IV, pp. 78–81, 95–97, 103–06, 110–11, 119–21.

ADVANCE AROUND DICK HILLS AND FLATTOP *was difficult. Above appear troops of the 382d Infantry, 77th Division, on Dick Baker supporting advance to Dick Right. Below, Flattop is seen receiving American tank fire.*

Colonel Nist, XXIV Corps G–2, summed up the action along the Shuri front during the first week following the attack of 11 May in these words:

> During the past week's action, as our troops continued to fight their way into the enemy's main defenses, the Japanese demonstrated a complete willingness to suffer annihilation rather than to sacrifice ground. There was no variation in this pattern during the period.[26]

Opening the East Coast Corridor

When an opening was finally made in the Shuri line it was on the extreme left, along Buckner Bay. This opening was made by an advance up Conical Hill on 13 May which, in the opinion of General Buckner, who watched it, was the most spectacular of the campaign. The break, when it came, was a twofold surprise. General Hodge had believed that the high ground east of Shuri would have to be taken before Conical Hill, which is farther to the south, somewhat lower, and one of the strongest natural positions on Okinawa, could be successfully assaulted. For his part, General Bradley, commanding the 96th Division, was convinced after his reconnaissance of the terrain that Conical Hill would have to be approached from the northwest, by advances down the ridge line of the chain of hills. As events turned out, Conical Hill was reduced before Oboe Hill and the high ground at Shuri, and by attack from another direction. Furious fighting was still in progress in the inner areas for many days after capture of Conical's eastern face had opened the way for American troops to pass down the coast to Yonabaru and spill out into southern Okinawa.[27]

Conical—the Million Dollar Hill

The Navy, pouring expensive shells into Conical Hill from Buckner Bay, marked it with a "Million Dollar" price tag. The peak rose 476 feet high above the Yonabaru coastal plain, less than two miles south of Hill 178. From it radiated six long, sharp ridges. A long eastern spur ran down toward Buckner Bay; a second jutted northeast to Gaja Ridge, and another due north. Others ran northwest to King Hill, due west to Love, and due south for 800 yards along the coast to end in a rounded knob called Sugar Hill, just northwest of Yonabaru. The flat plain between Conical Hill and Buckner Bay was about 400 yards wide, and Route 13, the important east coast thoroughfare, passed through it. (See Map No. XLII.)

---

[26] XXIV Corps G–2 Weekly Summary No. 10, 13–19 May 45.

[27] Interv 1st I & H Off with Gen Buckner, 15 Jun 45; 96th Div FO No. 21, 10 May 45; Mulford and Rogers, 96th Div History, Pt. IV, pp. 13, 14.

A mile northeast of Conical Peak on the coastal flat was the enemy's projected Yonabaru airstrip, grass-covered and barely distinguishable. Unaha lay west of the airstrip, and behind that village the ground rose steeply to Hill 178. This high ground formed the northern edge of a U-shaped bowl the open end of which faced the bay. A chain of hills known from north to south as Tare, William, Easy, Charlie, and King shaped the base of the U, while Conical itself was the southern arm. The enclosed area was flat and sometimes swampy, except for Gaja Ridge, which rose by the village of Yonagusuku (or Gaja) near the middle of the southern arm.

A valley running behind Fox, Charlie, King, and Conical Hills, the entire way down to the Naha–Yonabaru road, separated the Conical Hill sector from the inner ring of Shuri defenses. The Oboe Hill mass, guarding Shuri's eastern flank, lay a mile northwest of the peak of Conical, across the valley.[28]

About 1,000 Japanese, heavily armed with mortars and organic 75-mm. artillery, occupied positions on Conical Hill itself. Defense of the sector was entrusted to Col. Hotishi Kanayama's *89th Regiment* of the *24th Division,* reinforced by the *27th Independent Battalion,* one of a number of harbor construction battalions which had changed their designation to "Sea Raiding Battalions." Also attached were one company of the *3d Independent Machine Gun Battalion* and the *23d Antitank Company*. A captured Japanese map dated 8 May placed two battalions of the *44th Independent Mixed Brigade* as guarding the ground between the peak of Conical and Yonabaru, but it appears that these units were moved to the Dakeshi sector soon afterward. Their place was taken by the converted airdrome-maintenance squadron from the Naha airfield and also by the *29th Independent Battalion.*[29]

The Attack That Failed

The task given the 383d Infantry, 96th Division, when on 10 May it relieved the 184th Infantry, 7th Division, was the capture of Conical Hill. The 1st Battalion, which was to make the main effort, effected the relief on William Hill and the eastern slopes of Easy Hill. Easy was a symmetrical, oblong hill on a north-south axis, with steep sides. A deep, narrow cut separated Easy from Charlie Hill on the south. Charlie Hill on its eastern side was also steep. It was roughly circular and had three prominent noses: one to the northeast offering an approach, one on the southwest pointing to Love Hill, and a third

---

[28] Appleman, XXIV Corps History, pp. 385–87; Mulford and Rogers, 96th Div History, Pt. IV, pp. 7–10.

[29] The account of operations of the 96th Division at Conical Hill is taken from Mulford and Rogers, 96th Div History, Pt. IV; 96th Div Actn Rpt, Ch. VII; G–2 Periodic Rpts for the period.

running almost due south to a cut separating it from a U-shaped hill called King. Fox Hill lay to the west of Easy, its southern tip ending in a steep little rise west of Charlie known as Fox Pinnacle.

The big attack on 11 May started auspiciously. After a thorough mortar preparation Company B took Easy Hill without too much difficulty and then moved through the cut between Easy and Charlie to flank Fox from the southeast and gain positions on its crest. Company C, after jockeying for favorable jumping-off positions, managed to establish itself on top of Charlie Hill, though not at its summit. The Americans then began the first of a long series of grenade duels with Japanese dug into the reverse slope twenty or thirty yards away. Two days later Company B attacked the summit of Charlie from Fox, but it was stopped by withering fire from King Hill and from enemy positions close to those of Company C on Charlie. Machine-gun fire from Conical Hill and mortar fire from the reverse slopes of Love were added as four Americans moved over the skyline and attacked Charlie's reverse slope. Company B was forced to withdraw.

Some progress was made on 14 May. Company B attacked Charlie Hill again, securing a foothold on its northern end, and Company C extended its positions down Charlie's southern nose. Every man, however, in the platoon of Company A which attacked down the west side of Charlie was killed or injured. Another platoon from the same company tried unsuccessfully to take Fox Pinnacle. On the same day Company L, 3d Battalion, which on 13 May had taken up positions to seal the draw between Charlie and King Hills and thus close a gap between the 1st and 2d Battalions, attacked King and gained the entire crest.

Although the reverse slopes of Charlie and King had not been reduced, an attack on Love Hill, a low, bare ridge running generally east and west, was launched on 16 May as part of a plan which was intended to clean out Charlie and put Company L on the western end of King to supply a base of fire. From Love Hill, fire could reach the reverse slope positions on the southwest side of Conical Hill and support the 382d Infantry's attack on Oboe. Because of the inherent strength of Love's defenses the attack did not succeed; nor was progress made on Charlie's southern slopes against the large number of caves, swarming with Japanese. Tanks helped a platoon of Company C to reach Love Hill but ran out of ammunition and withdrew. A murderous barrage, from an estimated fifty machine guns firing from Love itself and from Conical and Oboe Hills and the reverse slopes of King and Charlie, then hit the platoon. Six men, all of them

CONICAL HILL *and adjoining enemy positions to the north and west.*

EAST COAST FLATLANDS, *over which the 184th Infantry, 7th Division, advanced to Yonabaru after capture of the east slope of Conical Hill.*

wounded, made their way back to the American lines that night; twenty were left on the objective.

Before dawn on 20 May five more survivors, who had spent the intervening four days behind enemy lines, returned. One of them, Sgt. Donald B. Williams, had hidden in a cave to tend a wounded comrade. Enemy soldiers had fired a bazooka into the cave, and Williams had killed a Japanese who had tried to enter. Williams returned only after his comrade's condition was hopeless and he himself was growing weak for want of food and water. The other four men, Sgt. R. D. Turner, Pvt. William Schweneger, Pvt. Keith Cochran, and Pvt. Kenneth Boynton, the first two of whom were wounded, had stayed in a tomb near the foot of Love Hill. Their attempts to escape at night were thwarted by machine-gun and mortar fire trained on the tomb's entrance. On the second night four Okinawans—an old man, two old women, and a 10-year-old girl—had moved into the tomb with them, and one of the women went out and filled two of their canteens with water. On the fourth day a heavy American air strike hit the hill, and an American machine gun poured lead at a 3-inch opening in the tomb from a distance of 700 yards. The four members of Company C made their escape that night when loud singing and women's voices indicated that the Japanese near by were having a party.

On 19 May Company E established itself on the western end of King Hill but was driven off by fire from Charlie and Love Hills and the reverse slope of King. Since the 96th Division had taken over this sector, more than 300 had been killed or wounded in trying to move down this series of hills. Constant attack and the use of tanks and demolitions had been unavailing, and the strain was beginning to tell on the troops. On 20 May an air strike was run against the reverse slopes of Charlie, toward the American lines, but, although the planes dropped their 500-pound bombs accurately from an altitude of only a few yards, the Charlie pocket continued to withstand assault. It was still alive with Japanese, and supporting fire from Love Hill was deadly. Charlie pocket was not to be finally eliminated or Love Hill taken until 30 May, after nineteen days of bitter struggle.

The Hole in the Dike

The 13th of May, hot and clear, was a turning point in the battle for Okinawa. On the two preceding days the 2d Battalion, 383d Infantry, had cleaned out Gaja Ridge and, by working south from Yonagusuku (Gaja) and the twin villages of Tobaru and Amaru, had opened the possibility of reaching Conical's peak from the north and northeast. On the 12th a toe hold had been gained on

Conical's northern spur, which ran down to Tobaru and Amaru, and Company G had made an extensive reconnaissance and destroyed many enemy positions up the draw on the west side of this spur. When General Hodge read the 96th Division's report that evening, he immediately telephoned its commander, General Bradley, and directed that the frontal assault on Conical Hill from the north be pushed. "We'll have the key to the Shuri line if he can make it," General Hodge told his associates.[30]

At 1100 on the 13th General Buckner arrived at the observation post of Colonel May, who had decided that the time was ripe for the assault on Conical Hill. Company F had spent the morning clearing Yonagusuku (Gaja) of Japanese who had infiltrated during the night; two platoons of tanks from Company B, 763d Tank Battalion, working with Company E, had pounded enemy positions in Conical's northern slopes all morning; but Company G, attacking strong points west of Conical's northern spur, was prevented from climbing to the crest by fire from Charlie Hill in its rear and from Conical itself. Colonel May ordered Lt. Col. Lee Morris, 2d Battalion commander, to attack Conical frontally with Companies E and F and to have tanks move with the infantry up the hill.

Two platoons of Company F on the left drove toward Conical's northeast spur and reached a series of boulders halfway up with surprising ease. The two platoon sergeants, T/Sgt. Guy J. Dale and T/Sgt. Dennis O. Duniphan, held a hasty consultation and decided to move up to the crest without waiting for orders from the company commander, 1st Lt. Owen R. O'Neill. By 1300 the men had reached the northeast crest of the ridge.

Japanese reaction was intense. Knee-mortar fire fell on the two platoons as they dug in, and at 1525 a counterattack of at least company strength struck frontally and on Company F's exposed left flank. Sergeant Duniphan stood up and emptied a BAR into enemy soldiers ten feet away, then grabbed a rifle and continued to fire at the attackers. Lieutenant O'Neill sent a runner down the hill to order 1st Lt. Richard W. Frothinger, leader of the 2d Platoon, to come up immediately. Lieutenant Frothinger led his platoon up the hill in a headlong dash through hostile machine-gun fire. An American artillery spotting plane flying over Conical watched the fight and called for fire. Suddenly an overwhelming concentration of artillery air bursts and 4.2-inch mortar fire splattered the area just beyond the crest. The fire was perfectly timed, and the Japanese were repulsed.

[30] Mulford and Rogers, 96th Div History, Pt. IV, p. 49.

Meanwhile Company E had climbed the eastern slopes of Conical's northern spur and the steep sides of the peak itself, taking positions on Company F's right, fifty yards east of Conical's peak. At dusk Company G dug in facing west along the northern spur; thus the lines extended continuously in a generally east-west direction high up on Conical's northern slopes. The eastern anchor of the Shuri line was weakening. The Japanese, having surmised correctly that the main effort against Conical Hill would be down the Charlie–King ridge line, had disposed their forces to meet the threat from that quarter. But the 383d Infantry had discovered and used a naturally stronger but less heavily defended avenue of approach; two American platoon leaders had taken the initiative and led their men up the hill at a moment of precious opportunity.

South to Sugar Hill

In what Colonel May called "the greatest display of courage of any group of men I have ever seen," two platoons of Company G, 383d Infantry, on 15 May moved up the northwest spur of Conical Hill from King Hill through extremely thick mortar fire. They dug in not far below Conical Peak. An earlier attempt by the company's reserve platoon to establish physical contact with the rest of the company from Conical's north spur around the base of the peak itself had been stymied when the six men engaged in the maneuver were all hit and tumbled seventy-five feet to the bottom of the peak.

Tanks worked over Japanese positions on Conical's eastern slopes and advanced as far south as the outskirts of Yonabaru on 16 May, and Company F secured slightly better positions, preparatory to a main attack down the east side of Conical Hill. On the following day the 3d Battalion, 381st Infantry, relieved Companies E and F of the 383d, placing all three regiments of the 96th Division in the line. If the fresh battalion succeeded in clearing the eastern slopes of Conical Hill, the 7th Division could be called from reserve to sweep down the coast and flank the Shuri line. (See Map No. XLIII.)

Sugar Hill, at the southern end of the 800-yard hogback that extended south from Conical's peak, was the objective of the 381st Infantry. On the eastern face of the hogback a number of finger ridges ran down into the Yonabaru coastal flats. Reducing the Japanese emplacements which covered the finger ridges from the west would be difficult, for the crest of the hogback would continue to be untenable because of fire from Love, Mike, and other hills to the west. It would be necessary to deny the crest to the enemy and to guard every inch of the military crest as soon as it was captured, to ward off Japanese attempts to establish positions on the skyline.

Second Lieutenant Leonard K. Warner, a Hawaiian, on 18 May led a platoon of Company K, 381st Infantry, down to the third finger ridge. On the way Lieutenant Warner had dashed up the second finger with two satchel charges and crossed the crest of the hogback to throw them into a heavy machine-gun emplacement. On the third finger the platoon was receiving heavy fire from its rear, chiefly from emplacements between the first and second fingers, when Lieutenant Warner's company commander called him and asked whether he could move on to Sugar Hill.

"Hell yes," said Warner. "The way the Japs are shooting me in the back they'll chase me all the way down there." [31]

Fire from Cutaway Hill, a peak shaped like an eyetooth and located on the hogback two-thirds of the way between Sugar Hill and Conical's peak, added to the platoon's troubles, and it had to withdraw under smoke. An outpost line on the first finger was held during the night. During the day, tanks working from the flats had had a difficult time and in the end had been forced to withdraw by heavy fire from Chinen Peninsula.

Lt. Col. Daniel A. Nolan, commander of the 3d Battalion, 381st Infantry, on 19 May sent fifteen men with demolitions to attack the enemy emplacements between the first and second fingers. After they failed in an attempt to climb the precipitous slope during the day, 2d Lt. Donald Walsh led the men after dark to the northernmost of the machine-gun positions. They killed its occupants and discovered that it commanded the Japanese defensive system on the reverse slopes of the Conical hogback. The enemy counterattacked persistently but unsuccessfully all night. On the next day the battalion engaged in fierce fighting southward to within 200 yards of Cutaway Hill, and Company L consolidated for the night between the second and third fingers. That night Company K secured the area between the peak of Conical Hill and the second finger, and fought bitter grenade battles with Japanese twenty yards away on the other side of the ridge line. On the 21st the company used 1,100 grenades in hanging on to its position.

On 21 May, while Company L was heavily engaging the enemy on Cutaway Hill and on the hogback to the north of it, Companies I and F attacked across the heavily serrated ground on the east side of the hogback toward Sugar Hill. The men paused at each ridge to set up a base of fire and pound the reverse slopes of the next fold with hundreds of mortar shells, then moved on with tanks to

[31] *Ibid.*, p. 101.

flush the Japanese from their caves and pillboxes. The company's 60-mm. mortars and heavy machine guns, giving heavy and effective support, were advanced from ridge to ridge just behind the troops. Artillery fire pounded the reverse slopes of Sugar Hill and broke up a strong attempt to reinforce this position by small groups of enemy advancing from the southwest across open ground. Company F, on the right, had to send its men by individual rushes across the open fields below Cutaway Hill to the north slopes of Sugar. This company consolidated its lines on Sugar Hill, but plunging fire from Cutaway was to plague the men for a week. Company I captured the eastern part of Sugar without much difficulty, and Company G came up to strengthen the line against the anticipated counterattack. Company F took the brunt of the attack that night and killed fifty Japanese. The day's gain had cost the 381st Infantry 56 casualties, but the regiment had disposed of 403 Japanese.[32]

All of Conical Hill's eastern slopes were now in American hands, and the 7th Division could proceed down the corridor by Buckner Bay without molestation from its right flank. The western side of Conical and the reverse slope of Cutaway remained firmly in the hands of the Japanese.

The month of May saw major changes in the chain of command, involving a transfer of additional responsibility to Tenth Army. On 17 May Admiral Turner was replaced as Commander Task Force 51 by Admiral Harry W. Hill, who was to control the air defenses of Okinawa and the naval forces in the area. The Commanding General of Tenth Army now reported directly to Admiral Spruance. General Buckner was given command of all forces ashore, direct responsibility for the defense and development of captured positions in the Ryukyus area, and, to assist in this mission, operational command of Task Force 51. On 27 May Admiral Spruance was relieved as Commander Fifth Fleet by Admiral William F. Halsey, who commanded the Ryukyus operation until 27 June, when, with the formation of the Ryukyus Force, Tenth Army came directly under CINCPOA.[33]

[32] Casualty figures from 381st Inf Jnl, Msg No. 65, 21 May 45.
[33] Tenth Army Actn Rpt, 7–III–21.

CHAPTER XIV

Battle in the Rain

At the end of the third week of May the fighting had penetrated to the inner ring of the Shuri defenses. The Tenth Army's hopes had been raised by the capture of the eastern slopes of Conical Hill, which, permitting the 7th Division to funnel through the corridor by Buckner Bay, opened up the possibility of an envelopment of the enemy forces. But the bid for envelopment was destined to fail. From 22 to 29 May, except for certain gains on the flanks, there was no appreciable progress against any part of the Japanese inner defense ring. The enemy line held with hardly a dent against every attack.

The stalemate was due in large measure to rain, mud, and the bogging down of all heavy equipment. The weather during April and thus far into May had been unexpectedly good; there had been far less rain than preinvasion meteorological tables had predicted. But now the days of grace from the skies were over: the heavens were about to open and the much talked-about "plum rains" of Okinawa were to set in and continue day after day. Mud was to become king, and it was impossible to mount a large-scale attack during this period.

Enemy Air Attacks

While the ground fighting was largely stalemated by rain, the air battle between the Americans on Okinawa and the enemy pilots from the Japanese home islands went on unceasingly. Despite their failure in April to destroy the invading American fleet, the Japanese air forces in May kept on unremittingly with their attacks. They were directed against two targets—the ships off shore and the airfields on Ie Shima and at Yontan and Kadena. During the latter half of May the Japanese air attacks on these targets reached a peak and included some of the severest strikes which the enemy delivered during the air fighting of the entire campaign. The American Tactical Air Force not only engaged in routine support of the ground forces—a support limited in effectiveness by the location of the enemy in deep underground positions—but also attempted to ward off the Japanese air attacks from the home islands. Thunderbolts and Corsairs of the Tactical Air Force made daily sweeps over the waters between Okinawa and southern Kyushu, intercepting enemy planes, and often continuing over Kyushu to bomb, rocket, and strafe targets there. From Guam, Saipan, and Tinian in the Marianas the strategic heavy bombing of the Japanese home islands went on concurrently without let-up.[1]

Japanese air raids reached a peak during the latter part of May. On the 20th, thirty-five planes raided the American fleet; twenty-three were shot down. On 22 and 23 May, Japanese planes came over Okinawa again. Beginning on 24 May, the enemy stepped up the tempo of the attack on American units ashore and afloat. The evening of the 24th was perfect bombing weather with a clear sky and full moon. The air alerts started about 2000 and it was 2400 before an all-clear sounded. In that interval there were seven distinct air raids on Okinawa. In the first raid planes penetrated through to bomb Yontan and Kadena. The third, fourth, and sixth groups of raiders also succeeded in dropping bombs on the airfields.

The seventh group consisted of five low-flying two-engine bombers, called "Sallys," that came in about 2230 from the direction of Ie Shima. Antiaircraft batteries immediately engaged them, and four planes crashed in flames near Yontan airfield. The fifth came in and made a belly landing, wheels up, on the northeast-southwest runway of Yontan. At least eight heavily armed Japanese rushed out of the plane and began tossing grenades and incendiaries into American aircraft parked along the runway. They destroyed 2 Corsairs, 4 C–54 transports, and 1 Privateer. Twenty-six other planes—1 Liberator bomber, 3 Hellcats, and 22 Corsairs—were damaged.

In the wild confusion that followed the landing of the Japanese airborne troops, two Americans were killed and eighteen injured. At 2338, forces arrived at Yontan to bolster the air-ground service units and to be on hand if enemy airborne troops made subsequent attempts to land. In addition to the thirty-three planes destroyed and damaged, two 600-drum fuel dumps containing 70,000 gallons of gasoline were ignited and destroyed by the Japanese. When a final survey could be made, it was found that ten Japanese had been killed at Yontan; three others were found dead in the plane, evidently killed

---

[1] The account of the air battles was taken from Comdr Fifth Amph Force, Report of Capture of Okinawa Gunto, 17 May–21 Jun 45, 4 Jul 45, II, 5–6; III, 9–44; IV, 2, 3; CINCPAC-CINCPOA Opns in POA, May 1945; Tenth Army G–3 Jnl and G–2 Periodic Rpts, 24 May–3 Jun 45; XXIV Corps G–2 Periodic Rpts, 23–31 May; G–2 Weekly Summary No. 11, 20–26 May 45; 53d AAA Brigade Unit Rpt No. 34, 25 May 45.

by antiaircraft fire. The other four "Sallys" each carried fourteen Japanese soldiers, all of whom died in the flaming wrecks. Sixty-nine bodies in all were counted. A Japanese soldier killed at Zampa Point the next day was thought to be the last of the airborne raiders. Yontan airfield was nonoperational until 0800 of 25 May because of the debris on the runway. This was the enemy's only attempt to land airborne troops on Okinawa during the battle.

While the attack on Yontan was in progress, twenty-three enemy planes conducted a raid against the field at Ie Shima. The bombing did not seriously damage the field itself but caused sixty casualties. During the night, antiaircraft fire shot down eleven enemy planes over Okinawa and sixteen over Ie Shima.

The air assault of 24–25 May was not confined to the airfields of Okinawa and Ie Shima. At the same time a large *Kamikaze* attack was under way against American ships. It was estimated the next day that 200 enemy planes had engaged in the attack. The enemy scored thirteen *Kamikaze* hits on twelve ships off shore. In repelling an attack during the morning of 25 May, American fighter planes intercepted and destroyed seventy-five enemy planes north of Okinawa. Altogether, on 24–25 May, more than 170 Japanese planes were brought down. During the week ending 26 May, the Japanese lost at least 193 planes in the Okinawa area.

The period of torrential rains was interrupted on 27–28 May by a night of clear weather with a bright moon. The Japanese air force and *Kamikazes* again came in force. Between 0730 of 27 May and 0830 of 28 May there were 56 raids of from 2 to 4 planes each, the total of enemy planes being estimated at 150. A vigorous effort was made by the enemy to penetrate the transport defense area and reach the heavy ships. The *Kamikazes* struck at both the Hagushi area and at Buckner Bay, which was now coming into use as an important anchorage. During the night of 27–28 May nine ships were hit by *Kamikazes*. One of them, the destroyer *Drexler,* hit at 0705 on 28 May, sank within two minutes. Including the *Kamikazes,* 114 enemy planes were destroyed during this attack. There were only two other *Kamikaze* attacks during the rest of the campaign, at the beginning and the end of June, both of much smaller scale than any preceding.

The total Japanese air effort was far greater than that encountered in any other Pacific operation. The proximity of airfields in Kyushu and Formosa permitted the employment by the enemy of all types of planes and pilots. Altogether, there were 896 air raids against Okinawa. Approximately 4,000 Japanese planes were destroyed in combat, 1,900 of which were suicide planes. The intensity and

JAPANESE AIR RAIDS ON OKINAWA *were stepped up the last week of May. Above, Japanese plane caught squarely by antiaircraft fire leaves a trail of smoke and flame as it falls toward the ocean. Picture below was taken after unsuccessful Japanese airborne raid on Yontan airfield the morning of 25 May. Bodies of the enemy "Commandos" are scattered around wreckage of their planes. Torn fuselage of one "Sally" is in left background.*

scale of the Japanese suicide air attacks on naval forces and shipping were the most spectacular aspects of the Okinawa campaign. Between 6 April and 22 June there were ten organized *Kamikaze* attacks, employing a total of 1,465 planes as shown below:[2]

Date of Attack	Total	Navy Planes	Army Planes
6–7 April	355	230	125
12–13 April	185	125	60
15–16 April	165	120	45
27–28 April	115	65	50
3–4 May	125	75	50
10–11 May	150	70	80
24–25 May	165	65	100
27–28 May	110	60	50
3–7 June	50	20	30
21–22 June	45	30	15
TOTAL	1465	860	605

In addition, sporadic small-scale suicide attacks were directed against the American fleet by both Army and Navy planes, bringing the total number of suicide sorties during the campaign to 1,900.

The violence of the air attacks is indicated by the damage inflicted on the American forces. Twenty-eight ships were sunk and 225 damaged by Japanese air action during the campaign. Destroyers sustained more hits than any other class of ships. Battleships, cruisers, and carriers also were among those struck, some of the big naval ships suffering heavy damage with great loss of life. The radar picket ships, made up principally of destroyers and destroyer escorts, suffered proportionately greater losses than any other part of the fleet. The great majority of ships sunk or damaged were victims of the *Kamikaze*. Suicide planes accounted for 26 of the 28 vessels sunk and for 164 of the 225 damaged by air attack during the entire campaign.

Stalemate in the Center

It was in the center, where during the preceding week the Americans had made least progress, that the impeding effect of the rains of the last week in May was most clearly shown. Having gained no break-through or momentum in the

[2] U. S. Strategic Bombing Survey (Pacific), Naval Analysis Division, *The Campaigns of the Pacific War* (Washington, 1946), Ch. XIV.

previous fighting, the troops found it impossible under the conditions to resume the offensive effectively.

On the morning of 22 May the 1st Marine Division held a line which extended over the northern and southern slopes of Wana Ridge, south through the village of Wana. To its left, holding the western flank of the XXIV Corps line, was the 77th Division, which had just secured Chocolate Drop. Left of the 77th Division, the 96th Division had recently completed the capture of Sugar Hill and was on the slopes of Oboe. (See Map No. XLIV.)

The 1st Marine Division at Wana Ridge and Wana Draw

When the heavy rains began the 1st Marines was on the northern slope of Wana Ridge, at the left (east) flank of the III Amphibious Corps. The 5th Marines was on the division right, holding the lower crest of Wana Ridge, with its line extending on over the southern slope into Wana village. Beyond the village of Wana lay Wana Draw, a broad, shallow basin, entirely bare, which dropped down from the coral heights west of northern Shuri to the Asa River and the coastal plain north of Naha. On the south side of Wana Draw a high coral ridge, similar to Wana Ridge on the north, climbed steeply to Shuri Heights at the southwestern corner of Shuri. Wana Draw was completely exposed to enemy fire from high ground on three sides.

The 1st Marine Division had been repeatedly thrown back since its first attack on Wana Ridge, 13 May.[3] Yet during most of this 9-day period the weather had been dry and the ground solid, making possible a coordinated attack of all arms—infantry, tanks, heavy assault guns, armored flame throwers, and airplanes. On 21 May the weather changed, with gusts of wind and an overcast that reduced visibility. Before dawn of the next day the rain began, and it continued throughout most of the day and on into the night. The prospects of success for the infantry alone, slogging through the mud without the support of other arms, were not encouraging.

The almost continual downpour filled Wana Draw with mud and water until it resembled a lake. Tanks bogged down, helplessly mired. Amphibian tractors were unable to negotiate the morass, and front-line units, which had depended on these vehicles for carrying supplies forward in bad weather, now had to resort to hand carrying of supplies and of the wounded. These were back-breaking tasks and were performed over areas swept by enemy fire. Mortar and

[3] The account of operations of the 1st Mar Div at Wana Ridge is taken from Stockman, 1st Mar Div Hist, and 1st Mar Div Special Actn Rpt, pp. 6–7.

artillery smoke was used as far as possible to give concealment for all movement. Litter cases were carried back through knee-deep mud.

Living conditions of front-line troops were indescribably bad. Foxholes dug into the clay slopes caved in from the constant soaking, and, even when the sides held, the holes had to be bailed out repeatedly. Clothes and equipment and the men's bodies were wet for days. The bodies of Japanese killed at night lay outside the foxholes, decomposing under swarms of flies. Sanitation measures broke down. The troops were often hungry. Sleep was almost impossible. The strain began to take a mounting toll of men.

Under these conditions the Marine attack against Wana Ridge was soon at a standstill. The action degenerated into what was called in official reports "aggressive patrolling." Despite inactivity, enemy mortar and artillery fire continued to play against the American front lines, especially at dusk and at night.

A break in the weather came on the morning of 28 May. The sky was clear. The 2d Battalion, 1st Marines, acting on a favorable report of a patrol that had reconnoitered the ground the day before, made ready to strike for 100 Meter Hill, or Knob Hill as it was sometimes called, at the eastern tip of Wana Ridge. As soon as this objective was gained, the 3d Battalion was to secure Wana Draw. Twice the 2d Battalion assaulted 100 Meter Hill, and by 0800 Company E reached the top. But the crest could not be held, and no gain at all was made down the southern and eastern slopes. Machine-gun fire from three directions hit the marines, mortar shells fell on them, and Japanese only a few yards away mounted satchel charges on sticks and flung them from close range. The attack failed, and smoke had to be employed to evacuate the wounded.

Meanwhile, on 28 May, the 5th Marines on the division right captured Beehive Hill, a strong enemy defense position on the lower end of Shuri Ridge south of Wana Draw.

The 77th Division Stands Still at Shuri

The 77th Division fared no better than did the 1st Marine Division. Its capture on 20 May of Flattop and the Chocolate Drop area was followed very quickly by the onset of the heavy rains. Thereafter the 77th Division made hardly any gains in its part of the line, directly in front of Shuri. Here the Japanese stood more stubbornly, if possible, than anywhere else, and held defiantly every muddy knob and slope. Jane (also called "Three Sisters"), Dorothy, and Tom Hills formed the main strong points directly north and east of Shuri from which the enemy faced the 77th Division across the rain-drenched country. Dorothy Hill was a fortress with several layers of caves and tunnels

WANA DRAW, *from east end of Wana Ridge, showing open ground over which marines advanced. Bottom of draw, with town of Wana 100 feet to the right, was flooded at time of the battle. Below is ground over which marines attacked 28 May. They captured "Beehive" but were unable to hold "Knob." Ruins of Ishimmi, east of the Marine zone, are at upper right.*

MUD AND FLOOD *increased the difficulties of fighting on Okinawa. Above, 77th Division infantrymen trudge toward the front lines past mud-clogged tanks. Below, 1st Division marines resort to hand carrying of supplies and wounded as roads are washed out by torrential rains.*

on its reverse slope and with heavy artillery and mortars concentrated behind its protecting bulk. The next objective of the 307th Infantry of the 77th Division was the Three Sisters, 400 yards across a low bare swale from Flattop. Farther to the west the 306th Infantry, which had relieved the 305th Infantry on 21 May, stood on Ishimmi Ridge and in front of the eastern end of Wana Ridge, which had proved so tough a barrier to the 1st Marine Division.

As a result of an ill-fated attack early in the morning of 21 May, Company A of the 307th Infantry was isolated along the bottom of the forward slope of Jane Hill, ahead of the rest of the troops back on Flattop and Ishimmi Ridge, with an exposed valley raked by enemy mortar and machine-gun fire between the troops and their base of supplies. All roads leading to the 307th front had become impassable, and over the last 1,000 yards everything had to be hand carried. As many men were lost in trying to bring supplies up to Company A across this muddy swale as were lost in the fighting on Jane Hill.[4] In these circumstances life was not pleasant on the lower slope of the hill, where foxholes were washed out in the yellow clay almost daily. Company A was virtually cut off at Jane Hill from 21 to 30 May.

The last week of May points up the importance of logistics to the battle. In this instance, mud defeated local logistics. Ammunition, water, and food had to be hand carried up from the rear for distances as great as a mile. Casualties had to be carried back, eight men struggling and slipping in mud up to their knees with each litter. Weapons were dirty and wet. In a second or two, mortar shells could be expended that had taken a man a half-day to bring to the weapon from the nearest vehicle or dump. Under these conditions there could be no attack. The men had all they could do to live. Their time was entirely taken in meeting the fundamental needs of existence. Hard fighting during the last third of May was impossible for men who were already exhausted. The troops simply tried to stay where they were. The front had everywhere bogged down in mud.

The 96th Division at Oboe

Like the 77th Division troops, elements of the 382d Infantry, 96th Division, holding positions at the foot of Hen Hill, just across the boundary from the 77th Division, were unable to move from their mud foxholes. The Japanese had perfect observation of this area from Tom Hill, just east of Shuri, and brought down mortar and machine-gun fire on any activity. There was little

---

[4] Appleman, XXIV Corps History, p. 442.

movement except for an occasional patrol. Mud, low supplies, and drooping spirits prevailed here too.

To the east the lines of the 382d Infantry crossed over the jaw-like clay promontory of Oboe, which stood like a rampart a thousand yards east of Shuri. On 21 May bitter fighting had placed elements of the 382d Infantry on the lip of Oboe. For the next week the crest of Oboe was a no-man's land, and around it, and even down the forward face, supposedly in American hands, a close and unending grenade and bitter hand-to-hand fight raged. Here, more than anywhere else on the cross-island line during the period of mud, action was always near at hand. Here it was hardest to maintain the status quo described by Lt. Col. Howard L. Cornutt, Assistant G–3 of the 96th Division, when he stated ironically: "Those on the forward slopes of hills slid down; those on the reverse slopes slid back. Otherwise, no change." [5]

An hour after midnight, in the morning of 24 May, a platoon of Japanese started through a gap between Companies C and L on Oboe and succeeded in knocking out the three right-hand foxholes of Company C. The light mortars of the 1st Battalion were at the base of Oboe, and when the attack developed they fired into the gap between the companies for the next four hours at the rate of a round and a half a minute. Communication lines were out: enemy mortars had cut every phone line, and the radio to the Navy had been drowned out by the rain. Artillery and illumination by the Navy could not be called over the area. By 0330 a full company of Japanese was attacking through the gap, and two platoons were assaulting Company A on the left of Company C. In the foxhole next to the three that had been knocked out by the Japanese, Pfc. Delmar Schriever, though wounded by mortar fire which killed the other two men in the foxhole with him, held his position single-handed until morning. Companies A and B were forced back off Oboe to the bottom, but the few men left in Company C remained near the top under the courageous leadership of Pfc. John J. Kwiecien, who took over command of the 1st Platoon when the platoon leader was wounded. In the 2d Platoon on the right only one man out of fourteen was unwounded when daylight came. These men on Oboe had used thirty-five cases of grenades during the night; only fifty rounds of 60-mm. mortar remained. By 0530 the foxholes on the right of Company C at the crest of Oboe had been won back from the Japanese. At this time Japanese were seen

---

[5] The account of operations of the 96th Division at Oboe Hill was taken from Mulford and Rogers, 96th Div History, Pt. IV, pp. 141–44; 96th Div Actn Rpt, Ch. VII; 382d Inf Actn Rpt, Ch. VII.

"THREE SISTERS," *photographed 6 May after the area had been saturated by American artillery fire. Radio towers (upper left) were destroyed later in May.*

OBOE *hill mass was under attack by 77th Division artillery when this picture was taken 23 May. Muddy reverse slope of Zebra (foreground) is pitted with foxholes; some shelters can be seen in defilade at foot of Oboe.*

forming for another attack, but a timely resupply of mortar ammunition enabled the embattled troops to repel this effort. During the Japanese counterattack against Oboe the 362d Field Artillery Battalion fired 560 rounds of shells in helping to stem the enemy onslaught.

When the Japanese attack subsided, 150 enemy dead lay on top of Oboe and on the slope immediately beyond. The Japanese dug in on the reverse slope of Oboe only twenty-five yards from the American foxholes. Between the two dug-in forces, on 24 May, there was an interchange of hand grenades all day long.

The heavy losses incurred by the 1st Battalion, 382d Infantry, in repelling this furious Japanese night assault compelled a reorganization of the battalion. The three rifle companies, A, B, and C, were combined into one company under the Company C commander, with a total strength of 198 officers and enlisted men. This is another example of how battalions were reduced to company strength at Shuri. On 24 May General Bradley, the 96th Division commander, ordered the 3d Battalion, 383d Infantry, to take over the left part of the line of the 2d Battalion, 382d, on Oboe. The ranks of the 2d Battalion had become too thin to withstand another attack like that of 24 May.

Efforts of the 383d Infantry to make inroads into the Love Hill system of defenses on the western side of Conical all failed during the period 22–28 May. Many men were killed during patrol action while searching for a weak spot in the enemy's lines. Nor could American troops move over the crest of the Conical hogback to the west slope without risking their lives. In the neighborhood of Cutaway Hill especially, the enemy constantly reinforced his lines and kept on the alert. No gains toward Shuri were registered in any part of this region lying west of the crest of Conical. The enemy held tight. Thus matters stood along the center of the XXIV Corps front at the end of the month of May.

The 6th Marine Division Occupies Naha

During the rainy period at the end of May, both flanks of the American line forged ahead of the center. This development was a continuation of a trend that had started in the third week of May. In that week two ramparts of the three hills that made up the integrated Sugar Loaf position—Sugar Loaf itself and the Horseshoe—had fallen after as bloody a period of fighting as the marines had ever encountered. However, the efforts of the 6th Marine Division to complete the reduction of Sugar Loaf, the left (west) anchor of the Japanese line, failed; on 21 May, after five days of fighting, they gave up their attempt to take the reverse (south) slope of the Crescent, the third and closest to Shuri of the Sugar Loaf hills.

For several days after Sugar Loaf fell, the 6th Marine Division continued its efforts to reduce Crescent, the easternmost strong point of the Sugar Loaf sector, but without success. The Japanese denied American troops control of the crest and retained complete possession of the crescent-shaped reverse slope. As long as this ground remained in Japanese hands there could be no swinging eastward by the 6th Marine Division for close envelopment of Shuri. After considering the prospect the division decided to abandon its efforts to force the fall of Crescent and instead to press on toward Naha and the Kokuba River. A strong defense force was left on the north face of Crescent to protect the left rear and to maintain contact with the 1st Marine Division to the east. The main effort of the Army's right (west) flank was now toward Naha and no longer immediately toward Shuri.[6]

The 6th Marine Division Crosses the Asato

The heavy rains had raised the Asato River when patrols on the night of 22–23 May waded the river upstream from Naha to reconnoiter the south bank. The initial reports were that it would be feasible to cross the stream without tank support. Between dawn and 1000, 23 May, patrols pressed 400 yards south of the river under moderate fire. At 1000 the decision was made to cross in force at 1200 by infiltration. An hour and a half after the movement began two battalions were across the Asato under cover of smoke. Casualties had to be evacuated back across the stream by hand, twelve men carrying each stretcher in chest-deep water.

Throughout the night of 23–24 May the 6th Engineer Battalion labored to build a crossing for vehicles. Borrowing from experience at Guadalcanal, five LVT's were brought to the stream and efforts made to move them into position to serve as piers for bridge timbers. Two of the LVT's struck mines along the bank and were destroyed, and the effort to bridge the stream in this manner was abandoned. At dawn a Bailey bridge was started, and by 1430 it had been finished. A tank crossing was ready before dark. The same day two squads of the Reconnaissance Company crossed the lower Asato and roamed the streets of northwestern Naha without meeting resistance.

[6] The account of operations of the 6th Mar Div was, unless otherwise indicated, taken from 6th Mar Div Special Actn Rpt, Phase III, pp. 11–15; Carleton, 6th Mar Div History, pp. 122–36.

CROSSING THE ASATO RIVER, *marines laid smoke to cover their advance at Machishi 23 May. Destroyed bridges (circled) had not been replaced at time picture was made. Eastern Naha and Kokuba estuary are at upper right.*

ENTERING NAHA, *Marine patrols move through deserted streets in the western part of town. The walled compounds around the houses, typical of Oriental urban structures, gave good cover for snipers.*

The Occupation of Naha

The unmolested patrols into Naha on 24 May led to the crossing of the lower Asato on 25 May by the Reconnaissance Company of the 6th Marine Division, which during the day penetrated deep into Naha west of the north-south canal that bisects the city. Only an occasional Japanese straggler was met; sniper fire was almost nonexistent. A few Okinawan civilians who were still hiding in the rubble of the city said they had seen only scattered 5- or 6-man Japanese patrols during the past week.[7] The rubble of Naha was deserted. The Reconnaissance Company dug in without packs and gear to hold the gain so easily obtained.

Naha had no tactical value other than to afford the Americans a route of travel southward to the next objective. The city was located in a wide coastal flat at the mouth of the Kokuba River; it was dominated by the high ground of the Oroku Peninsula across the channel to the south, and by a ridge that curved around the city and coastal flat from the northeast to southwest along the Kokuba estuary.

On 27 May one company of the 2d Battalion, 22d Marines, crossed the Asato, passed through the lines of the Reconnaissance Company, and pressed deeper into the western part of Naha. The next morning at daylight the marines moved on toward the Kokuba estuary; reaching it at 0900, they received hardly a shot as they picked their way among the demolished buildings and the heaps of debris. The effort of a platoon to press forward to scout the situation at the approaches to Ona-Yama Island, which lies in the middle of the Kokuba Channel opposite the south end of the Naha Canal, failed. The marines were met by heavy machine-gun fire, and in their withdrawal the platoon leader was killed. All of Naha west of the canal and north of Kokuba was now in possession of the marines. Steps were taken quickly to defend this portion of the city. Eight 37-mm. antitank guns were ranged along the sea wall bordering the north bank of the Kokuba estuary, and a line of marines took up positions behind the sea wall. The 1st Armored Amphibious Battalion held and patrolled the seaward side of the city.

During the night of 28 May engineers put three footbridges across the canal, and before dawn the 1st Battalion, 22d Marines, crossed to Telegraph Hill in east Naha, where a fight raged throughout the day without noticeable gains. On 30 May the 2d and 3d Battalions, 22d Marines, crossed the canal,

[7] Tenth Army G–3 Jnl, Msg No. 25, 28 May 45.

passed through the 1st Battalion, and took up the assault. Enemy machine guns emplaced in burial tombs on Hill 27 in east Naha temporarily checked the infantry. During most of the day tanks were unable to reach the position, but in the afternoon three worked their way along the road north of the hill, and their direct fire enabled the marines to seize it.

The Kokuba Hills

The Kokuba Hills extend eastward from the edge of Naha along the north side of the Kokuba estuary and the Naha–Yonabaru valley. They guard the southern and southwestern approaches to the rear of Shuri. With the 6th Marine Division pressing south along the west coast, defense of this terrain was vital to the enemy in preventing an envelopment of Shuri from Naha. On the night of 22–23 May the headquarters of the Japanese *44th Independent Mixed Brigade* moved from Shuri to Shichina village, in the Kokuba Hills, for better control of the operations on this flank.[8] The Japanese upon evacuating Naha took positions in the high ground in the eastern part of the city and the semicircle of hills beyond. There the fight on the enemy's left flank entered its next phase.

Since the crossing of the upper Asato on 23 May, the left (east) elements of the 6th Marine Division had encountered continuing opposition. The 4th Marines held this part of the line, and suffered heavy casualties as it tried to press forward in the mud of the flooded valley and low clay hills. By the night of 25 May Company E had been reduced to forty enlisted men and one officer. That day the 1st Battalion took the village of Machishi, but with bridges washed out and the torrential rains making the terrain impassable for tanks it was learned that infantry could go ahead only with heavy casualties. On 28 May the 29th Marines relieved the 4th Marines, and, although opposed by enemy small-arms fire, by the close of the day it had pressed to within 800 yards of the Kokuba River.

Both the 22d and the 29th Marines were now attacking east against the hill mass centering on Hill 46, west of Shichina village and north of the Kokuba estuary. After the fall of Hill 27 on 30 May there was a rapid advance of several hundred yards until the defenses of Hill 46 were reached. Then another intensive battle was fought in the rain and mud. Fourteen tanks clawed their way into firing position on the last day of the month and put direct fire into the enemy. Even then intense machine-gun and mortar fire denied the hill to a strong

[8] Tenth Army PW Interrog Summary No. 4, 1 Aug 45: The *44th Independent Mixed Brigade*.

coordinated attack, although large gains were made. Throughout the night American artillery pounded Hill 46. The next morning, on 1 June, the assault regiments took the hill, broke through the Shichina area, and then seized Hill 98 and the line of the north fork of the Kokuba.

The 7th Division Bids for Envelopment

When elements of the 96th Division seized the east face of Conical Hill and of Sugar Hill at the southern end of the Conical hogback, a path was cleared for the execution of a flanking maneuver around the right end of the Japanese line. The flanking force, once through the corridor and past Yonabaru, could sweep to the west up the Yonabaru valley and encircle Shuri from the rear. The main force of the Japanese army would then be trapped. This was the plan which the XXIV Corps was ready to put into effect when night fell on 21 May.[9]

Funneling Through the Conical Corridor

Strengthened by 1,691 replacements and 546 men returned to duty from hospitals since it left the lines on 9 May, the 7th Division moved up to forward assembly areas just north of Conical Hill and prepared to make the dash through the corridor. At 1900 on 21 May the 184th Infantry, chosen by General Arnold to lead the way, was in place at Gaja Ridge, at the northern base of Conical. The initial move of the envelopment was to be made in the dead of the night and in stealth.[10] General Buckner felt that "if the 7th can swing round, running the gauntlet, it may be the kill." [11]

Rain began to fall an hour before Company G, 184th Infantry, the lead element, was scheduled to leave its assembly area. The rain increased rapidly until it was a steady downpour. Up to 0200 on 22 May, the hour of departure, the men huddled under their ponchos listening to the dull, heavy reverberations of the artillery preparation, which sounded even louder and nearer in the rain. Then, in single column, the company headed south through the black night, the

[9] Appleman, XXIV Corps History, pp. 415ff. After the battle for Okinawa General Hodge stated that he had planned to use the 7th Division in such a maneuver even before the division had been relieved and before the attack of 11 May. See, however, Okinawa Diary, XXIV Corps, kept by Capt. Donald Mulford, 13–20 May 45, which indicates that General Hodge was even at that date somewhat uncertain about the maneuver.

[10] The account of operations of the 184th Infantry, 7th Division, through the coastal corridor was, unless otherwise indicated, taken from Gugeler, 7th Div History, pp. 292–313.

[11] Notes of Tenth Army Staff Meeting, 20 May 45, in Okinawa Diary kept by Lt Col Stevens and M/Sgt Burns.

rain, and the sludge. No one fired as two Japanese dodged into the shadows and the debris of Yonabaru, and at 0415 the company formed at a crossroads in the ruined town, platoons abreast, ready to push on to Spruce Hill. It accomplished this advance without incident. Once on the crest of Spruce Hill, Company G sent up a flare signaling Company F to come through and try to reach Chestnut Hill.

Daylight, a dull and murky gray, had come when Company F reached the crest of Chestnut, 435 feet above the coast 1,000 yards southeast of Yonabaru. Only one man was wounded in this phase of the assault. As Company F reached the crest of Chestnut and looked down over the southern slope, several enemy soldiers were spotted climbing the hill, apparently to take up defense positions. A soldier said as he looked at them that they "had better hold reveille a little earlier." Complete surprise had crowned the American effort. It was learned later that the Japanese command had not expected the Americans to make a night attack or to attack at all when tank and heavy-weapons support were immobilized by rain and mud.[12]

The 3d Battalion followed the 2d through Yonabaru. It then began advancing to the south toward Juniper and Bamboo Hills on a line southwest of Chestnut, the other high ground which the 184th was to seize before it would be considered safe for the 32d Infantry to come through the corridor and turn west to cut behind Shuri. The attack continued on the rainy morning of 23 May, with the 2d and 3d Battalions pressing forward to these initial objectives. At the end of the day, except for a small gap between Company G on Juniper Hill and Company L on Bamboo Hill, the 184th Infantry had won a solid line stretching from the seacoast across the southern slope of Chestnut Hill and then across to Juniper and Bamboo. In two rainy days the 184th had forced a 2,000-yard crack in the enemy's defenses south of Yonabaru and accomplished its mission. Now the 32d Infantry could begin the second and decisive phase of the enveloping plan.

The 32d Infantry Attempts an Envelopment

While the 184th Infantry held the blocking line from Chestnut to Bamboo and thus protected the left flank and rear, the 32d Infantry was to drive directly west along the Naha–Yonabaru valley to cut off Shuri from the south. The success of the entire plan of encirclement depended upon the 32d Infantry's carrying out its part.

[12] Interrog Yahara.

On 22 May, while the 184th Infantry was pressing south, Company F of the 32d Infantry moved to the southern tip of Conical Hill, just west of Yonabaru, to help protect the right side of the passage. The main body of the 32d Infantry, however, did not start moving until the morning of 23 May, after Colonel Green of the 184th Infantry radioed that his attack was going well and that it would be safe for the 32d to proceed. At 1045 on 23 May the 2d Battalion, 32d Infantry, passed through Yonabaru and headed west. Its initial objective was the string of hills west of Yonabaru and south of the Naha–Yonabaru road, centering on Oak Hill just below the village of Yonawa. By nightfall two battalions, the 2d and 3d, were deployed a mile southwest of Yonabaru facing west, ready to make their bid for envelopment. Already heavy machine-gun fire had slowed the advance and served notice that the enemy would bitterly oppose a drive up the Yonabaru valley. The continuing rains had by this time mired the tanks in their assembly areas north of Conical Hill, and the armor which commanders had counted on to spearhead the drive to the west was unable to function. Heavy assault guns likewise were immobilized. The infantry was on its own.[13]

During 24 May the 32d Infantry developed the line where the Japanese meant to check the westward thrust of the 7th Division. This line ran south from Mouse Hill (southwest of Conical Hill), crossed the Naha–Yonabaru road about a mile west of Yonabaru, and then bent slightly southwest to take in June and Mabel Hills, the latter being the key to the position. Mabel Hill guarded the important road center of Chan, which lay two miles almost directly south of Shuri. Oak Hill, an enemy strong point, was somewhat in front of this line. Tactically, it was apparent that this line protected the Shuri–Chan–Karadera–Kamizato–Iwa road net, the easternmost of two routes of withdrawal south from Shuri.

The Japanese reacted slowly to the initial penetration below Yonabaru. Mortar and artillery fire, however, gradually increased. The scattered groups of second-class troops encountered plainly did not have the skill and determination of the soldiers manning the Shuri line. On 23 May elements of the Japanese *24th Division* were dispatched from Shuri to retake Yonabaru.[14] This effort took shape in numerous counterattacks on the night of 24–25 May against the 184th Infantry, which had just secured a lodgment on Locust Hill, a high,

---

[13] The account of operations of 32d Infantry was, unless otherwise indicated, taken from Gugeler, 7th Div History, pp. 313–14, 320–27, 345–49, 362–66; 32d Inf Actn Rpt, pp. 23, 28.

[14] Interrog Yahara.

EAST COAST CORRIDOR, *looking north along Highway 13 from Yonabaru. Conical Hill is just to left of Gaja.*

YONABARU–NAHA VALLEY *highway, with Yonawa and Oak Hill in foreground. Picture was taken 26 May as 7th Division infantrymen pressed back the enemy's right flank below Shuri.*

broad coral escarpment half a mile south of Chestnut Hill. At 0230 the Japanese counterattack also struck elements of the 32d Infantry west of Yonabaru. The enemy made some penetration of American lines at this point, and fighting continued until after dawn, when the Japanese assault force withdrew, leaving many dead behind.[15]

On 25 or 26 May, the main body of the enfeebled *62d Division* left Shuri and made a circuitous march to the southeast to join the fight against the 184th Infantry below Yonabaru.[16] Its arrival on the Ozato–Mura front had no important effect except to strengthen the covering and holding force. The Hemlock-Locust Hill Escarpment area was cleared of the enemy on 26 May, and thereafter the 184th Infantry met no serious opposition as it pressed south to the vicinity of Karadera.[17] Patrols sent deep to the south reported encountering only scattered enemy troops. It became increasingly evident that the Japanese had pulled back their right flank, were fighting only a holding action there, and had no intention of withdrawing into the Chinen Peninsula as had been thought possible by American commanders.

It was on the right end of the 7th Division's enveloping attack that the Japanese brought the most fire power to bear and offered the most active resistance. The high ground at this point, where the southwest spurs of Conical Hill came down to the Naha–Yonabaru valley, was integrated with the Shuri fortified defense zone. American success at this point would cut the road connections south from Shuri and permit its envelopment; hence the Japanese denied to the 96th Division any gains in this area which would have helped the 32d Infantry in its push west.

The Japanese Hold

The bright promise of enveloping Shuri faded rapidly as the fighting of 23–26 May brought the 32d Infantry practically to a standstill in front of the Japanese defense line across the Yonabaru valley. The Japanese had emplaced a large number of antitank guns and automatic weapons which swept all approach routes to the key hills. Mortars were concentrated on the reverse slopes. Had tanks been able to operate, the 32d Infantry could perhaps have destroyed the enemy's fire power and overrun the Japanese defenders, but the tanks were mired. On 26 May torrential downpours totaled 3.5 inches of rain; the last ten

[15] XXIV Corps G–2 Periodic Rpt No. 55, 25 May 45.

[16] Tenth Army PW Interrog Summary No. 2, 2 Aug 45: The *62d Division*.

[17] 184th Inf Actn Rpt, pp. 16–17.

days of May averaged 1.11 inches daily.[18] General Hodge stated later that no phase of the Okinawa campaign worried him more than this period when the 32d Infantry was trying to break through behind Shuri.[19]

Decisive action in the Japanese holding battle took place in the vicinity of Duck and Mabel Hills, east of Chan. Here, on 26 May, the 32d Infantry tried to break the enemy resistance, but in a fierce encounter on Duck Hill it was thrown back with heavy casualties. The fighting was so intense and confused that five Japanese broke through and attacked T/5 William Goodman, the only medic left in Company I, who was bandaging wounded men in a forward exposed area. Goodman killed all five Japanese with a pistol and then held his ground until the wounded were evacuated. In the withdrawal from Duck Hill the dead had to be left behind. No gain was made on the 27th, and on the 28th there was no activity other than patrolling.[20]

The most significant gains of the 32d Infantry in its drive west were to come on 30 and 31 May, when all three of its battalions launched a coordinated attack. By the end of 30 May the 32d had taken Oak, Ella, and June Hills; the advance brought the regiment directly up against Mabel and Hetty Hills and the defenses of Chan. On the last day of the month the 32d Infantry seized Duck Hill, consolidated positions on Turkey Hill, north of Mabel, and occupied the forward face of Mabel itself. The enemy still held the reverse slope of Mabel and occupied the town of Chan. The Japanese encountered were not numerous, but they had to be killed in place. They were the rear-guard holding force.

In front of the 184th Infantry to the southeast, the enemy fought a delaying action on 28–29 May at Hill 69, commonly called Karadera Hill, just north of the village of the same name. When patrols of the 184th Infantry penetrated deep into the Chinen Peninsula on 30 May without encountering the enemy, it was obvious that this rugged region would not become a battlefield.[21]

By 30 May the XXIV Corps lines showed a large and deep bulge on the left flank below the Naha–Yonabaru road; here the American lines were approximately two miles farther south than at any other part of the cross-island battlefront. On the American left flank the envelopment of Shuri had almost succeeded in catching the Japanese army.

[18] Tenth Army G–4 Summary No. 99 in G–3 Jnl, Msg No. 35, 31 May 45.

[19] Interv XXIV Corps historian with Gen Hodge, 6 Jul 45.

[20] XXIV Corps G–3 Jnl, 29 May 45.

[21] Gugeler, 7th Div History, pp. 352–58; XXIV Corps G–2 Periodic Rpt No. 60, 31 May 45.

CHAPTER XV

The Fall of Shuri

As the end of May approached, conflict had been raging on the Shuri line nearly two months and many an American soldier wondered whether Shuri would ever be taken or whether he would be alive to witness its capture. While on 21 May the eastern slope of Conical Hill had been taken, after more than a week of further fighting the high belt of Shuri defenses still held firm all around the ancient capital of the Ryukyus. The American gains in southern Okinawa had been confined to a rather small area of hills and coral ridges which, aside from Yontan and Kadena airfields seized on 1 April, had no important value for the attack on the Japanese home islands. It is true that these airfields, the flat extent of Ie Shima, and certain coastal areas of central Okinawa suitable for air base development were already swarming with naval and army construction battalions, at work on the task of making the island over into a gigantic, unsinkable carrier from which to mount the final air assault on Japan. But this was just a beginning. Most of the big prizes—the port of Naha, the big anchorage of Nakagusuku Bay, Yonabaru, Shuri, Naha airfield, and the flat coastal ground of southern Okinawa—were still effectively denied to the Americans, long after they had expected to capture them.

By the end of May, however, the flower of General Ushijima's forces on Okinawa had been destroyed. The three major enemy combat units—the *62d Division,* the *24th Division,* and the *44th Independent Mixed Brigade*—had all been committed to the line and had all wasted away as a result of the incessant naval gunfire, artillery fire, air attacks, and the tank and infantry combat. Second-rate troops had for some time been present in the line, mixed with the surviving veterans of the regular combat units. By the end of May 62,548 of the enemy had been reported killed "and counted" and another 9,529 estimated as killed. As compared with 3,214 killed in northern Okinawa and 4,856 on Ie Shima, 64,000 of these were reported killed in the fighting in the Shuri fortified zone. According to division reports, about 12,000 were killed by the 1st and 6th Marine Divisions and 41,000 by the 7th, 27th, 77th, and 96th Army Divisions while in the line at one time or another under XXIV Corps. The largest number were killed by the 96th Division, credited with 17,000.[1]

Even though these reports of enemy losses are undoubtedly somewhat exaggerated, there is no question that Japanese forces, especially infantry combat units, had been seriously depleted. A conservative estimate would indicate that 50,000 of the best Japanese troops had been killed in the Shuri fighting by the end of May. The enemy's artillery also was weakening noticeably as piece after piece was captured or was destroyed by naval gunfire, counterbattery fire, and air bombing.

Nothing illustrates so well the great difference between the fighting in the Pacific and that in Europe as the small number of military prisoners taken on Okinawa. At the end of May the III Amphibious Corps had captured only 128 Japanese soldiers. At the same time, after two months of fighting in southern Okinawa, the four divisions of the XXIV Corps had taken only 90 military prisoners. The 77th Division, which had been in the center of the line from the last days of April through May, had taken only 9 during all that time.[2] Most of the enemy taken prisoner either were badly wounded or were unconscious; they could not prevent capture or commit suicide before falling into American hands.

In the light of these prisoner figures there is no question as to the state of Japanese morale. The Japanese soldier fought until he was killed. There was only one kind of Japanese casualty—the dead. Those that were wounded either died of their wounds or returned to the front lines to be killed. The Japanese soldier gave his all.

Casualties on the American side were the heaviest of the Pacific war. At the end of May, losses of the two Marine divisions, whose fighting included approximately a month on the Shuri front, stood at 1,718 killed, 8,852 wounded, and 101 missing. In two months of fighting, chiefly on the Shuri front, the XXIV Corps suffered 2,871 killed, 12,319 wounded, and 183 missing. The XXIV Corps and the III Amphibious Corps had lost a total of 26,044 killed, wounded, or missing. American losses were approximately one man killed to every ten Japanese.[3]

Nonbattle casualties were numerous, a large percentage of them being neuro-psychiatric or "combat fatigue" cases. The two Marine divisions had had 6,315 nonbattle cases by the end of May; the four Army divisions, 7,762. The most

[1] Tenth Army G–2 Periodic Rpt No. 67, 1 Jun 45; G–2 Summary, 1 Jun 45, in Tenth Army G–3 Jnl, Msg No. 5, 2 Jun 45.

[2] Ibid.

[3] Tenth Army G–3 Periodic Rpt No. 67, 1 Jun 45. For comparative figures see ASF Monthly Progress Rpt, Sec. 7, 31 May 45, pp. 17, 19; 30 Sep 45, p. 5.

"There was only one kind of Japanese casualty . . . ."

Our losses: "one man killed to every ten Japanese."

CASUALTIES

important cause of this was unquestionably the great amount of enemy artillery and mortar fire, the heaviest concentrations experienced in the Pacific war. Another cause of men's nerves giving way was the unending close-in battle with a fanatical foe. The rate of psychiatric cases was probably higher on Okinawa than in any previous operation in the Pacific.[4]

If Japanese artillery and mortar fire shattered nerves to such an extent among American troops, some idea may be gained of the ordeal experienced by the Japanese when they were exposed to the greatly superior American fire power delivered by artillery, naval gunfire, and planes. The Japanese, however, were generally deep underground during heavy bombardment; the Americans were usually in shallow foxholes, in defilade, or exposed on the slope or crest of some ridge that was under attack.

The fighting strength of the American combat units engaged in southern Okinawa at the end of May stood at 45,980 for the III Amphibious Corps and 51,745 for the XXIV Army Corps. The infantry divisions, especially those of the Army, were considerably below strength. On 26 May the 77th Infantry Division had a strength, exclusive of attached units, of only 9,628 enlisted men; the 96th Infantry Division, 10,993. At the end of May the American troops were exhausted. Out of 61 days the 96th Division had been in the line 50 days, the 7th Division 49, the 77th Division the last 32, the 1st Marine Division the last 31, and the 6th Marine Division more than 3 weeks. In the two months of fighting in southern Okinawa the 7th and 96th Divisions had seen the most continuous service. The 7th Division in that time had had one rest period of 12 days, the 96th Division one of 11 days.[5]

For the veteran combat troops of the Japanese army, there was no rest once they were committed. With few exceptions they stayed in the line until killed or seriously wounded. Gradually, toward the end of May, more and more second-rate troops from service units and labor groups were fed into the Japanese line to bolster the thinning ranks of the combat infantry.

American armor, which played so important a part in the ground action, had suffered heavily. By the end of May, not counting Marine tank losses, there had been 221 tank casualties in the four Army tank battalions and the one

[4] ASF Monthly Progress Rpt, Sec. 7, 30 Sep 45, p. 6; interv 1st I & H Off with Col F. B. Westervelt, Tenth Army Surgeon, 31 May 45.

[5] Tenth Army G-3 Periodic Rpt No. 67, 1 Jun 45; G-1 Periodic Rpt No. 8, 30 May 45, in G-3 Jnl, 2 Jun 45. The strength figures cited are confined to effective strength of organic and attached units of III Amphibious Corps and XXIV Corps only. For assigned strength of all forces in the Ryukyus, see Appendix C, Table No. 1.

armored flame thrower battalion. Of this total, 94 tanks, or 43 percent, had been completely destroyed. Enemy mines had destroyed or damaged 64 tanks and enemy gunfire 111. Such mishaps as thrown tracks or bogging down in bad terrain had accounted for 38, of which 25 were subsequently destroyed or damaged, mostly by enemy action. The 221 tank casualties constituted about 57 percent of the total number of Army tanks on Okinawa. At least 12 of the valuable and irreplaceable armored flame-throwing tanks were among those lost.[6]

Exodus From Shuri

American staff officers believed that the Japanese would fight at Shuri to the end. The struggle had gone on so long in front of Shuri that everyone apparently had formed the opinion that it would continue there until the last of the Japanese defenders had been killed. In a staff meeting at Tenth Army on 19 May Col. Louis B. Ely, intelligence officer of the Tenth Army, said that it looked as though the Japanese would fight at Shuri to the death. In another staff meeting, on the evening of 22 May, Colonel Ely, in commenting on the passage of the 7th Division down the Conical corridor, noted the absence of strong resistance to the move and interpreted this as supporting the view that the "Japs will hole up in Shuri." At the same time General Buckner remarked: "I think all Jap first line troops are in the Shuri position. They don't appear to be falling back." On 25 May the Tenth Army periodic intelligence report stated that "evidence of captured documents, POW [Prisoners of War] statements, and air photographs tends to indicate that the enemy intends to defend the Shuri area to the last." [7]

Actually, the Japanese had for some time been preparing to evacuate Shuri. About 20 May, even before the final stretches of the eastern face of the Conical hogback fell to the 96th Division, the pressure on both flanks and the American gains in front of Shuri forced the Japanese command to realize that a decision must be made whether to fight to the end at Shuri, bringing all remaining resources to that area, or to withdraw from Shuri to other positions farther south. The loss of ground on the west flank in the vicinity of Sugar Loaf Hill

[6] XXIV Corps G–2 Summary No. 12, 5 Jun 45, incls 2 and 7: Results of Enemy Action against Tanks as Submitted by 20th Armored Group; Tenth Army Ordnance Periodic Summary, 23 May 45, in G–3 Jnl, 24 May 45.

[7] Notes of Tenth Army Staff Meetings, in Okinawa Diary kept by Lt Col Stevens and M/Sgt Burns, 19 and 22 May 45; Tenth Army G–2 Periodic Rpt No. 60, 25 May 45.

and Naha was not, indeed, considered by the Japanese as endangering too greatly the defense of Shuri, as they believed that they could meet this threat by withdrawing the flank to positions south and southeast of Naha. But the loss of the remaining positions on the east and south of Conical Hill made the defense of Shuri extremely difficult and tipped the scales.[8]

Decision Under Shuri Castle

On 21 May, the very day when the 96th Division completed the seizure of the eastern face of Conical and carved out the corridor to the south, General Ushijima called a night conference in the command caves under Shuri Castle. It was attended by all division and brigade commanders of the Japanese *32d Army*. Three alternative courses of action were proposed: a final stand at Shuri; withdrawal to the Chinen Peninsula; and withdrawal to the south.[9]

The first plan was favored by the *62d Division*, which had fought so long in the Shuri area and looked upon that part of the island defenses as peculiarly its own. The argument of General Fujioka, the division's commander, was supported by the presence of large stores at Shuri and the general feeling that a withdrawal would not be in the best traditions of the Japanese Army. The second proposal, to retreat to the Chinen Peninsula, received little support from anyone; it was considered unfeasible because of the difficulties of transportation over mountainous terrain and poor roads. The third possibility, that of withdrawing to the south, had in its favor the prospect of prolonging the battle and thereby gaining time and exacting greater attrition from the American forces. Other considerations favoring the plan were the presence in the south of positions prepared earlier by the *24th Division* and the availability there of considerable quantities of stores and supplies.

For a time the trend of the discussion favored a final battle at Shuri, but it was generally conceded that this would result in a quicker defeat for the Japanese Army. The prospect of prolonging the battle by a withdrawal to the south was the determining consideration in the staff debate, and the decision was finally made to order a retreat to the south. The commanders present were directed to prepare for withdrawal from Shuri at the end of the month. The transport of supplies and wounded began the following night, 22–23 May. This final tactical deployment began silently, unsuspected by the Americans.

[8] Interrog Yahara; Tenth Army PW Interrog Summary No. 1, 5 Aug 45: *32d Army*.

[9] The account of the planning of the Japanese withdrawal from Shuri is based on Interrog Yahara; Interrog Shimada; Tenth Army PW Interrog Summary No. 1, 5 Aug 45: *32d Army;* Summary No. 2, 2 Aug 45: *62d Division*.

Discovery From the Air

From 22 May until the end of the month aerial observation over the enemy's rear areas was limited by the almost constant overcast and the hard rains. Planes, however, were over the enemy's lines for short periods nearly every day, and on 22 May groups of individuals, believed to be civilians, were observed moving south at dusk from Kamizato. The movement continued the following day. It was not believed that these people were soldiers since they were wearing white cloth. Leaflets had previously been dropped behind the Japanese lines telling the Okinawan civilians to identify themselves by wearing white and thus avoid being strafed and bombed. On 24 and 25 May aerial observation noted continued movement southward, but the impression persisted that it was civilian.[10]

The first doubt of the correctness of this view came on 26 May. In the afternoon the overcast lifted long enough for extensive aerial observation over the south end of the island. Movement extending from the front lines to the southern tip of the island was spotted. About 2,000 troops were estimated to be on the move between Oroku Peninsula and the middle part of the island below the Naha–Yonabaru valley. At 1800 from 3,000 to 4,000 people were seen traveling south just below Shuri. About a hundred trucks were on the roads in front of the Yaeju-Dake. At noon two tanks were observed pulling artillery pieces, and an hour later a prime mover towing another artillery piece was spotted. During the afternoon seven more tanks, moving south and southwest, were seen.

Pilots strafed the moving columns and reported that some of the soldiers seemed to explode when the tracers hit them—an indication that they probably were carrying satchel charges. Artillery and naval gunfire, guided by spotter planes, hit the larger concentrations of movement and traffic with destructive effect. Naval gunfire alone was estimated to have killed 500 Japanese in villages south of Tsukasan, and to have destroyed 1 artillery piece and 5 tanks.[11]

Just before dark, at 1902, a column of Japanese with its head near Ozato, just west of the Yuza-Dake, was seen in the far south of the island, moving north. Fifteen minutes later it was reported that this road was blocked to a point just above Makabe with troops moving north. The troop column extended over about 5,000 yards of road and was estimated to be in regimental strength.

[10] Appleman, XXIV Corps History, p. 464.

[11] Tenth Army G–2 Periodic Rpt No. 62, 27 May 45; CTF 51, Summary No. 80, 27 May 45, in Tenth Army G–3 Jnl, 28 May 45.

SECRET RETREAT *of the Japanese from Shuri was difficult for Intelligence to discover because of pitted, wooded terrain such as this. Where, however, enemy could be found, they were scattered or destroyed. These Japanese howitzers (below) were caught on road leading south from Shuri.*

This was the largest enemy troop movement ever seen in the Okinawa campaign.[12]

The reports of the aerial observers on the 26th were perplexing. Enemy troops were moving in all directions. The majority, however, were headed south; the main exception was the largest column, which was moving north. The heaviest movement was in an area about five miles south of Shuri. It was noted that artillery and armor were moving south. What did it all mean? One careful appraisal concluded that the Japanese were taking advantage of the bad weather, poor aerial observation, and the general stalling of the American attack to carry out a relief of tired troops in the lines by fresh reserves from the south. It was believed that artillery was being moved to new emplacements for greater protection and for continued support of the Shuri battle.[13]

The next day, 27 May, little movement was noted behind the enemy's lines in the morning, but in the afternoon from 2,000 to 3,000 troops were seen moving in both directions at the southern end of the island.[14]

After the reports of enemy movement on 26 May by aerial observers, General Buckner issued on 27 May an order directing that both corps "initiate without delay strong and unrelenting pressure to ascertain probable intentions and keep him [the Japanese] off balance. Enemy must not be permitted to establish himself securely on new positions with only nominal interference." [15] In view of the preponderance of other evidence it seems that this order was purely precautionary, and that there was no real conviction in the American command that the Japanese were actually engaged in a withdrawal from Shuri.

On 28 May the Tenth Army intelligence officer observed in a staff meeting that it "now looks as though the Japanese thinks holding the line around north of Shuri is his best bet. . . . It is probable that we will gradually surround the Shuri position." [16] General Buckner indicated at this meeting that he was concerned about the possibility of a Japanese counterattack against the 7th Division on the left flank. He asked, "What has Arnold in reserve against counterattack?" [17] On the following day, however, General Buckner said it looked as

---

[12] Tenth Army G–2 Periodic Rpt No. 62, 27 May 45; XXIV Corps G–2 Periodic Rpt No. 56, 27 May 45.

[13] Appleman, XXIV Corps History, pp. 466–67.

[14] XXIV Corps G–2 Periodic Rpt No. 57, 28 May 45. See also Tenth Army G–2 Periodic Rpt No. 63, 28 May 45.

[15] Tenth Army Actn Rpt, 7–III–24, 25.

[16] Notes of Tenth Army staff meeting in Okinawa Diary kept by Lt Col Stevens and M/Sgt Burns, 28 May 45.

[17] *Ibid.*

though the Japanese were trying to pull south but that they had made the decision too late.[18] On the day before, a total of 112 trucks and vehicles and approximately 1,000 enemy troops had been observed on the move to the south and southeast, in the vicinity of Itoman on the west coast, and around Iwa and Tomui in front of the Yaeju-Dake, a strong terrain position in the south.[19] On 28 May Marine patrols found evidence of recently evacuated enemy positions west of Shuri.[20] On 29 May there was almost no aerial observation because of a zero ceiling, and on 30 May practically no movement was seen behind the enemy's lines.

American opinion on the meaning of the Japanese movements crystallized on 30 May. After a meeting with III Amphibious Corps and XXIV Army Corps intelligence officers the Tenth Army intelligence officer reported at a staff meeting on the evening of 30 May that they had reached a consensus that the "enemy was holding the Shuri lines with a shell, and that the bulk of the troops were elsewhere." He estimated that there were 5,000 enemy troops in what he hoped would be the Shuri pocket, and stated that he did not know where the bulk of the Japanese troops were.[21] At a staff meeting held on the evening of 31 May, it was suggested that the enemy would make his next line the high ground from Naha-Ko and the Oroku Peninsula on the west to Baten-Ko below Yonabaru on the east. At this meeting General Buckner stated that "he [General Ushijima] made his decision to withdraw from Shuri two days too late." [22] During the following days it became clear that the Americans had underestimated the scope of the enemy's tactical plan and the extent to which it had been executed.

The Retreat South

Once the Japanese decision to withdraw had been made, steps were taken to carry out the withdrawal in an orderly manner. The major part of the transportation fell to the *24th Transport Regiment* of the *24th Division*. This unit had been exceptionally well trained in night driving in Manchuria, and as a result of its fine performance in the withdrawal from Shuri it received a unit citation from the *32d Army*. When the withdrawal from Shuri began only 80 of the 150 trucks of the transport regiment were left. One hundred and fifty Okinawan

[18] *Ibid.,* 29 May 45.

[19] Tenth Army G–2 Periodic Rpt No. 64, 29 May 45.

[20] III Amph Corps Actn Rpt, p. 56.

[21] Notes of Tenth Army staff meeting in Okinawa Diary (Stevens–Burns), 30 May 45.

[22] *Ibid.,* 31 May 45.

Boeitai helped to load the vehicles. The formal order from *32d Army* head-quarters to withdraw from Shuri was apparently issued on 24 May.[23]

The movement of supplies and the wounded began first, one truck unit moving out the night of 22 May. Communication units proceeded between 22 and 28 May to Mabuni and Hill 89, where the *32d Army* proposed to establish its new command post. The *36th Signal Regiment* left Shuri on 26 May and arrived at Mabuni by way of Tsukasan on 28 May. Other units moved out early. The *22d Independent Antitank Gun Battalion* left the Shuri area on the night of 24–25 May, withdrawing to the Naha–Yonabaru valley area, and at the end of the month continued on south to the southern end of the island. Remnants of the *27th Tank Regiment* began to withdraw from Shuri on 26 May, passing through Kamizato. At the same time the *103d* and *105th Machine Cannon Battalions* left the Shuri and Shichina areas and began the movement south, hand-carrying some of their guns.[24]

Of the major combat units of the *32d Army,* the *62d Division* left first. It began moving out of Shuri on 26 May, two days ahead of the original schedule, fighting delaying actions in the zone of the 7th Division, where the bulge had been pushed deep to the southwest of Yonabaru. The *44th Independent Mixed Brigade* on the left flank in front of the 6th and 1st Marine Divisions was to begin withdrawing from the front lines on 26 May, but, because of the failure of naval ground troops to arrive and take over the lines, the evacuation of the front positions by the brigade had to be delayed two days, and it was not until 28 May that the withdrawal began in the western part of the line. The units of the brigade assembled behind the lines and made the move south in mass on the night of 1–2 June. One battalion, the *3d,* withdrew directly from Shuri. The *24th Division* remained behind longest. Elements of the division fought in front of Shuri as late as 30 May, and the division headquarters itself did not leave Shuri until 29 May. The mortar battalions supporting the Shuri front had for the most part already left, their main movement south having taken place between 27 and 29 May.[25]

---

[23] Tenth Army PW Interrog Summary No. 3, 2 Aug 45: *24th Division;* No. 2, 2 Aug 45: *62d Division;* No. 19, 25 Jul 45: Air-Ground Units.

[24] Tenth Army PW Interrog Summary No. 8, 24 Jul 45: *27th Tank Regt;* No. 9, 24 Jul 45: Independent Antitank Gun Units; No. 12, 3 Aug 45: Army AAA Units on Okinawa; No. 15, 31 Jul 45: *36th Signal Regiment;* XXIV Corps PW Interrog Rpt No. 133 [n. d.]; 7th Div PW Interrog Rpt No. 47, 29 Jun 45.

[25] Tenth Army PW Interrog Summary No. 2, 2 Aug 45: *62d Division;* No. 4, 1 Aug 45: *44th Independent Mixed Brigade;* No. 3, 2 Aug 45: The *24th Division;* No. 10, 30 Jul 45: *1st* and *2d Light Mortar Battalions;* No. 11, 4 Aug 45: *1st Artillery Mortar Regiment.*

The evidence is conflicting concerning the date when the *32d Army* head-quarters left Shuri. The cook for the *32d Army* staff said that the *Army* headquarters left Shuri on 26 May and arrived at the Hill 89 headquarters cave near Mabuni on 29 May. Officers of the *62d Division* confirmed this, stating that the *Army* headquarters left Shuri on 26 May, the same day the division itself started to move south. On the other hand, Colonel Yahara, *32d Army* operations officer, and Mr. Shimada, secretary to General Cho, stated that the *Army* head-quarters did not move from Shuri until the night of 29 May. On the whole the evidence seems to indicate that the *Army* headquarters moved from Shuri before 29 May. On that day elements of the 1st Marine Division entered Shuri Castle, the *24th Division* headquarters left Shuri, and only the last of the rear-guard units were still in the line as a holding force. It seems improbable that the *32d Army* headquarters would have remained behind so long. It appears likely that the *Army* headquarters left Shuri at night between 26 and 28 May, possibly as early as 26 May.[26]

The main movement of *32d Army* combat units out of the inner Shuri defense zone took place from 26 to 28 May, some of the units, particularly the *62d Division,* fighting as they went. The *3d Independent Antitank Battalion,* the *2d Battalion* of the *22d Regiment* of the *24th Division,* and part of the *17th Independent Machine Gun Battalion* formed the principal components of the final holding force in front of Shuri, 29–31 May, after the *32d Regiment* withdrew.[27]

American Occupation of Shuri

As the battle lines tightened around Shuri at the end of May, the 1st Marine Division on the northwest and the 77th Division on the north and northeast stood closest to the town. Patrols reported no signs of weakness in the enemy's determination to hold the Shuri position. Invariably they drew heavy fire when they tried to move forward. There was one exception to the reports of the patrols. On 28 May a patrol brought back to the 5th Marines, 1st Marine Division, the news that Shuri Ridge, the high ground south of Wana Draw, seemed to be held more lightly than formerly. (See Map No. XLIV.)

---

[26] 7th Div PW Interrog Rpt No. 45, 26 Jun 45 (Nakamuta); Tenth Army PW Interrog Summary No. 2, 2 Aug 45: *62d Division;* Interrog Yahara; Interrog Shimada.

[27] Memo G–2 XXIV Corps for DCofS for Opns XXIV Corps [n. d.] cited in Appleman, XXIV Corps History, p. 475. The memo was prepared about the end of June 1945 and was based on PW interrogations and captured documents.

SHURI HEIGHTS, *at southwest corner of the city, was approached by the marines from the low ground at right. First building to be taken was the Shuri Normal School (upper left). (Photo taken 28 April 1945.)*

The Marines Take Shuri Castle

At 0730 on 29 May the 1st Battalion, 5th Marines, left its lines and started forward toward Shuri Ridge, where patrol action the previous day had indicated a possible weakness in the enemy's lines. The high ground was quickly occupied. The 1st Battalion was now on the ridge that lay at the eastern edge of Shuri. Shuri Castle itself lay from 700 to 800 yards almost straight west across the Corps and division boundary. From all appearances, this part of the Shuri perimeter was undefended and the castle could be captured by merely walking up to it. The battalion commander immediately requested permission from his regimental commander to cross the Corps boundary and go into Shuri Castle. The request was approved, and at midmorn Company A of the 5th Marines started toward the spot that had been so long a symbol of Japanese strength on Okinawa. At 1015 Shuri Castle was occupied by Company A.[28] The Marine unit entered Shuri through a gap in the covering forces caused by the withdrawal of the *3d Battalion, 15th Independent Mixed Regiment* of the *44th Independent Mixed Brigade,* in the course of the Japanese retreat from Shuri.[29] This seems to have been the only notable instance of confusion and mistake in the Japanese withdrawal operation as a whole. Everywhere else around Shuri the Japanese still held their covering positions in the front lines.

As a result of the unexpected entrance into Shuri, the 1st Marine Division at 0930 ordered the 1st Marines to bypass Wana Draw, leaving its position in the line next to the 77th Division, and to move around to the southwest to relieve the 1st Battalion, 5th Marines, in Shuri. This move was carried out with the 3d Battalion leading and the 1st Battalion following. Enemy positions were bypassed on the right, and by night the two battalions had established a perimeter in the south of Shuri.

The elements of the 1st Marine Division which entered Shuri Castle had crossed over into the 77th Division zone of action and line of fire without giving that unit notice that such a movement was under way. The 77th Division learned of the move barely in time to cancel an air strike on the Shuri Castle area which it had scheduled.[30]

The next day, the Marine units at Shuri Castle and south of Shuri did not move, except for small patrols that were turned back by heavy machine-gun

---

[28] The account of the capture of Shuri Castle is, unless otherwise noted, taken from 1st Mar Div Special Actn Rpt Phase III, pp. 7–8; Stockman, 1st Mar Div History, pp. 40–42; III Amph Corps Actn Rpt, p. 56.

[29] Tenth Army PW Interrog Summary No. 4, 1 Aug 45: *44th Independent Mixed Brigade.*

[30] 77th Div Actn Rpt Okinawa, p. 62; Leach, 77th Div History, II, 96–98.

and 47-mm. antitank fire a few hundred yards north of the castle. Vehicles could not reach the marines in Shuri and their supplies were critically low. Carrying parties of replacement troops formed an almost unbroken line from the west coast dumps all the way to Shuri. Many men collapsed from sheer exhaustion. Five air drops through heavy clouds to the marines in Shuri relieved somewhat their critical supply situation on 30 May.[31]

The entrances to the caves under Shuri Castle were still held by the enemy at 1330 on 30 May, and no additional ground had been taken in Shuri itself.[32] The two Marine battalions, dug in, merely formed a pocket within the Japanese perimeter on which the enemy's rear guard was fighting the holding battle around Shuri. The occupation of Shuri Castle did not cause these Japanese to withdraw from their covering positions or result in the occupation of Shuri itself; nor did it, so far as is known, affect the enemy's plans. The marines themselves had all they could do to get food and water and some ammunition up to their position in order to stay.

The Crust Breaks

Although the holding party at 100 Meter Hill repulsed the 306th Infantry on 30 May when it attacked across the Marine line, elsewhere across the Shuri front key positions were wrested from the enemy in what obviously was a breaking up of the Japanese rear-guard action. Now for the first time there was convincing proof along the front lines that the Japanese had withdrawn from Shuri. (See Map No. XLV.)

Dorothy Hill, a fortress directly east of Shuri and a tower of strength in the enemy's inner line for the past two weeks, was attacked by the 3d Battalion, 307th Infantry, 77th Division. The first platoon to reach the base of the hill was pinned down by heavy fire, the platoon leader and all noncommissioned officers being wounded. Other platoons maneuvered into position and finally one squad reached the crest at the right end. This entering wedge enabled two companies to reach the top, from which they discovered three levels of caves on the reverse slope. They went to work methodically, moving from right to left along the top level, burning and blasting each cave and dugout, the flame-thrower and satchel-charge men covered by riflemen. When work on the top level was finished, the second level of caves and tunnels received similar treatment, and then the third and lowest level. That night fifteen Japanese who had survived

---

[31] See also Tenth Army G–4 Periodic Rpt No. 66, 31 May 45.

[32] Tenth Army G–2 Summary, 30 May 45, in Tenth Army G–3 Jnl, 31 May 45.

the day's fighting crawled out of the blasted caves and were killed by Americans from their foxholes. A great amount of enemy equipment, including ten destroyed 150-mm. guns and twenty-five trucks, was found on the south (reverse) side of Dorothy Hill, testifying to the enemy fire power at this strong point. On 30 May, the 77th Division also took Jane Hill on its left flank and then almost unopposed took Tom Hill, the highest point of ground in the Shuri area, by 1700.[33]

For nine days elements of the 96th Division had been stalemated at the base of Hen Hill, just northeast of Shuri. On the 30th, Company F and one platoon of Company G, 382d Infantry, resumed the attack on Hen Hill. Pfc. Clarence B. Craft, a rifleman from Company G, was sent out ahead with five companions to test the Japanese positions. As he and his small group started up the slope, they were brought under heavy fire from Japanese just over the crest, and a shower of grenades fell on them. Three of the men were wounded and the other two were stopped. Craft, although a new replacement and in his first action, kept on going, tossing grenades at the crest. From just below the crest he threw two cases of grenades that were passed up to him from the bottom, those of the enemy going over his head or exploding near him. He then leaped to the crest and fired at point-blank range into the Japanese in a trench a few feet below him. Spurred by Craft's example, other men now came to his aid. Reloading, Craft pursued the Japanese down the trench, wiped out a machine-gun nest, and satchel-charged the cave into which the remaining Japanese had retreated. Altogether, in the taking of Hen Hill as a result of Craft's action, about seventy Japanese were killed, at least twenty-five of whom were credited to Craft himself. This daring action won him the Congressional Medal of Honor.[34]

To the left (east), Company F at the same time engaged in a grenade battle for Hector Hill, using ten cases of grenades in the assault on the crest. It was finally won after a satchel charge was hurled over the top and lit in the enemy trench on the other side, parts of Japanese bodies and pieces of enemy equipment hurtling into the sky in the blast. Hen and Hector Hills had fallen by 1400.[35]

On the 96th Division's left rapid advances were made on 30 May. Roger Hill was seized when the Japanese failed to man their combat positions quickly

[33] Leach, 77th Div History, II, 99; XXIV Corps G–2 Periodic Rpt No. 61, 1 Jun 45; Appleman, XXIV Corps History, p. 454.

[34] Mulford and Rogers, 96th Div History, Pt. IV, pp. 16 off; WA AGO No. 97, 1 Nov 45.

[35] Mulford and Rogers, op. cit., p. 163.

SHURI, *photographed 28 April (above) and 23 May 1945 (below). Ruins shown in lower picture include Methodist Church and a 2-story concrete structure (circle A). Dotted outline in photos indicates the castle wall.*

enough after an artillery barrage that had driven them to cover. They were killed to a man by the infantry, which surprised them when they tried to reach their fighting positions. Sgt. Richard Hindenburg alone killed six of the enemy with his BAR. The 3d Battalion, 381st Infantry, went down the western slope of the Conical hogback to find from 75 to 100 dead Japanese on the reverse slope of Cutaway Hill. At last the 2d Battalion, 383d Infantry, reached Love Hill and dug in, although scattered fire was still received from a machine gun in a nook of Charlie Hill and there were a few live Japanese on Love itself. In the afternoon the 3d Battalion, 383d Infantry, left its foxholes on Oboe, where it had experienced so great an ordeal, and proceeded down the reverse slope of the hill, finding only a few scattered Japanese. That night the 383d Infantry expressed a heartfelt sentiment when it reported "infinite relief to have Conical Hill behind us." Although there had been suicidal stands in a few places by the last of the holding force, the advances had been rapid.[36]

On 31 May the 77th Division walked over 100 Meter Hill at the eastern end of Wana Ridge and on into Shuri. The marines from the vicinity of Shuri Castle moved north without opposition to help in the occupation of the battered rubble. Overnight the enemy had stolen away. When darkness fell on 31 May the III Amphibious Corps and the XXIV Corps had joined lines south of Shuri and the 77th Division had been pinched out in the center of the line at Shuri. The troops rested on their arms before beginning the pursuit south with the coming of dawn.[37]

Crater of the Moon

Shuri, the second town of Okinawa, lay in utter ruin. There was no other city, town, or village in the Ryukyus that had been destroyed so completely. Naha too had been laid waste. Certain villages which had been strong points in the enemy's defense, such as Kakazu, Dakeshi, Kochi, Arakachi, and Kunishi, had been fought over and leveled to the ground. But none of these compared with the ancient capital of the Ryukyus. It was estimated that about 200,000 rounds of artillery and naval gunfire had struck Shuri. Numerous air strikes had dropped 1,000-pound bombs on it. Mortar shells by the thousands had arched their way into the town area. Only two structures, both of concrete— the big normal school at the southwestern corner and the little Methodist

[36] *Ibid.*, pp. 158–60; XXIV Corps G–2 Periodic Rpt No. 60, 31 May 45; 383d Inf Actn Rpt, p. 33; Appleman, XXIV Corps History, p. 455.

[37] 306th Inf Actn Rpt, Narrative Acct, p. 13; 1st Mar Div Special Actn Rpt, Phase III, p. 7; Leach, 77th Div History, II, 99–100.

SHURI CASTLE BELL, *with an American officer standing by.   Bell is a companion to one brought to U. S. Naval Academy by Commodore Perry.*

church, built in 1937, in the center of Shuri—had enough of their walls standing to form silhouettes on the skyline. The rest was flattened rubble. The narrow paved and dirt streets, churned by high explosives and pitted with shell craters, were impassable to any vehicle. The stone walls of the numerous little terraces were battered down. The rubble and broken red tile of the houses lay in heaps. The frame portion of buildings had been reduced to kindling wood. Tattered bits of Japanese military clothing, gas masks, and tropical helmets—the most frequently seen items—and the dark-colored Okinawan civilian dress lay about in wild confusion. Over all this crater-of-the-moon landscape hung the unforgettable stench of rotting human flesh.[38]

On a high oval knob of ground at the southern edge of the town, Shuri Castle had stood. Walls of coral blocks, 20 feet thick at the base and 40 feet in height, enclosed the castle area of approximately 290 acres. The castle in its modern form had been constructed in 1544, the architecture being of Chinese origin. Here the kings of Okinawa had ruled. Now the massive ramparts, which had been battered by 14- and 16-inch shells from American battleships, remained intact in only a few places. Inside the castle area one could discern the outline of the rubble-strewn and pitted parade ground. Magnificent large trees that had graced the castle grounds were now blackened skeletons on the skyline.

From the debris of what once had been Shuri Castle two large bronze bells, scarred and dented by shell fire, were dug out by the troops. One of them was about five feet in height, the other three and a half. Cast about 1550, they were inscribed with characters that may be translated as follows:

In the Southern Seas lie the islands of Ryukyu Kingdom, known widely for their scenic beauty. The Kingdom of Ryukyu embraces the excellent qualities of the three Han states of Korea and the culture of the Mings. Separated as it is from these nations by distance, still it is as close to them as lips to teeth. . . .

Behold! What is a bell? A bell is that which sounds far, wide, and high. It is a rare Buddhist instrument, bringing order to the routine of the monk. At dawn it breaks the long stillness of the night and guards against the torpidity of sleep. . . .

It will always ring on time, to toll the approach of darkness, and to toll the hour of dawn. It will startle the indolent into activity that will restore honor to their names. And how will the bell sound? It will echo far and wide like a peal of thunder, but with utmost purity. And evil men, hearing the bell, will be saved.[39]

[38] For the description of Shuri see Appleman, XXIV Corps History, pp. 458–62.
[39] Ibid., pp. 461–62.

CHAPTER XVI

Behind the Front

The stubborn and protracted defense by the Japanese of the fortified Shuri area affected every phase of logistic and other operations in support of the Okinawa campaign, adding unforeseen complications to the execution of a mission which in itself was of great complexity and magnitude. As time passed far beyond the limits set in the plans the quantity of supplies and equipment used increased in direct proportion, while the reduction of the elaborate defenses required the expenditure of inordinate amounts of materiel, especially ammunition. The planned capture of the ports of Naha and Yonabaru for the delivery of cargo failed to materialize and, as a result, the increased supplies required could not be unloaded in sufficient quantities. The carefully integrated shipping schedules for garrison and maintenance supplies were thereby upset. At the same time construction of base facilities was delayed. Difficulties were compounded when, in the last days of May and the early part of June 1945, the invading forces found themselves fighting the weather as well as the enemy. Steady and heavy rains severed land communications on Okinawa, and the motorized Tenth Army was bogged down in the mud. Only through the utmost use of all available resources, energetic improvisation, and resort to water and air transportation was it possible to keep the supplies rolling in to the appointed place in approximately the desired quantities and in time to defeat the enemy.[1]

As soon as the hilly terrain behind the Hagushi beaches was overrun by American troops, it became the scene of feverish activity. Roads were widened and improved, supply dumps established, antiaircraft guns emplaced, and hundreds of military installations constructed. Tent settlements sprang up everywhere, and the dark green of pyramidal and squad tents became as commonplace a feature of the landscape as the Okinawan tomb. Coral was chopped away from hills and laid on the roads and airfields. Bumper-to-bumper traffic raised clouds of dust on the main thoroughfares in dry weather and splattered along through deep mud in wet. Telephone service soon linked all Army and Navy

[1] Unless otherwise noted, the account of Okinawa campaign logistics was taken from Tenth Army Actn Rpt, Ch. 11, Secs. IV, XI, XIII, XIV, XVI; XXIV Corps Actn Rpt, pp. 26, 30, 31, 65–71, 80–83; Island Command Okinawa Actn Rpt, 30 Jun 45.

Large supply installation in Kakazu area

Route 1 near Kadena

Main west-coast telephone cable

SUPPLY AND COMMUNICATIONS INSTALLATIONS

installations, and Signal Corps troops also established an elaborate radio communication net and service to American bases in the rear. There were 170,000 Americans on the island a month after the landings, and about 245,000 on Okinawa and neighboring islands at the end of June.[2]

Supply Operations

Bringing the Supplies Ashore

Unloading of the assault shipping was nearly completed by 16 April, ahead of schedule.[3] (See Appendix C, Table No. 7.) Further progress was satisfactory through 6 May. Thereafter, however, the discharge of supplies failed to keep pace with unloading plans. Between 7 May and 15 June tonnage unloaded was more than 200,000 measurement tons behind schedule. However, this was largely offset by the earlier achievements, and the cumulative effect was not evident until 5 June. The chief difficulty was the failure to capture the port of Naha with its harbor and dock facilities as early as planned. Unloading continued for the most part over the reef and beaches in the Hagushi area long after it was expected that they would have been abandoned in favor of rehabilitated port facilities. (See Appendix C, Chart No. 3.) High winds, heavy rains, frequent air raids, and equipment shortages all contributed to the delays and the cumulative deficiencies. Particularly onerous was the necessity of selective discharge of cargo to bring ashore critical items of supply. Sometimes dock gangs had to be pulled off ships prior to unloading and placed on "hot" ships as emergencies developed. In the face of all these difficulties, more than 2,000,000 measurement tons of cargo were unloaded on Okinawa from 1 April to 30 June, an average of some 22,200 tons a day. (See Appendix C, Table No. 6.)

To supplement the tonnage unloaded at the Hagushi beaches, Tenth Army developed a number of unloading points at other places along the coasts of Okinawa. Such points were opened between 5 and 9 April in northern Okinawa for close support of III Amphibious Corps in its rapid advance northward during the early stages of the operation. After the marines moved south to take part in the drive against the main enemy position, work was rushed to develop unloading facilities at Machinato on the west coast. By 25 May LCT's were being unloaded at a temporary sand causeway. At the same time, temporary unloading

---

[2] Tenth Army G-4 Rpt No. 38, 3 May 45; No. 98, 2 Jul 45.   Figures are those for the ration strength of Tenth Army.

[3] See above, pp. 80–81.

points were developed on the coast between Machinato and Naha in further support of the III Corps. On 7 June, the port of Naha was opened for the use of LCT's and the rehabilitation of harbor and dock facilities was begun. It was planned that by the end of June the bulk of west-coast tonnage would be unloaded at Naha and that the Hagushi beaches would gradually be abandoned.

Unloading on the east coast of Okinawa began in the middle of April, and use was successively made of beaches at Chimu Bay, Ishikawa, Katchin Peninsula, Awase, and Kuba. Yonabaru was captured on 22 May and supplies were unloaded there on 1 June. A ponton pier was started there for LST's and smaller craft a week later and was completed on 12 June. In the last stages of the campaign an emergency unloading point was opened at Minatoga on the southeast coast on 9 June and was operated for two weeks.

By 30 June 1945 about 20 percent of all tonnage unloaded on Okinawa had been brought ashore at points other than the Hagushi beaches, amounting to nearly 400,000 measurement tons of cargo. In one respect, however, the use of unscheduled supply points contributed to the delays of unloading: as each new beach was opened in immediate support of the assault, available lighterage, trucks, and personnel were dispersed over a number of places, thereby materially slowing operations at the original unloading points. In addition, much of the cargo handled over the new beaches was not discharged directly from ships but from landing craft that had loaded at previously established dumps at Hagushi, Awase, and Kuba and had sailed down the coast.

As a result of slow unloading, ships awaiting discharge accumulated at the various anchorages and presented fine targets for Japanese air attacks. While strenuous efforts were continuously made to speed unloading operations and return the ships to safer areas, the originally planned schedule of resupply shipping could not be adhered to. Emphasis was placed on calling up ships loaded with supplies that were in great need on the island at the particular time. Calling up only the number of such ships which could be expeditiously handled was not always possible because the requirements were so great, particularly in the case of ammunition ships.[4]

Delivery of Supplies to the Front

Responsibility for supplying the assault troops passed smoothly, during the initial stages, from division to corps and then to the Island Command, the Army logistic agency, on 9 April. Depot and dump operations for the Island

---

[4] CTF 51 Actn Rpt, V–I–30.

Command were handled by the 1st Engineer Special Brigade until 24 May, when Island Command took over direct operational control of supply installations. All units normally drew supplies in their organic transportation from the Island Command supply points. These were first established in the area behind the Hagushi beaches, but forward supply points were opened farther south as the action moved toward that end of the island. Initially an ammunition supply point was established for each division, and, as operations progressed, these points were consolidated and new ones set up farther forward.

No unusual difficulties were encountered in moving up supplies to the troops until the latter part of May. When the heavy rains started on 20 May and continued day and night for two weeks, the main supply roads linking the forward and rear areas were washed out and movement of vehicles became impossible. The rainy period, moreover, coincided with the break-through at Shuri that started the troops moving rapidly south away from all established supply points. It became necessary to resort to water transportation to bring supplies to the forward dumps. In the interim the 7th Division, which was making the main effort in the sector at the time, was supplied by LVT along the coast. XXIV Corps established a supply point at Yonabaru on 31 May, and lighterage was made available by the Island Command and the Navy for the delivery of the necessary supplies. The first supplies arrived at Yonabaru on LCT's on 1 June. Several LCT's also ferried service troops and artillery forward and evacuated casualties.

As the pursuit of the retreating Japanese continued, the Corps turned the Yonabaru supply point over to Island Command and concentrated on a new forward unloading point at Minatoga, on the southern coast. To ensure the steady flow of ammunition to XXIV Corps units, a cargo ship and three LST's loaded entirely with that class of supply were anchored off Yonabaru and Minatoga and used as floating ammunition supply points. The 7th Division received some supplies by LVT at Minatoga on 6 June. The initial shipment of four LCT's loaded with rations and fuel and an LST with ammunition arrived on 8 June. Forty-four LVT's loaded with ammunition and bridging material were sent to Minatoga aboard an LST on 9 June. Shipments to the new supply point were continued from both east and west coasts of Okinawa by LST and LCT, with the LVT's being used as lighterage from ship to shore. During much of this time, supply of the assault elements on the line was almost entirely by hand carry. On the west coast III Amphibious Corps was being supplied ammunition by a cargo ship, an LST, and about seventy DUKW's making daily trips

Ship-to-shore supply causeway at Hagushi beaches

Handling supplies at 196th Ordnance dump

Supply trucks pulled through bad spot by 302d Combat Engineers

MOVING SUPPLIES

from rear areas, all unloading at Naha. Thirty-four LVT's also made a daily trip from the Hagushi beaches to advance Corps positions along the coast.

Air delivery was also utilized at this time to bring supplies forward. The Air Delivery Section of III Amphibious Corps was responsible for all air drops on the island. The section operated from CVE's until 18 April, and thereafter from Kadena airfield. Using torpedo bombers rather than C–47's, primarily because more accurate drops could thus be made, the section delivered a total of 334 short tons of supplies in 830 planeloads. Most of the air drops were to III Amphibious Corps units, particularly the 1st Marine Division, whose front-line elements were supplied almost exclusively by air between 30 May and 9 June, when the roads in its area were impassable even to tracked vehicles. The tonnage delivered by air to XXIV Corps in the week 2–9 June was small but, because of its emergency nature, important. Supplies thus dropped consisted in the main of ammunition and rations.[5]

Maintenance and construction of supply roads were impeded by the lack of good road-building material and by rapid deterioration from rainy weather and heavy traffic. In the XXIV Corps zone the limestone coral used for road building in the early stages of the campaign proved to be unsuitable, and extensive use had to be made of rubble from destroyed buildings and stone walls. A rock crusher was not available. As the Corps drove southward, the lack of adequate sources of coral limestone became acute and the use of building rubble had to be continued. When a rock crusher was made available at the end of the first week in June, it was set up and operated in a limestone quarry and then moved to a site where the excellent stone from the razed Shuri Castle could be used. It was at this time, moreover, that the problem of road maintenance became overwhelming. A 12-inch rainfall between 22 May and 5 June forced the abandonment of the two main supply roads serving the Corps. One of these, Route 13 along the east coast, was not reconstructed during the battle; the engineers concentrated on keeping Route 5, down the center of the island, in operation, as well as the roads running south from Yonabaru and Minatoga, to which supplies were moved by water. In the Marine zone on the west side of the island, only the continuous labor of all engineer units and rigid traffic control kept Route 1 open. By the end of June main supply roads had been developed from Chuda to Naha on the west coast (Route 1), from Chibana to Shuri in the center (Route 5), from Kin to Yonabaru on the east coast (Route 13), and at six intermediate points across the island.

_____
[5] III Amph Corps Actn Rpt, p. 128.

Approximately 164 miles of native roads had been reconstructed and widened for two-lane traffic, 37 miles of two-, three-, and four-lane roads had been newly constructed, and a total of 339 miles of road was under maintenance.

Supply Shortages

Providing an adequate supply of ammunition to support the sustained attacks on the Shuri defenses constituted the most critical logistical problem of the campaign. The resupply of ammunition beyond the initial five CINCPOA units of fire had been planned for a 40-day operation; the island was not officially declared secure until L plus 82 (22 June).[6] The sinking of three ammunition ships by enemy action on 6 and 27 April and damage to other ships resulted in a total loss of 21,000 short tons of ammunition. The unloading of ammunition was, moreover, never rapid enough to keep pace with expenditures, particularly by the artillery, and at the same time to build up ample reserves in the ammunition supply points. Further, it was found that the shiploads of all calibers balanced according to the CINCPOA unit of fire prescription did not fit the needs of a protracted campaign; the requirements for artillery ammunition far exceeded those for small-arms ammunition and resulted in hasty, wasteful unloading and constant shortages.

The ammunition situation first became critical when XXIV Corps developed the Naha–Shuri–Yonabaru defense line during the second week of April. The ammunition expenditures in the large-scale artillery attacks mounted rapidly. As the rate of discharge from the ships failed to keep pace, the supplies on hand dwindled. The plans for the Corps attack designed to penetrate the Japanese positions called for an expenditure of 14,800 tons of artillery ammunition plus supply maintenance of some 1,000 tons a day. To conserve supplies, command restrictions on artillery ammunition expenditures were imposed on 9 April. The Corps attack was delayed until 19 April, partly in order to accumulate sufficient stocks and reserves. This was accomplished in time by means of greater unloading efforts, making available all resupply ammunition, and diverting III Amphibious Corps' stocks to XXIV Corps.

After the attack of 19 April ammunition expenditures continued to mount. By the end of the campaign a total of 97,800 tons of ammunition had been expended. XXIV Corps alone consumed about 64,000 tons between 4 April and 21 June, and restrictions on daily expenditures were continuously in force in its zone until L plus 61 (1 June). In spite of restrictions an average of more than

---

[6] Interv 1st I & H Off with Brig Gen David H. Blakelock, G–4, Tenth Army, 22 and 27 May 45.

800 tons of ammunition was expended daily by Corps units. (See Appendix C, Table No. 10.)

About the middle of April a critical shortage of 155-mm. ammunition developed, and on 17 April Tenth Army had to call up four LST's loaded only with ammunition for 155-mm. guns and howitzers from the reserves in the Marianas. Subsequently, additional emergency requisitions on the reserves were necessary. CINCPOA was also requested to divert ammunition resupply shipments from canceled operations, as well as some originally intended for the European Theater of Operations, to Okinawa in order to alleviate the shortages. On 21 May Tenth Army had to request an emergency air shipment of 50,000 rounds of 81-mm. mortar ammunition, of which more than 26,000 rounds were received between 28 May and 9 June.

However, the expenditure of large-caliber ammunition (75-mm. and larger) on the average was within 1 percent of the over-all requirements estimated in the planning phase. Of the total of 2,116,691 rounds expended (including 350,339 rounds lost to the enemy), the greatest expenditure was in 105-mm. howitzer ammunition, with 1,104,630 rounds fired and an additional 225,507 rounds lost to the enemy. (See Appendix C, Table No. 8 and Chart No. 4.) Although this exceeded the total estimated requirements for 105-mm. howitzer ammunition by nearly 8 percent, the expenditure was well within the limits of available supply for the period.

Shortages of 4.2-inch chemical mortar ammunition, resulting in large part from an unusual percentage of defective fuses, were overcome by the use of surplus Navy stocks and by air shipments of replacement fuzes.

The supply of aviation gas on the island always bordered on the critical. Although no air missions had to be canceled, generally the two airfields barely had enough gas to carry out all scheduled missions. The relative scarcity of aviation gas was due principally to slow unloading and the lack of bulk storage facilities ashore. Gas tanks were not completed until the end of April; until then gas had to be brought ashore in drums and cans—a slow, laborious process. The use of DUKW's to take gas directly from the ships to the fields materially expedited unloading. Reserves on hand, however, were never plentiful, and, when a tanker failed to arrive on schedule at the end of April, Tenth Army had to call on the Navy to supply the gas for land-based aircraft from fleet tankers.[7]

[7] See Tenth Army Tactical Air Force Actn Rpt, 12 Jul 45, 6–IV–2, 3.

The loss of light and medium tanks during the campaign, much heavier than had been expected, caused another critical shortage and replacements could not be secured in time. Tenth Army reported the complete loss of 147 medium tanks and 4 light tanks by 30 June; replacements were requested from Oahu on 28 April but these had not arrived by the end of the campaign. As an emergency measure, all the medium tanks of the 193d Tank Battalion, attached to the 27th Division, were distributed to the other tank battalions on the island. XXIV Corps tank units received fifty of these tanks which contributed materially to combat effectiveness. The 193d, however, could not be reequipped and returned to combat.

Hospitalization and Evacuation

Hospitalization and evacuation facilities for battle casualties on Okinawa were also strained by the fierce and costly battle against the Japanese defenses, resulting in higher battle casualties than had been expected. (See Appendix C, Table No. 3.) The nonbattle casualties, however, were much lower than anticipated, and the low incidence of disease, with the corresponding reduction of the use of facilities for these long-term cases, provided welcome hospital and surgical facilities for the large number of wounded.[8]

In the normal course of events on Okinawa, a man hit on the battlefield was delivered by a collecting company, in a jeep ambulance, weasel, or weapons carrier, to a battalion aid station located from two to four hundred yards behind the lines. After treatment he was carried by standard or jeep ambulance to a collecting station, the first installation equipped to give whole-blood transfusions. The next stop was the division clearing station, to which portable surgical hospitals were attached. Finally, the patient would reach a field hospital, from four to six thousand yards behind the front. Evacuation to the field hospitals functioned satisfactorily on Okinawa until the end of May, when the heavy rains made the roads impassable. Evacuations from the divisions south of Naha–Yonabaru ceased. It became necessary to evacuate casualties by LST from Yonabaru on the east coast on 2 June and from Machinato on the west

---

[8] The account of medical activities on Okinawa is based on the following sources: Tenth Army Actn Rpt, 11–IV–28, 29, and Ch. 11, Sec. XV; Surgeon USAFMIDPAC, Administrative History of Medical Activities in the Middle Pacific, Block 18f: The Okinawa Operation, 1 Apr to 30 Jun 45, 2 vols; XXIV Corps Actn Rpt, pp. 72–79; Island Command Okinawa Actn Rpt, Ch. 8, Sec. XIV; 7th Div Actn Rpt, pp. 60–63, 74; 77th Div Actn Rpt Okinawa, pp. 73–76; 96th Div Actn Rpt, Ch. IX, pp. 19–21; interv 1st I & H Off with Col F. B. Westervelt, Tenth Army Surgeon, 31 May 45.

MOVEMENT OF WOUNDED *on Okinawa was difficult. Wounded had to be carried part of the way by stretcher before they could be placed on ambulance jeeps taking them to hospital ships or field hospitals.*

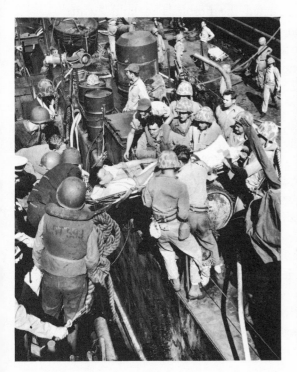
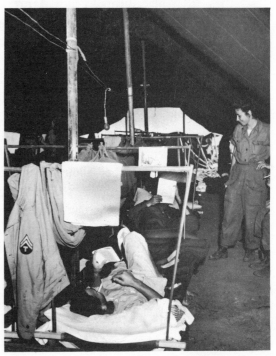

coast on 31 May. By 10 June water evacuation from XXIV Corps zone had been extended south to Minatoga. In the III Amphibious Corps sector at Itoman water evacuation was not feasible because of the reef and enemy fire. As a result, evacuation by L–5 artillery liaison planes was instituted. The planes landed on a stretch of concrete highway just north of Itoman and delivered the patients to Chatan. On 15 June air evacuation of XXIV Corps casualties from Minatoga was begun. By the end of June, 1,232 casualties had been evacuated by cub planes to the field hospitals.

By the end of April six field hospitals and one Marine evacuation hospital, with a total bed capacity of 3,000, were in operation. At the end of the campaign on 21 June available hospital beds for combat casualties had increased to only 3,929, in addition to 500 convalescent beds and 1,802 garrison beds. The small number of beds was chiefly responsible for the policy, applied in the first six weeks of the campaign, of immediately evacuating casualties to the Marianas. As a result of this policy many so-called "white" casualties, that is, casualties requiring two weeks or less of hospitalization, were evacuated from the island and lost to their units for considerable periods of time. On 16 May, in an attempt to stop this wholesale evacuation of a valuable source of trained replacements, Tenth Army instructed the hospitals to hold "white" cases to the limit of their capacity. Both corps tried to stem the losses by establishing convalescent camps—XXIV Corps on 6 May and III Amphibious Corps on 29 May. These camps alleviated conditions but hospital facilities continued to be strained after each of the great offensives. On 26 and 27 May all evacuation from Okinawa was suspended: the heavy rains made the airfields unusable, and no hospital ships were available for surface evacuation. The hospital bed situation was critical until air evacuation was resumed on 28 May. A total of 30,848 patients, or almost 80 percent of all battle casualties, was evacuated from Okinawa by 30 June—about half by air and half by ship.

Neuropsychiatric or "combat fatigue" cases were probably greater in number and severity in the Okinawa campaign than in any other Pacific operation. Such cases resulted primarily from the length and bitterness of the fighting, together with heavy hostile artillery and mortar fire. The influx of from three to four thousand cases crowded the field hospitals and resulted in needless evacuations from the island. Treatment was instituted as far forward as possible in the hope of making it more effective as well as of retarding the flow to hospitals. Rest camps for neuropsychiatric cases were established by divisions in addition to the corps installations. On 25 April Tenth Army opened one field hospital to handle only such cases. Early treatment produced good results. About half of the cases were finally treated in divisional installations; the other half, comprising the more serious cases, were treated in the field hospitals. About 80 percent of the latter were returned to duty in ten days, but half of these had to be reassigned to noncombat duties.

Fears that Okinawa was a disease-ridden island where the health of American troops would be gravely menaced proved unfounded. Surveys made in April revealed no schistosomiasis or scrub typhus and very little malaria; about 30 percent of the natives, however, were found to be infected with filariasis. Institution of sanitation control measures, such as DDT spraying from the air at 7- to 10-day intervals and the attachment of disease control units to combat organizations, helped, together with the general favorable climatic conditions, to prevent large-scale outbreaks of communicable diseases on the island. As a result the net disease rate for the troops on Okinawa was very low.

Military Government

One of the most puzzling questions confronting the planners of the Okinawa operation had been the probable attitude of the civilian population. It was very soon apparent that the behavior of the Okinawans would pose no problems. In the first place, only the less aggressive elements of the populace remained, for the Japanese Army had conscripted almost all males between the ages of fifteen and forty-five. Many of those who came into the lines were in the category of displaced persons before the invasion began, having moved northward from Naha and Shuri some time before. Others had been made homeless as the fighting passed through their villages. Casualties among civilians had been surprisingly light, most of them having sought the protection of the caves, and some, including whole families, having taken refuge in deep wells.

The initial landings brought no instances on Okinawa of mass suicide of civilians as there had been on the Kerama Islands, although some, particularly of the older inhabitants, had believed the Japanese terror propaganda and were panic-stricken when taken into American custody. While there appeared to be only a few cases of communicable diseases and little malaria, most civilians, living in overcrowded and unsanitary caves, were infested with lice and fleas.

A frugal and industrious people, with a low standard of living and little education, the Okinawans docilely made the best of the disaster which had overtaken them. With resignation they allowed themselves to be removed from

MILITARY GOVERNMENT *set up headquarters in Shimabuku at beginning of the Okinawa campaign. Tent City (upper left) was quickly established, and registration of military-age civilians was started (upper right). Many Okinawan men (lower left) were given jobs carrying supplies to American troops, while others (lower right) helped to distribute food supplies to displaced persons.*

their homes and their belongings to the special camp areas which soon supplanted the initial stockades as places of detention.[9] The principal areas chosen initially for civilian occupation were Ishikawa and the Katchin Peninsula in the north, and Koza, Shimabuku, and Awase in the south. Military Government supplied the minimum necessities of existence—food, water, clothing, shelter, medical care, and sanitation. Food stores sufficient to take care of civilian needs for from two to four weeks were discovered; additional quantities were available in the fields. Growing crops were harvested on a communal basis under American direction. Horses, cows, pigs, goats, and poultry, running wild after eluding the invading troops, were rounded up and turned over to the civilian camps.

There was no occasion for use of the occupation currency with which American troops had been supplied, in exchange for dollars, before landing; no price or wage economy existed in the zone of occupation. For a time the population had to devote its energies solely to the problems of existence.

Control of civilians on Okinawa was vested in a Military Government Section whose operation was a command function of Tenth Army. The organization provided for four types of detachments, each consisting of a number of teams. The first type accompanied assault divisions and conducted preliminary reconnaissance; the second organized Military Government activities behind the fighting front; the third administered the refugee civilian camps; and the fourth administered the Military Government districts. It proved difficult to secure adequate numbers of certain types of personnel for Military Government, especially interpreters who were sufficiently skilled in the Japanese language. Before the invasion seventy-five men were assigned for this duty; when it became apparent that this number was insufficient, an additional allotment of ninety-five interpreters was secured. As the campaign progressed, minor shortages of cooks, military police, and medical corpsmen developed in the camps for displaced civilians. In spite of these shortages, detachments that were originally designed to operate camps containing 10,000 civilians often found it necessary to care for as many as 20,000.

The number of Okinawans under control of Military Government rose rapidly in the first month of the invasion until by the end of April it amounted to 126,876. Because of the stalemate at the Shuri lines the increase during May was gradual, the total number of civilians at the beginning of June being 144,331.

[9] See above, p. 83.

DEVELOPMENT OF AIRFIELD *at Kadena (photographed 20 April 1945) was rapid.*

REHABILITATION OF PORT *at Naha was in progress when this picture was taken, 19 June 1945.*

But during the first three weeks of June, after the break-through on the Shuri line, the number again rose sharply until, at the conclusion of the fighting, the Okinawans under Military Government totaled approximately 196,000.[16]

Base Development

The purpose of the base development plans for Okinawa and Ie Shima was the construction of advance fleet and air bases and staging facilities for future operations. Initially, however, all construction work was directed to the support of the assault troops. Main supply and dump roads were improved, Yontan and Kadena airfields were put into operation, and work was begun on the construction of bulk storage facilities for gasoline with offshore connections to tankers.[11]

In the original plans many more islands in the Ryukyus chain had been selected for capture and development as American bases, particularly for aircraft. No less than five additional islands—Okino Daito, Kume, Miyako, Kikai, and Tokuno—had been scheduled for invasion in Phase III of ICEBERG and were to be developed as fighter and B–29 bases and radar stations. In the course of time, as reconnaissance revealed that some of the islands were unsuitable for the purposes intended, plans for their capture were canceled. Of the five, only Kume was taken, on 26 June, and not for use as an air base but in order to enlarge the air warning net for the Okinawa island group.

The cancellation of the Phase III projects greatly affected the plans for base development on Okinawa and Ie Shima. In some cases most of the resources and troops intended for the abandoned operations were made available for the work on Okinawa. At the same time, however, some of the airfield construction projects were also transferred, thereby sizeably increasing the task of the Okinawa construction troops. In one case favorable estimates of construction possibilities on Okinawa and Ie Shima were responsible in large part for the decision to abandon one of the most important operations planned for Phase III—the Miyako operation. On 9 April Tenth Army reported to Admiral Nimitz that a detailed reconnaissance of the terrain of Okinawa revealed excellent airfield sites for Very Long Range bombers (VLR) on the island. As a result, Admiral

---

[10] Tenth Army, G–4 Periodic Reports, Ryukyus Campaign, for the following dates: 4 and 10 May 45, 4 and 25 Jun 45.

[11] Sources for the discussion of base development problems are as follows: Tenth Army Actn Rpt, 1–0–2, 3; 11–IV–6, 7, 24–28; 11–IX–10, 13; USAFPOA Participation in Okinawa Operations, I, 45–46, 167; USAFMIDPAC G–5 History, pp. 235–61; Island Command Okinawa Actn Rpt, Ch. 8, Sec. X; interv 1st I & H Off with Commodore A. G. Bissett, Commander Island Command Construction Troops, 19 May 45.

Nimitz recommended to the Joint Chiefs of Staff that the seizure of Miyako Island for development as a VLR bomber base be abandoned in favor of a more intensive construction program for Okinawa and Ie Shima. The Joint Chiefs approved and the Miyako operation was canceled on 26 April. Accordingly, base development plans were changed to provide for 18 air strips on Okinawa and 4 on Ie Shima, instead of the 8 and 2 originally planned respectively for the two islands. Construction of fields on Okinawa was to center on the provision of facilities for B–29 operations, while Ie Shima was to be developed primarily as a base for VLR fighter escorts.

There was concern over interruptions to the progress of the greatly expanded Okinawa program. The extremely heavy rains at the end of May practically stopped all construction work until about 15 June, as troops working on the airfields had to be diverted to maintenance of the main supply roads to the assault troops. Although the cancellation of the Miyako project made available more men for the base program on Okinawa, only 31,400 of the 80,000 construction troops needed had reached the island by 22 June 1945. It was impossible to keep abreast of scheduled dates of completion. The delays in unloading and failure to uncover airfields and ports on schedule also contributed to the delay in the base development program.

Work on fighter airfields was initially given the highest priority in order to provide land-based air cover during the assault. By 10 April Kadena and Yontan airfields had been reconditioned for successful operations. American engineers found that the Japanese airfields were poorly constructed, being surfaced with only a thin layer of coral rock and lacking adequate drainage. The runways had to be completely rebuilt, with a foot of coral surfacing added. By the end of May construction was in progress on ten different bomber and fighter strips on Okinawa and Ie Shima. Of these only the fields at Yontan and Kadena and one of the fighter strips on Ie Shima were near completion. The first American air strip built on Okinawa was the 7,000-foot medium bomber runway at Yontan, completed on 17 June. By the end of June a 7,500-foot VLR strip at Kadena was 25 percent complete, two 5,000-foot fighter strips at Awase and Chimu were ready for operation, an 8,500-foot VLR strip at Zampa Point was 15 percent complete, and construction was under way for VLR and medium-bomber strips at Futema and Machinato.

Harbor development began at the end of April with the construction of a 500-foot ponton barge pier on the Katchin Peninsula at Buckner Bay. Temporary ponton barge piers were built at other sites on the bay—at Kin on Chimu Bay, at Machinato, and at the mouth of the Bishi River. By the end of June an 800-foot ponton barge pier was under construction at Yonabaru. Preparations for building permanent ship piers and cargo berths were also under way. At Naha troops had begun clearing the harbor of wrecks and debris at the beginning of June; several months would be required before this work would be completed and Naha could serve as a major port.

By the end of the Okinawa campaign the full realization of the plans for the development of major air and naval bases in the Ryukyus still lay in the future. Most of the airfields would not be completed for two or three months, although fighters were flying from some to attack Kyushu. The naval base in Buckner Bay was far from complete when the war ended. It was not until the last night of the war that Okinawa-based B-29's carried out their first and last offensive mission against the Japanese homeland.

CHAPTER XVII

The Enemy's Last Stand

"Ushijima missed the boat on his withdrawal from the Shuri Line," General Buckner declared on 31 May as he re-formed his ranks for the pursuit and final destruction of the *32d Army*. "It's all over now but cleaning up pockets of resistance. This doesn't mean there won't be stiff fighting but the Japs won't be able to organize another line." Other officers also did not credit the enemy with the ability to execute an orderly withdrawal.[1] This optimism proved soon to be largely unfounded. It was to be learned that the enemy had withdrawn his forces from Shuri effectively and in time to organize a new line in the south. The enemy's maneuver, though it did not result in setting up a formidable line of defense, was to necessitate more than three crowded weeks of pursuit and fighting by the American troops to bring organized resistance to an end.

The Push South to the Yaeju-Dake–Yuza-Dake Barrier

On 31 May General Buckner extended the Army boundary along the road joining the villages of Chan, Iwa, and Gushichan. He ordered his two corps to complete the encirclement of Shuri in order to cut the remaining Japanese troops into large segments. General Buckner and his staff still hoped to isolate a large portion of the *32d Army* and prevent its withdrawal from Shuri; thus the two corps were directed to converge at Chan "in order to pocket enemy north this point." III Amphibious Corps was then to secure Naha and its airfield while XXIV Corps drove rapidly southeast to prevent the enemy from retiring into the Chinen Peninsula. General Buckner expected the Japanese, without skilled men or adequate transportation or communications, and hindered by boggy roads, to experience trouble and disorder during their mass retreat.[2]

Mud was a major concern of American commanders. Nearly twelve inches of rain had fallen during the last ten days of May and more was expected during the first part of June. Although 400 trucks had been used on 30 May to dump coral and rubble into the mudholes on Route 5, the main north-south

---

[1] Notes of Tenth Army Staff Meeting, in Okinawa Diary kept by Stevens and Burns, 31 May 45.
[2] *Ibid.,* 30 May 45; Tenth Army Opns Order No. 12–45, 31 May 45.

road through the center of Okinawa, it was closed the following day to all but the most essential traffic. Other supply routes along the east and west coasts were in almost impassable condition. At the time when General Buckner ordered his troops to "drive rapidly," supply trucks were moving toward the front only as fast as they could be dragged by winches or bulldozers through the numerous quagmires. Units on each flank were using boats or amphibian tractors to transport supplies from rear areas to forward dumps, but they still faced the problem of moving food and ammunition from the beaches to the front-line foxholes. Center divisions were under a still greater strain. Much of the ammunition, food, and water was carried forward by reserve units—sometimes by men from the assault companies.

"We had awfully tough luck," said General Buckner, "to get the bad weather at the identical time that things broke." His deputy chief of staff considered the mud to be as great a deterrent to the attack as a large-scale enemy counterattack.[3]

The Japanese Make Their Escape

The XXIV Corps occupied the southernmost positions of the American front. General Hodge shifted the 7th Division toward the east and ordered the 96th to move south, relieve the 32d Infantry, and take up the western end of the Corps line. The 77th Division became responsible for protecting the rear of the 96th and for mopping up the part of the Shuri line which was in the XXIV Corps sector. By evening of 31 May, the 7th and 96th Divisions reached the Corps' objective, and they were ready to start south on the following morning.[4]

The lines of the III Amphibious Corps stretched from Shuri to a point 1,000 yards southeast of Naha; its nearest position was more than 3,000 yards from the dominating ground near Chan where General Buckner still hoped to converge spearheads of his two corps and to reduce Ushijima's force to segments. This hope disappeared by the night of 31 May, when the performance of the 96th and 7th Divisions indicated that General Ushijima had already accomplished his sly withdrawal despite the difficulties of mud and communications. When it became apparent that the Japanese withdrawal had frustrated American hopes of splitting the enemy forces, Tenth Army revised its plans

[3] Appleman, XXIV Corps History, p. 496; Notes of Tenth Army Staff Meeting, in Okinawa Diary kept by Stevens and Burns, 30 and 31 May 45.

[4] XXIV Corps FO No. 52, 31 May 45; Appleman, XXIV Corps History, p. 490; XXIV Corps G–3 Periodic Rpt, 31 May 45.

and permitted the III Amphibious Corps to attack down the west coast and the 7th Division to proceed down the east flank.[5] (See Map No. XLVI.)

When the attack toward the south began on the first day of June, it was planned that the Marines should destroy the remaining Japanese rather than isolate them. Patrols from the III Amphibious Corps soon discovered that only a thin shell of defenses remained near Shuri. General Geiger decided, therefore, to push the 1st Marine Division directly south to seal the base of Oroku Peninsula, and he also made plans for an amphibious landing by the 6th Marine Division on the tip of the peninsula.[6]

Four miles south of the front line loomed another coral escarpment, the largest on the Okinawa battlefield. This was the Yuza-Dake–Yaeju-Dake, which formed a great wall across the southern end of the island that had been visible since the early days of the campaign. The central part of the island between the American front lines of 31 May and the Yaeju-Dake consisted of a series of comparatively small rounded hills and uneven low ridges; a few larger hills stretched across the base of the Oroku Peninsula on the west side of the island. The highest hills south of the landing beaches were on the east side of southern Okinawa and on Chinen Peninsula, which consisted entirely of hilly ground except for the narrow strip of flat land at the shore.

Pursuit in the Mud

Dense fog banks covered southern Okinawa on the morning of 1 June. Visibility extended for only a few yards and mud was ankle-deep as the Americans attacked south to catch up with Ushijima's escaped army before it should have time to burrow into a new defensive line. On 1 June the Japanese defended two hills in front of the 7th Division, and during 1–2 June they made a solid stand in the zone of the 96th near Chan. Otherwise there was only spotty resistance of delaying and nuisance value until 6 June. On that day the pace of the American troops was retarded by vigorous enemy action to the front and by the overextension of the supply lines of the front-line units.[7]

Most of the hills were either defended by thin enemy forces or had been completely abandoned, and a lack of skill was noticeable among the enemy troops encountered. As American troops approached their positions the Japanese of-

[5] Interv 1st I & H Off with Lt Col J. R. Weaver, ACofS, G–2, Tenth Army, 5 Jun 45.

[6] The III Amph Corps Opns Ord No. 15–45, 1 Jun 45, in accordance with Tenth Army Opns Ord No. 12–45, 31 May 45, directed the marines to join with XXIV Corps elements near Chan. This was not done, however, when it was realized that the bulk of enemy troops had escaped to the south. Statement of Capt James R. Stockman, USMC, Marine Corps Historian, 6 May 46.

[7] Gugeler, 7th Div History, pp. 381–84; Mulford and Rogers, 96th Div History, Pt. IV, pp. 171–72.

fered ineffectual fire until the attack drew close, and then frequently tried to escape by running across open ground. They became easy targets for riflemen and machine gunners, who were quick to see and respect skill in their opponents and as quick to feel disdain for spiritless mediocrity. S/Sgt. Lowell E. McSpadden, a member of the 383d Infantry, expressed the attitude of the infantrymen toward these inferior troops when he stepped up behind two Japanese soldiers without being seen, tapped one on the shoulder, and then shot both with a .45-caliber pistol which he had borrowed for the purpose.[8]

After the first day of the pursuit, rain was more troublesome and constant than enemy interference. The 184th Infantry waded south and east over the green and rain-soaked hills on Chinen Peninsula against light opposition that indicated an absence of enemy plans for a defense of that area. General Arnold, moving to speed up operations, committed the 32d Infantry to patrolling the northern part of the peninsula.[9] Late in the afternoon of 3 June, patrols from the 1st Battalion, 184th, reached the southeast coast of Okinawa near the town of Hyakuna and completed the 7th Division's first mission. It had been, General Buckner said, a magnificent performance.[10]

General Hodge doubted that his corps could have continued its pace had it not been for previous experience in the marshes of Leyte.[11] Only flimsy resistance faced the 1st Marine Division, but its supply system had collapsed and the battalions had to rely upon air drops or carrying parties. By 3 June the gap in depth between the two corps had increased to 3,000 yards, and the 383d Infantry was subjected to harassing fire from its exposed right flank. To protect his corps' flank, General Hodge sent the 305th Infantry, 77th Division, south to fill the increasing void.[12]

Toward the Yaeju-Dake

In the meantime the 2d Battalion, 5th Marines, crossing the Corps boundary north of Chan, attacked southwest through Tera and secured Hill 57 and the high ground south of Gisushi, thus reducing the gap to 1,000 yards.

With the elimination of possible defensive terrain on Chinen Peninsula and in central southern Okinawa, it was becoming evident by the evening of 3 June that General Ushijima intended to stage his final stand on the southern

---

[8] Mulford and Rogers, 96th Div History, Pt. IV, p. 173.

[9] Gugeler, 7th Div History, p. 384.

[10] Notes of Tenth Army Staff Meeting, in Okinawa Diary kept by Stevens and Burns, 4 Jun 45.

[11] Appleman, XXIV Corps History, p. 515.

[12] Stockman, 1st Mar Div History; III Amph Corps G–3 Periodic Rpt, 1 Jun 45; Appleman, XXIV Corps History, p. 503.

MUD AND SUPPLY *were major problems in pursuing the Japanese southward from Shuri. Success depended largely on ability to move American supplies over bad roads. Tractor (above) is pulling a reconnaissance car uphill from portable bridge in the hollow. When roads became impassable to motor vehicles (below), horses were used.*

tip of the island, almost certainly on the Yaeju-Dake Escarpment, which lay within the zone of the III Amphibious Corps. Moreover, if the XXIV Corps maintained its pace for one or two days longer, as seemed likely, it would have secured its portion of southern Okinawa. In order to deny the enemy a breathing spell before the final period of combat, General Buckner shifted the Corps' boundary to the west so that the entire escarpment fell within the zone of the XXIV Corps. Effective at noon on 4 June, the boundary between the corps changed from the road connecting Iwa with Gushichan to the road connecting Iwa with Yuza, Ozato, and Komesu.[15] (See Map No. XLVII.)

Shifting their direction of attack on 4 June to the southwest, General Hodge's troops moved across the small, tidy fields, the rice paddies along the sea, and the hills luxuriantly green from the continuing spring rains. By midafternoon the 7th Division had secured more than 6,000 yards of coast line and had reached the soggy banks of the Minatoga River. Infantrymen waded the swollen stream, the only bridge having been destroyed. The 96th joined on the west to extend the Corps line from Minatoga to Iwa. To the south the Japanese had prepared the outposts of their next important line, which was to be their last. Behind the American lines the supply routes, now stretched beyond an unbridged river, were strained to the limit. Commanders immediately explored the possibilities of landing supplies at Minatoga. During the several days that followed, the American troops crowded steadily but more cautiously forward against a heavy and determined opposition that was reminiscent of previous fighting and suggested that the enemy's last line was close at hand.[14]

The Capture of Oroku Peninsula

It was only by chance and whim that the Oroku Peninsula was defended by the Japanese after the Shuri line was abandoned. Before 1 April enemy naval units were responsible for this two-by-three-mile peninsula and the installations emplaced there to protect the airfield and the city of Naha. A few days before the American landings took place, but after the threat of invasion made it either impossible or unnecessary for the naval units to continue with their more specific missions, they were consolidated under the *Okinawa Base Force*. Most of the Navy personnel congregated on Oroku Peninsula. The *Okinawa Base*

[13] Tenth Army Opns Ord No. 13–45, 4 Jun 45; Appleman, XXIV Corps History, pp. 503–04.
[14] Gugeler, 7th Div History, p. 386.

Force, commanded by Rear Admiral Minoru Ota, was in turn responsible to the *32d Army,* toward which Ota adopted a policy of complete cooperation.[15]

The total strength of enemy naval units on Okinawa was originally nearly 10,000 men; less than a third of that number, however, belonged to the Japanese Navy, the majority being either recently inducted civilians or Home Guards. Of the men who made up the construction units, the naval air units, the *Midget Submarine Unit,* and the other organizations that became a part of the *Base Force,* only two or three hundred had received more than superficial training for land warfare. None of these naval units participated in combat until the counterattack of 4 May, when a limited number of naval troops were sent to the front line and sustained very high casualties. Other units were subsequently fed into the front lines. The *37th Torpedo Maintenance Unit* was almost completely destroyed when, with three times as many men as rifles, it entered the fighting at Shuri and Yonabaru toward the end of May.

The greatest misfortune affecting the ultimate fate of the enemy naval forces occurred at the time of the mass exodus from Shuri. The *32d Army* headquarters directed all naval troops to fall back on 28 May to a new defense area, near the coastal town of Nagusuku. Because of an ambiguously worded order, the remaining men of the *Base Force* destroyed most of the weapons and equipment which they were unable to carry; they then moved south on 26 May, two days before they were scheduled to withdraw. When they arrived at their assigned area they found it totally unsuited to the type of fighting for which they were prepared, as well as inferior to the area they had just left. Disgusted with their new sector, the young officers asked Ota for permission to return to Oroku "to fight and die at the place where we built positions and where we were so long to die [*sic*] in that one part of the island which really belonged to the Navy." Advocates of independent action by the Navy succeeded in persuading Ota of the advisability of returning the troops to Oroku. Without consulting the Army Ota ordered the troops back on 28 May, and the return was effected that night. Naval troops numbering about 2,000 returned to their former positions. Some Navy personnel stayed in the south to fight on the Yuza-Dake or Yaeju-Dake line; the rest of the original 10,000 had been used up in the previous combat.

Naha airfield, the largest and most important which the Japanese had constructed on Okinawa, was at the northern end of a strip of flat land on the

[15] The account of the disposition of Admiral Ota's forces is taken from Tenth Army PW Interrog Summary No. 16, 28 Jul 45: Naval Units on Okinawa; Int Monograph, Pt. II, Sec. A: Oroku Hanto.

ADVANCING TO YAEJU-DAKE *through the Iwa area, American tank passes burning native house, fired to lessen danger from snipers.   Below is seen a patrol of the 381st Infantry, 96th Division, moving south toward Yaeju-Dake.*

LAST POINT OF RESISTANCE *in the Oroku Peninsula was Hill 57, shown above in* *panorama. Below is a close-up of a concrete emplacement (dotted outline in photo above)* *after it had been blasted open by Marine artillery fire.*

west side of Oroku Peninsula. The rest of the peninsula was wrinkled with ridges and hills up to 200 feet in height but was lacking in any pattern or dominant terrain features. Between the hills were valleys planted in sugar cane and other dry crops; the valleys had been sown with mines and were carefully covered by automatic weapons firing from camouflaged cave openings.

An Amphibious Assault

A shore-to-shore movement would offer suitable landing beaches and orient the American attack in the direction that afforded the best use of supporting artillery. This plan of attacking from the sea would also provide for supply by sea, made necessary by the break-down of roads. Therefore General Shepherd, commander of the 6th Marine Division, ordered the 4th Marines, followed by the 29th, to make a landing. Planning and organization had been completed by the evening of 3 June. At 0445 on the following morning supporting artillery began an hour-long preparation during which 4,300 shells fell on the high ground in front of the landing beaches. With amphibian tanks in the lead the 1st Battalion, 4th Marines, embarked from the assembly area north of the Asato River and headed south toward the northern point of the Oroku Peninsula. The formation was partially broken when some of the amphibian tractors, which had been used by the marines to haul supplies to the front during the rainy period, failed after getting under way, leaving elements of the assault force stranded in the water. There was only light fire, however, when the first troops stepped ashore a few minutes before 0600 and the men hurried inland to carve out a beachhead sufficiently large to warrant landing the remainder of the force. An hour and a half after the landing the two assault battalions were 900 yards inland, and twenty-four tanks and four self-propelled guns were ashore; by 1000 the 29th Marines was ordered to land and take up the north end of the division line. The landing was proceeding satisfactorily.[16]

As the 4th Marines landed on the north point of Oroku the 6th Reconnaissance Company seized Ono-Yama, a small island in the center of the Naha Inlet which formed the anchor for two destroyed bridges linking Naha to the peninsula. A few defenders were killed, and the island was in American hands an hour after the assault commenced. Replacement of the bridges, necessary to provide adequate logistical support, was hindered by Japanese machine-gun and 20-mm. shell fire, and it was not until the following day that the final sections of a ponton bridge were floated into place.

---

[16] The account of the operations of 6th Mar Div on Oroku is taken from 6th Mar Div Special Actn Rpt Phase III, Ch. III and App. III; and Carleton, 6th Mar Div History, Ch. III.

Mud, Mines, and Machine Guns

At the end of the first day assault battalions, 1,800 yards beyond the point of the landing, faced stabilized enemy fire power from a wealth of automatic weapons varying from light machine guns to 40-mm. cannons. It was later learned that many of these weapons had been stripped from damaged planes, adapted for use by ground troops, and, with painstaking care, hidden underground behind narrow, camouflaged firing ports that overlooked the mine-sown valleys and other approaches to the defended hills. The 10-day battle for Oroku Peninsula is the story of a half-trained enemy force, poor in standard weapons, organization, and hope of eventual success, but possessed of abundant automatic fire power, a system of underground positions larger than they could man, and a willingness to die in those positions in order to make the Americans pay dearly for the ground.

Gains were slowed down on the second day and came to an abrupt halt when the 29th Marines, on the northern flank, hit a hard core on Hill 57 near the center of the peninsula. With progress least difficult on the right (south), General Shepherd tried to crowd the 4th Marines forward to outflank the enemy's positions. The southern end of the line yielded as far as the village of Gushi; then the entire line, 4,000 yards long, faced a tight ring of Japanese defenses that held the marines to slight gains for two more days, 7 and 8 June. Use of tanks was restricted by mud and the widely scattered mine fields, which were protected by abundant machine-gun fire. Three platoons of tanks helped in the capture of Hill 57 on 7 June, but usually the tanks were bogged in mud or fenced off beyond direct-support range by mine fields. In three instances when men from the 2d Battalion, 4th Marines, were unable to fight their way to the top of a hill, they used the extensive tunnel systems and went through the hills rather than over them.

Meanwhile, the 1st Marine Division had freed itself from the mud, and on 6 June it was halfway across the base of Oroku Peninsula, closing the gap between the two corps but exposing its own west flank. General Shepherd committed the Corps reserve, the 22d Marines, sending them south to establish a line across the base of the peninsula. This placed elements of the division on opposite sides of the Japanese troops on Oroku, and General Shepherd, recognizing that the logical avenues of entry to the Japanese hill positions were from the south and southeast, ordered the 22d to patrol to the northwest and then to attack in that direction. The 4th Marines was ordered to attack on the left of the 22d's line.

With three regiments thus engaged in the fight, the division continued to concentrate on an encircling move to compress the Japanese on the high ground near Tomigusuki. There were no soft spots along the enemy line, and each slow advance the marines scored was against machine-gun and 20-mm. and 40-mm. antiaircraft fire. Fighting proceeded with the same sustained effort by both sides through 10 June, when the remaining Japanese were confined in an area no larger than 1,000 by 2,000 yards. Subjected to extreme pressure, the Japanese during the night of 10 June erupted in a series of local counterattacks along the entire front. Two hundred enemy dead were scattered along the front lines on the following morning.

End of the Okinawa Base Force

General Shepherd struck back at the Japanese at 0730, 11 June; he employed the greater part of eight battalions and supported them with tanks, which after several days of clear weather were no longer restricted by mud. This was planned as the final blow to break through the enemy resistance. The 29th Marines attacking from the west, and the 4th moving from the south, made only slight headway; the 22d Marines, after an intense artillery barrage, drove toward Hill 62 from the southeast. The first attack stopped short of the objective, but, about noon, the 2d Battalion, 22d Marines, rammed another assault against Hill 62 while the 3d Battalion moved off for Hill 53, about 300 yards north. The first of these objectives fell by 1330, and Hill 53, which afforded observation of the remainder of the enemy-held ground, soon afterward. The three regiments held a tight ring in an area 1,000 yards square.

A break-up in the Japanese forces occurred on the following day. As the converging forces closed in on the remaining pocket, the Japanese were forced from the high ground onto the flat land near the Naha Inlet. Some chose to fight until killed; others, including several who lay down on satchel charges and blew their bodies high in the air, destroyed themselves. On 12 June and the day following, 159 surrendered—the first large group of Japanese taken prisoner.

When the destruction of his force was nearly complete, Admiral Ota committed suicide. On 15 June, as patrols sought out the last of the Japanese on Oroku, the marines found Ota's body and those of five members of his staff lying on a raised, mattress-covered platform in one of the passages in the underground headquarters. Their throats had been cut, and, from the appearance of the room, it was apparent that an aide had carefully arranged the bodies and tidied up after the self-destruction of the Japanese officers. Nearly 200 other bodies were found in the headquarters, one of the most elaborate underground systems on the island. More than 1,500 feet of tunnels connected the office rooms, which were well ventilated, equipped with electricity, and reinforced with concrete doorways and walls.[17]

The slow and tedious battle for Oroku Peninsula had lasted for ten days. The total number of marines killed or wounded was 1,608, a cost in casualties proportionately greater than the American forces suffered during the fighting for Shuri, where they were opposed by General Ushijima's infantrymen.

Six days before the 6th Marine Division wiped out Admiral Ota's force, and four days after the XXIV Corps separated Chinen Peninsula from the rest of the battlefield, the 1st Marine Division reached the west coast above Itoman. Besides straightening Tenth Army front lines between that village and Gushichan, this advance opened a water supply route for the advance elements of the III Amphibious Corps.[18]

Assaulting the Last Defense Line

When the rainy period on Okinawa ended on 5 June, troops of the XXIV Corps occupied a solid line across 6,000 yards of soft clay. Supply was critical and was partially dependent upon air drops. Tanks could not operate, and to the front, 1,000 or 1,500 yards away, stood the craggy Yaeju-Dake and Yuza-Dake hill masses—physical barriers which, together with Hill 95 on the east coast, formed a great wall across the entire XXIV Corps sector from Gushichan to Yuza. The highest point of this 4-mile-long cliff was the Yaeju-Dake Peak, which rose 290 feet above the adjoining valley floor. Because of its shape the troops who fought up its slopes named it the "Big Apple." The Yuza-Dake stood at the west end of the line and then tapered off into Kunishi Ridge, which extended across the III Amphibious Corps' sector. Hill 95, which paralleled rather than crossed the direction of attack, formed the eastern anchor. On the seaward side of Hill 95 there was a 300-foot drop to the water; on the side next to Hanagusuku village there was another sheer drop of about 170 feet to the valley floor. The only break in this defensive wall was in the 7th Division's sector, where a narrow valley pointed south through Nakaza. This approach to the high tableland beyond the escarpment cliff was subject to fire and observation from both flanks.

Between this redoubtable terrain and the front occupied by XXIV Corps on the evening of 5 June were a few grassy knolls and numerous small hills scattered

[17] Tenth Army Int Monograph, Pt. II, Sec. A: Oroku Hanto.
[18] 1st Mar Div Special Actn Rpt, Assault Narrative, Phase III, p. 12.

BASE OF OROKU PENINSULA, *where* Okinawa Base Force *made its last stand*.

over a generally flat valley. After two weeks of almost continual rain, the valley was rich with verdure and thus far only slightly torn by shells and combat.

General Ushijima's army reached this new defensive area several days ahead of the Americans and, by 3 or 4 June, was deployed in the caves and crevices in and behind the escarpment wall. The combined strength of *32d Army* infantry units was about 11,000 men. Total enemy strength, however, amounted to nearly three times that number. It included personnel from artillery or mortar units which no longer possessed weapons; signal, ordnance, airfield construction, and other units whose normal duties were no longer necessary; and conscripted Okinawans whose ability and will to fight did not equal those of the regular Japanese soldiers.[19]

About 8,000 men made up the Japanese *24th Division,* which, as his strongest unit, General Ushijima stationed in the center and across the west flank from Yaeju-Dake to the town of Itoman. The *62d Division,* originally the *32d Army's* best but now reduced to two or three thousand men, took up reserve positions near Makabe. This left only the *44th Independent Mixed Brigade* to defend the eastern part of the enemy's final line facing the 7th Division. Around these three original major combat units General Ushijima grouped the remaining service and labor troops, scattered naval personnel, and Okinawan conscripts. Thus, with a heterogenous army lacking in adequate training, artillery support, communications, and equipment and supplies, General Ushijima waited for the final battle. His headquarters took only a 20-day supply of rations when it moved from Shuri to the southern tip of the island—an indication of his own appraisal of his army's capabilities.

Both sides watched warily and prepared for the Americans' next assault. The state of supply, the condition of the narrow roads linking assault elements with supply dumps at Yonabaru, and the lack of armored and direct-fire weapons prevented an immediate large-scale attack by the XXIV Corps. American commanders probed the enemy line with patrols, regrouped their forces, and assembled necessary supplies through the little port of Minatoga, which was in operation by 8 June.[20]

[19] The account of Japanese strength on southern Okinawa at this time is taken from Tenth Army Int Monograph, Pt. I, Sec. B; Interrog Yahara; Interrog Shimada; Appleman, XXIV Corps History, pp. 493–96, 518–19; and Gugeler, 7th Div History, pp. 376–77. The Japanese strength as given in the text is only an estimate; accurate statistics are not available. While the figures for the *62d* and *24th Divisions* and the *44th Independent Mixed Brigade* are reasonably accurate, the number of other enemy troops was roughly estimated.

[20] XXIV Corps Actn Rpt, p. 32.

YAEJU-DAKE *was brought under American artillery fire shortly before the infantry attempted its first advance to the escarpment. Burst at upper left is white phosphorus.*

HILL 95, *near Yaeju-Dake, with Gushichan in foreground.*

Locating Enemy Strength

One of these probing actions made a slight penetration of the enemy's line and soon revealed the nature and volume of the enemy fire power protecting the final Japanese line. Nearest the Big Apple Peak was the 381st Infantry, first to venture into the Yaeju-Dake and the first to be driven back. West of the Big Apple was a secondary escarpment, like a step, about halfway to the top. Col. Michael E. Halloran ordered the 1st Battalion to explore this area and, if possible, to seize a lodgment on the lower part of the escarpment which would permit an attack against the Big Apple from the west and against the flank of the enemy's most dominating fortification.[21]

On the morning of 6 June the battalion commander, Maj. V. H. Thompson, leapfrogged his companies through Yunagusuku against only half-hearted opposition and then sent Company B, under Capt. John E. Byers, forward to test the escarpment wall. Three squad-sized patrols crept through bands of fire from machine guns, some of which were so far inside caves that they could not be destroyed with grenades, and reached the lower of the two escarpments. The rest of the company followed, and Thompson ordered Company C to move abreast and left of Byers' men. It was midafternoon, and the first attempt at penetration of this largest escarpment on Okinawa was proceeding with promise of success. Company C started across the open rice paddies to the base of the cliff, and Company B moved up a steep trail leading to the intermediate level of the escarpment. This movement went beyond the line of enemy delaying action and into the area where General Ushijima had ordered his army to "bring all its might to bear" to break up the American attack and exact a heavy toll of the attacking force. "To this end," he instructed, "the present position will be defended to the death, even to the last man. Needless to say, retreat is forbidden." [22]

The Japanese waited patiently until both companies were in a belt of pre-registered fire, then opened up with machine guns and 20-mm. dual purpose guns in sufficient quantity to lace both companies with beads of automatic fire. Major Thompson immediately started to organize a withdrawal and employed ten battalions of artillery to drop smoke shells in front of his trapped men. Even this was inadequate and many of the troops did not return until after dark. Company C lost five men killed and as many wounded. Casualties in Company B for the day totaled 43, including 14 missing. Of the missing men, 4 were dead,

[21] Mulford and Rogers, 96th Div History, Pt. IV, pp. 185–89.

Appleman, XXIV Corps History, p. 528.

2 returned the following morning, and the other 8 were trapped behind enemy lines. Three of the trapped men were subsequently killed by friendly or enemy fire, and the remaining five stayed in enemy territory until the morning of 14 June, although they tried to escape on each of the eight intervening nights.

For the next three days the 96th Division blasted the coral escarpment with artillery and air strikes and watched it closely for possible gun positions and strong points. The heaviest fighting occurred on the extreme eastern flank of the 7th Division, where Company B, 184th Infantry, faced unyielding opposition on a tapered ridge that pointed northeast from the tip of Hill 95. One of the roughest single terrain features on Okinawa, this 800-yard-long ridge was a jumbled mass of coral that was as porous as sponge and as brittle and sharp as glass. There were several fortified positions on the ridge as well as numerous cavities which protected individual enemy riflemen. The entire ridge was also under fire and observation from other positions on Hill 95. The advance was tedious, and the company made only slight progress. The largest gain from 6 to 9 June was in the zone of the 17th Infantry, which forced advances up to 1,800 yards and occupied the green knolls at the base of the escarpment. These small hills were not heavily defended but they were exposed to enemy fire from the face of the Yaeju-Dake and from the tableland above.[23]

The 32d Infantry, which had rounded up about 10,000 Okinawa civilians during six days of patrol activity on Chinen Peninsula, moved south on the afternoon of 8 May and effected relief of the 184th. Road conditions were improved and a large quantity of supplies reached Minatoga on 8 June; two companies of medium tanks were near the front lines and others were moving forward. General Arnold planned to strike the first blow against the new Japanese line and ordered the attack to commence at 0730 on 9 June. There were two immediate objectives. The task of reducing Hill 95 and the rough-hewn coral ridge that lay in front fell to the 1st Battalion, 32d Infantry, commanded by Lt. Col. Robert C. Foulston; the 3d Battalion, 17th Infantry, under Lt. Col Lee Wallace, was to secure a lodgment on the southern and low end of the Yaeju-Dake at a point just north of the town of Asato.

First Break in the Japanese Wall

Dawn patrols proceeded unmolested toward the coral ridge in front of Hill 95, but the Japanese reacted quickly before the remainder of Company C of the 32d Infantry, which carried the burden of the attack, had moved 100 yards.

[23] *Ibid.,* p. 500; Gugeler, 7th Div History, pp. 393-419.

As long as the men kept their heads down the enemy fire subsided, but any attempt to move forward attracted rifle and machine-gun and knee-mortar fire which blasted sharp chips from the coral formation. The company commander, Capt. Robert Washnok, held up the frontal assault, placed artillery shells on Hill 95, used about 2,000 mortar shells on his objective, and then tried working a platoon forward on the Gushichan side to eliminate two strongly defended knobs near the end of Hill 95. This effort was partially successful; the men killed thirteen Japanese and located the source of the most troublesome automatic fire, but toward evening they had to be recalled.

The first and greatest obstacle confronting Wallace's attack was the open ground over which both assault companies had to move. Wallace used all available support and the men camouflaged themselves with grass and rice plants, but enemy fire began almost as soon as the leading platoons moved into the open. The infantrymen crawled through the slimy rice paddies on their stomachs. Within an hour Company I was strung from the line of departure to the base of the objective which two squads had reached. About this time the Japanese opened fire with another machine gun, separating the advance squads with a band of fire. This left one squad to continue the attack; the remainder of the company was unable to move, cut off by fire or strung across the rice paddies.

Those men in the squad still free to operate lifted and pulled each other to the edge of the cliff and crawled quietly forward through the high grass on top. Pfc. Ignac A. Zeleski, a BAR man, moved so stealthily that he almost touched the heels of one Japanese. Zeleski killed him, and the other men killed eight more Japanese within the first ten minutes. Another squad reached the top of the escarpment about an hour later but was caught in cross and grazing fire from three machine guns, and the entire 8-man squad was killed. Gradually, however, a few more men reached the top, and by evening there were twenty men from Company I holding a small area at the escarpment rim.

Company K had a similar experience. Accurate enemy fire killed one man, wounded two others, and halted the company when it was from 200 to 300 yards from its objective. For forty-five minutes the attack dragged on until S/Sgt. Lester L. Johnson and eight men maneuvered forward through enemy fire, gained the high ground, and concentrated their fire on the enemy machine gun that was firing on the remainder of the company. This did not silence the gun but did prevent the gunner from aiming well, and Johnson waved for the rest of the company to follow. By 1330 of 9 June Company K was consolidated on the southeastern tip of the Yaeju-Dake. That evening, three small but determined counterattacks, with sustained grenade fire between each attempt, hit the small force from Company I, which held off the attackers with a light machine gun and automatic rifles.

Tanks stirred dust along the narrow roads when, at 0600 on the morning of 10 June, they started for the front lines. A full battalion was on hand to support the 7th Division; two companies operated with the 96th Division, which began its assault on the Yaeju-Dake that morning. The character of warfare on Okinawa changed, and until the end of the campaign there was a freer, more aggressive use of tanks. Weather and terrain were more favorable, and flame tanks became the American solution to the Japanese coral caves; interference from enemy shells became less with the destruction of each Japanese gun; and, more important, through experience the infantrymen and tankers developed a team that neared perfection. Improved visibility also aided observation of artillery fire and air strikes. The battle for the southern tip of Okinawa blazed with orange rods of flame and became a thunderous roar of machine guns, shells, rockets, and bombs.[24]

Pumping Flame Through a Hose

Company C, 32d Infantry, still bore the responsibility of destroying the Japanese in front of Hill 95. When the fighting flared again on the second day of the attack, Navy cruisers fired on the seaward side of the ridge; artillery and tanks shelled and machine-gunned the top and sides of Hill 95; and the 2d Battalion attacked toward the village of Hanagusuku. Captain Washnok and his men crept cautiously over the coral. The Japanese did not withdraw; Company C killed them as it advanced. By early afternoon the men had eliminated all enemy fire except that from a few scattered rifles and several fortified caves in two rocky knobs near the northeast end of Hill 95. Colonel Finn advocated the use of flame. Washnok held his company in place, and Capt. Tony Niemeyer, 6-foot 4-inch commander of Company C, 713th Armored Flame Thrower Battalion, moved one tank to the base of the two knobs. Then he attached a 200-foot hose, a special piece of equipment for delivering fuel to an area inaccessible to the tank. S/Sgt. Joseph Frydrych, infantry platoon leader, Captain Niemeyer, and Sgt. Paul E. Schrum dragged the hose onto the high rock and sprayed napalm over the two strong points, forcing out thirty-five or forty enemy soldiers whom the infantryman killed by rifle or BAR fire. Except for stray rifle fire, all enemy opposition in the coral ridge was gone when the 1st Battalion set up

---

[24] 763d Tk Bn S–3 Periodic Rpt, 10 Jun 45; 711th Tk Bn Actn Rpt, p. 18.

defenses for the night. The Japanese came back, however, during the night; they harassed Company C with mortars and grenades and prowled in the open in front of the other advanced companies. Two days of fighting through the rough terrain had cost Company C forty-three casualties, ten of whom were killed.

Niemeyer was active again on the morning of 11 June, when the 32d Infantry proceeded against the high end of Hill 95. Company B had taken the lead and pushed against the northeast end of the hill; although tank and artillery fire on Hill 95 was so heavy that the hill was partially obscured with haze, several machine guns fired from caves which could not be reached, and the men were temporarily stopped. When this approach failed, Niemeyer, Colonel Finn, and Capt. Dallas D. Thomas, Company B commander, decided to use the flame-thrower tanks to burn a path to the top of the 170-foot coral cliff. Captain Niemeyer, a daring soldier who was enthusiastic over the capabilities of his flame-thrower tanks, moved them to the Hanagusuku side of Hill 95 and forced streams of red flame against the portion of the cliff where the infantrymen expected to make the ascent. This flame eliminated any threat of close-quarters resistance from caves in the face of the escarpment. The next step was to reach the flat top of the hill and secure a toe hold on the high ground. At 1100 Niemeyer and a platoon under 1st Lt. Frank A. Davis fastened one end of a hose to a flame tank and began dragging the other end up the almost vertical side of the hill. The tanks, artillery, mortars, and machine guns stepped up their rate of fire to keep down enemy interference, the men being as exposed as spiders on a bare wall. This spectacular attack was also slow, and it was forty-five minutes before the men reached a small shelf just below the lip of the escarpment. They stopped here long enough to squirt napalm onto the flat rocks above them in case any Japanese were waiting for them there, then scrambled over the edge and poured flame onto the near-by area. Davis and his men fanned out behind the flame. The remainder of Company B followed immediately; the company quickly expanded its holding across the northeast end of the hill and then pushed south, still using flame against suspected enemy strong points. When the fuel from one tank was exhausted the hose was fitted to another tank.

Colonel Foulston reinforced his attacking company with two platoons from Company A. When evening came the 1st Battalion had destroyed the enemy force on the northeast end of the tableland. The men were involved in close-in fighting with Japanese hiding in rocks and crevices but their grip on the tableland was firm.

When it was time for front-line troops to dig in on the evening of 11 June, one battalion from each of the 7th Division's attacking regiments held a small corner of the enemy's main line on southern Okinawa. During the three days since the assault against Hill 95 and the Yaeju-Dake began on 9 June, the right (western) end of the XXIV Corps line had remained relatively unchanged. The 1st Battalion, 17th Infantry, softened its end of the Yaeju-Dake with lavish use of artillery, to destroy enemy strong points on the plateau above the escarpment, and employed tanks and cannon company weapons directly against caves in the face of the cliff.[25]

The 96th Attacks in the Center

Meanwhile, the 381st and 383d Infantry Regiments hammered away at the high peaks of Yaeju-Dake and Yuza-Dake. On 10 June the 383d attacked toward the town of Yuza, which it reached the following day. There was heavy fighting from one wall to the next in the battered town and, in addition, constant fire from Yuza-Dake, which towered over the southern edge of the town. The troops withdrew that evening when enemy fire increased.[26]

With its approach blocked by the highest and steepest section of the Yaeju-Dake wall, the 381st Infantry struck toward the saddle between the Big Apple Peak and the Yuza-Dake, where the escarpment rose in two levels. Major Thompson's 1st Battalion had unsuccessfully explored this route on 6 June when Companies B and C reached the intermediate level, immediately drew preregistered fire, and were forced to abandon their gains under smoke. After shelling the Japanese emplacements for four days these two companies attacked over the same route, this time with tank support. Difficult terrain and mines prevented effective use of the tanks, but Companies B and C pushed ahead without them and, by 0900 of 10 June, three of the attacking platoons were back on the ledge where the previous attack had stalled. Japanese machine guns opened fire as promptly and accurately as before, and the advance again ended suddenly with half of the men on the first ledge of the escarpment and the rest scattered in the rice paddies to the rear.

Throughout the day the company commanders tried to maneuver the trailing elements of their units forward. Each effort failed until, late in the afternoon, another smoke screen was laid down, this time to cover the advance of the rear elements and the preparation of defensive positions for the night. When the smoke had cleared, both companies were in place. A few minutes later about a

[25] Gugeler, 7th Div History, pp. 405–11, 420.
[26] Mulford and Rogers, 96th Div History, Pt. IV, pp. 191–99.

Flame-throwing tanks advance to Hill 95.   *Flame hose is stretched up the hill.*

Flame from hose hits hill.   *Burned, bewildered survivor is captured.*

Enemy position burned out by Capt. Tony Niemeyer's team.

FLAME THROUGH A HOSE

hundred Japanese troops, believing the smoke had covered a withdrawal as on 6 June, emerged from their holes and gathered near a building at the southern end of the flat area, where they began to change to civilian clothes for their customary night infiltrations. Capt. Philip D. Newell, commanding Company C, adjusted artillery fire in their midst and most of them were killed.

An ammunition-carrying party took supplies to the forward companies that night, enabling the men to defend their gain successfully against a counterattack that came early the next morning. Just before dawn on 11 June the remainder of the battalion joined the two advance companies. The 381st Infantry made no attempt to extend its holdings on 11 June but conducted heavy tank and artillery fire against the cave openings on the Big Apple Peak. The next important thrust against the Japanese line was to occur in the sector of the 17th Infantry where Col. Francis Pachler was planning a night attack against his portion of the Yaeju-Dake.

Night Move Onto the Yaeju-Dake

Colonel Pachler had good reasons for favoring a night move. The advantages of observation belonged almost completely to the defending force, and this had seriously interfered when the 3d Battalion, 17th Infantry, seized the southeast end of the escarpment. The coral wall of the escarpment in front of the 1st Battalion was higher at this end; at the same time the two suitable routes leading to the high ground were narrow and could be easily controlled by Japanese fire. The troops had held positions at the base of the 170-foot cliff for several days and were familiar with the terrain. They had, in fact, been looking at the escarpment so long that, as their commander, Maj. Maynard Weaver, said, they were anxious to get on top so that they could look at something else.[27]

Although the night attack was planned principally for the 1st Battalion, Colonel Pachler also decided on a coordinated move to enlarge the area held by the 3d Battalion. The final plan included three assault companies: Company A was to occupy a cluster of coral about a hundred yards beyond the edge of the escarpment and next to the boundary between the 7th and 96th Divisions; Company B had a similar objective about 200 yards to the southeast; and Company L was directed against the small hill between the 1st Battalion's objectives and the positions occupied by the 3d Battalion on 11 June. Each company was to take a separate route. Company A's path led directly up the face of the cliff to its objective. Company B had to travel south to a break in

[27] Gugeler, 7th Div History, pp. 421–29.

the escarpment face and then, once on the high ground, turn right toward its objective. The objective of Company L was near the edge of the escarpment and easily approached.

Movement was to begin at 0400 on 12 June. Since the attack was based on stealth, no artillery preparation was used. However, 2 battalions of 105-mm. artillery, 1 battery of 155-mm. howitzers, and an 8-inch howitzer battalion were scheduled to deliver heavy harassing fires during the early part of the night. Also a total of 21 batteries registered their fires on the afternoon of 11 June and were prepared to surround the objectives with protective artillery fire if trouble developed after they were reached. One section of heavy machine guns was attached to each assault company.

Colonel Pachler had planned the attack carefully and insisted that every man participating know all details of the movement. Reconnaissance patrols had examined the trails leading to the high ground, and demolition teams had satchel-charged known cave positions in the face of the cliff. Nevertheless, everyone concerned with the attack dreaded the possibility of confusion that might result from the unknown conditions during darkness. This apprehension increased at 2000 on the night of 11 June when the 7th Division G-2 Section reported interception of an enemy radio message that evening which said, "Prepare to support the attack at 2300." A little later another intercepted message read: "If there are any volunteers for the suicide penetration, report them before the contact which is to be made one hour from now." [28] At the same time, from dusk until nearly 2300, the Japanese fired an extremely heavy concentration of artillery which front-line troops fully expected to be followed by a counterattack. The counterattack came but was aimed against the 1st Battalion, 32d Infantry, which had reached the top of Hill 95 that afternoon, and against the 96th Division. There was no enemy activity in the 17th Infantry's sector.

Night illumination and harassing shell fire ceased shortly before 0400, and thereafter the execution of the attack followed the plan almost without variation. The attacking companies moved out in single file. As promptly as if it had been scheduled, a heavy fog settled over southern Okinawa. It was of the right density—allowing visibility up to ten feet—to provide concealment but still allow the men to follow their paths without confusion. On the high ground Company A found a few civilians wandering about, and the leading platoon of Company B met three Japanese soldiers just after it reached the shelf of the

[28] 7th Div G-2 Jnl, Msg Nos. 31, 32, 39, 11 Jun 45.

escarpment. The men ignored them and walked quietly on. Nor did the enemy open fire. By 0530, a few minutes after dawn, Companies A and B were in place and no one had fired a shot. (See Map No. XLVIII.)

Without incident Company L reached its objective and then, anxious to take advantage of the fog and the absence of enemy fire, its commander sent his support platoon to another small hill fifty yards beyond. This objective was secured within a few minutes, after two enemy soldiers were killed. The platoon leader called his company commander to report progress and then frantically called for mortar fire. Walking toward his position in a column of twos were about fifty Japanese. The Americans opened fire with rifles and BAR's, broke up the column formation, and counted thirty-seven enemy soldiers killed; the others escaped.

Men in the 1st Battalion were pleased no less with the success of the night attack. A few minutes after Company A was in place, four enemy soldiers came trudging up toward them. They were killed with as many shots. Four others followed these at a short interval and were killed in the same way. Company B was not molested until about 0530, when some Japanese tried to come out of several caves in the center of the company's position. Since the cave openings were reinforced with concrete they could not be closed with demolition charges, but the men guarded the entrances and shot the Japanese as they emerged. Soon after daylight Company C began mopping up caves in the face of the escarpment, and later it joined the rest of the battalion on the high ground. By 0800 the situation was settled and the 17th Infantry held strong positions on the Yaeju-Dake. The Japanese had withdrawn their front-line troops from Yaeju-Dake during the night in order to escape harassing artillery, but they had expected to reoccupy it before "the expected 0700 attack." Fifteen hours after the 32d Infantry burned its way to the top of Hill 95, the 17th Infantry had seized its portion of the Yaeju-Dake in a masterfully executed night attack.

The 2d Battalion, 17th Infantry, relieved Companies I and K during the day, and, with Company L attached and supported by medium and flame tanks, continued the attack. The 1st Battalion held its ground and fired at enemy soldiers who, slow to realize that their defensive terrain had been stolen during the night, tried to creep back to their posts. Company B alone killed sixty-three during the day.

Progress in the Center

At 0600 on the same day, 12 June, Colonel Holloran's 381st Infantry delivered the next blow against the Japanese main line of resistance. Since 10 June,

NIGHT ATTACK ON YAEJU-DAKE *by the 17th Infantry, 7th Division, on 12 June resulted in capture of the section shown in picture above. Company A went up the path shown near center and occupied the coral ridges appearing in center. Company B moved up the slope at left and swung back to right on top of the escarpment. Below are infantrymen on Yaeju-Dake the morning of 13 June. Litter team evacuating wounded can be seen on the road.*

when the 381st launched its attack against the escarpment, the 1st Battalion had gained a toe hold on the intermediate level in the saddle between the Yaeju-Dake and the Yuza-Dake Peaks. The 3d Battalion had cleaned the enemy troops out of Tomui but was unable to proceed against the blunt and steep segment of the escarpment that lay in its zone. For 12 June Colonel Halloran committed his reserve battalion, the 2d, on the west end of his flank to fight abreast of the center salient and, at the same time, close a gap between his regiment and the 383d. Then, depending upon the success of the 17th Infantry's night attack, the 3d Battalion was to press its attack against the adjoining portion of the escarpment.[29]

Despite extensive use of artillery and tanks on previous days to batter cave openings in the face of the cliff, enemy fire flared as briskly as ever when the 3d Battalion, under Lt. Col. D. A. Nolan, Jr., reached the base of the escarpment on the morning of 12 June. Realizing that a frontal assault against this defended wall would be both slow and costly, Colonel Nolan left Company K to contain the enemy and to mop up near the bottom of the cliff; he ordered Capt. Roy A. Davis to take Company L around to the southeast, climb the escarpment in the 7th Division's zone, and then move back along the edge of the cliff to a position above Company K.[30]

It was nearly midafternoon before Davis and his men were in place on the high ground. Company K, meanwhile, worked along the base of the cliff under a steady volume of rifle fire but with protection of smoke. An effort to join the two elements of the battalion for the night failed, but the 381st Infantry had broken a 3-day stalemate at the steepest part of the escarpment and was now ready to pry the next section from Japanese control.

Japanese troops still controlled the Big Apple Peak, which rose about sixty feet above the general level of the plateau, but by evening of 12 June the 7th and 96th Divisions had forced the reconstituted *44th Independent Mixed Brigade* from the southeastern end of the enemy's line.

General Ushijima acted as quickly as his shattered communication system and the confusion of his front-line units would permit. With his artillery pieces shelled and bombed into near-silence, and his supplies and equipment diminishing even faster than his manpower, his only hope was to send more troops into the shell fire and flame with which the American forces were sweeping the front-line area. His order read:

[29] 381st Inf Unit Jnl, Msg No. 45, 11 Jun 45.
[30] Mulford and Rogers, 96th Div History, Pt. IV, pp. 204–06.

The enemy in the 44th IMB sector has finally penetrated our main line of resistance. . . . The plan of the 44th IMB is to annihilate, with its main strength, the enemy penetrating the Yaeju-Dake sector.

The Army will undertake to reoccupy and hold its Main Line of Resistance to the death. The 62d Division will place two picked infantry battalions under the command of the CG, 44th IMB.[31]

The *64th Brigade*—the part of the *62d Division* which had moved from Shuri to reserve positions near Makabe—did not issue this order until late on 13 June, fully thirty hours after its need arose. Moreover, piecemeal commitment of reserve troops was inadequate. By 13 June the *44th Brigade* was so close to destruction that when the reinforcements arrived the remnants of the *44th* were absorbed by the reinforcing battalions and there were still not enough men to hold the line. The enemy then committed the main strength of the *62d Division,* his last reserve and hope, with a plea for cooperation and orders to "reoccupy and secure the Main Line of Resistance."

By the time the *62d Division* could move onto the line, however, it ran squarely into General Hodge's men attacking south across the coral-studded plateau. The Americans were moving behind the fire of machine guns and tanks and over the bodies of the Japanese who had defended their last strong line "to the death."

The Battle of Kunishi Ridge

Only the eastern end of the Japanese line collapsed. On the western side of the island troops of the *24th Division* fought to a standstill one regiment of the 96th Division and the 1st Marine Division from 12 until 17 June. This slugging battle of tanks and infantrymen, with heavy blows furnished by planes and by naval and ground artillery, was for the possession of Yuza Peak and Kunishi Ridge. Yuza Peak, approximately 300 feet higher than the surrounding ground, dominated this part of the fortified line and was the source of most of the enemy fire. Its capture was the responsibility of the 383d Infantry, 96th Division. The western side of Yuza Peak tapered off toward the sea and formed Kunishi Ridge, a 2,000-yard-long coral barrier lying athwart the 1st Marine Division sector. Movement toward the Peak was restricted by extensive mine fields.

On three successive days the 383d Infantry drove the enemy troops from the town of Yuza, but each time machine-gun fire plunging from the coral peak beyond forced the men to withdraw to defensive positions at night. The Japanese reoccupied the town each night. Real progress was first made on 15 June when

---

[31] Cited in Appleman, XXIV Corps History, pp. 564–65.

the 2d Battalion, 382d Infantry, having relieved the center battalion of the 383d, gained the northern slope of the peak. The remainder of the 383d, weary from thirty-five days of continuous combat, passed into reserve on the following day, and Colonel Dill's 382d Infantry proceeded against the hard core of the Yuza line.[32]

Kunishi Ridge was the scene of the most frantic, bewildering, and costly close-in battle on the southern tip of Okinawa. After reaching the west coast of the island above Itoman and isolating Oroku Peninsula from the rest of the southern battlefield, the 1st Marine Division edged forward against slight resistance until the front lines were 1,500 yards north of Kunishi Ridge and subject to fire and observation from the heights of Yuza Peak. Two regiments, the 1st and 7th, were abreast. The 1st Marines, on the left, were the first to go beyond the guarded approaches of the Japanese line and the first to pay heavily with casualties. On 10 June the 1st Battalion lost 125 men wounded or killed during an attack against a small hill west of Yuza town. Seventy-five of these were from Company C. On the same day the 7th Marines reached the high ground at the northern edge of Tera, a long ridge contested almost as vigorously. The left flank swung ahead again on 11 June to Hill 69, west of Ozato, against steady and heavy opposition.[33]

A 1,000-yard strip of low and generally level ground separated the 1st Marine Division's line between Tera and Ozato from Kunishi Ridge, the next step in the advance. The 7th Marines ventured onto this open ground on 11 June and was promptly driven back by Japanese machine guns which covered the entire valley. As a result of this experience, General del Valle and the commander of the 7th Marines, Col. Edward W. Snedeker, decided to make the next move under cover of darkness. Each of the assault battalions was to lead off with one company at 0300 on 12 June, seize the west end of Kunishi Ridge and hold until daylight, and then support the advance of the remainder of the battalions.

Companies C and F walked onto the ridge with surprising ease, but the illusion of easy victory ended at dawn. Company C opened fire first, killing several enemy soldiers just as the two companies reached their objectives. This disturbance was the signal for immediate enemy action. Mortar shells began falling within a minute or two, and, as daylight increased, the Japanese sighted

[32] Ibid., pp. 552–57.
[33] Stockman, 1st Mar Div History, pp. 123–44.

their guns along the length of the coral ridge and began shelling and machine-gunning the valley of approach to prevent reinforcement. Colonel Snedeker challenged the enemy guns with two tanks, but one of these was knocked out and the other driven back by the fury of the shell fire. Both forward companies were suffering casualties and asked for help, but the other companies of the two battalions could no more move across the valley with impunity than the assault companies could expose themselves on Kunishi Ridge.

An attempt to cross under smoke failed when the Japanese crisscrossed bands of machine-gun fire through the haze and forced the two companies and their tank support to withdraw. In the afternoon, with Companies C and F still asking for help, several tanks succeeded in reaching Kunishi Ridge with a supply of plasma, water, and ammunition and brought back the seriously wounded. After this successful venture the battalion commanders evolved a plan for ferrying infantrymen, six in each tank, across the 1,000-yard strip of exposed ground. Before nightfall fifty-four men had dropped through the tank escape hatches onto Kunishi Ridge, and twenty-two casualties were evacuated on the return trips. This method of transporting both supplies and men was used throughout the fighting for Kunishi Ridge.[84]

The difficulties of 12 June were only the beginning of trouble. With the return of daylight on 13 June six companies occupied the lower end of Kunishi Ridge, and none of them could move. All were dependent upon tanks for supplies and evacuation. Twenty-nine planes dropped supplies, but with only partial success since a portion of the drops fell beyond reach and was unrecoverable. One hundred and forty men from the two battalions were casualties on 13 June; the seriously wounded were returned in tanks, men with light wounds stayed on the ridge, and the bodies of the dead were gathered near the base of the ridge.

The burden of offensive action fell upon the tanks on 13 June and the three days following. Flame and medium tanks moving out on firing missions carried supplies and reinforcements forward and then, on the return trip for more fuel or ammunition, carried wounded men to the rear. Soft rice paddies made it necessary for the tanks to stay on the one good road in the sector, and this road was effectively covered by Japanese 47-mm. shells and other artillery, which destroyed or damaged a total of twenty-one tanks during the 5-day battle.

[84] 1st Mar Div Special Actn Rpt, Assault Narrative, Phase III, p. 14; Tank Support Annex, pp. 37–38, 49, 50; III Amph Corps G–3 Periodic Rpt, 13 Jun 45, par. 3.

YUZA PEAK, *under attack by the 382d Infantry, 96th Division. Tanks are working on the caves and tunnel system at base of ridge.*

KUNISHI RIDGE, *with Yuza-Dake and Yaeju-Dake Escarpments in background. From the ridge the enemy fired on troops attacking Yuza peak. (Photo taken 10 October 1944.)*

Most enemy fire on Kunishi Ridge came from the front and the left flank. To relieve this pressure from the left, the 1st Marines ordered the 2d Battalion to seize the eastern and higher end to the left of the 7th Marines. This attack was similar to the first both in plan and in result. At 0300 on 14 June Companies E and G moved out. Two hours later the assault platoons were in place, but at dawn a sudden heavy volume of enemy fire interrupted further advance. The leading men were cut off, the rear elements could not move, and all the men were receiving rifle, mortar, and machine-gun fire from the front and left flank and rifle fire from bypassed Japanese in the rear. No one could stand up on the ridge, and even the wounded had to be dragged on ponchos to the escape hatch underneath the tanks upon which, as did also the 7th Marines, these two companies depended for supply and evacuation. It was not until dark that the battalion was able to consolidate its position.

The two regiments held grimly to Kunishi Ridge although making no appreciable gains until 17 June, after the tanks, planes, and artillery had destroyed the enemy's ability and will to resist. The 7th Marines attempted to expand their hold on 15 June but, although fifteen battalions of artillery supported the effort, it resulted in an additional thirty-five casualties in the attacking companies. Two days on Kunishi Ridge had cost the 2d Battalion of the 1st Marines nearly 150 casualties and, after dark, it was relieved by the 2d Battalion, 5th Marines.

Signs of weakening enemy strength appeared first on 16 June and the 7th Marines made some headway on each of its flanks. The zone of the 2d Battalion was taken over by the 22d Marines before dawn of the 17th. Most of the enemy resistance disappeared when these comparatively fresh troops took up the attack and gained ground on 17 June. During the five days of savage fighting, tanks had carried 550 reinforcing troops and approximately 90 tons of supplies to Kunishi Ridge and had evacuated 1,150 troops to the rear, most of whom were casualties.

CHAPTER XVIII

The Battle Ends

"We have passed the speculative phase of the campaign and are down to the final kill." This was General Buckner's appraisal of the battle for Okinawa on 15 June.[1] Infantrymen on the front lines also sensed the impending disintegration of General Ushijima's *32d Army,* not because of any noticeable weakening in the individual's will to fight but because, destitute of the supplies and tools of war, of the coordination, communications, and skill necessary to a fighting machine, the Japanese collectively lacked the power of adequate resistance.

End of Organized Resistance

Most of General Ushijima's crack troops were rotting in the rubble of the Shuri battlefield. Of the combat and service troops who had escaped to the south, a thousand were being killed each day.[2] Those who lived had become a mass of uncoordinated troops fighting to the death but presenting no integrated defense against the Tenth Army attack ranging south toward the last prominent hills left to the Japanese.

Fight Before the Caves

After gaining the top of Hill 95 and the rim of the Yaeju-Dake, only a generally level plateau separated the XXIV Corps front lines from the cave headquarters of General Ushijima's army which, according to prisoners of war, was located in a great coral ledge at the southern extremity of the Corps sector. This entire tableland, although evenly contoured, was liberally covered with coral heads. Some were grouped densely and formed a partial barrier; others were little larger than stumps or bushes and appeared to have grown from the earth. A few coral bulges were large and prominent enough to afford the Japanese strong positions. The largest of these were the Big Apple and Yuza-Dake Peaks

---

[1] This statement was made by General Buckner at a staff meeting at Tenth Army headquarters. See Colonel Stevens' Diary for 15 Jun 45.

[2] Enemy casualty figures listed in Par. 3, G–2 Periodic Rpt No. 68, 2 Jun 45, and No. 81, 15 Jun 45. Because of the exaggerated figures on enemy casualties, only the killed who were actually counted are considered in this estimate.

at the north end of the 96th Division's sector. Within the zone of the 7th Division were Hills 153 and 115, jagged protuberances of coral which, after the fall of the Yaeju-Dake and Hill 95, became General Ushijima's last hope of defending the eastern end of his line.

The 5-day battle for these hills and the fields of coral outcroppings on the surrounding plateau, lasting from 13 to 17 June, was as much like hunting as fighting. It was a battle of massed tanks which operated ahead of the usual infantry support, blasting the coral rocks with shell bursts and almost constant machine-gun fire. The battlefield was perfect for armored flame throwers, which poured flame into the caves and clusters of rocky crags and wooded areas, either killing the Japanese at once or forcing them into lanes of machine-gun fire. In five days flame tanks of the 713th Armored Flame Thrower Battalion directed more than 37,000 gallons of burning gasoline at the enemy.[3] It was also a battle of infantry platoons or individual infantrymen against disorganized but desperate enemy soldiers.

Some of the largest cave defenses in southern Okinawa were in the Yaeju and Yuza Peaks. Infantrymen of the 96th Division destroyed these positions with hand and rifle grenades, satchel charges, and portable flame throwers. For the infantrymen it was a search for the enemy's hiding places, often followed by a few minutes of reckless combat. Troops of the 381st Infantry occupied the commanding ground on the Big Apple Peak on 14 June but, for lack of enough explosives to seal the numerous caves in the area, were forced into a night-long fight with Japanese who emerged from the caves after darkness.[4] Yuza Peak fell two days later, on 16 June. On the same day the 17th and 32d Regiments reached Hill 153 and Hill 115, but another day of bitter fighting was required before the Japanese forces were completely destroyed.

Collapse of the 32d Army

By the evening of 17 June, Tenth Army troops held a solid front line along the crests of Kunishi Ridge, Hill 153, and Hill 115, and, for the first time, could look south over the entire enemy-held territory, covering about eight square miles. Forced from its last defensive terrain and obliged to realize that nothing could prevent its destruction, General Ushijima's army suddenly collapsed. Its discipline and morale, weakened by nearly eighty days of defeat, now broke completely and the *32d Army* degenerated into a mob.

---

[3] Actn Rpt, 713th Tank Bn, Armored Flame Thrower, Prov, pp. 23–29.
[4] The action on the Big Apple is described in Mulford and Rogers, 96th Div History, pp. 213–24.

FIGHTING TOWARD HILL 89, *tanks of the 769th Tank Battalion attack a bypassed Japanese strong point. On top of Yaeju-Dake 18 June, 96th Division infantrymen (below) probe hidden enemy pockets. Yellow cloth (right) marks the front lines for American bombers and fighters.*

As a unit, the *44th Brigade* was destroyed when its command post on Hill 115 fell to the 32d Infantry; only a few stragglers escaped. Enemy soldiers who had served in the *62d Division* fell back to defend the army headquarters at Hill 89. Approximately 400 members of the *24th Division*—all that remained of the Japanese *32d Regiment*—were scattered through the caves near Kunishi Ridge, where they remained in hiding as the battle passed on to the south. The rest of the *24th Division* retreated to its headquarters near Medeera, less than half a mile southwest of Hill 153.[5]

"Hill 153," said General Ushijima in an order written a few hours after that hill fell to the 17th Infantry, "is the essential point at which the final destiny of the entire army must be decided. It is very painful to the Commanding General of the Army that the orders sent out from time to time . . . concerning that hill have been disregarded." He ordered one battalion to recapture the hill before morning. A copy of this order was found the following morning on the body of one of the from 100 to 200 soldiers who tried to recapture Hill 153. On the back were notes written by the commander of the battalion:

> The contents of the first paragraph of this Army Order were utterly unexpected by this battalion; it is, indeed extremely unfortunate.
> The units which are to retake Hill 153 will carry out the Battalion orders without thought of losses, thereby bringing fame to the battalion.
> When the hill is retaken, report its seizure immediately.[6]

An hour after daylight, 18 June, the Japanese soldiers who were to report the capture of Hill 153 lay dead and scattered through the coral pinnacles. Their attack had not even alarmed infantrymen of the 184th Infantry, which had replaced the 17th on the previous evening. The Japanese massed on the south side of the hill and milled about until they were killed.

On 18 June, in the last written official order of the *32d Army,* General Ushijima appointed an officer to lead the "Blood and Iron Youth Organization" and conduct guerilla warfare after the cessation of organized combat. At the same time he ordered remaining troops to make their way to the mountains in the northern end of Okinawa where a small band of guerillas was supposedly

[5] This information was obtained from Capt Howard Moss, Language Officer with the 7th Division. After the end of the fighting, Captain Moss and members ot his team induced several hundred Japanese soldiers to surrender and from them he obtained information as to the disposition of enemy forces. On 29 August 1945, Col Kikuji Hongo, commander of the Japanese *32d Regiment,* surrendered between 400 and 450 men to Captain Moss. Hongo explained that these men, disorganized by the battle for Kunishi Ridge, had hidden in the caves on Kunishi until induced to surrender.

[6] Tama Opnl Ord A–91, G–2 Periodic Rpt No. 79, Hq 7th Inf Div, 18 Jun 45, Incl No. 4, p. 18.

already operating. The migration was to extend over several days; soldiers were to travel in groups of from two to five and were urged to wear civilian clothes and avoid conflict if possible.

This infiltration of Japanese was detected during the night of 18–19 June and both the front lines and rear installations burst into activity. Illumination flares hung over the southern tip of Okinawa between darkness and dawn, and the sound of machine-gun fire was almost constant through the night. This nighttime movement reached a peak several nights later, when one division, the 7th, killed 502 enemy soldiers. The infiltrating Japanese were not aggressive and carried weapons only for their own protection, their chief concern being to escape to the north or, in some instances, to submerge their identity in the civilian population.[7]

While some Japanese chose to chance the hazards of moving north, a great many fought savagely and were determined to take as many Americans as possible to death with them. The two divisions on the flanks found spotty and unpredictable resistance. On 18 and 19 June, the 6th Marine Division leapfrogged attacking battalions forward and plunged across the southwestern tip of the island. This fast-moving assault, and the advance of the 7th Division on the east, were opposed by machine guns and mortars but there was no integrated scheme of defense; the mass of civilians encountered delayed the troops almost as much as did enemy resistance. In the center, however, the 1st Marine and the 96th Infantry Divisions and the 305th Infantry, 77th Division, were opposed by the cornered remnants of the *24th Division*, which made its last desperate stand near its command post at Medeera. The 5th Marines attacked Hill 81 in this area on four successive days before it fell on 21 June, and Hill 85 in the XXIV Corps sector was defended with the same die-hard determination.[8] (See Map No. XLIX.)

In spite of the active role which tanks played in the fighting, a role which served to accelerate the battle, infantry combat went on as usual. One of the more conspicuous displays of recklessness occurred on 19 June when Company E, 305th Infantry, attacked several machine-gun nests. T/Sgt. John Meagher mounted a tank and was pointing out targets to the tank gunners when a Japanese raced toward the tank with a satchel charge. Meagher jumped from the tank, bayoneted the enemy soldier, and returned to the tank for a machine

[7] Appleman, XXIV Corps History, pp. 587–90; Gugeler, 7th Div History, pp. 500–01.
[8] Appleman, XXIV Corps History, pp. 596–97; III Amph Corps G–3 Periodic Rpts Nos. 79–82, 18–21 Jun 45.

LT. GEN. SIMON B. BUCKNER, *Commanding General, Tenth Army (foreground), holding camera, photographed while observing action on the Marine front during the latter part of the campaign. With him, holding walking stick, is Maj. Gen. Lemuel C. Shepherd, Jr., Commanding General, 6th Marine Division.*

gun. Firing from his hip, he then moved through enemy fire toward the nearest pillbox, killed six enemy gunners there, and proceeded toward another machine gun. His ammunition gave out just as he reached the second pillbox. Meagher grabbed his empty gun by the barrel and beat the enemy crew to death. For this daring, one-man assault, Meagher was awarded the Congressional Medal of Honor.

Except for the Medeera pocket, front lines had almost disappeared by the evening of 21 June. Enemy troops, numbering between 15,000 and 18,000, were hiding in crevices in the great cliffs that walled the southern coast, in caves and ruined buildings, or in the brush, ditches, or coral. Some were waiting for an opportunity to surrender or were simply trying to evade American troops and prolong their own existence. Others, surrounded near Medeera, were fighting desperately with mortars and machine guns. Many of the Okinawa conscripts hoped to rejoin their families.

Although the ratio of Japanese killed to American casualties increased favorably, the latter remained relatively high as infantrymen combed the tip of the island for snipers or fought through the streets of Medeera and Makabe. Disorganization of the enemy force did not lessen the need for aggressive action, although the same effort by the troops usually resulted in a greater number of enemy casualties than in the Shuri area. From the fall of Shuri until front lines disappeared, Tenth Army lost 1,555 men killed in action and 6,602 wounded.[9]

Among those killed was General Buckner. Early in the afternoon of 18 June, General Buckner stopped at a forward observation post of the 8th Marine Regiment, 2d Marine Division, near the southwest tip of Okinawa. Although this division staged a feint on 1 April and 19 April, none of its elements came ashore till June, when the 8th, after taking Theia and Iguni Islands, joined in the final battle.[10] While General Buckner watched the progress of the fighting, at 1315, a shell from a Japanese dual purpose gun exploded directly above the observation post. A fragment of coral, broken off by the explosion, struck General Buckner in the chest. He collapsed immediately and died ten minutes later. Maj. Gen. Roy S. Geiger, senior commander on Okinawa, assumed command of Tenth Army.[11] He was succeeded on 23 June by Gen. Joseph W. Stilwell.

Brig. Gen. Claudius M. Easley, assistant commander of the 96th Division, was killed the day after General Buckner's death. General Easley, known by all as

[9] See casualty reports in Tenth Army G–3 Jnl for period 22 May–21 Jun 45.

[10] III Amph Corps G–3 Periodic Rpt No. 76, 16 Jun 45.

[11] Appleman, XXIV Corps History, pp. 584–85.

a front-line soldier, was pointing out the location of a machine gun when two
bullets from the gun struck him in the forehead. The lives of these two generals
were added to more than 7,000 others of the Tenth Army as part of the cost of
victory on Okinawa.[12]

Surrender and Suicide

Deterioration of Enemy Discipline and Morale

Until American troops occupied the last of its defensive terrain, the Japanese
Army, in spite of adversities and broken fortunes, had maintained discipline and
organization astonishingly well. When the process of dissolution began, however,
it spread like an epidemic. Most Japanese soldiers lost hope of eventual victory
when they abandoned Shuri. As early as 12 June the sound of their artillery had
faded from its April rumble to a faint whisper, and small weapons were scarcer
than men. "If hand grenades, explosives, etc., are dropped on the battlefield," a
Japanese general ordered, "every single item will be picked up; the man doing the
salvaging will arm himself with them." [13]

There was dissension among troops and officers. One prisoner said it was
common for men to join other units without knowing the names of the unit and
of its officers. Others reported that medical supplies were so low that treatment
was limited to bandaging, and many of the wounded were left to die or to
commit suicide. About half the troops were fighting in a daze, and rape was
common since the soldiers felt that they had only a short time to live.[14] These
conditions existed even before Kunishi Ridge and Hill 153 were in American
hands. After they fell the Japanese soldiers realized that no action in which they
participated could have even momentary success.

Faced with these wretched conditions, Japanese officers had maintained
discipline by assuring their soldiers that there was no alternative to death since
the Americans would kill them if captured. On the other hand, Japanese officers
promised their troops a counterlanding, an airborne invasion, and a general
all-out attack toward the latter part of June. According to prisoners of war who
told of this persistent rumor, the *9th Division* was to come from Formosa, and
500 planes and the remains of the Imperial Fleet were to participate in the great
attack. One proviso of this grandiose plan, however, was that, if the Japanese

---

[12] Mulford and Rogers, 96th Div History, Pt. IV, p. 257.
[13] Transl No. 47, Incl No. 4 to G–2 Periodic Rpt No. 79, Hq 7th Inf Div, 18 Jun 45.
[14] Appleman, XXIV Corps History, pp. 572–74.

Army on Okinawa were destroyed by 20 June, the counterlandings would be canceled and the remaining troops would launch an all-out attack.[15] The reports incidentally made Tenth Army troops chary and watchful for a banzai charge which many believed would come at the end of the battle.[16]

American Psychological Warfare

Decline of enemy morale may have resulted in part from a campaign of psychological warfare which General Buckner started before the April landing and intensified as the assault against the Yaeju-Dake began. From 25 March until the end of organized fighting, planes dropped about 8,000,000 propaganda leaflets on the island. Until mid-June these leaflets were aimed at winning the confidence of the civilians and soldiers and at spreading defeatism. Through a letter addressed to General Ushijima and dropped behind enemy lines on the morning of 10 June, General Buckner hoped to initiate mass surrender by the Japanese:

> The forces under your command have fought bravely and well, and your infantry tactics have merited the respect of your opponents. . . . Like myself, you are an infantry general long schooled and practiced in infantry warfare. . . . I believe, therefore, that you understand as clearly as I, that the destruction of all Japanese resistance on the island is merely a matter of days. . . .[17]

General Buckner then invited Ushijima to enter negotiations for surrender.

No one seriously expected Ushijima to respond to this bid for surrender. Two days later planes scattered another 30,000 leaflets over enemy ground, this time emphasizing Ushijima's refusal to negotiate for surrender and his selfish determination to commit his entire army to destruction, and calling upon his subordinate officers and men to quit of their own accord. Another appeal was made on 14 June.

Actually, it was later learned, General Ushijima did not receive the original message until 17 June, the delay resulting from the lack of communications and the general confusion existing among his troops. Both he and his chief of staff, General Cho, considered the message hilariously funny and said that it would not be consonant with their honor as Samurai to entertain such a proposal.[18]

---

[15] *Ibid.*, pp. 526–27.

[16] G–2 Periodic Rpts, Tenth Army and Its Units, 10–20 Jun 45.

[17] Joint Intelligence Center, POA Commandant Navy 128, Report on Psychological Warfare Activities Okinawa Operation, 15 Sep 45.

[18] Appleman, XXIV Corps History, p. 558.

OVERCOMING THE LAST RESISTANCE *on Okinawa was aided by propaganda leaflets, one of which (above) is being read by a prisoner awaiting transportation to the rear. Many civilians gave up at the same time. At numerous points, however, severe fighting continued. Below, tanks are shown reducing an enemy position. Center tank was knocked out but was protected from capture by others. Shell bursts mark location of Japanese.*

During the last days of the battle hundreds of thousands of "surrender leaflets" fell among Japanese soldiers who, caught between the sea and American front lines, were beginning to doubt the promises of their own government and army and to ponder the truth of American promises of humane treatment to those who came into American lines. A more direct appeal for surrender was made by the 7th Division on 17 June when all of its units ceased firing for an hour while interpreters broadcast pleas of surrender over portable loudspeakers. Several enemy soldiers walked toward the lines, watched for a few minutes, and then disappeared. One American soldier was wounded, and the Japanese put three holes through one of the loudspeakers. The appeal was wholly ineffective. On the same day, although firing continued, interpreters of the 7th Division set up a loudspeaker at the cliff southeast of Nakaza and coaxed between 500 and 600 civilians from natural caves in the rocky sea cliff. From this group the interpreters culled more than seventy enemy soldiers who had previously deserted their army and hoped to pass as civilians.[19]

Surrender and Suicide at the Water's Edge

Mass surrender of Japanese soldiers did not begin until the Tenth Army crowded them almost to the water's edge. There was a noticeable increase, however, after the intensification of the psychological warfare program. During the first seventy days of battle, prisoners captured by Tenth Army averaged less than four a day. This average increased to more than fifty a day between 12 and 18 June; and on 19 June, as the 6th Marine and 7th Infantry Divisions rolled forward near the east and west coasts, 343 enemy soldiers voluntarily surrendered. On the afternoon of 20 June the 32d Infantry seized the east end of Hill 89, a coral bulge next to the sea which housed General Ushijima's staff and headquarters. On the same day 977 prisoners were taken—an unprecedented accomplishment in the Pacific war.[20]

Even among these destitute and disorganized soldiers, less than a third chose to surrender rather than die, although prisoners claimed that others wanted to surrender but could find no opportunity. Casualties among the Japanese averaged about a thousand a day during the first half of June, jumped to nearly 2,000 on 19 June, to 3,000 the next day, and reached more than 4,000 on 21 June.[21] This tremendous rise in enemy deaths resulted from the sudden and complete unbalance of power between the opposing forces and from the

[19] Gugeler, 7th Div History, pp. 483–84.
[20] See Tenth Army G–2 Periodic Rpts for the period.
[21] *Ibid.*

SURRENDER *instructions to the enemy were broadcast by this "converted" Japanese from an LCI standing off the rocky cliff near Hill 89. Below is seen a group of prisoners who preferred capture to suicide. They are waiting to be questioned by American officers.*

resignation of many Japanese to death. When cornered or injured, many of them would hold grenades against their stomachs and blow themselves to pieces—a kind of poor man's hara-kiri. During the last days of the battle many bodies were found with the abdomen and right hand blown away—the telltale evidence of self-destruction. Men in the 184th Infantry counted at least sixteen separate explosions when an armored flame thrower threatened a troublesome source of enemy fire. One Japanese soldier approached a field artillery outpost, jumped into plain view, and yelled in understandable English: "Watch out! I'm going to blow my head off!" He fulfilled his promise, but a companion with him had to be killed. Many others hid among the brush and rocks until the Americans were almost upon them. Then they would suddenly jump up, throw a grenade or fire a few aimless shots, and wait to be killed.[22]

Sometimes the conditions under which the Japanese met defeat were less tragic. A small landing craft idled along the southern coast one or two hundred yards from shore and, through a loudspeaker mounted on its deck, a "converted" prisoner of war shouted appeals for surrender to other Japanese soldiers who had retreated to the water's edge and now lurked among the boulders at the foot of the cliff or in caves in its face. The prisoner, a sergeant in the Japanese Army, was a persuasive speaker who was convinced of good treatment in the hands of Americans and tried to save his comrades from needless death. Sometimes he would order the soldiers to leave their hiding places, strip to their loin cloths, and follow the coast north to the American lines; as a sergeant, he was often obeyed.[23]

Interpreters or prisoners broadcast pleas of "cease resistance" over other portable loudspeakers set up in the southern tip of the island. The Japanese surrendered by twos or threes, apprehensive and hesitant and with curious expressions of hope and fear. Many prisoners offered to return to induce their comrades to surrender. Usually they were given cigarettes to take back to the caves as proof of American promises. Two such "bait-boys," known as "Murrymoto" and "Goto," brought back several hundred prisoners and were so faithful that their captors allowed them to carry weapons and live in the company perimeter during the night. In this manner 7,401 Japanese soldiers, including more than 200 commissioned officers and 3,339 unarmed laborers, surrendered to Tenth Army troops.[24]

[22] Gugeler, 7th Div History, p. 488; Appleman, XXIV Corps History, p. 574.
[23] Gugeler, 7th Div History, pp. 501–02.
[24] *Ibid.*, p. 503; Tenth Army Actn Rpt, 11–II–22.

Okinawa Civilians

Civilians became a nuisance to combat units after the assault on the final enemy lines began, and remained a burden until front lines no longer existed. More than 10,000 civilians stayed on Chinen Peninsula and were relatively unharmed by the battle. A much larger number, forced south by the advancing lines, hid in caves or stone huts until they were overtaken. Then they tried to pass through the machine-gun and shell fire to enter American lines or attempted the even more hazardous feat of slipping through the front lines during darkness. Infantrymen helped these unfortunate civilians as much as possible and often interrupted the fighting to collect and guide them through the front lines. During the last days of the fighting there were always groups of civilians sitting just behind the front lines, waiting for help, instructions, or, as many of them believed, death.[25]

Eighty thousand Okinawa civilians, between a third and a half of whom were wounded, crawled from caves at the south tip of the island during the last two weeks of June. These were either children, the very old, or women; there were few able-bodied men among them. In long columns they walked toward the rear. Most of the women carried babies on their backs and bundles of clothing, food, dishes, and kettles on their heads—all they owned. They chewed stalks of sugar cane when they could find them. The bodies of many thousands of other civilians lay scattered in the ditches, in the cane fields, and in the rubble of the villages, or were sealed in caves.[26]

The Death of Generals Ushijima and Cho

As General Ushijima and his staff concluded the activities of the *32d Army* in the system of caves within Hill 89, near Mabuni, the 32d Infantry attacked across the broad and flat top of the hill. One entrance to the cave was on top and near the center of the 500-yard-long hill; another entrance opened on the face of the 290-foot cliff facing the sea. It was about noon on 21 June when the front lines reached the first of these entrances. An officer prisoner had volunteered to deliver another offer of surrender to Ushijima but, when he and the infantrymen gathered near the opening, the Japanese closed the entrance by blasting it from the inside. Enemy resistance on top of Hill 89 was strong, and flame tanks used

[25] Appleman, XXIV Corps History, pp. 595–96; Mulford and Rogers, 96th Div History, pp. 251, 259, 265, 269; Gugeler, 7th Div History, pp. 482–86.

[26] Tenth Army Mil Govt Opns Rpt Ryukyus Area, 1 Aug 45, App. V, Pt. IV: Table of Population Changes. The estimate of the number of civilians wounded during the last few days of the campaign is that of Capt. Russell Gugeler, 7th Div Hist Off. See also XXIV Corps Actn Rpt, pp. 97–99.

LAST JAPANESE COMMAND POST *on Okinawa was Hill 89. The 32d Infantry, 7th Division, attacked up lower east end (left). Below appears the still smouldering reverse slope of Hill 89, where Generals Ushijima and Cho committed suicide.*

nearly 5,000 gallons of gasoline before the entire top was free of Japanese soldiers that evening.[27]

General Ushijima radioed his last message to Imperial Headquarters on the evening of 21 June. The impetuous General Cho made a last appeal for all units to fight to the utmost. He also prepared several messages which he hoped his secretary could eventually deliver in Japan. "Our strategy, tactics, and technics," he explained, "all were used to the utmost and we fought valiantly, but it was as nothing before the material strength of the enemy." [28] Realizing that they could hold out no longer, Generals Ushijima and Cho made ready for death. Their cook prepared an especially large meal to be served shortly before midnight. When the meal was finished, the two generals and their staff drank numerous farewell toasts with the remaining bottles of Scotch whisky which had been carried from Shuri. The rest of the story is told by a prisoner who learned the details of the death of Ushijima and Cho from other prisoners:

Alas! The Stars of the Generals have fallen with the setting of the waning moon over Mabuni. . . .

The pale moon shimmers bluish white over the waters of the southern sea, but on Hill 89 which juts abruptly from the reefs, the rocks and boulders are dyed crimson by the blood of the penetration unit which, with burning patriotism, rush the American positions for the last stand. The surrounding area displays a picture of concentrated fireworks; bursts of naval gun fire, flashes of mortar and artillery fire, to which is added the occasional chatter of machine guns. . . .

Gathered around their section chiefs, members of each section bow in veneration toward the eastern sky and the cheer of "long live the Emperor" echoes among the boulders. . . . The faces of all are flushed with deep emotion and tears fall upon ragged uniforms, soiled with the dirt and grime of battle. . . .

Four o'clock, the final hour of Hara-kiri; the Commanding General, dressed in full field uniform, and the Chief of Staff in a white kimono appeared. . . . The Chief of Staff says as he leaves the cave first, "Well, Commanding General Ushijima, as the way may be dark, I, Cho, will lead the way." The Commanding General replies, "Please do so, and I'll take along my fan since it is getting warm." Saying this he picked up his Okinawa-made Kuba fan and walked out quietly fanning himself. . . .

The moon, which had been shining until now, sinks below the waves of the western sea. Dawn has not yet arrived and, at 0410, the generals appeared at the mouth of the cave. The American forces were only three meters away [sic]. Four meters away from the mouth of the cave a sheet of white cloth is placed on a quilt; this is the ritual place for the two Generals to commit Hara-kiri. The Commanding General and the Chief of Staff sit down

---

[27] Gugeler, 7th Div History, pp. 494–95.
[28] Interrog Shimada; see also Appleman, XXIV Corps History, p. 611.

on the quilt, bow in reverence towards the eastern sky, and Adjutant J. respectfully presents the sword. Finally, the time for the honored rites of Hara-kiri arrives. At this time several grenades were hurled near this solemn scene by the enemy troops who observed movements taking place beneath them. A simultaneous shout and a flash of a sword, then another repeated shout and a flash, and both Generals had nobly accomplished their last duty to their Emperor. . . .

All is quiet after the cessation of gunfire and smoke; and the full moon is once again gleaming over the waves of the southern sea. Hill 89 of Mabuni will live in memory forever.[29]

The death of General Ushijima and his Chief of Staff, General Cho, marked the end of the Okinawa campaign and the *32d Army*. Organized fighting on Okinawa had lasted eighty-three days, for it was not until 22 June that Hill 85 between Medeera and Makabe fell to the 305th Infantry. That the Japanese defense had been longer and stronger than could reasonably have been expected was not, it appeared, sufficient for the Japanese commander. Following the ancient code and ritual of the Samurai, he made the only acceptable atonement to his emperor for his failure to defend Okinawa successfully.

At Tenth Army headquarters on the same morning, 22 June, representatives of the Tenth Army, the two corps, and the divisions stood in formation, the band played "The Star Spangled Banner," and the color guard raised the American flag over Okinawa. Near the top of the pole a sudden breeze swept the flag out full against a blue and quiet sky.[30]

Final Mop-up

On 23 June 1945 Tenth Army began a thorough and coordinated mop-up campaign to eliminate the disorganized remnants of the *32d Army* in southern Okinawa. The plan assigned XXIV Corps and III Amphibious Corps their respective zones of action and fixed three phase lines for the completion of the task, which was to take ten days. After reaching the first phase line at the southern end of the island, the two corps were to turn and advance northward through two successive phase lines until they reached the Naha–Yonabaru valley. A blocking line was established along the Naha–Yonabaru cross-island road to prevent any Japanese soldiers from infiltrating to the northern part of the island.[31]

[29] Gugeler, 7th Div History, pp. 496–98.
[30] Okinawa Diary kept by Stevens and Burns, 22 Jun 45.
[31] Tenth Army Opns Ord 15–45, 19 Jun 45; Actn Rpt, 7–III–34, 35.

RAISING THE AMERICAN FLAG *on 22 June denoted the end of organized resistance.*

The mop-up was successfully completed on 30 June, in less than the allotted time. The troops first cleaned out some strong pockets of unorganized resistance in the sweep to the first phase line in the south. Cave positions were systematically sealed up by flame throwers and demolitions, with hundreds of Japanese entombed within. Several bloody skirmishes ensued when well-armed groups of the enemy attempted to infiltrate the American lines and make their way to the north. Extensive patrolling ferreted out individual Japanese soldiers hiding in cane fields and rice paddies. Once the American troops turned northward, fewer and fewer of the enemy were found, and the third and final phase line was reached with comparative ease. By the end of the month the mop-up had yielded an estimated total of 8,975 Japanese soldiers killed, 2,902 military prisoners taken, and 906 labor troops rounded up. Large quantities of enemy supplies and equipment were captured.[32] American battle casualties between 23 and 30 June came to 783, most of which were incurred in the first three days of the mop-up. On 2 July the Ryukyus campaign was declared ended.

Victory: Cost and Value

The price paid for Okinawa was dear. The final toll of American casualties was the highest experienced in any campaign against the Japanese. Total American battle casualties were 49,151, of which 12,520 were killed or missing and 36,631 wounded. Army losses were 4,582 killed, 93 missing, and 18,099 wounded; Marine losses, including those of the Tactical Air Force, were 2,938 killed and missing and 13,708 wounded; Navy casualties totaled 4,907 killed and missing and 4,824 wounded. Nonbattle casualties during the campaign amounted to 15,613 for the Army and 10,598 for the Marines. The losses in ships were 36 sunk and 368 damaged, most of them as a result of air action. Losses in the air were 763 planes from 1 April to 1 July.

The high cost of the victory was due to the fact that the battle had been fought against a capably led Japanese army of greater strength than anticipated, over difficult terrain heavily and expertly fortified, and thousands of miles from home. The campaign had lasted considerably longer than was expected. But Americans had demonstrated again on Okinawa that they could, ultimately, wrest from the Japanese whatever ground they wanted.

The cost of the battle to the Japanese was even higher than to the Americans. Approximately 110,000 of the enemy lost their lives in the attempt to hold

[32] Tenth Army Actn Rpt, 7–III–34, 35; G–1 Casualty Rpts, 23–30 Jun 45, in G–3 Jnl, 23–30 Jun 45.

Okinawa, and 7,400 more were taken prisoners. The enemy lost 7,800 airplanes, 16 ships sunk, and 4 ships damaged. More important, the Japanese lost 640 square miles of territory within 350 miles of Kyushu.

The military value of Okinawa exceeded all hope. It was sufficiently large to mount great numbers of troops; it provided numerous airfield sites close to the enemy's homeland; and it furnished fleet anchorage helping the Navy to keep in action at Japan's doors. As soon as the fighting ended, American forces on Okinawa set themselves to preparing for the battles on the main islands of Japan, their thoughts sober as they remembered the bitter bloodshed behind and also envisioned an even more desperate struggle to come.

The sequel to Okinawa, however, was contrary to all expectation. In the midst of feverish preparations on the island in August 1945, with the day for the assault on Kyushu drawing near, there came the almost unbelievable and joyous news that the war was over. The battle of Okinawa was the last of World War II.

Appendix A

Major Tactical Units of Tenth Army in the Ryukyus Campaign

The following list shows the organization of Tenth Army and its major tactical components as they entered combat. The components omitted are the Island Command, which had a nontactical mission; the 81st Infantry Division, which did not participate in the battle; and the 2d Marine Division, of which only the 8th Marine Regiment landed on Okinawa, late in the campaign.

The list was compiled from Tenth Army Action Report, Ryukyus. Discrepancies found in this Action Report have been eliminated, but, despite careful research and checking, other minor errors may still exist. Such errors will be corrected in the Order of Battle of the United States Army, World War II, now being prepared for this series.

Tenth Army

Hq Tenth Army

SPECIAL TROOPS

Hq & Hq Det, Sp Trs, Tenth Army
 163d Liaison Sq (AAF)
 1st Depot Unit (AAF)
 3236th, 3240th Sig Serv Dets (FA)
 3040th QM Car Co (–2 Plats)
 Psychological Warfare Tm
 143d–152d Photo Interp Tms
 Base Censorship Det
 32d, 33d Japanese Ord of Btl Tms
 1st Info & Hist Serv
 K Hist Unit
 Civ Correspondent Gp
 303d, 304th Hq Int Dets
 105th, 901st, 902d, 903d Army Postal
  Units
 357th Provisional Army Postal Unit

310th Counter Intelligence Corps Det
Ten Counter Intelligence Corps Opns
 Tms
Two Counter Intelligence Corps Hq &
 Adm Tms

ARMORED

20th Armored Gp

COAST ARTILLERY (AA)

Hq & Hq Btry, Tenth Army (AAA)
Hq & Hq Btry, 53d AAA Brig
Hq & Hq Btrys, 43d, 44th, 97th, 136th,
 137th AAA Gps
96th, 98th, 369th, 503d, 505th, 948th AAA
 Gun Bns, Semimobile
834th AAA Auto Wpns Bn, Self-propelled
866th AAA Auto Wpns Bn (–A, B, & C
 Btrys)

779th, 870th AAA Auto Wpns Bn, Semimobile
294th, 295th, 325th AAA Searchlight Bns
Hq & Hq Btry, 230th AAA Searchlight Bn
  A Btry, 230th AAA Searchlight Bn
    1st Plat, C Btry, 230th AAA Searchlight
    Bn
162d AAA Opns Det

COAST ARTILLERY (HD)

Hq & Hq Btry, 144th CA Gp (155mm
Gun)
38th, 179th, 282d CA Bns (155mm Gun)

ENGINEER

1746th Engr Map Det

SIGNAL

3d, 82d Sig Construction Bns, Light
85th Sig Opn Bn
3181st Sig Serv Bn, Mobile
  3161st Sig Serv Co
  241st Sig Opn Co
Det, 585th Sig Depot Co
Det, 57th Sig Repair Co
529th Sig Opn Co

3385th Sig Serv Tm, Bn Hq
3373d Sig Serv Co (SIAM)
Provisional Radio Int Co
8th, 108th, 110th, 111th, 274th Sig Radar
  Maintenance Units
279th Pigeon Combat Plat

MEDICAL

Hq Provisional Serv Unit
  366th Orthopedic Tm
  376th, 377th Surgical Tms
  390th Neuro Surgical Tm
  341st, 342d, 343d Surgical Dets
Hq & Hq Det, 80th Med Gp
  Hq & Hq Dets, 96th, 153d Med Bns
    665th, 668th Clearing Cos
    386th, 444th, 541st, 646th Collecting
    Cos
    843d, 847th Supply Tms
    176th Malaria Control Unit
    215th Malaria Survey Unit

MISCELLANEOUS

713th Armd Flame Thrower Bn
Air Delivery Sec, III Phib Corps
2d Landing Force Air Support Control
Unit

XXIV Corps

Hq XXIV Corps
CORPS TROOPS
Hq Co, XXIV Corps
  XXIV Corps Military Police Plat
  519th Military Police Bn (–Cos A & B)
  235th Army Postal Unit
  139th–142d, 161st Photo Interp Tms
  3231st Photo Unit
  306th, 307th Hq Int Dets
  L Hist Unit
  29th Japanese Ord of Btl Tm
  Base Censorship Det
  224th Counter Intelligence Corps Det
  Civ Correspondent Gp

MEDICAL

Hq & Hq Det, 71st Med Bn, Separate
  594th QM Laundry Co (–3 Plats)
  556th Ambulance Co, Separate, Motorized
  394th Clearing Co, Separate
  644th, 645th Collecting Cos
  214th Malaria Survey Unit (FB)
  2d Supply Tm Type #4, 726th Med Det
  377th Surgical Det
  366th Orthopedic Tm (EB)

MILITARY GOVERNMENT UNITS

Three Military Govt Dets

1st–3d G–10 Dispensaries (USN)

2d G–6 Hospital (USN)

FIELD ARTILLERY

Hq & Hq Btry, XXIV Corps Arty
   Hq & Hq Btry, 419th FA Gp
      145th, 198th, 225th FA Bns (155mm
        How)
      287th FA Observation Bn

ENGINEER

Hq & Hq Co, 1176th Engr Construction
   Gp
   47th, 1397th, 1398th Engr Construction
     Bns
Provisional Engr Topographic Plat
1445th Engr Searchlight Maintenance Co
968th Engr Maintenance Co
1088th Engr Depot Co (–1st & 2d Plats)
1901st Engr Aviation Bn

QUARTERMASTER

Hq & Hq Det, 521st QM Gp
   Hq & Hq Det, 187th QM Bn, Mobile

Hq & Hq Det, 492d QM Bn
   247th QM Depot Supply Co (–3d
     Plat)
   244th QM Depot Supply Co (–1st &
     2d Plats)
   4342d QM Serv Co (–2d Plat)
   3063d QM Graves Reg Co (–3 Plats)
   3008th QM Graves Reg Co (–4
     Plats)
   3754th QM Truck Co (–3 Plats)

SIGNAL

101st Sig Bn

MISCELLANEOUS

3d Landing Force Air Support Control
   Unit
Det, Air Warning Sq #7
Hq & Hq Co, 504th Port Bn
88th Chem Mortar Bn (–Cos A & B)
866th AAA Auto Wpns Bn

III Amphibious Corps

CORPS TROOPS

Hq & Serv Bn, III Phib Corps
Sig Bn, III Phib Corps
Med Bn, III Phib Corps
Hq Btry, III Phib Corps Arty
11th Mil Transport Bn, Fleet Marine
   Force, Pacific
1st Provisional Military Police Bn, Fleet
   Marine Force, Pacific
Co A, 51st Military Police Bn (USA)
2d, 3d Corps Evacuation Hospitals
456th Amphibious Truck Co (USA)
1st Bomb Disposal Co (–2 Plats)
3d Separate Radio Int Plat
1st Landing Force Air Support Control
   Unit
43–D Mobile Communication Unit

Det, Air Warning Sq
Two Military Govt Dets (USA)
12th G–10 Dispensary (USN)
1st G–6 Hospital (USN)
1st Laundry Co (–1st, 2d, & 3d Plats)
Hq Corps Shore Party
7th Field Depot
   Hq Co
   Guard Co
   Sig Co
   Engr Co
   Ord Co
   General Supply Co
   Military Transport Co
   Six Depot Cos
   3d, 12th Ammunition Cos

2d Plat, 2d Laundry Co
Fumigation & Bath Co
1st Provisional AAA Gp
   2d, 5th, 8th, 16th AAA Bns
2d Provisional FA Gp, Hq Btry

1st, 3d, 6th 155mm How Bns
7th, 8th, 9th 155mm Gun Bns
802d Engr Aviation Bn (USA)
1st Separate Engr Bn
71st, 130th Naval Construction Bns (USN)

7th Infantry Division

ORGANIC UNITS
Hq 7th Inf Div
Special Troops, 7th Inf Div
   Hq Co, 7th Inf Div
   Military Police Plat, 7th Inf Div
   Band, 7th Inf Div
   7th QM Co
   7th Cav Rn Tr (Mechanized)
   7th Sig Co
   707th Ord Light Maintenance Co
   7th Med Bn
   13th Engr (C) Bn
Hq & Hq Btry, Div Arty
   31st, 48th, 49th, 57th FA Bns
17th, 32d, 184th Inf Rgts

ATTACHED UNITS (AS OF L DAY)
Antiaircraft Artillery
   502d AAA Gun Bn
   861st AAA Auto Wpns Bn
      1st Plat, A Btry, 295th AAA Search-
         light Bn
      Det, Air Warning Sq #8
Armored
   711th Tank Bn, Medium
   718th, 536th Amph Tractor Bn
   776th Amph Tank Bn
Chemical
   91st Chem Co
   Supply Tm, 1st Provisional Chem Det
Engineer
   Hq & Hq Co, 1140th Engr (C) Gp
      50th, 104th, 110th Engr (C) Bns
      1st Plat, 1088th Engr Depot Co
Medical
   69th Field Hospital

52d, 66th Portable Surgical Hospitals
One Orthop Tm, 366th Med Serv Det
376th Surgical Tm
390th Neuro Surgical Tm
5th Museum & Med Arts Det
Ordnance
   644th Ord Ammunition Co
   Det, 196th Ord Depot Co
   204th Ord Bomb Disposal Sq
   284th Ord Heavy Maintenance Co,
      Tank
Quartermaster
   40th QM War Dog Plat
   3260th QM Serv Co
   191st QM Gas Supply Co
   1st & 3d Plats, 3754th QM Truck Co
   1st Sec, 2d Plat, 4342d QM Serv Co
   472d, 481st Amph Truck Cos
   1st & 2d Plats, 244th QM Depot Supply
      Co
   2d Plat, 3008th QM Graves Reg Co
Transportation
   200th, 291st Port Cos
Miscellaneous
   7th Counter Intelligence Corps Det
   156th Photo Interp Tm
   Base Censor Det
   Civ Correspondent Gp
   310th Hq Int Det
   News Tm A, 1st Info & Hist Serv
   Two Military Govt Dets
4th, 5th G–10 Dispensaries (USN)
32d, 33d Photo Assignment Units
Co A, 519th Military Police Bn
   74th Joint Assault Sig Co

77th Infantry Division

ORGANIC UNITS

Hq 77th Inf Div

Special Troops, 77th Inf Div

    Hq Co, 77th Inf Div

    Military Police Plat, 77th Inf Div

    Band, 77th Inf Div

    77th QM Co

    77th Cav Recon Tr (Mechanized)

    77th Sig Co

    777th Ord Light Maintenance Co

    302d Med Bn

    302d Engr (C) Bn

Hq & Hq Btry, Div Arty

    304th, 305th, 306th, 902d FA Bns

305th, 306th, 307th Inf Regts

ATTACHED UNITS (AS OF L MINUS 5)

Antiaircraft Artillery

    93d AAA Gun Bn

    204th Radar Maintenance Unit

    7th AAA Auto Wpns Bn

    2d Plat, Btry A, 295th AAA Searchlight Bn

Armored

    706th Tank Bn (Medium)

    708th Amph Tank Bn

    715th, 773d Amph Tractor Bn

Chemical

    Supply Tm, 1st Provisional Chem Det

    Co A, 88th Chem Mortar Bn

Engineer

    Hq & Hq Co, 1118th Engr (C) Gp

        132d, 233d, 242d Engr (C) Bns

Ordnance

    693d Ord Ammunition Co

    92d Bomb Disposal Sq

    Det, 196th Ord Depot Co

Medical

    36th Field Hospital

    68th, 95th Portable Surgical Hospitals

    Det, 75th Station Hospital

Quartermaster

    43d QM War Dog Plat

    2d Plat, 3063d QM Graves Reg Co

    477th, 828th Amph Truck Cos

    203d, 292d Port Cos

Military Government

    Three Military Govt Dets

    6th, 7th G–10 Dispensaries (USN)

Field Artillery

    Hq & Hq Btry, 420th FA Gp

        531st, 432d FA Bns (155mm Gun)

Miscellaneous

    36th Japanese Ord of Btl Tm

    292d Joint Assault Sig Co

    Co B, 724th Military Police Bn

    Provisional Radio Intelligence Co

    Det 62d, 7th Weather Sq

    Det, Air Warning Sq #8

    Amphibious Recon Bn, Fleet Marine Force, Pacific (–Co B)

    3234th Photo Assignment Unit

    158th Photo Interp Tm

    312th Hq Intelligence Det

    Base Censor Det

    77th Counter Intelligence Corps Det

    Civ Correspondent Gp

    News Team Co, 1st Info & Hist Serv

96th Infantry Division

ORGANIC UNITS

Hq, 96th Inf Div

Special Troops, 96th Inf Div

    Hq Co, 96th Inf Div

    Military Police Plat, 96th Inf Div

    Band, 96th Inf Div

    96th QM Co

    96th Cav Recon Tr (Mechanized)

    96th Sig Co

    796th Ord Light Maintenance Co

    321st Med Bn

    321st Engr (C) Bn

Hq & Hq Btry, Div Arty

    361st, 362d, 363d, 921st FA Bns

381st, 382d, 383d Inf Regts

ATTACHED UNITS (AS OF L DAY)

Antiaircraft Artillery

    504th AAA Gun Bn

    485th AAA Auto Wpns Bn

    Btry C, 294th AAA Searchlight Bn

    (−1 Plat)

    Det, Air Warning Sq #8

Armored

    763d Tank Bn

    780th Amph Tk Bn

    728th, 788th Amph Tractor Bn

Chemical

    Supply Tm, 1st Provisional Chem Det

    Co B, 88th Chem Mortar Bn

Engineer

    Hq & Hq Co, 1122d Engr (C) Gp

    170th, 173d, 174th Engr (C) Bns

    2d Plat, 1088th Engr Dep Co

Medical

    31st Field Hospital

    51st, 67th Portable Surgical Hospitals

    Det, 233d General Hospital

Ordnance

    632d Ord Ammunition Co

    206th Ord Bomb Disposal Sq

    Det, 196th Ord Depot Co

Quartermaster

    41st QM War Dog Plat

    3240th QM Serv Co

    2d Sec, 2d Plat, 4342d QM Serv Co

    3d Plat, 3008th QM Graves Reg Co

    3d Plat, 3063d QM Graves Reg Co

    474th, 827th Amph Truck Co

    204th, 293d Port Cos

Military Government

    Two Military Govt Dets

    8th, 9th G−10 Dispensaries (USN)

Miscellaneous

    160th Photo Interp Tm

    3235th Photo Assignment Unit

    314th Hq Intelligence Det

    38th Japanese Ord of Btl Tm

    Base Censor Det

    Civ Correspondent Gp

    News Tm B, 1st Info & Hist Serv

    96th Counter Intelligence Corps Det

    Co C, 519th Military Police Bn

    593d Joint Assault Sig Co

27th Infantry Division

ORGANIC TROOPS

Hq 27th Inf Div

Special Troops, 27th Inf Div

    Hq Co, 27th Inf Div

    Military Police Plat. 27th Inf Div

    Band, 27th Inf Div

    27th Cav Rcn Tr (Mechanized)

    27th QM Co

    27th Sig Co

    727th Ord Light Maintenance Co

    102d Med Bn

    102d Engr (C) Bn

Hq & Hq Btry, Div Arty

    104th, 105th, 106th, 249th FA Bns

105th, 106th, 165th Inf Regts

ATTACHED UNITS (AS OF L PLUS 14)

Armored
    193d Tank Bn (Medium)
Engineer
    Hq & Hq Co, 1165th Engr (C) Gp
        34th, 152d, 1341st Engr (C) Bns
Medical
    68th Field Hospital
    96th, 98th Portable Surgical Hospitals
    219th Malaria Survey Unit
    122d Malaria Control Unit
Ordnance
    61st Ord Ammunition Co

Quartermaster
    45th QM War Dog Plat
    1st Plat, 3063d QM Graves Reg Co
Military Government
    15th, 16th G–10 Dispensaries (USN)
    One Military Govt Det
Miscellaneous
    157th Photo Interp Tm
    311th Hq Intelligence Det
    Civ Correspondent Gp
    35th Japanese Ord of Btl Tm
    News Team E, 1st Info & Hist Serv
    27th Counter Intelligence Corps Det
    594th Joint Assault Sig Co

1st Marine Division

ORGANIC UNITS

Hq Bn, 1st Marine Div
1st Tank Bn
1st Pioneer Bn
1st Engr Bn
1st Serv Bn
1st Med Bn
1st Motor Transport Bn
11th Marines (Arty Regt)
1st, 5th, 7th Marines (Inf Regt)

ATTACHED UNITS (AS OF L DAY)

4th Joint Assault Sig Co

Det, Air Warning Sq
Co B, 51st Military Police Bn (USA)
3d, 454th Amph Truck Cos
3d Provisional Armd Amph Bn
1st, 8th Amph Tractor Bns
4th War Dog Plat
4th Provisional Rocket Det
3d Marine Observation Sq
2d Plat, 1st Bomb Disposal Co
2d Plat, 1st Laundry Co
Two Military Govt Dets (USA)
17th, 18th G–10 Dispensaries (USN)
145th Naval Construction Bn (USN)

6th Marine Division

ORGANIC UNITS

Hq Bn, 6th Marine Div
6th Tank Bn
6th Pioneer Bn
6th Engr Bn
6th Serv Bn
6th Med Bn
6th Motor Transport Bn
15th Marines (Arty Regt)
4th, 22d, 29th Marines (Inf Regts)

ATTACHED UNITS (AS OF L DAY)

6th Joint Assault Sig Co
Det, Air Warning Sq
Co C, 51st Military Police Bn (USA)
6th, 814th Amph Truck Cos
1st Armd Amph Tractor Bn
4th, 9th Amph Tractor Bns
1st War Dog Plat
5th Provisional Rocket Det

6th Marine Observation Sq
3d Plat, 1st Bomb Disposal Co
3d Plat, 1st Laundry Co
Two Military Govt Dets (USA)

10th, 11th G–10 Dispensaries (USN)
58th Naval Construction Bn
11th Spec Naval Construction Bn
   (–Hq Det & 3 Cos)

Tactical Air Force

ARMY

Hq & Hq Sq, 301st Fighter Wing
  318th Fighter Gp
    19th, 73d, 333d Fighter Sqs
    548th Night Fighter Sq
  413th Fighter Gp
    1st, 21st, 34th Fighter Sqs
  507th Fighter Gp
    463d, 464th, 465th Fighter Sqs
  337th Air Serv Gp
    Hq & Base Serv Sq
    371st Engr Sq
    577th Materiel Sq
  364th Air Serv Gp
    Hq & Base Serv Gp
    612th Engr Sq
    622d Materiel Sq
  557th Air Serv Gp
    Hq & Base Serv Sq
    987th Engr Sq
    992d Materiel Sq
  342d Station Complement Sq
  460th Aviation Sq
Hq & Hq Sq, VII Bomber Command
  11th Bomb Gp, Heavy
    26th, 42d, 98th, 431st Bomb Sqs
  494th Bomb Gp, Heavy
    864th, 865th, 866th, 867th Bomb Sqs
  41st Bomb Gp, Medium
    47th, 48th, 396th, 820th Bomb Sqs
  13th Air Serv Gp
    Hq & Base Serv Sq
    489th Engr Sq
    610th Materiel Sq
  57th Air Serv Gp
    Hq & Base Serv Sq
    613th Engr Sq

  619th Materiel Sq
  389th Air Serv Gp
  Hq & Base Serv Sq
  593d Engr Sq
  594th Materiel Sq
MARINE
Hq Sq, Marine Air Wing—2
  Marine Air Gp—33
    Hq Sq—33
    Serv Sq—33
    VMF—312, 322, 323 (Marine Fighter Sqs)
    VMF—543 (Marine Fighter Sq, Night)
    VMTB—232 (Marine Torpedo Bomber Sq)
  Marine Air Gp—31
    Hq Sq—31
    Serv Sq—31
    VMF—224, 311, 441 (Marine Fighter Sqs)
    VMF—542 (Marine Fighter Sq, Night)
  Marine Air Gp—14
    Hq Sq—14
    Serv Sq—14
    VMF—212, 222, 223 (Marine Fighter Sqs)
  Marine Air Gp—22
    Hq Sq—22
    Serv Sq—22
    VMF—113, 314, 422 (Marine Fighter Sqs)
    VMF—533 (Marine Fighter Sq, Night)
  Marine Observation Sq—7

Appendix B

Japanese 32d Army Units in the Ryukyus Campaign

This list of *32d Army* units was compiled by G–2, Tenth Army, from captured documents and prisoner of war interrogations. While information on enemy units is more complete for the Okinawa operation than for any other Pacific campaign, it is not possible to reconstruct the troop list of the *32d Army* without gaps and uncertainties as to both units and their strengths. The following list may omit some units which were destroyed during the battle and others which were disbanded in order to transfer their personnel to other units depleted in combat.

Uncertainty with regard to the strength of the units arises chiefly from the fact that there exist only the roughest estimates of the total number of Okinawans brought into the *32d Army*. These Okinawans fall into three classes, of which only the first can be estimated with reasonable accuracy: (1) the *Boeitai* (*Okinawan Home Guard*), comprising an estimated 20,000 men; (2) the Okinawans used to supplement the Japanese forces in old units, most of which had arrived at Okinawa understrength; (3) the Okinawans employed in a few instances to form new units with a Japanese nucleus. Since the full extent to which Japanese forces were augmented by Okinawans is not known, the following list gives only the estimated strength of the various units in respect to their Japanese elements.

Unit	Estimated Strength (Japanese Only)
32d Army Hq...	1,070
Infantry [a]	
24th Div (including 22d, 32d, 89th Inf Regts).............................	14,360
62d Div (including 11th–15th, 21st–23d, 272d, 273d Independent Inf Bns)....	11,723
44th Ind Mixed Brig (including 2d Inf Unit of 3 Bns and 15th Independent Mixed Regt)..	4,485
1st–3d, 26th–29th Independent Bns (converted from Sea Raiding Base Bns).....	6,242
223d, 224th, 225th Special Garrison Cos....................................	600
3d, 4th Commando Units...	900
Total Infantry...	38,310
Armored	
27th Tank Regt...	750
Artillery and Automatic Weapons (Attached Units)	
5th Arty Command...	147
1st Medium Arty Regt (2d Bn only)......................................	856
23d Medium Arty Regt...	1,143
7th Heavy Arty Regt (3 Btrys)..	526
100th Heavy Arty Bn..	565
1st Ind Arty Mortar Regt (1st, 4th, 5th Cos only)......................	613
1st Light Mortar Bn (3d–6th Independent Mortar Cos)....................	633
2d Light Mortar Bn (7th–10th Independent Mortar Cos)...................	615
3d, 7th, 22d Ind Antitank Bns..	1,015
18th, 22d, 23d, 32d Independent Antitank Cos...........................	569
27th Independent AA Arty Bn..	505
21st AA Hq...	71
79th, 80th, 81st Independent AA Arty Bns...............................	1,544
103d, 104th, 105th Machine Cannon Bns..................................	1,011
3d, 4th, 14th, 17th, 23d Independent Machine Gun Bns...................	1,663
Total Artillery and Automatic Weapons..................................	11,476
Shipping and Engineers	
23d, 26th Shipping Engr Regt (minus 1 co each).............................	1,600
66th Independent Engr Bn...	865
7th Shipping Hq, Naha Branch...	300
Field Shipping Main Depot, Okinawa Branch..................................	100
11th Shipping Group..	100
101st, 102d Sea Duty Cos (Koreans)...	1,500
Total Shipping and Engineers...	4,465

[a] Strengths of the 1st and 2d Provisional Brigs (1st–6th Special Established Regts) and of the 6th and 50th Special Established Bns are omitted because the service units from which they were formed are itemized individually in this list.

Unit	Estimated Strength (Japanese Only)
Air Force (Ground)	
19th Air Sector Command Hq..	41
44th, 50th, 56th, 158th Airfield Bns..................................	1,487
3d, 75th Airfield Cos..	458
2d Air Sig Regt (elements)...	500
6th Air Fixed Sig Unit...	50
21st Air Sig Unit..	100
25th, 26th AA Radio Units...	150
3d Independent Air Maintenance Unit...................................	120
118th Independent Maintenance Unit....................................	130
29th Field Airfield Construction Bn....................................	750
5th Field Air Repair Depot Bn...	300
502d, 503d, 504th Special Garrison Engr Units.........................	2,850
Total Air Force (Ground)..	6,936
Line of Communications Troops	
36th Sig Regt (including 106th, 126th, 127th Independent Wire Cos; 100th, 109th, 113th–116th, 131st, 132d Independent Radio Plats)...............	1,912
49th L of C Sector Unit..	1,400
32d Army Field Freight Depot..	1,167
32d Army Field Ord Depot...	1,498
27th Field Water Purification Unit.....................................	244
14th, 20th Field Well Drilling Cos.....................................	400
Okinawa Mil Hosp...	204
72d Land Duty Co..	508
Total Line of Communications Troops..................................	7,333
Naval Units...	3,500
Miscellaneous Units	
5th Sea Raiding Base Hq...	42
1st–3d Sea Raiding Sqs..	312
3d Independent Sea Transport Unit.....................................	250
7th Field Shipping Unit..	700
11th Sea Transportation Bn..	400
46th Independent Airfield Co..	120
2d Field Construction Duty Co...	366
6th, 7th Construction Duty Cos..	662
32d Army Ord Duty Unit...	150
32d Army Det Construction Unit.......................................	357
Total Miscellaneous Units...	3,359
Total Strength..	77,199

Source: Tenth Army G–2 Intelligence Monograph, Ryukyus Campaign, Pt. 1, Sec. B: Order of Battle, p.3.

Appendix C
Statistics of the Ryukyus Campaign

The following tables and charts are included to illustrate certain quantitative aspects of the Ryukyus campaign. Unfortunately, data are not available to permit a complete statistical summary of all phases of the campaign. Nevertheless, the data presented serve to indicate statistically the intensity of the fighting on Okinawa and the magnitude of the logistical effort necessary to support this operation.

The material shown in this appendix has been drawn from the most reliable sources. In instances where figures were available from more than one source, and were in conflict, all data were carefully weighed to ensure that the most reliable were used. Figures included in the text, however, were not always given in such sources, since refined summary data usually do not reflect the status of operations as of a given date or at the conclusion of a specific engagement. In such instances the only recourse was to periodic reports, prepared under the stress of battle and subject to revision as more details were learned. For this reason, sources cited in the text, while representing the best available for the data shown, will not always agree with those cited in appendix tables.

TABLE NO. 1

Strength of Army, Marine, and Naval Forces of Tenth Army in the Ryukyus Campaign, 30 April–30 June 1945 [a]

Command and Unit	30 April			31 May			30 June		
	Total	Offi-cers [b]	Enlisted men	Total	Offi-cers [b]	Enlisted men	Total	Offi-cers [b]	Enlisted men
ARMY............	102,250	6,379	95,871	167,971	10,991	156,980	190,301	13,810	176,491
7th Division.............	15,483	794	14,689	17,263	800	16,463	15,584	798	14,786
27th Division.............	13,488	722	12,766	12,404	679	11,725	11,624	652	10,972
77th Division.............	12,000	656	11,344	15,185	766	14,419	12,853	824	12,029
96th Division.............	13,146	798	12,348	14,220	706	13,514	13,140	751	12,389
Nondivisional Ground Force Units [c]............	38,200	2,591	35,609	55,607	3,512	52,095	60,501	3,847	56,654
Service Forces.............	8,918	643	8,275	30,053	2,107	27,946	36,764	2,688	34,076
Other [d]..................	1,015	175	840	23,239	2,421	20,818	39,835	4,250	35,585
MARINE [e]	88,500	n. a.	n. a.	58,894	n. a.	n. a.	2,489	n. a.	n. a.
NAVY [e]............	18,000	n. a.	n. a.	21,793	n. a.	n. a.	1,225	n. a.	n. a.

[a] Figures represent assigned strength rather than actual effective strength. In accordance with WD Circular No. 280, 6 July 1944, hospital patients in the Ryukyus were carried on the rolls of their respective organizations during hospitalization or until completion of the prescribed period of 60 days of total hospitalization.

[b] Includes warrant officers, flight officers, nurses, dieticians, and physical therapists.

[c] Includes armored forces, artillery, service units, and headquarters troops that were not specifically assigned to infantry divisions.

[d] Includes air-force-type units, overhead, replacements, and other miscellaneous units and personnel assigned to the Ryukyus operation and all theater-attached strength.

[e] Figures shown represent total strength of Marine and Navy units attached to the Tenth Army for the Ryukyus campaign. The marked decline shown for June is the result of reassignment of the units involved rather than of large-scale evacuation of personnel.

n. a. Not available.

Source: U. S. War Department Monthly Strength Reports.

TABLE NO. 2

Comparative American and Enemy Major Losses in the Ryukyus Campaign, 1 April–30 June 1945

Nature of Loss	American	Enemy
PERSONNEL		
Killed, Total...	12,281	[a] 110,071
Army...	[b] 4,582	n. a.
Marine...	[b] 2,792	n. a.
Navy...	4,907	n. a.
Captured..	n. a.	[c] 7,401
AIRCRAFT		
Planes Lost, Total......................................	[d] 763	[e] 7,830
Combat..	458	4,155
Operational...	305	2,655
Destroyed on Ground....................................	([f])	1,020
SHIPS		
Sunk...	[g] 36	16
Damaged..	[h] 368	4

[a] Data are from USAFWESPAC G–2 Periodic Report No. 15, 26 November–2 December 1945. The figure shown includes an unknown number of Okinawan conscripts and civilians. This, together with possible errors in counting the dead, accounts for the apparent discrepancy between total Japanese casualties and the total Japanese strength of 77,199 at the beginning of the campaign, as shown in Appendix B.

[b] Data are from U. S. Tenth Army Action Report Ryukyus, 26 March to 30 June 1945, Vol. 1, Ch. 11, Sec. I, p. 12. Figure for Marine personnel killed includes data for Tactical Air Force.

[c] Does not include 3,339 unarmed laborers and 15 combat civilians captured. Additional prisoners of war captured after the campaign raised the total to 16,346 by the end of November 1945.

[d] Includes 98 from British carriers (26 combat and 72 operational).

[e] Comprises 3,605 army planes and 4,225 navy planes, of which 850 and 1,050, respectively, were suicide planes.

[f] Data are not available to indicate the total number of American planes destroyed on the ground. However, authenticated reports of at least 7 such losses are available (see p. 361).

[g] Includes 26 sunk by suicide planes.

[h] Includes 164 damaged by suicide planes.

n. a. Not available.

Source: United States Strategic Bombing Survey, *The Campaigns of the Pacific War,* Ch. XIV, Appendix 99, p. 331 except as otherwise indicated.

TABLE NO. 3

Casualties Sustained by Tenth Army, 1 April–30 June 1945 [a]

Unit	Total	Battle Casualties				Non-battle Casual-ties
		Total	Killed[b]	Wound-ed [c]	Miss-ing	
ALL UNITS...........	65,631	39,420	7,374	31,807	239	26,211
XXIV Corps...............	34,736	22,182	4,412	17,689	81	12,554
7th Division......................	10,893	6,068	1,122	4,943	3	4,825
27th Division.....................	5,224	3,255	711	2,520	24	1,969
77th Division.....................	7,126	5,026	1,018	3,968	40	2,100
96th Division.....................	10,247	7,430	1,506	5,912	12	2,817
Corps Troops....................	1,246	403	55	346	2	843
III Amphibious Corps.......	26,724	16,507	2,779	13,609	119	10,217
1st Division......................	13,002	7,901	1,115	6,745	41	5,101
2d Division [d]......................	95	94	7	26	61	1
6th Division......................	12,815	8,326	1,622	6,689	15	4,489
Corps Troops....................	812	186	35	149	2	626
Tactical Air Force...........	520	139	13	99	27	381
Army Garrison Forces [e]......	2,636	383	110	261	12	2,253
Tenth Army troops [f].........	1,015	209	60	149	....	806

[a] Data are preliminary. Official casualty data will be released at a later date by the U. S. War Department and the U. S. Marine Corps. Figures shown include data for attached units.

[b] Includes number that died from wounds.

[c] Includes number injured in action.

[d] Except for diversionary activities in the south on 1–2 April, the 2d Marine Division was not actively engaged in the campaign. However, on 16 June, the 8th Regimental Combat Team of the division was landed to provide reinforcement.

[e] Comprises AGF 331 (Island Command, Okinawa) and AGF 245 (Ie Shima).

[f] Includes data for Medical Service, distributed as follows: 1 killed, 17 wounded, and 254 nonbattle casualties.

Source: U. S. Tenth Army Action Report Ryukyus, 26 March to 30 June 1945, Vol. 1, Ch. 11, Sec. I, p. 12.

CHART NO. 1

Tenth Army Weekly Battle Casualties, 1 April–30 June 1945

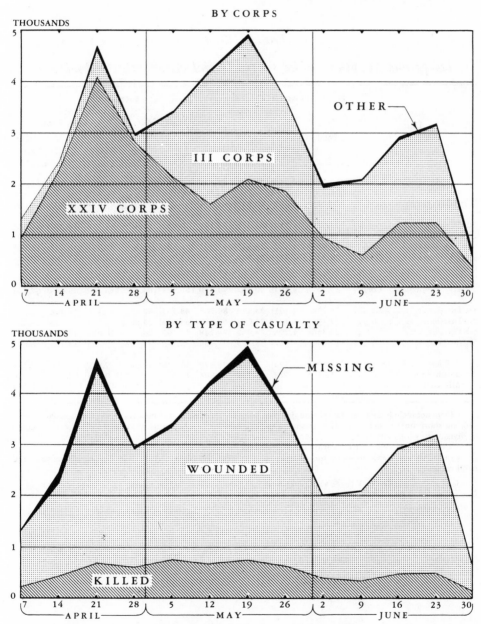

BY CORPS

THOUSANDS

OTHER

III CORPS

XXIV CORPS

BY TYPE OF CASUALTY

THOUSANDS

MISSING

WOUNDED

KILLED

Source: U. S. Tenth Army, G–1 Periodic Reports.

TABLE NO. 4

Troops and Supplies Loaded for the Initial Assault on the Ryukyus [a]

Unit	Number of Assault Troops			Supplies					
				Measurement Tons [b]			Short Tons		
	Total	Officers	Enlisted Men	Total	Vehicles	Cargo	Total	Vehicles	Cargo
ALL UNITS..........	182,821	10,746	172,075	746,850	503,555	243,295	286,635	129,917	156,718
XXIV Corps............	88,415	5,087	83,328	385,691	282,093	103,598	142,634	72,695	69,939
7th Division.................	21,929	1,150	20,779	95,789	70,382	25,407	34,856	18,272	16,584
27th Division...............	16,143	970	15,173	62,151	38,737	23,414	23,739	10,445	13,294
77th Division...............	20,981	1,170	19,811	99,999	76,698	23,301	34,936	18,271	16,665
96th Division...............	22,330	1,256	21,074	85,066	63,708	21,358	34,302	17,381	16,921
Corps Troops...............	7,032	541	6,491	42,686	32,568	10,118	14,801	8,326	6,475
III Amphibious Corps..	85,247	4,595	80,652	294,430	189,934	104,496	112,240	49,449	62,791
1st Division.................	26,274	1,401	24,873	80,765	48,585	32,180	31,463	14,226	17,237
2d Division.................	22,195	1,183	21,012	57,883	36,833	21,050	22,971	9,554	13,417
6th Division.................	24,356	1,294	23,062	78,748	52,267	26,481	28,031	12,564	15,467
Corps Troops...............	12,422	717	11,705	77,034	52,249	24,785	29,775	13,105	16,670
Tactical Air Force........	3,172	390	2,782	23,879	11,578	12,301	9,849	2,296	7,553
Tenth Army Troops......	5,417	628	4,789	21,806	13,091	8,715	9,533	4,157	5,376
Miscellaneous Units [c]	570	46	524	21,044	6,859	14,185	12,379	1,320	11,059

[a] Does not include data for first echelon garrison force comprising 11,031 men and 77,717 measurement tons (26,160 short tons) of supplies. Figures shown include data for attached units, grouped according to the corps or division to which assigned.

[b] Unit of volume used for measuring cargo, based on 40 cubic feet of shipping space per ton.

[c] Includes units and supplies for Military Government, Naval Air Base, Air Defense Command, and naval resupply.

Source: Commander Task Force 51, Commander Amphibious Forces U. S. Pacific Fleet, Report on Okinawa Gunto Operation from 17 February to 17 May 1945, Pt. V, Sec. 1.

TABLE NO. 5

Personnel and Supplies Loaded for Assault and for First Echelon Garrison in the Ryukyus Campaign, by Point of Embarkation [a]

Point of Embarkation	Number of Ships	Number of Troops	Supplies	
			Measure-ment Tons	Short Tons
TOTAL.........................	458	193,852	824,567	312,795
Leyte..................................	186	71,163	320,148	117,884
Guadalcanal–Espiritu–Russells	159	74,970	285,279	108,435
Saipan–Tinian–Guam	61	31,771	119,673	47,446
Oahu..................................	39	12,837	69,423	26,762
San Francisco–Seattle [b]..................	13	3,111	30,044	12,268

[a] Includes data for first echelon garrison force comprising 21 ships carrying 11,031 men and 77,717 measurement tons (26,160 short tons) of supplies.

[b] Includes minor quantities loaded at Roi.

Source: Office of the Chief of Naval Operations, Amphibious Operations—Capture of Okinawa (Ryukyus Operations), 27 March to 21 June 1945, Ch. VII, "Logistics," p. 7–24.

TABLE NO. 6

Comparison of Estimated Capacities for Unloading at Okinawa Beaches and Quantities Actually Unloaded, 1 April–30 June 1945 [a]

Period	Estimated Capacities [b] (M/T's)	Actual Discharge (M/T's)	Percent Deviation from Estimates	
			Each Period	Cumulative
TOTAL......................	1,981,495	2,016,490	+1.8	+1.8
1–16 April.........................	529,995	577,040	+8.9	+8.9
17–26 April........................	98,500	202,085	+105.2	+24.0
27 April–6 May.....................	169,000	200,877	+18.9	+22.9
7–16 May..........................	205,500	166,870	−18.8	+14.3
17–26 May.........................	239,000	170,886	−28.5	+6.1
27 May–5 June.....................	261,000	159,274	−39.0	−1.7
6–15 June..........................	189,000	163,863	−13.3	−3.0
16–25 June.........................	193,000	188,046	−2.6	−3.0
26–30 June.........................	[c]96,500	187,549	+94.4	+1.8

[a] Does not include 206,598 measurement tons unloaded at Ie Shima from 16 April through 30 June.

[b] Estimates of capacities varied with the expected progress of the campaign and the consequent expansion of unloading facilities at some beaches and partial or complete abandonment of others.

[c] No estimate available beyond 25 June. Figure shown is interpolated, based on estimate for 16–25 June.

Source: U. S. Tenth Army Action Report Ryukyus, 26 March to 30 June 1945, Vol. 1, Ch. 11, Sec. IV, pp. 43 ff.

CHART NO. 2

Comparison of Estimated Capacities for Unloading at Okinawa Beaches and Quantities Actually Unloaded, 1 April–30 June 1945

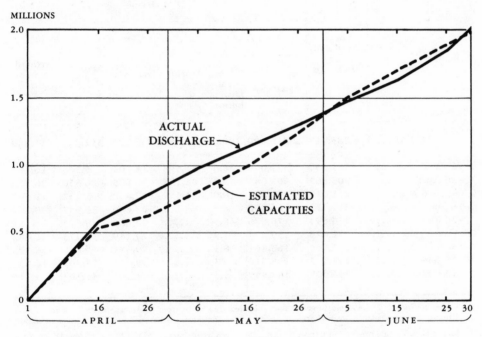

Source: U. S. Tenth Army Action Report Ryukyus, 26 March to 30 June 1945, Vol. 1, pp. 43 ff.

TABLE NO. 7

Cargo Unloaded at Okinawa Beaches, 1 April–30 June 1945 [a]

(*Measurement Tons*)

Period	Cargo Available for Discharge [b]	Discharged					
		All Types		Assault	Garrison	Maintenance	Ground Ammunition
		Quantity	Percent Distribution				
TOTAL....	2,883,917	2,016,490	100.0	673,067	839,190	352,353	151,880
1–16 April.........	917,056	577,040	28.6	537,568	18,104	5,264	16,104
17–26 April........	203,861	202,085	10.0	104,144	50,875	26,350	20,716
27 April–6 May.....	211,918	200,877	10.0	31,355	117,800	31,732	19,990
7–16 May..........	211,728	166,870	8.3	....	102,646	33,957	30,267
17–26 May.........	274,894	170,886	8.5	....	96,680	48,625	25,581
27 May–5 June......	252,873	159,274	7.9	....	114,119	34,473	10,682
6–15 June..........	267,550	163,863	8.1	....	99,624	55,846	8,393
16–25 June........	248,132	188,046	9.3	....	98,011	74,002	16,033
26–30 June........	295,905	187,549	9.3	....	141,331	42,104	4,114

[a] Does not include 206,598 measurement tons unloaded at Ie Shima from 16 April through 30 June.

[b] Includes cargo available for discharge in the target area and cargo loaded on ships at the regulating station.

Source: U. S. Tenth Army Action Report Ryukyus, 26 March to 30 June 1945, Vol. 1, Ch. 11, Sec. IV, pp. 51 ff.

CHART NO. 3

Average Daily Volume of Supplies Unloaded in the Ryukyus,
1 April–16 May 1945

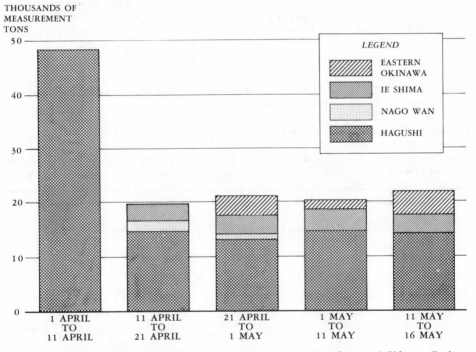

THOUSANDS OF
MEASUREMENT
TONS

LEGEND

EASTERN OKINAWA

IE SHIMA

NAGO WAN

HAGUSHI

Source: Office of the Chief of Naval Operations, Amphibious Operations, Capture of Okinawa (Ryukyus Operations), 27 March to 21 June 1945, p. 7–46.

TABLE NO. 8

Ammunition Expended by Tenth Army Field Artillery, 1 April–30 June 1945

(*Number of Rounds*)

Type of Weapon	Estimated Require-ments	Supply Available [a]	Quantity Expended		
			Total	Fired	Lost to Enemy Action
TOTAL............	2,119,760	3,315,209	2,116,691	1,766,352	350,339
Howitzer, 75-mm..........	266,640	612,020	230,067	166,068	63,999
Howitzer, 105-mm.........	1,236,700	1,889,452	1,330,137	1,104,630	225,507
Howitzer, 155-mm........	400,980	566,574	390,996	346,914	44,082
Gun, 155-mm..............	190,400	212,235	142,783	129,624	13,159
Howitzer, 8-inch..........	25,040	34,928	22,708	19,116	3,592

[a] Represents total quantities on hand during the period 1 April–22 June; does not include quantities in transit on 22 June.

Source: U. S. Tenth Army Action Report Ryukyus, 26 March to 30 June 1945, Vol. 1, Ch. 11, Sec. VI, p. 78.

CHART NO. 4

Ammunition Expended by Tenth Army Field Artillery, 1 April–30 June 1945

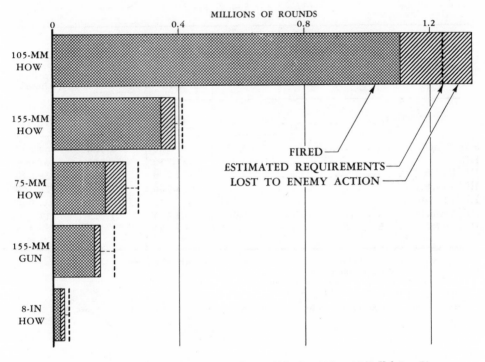

MILLIONS OF ROUNDS

FIRED
ESTIMATED REQUIREMENTS
LOST TO ENEMY ACTION

Source: U. S. Tenth Army Action Report, Ryukyus, 26 March to 30 June 1945, Vol. 1, p. 78.

TABLE NO. 9

Ammunition Expended by the U. S. Navy in the Ryukyus Campaign,
March–June 1945

(*Number of Rounds Fired*)

Type	Total	Period		
		Prior to 1 April	1 April	2 April– 24 June
ALL TYPES....................	600,018	41,543	44,825	513,650
Star, 5-inch..........................	66,653	500	1,500	64,653
HC, 5-inch ᵃ	ᵇ 432,008	27,750	36,250	368,008
HC, 6-inch...........................	46,020	4,200	3,000	38,820
HC, 8-inch...........................	32,180	3,700	2,100	26,380
HC, 12-inch..........................	2,700	575	175	1,950
HC, 14-inch..........................	16,046	3,275	1,325	11,446
HC, 16-inch..........................	4,411	ᶜ 1,543	475	2,393

ᵃ Includes AAC shells. Proximity-type fuzes were not used in shore bombardment. The HC (High Capacity) fragmentation shells detonated on impact.

ᵇ Includes approximately 20,000 rounds of antiaircraft fire.

ᶜ Includes 518 rounds fired by fast battleships.

Source: Tenth Army Action Report Ryukyus, 26 March to 30 June 1945, Vol. 1, Ch. 11, Sec. V, p. 19.

TABLE NO. 10

Ammunition Expended by XXIV Corps, by Type of Weapon, 4 April–21 June 1945 [a]

Weapon	Total		April		May		June	
	Number of Rounds	Short Tons	Number of Rounds	Short Tons	Number of Rounds	Short Tons	Number of Rounds	Short Tons
ALL TYPES.........	....	64,324	....	24,438	....	28,977	....	10,909
Howitzer, 8-in	19,008	2,224	6,077	684	9,154	1,031	3,777	509
Gun, 155-mm...............	79,888	5,891	32,156	2,362	34,387	2,529	13,345	1,000
Howitzer, 155-mm..........	278,946	16,702	114,770	7,292	113,636	6,907	50,540	2,503
Howitzer, 105-mm..........	792,371	28,152	284,695	10,427	377,436	12,799	130,240	4,926
Howitzer, 75-mm	179,977	2,429	68,081	919	91,126	1,230	20,770	280
Gun, 75-mm................	104,893	1,521	33,013	479	43,808	635	28,072	407
Gun, 57-mm................	21,997	231	7,118	74	5,682	58	9,197	99
Gun, 37-mm................	87,193	204	39,362	93	25,066	58	22,765	53
Mortar, 81-mm..............	443,589	3,672	146,385	1,181	241,853	2,054	55,351	437
Mortar, 60-mm..............	521,301	1,626	98,117	307	311,722	974	111,462	345
Rocket Launcher, 2.36-in......	20,359	62	10,263	31	7,956	24	2,140	7
Grenade, Hand..............	366,734	365	111,815	96	181,841	192	73,078	77
Grenade, Rifle.............	25,670	40	15,220	25	8,254	12	2,196	3
Submachine Gun, cal. .45 [b]...	1,461,180	35	612,958	16	683,732	15	164,490	4
Carbine, cal. .30............	2,009,597	34	926,778	16	773,824	13	308,995	5
Rifle, cal. .30................	9,267,923	372	3,569,182	143	4,545,337	183	1,153,404	46
Machine Gun, cal. .30.........	16,285,499	627	6,091,400	234	5,745,989	221	4,448,110	172
Machine Gun, cal. .50.........	786,754	137	394,108	59	203,456	42	189,190	36

[a] Data for 1–3 April are not available; expenditures after 21 June were negligible.

[b] Includes relatively minor expenditures of cal. .45 ball ammunition for pistols and revolvers.

Source: Personal records of Col. G. F. Powell, Ordnance Officer, XXIV Corps, U. S. Tenth Army.

Bibliographical Note

The sources used for this volume are of three main types: (1) manuscript histories of the major Army and Marine units taking part in the action; (2) interviews; (3) official records, including Japanese records and prisoner of war interrogations. By far the largest part of the narrative of combat on Okinawa is based on the histories of the combat divisions written by combat historians in the field. This central body of combat narrative has been expanded by resort to records of Army, corps, and division headquarters and by interviews with senior Army, Navy, and Marine commanders and staff officers. Official records of the major Marine units engaged in the campaign were used to verify and elaborate material in the combat histories of Marine divisions. The account of the Navy's participation is based on naval planning and intelligence records and action reports. Information on Japanese plans and actions was drawn from a great body of enemy intelligence material found in the G–2 records and reports of Army, corps, and divisions, and from enemy interrogations. The capture of high-ranking Japanese officers enabled historians to secure first-hand information as to enemy plans and operations; in some cases the aid of the captured officers was even enlisted in reconstructing engagements at the scene of action. All this material on the enemy has made it possible to describe the tactics and operations on both sides of the fighting line on Okinawa to a far greater extent than in any other battle in the Pacific. For the general background of the campaign and for high-level decisions, the main sources are the records of the Joint Chiefs of Staff and the published reports of the Chief of Staff, U. S. Army, and the Chief of Naval Operations, U. S. Navy.

Manuscript Histories

The manuscript histories of participating corps and divisions were written by combat historians attached to the units during the campaign. The combat historians relied heavily on systematic interviews with commanders, from the highest to the lowest echelons, and with groups and individuals who took part in the various actions. These interviews supplied information on details of combat that are seldom recorded in official documents and made clear the reasons why decisions were made. The division historians also participated in critiques of small actions, often held within forty-eight hours after the action occurred, and in critiques of the campaign as a whole. Whenever necessary, the facts were checked against regimental and battalion journals and message files, together with other records kept by divisions in combat. Often the historians themselves observed the actions at first hand; and they walked, rode, and flew extensively over the terrain. All of the histories were written under the direction of the Tenth Army historian, Lt. Col. John Stevens. The manuscript histories used, which are on file in the Historical Division, WDSS, are as follows:

> Maj. Roy E. Appleman, The XXIV Corps in the Conquest of Okinawa (1 Apr–22 Jun 45), 4 vols., Dec 45.
>
> Capt. Donald Mulford and 1st Lt. Jesse Rogers, The 96th Division on Okinawa, 4 parts, n. d. Captain Mulford wrote Parts I, III, and IV.
>
> Capt. Russell A. Gugeler, The Operations of the 7th Infantry Division on Okinawa, 1 April to 22 June 1945, 3 vols., n. d.
>
> Capt. Edmund G. Love, The 27th Division on Okinawa, n. d.
>
> 1st Lt. Paul R. Leach, Narrative of the Operations of the 77th Division on Okinawa, 3 vols., n. d. Vol. I covers the Kerama Islands; Vol. II, Okinawa; and Vol. III, Ie Shima.

For the coverage of Marine Corps actions, the following two manuscript histories were used:

> Capt. Phillips D. Carleton, USMC, The 6th Marine Division on Okinawa, 2 parts, n. d.
>
> Capt. James R. Stockman, The First Marine Division on Okinawa, 1 April–30 June 1945, published by the Historical Division, Headquarters, U. S. Marine Corps, 1946.

Interviews

Interviews constituted one of the most important sources for the account of the Okinawa campaign. The extent of this use may not be fully indicated in the footnotes as reference is often made to the division histories, which are based largely on interviews. Numerous interviews which cover issues not touched on in the division histories are, however, referred to directly. In particular, interviews with the commanding general and staff officers of Tenth Army were used in constructing the broad framework of the narrative. These were supplemented by notes of Tenth Army staff meetings made by the Tenth Army historian, by written statements supplied to the historian by the staff officers in answer to questions, and by notes of press conferences made by the historian. All facts adduced by interview or written statement have been carefully checked against available documents. These interviews and notes are recorded in diaries and journals kept by the Army, corps, and division historians, which contain also details of crucial actions as related by participants while the events were freshly remembered. The diaries and journals of the historians are on file in the Historical Division, WDSS.

Official Records

U. S. Army

The most important Army records used are listed below according to major headquarters. These records were consulted in the field and in the Historical Division, WDSS. They will be deposited with the Historical Records Section, War Department Records Branch, Adjutant General's Office, Washington, D. C.

U. S. ARMY FORCES, MIDDLE PACIFIC

Participation in the Okinawa Operation, 2 vols., 15 Mar 46.

History of G–5 Section, n. d.

G–2 Study of Okinawa Gunto, 1 Feb 45.

Administrative History of Medical Activities in the Middle Pacific, Block 18f: The Okinawa Operation, 1 April to 30 June 1945, 2 vols., n. d.

TENTH ARMY

Action Report Ryukyus, 26 March to 30 June 1945, 3 vols., 3 Sep 45. The first volume contains the text of the report; the other two, the map and pictorial supplements. The history is generally reliable but of little use for combat action. It contains good summaries of staff section activities, particularly those concerned with logistics.

Tentative Operations Plan 1–45, 6 Jan 45. The Army over-all plan for the initial assault.

Operations Orders 2A–45 to 16–45, 26 Mar–21 Jun 45.

Field Orders Nos. 9–59, 21 Apr–3 Jul 45. Concerned with attachment of units.

Administrative Orders Nos. 1–3, 28 Apr–20 May 45. Supplements to Operations Orders.

Operational Directives Nos. 1–12A, 1 Jan–1 Jun 45. Broad logistical procedures.

G–1 Journal and Messages, Daily Reports.

G–2 Journal, Message File, Periodic Reports.

G–2 Weekly Summary Nos. 1–3, 5, 28 May–25 Jun 45. Good general expositions of enemy order of battle and weapons.

G–2 Intelligence Monograph, 5 parts. Excellent studies of enemy plans, defenses, order of battle, and weapons. Based on interrogations of prisoners, captured documents, and ground reconnaissance after the battle.

G–2, Combat Intelligence Collecting Agency Subsection, Prisoner of War Interrogation Summaries Nos. 1–19, Jul–Aug 45. Excellent and accurate summaries of hundreds of interrogations of Japanese prisoners. Fuller and more accurate than the G–2 Intelligence Monograph.

G–2 Prisoner of War Interrogation Reports, Nos. 9–28, 8 Jun–6 Aug. 45. Individual interrogations. Nos. 27 and 28 of Colonel Yahara and Mr. Shimada are the most important.

G–2, Combat Intelligence Collecting Agency Subsection, Translations Nos. 4–308, 17 Apr–11 Jul 45. Translations of captured documents.

G–3 Journal and Message File, Periodic Reports. The most important Tenth Army journal. Valuable for naval operations. Almost all important staff documents will be found in the G–3 Journal file.

G–4 Journal and Message File, Periodic Reports.

Other staff section periodic reports and papers. Those of the Artillery, Engineer, and Antiaircraft Sections are particularly useful.

Military Government Section, Operations Report, 1 Aug 45. A brief narrative with a good documentary appendix.

After Action Reports of the numerous combat and service units attached to Tenth Army. The most important are those of 713th Armored Flame Thrower Battalion, 53d AAA Brigade, 144th Coast Artillery Group, and 20th Armored Group.

Island Command Okinawa, Action Report 13 Dec 44–30 Jun 45, 30 Jun 45.

Tactical Air Force, Action Report, Phase I, Nansei Shoto, 8 Dec 44 to 30 Jun 45, incl., 12 Jul 45.

XXIV CORPS

Action Report Ryukyus, 1 Apr–30 Jun 45, n. d. This report contains a good digest of combat intelligence, but there are some important omissions. It is particularly useful for logistical activities and the general course of the campaign.

Chief of Staff Journal. This journal contains many significant entries but is incomplete and fragmentary in many places.

Field Orders Nos. 45–53, 8 Feb–22 Jun 45.

Administrative Orders Nos. 10–17, 10 Feb–19 Jun 45.

G–1 Journal, Periodic Reports.

G–2 Journal and Message File.

G–2 Summary Nos. 4–15, 12 Apr–26 Jun 45. A weekly review of enemy intelligence with good order of battle discussions.

G–2 Intelligence Service Organization, Prisoner of War Interrogation Reports Nos. 68–206, 15 Apr–19 Jun 45.

G–2 Intelligence Service Organization, Translations, Batch Nos. 2–624, 7 Apr–23 Jun 45.

G–3 Journal, Periodic Reports.

G–4 Journal and Message File.

Other staff section journals and reports, including Signal, Ordnance, Military Government, Engineers, Chemical Warfare, Surgeon, and Artillery. Those of Artillery are rather voluminous.

After Action Reports of combat and service units attached to XXIV Corps. The most important are those of 419th and 420th Field Artillery Groups, 97th AAA Group, and 20th Armored Group.

7th, 27th, 77th, and 96th Divisions. Action Reports and supporting documents of division and subordinate headquarters. These include reports of staff sections of division headquarters and files of journals, messages, periodic and special reports, orders, maps, and overlays maintained by division, regimental, and battalion headquarters.

U. S. Navy

The naval records used include the operation reports of naval commanders, their operation plans, and important intelligence records. These are on file in the Navy Department, Office of Naval Records, Washington, D. C.

Office of the Chief of Naval Operations, Amphibious Operations—Capture of Okinawa, 27 March to 21 June 1945 (OPNAV 34–P–0700), 22 Jan 46.

A composite and general account consisting of extracts from the operational reports of the Army and Navy commanders.

————, Civil Affairs Handbook, Ryukyu (Loochoo) Islands (OPNAV 13-31), 15 Nov 44.

Commander in Chief, U. S. Pacific Fleet and Pacific Ocean Areas (CINC-PAC-CINCPOA), Operations in the Pacific Ocean Areas during the Month of ————. A monthly report, used for the period from October 1944 to June 1945 for coverage of naval operations.

————, Operation Plan 14-44, serial 0001193, 31 Dec 44.

————, Joint Staff Study ICEBERG, serial 000131, 25 Oct 44.

————, Base Development Plan LEGUMINOUS, serial 000221, 10 Feb 45.

————, Okinawa Gunto, Second Supplement to Information Bulletin No. 161-44. (Bulletin No. 53-45), 28 Feb 45.

————, Information Bulletin Okinawa Gunto (Bulletin No. 161-44), 15 Nov 44.

————, Translations Interrogations Nos. 28, 32, 35, 37 (Bulletins Nos. 107-45, 147-45, 170-45, 186-45), 14 May-24 Jul 45.

Joint Intelligence Center, Pacific Ocean Areas, Report of Psychological Warfare Activities, Okinawa Operation, 15 Sep 45.

Commander Fifth Fleet, Operations Plan 1-45, 3 Jan 45.

Commander Amphibious Forces Pacific Fleet, Operations Plan A1-45, 16 Feb 45.

Commander Task Force 51 (CTF 51), Commander Amphibious Forces U. S. Pacific Fleet (COMPHIBSPAC), Report on Okinawa Gunto Operation from 17 February to 17 May 1945, 25 Jul 45.

Commander Task Force 58, Action Report 14 March to 28 May 1945, 18 Jun 45.

Commander Amphibious Group One, Commander Task Force 52, Action Report Okinawa, March-April 1945, 1 May 45.

Commander Amphibious Group Four, Pacific Fleet (CTF 53), Report of Participation in the Capture of Okinawa Gunto, 20 Jul 45.

Commander Amphibious Group Twelve, Commander Task Force 55, Report on the Capture of Okinawa Gunto, Phases I and II, 14 March-9 June 1945, 31 Jul 45.

Amphibious Group Seven, Action Report of Commander Western Islands Attack Group for Capture of Okinawa Gunto, 9 March 1945 to 2 April 1945, 26 May 45.

Commander Fifth Amphibious Force (CTF 51 and 31), Report of Capture of Okinawa Gunto, Phases I and II, 17 May 1945–21 June 1945, 4 Jul 45.
Commander Second Carrier Task Force, Pacific, Commander Task Force 38, Action Report 28 May–1 July 1945, 7 Jul 45.

U. S. Marine Corps

The use of Marine Corps documents has been limited to the action reports of the major participating units. These may be consulted at the Historical Division, Headquarters, U. S. Marine Corps, Washington, D. C.

III Amphibious Corps Action Report Ryukyus Operation Phases I and II, 1 Jul 45, with Appendices. Appendices 8 and 9 contain G–3 Periodic Reports and Operation Orders.
1st Marine Division Special Action Report Nansei Shoto.
6th Marine Division Special Action Report Nansei Shoto.

UNITED STATES ARMY IN WORLD WAR II

The following volumes have been published or are in press:

The War Department

Chief of Staff: Prewar Plans and Preparations
Washington Command Post: The Operations Division
Strategic Planning for Coalition Warfare: 1941–1942
Strategic Planning for Coalition Warfare: 1943–1944
Global Logistics and Strategy: 1940–1943
Global Logistics and Strategy: 1943–1945
The Army and Economic Mobilization
The Army and Industrial Manpower

The Army Ground Forces

The Organization of Ground Combat Troops
The Procurement and Training of Ground Combat Troops

The Army Service Forces

The Organization and Role of the Army Service Forces

The Western Hemisphere

The Framework of Hemisphere Defense
Guarding the United States and Its Outposts

The War in the Pacific

The Fall of the Philippines
Guadalcanal: The First Offensive
Victory in Papua
CARTWHEEL: The Reductions of Rabaul
Seizure of the Gilberts and Marshalls
Campaign in the Marianas
The Approach to the Philippines
Leyte: The Return to the Philippines
Triumph in the Philippines
Okinawa: The Last Battle
Strategy and Command: The First Two Years

The Mediterranean Theater of Operations

Northwest Africa: Seizing the Initiative in the West
Sicily and the Surrender of Italy
Salerno to Cassino
Cassino to the Alps

The European Theater of Operations
  Cross-Channel Attack
  Breakout and Pursuit
  The Lorraine Campaign
  The Siegfried Line Campaign
  The Ardennes: Battle of the Bulge
  The Last Offensive
  The Supreme Command
  Logistical Support of the Armies, Volume I
  Logistical Support of the Armies, Volume II

The Middle East Theater
  The Persian Corridor and Aid to Russia

The China-Burma-India Theater
  Stilwell's Mission to China
  Stilwell's Command Problems
  Time Runs Out in CBI

The Technical Services
  The Chemical Warfare Service: Organizing for War
  The Chemical Warfare Service: From Laboratory to Field
  The Chemical Warfare Service: Chemicals in Combat
  The Corps of Engineers: Troops and Equipment
  The Corps of Engineers: The War Against Japan
  The Corps of Engineers: The War Against Germany
  The Corps of Engineers: Military Construction in the United States
  The Medical Department: Hospitalization and Evacuation, Zone of Interior
  The Medical Department: Medical Service in the Mediterranean and Minor Theaters
  The Ordnance Department: Planning Munitions for War
  The Ordnance Department: Procurement and Supply
  The Ordnance Department: On Beachhead and Battlefront
  The Quartermaester Corps: Organization, Supply, and Services, Volume I.
  The Quartermaster Corps: Organization, Supply, and Services, Volume II
  The Quartermaster Corps: Operations in the War Against Japan
  The Quartermaster Corps: Operations in the War Against Germany
  The Signal Corps: The Emergency
  The Signal Corps: The Test
  The Signal Corps: The Outcome
  The Transportation Corps: Responsibilities, Organization, and Operations
  The Transportation Corps: Movements, Training, and Supply
  The Transportation Corps: Operations Overseas

Special Studies

Chronology: 1941–1945
Military Relations Between the United States and Canada: 1939–1945
Rearming the French
Three Battles: Arnaville, Altuzzo, and Schmidt
The Women's Army Corps
Civil Affairs: Soldiers Become Governors
Buying Aircraft: Materiel Procurement for the Army Air Forces
The Employment of Negro Troops
Manhattan: The U.S. Army and the Atomic Bomb

Pictorial Record

The War Against Germany and Italy: Mediterranean and Adjacent Areas
The War Against Germany: Europe and Adjacent Areas
The War Against Japan

Index

☆ U.S. GOVERNMENT PRINTING OFFICE: 1991 272-035